AMERICAN ENVIRONMENTAL HISTORY

Second Edition

JOSEPH M. PETULLA

University of San Francisco

Merrill Publishing Company
A Bell & Howell Information Company
Columbus   Toronto   London   Melbourne

The cover photo is an 1868 Currier and Ives print drawn by E. F. Palmer, which represents a composite of nineteenth century America. Its subtitle, "Westward the Course of Empire Takes Its Way" comes from a poem written by English philosopher Bishop George Berkeley in 1752.

In 1868 the most exciting phenomenon of the relentless "course of empire" was the proliferating American railroad, which splits the picture into two diagonal sides of opposition—civilization and wilderness. The railroad is seen in this book as the technological culmination of the steam age, precipitating rapid expansion in the process of urbanization, industrialization, commercialization and national integration. The railroad can further be viewed as the conveyor of civilization to the unforeseen horizons of the future. Log houses, simple axes, and covered wagons on narrow dirt roads would soon give way to bustling towns and cities with frame houses, factories and eventually eight-lane interstate highways. The landscape with its mountains, lakes (and Indians) would also dissolve into the face of "imperial" civilization. How this happened is the story of American environmental history. (Print courtesy of The Bancroft Library)

Those who find the context of the book discouraging should turn to the engraving by William Blake (ca. 1774) at the end of the text. His moon ark, peace dove, and bow in the clouds are classic symbols of hope, more and more necessary for survival for dwellers of the ark.

Published by Merrill Publishing Company
A Bell & Howell Company
Columbus, Ohio 43216

This book was set in Zapf Book.

Administrative Editor: David Gordon
Production Editor and Text Designer: Jeffrey Putnam
Art Coordinator: Lorraine Woost
Cover Designer: Cathy Watterson

Library of Congress Catalog Card Number: 87-61585
International Standard Book Number: 0-675-20885-8
Printed in the United States of America
1 2 3 4 5 6 7 8 9 – 92 91 90 89 88 87

Contents

To my mother, Jennie Ruby Petulla
and to my late father, Louis Petulla

Preface

In the years since the first edition of *American Environmental History* was published (or more pointedly since I began the book in 1972), a great deal has happened in the history of the country's environment. At the same time, not much has changed. The greatest changes have occurred to the consciousness of the American people. On Earth Day in 1970, very few people had the vaguest notion of the meaning of ecology and even fewer were interested in doing anything about the country's half-concealed environmental timebombs. The timebombs began their intermittent explosions: smog disasters and smog alerts, not only in New York and Los Angeles but also in most large cities; major fish kills and water pollution crises; and, finally, toxic waste and industrial toxic emissions. It dawned on both rural and urban Americans that the country's land, air, and water were imperiled and becoming unsafe. In the early 1980s, the majority decided that the government should do something about environmental problems, even at great cost or loss of economic growth. This development of consciousness has complicated the questions I posed when I began the book in the early 1970s. How could events change so quickly?

The seventies were a monumental struggle between many different environmental groups and their enemies. The federal government passed laws and the EPA developed rules, and no one seemed to keep them. Industry sometimes overpowered local agencies entrusted to enforce the rules. Sometimes the EPA didn't even develop the rules until some environmental groups sued the agency.

Recently I concluded that not much has changed in the structure of things, despite the raised environmental consciousness. In 1982 I began a study on pollution control technologies in industry, mainly to find out if industry was saving any money by recyling hazardous waste or conserving energy. I spent four years on the study and took one very long trip around the country, but I didn't find a very clear answer to the question. I did find that people in industry and agencies who are trying to improve the country's environment struggle daily. That is another story, told in *Environmental Protection in the United States: Industry, Agencies, Environmentalists* (San Francisco Study Center, 1987). I bring up the subject because the experience has sobered my optimism. Despite the popular support for environmental quality, the economic, social, and political institutions of this country do not sustain a clean and healthy environment. The reasons, as ever, are rooted in history. *American Environmental History* is more relevant than ever.

The industry experience also influenced how I updated and revised this book. The first major addition is a new final chapter on environmental legislative history since World War II that emphasizes air, water, and hazardous waste problems. Contemporary consciousness is focused on "environmental" as opposed to natural resource issues, which received the primary emphasis in the first edition. Of course, land, air, and water are natural resources and closely connected to pollution questions. To clarify the connection, I added a second new chapter to the middle of the book to highlight urban environmental problems, which have a somewhat different character and history. Both of these new chapters fit well into the purposes of the book but broaden it to the extent that the former subtitle, "The Exploitation and Conservation of Natural Resources," has been dropped.

I also updated the bibliographical sections at the end of each chapter. Much has been written on environmental history since the book originally appeared, and I have attempted to include most of the recent books that concern the text. The field of environmental history is attracting both young scholars and established historians. The many choices allow students a variety of supplementary subjects and approaches. Finally, I updated the natural resource data in the later chapters, particularly on agriculture and timber use, and included other new sections as I saw fit.

I am grateful to David Gordon of Merrill for his interest in environmental history, and particularly this book. My debt to the dozens of scholars whose names appear in the reference lists has become deeper over the years. And Maggie, my transcendentalist ms., has become a bit more militant with time and is still helpful with comment and inspiration.

Preface to the First Edition

If English historian George Unwin was correct when he said, "History is an account of the things that mattered most in the past, and it derives its chief interest from the assumption that those things were largely the causes of what matters to us now," then he has provided my excuse for the present volume. Natural-resource questions have mattered very much in the past few years. They have involved just about everyone: workers trying to get to their jobs; industrialists looking for low-sulfur fuel; legislators in every level of government; environmentalists; union leaders; public agency officials, and many more.

The idea for this book came from a course, "The History of Resource Use in the United States," at the University of California at Berkeley, intended mainly for students in the Department of Conservation and Resource Studies. We had found that the students' understanding of contemporary resource and environmental problems was often limited by an inadequate historical perspective. We tried to enrich their purview with a historical account which draws on many disciplines. These students have in many ways contributed to the shape of the book. Through evaluations and comments, they have indicated the weaknesses of the course as well as their own personal needs. Some appreciated the connection with economic history; they even reported that the course helped them to understand something about economics, especially in its relationship to natural resources. Others were happy for a history course that kept them interested. A few particularly liked what they learned about the history of technology and historical geography. The negative comments kept me honest, but all of the evaluations strengthened our belief that natural resources cannot be studied in isolation from economic, political, social, and technological developments in past or contemporary history. My experience in teaching the course confirmed earlier suspicions that conservation history is best understood in the context of the nation's economic, social, and political growth.

Most of the work in this field was accomplished a generation or two ago by such superb scholars as Paul Gates, Fred Shannon, John Ise, Roy Robbins, Edward Kirkland, Everett Dick, Percy Bidwell and John Falconer, Lewis Gray, and Ralph Brown, though it is somewhat brash to list only a few of the authorities who have so much depended on each other's work for the past hundred years. Even as I wrote the above names more recent authors, such as Clarence Danhof, Roderick Nash, John Schlebecker, and environmentalists such as Barry Commoner came to mind. I shall simply acknowledge a great debt to all of them and many more.

Thus this book is not so much an original piece of scholarship as a new organization of hundreds of disparate pieces of information, mainly from secondary sources but also from monographs, original documents and statistical sources. Geography books, engineering manuals, and geological archeology studies have proved as helpful as economic history texts, statistical abstracts, histories of technology and political and social histories. The focal point and distinguishing feature of the book is its discussion of the central variable, natural-resource use as a major determinant of the United States natural environment.

I have attempted to produce a simply-written synthesis showing the development of resource exploitation and conservation in the United States for those interested in the problems of the natural environment. I have assumed that the reader has little technical knowledge of the subject. However, I have also attempted to fill in the background of those who might have had environmental or conservation concerns for a long period of time. The overriding difficulty in writing a book like this one is the problem of selecting the content from the massive collection of available, often contradictory, data. In general I concur with Walter Lippmann's dictum, "we have to select some facts rather than others and in so doing we use our selective judgment of what is interesting or important or both." I have included what I consider to be interesting or important but preferably both.

Whenever my opinion is registered in the text, it is, of course only one of many possible interpretations. At the end of each chapter I have included a section entitled "References for Further Reading" for those who would like to explore a particular question or period in further depth. I cite these particular works because the data, interpretations and bibliographies of the authors have been especially helpful to me. Of course, there are many more sources and cross-references, some of them more recent, but I preferred the data and interpretations of the authors cited. For instance, I sometimes chose traditional economic historians over recent econometricians, sometimes the opposite; occasionally I took the traditional over the revisionist historian, sometimes the opposite; often I used the radical interpretation. In a few cases the very latest secondary source of the subject was published in the 20s or 30s. Monographs and important historical source books—e.g., the very useful *Historical Statistics of the United States: Colonial Times to 1970*—also have been cited, but a comprehensive survey has not been compiled. The references are provided for further study; they themselves contain exhaustive bibliographies.

Introduction

In one of his "Peanuts" cartoons, Charles Schulz has dressed Snoopy in hiking gear and sent him into the woods. Snoopy marveled at the wonders of nature and its complex web of interrelationships. He was most pleased that the web of nature was doing its bit in the material betterment of Beagledom.

Snoopy's relationship to nature seems accurately to mirror the collective attitudes of the American people. In fact, the idea that nature and its resources exist solely to be used for the material benefit of humans and for the particular profit of those who own them constitutes the very definition of natural resources in the world today: A resource is apparently considered to be something that supports human life and its needs, real or imagined, individual or social.

As a consequence the natural environment and resources have been transformed into commodities and marketed like eggs, beans, automobiles, tennis rackets, and counseling or lawyering. The phrase "exploitation of natural resources" in this book refers to the process of progressively quantifying them in monetary terms. That is, "exploitation of natural resources" means applying more refined economic rationality in successive epochs to the natural resources of the United States—land, agriculture, timber, and mineral ores—or, as Snoopy might say, "sunlight, air, plants, water, soil, birds, micro-organisms." The goal of economic rationality is, by definition, to gain further profits through a variety of means. It has generally characterized the capitalism of the western world. Snoopy's web of nature might have made a good life for some beagles, but it has made an even better life for the few who gained control over the water and soil.

An important part of the story of resources in America deals with the stages of their quantification and control. During much of the nation's history, its leaders have struggled for a way to measure out and put a price tag on the country's vast and rich natural resources. It was a special problem after the Revolution when Congress applied the grid system to their newly acquired territory, whereby all America was to be divided into townships six miles square, then sold. Speculating and subdividing arrived early in American history.

Natural resources came to be considered almost exclusively for their market profitability. One half of the double-entry bookkeeping system came easily to Americans in these early periods, for resources were quite cheap. As entrepreneurs found markets, entries on the opposite side of the page enabled them to determine profitability. The tension between the two sides of the ledger precipitated the trend toward advanced technologies and scientific knowledge, more sophisticated systems of exchange and banking, wider trading areas and better transportation routes, bigger companies and more centralized governments. Material comforts came willy-nilly in the wake of these developments, but they took their toll from the natural environment, and the price is steadily rising.

So another principle—that natural resources should be conserved and the natural environment protected—has been introduced into the American social fabric. The impetus originally came from foreign visitors and immigrants who had seen their own European resources exhausted or depleted because of centuries of wasteful management. It also came from scientists, native or trained in Europe—naturalists and transcendentalists who joined forces in the American conservation movement at the end of the nineteenth century. "Conservation of natural resources" here refers to the protection of the natural environment for the preservation of its inherent values or for the protection of its resources for future generations. Conservationists stressed the natural and social values over economic considerations of marketability and profitability, but the scientific-minded conservationists interested in future utilization of resources were no less "rational" and "efficient" than the more enlightened business-men of their time in efforts to implement policies that would conserve resources for long-term use.

How resource use has changed as people came to depend on different resources or as their life style changed is another part of the story of the American natural environment. Yesterday's luxuries—a gas or electric stove and running water—became today's necessities. The evolution involves not only land, soils, climate, mineral resources, but also labor and capital necessary for industrialization, transportation facilities, technology, government policies, managerial skills, banking arrangements and even the attitudes of the people toward economic growth, change and resource use.

It is almost an understatement to assert that Americans have been all too willing to exploit natural resources to their limits for personal gain. But to decry America's materialism and greedy profit-seeking, its collective attitudes of waste, would be an over-simplified moralization. Attitudes—materialistic or otherwise—are born in history. Economic, political and social institutions create a culture and a mentality which in turn live long after those institutions have given way to new structures. With them technologies are developed to meet new needs and engender habits, even new cultures of their own. Economics and politics, attitudes and beliefs, technologies and habits—these variables interact in a complex web of relationships in the creation of a culture.

Different periods of time will necessarily be characterized by a different mix of the variables, and as one era builds upon the preceding one, social change proceeds from the possibilities inherent in the former society. If environmental change is to occur, an understanding of American history with a special view of the way natural resources have been exploited or conserved is important. Awareness of past and present institutional structures is needed before the first step toward environmental and social change can be taken.

The American land and its principal natural resources have been utilized in the past 350 years in ways which have depended on American political and economic institu-tions, technologies and habits. When the English Crown and Parliament determined what would be encouraged for production and export from the American colonies, imperial desires for raw materials (or preferably gold and silver) limited the options of the colonists. Political struggles later played an important role in resource and land distribution after America won its independence; without a federal constitution, a national land policy and governmental encouragement of social capital, sectional sentiments would no doubt have prevailed and resource exploitation would have remained at a primitive level for generations after the War.

Likewise economic considerations have been paramount through American history: which resources would be most profitable for exploitation, and to whom? Entrepreneurs with sufficient capital have done well with exploitable American natural resources: northern timber and fish, southern tobacco and cotton, western wheat and cattle, omnipresent land speculation, gold, silver and a host of later mineral ores and fossil fuels. In America, capital investment, of course, has flowed to the resources of highest profitability. With only a negligible amount of capital and transportation to expanding markets, a man of moderate means could become very rich in a short time if he was lucky enough to make his fortune between periods of depression.

When technical obstacles stood in the way of more rapid exploitation of resources—a crude plow or inefficient power source—new technologies were borrowed from the old country and improved, such as the steam engine (as applied to steamboats and locomotives) or steel plows and harvesters. Technological innovations, however, presupposed markets and eager entrepreneurs, cooperative governments, and most of all, resources available to be exploited. Mass production methods and automation of resource processing were the logical results of economic rationality and cost-cutting.

Thus American exploitative attitudes were derived from the specific historical situations. Natural resources were available for the taking; social status came from rapid material advancement and affluence; economic opportunities encouraged risk and the plunder of nature; national policy opened increasingly larger areas of land and subsequent markets; technologies to exploit and move resources followed the need; the "good life" and economic security seemed to require an ever-increasing rate of resource exploitation.

Changes in the utilization of resources have generally occurred after every major American war—the Revolutionary, Civil, World War I, World War II, Vietnam—and these milestones signaled new relationships among economic, social, political and technological factors with natural resources. Social life and labor with a primitive resource technology before the Revolutionary War scarcely could be distinguished from peasant life in the High Middle Ages. Differences in agriculture stemmed primarily from regional, soil and climatic conditions, and also of course the demands of the English Crown for the goods that would turn a profit: *e.g.*, tobacco, rice, indigo, timber. New England could provide the motherland mainly timber and naval stores; it turned to Indian corn for its own staple. The South became most valuable to England, and later the Middle Colonies concentrated on wheat production. Every area was largely self-sufficient, growing whatever food the area would produce; it made its own tools, clothing, and other necessities. Only those who lived near a navigable river or a decent road or on the coastline could begin to specialize for trading purposes.

After the Revolution, technology did not change dramatically, but political and economic conditions—the Federal Constitution and expanding markets—occasioned later technical innovations which encouraged further economic and social developments. The Constitution centralized the power to mint money in the hands of the federal government and established the possibility of a nationally-integrated economy; its tariffs, taxes and land policies gave the entrepreneurial class and landowners a mighty financial boost along with the security they desperately craved. The race for ownership of land, control of natural resources and capture of commercial enterprises accelerated at the turn of the century when the Louisiana Territory was added to the new nation. At this time, when the supply of natural resources appeared limitless, the question for John Jacob Astor, the southern cotton growers, the land speculators and their minions of imitators lay only in who would be the first to reap the fortunes which were to come from the bountiful American land.

By 1840, the new roads, canals and railroads had opened up markets and the beginnings of regional specialization. The first flush of affluence settled on a people who bought and sold their resources at a profit, especially in the South. Because of the genius of Eli Whitney, cotton was raised and sold to burgeoning New England textile mills and around the world with such great returns that growers expanded into every region of the South and Southwest, including Indian lands. The Northern cities needed food, which was supplied by a new wave of farmers west of the Appalachians. By the time of the Civil War, American agriculture had a technology which could increase its productivity a hundredfold, and American mining had transformed itself from an insignificant avocation to a major industry.

With increased industrialization after the Civil War, resource demand reached increasingly greater heights as new methods in the manufacture of iron and steel led to a frantic search for additional supplies of ore. The Union government initiated the process by its purchase of arms, food and clothing during the war with unprecedented printings of millions of "greenback" dollars. The railroad also played a crucial role in the new phase of resource exploitation because it enabled men like Rockefeller and Carnegie to integrate their production, processing and marketing. In 1890, about 170,000 miles of railroads connected agricultural regions with large, expanding cities and ports to take their crops to Europe; they also joined iron and copper (for electricity) mining areas of Lake Superior and the West with blast furnaces, coal fields and markets of the East. Coal heated most homes and buildings and generated the steam power for locomotives and factories. Its coke and the revolutionary Bessemer process created tough steel for high-rise buildings and bridges. But while steel flourished, agriculture began to languish from overproduction, over capitalization and railroad domination. Foreign markets were sought to solve the farmers' problems, and America began to flex its military muscle to protect those markets.

At the turn of the century, the big corporations centered their operations close to their financial and banking operations in New York, where they coordinated markets with production through telephone, telegraph and the railroad. Electricity and the efficiency of the new corporations were the marvels of the decade so that capitalists with huge financial resources began to buy out the hundreds of little firms through holding companies in order to "rationalize and stabilize" the economic life of the country. The flow of capital investment into profitable enterprise intensified. The age of monopoly had begun. And the growing cities were beginning to choke on their own congestion, smoke, and sewage. Typhoid, dysentery, and cholera epidemics were common.

Meanwhile the conservation movement had grown from a small group of scientists, naturalists and transcendentalists to a powerful force in government, especially under Theodore Roosevelt. Much to the chagrin of western sectionalists and big logging firms, millions of acres of timber had been set aside as national forests and parks. When the time came to decide how these forests were to be used, clashes within the conservation movement led to its ideological split into "utilizers" and "preservers."

After World War I, the internal combustion engine dominated economic and social life. Roads, suburbs and booming oil, steel, and auto industries characterized the roaring twenties, and a new affluence was spread across the land. Even thousands of tractors were sold in the decade, though agriculture was suffering another round of overproduction and low prices.

The bottom fell out of the whole economy during the Great Depression. Roosevelt and his Brain Trust tried but could scarcely get the nation's economic engine going again. Only World War II could accomplish that feat, aided and abetted later by American expansionist imperialism. Continued economic expansion and material wealth meant an equal amount of exponential environmental degradation.

The economy continued to soar after the war, and some of the benefits of wealth filtered down to the working classes. The new widespread abundance was built on the productivity of agriculture, cheap raw materials, and energy for a nation geared to industrial growth. By the 1950s, many of the natural-resource industries, especially oil and steel, were monopolized. Agribusinesses had much earlier been able to set up processing and marketing organizations between the farmer and the consumer, setting the stage for the monopolization of several basic foods. After the war, exponential growth of energy consumption in every industry, especially the new synthetics, led to increased air and water pollution and environmental degradation. The automobile culture added the exclamation point to the era's environmental pollution. At the end of the sixties a new wave of environmental concern awakened the country again. While early conservationists attempted to effect policies of "wise use" or preservation, latter-day environmentalists have tried to protect the quality of man-made or natural environments from the many sources of pollution.

The war in Vietnam made economic matters worse as the supply of resources and dollars backed by gold began to wane. After the oil-producing nations of the Middle East cut off their contribution to the country's oil supplies, an energy crisis was contrived, and subsequent skyrocketing prices for petroleum-based products brought home the realization that natural resources could no longer be taken for granted. By this time, agricultural machinery and fertilizers as well as a myriad of industries from steel to synthetics depended on the steady flow of petroleum; a dispersed business and labor force also depended on automobiles and trucks to get to work or to carry on its daily business. Industrialization, spurred by military demands and new consumer-product industries, as well as pollution from automobiles and urbanization, brought widespread negative reactions from a people beginning to suffer from its own abundance.

So, the American nation passed from a near-subsistence, localized use of natural resources to a highly integrated, national and international specialized economy. The basic fact is not so interesting as the way in which the present situation was reached: How did it happen that a powerless federal government came to control so many of the natural resources of the country? How were seemingly insuperable obstacles of geography and technology overcome to tie the nation's resource networks together? How did a few corporations manage to control resources so widely scattered and abundant, such as oil and iron? Why did the technology that had served the country so well for so long begin to devour the people who created its apparatus? In other words, how did the nation arrive in the semi-sorry environmental state that now pervades it?

The major themes of this book are not difficult to isolate. First, I suggest that the economic rationality of American democracy has tended to lead to economic concentration, a waste of natural resources, and environmental degradation (also an inequitable distribution of wealth, but this subject is scarcely touched upon). Second, business imperatives, rather than environmental or social concerns, and technological developments have increased the exploitation and processing of natural resources. Third, at the same time, the nation has become increasingly tied together through cheap transportation and regional specialization of resource extraction or processing. Fourth, American political policy and legal institutions have generally supported the logic of private enterprise development, promoting and defending individual private property rights over social and environmental concerns, eschewing control of private lands even for purposes of conservation; and also providing abundant government assistance for the profitable purposes of agriculture, lumber, oil, and mining interests. The government has increasingly underwritten the needs of the larger companies representing the more "rationalized," efficient sectors of their respective industries.

Nonetheless, sharp criticism of both the economic rationality and the corresponding political policy has surfaced in every age of American social life. This theme is also a small but important aspect of the book. Very often voices of conservation have been muffled in the roar of industrial progress, or have been so rare as to be insignificant forces; sometimes the entire conservation movement has been coopted and defanged by corporate interests. But the critical voices and collective environmental protest have returned, just as the great social movements continually come back after seemingly irreparable setbacks.

The modern environmental movement, begun after World War II, gradually accelerated for a generation until the 1970s; its momentum created a wave of federal environmental legislation. Just as the movement's political power seemed to wane, the effects of 100 years of industrial toxic waste dumping were made painfully obvious to Americans. Chemicals suspected of causing cancer and other diseases had seeped into underground drinking water supplies and were causing serious environmental health problems. This national scare gave new impetus to the environmental movement and, importantly, to the general environmental consciousness of the American people.

When I began research for this book in 1972, the modern environmental movement was struggling, and few believed it could match the power and financial strength of its traditional adversaries. Although the final outcome of the struggle between overexploitation and conservation is uncertain, the odds have evened over the years. I hope this thought offers comfort to those struggling for a better environment.

Part One

THE
COLONIAL PERIOD

Chronology of Major Events

1607	Jamestown settled by the London Company.
1609	Jamestown settlers learn corn cultivation from Indians.
1612	First successful Virginia tobacco crop.
1619	First export of Virginia tobacco to England. Headright system introduced in Virginia. First black slaves imported into Virginia.
1620	Pilgrims land at Plymouth.
1623	Plymouth colonists learn corn cultivation from Indian, Squanto.
1624	New Netherland settled by the Dutch.
1626	Wheat successfully cultivated in New Netherland. First flour mill in colonies at New Netherland.
1629	Patroon system of large landholdings established in New Netherland.
1630	Settlement of Massachusetts Bay begun.
1634	Maryland settled.
1635	Connecticut River Valley settled.
1643	First colonial woolen mill founded at Rowley, Mass. First important iron works set up at Lynn, Mass.
1644	First Boston ship built.
1650	Fifty-one tanneries in Massachusetts Bay Colony.
1651	Navigation Act passed by Parliament. (Four more passed in 1660, 1663, 1673, 1696.)
1653	North Carolina settled.
1660	Estimated colonial population: 84,800.
1664	New Netherland seized by the English.
1670	Charleston, S.C., founded.
1670-1690	Sharp growth in Virginia aristocracy.
1682	Pennsylvania founded by William Penn. In the 1680s Penn introduced the practice of selling land in the colonies.
1691	Broad arrow policy of the Crown reserves trees for ship masts in Massachusetts.
1695	Rice introduced in the Carolinas.
1696	Colonial merchants' triangular trade established between West Africa and West Indies.
1699	Woolens Act forbids export of raw or manufactured wool.
1700	Fifteen hundred tons of iron produced in the Colonies. Frontier extends beyond the Fall Line to the crest of the Appalachians.
1708	First Germans settle in Pennsylvania.
1709	Englishman Abraham Darby smelts iron with coke.
1717-1730	Heavy migration of Scotch-Irish, who introduce potato at Londonderry, N.H.
1720	Lead mines opened in Missouri.
1725	Estimated colonial slave population: 75,000.

1730	Estimated colonial population: 654,950. Furs and skins sold in South Carolina: 255,000.
1733	Molasses Act passed by Parliament.
1742	Indigo domesticated by Eliza Lucas. Sugar cane introduced into Louisiana by Jesuit priests.
1743	American Philosophical Society organized to promote scientific agriculture.
1750	Iron Act prohibits production of finished ironware. Ten thousand tons of iron produced in colonies (one-seventh of world production).
1756-1763	French and Indian War.
1763	Treaty of Paris cedes the French territories in Canada, the West and the Spanish Floridas to England. Estimated colonial population: 1,650,000.
1764	Largest colonial iron works set up in northern New Jersey. Sugar Act passed by Parliament.
1767	Sea Island cotton grown in Georgia and South Carolina. Townshend Acts passed by Parliament.
1769	Englishman James Watt patents his steam engine.
1776	American Declaration of Independence and Revolution. Spanish found missions and presidios in California.

Chapter 1

THE LAND AND
ITS IMPERIAL SUITORS

*T*he history of natural resources in the United States has largely been determined by the demands of human institutions, e.g., as will be seen later in
this chapter, the explorers' search for gold or other tradable commodities.
But the American land itself has undergone a long and eventful history. Pushed and
pulled by wind and water, shifting under powerful intra-terrestrial tectonic forces,
oxidized, hydrated, its surface has been transformed from naked mineral rock to
richly forested land with help from microbes and primitive vegetation. Ice also entered
into the picture. The last Continental glacier stopped its advance where northern
Pennsylvania now stands, down in a sweeping arc to the present St. Louis area,
up again to northern Montana and along the northern border of the country.

What remained of the melted glacier's rocks and river beds left more than a passing
mark on later ages. The Great Lakes' immense ponds trapped between high land and
the receding glacier became important water routes. Nantucket, the home port of a
flourishing whaling industry, Cape Cod, and Long Island were built up from the gravel
of retreating ice. Immense glaciers dropped rocks and pushed soil, trees, and plants
to dramatically different climates and created the possibilities of new geographies and
ecological relationships. In some places like the areas near Pyramid Lake, Nevada, or
the Great Salt Lake of Utah the climate changed dramatically over centuries, and lakes
have subsequently evaporated into deserts.

Geography

First it is important to describe, at least superficially, this land that greeted its sixteenth
and seventeenth century suitors, and which its eighteenth and nineteenth century
settlers sought to conquer. The continent stretches three thousand miles from Atlantic
to Pacific and twelve hundred miles from the Gulf of Mexico to the Canadian border.
The contemporary United States embraces about 2.3 billion acres. Two mountain
ranges, an ancient cordillera in the east reaching from Maine to Georgia and Alabama
and a high, rugged blanket spreading over most of the West, enclose the Great Plains
and Central Prairie lowlands from the Rockies to the Appalachians.

In the East a coastal plain borders the Atlantic and reaches inland through three
main arteries to the plateaus beyond the Appalachians: in the North down the St.
Lawrence Valley to the Great Lakes; up the Hudson River Valley and over the Mohawk
Valley to Lake Ontario; or south around the foot of the range in southern Georgia.
The Appalachians reach around 6,000 feet above sea level and offer no significant

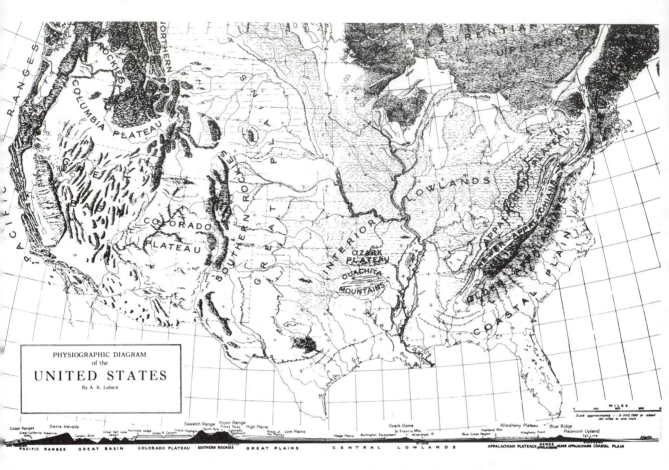

PHYSIOGRAPHIC DIAGRAM
of the
UNITED STATES
By A. K. Lobeck

obstacles to the weather systems coming from the Atlantic Ocean. The temperature is moderate in the East, and abundant rainfall is spread throughout the year.

In the West, on the other hand, parallel strips of towering mountains effectively shield inland regions from the moisture of the Pacific. The two ranges—the Coast range and the Cascades joining the Sierra Nevada—are connected in southern Oregon and northern California by the Klamath Mountains. Between the two mountain chains lie the Willamette Valley in the Northwest and California's fertile Central Valley. A high and arid plateau region, from 4,000 to 6,000 feet above sea level, lies east of these ranges; the Columbia in the North, the Great Basin around Great Salt Lake, and the Colorado plateau are the largest of these areas. Beyond the Continental Divide in the Rockies little moisture from westerly oceanic air penetrates. Neither is there low and easy access through the high mountain ranges of the far West.

Just east of the Rockies, the Great Plains begin their sweep eastwards. At about the hundredth meridian, precipitation increases, changing the physical geography and agricultural potential as well. The region east of the hundredth meridian is geographically distinguishable from the Great Plains and known as the Central Lowlands. Since temperature drops about 1.6°C per thousand feet of elevation, the entire central plains

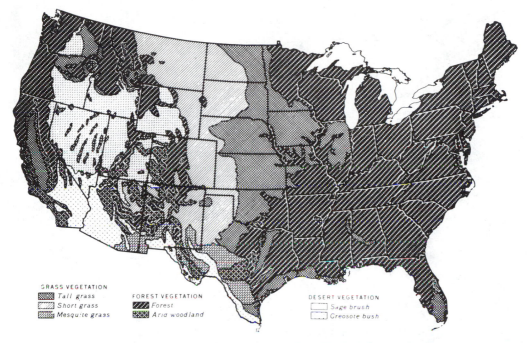

Figure 1–1. Native vegetation of continental United States. Forests and other vegetation depend on the entire ecological system of its region: soil materials and texture, amount of precipitation, climate and other geographical factors.

region, elevated no more than a thousand feet, should not be inclined toward cold weather. However, no mountain range impedes cold polar air from the north, nor is there any impediment to warm moisture coming from the Gulf in the south. The intermingling of the two weather systems often creates swift and dramatic climatic changes.

Vegetation and Wildlife

Such diversity of climates on the American landscape assures the land of a rich variety of natural vegetation and animal life. Originally America's virgin forests covered almost half of the country's surface, extending inland from both oceans. In the East the land was overlaid with mixed broadleafed (deciduous) and pine (coniferous) forests virtually all the way to the prairies. In the West the coniferous forests on the western rainy slopes of the mountain ranges were broken by drier intermontane plateaus. Huge sequoia, redwood, Douglas fir and Sitka spruce in the West dwarfed many of the eastern varieties—maple, oak, hickory, sycamore, cherry, ash, chestnut, black walnut, tulip poplar, white pine, elm. Western giants were from sixty to one hundred feet around above the trunk swell, but even the eastern trees grew to enormous proportions: Ohio's white oaks could get to be twenty feet around, and the largest deciduous tree in the Americas, the giant sycamore, often doubled the size of the

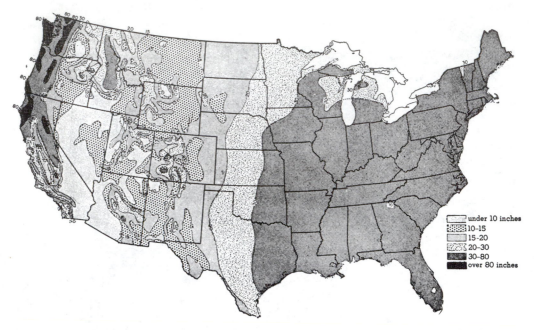

Figure 1–2. Average precipitation of continental United States. Rainfall at different seasons and in different sections of the country determines agricultural production and even more fundamentally—along with climate, parent materials, and geographical factors—the quality of the soil itself.

white oaks; it was found in the eastern climax forest. In all, dozens of species of huge native trees astounded the earliest explorers and European immigrants.

Between the forests were grasslands, long and luxuriant east of the hundredth meridian, short and sturdy in the Great Plains. Thousands of species of wild flowers dotted the plains with color in the spring during those primeval days. In the arid West and Southwest, sagebrush cactus and bunch perennial grasses held the soil in place for their own exotic wild flowers each spring.

Great herds of buffalo—probably 60,000,000 of them before the Europeans arrived—not only roamed the plains but even cut wide trails into eastern forests, over which later settlers could find their way west. Deer, elk, moose, bear and hundreds of smaller species lived in the forests. Antelope shared the plains with the buffalo. Tens of thousands of beaver populated thousands of streams from east to west. In the high regions, goats and mountain sheep grazed. The marshes swarmed with wild turkey, duck, swan, grouse and crane, and in the air millions of wild geese and passenger pigeons carved flyways out of the sky. The streams and rivers of the land were brimming with myriads of fish—salmon climbing western coastal rivers to spawning nests, shad in the East, and bountiful crops of shellfish off coastal waters.

Soils and Water

The variety of trees, plants and animals, along with the more fundamental forces of heat, wind and water on rock, all had contributed to make qualitative gradations in the soil. Thousands of years of growth, death, and disintegration prepared a rich soil over most of the country, as different temperatures, moisture, drainage patterns, plants, chemicals, worms, and microorganisms in various sections broke down plant refuse into humus. When heat, moisture, and aeration are present in the correct balance, billions of microorganisms and many worms can live in a handful of pasty humus. Humus, along with mineral particles, determines soil structure. Because of countless possible variations of climate, minerals, decaying organic matter, and microorganisms, a great variety of soils can be found in what is now the United States.

Once again the hundredth meridian boundary offers an example of the difference the rain makes. West of it are the pedocal (lime-accumulating) soils, where less than 20 inches of rain per year falls. On the eastern side, rainfall exceeding 20 inches is indirectly responsibile for the pedalfer (non-lime-accumulating) soils. Particularly in the East, more decomposition and fermentation of the leaf-litter cover takes place, with increasing rainfall and warmer temperature tending to carry minerals into the earth and leaving the topsoil more acid. Without the decomposition and fermentation encouraged by rain, the soils tend to be alkaline, richer in minerals. The neutral prairie soils, developed under tall grass vegetation, offer the best possibilities for farmland. Deep grass roots die and rot, forming an excellent humus with thousands of years worth of overlaid tall grass stalks. Grasses also strengthen the soil by retaining clay crystals and organic nutrients, while they open up "pores" for infiltration of rain water.

Each region of the United States is characterized by its own type or types of soils. The pedalfer soils that developed under forest cover in the East, called podzols, vary in their fertility. The gray-brown podzolic soils of the northern Appalachian broadleafed forests encourage fair productivity. Cold temperatures limit fast decomposition and fermentation of organic material, leaving a small supply of minerals in the ground. The warm temperatures, heavy rainfall and high humidity of the South cause faster leaching of minerals from the leaf litter to form acid red-yellow podzolic soils. Throughout the East, the soils generally lack free lime (calcium carbonate) because of climatic conditions. In the Northwest, volcanic lava flows have enriched the ground, but the climates of mountain areas have not permitted a dense and mature soil structure (and vegetation cover) to develop in higher regions.

A final and all-important resource of the land is its watershed system. The great Mississippi Basin drains more than half of America's land area, from the Appalachians to the Rockies. The eastern tributaries of the Mississippi—the Ohio, the Wabash, the Cumberland, the Tennessee—are fed by shorter, faster streams and rivers in the eastern hills and mountains. Out of the West into the Mississippi come the Missouri, the Platte, the Arkansas, and the Red River. These rivers and their sources create an immense, swelling outflow into the Gulf of Mexico.

The largest, but certainly not the only, great watershed of the country is that of the Mississippi. The St. Lawrence drains the Great Lakes. In the Southwest, the Rio Grande separates two countries, and the Colorado passes through seven states and Mexico on the way to the Gulf of California. In the Northwest, the Columbia collects waters from the Cascades, as do the Sacramento and the San Joaquin from California's Sierras; all three rivers connect inland valleys with the Pacific. At least eight vast Continental artesian basins store water which has soaked through the first layers of the earth to bedrock. These waters, along with the land's marshes, ponds and lakes, constitute the reservoir of Continental America. Life ultimately depends upon their maintenance.

Native Americans

The land and its rivers probably supported about 10,000,000 Native Americans north of the Rio Grande when Europeans first set foot on its coasts. Most tribes lived in regions where game, fish, berries, fruits, and nuts provided a substantial diet for their people. Great Lakes Indians hunted, fished, and lived in houses. These and many other Indian tribes east of the hundredth meridian also grew corn, beans, squash, and sweet potatoes, depending on the climate and local diet. Yet even the Southwest Indians developed irrigation systems that supported agriculture in an arid climate.

But there were exceptions too. In the deserts of the Great Basin, for example, the land scarcely afforded enough to live on—only roots, insects, and rodents—but the Piutes developed a culture within these trying conditions. The Plains Indians, especially after they acquired horses from the Spaniards, thrived on buffalo meat. The cultures of Indian tribes from east to west were quite distinct from each other.

The grasslands of North America were greatly enlarged by Native Americans who burned forests for agricultural cultivation or for flushing animals in the hunt. On both eastern and western coasts, explorers and settlers found large grassland areas. The newcomers sometimes told of Indian fire-drives. It is probable that the Native Americans also fired those lands which settlers found as prairies—parts of such lands lying in what are now the states of Kentucky, Ohio, Indiana, Illinois, Michigan, Wisconsin, and Texas. (Some of these lands have once again become forested.)

Explorers of the New Land

To the sixteenth century Spanish and Portuguese explorers looking for a new trade route to the east, the American land was more of a bugaboo than anything of value. Actually, the earlier explorers were convinced that America *was* the Orient. They merely sailed the Continent's extensive coastline seeking suitable trading ventures. In the process, Spanish colonists exploited alternative sources of value, chiefly the labor of the natives who cultivated tropical crops and who were later enslaved to mine silver and gold. The West Indies were chosen as the first Spanish colonial base where tropical plantations could be developed. From there conquistadores spread into Central America and Mexico.

By the middle of the 1500s, Spain had secured bases not only in the West Indies, but also in Mexico, Central America and as far south as Peru. Outposts protected Spanish interests so that gold plundering and mining operations could be maintained. Traders no longer cherished tea and spices of the Far East as their chief commodities. Gold was the new prize; it attracted adventurers and gentlemen from every part of Spain. The boom towns which these men—Cortes, Guzman, Ibarra, Carbajal and scores more attracted by the gold and silver treasures in Aztec temples—set up in northern Aztec country soon stretched all the way to Peru. They provided Spain with an unmatchable source of wealth for a century and a half. To this day those towns—Zacatecas, Durango, Guanajuato, Monterrey, Mexico City—survive as thriving capitals of large Mexican states. Charles V and Philip II of Spain had few concerns about revenue.

They merely collected huge percentages from the traders, who dispatched armadas each year to Vera Cruz and Puerto Bello with a few scarce commodities and a new supply of settlers in return for gold, silver and tropical goods.

Spain's position of strength among the world powers began to slip toward the end of the 1500s because of its efforts to subjugate the people of the European Low Countries and also because of warfare with the English. Furthermore, the accumulated stocks of Indian gold and silver treasure were exhausted by this time, and the better-grade, easily accessible ores in their colonies began to decline. A century of luxury, however, drove Spain's adventurers to continue the search for precious metals. But their lucky stars were on the wane.

Spain was not alone in its desire to exploit the East for gold, silver, exotic spices or trading wares. Although France, England and the Netherlands established no permanent colonies in North America during the sixteenth century, all were striving mightily to break Spain's monopolistic hold on the Americas. At the beginning of the 1600s all three set up permanent colonies in North America and the Caribbean. But by this time Spain and Portugal had control of two-thirds of the hemisphere.

Furs and Trading

Samuel de Champlain established Quebec for France in 1608. His treasure was delivered to the mother country in the form of furs extracted from the plentiful wildlife of the St. Lawrence Valley. Traders soon colonized Acadia (New Brunswick and Nova Scotia) to act as a buffer region between their outposts and the New England colonies. Jesuit missionaries quickly were sent to convert the Native Americans, and together with the traders they prepared for the final exploration of the legendary Mississippi Valley. Until 1656, however, the Iroquois' adamant blockade served to contain the French advance.

Beginning about 1670, from their southern and northern military and trading bases, the French entered the Mississippi Valley. Explorers, tradesmen, fur men, and missionaries traveled the lakes, rivers and portages, pushed on by rumors of gold regions, or of unsurpassed beaver country and unparalleled profits, or of Indian settlements ready for conversion. Settlers in Louisiana worked their way to Illinois and all the way to the northern Red River. Mobile became Louisiana's capital, and its leaders called for increased French populations to meet competition from the Spanish in Florida and the English in South Carolina and Georgia. French trading posts were sprinkled along all the large waterways from the Gulf to as far as the Kansas River and around the Great Lakes. Some explorers trekked to the Rocky Mountains and Santa Fe. No gold enriched these hopeful adventurers, but businessmen cultivated the thriving fur trade and enriched themselves as they formed a growing entrepreneurial class.

Most sought-after were the beaver pelts which were taken for a seemingly insatiable European hat industry. Deerskins were also much in demand locally as well as for export. Other wildlife was hunted mainly to be eaten by the local inhabitants. Indians traded freely with the settlers—beaver, deer, otter and lynx in exchange for blankets, clothing and even European cooking ware, knives, axes, and iron arrowheads. Of course all the fur trading had a drastic impact on Indian life and culture. Many tribes became dependent upon regular supplies from the trading posts, and in return for substantially increased prices measured in terms of numbers of beaver pelts, the trading posts would grant loans and easy credit to their Indian customers. When the white man's musket became widely available in the colonies, and began to be traded to the Indians, it was easier for the Indians temporarily to meet their rising costs, but deer and beaver populations in hundreds of areas were decimated. Neither did the trading posts usually offer their Indian customers quality goods. The guns often misfired and the textiles, hardware, and liquor often had already been rejected by white settlers themselves quite accustomed to second class goods. Furthermore, once the Indians were dependent on the musket, they were in continual need of the gunpowder monopolized by the white traders.

The Dutch West India Company carried its country's flag to the Americas soon after the Netherlands shook off the yoke of Spain. In 1609 the Dutch began their gradual conquest of the Hudson River region, beginning with Manhattan Island and Albany, later proceeding to Connecticut, west up the Mohawk, and south to the Delaware River. The fur trade made colonization profitable for the Dutch traders as well as the French. An earlier Swedish settlement on the Delaware was absorbed in 1655 by the Dutch, who were in turn conquered in 1664 by the English.

Perhaps the most significant legacy from the Dutch was their innovative triangular trade arrangements in the early 1600s. Their traders shipped Dutch goods to the African gold coast, where they picked up slaves to trade for sugar and molasses in the West Indies. From the Caribbean they proceeded up the coast, trading some sugar and European goods for beaver pelts at New Amsterdam before returning home. The route proved exceedingly profitable for its backers, as much for reasons of navigation as of economics. To travel directly to the west meant heading straight into the Atlantic Westerly winds. It was almost as fast to travel south with the help of the Northeast Trade winds, then cross the South Atlantic and pick up the Gulf Stream north, returning home with the Westerlies pushing. And they made money on the entire route.

The English Colonies

English expansion took place comparatively late, mainly because during the sixteenth century her sea power and commerce were still in their take-off period. The fast-sailing Elizabethan sea dogs achieved some notoriety by plundering and smuggling during this era, and a few of them successfully employed themselves in the slave trade between Africa, Brazil and the Caribbean. The English reached their maturity as sea competitors of Spain under Francis Drake when they humiliated the Armada and mastered the Atlantic sea-ways at the end of the sixteenth century. By this time London merchants had amassed enough capital to cooperate in joint stock companies looking for new sources of trade and enterprise.

In 1606, merchants of the London and Plymouth stock companies received patents from the crown to settle "Virginia." The London, or South Virginia, Company was given permission to settle on an area located between what is now Washington, D.C., and New York City; the Plymouth, or North Virginia, Company to settle New England. But they were to keep their colonies at least 100 miles separated from each other. Within a hundred years over twenty English colonies and trading posts in America with about 200,000 colonists were spread from the Hudson Bay to Barbados and Guiana. For the English, however, the motivations included religious commitments (New England and Maryland) and political goals (supremacy over the Dutch in New Amsterdam) as well as commercial enterprises (Virginia, Maryland, Pennsylvania). Private ventures financed the English colonies, either as chartered trading companies or as proprietary grants to individuals.

In the Caribbean, England tried to make up for a lost century. Bermuda was founded from Jamestown. Guiana, Barbados, the Leeward Islands and Old Providence were colonized in the early part of the seventeenth century. The Bahama Islands were related to the Carolinas in their origins. Jamaica was taken from Spain, the Windward Island colonies from France.

The English raised sugar and tobacco on the plantations of the Caribbean colonies. Labor was supplied by enslaved blacks in increasing numbers as the century passed and the slave trade expanded. English buccaneers utilized British ports on their way to and from Spanish ships and colonies. The colonial ports in the Caribbean were also important to the British navy as strategic bases during perennial intercolonial wars.

On the mainland, cultivation of tobacco developed by John Rolfe from West Indian varieties saved the Virginia colony from extinction ten years after its establishment. Rice and indigo plantations dominated in the Carolinas and Georgia. Indentured servants, rather than black slaves, provided most of the work force of the southern mainland plantations in the 1600s. In the latter quarter of the century, when plantation sizes doubled and tripled and indentured servants could not supply the needed labor in sufficient numbers, slavery became institutionalized.

Massachusetts was the hub of New England activity, the earlier settlements of Maine, New Hampshire and Plymouth having been absorbed by it. New England economic vitality stemmed from fishing and fur trading. The Hudson Bay Company set up northern outposts on the James Bay and Hudson Bay in order to compete with the French for the fur trade of the St. Lawrence. Very soon they sent home 75% dividends to their London stockholders. The Indians preferred the wool blankets and steel knives of the English to those of the French. Beaver pelts and deerskins continued to be the major source of contention between the British and the French for a hundred years before the French and Indian Wars.

Land Disposal in the Colonies

Related to colonization was the problem of land distribution during these early colonial days. No uniform method predominated throughout the colonies, primarily because each settlement was established for its own unique purpose and was subject to unique geographic, political, social and economic limitations. It is true that all the colonies were expected to turn a profit for someone, or some company, but it is not true that the economic motive was always the primary or exclusive motive. The proprietors of New Jersey or the Carolinas wanted to sell land to or to collect yearly quitrents from their settlers, but in order to sell undeveloped land, they had to offer it at inexpensive prices. And in order to attract settlers, the quitrents had to be very low. Likewise, the companies made offers which were quite attractive to potential settlers of formidable wilderness areas. Colonies were competing with each other for settlers. The history of the early colonies abounds with examples of people who packed up and moved to a more hospitable, and less expensive, neighboring colony.

In New England, although the settlements were organized as corporations with patents from the British Crown and were expected to make money for the company, economic considerations were temporarily subordinated to a methodical occupation of the land. When a group of heads of families wanted to move from an older community, they would petition for or purchase a tract of land just beyond the older settlement. The size of the new tract could extend from four to ten square miles. Near the center of the land a village was laid out, complete with meeting-house, house lots and village green. The individual house lot included a garden and sometimes a small enclosure for feeding livestock. These lots could be as small as a quarter acre and as large as ten or twenty acres, depending on individual family needs and status.

The "uplands," large arable fields of several hundred acres each, were divided into long strips, in the manner of medieval tillage, and granted to individual families by "lots." The "allotments" were surrounded by a common fence, built and maintained collectively to keep out livestock and wildlife, and decisions regarding planting and harvesting were also made in common. After the harvest, cattle fed on the crop stubble and added manure to the soil of the field. Members of the settlement usually received an apportioned measure of meadowland and wood lots, also jointly managed. Settlers from religiously-oriented communities received lands of equal size; other communities determined allotments by size of individual investment and ability to use the land (e.g., number of members in the family, etc.).

Besides the uplands and meadows allotted to proprietary members of a community, other common fields—lands left over from the original purchase or grant—were made available to everyone who lived in the settlement. Townspeople could pasture their animals there and extract timber and stone for personal needs from the common fields. Latecomers and squatters often received strips of land from the commons. The overall result of the New England land system was a compact community with land distribution fairly equally proportioned among its inhabitants. Although some land concentration occurred among older inhabitants of the early townships through inheritance and purchase, land speculation was virtually unknown during the 1600s in New England. The compactness of New England towns did not begin to break down until the middle of the following century.

Proprietary Colonies

In proprietary colonies—lands granted to individual proprietors by the king—just the opposite kind of land settlement and distribution took place. Since the lands were received as private estates to be sold, leased or mortgaged, the proprietors were essentially land investors or speculators, with whom the final privileges of government rested. It remained only for them to decide how to attract settlers and collect revenues, even when lofty motives of religious toleration were involved.

New Jersey proprietors granted English freemen 150 acres, plus another 150 acres for each able-bodied servant, if they could muster for themselves six months of provisions, musket and ammunition and be on the land within a year of the first allotting of the land, 1669. Male servants were given seventy-five acres after the terms of their service expired. Later settlers received lesser amounts of land in New Jersey. A quitrent, i.e., a fixed annual tax, was to be paid to the lords' proprietors, a custom which carried more than symbolic vestiges of medieval practice. All the middle and southern colonies utilized the practice known as the headright system, of granting allotments of land to those who paid their own way or who paid to transport others to America for settlement in Pennsylvania, New Jersey, Maryland, Virginia, the Carolinas and Georgia.

William Penn not only adopted the headright system in Pennsylvania, but also had the opportunity to sell over 300,000 acres of land in lots of from 250 to 10,000 acres to wealthy English Quakers. Selling land in the colonies was a novel innovation in the 1680s when Penn introduced the practice, but within a generation it was widespread and proved to be the quickest route to land engrossment or monopolization. Penn also received quitrents. The quitrent system proved to be a less than satisfactory source of revenue to most proprietors. Very often quitrents were completely evaded; practically always payments were tardy; and quitrents were even the source of many violent uprisings and disorders in agrarian communities. Taxes always seem to have been unequally applied and just as commonly resented.

In contrast to the compact communities of New England, the proprietary system fostered an individualistic, random type of settlement in the middle colonies. Farms and plantations followed rivers and streams and neighbors were rarely interested in forming an intentional community. Only after a generation or two when a number of scattered farms had been cleared was a local government organized in order to provide for roads, protection, etc., where water transportation was lacking. The size of individual holdings in the middle colonies varied greatly, even in the same regions, but the normal allotment fell between 100 and 200 acres, somewhat larger than New England holdings. After 1700 when land began to be bought and sold more commonly, much wider discrepancies of land-holdings became visible. Local government attempted to curb these tendencies in early New England, but no such community government existed in the middle colonies.

In New York some very large early estates—holdovers from the Dutch Patroon colonies—of up to 840 square miles were scattered up the Hudson. The patroonships of New Netherland were legally recognized by the English governors, and the number of thousand- to two-thousand acre estates in New York was a visible reminder of the old colonies.

Virginia

In Virginia, the headright system was functioning as the usual method of receiving land by 1625 when the Virginia (London) Company reluctantly relinquished its charter to the Crown. At this time the average size estate for most settlers was about 100 to 200 acres per family, except for a few families which owned 1,000 to 2,000 acres each and one family which had an estate of 800,000 acres. For the rest of the century the average size grew slowly. Many questionable claims were honored during this period: planters claiming the same new settlers; outright forgery with sea-captain's complicity, etc. However, land was not sold in Virginia until the beginning of the 1700s, and then it was done over the veto of the Crown.

It is possible that the headright system in Virginia had almost as much to do with the beginnings of large holdings and plantations as geographic and climatic factors of the region. Since more land was granted to planters who transported indentured servants to the New Land, and more land with cheap labor led to greater profits, the practice grew in popularity there.

Ship captains looked for every opportunity to carry indentured servants to the colonies. The cargoes of manufactured goods from England took much less space than bulky loads of sugar, molasses and tobacco on the return trip from the colonies. Extra passengers brought lucrative profits from labor-hungry planters. Thus captains or their agents scanned taverns and fairs, debtor's prisons or homes of the down-and-outers for potential indentures. They bally-hooed and shanghaied men, women and children alike; neither were they adverse to bribing judges for the privilege of "rehabilitating" offenders.

However, the headright system also provided that land be given to the servant after his period of servitude. This pressured the plantation owner to obtain new workers when the indenture period was completed. This difficulty was resolved as the institution of slavery was incorporated into the mainland's social and economic life at the end of the century. By that time the majority of Virginia's 100,000 population was composed of freed indentured servants.

Land concentrations were inevitable after land sales in Virginia superseded the headright system in the beginning decades of the eighteenth century. Those who had the means to pay developed huge plantations.

Virginia—and the proprietary colonies in general—did not dispose of the land in rectangular shapes as was the case in New England townships. Rather, the bounds were determined by natural objects, such as hills, trees, and streams. From a geographical point of view, the southern system was often preferable, but the fall of a tree or the change of a stream bed could lead to endless litigation. Because of the dispersal of planters over the countryside, the county system of government prevailed in the South and also in other proprietary colonies, rather than the New England township type of government.

New England Colonies

Government and land patterns of the Puritan settlements of New England reflected their Calvinist theology, which emphasized congregational participation in church affairs. Compact community settlement was necessary for church governance even though it meant that Puritans had to walk considerable distances to and from their widely scattered land holdings. New England town government usually forbade its residents to sell land to outsiders without the prior permission of the community, and even attempted to forestall any family from garnering a large amount of property. These rules were forgotten, however, by the mid-1700s when non-Calvinist ideals prevailed.

Survival in the Colonies

Basic necessities of life appeared to be the same in all of the colonies, north and south. Settlers depended first of all on natural food resources to survive: indigenous plants, wild animals, fish, wild geese and ducks, many varieties of berry bushes, even wild cherries, grapes and crab apples. They ate wild game and fish with gladness. Most of all it was Indian helpfulness which carried the first settlers through their initial decades on the land. Indians taught the neophytes to hunt, gather, fish; to plant maize, pumpkins, sweet potatoes, beans, and squash; and to fertilize with fish or seaweed.

Settlers on the coast found much of the land already cleared by the Indians, who fired the land sometimes to grow corn, sometimes to drive out wild game in order to facilitate the hunt. Although fewer than 250,000 Indians lived along the Atlantic coast from the St. Lawrence to Florida, they exercised a potent impact on the land, mainly because of their land-clearing practices. Whenever the soils appeared to be exhausted and yielded fewer crops, the Indians moved inland, cleared more land, and allowed old cultivated land to restore itself. The move inland had the additional advantage of opening up new supplies of wild fruits, berries, and game.

One of the most formidable stumbling-blocks for the early settlers was the thick, inland forest. Trees either had to be cut down, burned, or used for building and fencing; or girdled by deep cutting in a circle around the bottom of the tree. The former was the more useful practice, but it took more time and labor than the colonists had to spare. Girdling, or "deadening," was an Indian practice that well served its function. Dead leaves fell from the girdled tree, contributing minerals to the topsoil. Smaller trees and underbrush were burned around it, adding more nutrients, and the summer sun was able to shine unhindered on the newly planted corn. Trees were also girdled in areas which were to be opened for livestock grazing.

Although Indians used fire to drive game out of the forest, the purposes of clearing the forests by this device were not limited to hunting. Broadcast burning of forests also prepared land for cultivation by reducing brush, weeds, and potential pests; it also provided ash nutrients to the Indian crops of maize (corn), squash, and beans. The Indians also noticed that some types of wild game, desirable for eating, increased their populations in open fields, as did the yields of wild berries and seeds.

Besides following Indian agriculture, settlers soon began to plant some European grains: wheat, rye, barley, and oats. They also planted peas. A major problem after plantings was the protection of seedlings from wild game and domestic livestock. Building fences was a difficult task for the individual farmer of the middle and southern colonies, but one efficiently accomplished by New Englanders in common fields and by collective effort.

The first colonists tilled their fields with the crudest of tools. The small oxen, which were left to fend for themselves in the wild when they were not working, and which therefore were often undernourished, weak, and almost frail, could barely draw the heavy wooden plows, hardly distinguishable from their medieval counterparts. Farmers seeded by hand, reaped with sickles and scythes, and threshed with wood flails, much as in biblical times. Farm families worked hard for every pound of wheat, rye, corn, or barley, all critically important to the colonists' diet. Because of the enormous amount of energy demanded of them, typical English farmers each were used to about 6,000 calories a day. A diet of wild game, fowl, fish and berries simply did not supply enough energy for them.

According to archeologist-ethnogastronomists James Deetz and Jay Anderson, English settlers strove to acquire their prodigious calorie needs by consuming "a normal daily diet of one pound of meal or peas cooked up in a porridge, pudding, or bread, over half a pound of butter and cheese, and a full gallon of strong, dark ale."

Types of Resource Exploitation

Even in the earliest stages of European settlement of the land, it bore the imprint of a variety of physical and cultural forces. Indians had already opened up many of the forests through burning. The Spanish plundered and mined gold and silver. Europeans began their long siege on North American wildlife. Rival nations struggled over territory, which was meted out or sold as colonies, plantations, lots, squares, or strips. Immigrants settled on it and began their battle with the forest and climate, with the quickly-depleted, often-rocky soils or malarial insects, sometimes with Indians, and eventually with American or English merchants.

Broadcast burning created problems when it was not done with care, as Eugene Hilgard pointed out in his 1860 *Report,* which showed the difference between Indian and American burning. Careless burning, such as that done by settlers after quick profits, left land exposed to destructive winds and rains. When the settlers moved on to clear and cultivate another stretch of land, the old land lost its topsoil through erosion.

Something like the burning wastage occurred where mining was done. Immense quantities of wood were required to smelt minerals. For example, around an old mining region in Zacatecas, Mexico, where large areas of oak, pine, and mesquite once stood, only sparse vegetation now remains. Incidentally, but no less destructively, the domestic animals used for hard work in the mines were kept fairly close to the mines. They grazed and foraged, stripping away grasses and underbrush, and leaving the land bare to the elements, which promptly began to erode the land.

Thus natural-resource use and misuse were tied in with climatic, economic, political, social, and religious factors even in the first century of European settlement in America. As the years passed, these factors became stronger determinants of resource use. One task we take up in the following pages lies in unravelling the strands of physical and cultural exploitation and conservation.

References for Further Reading

Most books on the geography or physiography of North America, e.g., J. H. Paterson's *North America* (1960), supply important data on the "given" physical resources of the continent. W. D. Thornbury's *Principles of Geomorphology* (1969) shows the development of American landforms, along with the influences of climate, vegetation, etc. Many books on the political history of the United States touch on the explorers of the country as well. C. P. Nettels covers the explorations topically in his *The Roots of American Civilization* (1938). The most comprehensive and readable study on the beginnings of land disposal in the country is Marshall Harris' *Origin of the Land Tenure System in the United States* (1953). A book which brings together most of the above themes is Ralph H. Brown's *Historical Geography of the United States* (1948). A superb insight into seventeenth-century subsistence farming is given in *Husbandmen of Plymouth: Farms and Villages in the Old Colony, 1620-1692* by Darret B. Rutman (1967). The well-known collection of essays in *Man's Role in Changing the Face of the Earth*, edited by William L. Thomas (1956), contains good material on North America, particularly on the themes by Carl O. Sauer. For a discussion about the relationship of Indians to the natural environment, see *American Indian Environments, Ecological Issues in Native American History*, edited by Christopher Vecsey and Robert W. Venables (1980). Good original sources for this chapter include William Bradford's *Journal of Plymouth Plantation* and Jonathan Edwards' *Personal Narrative*, on the initial Puritan reaction to the American environment as a hostile environment; as well as the poems of the first American poet, Ann Bradstreet, especially "Contemplations," which views nature as God's creation.

Chapter 2

MERCANTILISM
AND COLONIAL RESOURCES

*I*n their pursuit of profit and power, the great European nations, from the sixteenth to the eighteenth centuries, placed their faith in the economic religion of the time, mercantilism—at once a way of life and a self-fulfilling prophecy. They believed that only a given amount of wealth existed in the world and that one nation could increase its share of the pie of wealth only by slicing it out of another's share.

In one sense, of course, this might be true. There are fixed amounts of the world's basic non-renewable resources—oil, coal, gas, gold, silver. When these are depleted or monopolized, nations that lack them or substitutes of equal utility will suffer. But mercantilist theorists, particularly the British, were not referring to non-renewable sources of wealth. They had in mind commercial or industrial wealth, i.e. processed natural resources, which they sought to protect with tariffs and which they strove to market abroad in order to achieve a favorable balance of trade.

Mercantilism

Mercantilism was essentially a happy union between merchant and nationalist. The two considered their interests to be identical. Mercantilist theorists like Charles Dovenant, Sir Thomas Mun, Sir Josiah Child or Sir William Petty (even the thought of John Locke was influenced by the mercantilists) wanted above all to garner as much bullion or specie—gold and silver used as money—as possible for their country. Mercantilists claimed that it didn't matter who owned the bullion of the country so long as it was *in* the country; in fact, however, royalty and bourgeoisie squabbled over the precious metals. National power was considered to be synonymous with specie, necessary to build strong armies and navies which protected the national power. This was an argument kings used on their merchants when they were about to raise taxes.

Thus either a country needed mines of gold and silver, as Spain enjoyed, or lacking these, needed at least the equivalent in industrial wealth, which could be used to trade favorably for specie. (Or a country could plunder vessels carrying precious metals, a practice not officially preached but unofficially fostered by a few English mercantilists.)

The reason industrial wealth was favored over agriculture or other raw materials was simply that more profit could be realized from it, and thereby a more certain likelihood of a favorable balance of trade. Colonies were important because they provided industrial raw materials for the mother country to process and sell back to the colonies or abroad at a handsome profit. With the surplus specie derived from advantageous trading, stronger armies and navies could be outfitted to penetrate more remote regions for further colonization. A strong military could also be used to preserve home government.

The mercantilist prophecy was self-fulfilling because colonial adventurers usually bumped into those of other nations pursuing the same course and sea lanes, especially if both parties believed in the same economic values. In the frantic effort to monopolize the sources of a so-called limited supply of wealth, wars were inevitable and much bullion was needed to pay for them.

The English merchant classes liked the idea of accumulating bullion, but they could not have accomplished the mercantilist program without complete governmental cooperation. Over a period of several generations the English crown and Parliament assumed pervasive control of the economy. They worked to create a self-sufficient empire by colonizing, stimulating domestic production, granting bounties for needed raw materials, imposing high duties on foreign manufactures, granting monopolies to trading companies, regulating the wages of domestic workers, and at the same time enforcing thrifty living (they didn't want to consume their potential exports at home), and in general building the foundations of the Industrial Revolution. Later the merchants felt the weight of so many governmental rules and wanted to be left alone, but they needed a strong alliance with government prior to the 1880s.

England codified many of her mercantilist restrictions and laws in the Navigation Acts during the mid-1600s and supplemented these laws with others during the next hundred years. In general they required:

1. That all trade between England and her colonies be carried in English or colonial ships with crews three-fourths English or colonial

2. That the colonies receive their imports, with negligible exceptions, from England, forcing colonial ships trading with other European nations to pass through English ports to pay duties on their way back to their home ports in the colonies

3. That the colonies trade certain "enumerated" articles (first tobacco, then dozens more added gradually) only with England.

This was the mercantilist design for the American colonies. The arrangement was beneficial to the colonists in the beginning, since they needed military and naval protection as well as financial support and other material assistance. As England became more demanding in her mercantilist policies, more damage was inflicted on the economic independence of the colonies. Gradually smuggling became another semi-respectable business which grew as long as the mother country was preoccupied with internal conflicts or imperialist struggles. These lasted until the end of the French and Indian War in 1763.

Southern Agriculture: Tobacco

In the American South, the mercantilist system seemed to work well for both colonial planters and English merchants, who provided easy credit for goods and capital loans to develop plantations. Given their status as enumerated goods, tobacco and later rice and indigo were permitted to be shipped only to England; the mother country could in turn trans-ship these highly prized goods to the Continent for specie. The southern colonies possessed all the qualities that made colonization desirable. Their goods were easy to transport, were not perishable, and didn't compete with those of England. Even after the soil along the coast was exhausted and coastal ports were in the control of colonial merchants or competitive middlemen, the wide estuaries of Maryland and Virginia enabled the English merchants to take their vessels directly to plantation wharves miles inland.

The South eclipsed all other colonial areas in economic value during the colonial period. In the beginning of settlement in the South, conditions for farming were primitive, but tobacco needed only a long growing season, fertile soil, and long, long hours of care. The land did not have to be completely cleared, nor were expensive farm implements necessary. The Continental demand for tobacco was already high.

The English were smoking Spanish tobacco long before settlers arrived on the Virginia coast. The Stuart King James I deplored its use in *A Counterblaste to Tobacco*, claiming that its smell was enough proof of its poisonous, "vile and stinking" character. Others praised its medicinal and sociable qualities. Mercantilists fought against its use on economic grounds, pointing out that the amenities of English gentlefolk were costing the country huge trade deficits to Spain.

The Virginia colony eventually quieted the debate by presenting its own answer to the bullion-draining Spanish import. There were two major varieties of tobacco in the Americas: the kind that the North American Indians grew and were smoking at the time of the first settlers' arrival, *Nicotiana rustica*, a coarse, rough tobacco which was tried and rejected very soon by white experimenters; and a milder variety, *Nicotiana tabacum*, which John Rolfe, husband of Pocahantas, discovered on a British Caribbean island and cultivated in Virginia as a cash crop. By the end of the century this precious weed spread from the James River and Chesapeake Bay north and west along virtually every river valley—the York, the Rappahannock, the Potomac—into Maryland, and south into the Carolinas. First the heavy-leafed *Orinoco* was grown on the fertile bottom lands of the colonies; much of it was exported from England to German and French customers. Then a finer, sweeter strain with a smaller leaf which grew well only on sandy soils was developed for those who preferred a faster-burning, sweeter tobacco. Hundreds more have been tried since those early days of experimentation, few standing the test of changing tastes.

Tobacco production was a long and arduous process. Tobacco seedlings need protection from the burning rays of the sun; therefore tobacco seeds were sown in January under the shade of forest sections of the plantation. In early May thousands of young plants were taken to the fields and re-planted on specially prepared hills. While they grew toward maturity, tobacco plants were given meticulous care—weeding, inspections for the dreaded hornworm, cultivating, pruning and topping (pinching off by hand the top of the plant to eliminate flowering or small leaves and to encourage the growth of full bodied tobacco). Finally, on a dry day, mature stalks of eight to twelve leaves could be cut. Leaves wilted on the stalks, which were threaded and hung in tobacco barns to be cured. In the beginning of tobacco cultivation it took months to complete the curing process, during which time the humidity and temperature of the barns were regulated by opening and shutting the windows; later the process was speeded up in small windowless mud and log barns, outside of which fires were kindled in stoves. Heat was then sent into the structures through pipes or flues. After stripping the leaves from the stalks, planters sorted leaves for quality. Finally the tobacco was packed in casks called hogsheads and stored in a warehouse near the docks. If the farmer's fields happened to be located far from the wharf or port, the heavy hogsheads had to be rolled by hand to shipping facilities. A special hook-up was later designed to enable oxen and horses to pull the hogsheads. In the meantime the soil had to be prepared for the next crop. Virgin soil would yield about 1,000 pounds of tobacco per acre, and a man needed helpers or slaves if he wished to plant more than three acres.

Labor on the Plantation

Indentured servants, replaced by black slaves later, performed the arduous labor of the plantations. A servant was considered fortunate if he survived the voyage across the seas, but many rued the day they lived to step down on the land that became their home. If they were not stooping over tobacco in the hot sun from morning to night, they were clearing gigantic trees for an expanded planting. Malaria from mosquitos in the estuarine climate wiped out servants almost as fast as they arrived by ship. Those who lived through the five or more years of perilous toil were entitled to freedom, a year's supply of grain, clothing, and sometimes a rifle, land and tools. However, only about one in five did survive during the first decades of colonization.

All the colonies promised land to freed servants at one time or another, but this generosity was often repealed or withheld. Sooner or later, though, freedmen usually acquired land, either on credit or through tenancy and personal savings, sometimes even having it willed to them by their former masters. During colonial times the price of land was quite low. If the new landowner cultivated tobacco during a few good years, he could purchase an indentured servant of his own. If his operation grew large enough to remain viable during the depressions of the latter part of the 1600s, he might have seen his son become a wealthy planter with a few dozen slaves.

Land Holdings and Economics

The small freeman planter class acted as the solid backbone of Virginia life during most of the 1600s. Although their holdings averaged 500 to 1,000 acres, much of the land was forested. Fortunes made on tobacco could be lost overnight because of year-to-year overproduction and price fluctuations, and the hard reality of this fact compelled most planters to grow their own food and raise cattle, hogs and poultry. Even in lean years the hard-hit Virginia yeoman probably had enough meat, butter, cheese, corn, grain, and berries to feed himself and his family. Since farms were widely separated, the farmer learned quickly that he should acquire a degree of self-sufficiency.

As the seventeenth century wore on and the years of tobacco oversupply and of falling prices began to outnumber years of high prices, smaller agricultural units gave way to the large plantations which could absorb the losses. Because it became more necessary to build large plantations with a large black labor force in order to stay in the tobacco business, many small planters gave up and migrated to other colonies or to the frontier. Some specialized in grains or in high quality tobacco. There were even some small operations which made it into the 1700s. By this time, however, the landscape had changed. Large holdings with several thousand acres each became the normal agricultural unit. Our images of southern gentility come from eighteenth and nineteenth century brick mansions and beautifully landscaped lawns, with black coachmen in elaborate carriages, rather than the simple frame farmhouses of the small planter class of the 1600s.

The Rice and Indigo Crops

The British mercantilists were by no means satisfied with one-commodity support from the American colonies. The proprietors of the Carolinas intentionally sought new exportable goods, and, in 1695, rice was introduced, probably brought from Madagascar.

The moist regions of the southern coastal plains were well suited for rice culture. In the beginning of colonization, planters farmed rice on inland swamp areas, although rice need not be flooded to grow well. Each spring rice was sown in shallow trenches dug by black slaves using short-handled hoes. The rice demanded constant hand weeding and hoeing until it reached about two feet. The rice was sickle-harvested in September and stored in sheaves for curing. It was loosened from its outer husks with wooden hand flails or occasionally by treading by ox or horse.

Irrigation techniques were employed beginning about 1724 by using simple damming techniques on ponds and springs. After it supplied moisture to the crops, the water was drained into adjoining streams. It wasn't until late in the eighteenth century that tidal flooding was utilized from swamps bordering the rivers of the coastal plain. Planters found that flooding destroyed weeds and insects, fertilized the fields, and protected the rice stands during high tide, which pushed the fresh water of the rivers into their fields, where it was retained during each flooding period. The water was drained out several times for dry hoeings until the crop reached a suitable height. The final inundation remained for two or three months. (Plows were rarely used in the South during the colonial period. Field workers cultivated with hoes and weeded by hand. After the American Revolution, some attempts were made to introduce plows and horse hoes.) Floodings on rice fields greatly increased productivity, but no suitable substitute for the sickle and the wood flail was found until the Civil War, when scythes or cradles and wooden mills became common in harvesting and threshing. By that time, however, planters had already found a way to speed up winnowing. They applied a fan to blow the lighter stalks away from the heavier grains. Earlier they had used the centuries-old method of tossing the stalks in the air and letting the wind do the work.

The rice grain is also covered by an inner thin brown skin, now known to contain vitamins. To colonial planters the removal of this cuticle—the rice "cleaning" and polishing process—presented a major problem. They removed the skin by hand pounding the rice with wooden pestles, then sifting it out. After the Revolution, ox or horse power moved similar pounding pestle devices, which were set in large wood blocks.

The third great southern staple, indigo, was not developed until the middle of the 1700s. In 1742 Eliza Lucas, the daughter of the governor of Antigua, succeeded in domesticating the wild plant, valuable throughout the Continent for its dye extract. Unsuccessful efforts had been made to launch the indigo industry in the colonies for at least fifty years prior to Miss Lucas's efforts. As soon as British Parliament received word of her achievement, they offered a bounty of sixpence per pound of the dye.

Like the other chief crops of the South, indigo was highly labor intensive. It needed hand planting, cultivating, harvesting at the proper time before the wood got too hard, and careful handling so as not to rub off the bluish color from its leaves. The production of its dye was perfected over a period of years. First the leaves were soaked in vats, the fermented water being drawn into a second set of vats where it was agitated by beater paddles. Lime water was found to precipitate the dyestuff, which then required further purification through brewing and settling. After the water was once again carefully drawn out of the vats, the dye residue was collected into sacks, pressed, dried and packed in barrels for shipment.

The advantage of growing rice and indigo together was that the labor force of slaves could be busily employed throughout every season of the year. Indigo could be harvested in June or July and also in August or September during floodings of the rice fields.

Ingenious overseers managed to find something for the farmworkers or slaves to do every minute of the day and year. Neither malarial conditions nor back-breaking labor in a semi-tropical climate made agricultural labor a pleasant occupation. Only a slave labor force could be expected to accomplish the arduous tasks of southern agriculture for as long as its crops were economically valuable to planters, merchants, mercantilists, or pre-Civil War aristocracy.

The Fur Trade

The northern colonies generally disappointed the more rabid English mercantilists. Only the fur trade—more precisely the fur and skin trade—and abundant timber products seemed to justify British presence at all. Every other occupation of the North was either useless to the homeland or, what was worse, it competed with her. Beaver fur commanded a good price because beaver underfur possessed microscopic barbs used in the felting of the beaver hats then popular in Europe. In 1638, King Charles I decreed that all hats manufactured in England had to be made of beaver fur. This was a severe blow to the North American beaver but a mighty boost to the merchant class and mercantilism. Deerskins also became increasingly utilized as clothing in the colonies.

The wild game fur and skins near colonial settlements on the coast were quickly exhausted by extensive hunting and trapping. Very soon after the founding of the English colonies, most of the trade was done directly with the Indians, and English traders went farther and farther inland to barter for furs. By the end of the 1600s the Hudson Bay Company had secured the privileged position of exclusive dealing with the Indians over other English trading companies, but it took thirty years of war with the French to secure these privileges for the English Crown. In similar fashion the English took over the Dutch trading post at Fort Orange, which became Albany in New York, at the junction of the Hudson and the Mohawk Rivers, where they dealt for furs and skins with the Iroquois. After the wild game in their own region had been depleted, the Iroquois procured furs from Indians farther west and continued to trade them with the English. This was one reason the Iroquois allied themselves with the English against the French, who traded with the Indians at their western trading posts. Later English traders began to penetrate the western regions themselves and deal directly with the western tribes.

The frontier was a continual battleground for these furs, English against French with Indians in the middle, from western Pennsylvania through the Ohio Valley west to the Mississippi and south to Mobile and New Orleans. In the South, the English outbid their competitors for Cherokee friendship. During the 1700s, English fur traders poured into the frontier regions around the southern edges of the Appalachians. Hundreds of expeditions emerged from the hinterland every year in Charleston and Augusta to turn over furs and skins to local merchants or representatives of English houses. In 1706-07, over 121,000 deerskins were packed out of the Carolinas alone. By 1730 the annual total reached 255,000 in South Carolina. A Hudson Bay Company sale in November 1743 recorded the disposal of 26,750 beaver pelts, 14,730 martens and 1850 wolves; in the same year 127,080 beaver, 30,325 martens, 1267 wolves, 12,428 otters, 110,000 raccoons and 16,512 bears were received in the French port of La Rochelle. By 1750, 2,000,000 beavers had been killed in eastern North America by whites and their Indian associates.

The beginning of a fur and skin transaction would take place in the office of a London merchant. He would send to a colonial trading house goods to be traded to Indians for skins and furs. These articles would include muskets, gunpowder, blankets, iron goods such as kettles, traps, knives and tools, and ornaments such as rings, bells, and jewelry. The American merchant would hire a fur trader to cart the goods and plenty of American rum inland to the firm's storehouse at the edge of civilization. The trader there picked up and saddled pack-horses, often in trains of twenty with at least 150 pounds of goods each, and started his long trek through the wild interior. He negotiated with Indians at designated places, then returned to his eastern terminus. The business remained extremely profitable for as long into the 1800s as the game lasted on the retreating western frontier.

America's wild game and deer trade also gave a start to hundreds of colonial tanners. As early as 1650, 51 of them were kept busy in the Massachusetts Bay Colony. Tanners prepared deerskins to be worn, just as Indians had for generations made hunting shirts, moccasins and tepees by scraping, soaking and tanning the hides with the dust of decaying tree stumps. Indians used animal fat to soften the skins. Early tanners had similar methods but preferred the tannin or tannic acid of the crushed bark of oaks, hemlocks and other trees, and lime with soaking water, and hard tallow for softening. Leather "fulling" shops where leather was beaten into greater pliability completed the process before sewing. Most of this work was done for local trade rather than for exporting.

Forest Resources

Wars with Spain and France during the seventeenth and eighteenth centuries occasioned a strong British preference for colonial forest products to keep her shipwrights supplied with materials. During this time England depended on Baltic countries for lumber and naval stores of tar, pitch and resin. Although it was much less expensive for her to transport lumber and stores from Continental sources than from the American colonies, the supply of naval materials was often interrupted and monopolized by one firm which raised prices beyond British willingness to pay. Mercantilists insisted on utilizing the seemingly inexhaustible supply of colonial timbers and naval stores.

Maritime Uses for American Forest Products

The white pine regions of New England provided masts of unexcelled quality. Concerned that colonial interests might begin to control this important resource, the authors of the new charter of Massachusetts in 1691 reserved to the Crown all trees more than twenty-four inches in diameter which could be used for masts. Called the "Broad Arrow" policy, it was to be enforced by a small number of the king's deputies in America, and it was applied only to trees on non-private lands. The trees were designated by marking or branding with the broad arrow of the king, an action which goes down in American history as its first official conservation policy. But few colonists paid any attention to the regulation. It was difficult to enforce any law on the American frontier, the king's broad arrow notwithstanding.

Oak lumber made superb ship frames, and from the pine forests tar, pitch, and resin could be extracted. Tar preserved and protected the ropes aboard ship; pitch sealed its seams; and resin was needed with pitch to protect the underwater parts of the vessel.

Lumber Processing

The lumber industry in America commenced with the first settlers, who year by year cleared more of the forest as they moved westward. It took only a generation or two for the major forest areas to be located a considerable distance from the coast. The distance presented no insuperable obstacle so long as water flowed into the sea. Logs were rolled into streams and rivers and floated to hundreds of sawmills located where navigation stopped on the Fall Line from Maine to the Carolinas. Here huge water wheels powered saws which fashioned timbers, planks and barrel staves. A crank attached to the water wheel moved the saw up and down. The water wheel saw was nothing but a pit saw connected to a frame; saws like it had been operating in Scandinavian countries since the 1400s.

Figure 2–1. Large square beams commonly used in colonial and early American building were often cut in pits. The sawing stroke was made by the sawyer below, who pulled the saw toward him, while the man or boy on the work retrieved the saw. The cut was held open with a wedge, which may be seen at left. The man in the pit was not spared regular showers of sawdust. Sawed timber replaced rough-hewn logs early in this country. Courtesy The Bettmann Archive.

Gang saws, parallel saws set in a frame, a later colonial development, sometimes could cut a whole tree trunk in one pass through the saw. Neither apparatus was extremely efficient but both represented substantial progress over the long sash sawyers, one worker in a pit and one above—who had to push and pull their crude saws through thick hardwoods. The early pit saws cut only on the downward thrust, pulled down by the man in the pit and brought up by the man above who guided its path. (The crosscut saw, which cut both ways, was not developed until after the Civil War.) Pioneers used the hoe-like adze for squaring timbers and the short-handle frow, a blade set at a right angle with its handle, for splitting shakes when they were ready to build their permanent dwellings.

But most of the lumbering in colonial America settled down to a duel between the settler's ax and the myriads of trees. Although the hatchet, iron wedge, wood plane and crowbar had been used for generations in Mediterranean countries, the "American axe" was not developed until the first part of the eighteenth century. It weighed four to seven pounds. Ben Franklin timed two men in Gnadenhutten, Pennsylvania, and claimed they cut down a fourteen-inch tree in six minutes.

Naval Stores and Cooperage

Ships were comparatively diminutive in those days, so that transporting the American forest to England was not a practical undertaking, even if the logs were ready to be assembled. So Parliament settled for white pine masts and naval stores and offered bounties for their production. Turpentine, one of the stores, was drawn from incisions in long-leaf pine trees. Resin is left after distilling the oil of turpentine. Tar was sweated from pine wood in an enclosed kiln fired from the top. Pitch was made by boiling the tar.

It took a long time for neophyte tar-makers to develop the knack of producing quality naval stores. British shipwrights often complained about improper naval-stores consistencies from America; yet colonists increased exports year by year. Slave labor in North Carolina enabled that colony to send great quantities of naval stores back to England. The production of naval stores, like that of the rest of the commodities desired by the mother country, was highly labor-intensive.

Cooperage production, the making of barrels, hogsheads, and casks, employed another large segment of the population of many coastal towns. The entire export trade, from tobacco to fish, needed cooperage in quantity. Beyond the colonies Continental fishermen, English merchants and West Indian plantations sought barrels of one sort or another from the Americans. Most large plantations employed their own coopers to produce an adequate stock of hogsheads in which to ship goods. (They also employed blacksmiths, tanners, carpenters, shoemakers, distillers, and sometimes spinners and weavers.)

Other Forest Products

Practically all settlers utilized forest products from their lands for trading. Potash and pearl ash, made from hardwoods, were particularly valuable items for trade. In the extraction of potash, wood was burned and water was leached through the ash. Then the water was boiled off, leaving the potash powder in the form of lye. This could be further refined and purified by baking out the carbon; the resulting powder was called pearl ash. Merchants were always happy to trade for these products, much in demand in England for bleaching cloth and making soap or glass. Colonists used the ash as a fertilizer or boiled it with farm fats to make soft soap or tallow candles. The accrual of these marginal economic benefits from the land was obtained only by the investment of an inordinate amount of labor, however. It took a lot of burning and leaching to make enough potash to sell.

Shipbuilding

Forest products from New England and the middle colonies also supported an incipient shipbuilding industry. On the beaches of growing coastal cities, industrious shipwrights working on hundreds of partially constructed hulks on rough shipways beside piles of lumber were a common sight. In the very early days of the colonies, vessels were constructed at the forest's edge and rolled on tree trunks into the ocean or navigable rivers. By the mid-eighteenth century inland cities along these rivers encouraged their settlers to engage in shipbuilding because the industry became the focal point for dozens of other activities.

The British were chagrined at shipbuilding in the colonies because it competed with so many of their industries, not only shipbuilding itself but all the auxiliary trades—sail and rope production from flax, iron forging of anchors, rudders, spikes, etc. It inevitably happened that English merchants themselves supported colonial enterprise by buying and operating colonial-built ships as well as by procuring provisions from colonials. For the merchants it was more profitable to ignore mercantilist philosophy.

As more and more ships were bought by colonial merchants and captains—the number of non-fishing colonial vessels reached over 2,000 by the time of the American Revolution—American shipping became more than a minor threat to British capitalist interests. It was bound to happen that colonial merchants and ship captains would want to own their own ships. They could avoid inflated shipping and freight charges and maneuver their vessels in the Caribbean at will to find better trades. Shipbuilding was soon a going concern in the colonies.

The Fishing Industry

It was the fishing industry, though, that represented the major challenge to mercantilist policy, for in time colonial fisheries all but drove the British out of their territory, the Grand Banks of Newfoundland. The Banks were formed on the continental shelf between Newfoundland and the tip of Long Island. Icebergs from the cold Labrador current meet the warm Gulf current, depositing earth from the melting icebergs on the shelf. The shallow banks and constant mixing of waters of different temperatures and salinity have made the area a natural home for a hundred kinds of fish. During the 1500s, fishermen from practically every European port made for the Grand Banks every spring to "collect" codfish. (So great was the abundance of cod, hake, haddock, mackerel and other species that their work was more like collecting than fishing.) Each vessel carried about a dozen men, who fished by hand with hempen line and hook. During most of that century, the fish were partly cleaned and immediately stored in salt in the hold of the ship for the return trip home. Cod were then dried at home fisheries.

Some fishermen, more and more of them as time passed, found it convenient to put ashore on the beaches of Newfoundland or on one of the islands near the Grand Banks to make repairs and procure fresh provisions. Soon they began the process of drying cod on the islands and making temporary settlements. They set up wharves; built huts or "stages" for dressing and curing the fish; and made shelves for drying fish (called "flakes"), presses to extract oil from codfish livers, and shelters for themselves. They remained only as long as the summer, for they feared the Atlantic winter storms on their return trip.

Development of North American fisheries did not figure in the plans of the English mercantilists, since they had their own English fishing industries and did not need more fish or fisheries, but fishing was an obvious move for the settlers of northern colonies. In fact, it was the only practical road to economic security. Some northern colonists tried cash crops with little or no success, the Pleistocene glacier having deposited more than a moderate share of its boulders and rocks on their soil. But this same glacier left them a comparative advantage with excellent bays and harbors and a continental shelf which had remained under water rather than rising into a coastal plain, as happened in the South where no massive glacier ice had pressed the land. The very geography of the northern colonies impelled the settlers to exploit the region's strength. Then too, there was a continued high demand for fish on the Continent, even in England where Parliament had retained the fish-eating religious days after the Reformation. In the West Indies, poor quality fish were sought for the slaves and high quality fish for the planters.

Boston, Salem, Gloucester and Marblehead became the most important fishing centers of New England, but fishing also occupied all the villages down the coastline. These communities became the flourishing successors to the early temporary fishing settlements around the Grand Banks. They were equipped with similar adornments. Occasionally New England fishermen proceeded directly to their Mediterranean and African customers with "green" or undried cod. Usually, however, they returned to their home ports and processed the fish before shipping it out.

The fishing industry required enormous amounts of salt to preserve the catch, more for "green" shipping than dried, but many years passed before even a small salt industry emerged. Salt water was pumped from the sea into vats where it evaporated under the sun and over fire. Near the end of the 1700s, salt springs were discovered in upstate New York, adding to the supply. Neither of these sources, however, covered the need of American fisheries, which simply traded some of their catch to Mediterranean countries for thousands of bushels of salt each year.

Whaling

By 1700 New Englanders exported over ten million tons of fish annually and the industry continued to rise in prominence during the century. At the same time whaling was assuming greater importance for the New England colonies. Whaling began at Southhampton, Long Island, in 1650 as a shore pursuit. Whales were occasionally caught on the beach at low tide; settlers sometimes hired Indians to help them bring in whales from offshore. Imitating the Indian practice, watchers were stationed on the beaches. When a whale appeared, a crew set out in a small boat to harpoon it and drag it in. Another crew would immediately cut it up to render its blubber into oil and other products.

Whale oil was prized as an excellent illuminant for lamps, but it was also used for soap-making and lubrication. Whalebone or baleen from the huge mouths of the right whales became important for corset stays, handles, and thousands of carved artifacts (scrimshaw). The sperm whale was sought after for the high quality of the blubber oil and spermaceti, a waxy solid substance in its head which made superb candles and ointments. Sperm whales are distinguished from the right whales by their spermaceti and free, toothed jaws; right whales fed simply by opening their jaws and straining millions of sea plankton through hairy fringes on the inner edges of their baleen.

Figure 2–2. The perils of whaling. This 1850 woodcut dramatizes one of the whaler's most persistent fears—that of being capsized by a sounding whale. Boats had to approach the whales near enough to allow the harpoon to be thrown. A large whale, fighting for its life, could then overturn the whaleboat with its flukes. Few sailors could swim, and even swimmers could be stunned or killed by the violence of the capsizing. Note the cloud of smoke issuing from the mother ship. Apparently this vessel had caught some whales and was boiling out the oil. Also note the line tub in the foreground. Harpoon line was coiled in such tubs to play out smoothly—if the whalers were lucky. Courtesy The Bettmann Archive.

In the early years of whaling, the right whale was pursued because it was the "right" whale to hunt; it inflated when killed rather than sinking as the "wrong" one would do. A large right whale weighed about ninety tons, thirty times as much as an elephant, and was often over 100 feet in length. The right whale came close enough to the coast for the early whalers to pursue in small boats.

Gradually American whalers took to the high seas to seek out the sperm whale. The seaman who was posted on the mast-head to keep on the lookout for whales shouted "A-A-A-A-H Blows" when a whale was sighted spouting water as it came up for air. Seamen jumped for the whaleboats which immediately were let over the side. Each boat had a crew of six, four oarsmen, a steersman at the bow and a mate shouting threats and encouragement to the rowers, whose backs were to the whale. The pursuit could last for hours, until the time when, drawing close to the giant, the mate would instruct the steersman to drive in the harpoon. His thrust fastened the whaleboat to the huge black flank, but with 300 fathoms of rope between iron and boat.

Next followed another ride, "the Nantucket sleigh ride," this time with the boat pulled by the whale fleeing for its life, down into the deep or through the waters at a dizzying speed, often reaching twenty-five miles an hour at about 140 horsepower. When the whale tired, the boat was drawn close and the mate, who had changed places with the steersman at the bow, plunged another long iron into the beast's heart or lungs with an unmerciful twist. The whale would spew blood and thrash to its death. Sperm whales were far less docile than baleen whales.

The occupation was not without its dangers. Whales were known to have utterly demolished pursuing whaleboats, and tales have been told of their ability to take towropes in their mouths and spin the boats around themselves or to whip the boats high into the air before freeing themselves of their tormentors. Once in a great while even a whaleship was said to have been sunk by an avenging whale.

After towing the dead animal back to the ship, the crew lashed it to the vessel's side and began the long labor of rendering the blubber and storing its products. A narrow platform was lowered beside the whale. On it the captain and mates stood while they carved the hulk into pieces and sent them up part by part to be transformed into consumer goods. Fires under great iron pots burned day and night until every ounce of oil was rendered; it was stored in barrels below deck. The entire crew worked hard, for they were paid a variable fraction of the profits according to their position on the expedition. The bigger the catch, the more each would earn.

It is not difficult to understand why settlers from the New England and middle colonies were heavily engaged in fishing activities. Even inland residents enjoyed abundant stocks of fresh fish, but it was in New England that the fishing industry early grew to international prominence. Whaling did not reach its peak until the nineteenth century; it continues to this day, except that the whales enjoy less than an equal chance to survive under stresses from Russian and Japanese fleets equipped with radar and powerful harpoon guns.

Mercantilist Trade Patterns

Mercantilism shaped many of the contours of colonial resource development and use. Yet although the colonies were valuable insofar as they contributed to the self-sufficient supremacy of the motherland, the trade which promoted the material progress of England did the same for the colonies. With increasing production of their export goods, colonial entrepreneurs turned their attention to expanding European markets.

The three big colonial money-makers—tobacco, rice and indigo—had to be sent directly to Great Britain, with the exception of half of the rice crop, which the colonies were allowed to send directly to southern Europe and the West Indies. By the end of the colonial period, the five southern colonies exported and imported well over half of all the goods that went out and came into all thirteen colonies. More important, their exports usually exceeded their imports in value.

England wanted furs, lumber and naval stores from the northern colonies, but the North found ways to export these goods plus fish, wheat, and flour to many other European countries and the West Indies. Naval timbers and stores were enumerated in 1704, but this regulation did not stop northern ships from sailing directly to Mediterranean ports and returning directly to the colonies with wine and salt, rarely obeying the requirement of the navigation laws to stop in England on the way home.

Northern exporters also sent forest products to the West Indies, which, like European countries, needed large supplies of cooperage in which to transport their own exports. Often a cooper went on board ship to assemble staves, hoops, and heads during the trip south. The West Indies imported wheat, bread, flour and fish from the north as well, along with dozens of miscellaneous commodities like candles, shoes, soap, and livestock.

In return, the Caribbean Islands sent back north sugar, molasses and rum, the central ingredients of further industry and trade. Sugar was refined, and molasses was distilled into rum. Rum not only gained increasingly as the most popular beverage of the colonies, but it also was the key commodity in the Indian trade and the notorious African triangular trade. New England ships carried the watered-down, home version to Africa for slaves, who were traded for sugar and molasses at the West Indies, and then these ships would complete the cycle by returning up the coast to Newport, the capital of the slave trade in the colonies.

What complicated West Indian trade was the imperial British presence there. Goods were cheaper from the French Islands and not subject to English export duties. The French also paid higher prices for a greater quantity of miscellaneous northern goods from each shipment. Although there was nothing strictly illegal about the northern trade with the French, Spanish, Dutch, and Danes in the West Indies, it enriched New rather than Old England, and encouraged non-loyalist sentiments, as well as surplus agricultural and manufacturing production, in the colonies.

Thus the British West Indies lost part of their sugar trade with the colonies because of the comparative disadvantage of prices. Soon their English plantation owners convinced Parliament to levy high taxes on non-British West Indian products imported into the American colonies. Parliament acquiesced by passing the infamous Molasses Act of 1733. The Act was actually a mercantilist attempt to strike a blow at the major British enemy of the day, the French, by depriving them of colonial goods traded for French sugars, rum, and molasses. From this time till the Revolution, smuggling became a way of life among northern shippers, brazenly trading with France even during the French and Indian War—a conflict supposedly fought by the British in behalf of colonial rights.

Conservation

Although the beauties of wilderness were not lost on many early American settlers, it was the seemingly limitless resources of land, timber, fishing, and perhaps gold or silver that captured their total attention. Because these pioneers had to tame, conquer and subdue an inexhaustible supply of land before they would reap their material rewards, conservation of resources seemed irrelevant. William Penn, who prescribed that for every five acres of forest cleared on his lands one acre was to be left standing, was a notable exception to the rule.

Virginia tobacco planters exemplified the more common practice of "using up" the land. Their tobacco quickly drained nitrogen and potassium from the soil so that tobacco could not be grown on the same piece of land for more than four years. Rather than attempting to find ways to replenish the soil, they found it easier simply to begin tobacco cultivation on a new stretch of land. Occasionally they tried to squeeze out some corn or wheat from the old fields before allowing them to grow wild.

Yet because of the nature of tobacco cultivation, even before these fields were abandoned they were subject to erosion. No weeds were permitted to grow between the straight and even rows, which aided the formation of gullies during the violent rainy seasons when topsoil was washed away. Sheet erosion was also common after every season when the surface of the ground was left bare; no cover protected the soil from the impact of rain, which created its own surface over the water-soaked fields and carried off soil first in sheets, then forming rills and gullies. Very often the process was hastened because it was necessary for planters to use the thin soils on the woodland hillsides to cultivate enough tobacco to satisfy demanding merchants in England. The first serious soil erosion of the country occurred in Virginia, Maryland, and North Carolina because of intensive tobacco cultivation, but the pattern continued as the settlers moved west. The later cultivation of cotton in the Piedmont regions resulted in tens of thousands of gullies, some in Georgia over 150 feet deep.

Pressure to produce increased quantities of tobacco and timber products came from the mercantile system in England, locked in the European struggle over who would gain ultimate supremacy of power and profits. Control of international waterways and strong shipbuilding and shipping industries were the foundation of mercantilism. The American colonies were called upon to support the mother country in their design by providing abundant supplies of white pine masts and naval stores so that their collective interests could be protected from the rival nations and pirates. At the same time English merchants accepted colonial tobacco, sugar and indigo for use in further trading with friendly European neighbors, thereby increasing their stocks of bullion. Mercantilism demanded intensive cultivation, and by the end of the 1700s the dark brown forest soils had turned to lighter shades, indicating exhaustion and deteriorating soil structure.

As the system developed, the State put controls and regulations on more and more spheres of everyday life in the colonies. These residents soon understood that the purpose of these restrictions lay in transferring their wealth to England. They learned the lesson of the age: that there were profits to be made, but they were chagrined that their English cousins were garnering them. Even the small farmers were squeezed out of the small surpluses they were able to gain because of the exigencies of the economic system. The colonies were thus drawn into economic and political conflict that was to lead to the American Revolutionary War.

References for Further Reading

For excellent general references on the economic history of the United States from colonial times, yet with considerable detail on specific resources, see *A History of American Economic Life* by Edward C Kirkland (1969), *America's Economic Growth* by Fred A Shannon (1954) and Harold U Faulkner's *American Economic History* (1960). Most statistical material in this chapter (as well as for succeeding ones) is derived from *Historical Statistics of the United States: Colonial Times to 1970 (1976)*, published by the US Department of Commerce. The classic treatment of early southern agriculture with extensive data on tobacco, rice and indigo is Lewis C Gray's *A History of Agriculture in Southern United States to 1860* (1933). Likewise, the *History of the Lumber Industry of America* by James K Defebaugh (1906-07), answers most questions about the early lumber industry. Thomas R Cox's more recent synthesis, *This Well-Wooded Land: Americans and their Forests from Colonial Times to the Present* (1984), places lumbering in the context of conservation and other uses of the forest. Peter Matthiessen's *Wildlife in America* (1964) presents an informative history of man's effect on the wildlife of the North American continent. Arthur J Ray's *Indians in the Fur Trade* (1974) is an interesting and scholarly account of the Indian role of hunter, trapper and middleman southwest of Hudson Bay. The American Heritage publication *Seafaring American* by Alexander Laing (1974) offers a popular and interesting version of the early fishing and whaling industries along with other seafaring lore of the era. For a good general background of the period see Daniel J Boorstin's *The Americans: The Colonial Experience* (1958).

Chapter 3

EVERYDAY LIFE AND
REVOLUTIONARY DEVELOPMENTS

*E*very great revolutionary movement needs the support of ordinary people if
it is to gain momentum. In the American colonies, this support was slow in
coming, but by the eve of the Revolution pioneer families were ready to join
southern aristocrats, merchants and entrepreneurs in an effort to throw the King's
ministries out of the colonies for good. The connection between the everyday life
of the northern farmer and that of the traditionally conservative southern planter,
merchant or entrepreneur can be found in the tightening grip of British mercantilist
policy. The ultimate question, however, dealt with natural resources: who would reap
the fruits of America's land and labor?

The Northern Farmer

In New England and the middle colonies, small settlements on the seaboard were
established originally in order to set up trade relationships with the mother country.
Farmers gradually separated themselves from these communities and attempted to
provide for the agricultural needs of the small trading cities. By the 1720s the process
of orderly settlement of New England towns had almost universally broken down. New
grants were sold to proprietors for speculative purposes, and the land was resold to
individual families. The land close to the older settlements went for higher prices,
generally in lots of 10 to 100 acres. Land closer to the frontier was much cheaper, but
transportation and Indian problems were compounded. In either case farmers were
separated from each other and from a close-knit community.

In the middle colonies, land speculation was accepted and operated from their
inception. By the mid-eighteenth century, hundreds of square miles had been bought
up by land companies for speculative purposes. But although the 1700s ushered in
widespread buying and selling of land, not everyone bothered to buy his piece of
property. All along the frontier from Massachusetts to Georgia, independent-minded
squatters—indentured servants, slaves, small farmers forced to leave their tobacco
holdings, as well as Scots who had emigrated from Northern Ireland—cleared the
land that suited their fancy and worked it. Land deeds were the least of their worries
on the frontier. Beginning in 1708, wave after wave of Scotch-Irish fled Ulster because
of rackrenting of land and economic hardships associated with British imperialist
policy. Most of these lower-middle-class immigrants fought their way to the frontier,

refused to pay taxes or quitrents, and made trouble with the Indians. By 1775 there were 350,000 Scotch-Irish in the American colonies.

The way to the frontier was opened for the settler by traders whose pack-horses widened Indian paths into trails. Most pioneering families were young, ready to endure the sacrifices of the frontier. They did not need large sums of money to get their farms started; perhaps the equivalent of $50 to $100 in English currency would do, but this amount represented more than most young families possessed, and it had to be borrowed. Horses or oxen, a plow, a gun, a few tools, a cart or wagon, a cow, some hogs, chickens, and seed—these items would be sufficient in the beginning, but it took about two years for the average pioneer farm to become self-supporting. The bare essentials were the axe and oxen, most important for clearing, plowing, hauling and, finally, eating.

Clearing the Forests

Sometimes the frontier was located just a few miles west of town. For most, however, the trip to the new land took several days. Since the forest represented the most the most pressing obstacle to the farmer, clearing of about three acres was begun immediately. Girdling, or deadening the trees, was popular because the leaves fell quickly, a crop could be planted, and within a few years the wind often did the work of blowing over the trees. Time was precious on the frontier. Girdling brought problems with it, though. Trees and branches fell on crops, livestock, and more than a few passersby, and plowing or cultivating around the deadened trees was a difficult and time-consuming task. After 1700, most New Englanders and the Pennsylvania Germans preferred the "Yankee" cut-and-burn method, requiring strenuous labor but also yielding immediate return from the sale of potash and pearl ash.

Unfortunately, a hot burn during a dry period often robbed the soil of its rich humus and leaf mold, depriving the farmer of nature's thousand-year legacy. It is unlikely that the farmer realized what the time-honored Yankee system did to his soil. He wanted unencumbered, cleared fields. He found that wood ashes from the burning of brush, rails and saplings were known to have some good effects on the soil. Over a period of two centuries most of the woodlands of eastern America were burned to the ground for agricultural use.

The Pioneer Farm

Pioneers usually planted corn and some vegetables first, and within a few years wheat or rye. Corn, or "Indian corn" as the first settlers named it, was prized as the premier crop. It competed well with wild growth, it could be eaten by both settlers and livestock, and its stalks provided winter fodder for farm animals. If he was blessed with good soil a farmer could get yields of 50 to 100 bushels of corn an acre, as the Indians did. The ground was turned over, if omnipresent roots did not make it impossible, by a crude plow that took two men and four to six oxen to operate. With hard work they could turn over a few inches of an acre or two in a day. The thick wooden plow was redesigned often during the colonial period, but with little success. The wood mouldboard, plated with scraps of metal, created too much friction with too blunt a wedge to cut either deeply or smoothly.

Whenever a plow with more graceful lines was constructed, it stayed intact only until it hit the first boulder or root. Thus, for decades on the colonial farm, one man or boy bore down on the beam while the second steered and prodded the oxen or horses. Cast iron shares (points) were not introduced until the beginning of the 1800s, and even then many farmers refused the innovation, believing that iron poisoned the soil.

Often the farmer didn't even try to plow the newly-cleared land but simply harrowed his fields. Harrows, triangular beams with iron or wooden teeth, loosened the soil with or without previous plowing.

The grains were reaped with a sickle and threshed with a flail or treading by oxen or horses. For winnowing, the grain was thrown into the wind, which carried the stalks away while the grain fell through sieves.

Farm animals scavenged for food in the woods or meadows. Every few years the meadow diet was supplemented by a grass crop of timothy or red clover, introduced from Europe and planted in regular intervals between grain crops. Hay was scarce both in the natural meadows and from the sown crops until settlers began to plant it regularly. Livestock from several farms in an area tended to converge on the same limited open acreage, subjecting the fields to overgrazing. The Pennsylvania German farmers, with larger cattle herds, not only sowed in larger fields of hay but also drained swamps for meadows and irrigated higher unwatered fields for additional grazing space.

Most frontier farms kept only a few cattle and milk cows, a few dozen sheep, some hogs, and chickens. The Pennsylvania Germans ("Dutch" from "Deutsch"), who first settled near Philadelphia in 1683 and whose numbers increased yearly in eastern and central Pennsylvania, specialized early in the cattle industry to meet the demands of a growing domestic market, and because of the burgeoning industrial revolution in England. They took advantage of new export possibilities as well. They pickled the meat in a salt-water solution, brine, which acted as a preservative. In general the Germans took much better care of their farms and livestock than their Yankee neighbors to the north. They built beautiful large stone barns which kept the animals warm during the winter months and which stored hay and grain as well. Often the German barns were constructed on the sides of hills so that wagons or carts could pull into the second level to unload and store the grain and hay while the horses and cattle were fed in their stalls underneath. Almost 400,000 German immigrants were in the colonies by 1775, most of them in Pennsylvania.

One of the first tasks of the pioneer family was the selection of the best timbers of the land for their log home. Introduced by Swedish settlers in 1638 in the Delaware regions, log cabins spread along the frontier in every colony. The logs were interlocked and the hut insulated between the logs with what later was called chinking (chips, sticks, and moss) and daubing (clay or mud). The roof formed an inverted V; it was layered with poles and bark or thatching (bound bundles of straw). Settlers improvised from this framework. Shakes or shingles were sometimes cut for the roof and brick

fireplaces were built to lessen fire danger. Varieties of skins, lattices, or wooden coverings were used as door and window shutters. Where newcomers were lucky enough to live near other settlers, log houses were "rolled up" in short order through log-rolling bees or other community efforts.

The simple log cabin became the basic design for later country homes. In New England it was embellished as a one-story, two- or three-room farmhouse, followed later by the more elaborate two-story "salt box" structure, with a lean-to, steep-sloping roof in the rear added on, first perhaps to house animals in the winter, then to serve as a summer kitchen. The New England salt box home remained a dominant part of the landscape for well over a hundred years.

After planting came fencing to protect the crops from wildlife and livestock intruders. Fences were made from material at hand. New Englanders built stone fences from the abundant rocks in their fields. In the middle colonies, farmers rolled chestnut or oak trees to the field's edge, split them into rails of a few inches thick, and laid them overlapping at the ends in a zig-zag fashion, perhaps eight feet high. This "worm" fence needed no braces, although some farmers supported the connections with two poles in an X position; the latter were called "snake" fences. The worm and snake fences did the job, but consumed an extravagant number of hardwood rails. Where communities became more densely settled and the supply of wood was rationed, hedges or post-and-rail fences were substituted.

Fences could wall out cattle, but wildlife was not so easily tamed. The presence of wildlife was a mixed blessing, or curse, since venison, bear, moose, beaver and fowl had become important staples for the pioneer family. Freshwater fish from inland streams supplemented their diets; passenger pigeons, which migrated each spring in flocks numbering in the millions, were killed by the hundreds, then cleaned, salted, and preserved as winter delicacies. (In later generations they would be shot for sport.) It didn't take too many years for the forest to be drained of its offerings, if for no other reason than that most of the trees were gone. The newly-cleared lands invited new smaller game—squirrels, rabbits, grouse, quail and groundhogs—but settlers often had to fall back on their own hogs, cattle and chickens for fresh meat. With the decline of woodland wildlife came the rise of cattle, sheep, and hog raising. Hams were cured over the flames and fumes of hickory, sassafras, hard maple, or corn cobs, depending on the taste and the region of the settlers. Beef was dried and "salted-down" for its preservation.

Figure 3–1. Colonial agricultural tools. The farm tools illustrated here show the essentially medieval nature of colonial agriculture. Sickles, shown in the woodcut being used by a team of reapers, have been used to cut grain for centuries. The brush harrow, made by attaching many-branched bushes or treetops to a long drag log, was pulled by a single draft animal. Harrows made with wooden or (later) iron teeth were more efficient in pulverizing the ground before seeding. On early colonial farms, because of small harvests, most threshing was done with hand-flails on barn floors. Sickles and such home-made devices as flails and brush harrows were inexpensive to produce and to maintain. The Old Colony strong plow was built of wood sheathed in iron about 1735. The beam is about six feet long. This plow was used in the rocky soil of New Hampshire. New England soils wore or broke the iron plowshares—but even in such instances the local blacksmith knew how to forge a new share, using the materials readily available. Courtesy The Smithsonian Institution.

With the exception of some butter and cheese making (which was the only way milk could be preserved) for home consumption, milk was not an important food item on the frontier. Drinks from other staples were more popular: whiskey from corn; hard cider from apples; perry from pears; mead from honey; beer from persimmon and maple sugar; and anything else that would ferment from wild berries and honey.

Pioneer Self-Sufficiency

It is obvious that the pioneer farmer could put meat and bread on his table. The following quotation from a Suffolk County bicentennial publication (in Bidwell and Falconer), although omitting the vital role played by the early farmer's wife, indicates how far the farm's self-sufficiency extended:

From his feet to his head the farmer stood in vestment produced on his own farm. The leather of his shoes came from the hides of his own cattle. The linen and woolen that he wore were products that he raised. The farmer's wife or daughter braided and sewed the straw hat on his head. His fur cap was made from the skin of a fox he shot. The feathers of wild fowl in the bed whereon he rested his weary frame by night, were the results acquired in his shooting. The pillowcases, sheets, and blankets, the comfortables, quilts and counterpanes, the towels and table cloth, were home made. His harness and lines he cut from hides grown on his farm. Everything about his ox yoke except staple and ring he made. His whip, his ox gad, his flail, axe, hoe and fork-handle, were his own work. How little he bought and how much he contrived to supply his wants by home manufacture would astonish this generation.

Sheep were raised for wool rather than mutton. A patch of flax was planted soon after the grains, for along with wool from the sheep, thread and yarn could be woven into cloth and knitted into "linsey-woolsey" clothing. Even Alexander Hamilton, in his *Report on Manufactures*, praised the farm families for the varieties of clothing and cloth products produced in their homes: "Great quantities of coarse cloths, coatings, serges, and flannels, linsey woolseys, hosiery of wool, cotton, and thread, coarse fustians (cotton and flax), jeans (wool and cotton), and muslins, checked and striped cotton and linen goods, bed ticks, coverlets and counterpaines, tow linens, coarse shirtings, sheetings, towelling and table linen, and various mixtures of woolen and cotton and of cotton and flax. . . ."

Many stages intervened before colonial farm families enjoyed the results of their time-consuming labors. Sheep had to be hand-sheared; wool had to be washed of its natural grease and dirt, carded and combed by hand to straighten the fibers for spinning into yarn and thread. Berries and bark in many combinations made colorful dyes; indigo had to be imported.

Flax, a blue-flowered prized textile plant, was grown for its fibers that can be woven into linen. Children on the farm weeded and cared for the flax patch. When the flax ripened and was pulled out (not cut), it was dried and bleached in the meadow, then rippled with a wire comb to break off the seed-bolls. Flax stalks were soaked to soften the inner wood of the stem before the farmer's family separated out the fibers in the difficult process of breaking the brittle stalks, swingling (cleaning off broken bits of woody stalk) and hackling (further cleaning and straightening the flax with the steel teeth of a comb). These processes changed the fibers into strands of soft, gray material. Instruments called the flax-brake, swingling knives, and hackle were used for the long and difficult task. Then the flax could be spun into thread and combined with wool in linsey woolsey.

Farms were never completely independent. At the very least they needed salt both for themselves and their livestock and they usually wanted to trade their small surpluses for money or other necessities. At least once a year every outer neighborhood sent a pack-horse or wagon expedition to the nearest trading settlement to procure salt, gunpowder, and iron goods such as nails, kettles and tools. They bartered with furs, skins, whiskey, cider, ginseng, potash and pearl ash, maple syrup and other farm products. In many years, however, particularly during the depression in the late 1760s, prices for their products were depressed and salt was very scarce and expensive.

Problems for Colonial Farmers

The farmer's perennial problems were a chronic labor shortage; the weather; a colonial economy structured against his interests; and Indians who were not ready to forgive him for taking their land. A farm household had only a few hands to do an enormous amount of work. A death in the family or even of a cow could spell disaster. Occasionally a string of yearly wheat crops could be wiped out by either drought, the "blast" or mildew, or the Hessian fly.

In this context, it is easy to understand why northern farmers hardly had the time to think about soil conservation measures, much less the extra money to buy supplemental fertilizers. They could have tried crop rotation or the application of fish, rockweed or limestone if these nutrients were locally available, but even these measures took time away from more pressing daily needs. Often the frontiersmen didn't know why the lands yielded less and less each year. They simply let failing land lie fallow and cleared more acreage. In a letter to Arthur Young (quoted in Boorstin), George Washington said that he was embarrassed by the way his fellow American farmers ("if they can be called farmers," he emphasized) treated the land, but their aim was "not to make the most they can from the land, which is . . . cheap, but the most of the labour, which is dear; the consequence of which has been, much ground has been scratched over and none cultivated or improved as it ought to have been. . . ."

Europeans who traveled through the colonies at the time deplored the wasteful practices of American farmers. In the mid-eighteenth century, Swedish botanist Peter Kalm stated that the very richness of the American soils spoiled the farmers and made them sloppy in their farming habits. After a four-year journey through the middle colonies and Quebec, Kalm wrote his *Travels Into North America*, observations which include astute comments on American farming habits:

The rye grows very poorly in most of the fields, chiefly because of careless agricultural practices and the poor soil, which is seldom or never manured. After the inhabitants have converted into a tillable field a tract of land which was forest for many centuries, and which consequently had a very fine soil, they use it as long as it will bear any crops. When it ceases to bear any they turn it into pastures for the cattle, and take new grain fields in another place, where a rich black soil can be found that has never been used. This kind of agriculture will do for a time; but it will afterwards have bad consequences. A few of the inhabitants, however, treat their fields a little better.

Their eyes are fixed upon the present gain, and they are blind to the future. Their cattle grow poorer daily in quality and size because of hunger. On my travels I observed several wild plants which horses and cows preferred to others, and which grew well on the driest and poorest ground where no others would thrive. But the inhabitants did not know how to turn this to their advantage, owing to the *slight respect for natural history*, that science being here, as in other parts of the world, looked upon as a mere trifle and the pastime of fools. . . . I found everywhere the wisdom and the goodness of the Creator; but too seldom saw any inclination among men to make use of them.

Life on the frontier was precarious, especially if payments had to be made on the land; these considerations had to be taken care of before land conservation. If the land was of marginal quality to begin with and if other difficulties forced the farmer to borrow from merchants at six to eight percent interest, his financial problems were apt to compound themselves year by year. Debts were listed in English pounds and shillings but were paid in farm produce. If prices on farm items fell, more corn or wheat had to be repaid than originally borrowed on. Furthermore, taxes had to be paid in some localities for road improvement or Indian protection.

The money problem—fluctuating prices, currency shortages, indebtedness—plagued farmers throughout the colonial period and afterward. Provincial governments attempted to alleviate their plight by establishing land banks which made loans at low interest rates against rural land mortgages. In effect land replaced gold or English money as the ultimate security for the payment of bills. Although many land banks, mostly private undertakings, failed, the more stable institutions provided a valuable service to debt-ridden farmers who needed low-interest money in times of financial distress. One of these land banks, organized in Massachusetts in 1740, had granted 3% loans to about 1,000 farmers in one year when Parliament forced it to liquidate and close its doors. English merchants and creditors feared that the "bills of credit" issued by the banks would undermine the value of hard money.

The colonial governments themselves needed a supply of money to discharge their own obligations. They issued local bills of credit, backed by taxation. The bills came to be utilized as legal tender in many places so that even private debts could be paid by them. But again in 1751, Parliamentary statute forbade any New England colony from issuing legal tenders for private transactions. The Currency Act of 1764 extended the prohibition to all of the colonies. The outcry against these statutes did not arise solely, or even primarily, from the small farmers. Great Virginia planters joined with merchants and entrepreneurs in the protest. Each of these groups wanted to enlarge its supplies of currency. Further, each group had political complaints against the Crown for infringement of its freedom.

The Southern Planter

The southern coastal plain, geophysically lifted from the Atlantic's Continental shelf, gave the earliest colonial settlers many productive years. The soil's inevitable decline in productivity came after yearly tobacco crops exhausted its minerals. Land failure was accelerated because brush was burned over the soil to sterilize it of wild growth, which often burned out the humus and weakened the soil structure that had kept it intact. Heavy coastal rains were then more easily able to wash away the topsoil of the plain.

Patterns of Land Use

The fields were abandoned to small, independent farmers who tried to raise wheat, corn, and cattle. Few of them tried to replenish the soil's mineral supply, however, so that by the end of the 1700s farming became nearly impossible on the coastal plain. In the meantime the process was repeated on the Piedmont plateau, low rolling hill areas between the Fall Line (the upper limits of navigation) and the mountains. Tobacco farmers cleared new lands and again mined the soil. A few innovative farmers (including George Washington and Thomas Jefferson) experimented with lime, marl, plaster, and other fertilizers or rotated clover, winter vetch, peas, and grass crops with tobacco. Many of the wealthy planters hardly bothered with their inland Piedmont plantations, preferring to remain at their residences in the older communities where older cultural and social life thrived. They left the management of the newer plantations to overseers.

Control from London

Although the southern economy in general was flourishing, tobacco prices, controlled by English merchants, stayed quite low during the 1700s. Southern tobacco plantation owners could maintain their extravagant life style because they enjoyed other income and investments, notably in large tracts of western lands from which they derived rents from tenants or which they could later sell at large speculative profit.

In Virginia, the Governor's Council and the House of Burgesses, both dominated by the wealthy men of property, held distributive power over coveted western land. Fortunes were made or lost through the decisions of the Williamsburg legislators and government bureaucrats. Aggressive landseekers like George Washington uncovered prime virgin lands for future plantations or speculative purposes. Boorstin quotes Washington's advice to his debt-ridden friend Captain John Posey to "look to Frederick, and see what fortunes were made by the Hites and the first takers up of those lands; Nay, how the greatest estates we have in this Colony were made. Was it not by taking up and purchasing at very low rates the rich back lands that we possess?" Often government approval of land sales was obtained more easily if groups of influential Virginians organized themselves into land companies like the Great Dismal Swamp Land Company.

Nonetheless many planters fell deeply into debt. The reason lay in their complete dependence on the London merchant, who picked up and sold the crop, deducting from the sale all his expenses and the cost of goods ordered by the planter, plus other commissions, freight charges, duties, insurance, and other charges. Since revenue from the crop often did not cover these costs, the merchant would lend the difference at the rate of 6% to 8% against the following year's crop. After a number of years of indebtedness, the planter's situation, for completely different reasons, became nearly as precarious as that of the northern farmer. Even the prosperous northern farmer, as he became more involved in international trade in wheat and meat exports, began to smart under mercantilist restrictions, heavy taxes, and additional freight charges.

The southern planters' difficulties loomed even larger after the French and Indian War and the Royal Proclamation of 1763. The proclamation stipulated that colonial governors were not permitted to sell lands west of the sources of the rivers flowing into the Atlantic, and that no fur trader was to go beyond that point without permission of a new centralized trading commission in Montreal. The change in policy came as a surprise to most colonists because earlier the government sought to fill in unoccupied lands quickly as buffers against the French and Spanish. More western settlers also meant more furs and skins for English trade. As the problem of imperial control subsided after the Seven Years' War, the Indians became more militant. At first sight the new regulations, which set aside the western lands as Indian territory, seemed like a magnanimous gesture to the Indian tribes.

Most likely, though, more mundane considerations led to the new policy. A firmer grip on the economic and political activities of the colonial subjects could be exercised if they were consolidated on the seaboard. Next, it became apparent that western lands were increasing in value, and wealthy English investors and speculators wanted these lands protected from squatters' invasions. Third, the English wanted to regulate the number of frontier fur men who dealt with the Indians. Finally, the British government wanted to obtain revenues from western lands for itself, rather than let them go to provincial governments, and to open these lands up piece by piece. Unfortunately for the southern planters, their needs were not recognized in the Royal Proclamation. One of their major protections against financial ruin and increasing indebtedness had been the enhanced values of western lands, which they bought for practically nothing. After the proclamation, neither their yearly crop sales, nor their rents from tenants living on the Piedmont plateau, nor even the merchandizing of goods produced for their English contacts could carry them over their chronic indebtedness.

The new policy also affected poor farmers of both North and South. Bad times were driving many of them to the free western lands. Now there was no refuge for the insolvent pioneer farmer.

English and American Merchants

The financial fate of American planters and farmers was intertwined with that of the people who marketed their products and extended them credit, merchants in England or the port cities of the colonies. Planters in the South dealt directly with English merchants, most of whom had local representatives who collected debts from planters, advised the English firm of market conditions, and sold goods of the English company from a port warehouse. Although the colonial representatives earned considerable commissions for their efforts, they were clearly subordinate to the English merchants, who preferred to negotiate directly with the planters and send their ships directly to plantation wharves. The colonial representatives often set up their own tobacco plantations, but were less successful economically than either established planters or their superiors in London.

The planters habitually complained about the English merchants' high commissions and merciless demands for unpaid bills, as well as their lack of foresight in providing enough vessels to ship their crops. None of these annoyances, however, seemed to cause extreme pressure on the planter until the mid-eighteenth century, when debts began piling on debts; sometimes crops for two or three years in advance had liens placed on them for unpaid bills. The credit system was ready to break down by the time of the Revolution.

American Merchants

American colonial merchants, starting small in commercial seaboard cities, within a generation rose to the ranks of the wealthy upper classes in the colonies. To begin their operation they needed only good English connections, i.e., friends or relatives in an English export house that would extend long-term credit. American merchants were able to monopolize the goods generally unavailable in the colonies until well into the 1700s—salt, guns, kettles, cloth, nails and hundreds of other manufactured items. Merchants set prices and reaped large profits from small farmers and fishermen. The merchant class usually controlled local enterprises that demanded significant capital investments. They built their own ships and sent them around the globe, lent money, set up distilleries and slaughterhouses, bartered guns and liquor with the Indians for furs, and in general determined local political policy. Stories of corrupt merchants fill accounts of contemporary histories of the period.

The merchant's local transactions were arranged by "book credit" and bartering. A farmer would drive his cart filled with corn or flour, perhaps with a calf or other livestock trailing on a rope, to the merchant's shop and trade these goods for some salt, a gun, molasses, and nails. If the trade didn't even out, debt or credit would be extended until the next trade.

The merchant could achieve larger financial rewards through international trade. He might slaughter and pickle the livestock of local farmers and, along with a load of fish and timbers or barrels, send the shipment to the West Indies with instructions to his captain to strike the best bargain at whatever port he could find it. From the Caribbean he could recover valuable specie (hard money) and sugar and molasses. Or he could send beaver in exchange for hats and manufactured goods in London. Or codfish and timbers for salt at Barcelona. Some of his vessels touched a half dozen or more ports, picking up goods, trading them, bringing others home. Most of the merchant's business was carried on with London because of the availability of credit and manufactured goods; the specie which the merchant won from the West Indies ended up in that city. The English firm also granted the colonial merchant bills of credit with which he could pay debts incurred at other ports. (Until the new mercantilist policy after the Seven Years' War, American merchants generally ignored the Navigation laws.)

Threat to Merchants' Prosperity

American merchants remained prosperous as long as they could pay off their English contacts with specie recovered in the West Indies. A series of events beginning in the middle of the eighteenth century threatened the American merchant's privileged position. First, many European nations, becoming more militant mercantilists because of increasing losses of bullion, closed their ports to foreign ships. At the same time, Britain was expanding its industrial capacity and striving to find new markets in the colonies for its goods. The mother country demanded payment in English currency, specie or specific items—not surplus American products like agricultural goods, livestock or fish, because these competed with British products. Americans would no doubt have been delighted to buy English manufactured products had they the money to buy them. Even with large amounts of bullion going to the colonies from the West Indies, the Americans were suffering a greater unfavorable balance of trade with England every year after 1750.

After the War in 1763, the Americans' last source of solvency from the Caribbean was cut off by the British government, which set out in earnest to enforce the Navigation laws. That year the British navy was given powers to search to ferret out colonial smugglers, who were trading enumerated goods to foreign nations and avoiding the stop in England to pay duties on goods from these countries. Customs service staff was increased, as were the number of local admiralty courts, empowered to enforce the Navigation laws. By 1768 an entire new bureaucracy of inspectors, agents, prosecutors and judges to register and inspect American vessels and to prosecute violators was well established. Their salaries, and bounties to informers, were paid from the cargoes of seized vessels and customs revenues. A substantial surplus was sent home across the ocean. John Hancock was one of a bevy of smugglers who created an uproar of protest against these laws and writs of assistance (search warrants).

What the new apparatus meant in practical terms was that sugar (an enumerated good), which the Americans picked up at French or Spanish Caribbean Islands for a 25% to 40% cheaper price than at British Islands, had to go to England for the payment of heavy duties before reshipment home, a very uneconomic transaction for the colonial merchant. In 1764, the Sugar Act was passed, banning colonial importation of foreign island rum and raising the duty on sugar but reducing the duty on molasses. The act also required American customs officials to keep full records on all imports and exports for possible examination by admiralty officials.

The list of enumerated articles to be traded only with England was expanded in 1764, including lumber, hides and skins, pig and bar iron, and potash and pearl ash. Higher duties were imposed on colonial imports from foreign countries; many goods were forbidden, and in 1766 all goods not already on the enumerated list (e.g., flour and fish) bound for ports north of Cape Finisterre had to stop first at an English port to pay fees. In sum, the logic of mercantilist policy was applied to every commercial situation.

The Colonial Iron Industry

As early as 1699, colonial interests were forbidden to export any wool, raw or manufactured, to another American colony or "to any other place whatsoever." The same restriction was applied to hats in 1732. But another kind of control was placed on iron in 1750. The production of crude or pig iron was encouraged with bounties but further production into finished iron or steel hardware was forbidden. The Iron Act of that year banned the construction of new slitting and rolling mills, plating forges, or steel furnaces. In 1764, iron was placed on the enumerated list.

This development underlined mercantilist policy but carried with it more significant overtones. Manufacture of iron and steel was an increasingly critical industry, particularly in waging war, for any country coveting industrial supremacy. Since the depletion of its forests for making charcoal, England had been largely dependent upon Sweden for bar iron to convert to manufactured goods. From 1760 onward, England needed all the crude iron she could acquire to continue her industrial revolution.

Natural Resources

Like other natural resources, iron ore was plentiful in the New World; early settlers noticed the reddish bog ore in or around dozens of waterways along the seaboard. Some types of iron dissolve in water and are deposited in the form of fine powder on the bottoms of lakes, ponds, streams or rivers, usually because an agent such as evaporation or a carbonate (particularly calcium carbonate, i.e., limestone) brings about its precipitation. That is, whenever water containing iron (in the form of ferrous oxide) meets water with dissolved calcium salts, or when water with iron flows over limestone, the iron will be deposited as ferric oxide. Iron powder precipitated in or along water courses is called bog ore; in addition, rock ore was found later on many land sites in the colonies, including western Connecticut, southwestern Massachusetts, New Jersey, Pennsylvania, and Maryland.

The smelting, or reduction, of iron ore is based on the reaction of oxygen to carbon at certain high temperatures. If iron ore is heated along with a carbonaceous material like charcoal, it will yield some of its oxygen, which combines with the charcoal to form carbon monoxide gas. At a still higher temperature, the iron becomes porous, and when even more heat is applied it absorbs carbon and melts. Carbon from the charcoal takes the place of the oxygen in the ore. Large quantities of charcoal are needed both to heat the iron and to remove the oxygen from the ore.

Many methods of charcoal-making were employed in the days of early America, but the purpose of all of them was to get timbers smoldering in a state of oxygen deficiency. Piles of wood (elm was considered especially desirable) were thickly covered with earth and sod, except for a few openings to allow for a draught at the beginning of the fire. Burning poles were pushed into the pile, and when the fire was started, earth was thrown over the air openings. Wood piles had to be carefully watched lest they turn into bonfires. The same principle was later applied to coke-making when bituminous coal, cooked in the absence of air, was used to smelt iron.

The American colonies enjoyed not only large deposits of bog and rock ore but, just as important, vast stretches of timber which could supply charcoal for the reduction of the ore. Fast-running streams through the forests could power waterwheels to drive the large leather bellows at the furnaces, and the water could also be diverted to cool the metals at the forges. A limestone flux, necessary to reduce melting temperatures and to remove impurities, was found in seashells as well as in limestone itself.

The Early Iron Industry

The earliest forges in the colonies, called "bloomeries," were quite primitive by later standards, but those in remote areas stayed in operation for generations to supply local needs. Bog ore was treated with charcoal, which absorbed the oxygen in the ore. A small, spongy ball of incandescent metal lacking in carbon fell to the bottom of the furnace, and white-hot it was removed and hammered by hand to remove the slag. The wrought iron was sold to a blacksmith who reheated and worked the soft iron into finished articles. Unless the iron is heated red-hot or hotter, it cannot absorb enough carbon to become molten and flow into iron "pigs."

Later, as the colonial population moved westward large quantities of rock ore were discovered. New blast furnaces were built to smelt down the rock ores. Most were twenty-five-foot trapezoidal stone structures, often built onto the side of a hill so that the mixture of charcoal, ore and a limestone flux or crushed seashells could easily be layered in from the top. The bellows usually were worked by water power; every blast of air heightened temperatures and sent jets of sparks through the furnace stack. Alloyed with charcoal, the molten iron ran from the hearth to be cast into molds scraped out of scorched sand. The cast pig iron bars thus produced were made at a relatively low temperature—only slightly higher than that of smelted copper. This meant that the iron contained a high carbon content and therefore was quite brittle.

Next, the iron pigs were converted into more malleable wrought iron at a separate hearth and forge. (The word "wrought" is the past participle of "work"; thus "wrought iron," is iron that has been "worked.") At the wrought-iron forge, the carbon was removed at higher temperatures by a current of air. The air burned out the excess carbon in the iron, forming carbon monoxide and carbon dioxide. Freed of its carbon, the iron became malleable; it could be worked without shattering.

The later forges used waterwheels to activate trip-hammers with long wooden arms and giant iron heads as the iron was placed alternately into the fire and onto the anvil. From the bar iron, blacksmiths made tools, implements, wheel supports, stone plates, pots, and dozens of other ironware articles. Since cast iron was cheaper to produce, it was used widely in products such as pots, pipes, rails, and firebacks—products that did not suffer if the iron was brittle. These items were cast in sand molds in boxes. Iron was poured directly from the furnaces into these molds.

The first iron smelted in America came from Massachusetts. In 1643, John Winthrop II convinced a group of English capitalists to invest in furnaces and forges in the bog ore regions of the Bay Colony of Saugus at Lynn on the Saugus River and also at Braintree. Winthrop's ten-foot dam across the Saugus River flooded about 1,000 acres but gave thirty feet of head to the thirty-foot waterwheel. Although Winthrop grievously misjudged the quantity of ore in the region, and although his successor just as grievously mismanaged the finances of the operation, the iron works eventually started to produce iron. They lasted more than fifty years. The plant included a large blast furnace, a forge with a 500-pound trip-hammer, and a rolling and slitting mill for making sheets of iron and nails. This Massachusetts plant compared favorably with any iron works in England or on the Continent. By the time America signed its treaty with England after the Revolution, seventy-six other iron works were producing metal

Figure 3–2. Colonial power source. This overshot water wheel, part of a Virginia mill which has been traced back as far as 1777, is typical of such colonial power sources. Water was delivered to the wheel through the boxlike flume at the upper right. The flow of water could be controlled by a box gate valve. In the illustration the miller is propping up a beam which connects to the flume valve by a linkage. In some mills energy from the turning wheel was converted from vertical to horizontal by a series of peg-tooth gears; in others, possibly this one included, the power was taken off by belts to operate saws and other vertical rotary equipment. (A circular saw blade of later design appears to be standing upright behind the miller.) Wherever abundant supplies of sharply falling water were to be found, the colonists capitalized upon the energy given them and built mills. Courtesy U.S. Forest Service.

in Massachusetts. The glacial lakes and ponds of the region were replete with bog ore and the streams were right for waterwheels.

Numerous ponds with bog ore in central New Jersey, rock ore in northern New Jersey, good streams, timber, and the nearby New York market pushed New Jersey into the iron industry by the end of the 1600s. The Pennsylvania industry started later; there were about twenty bloomeries operating near Philadelphia in 1734, but shortly after this time the colony converted most of its bloomeries into blast furnaces making cast iron.

Growth of the Iron Industry

By the time of the Revolution, iron works had been built in every colony except Georgia. In 1700, utilizing mainly bog ore, the seaboard colonies produced about 1,500 tons; fifty years later 10,000 tons, one-seventh of the world's production. By 1775, the industry had pushed well inland and upped its output to 30,000 tons, third in the world behind only Russia and Sweden.

The plentiful supplies of land, ore, timber and water were combined in gigantic iron plantations of colonial days. Martha Furnace iron plantation in the Pine Barrens of southern New Jersey encompassed 20,000 acres, but dozens of other plantations were as small as a few hundred acres.

Acreage was important because of the need for charcoal. A typical blast furnace devoured about five to six thousand cords of wood or approximately 250 acres of woodland a year, with many more hundreds of cords used by forges and blacksmith shops. The Hopewell Village iron plantation in Pennsylvania used 15,000 cords of wood a year for its charcoal supply. The plantations employed large crews of woodcutters, charcoal burners, furnacemen and forgemen, blacksmiths, and farmhands. The plantations also provided themselves with gristmills, sawmills, general stores, sometimes even churches and schools. Cottages and huts were clustered around the furnace and forges. A little farther away, one could find a vegetable garden. The ironmaster very likely overlooked the scene from his Georgian mansion on a nearby hill. The iron plantation contained elements of the feudal village as well as the company town.

By 1770, the plantations were producing more iron products than England and Wales. The pig iron from their blast furnaces could be cast directly into pots, pans, stove plates or many other iron goods. The larger operations had rolling and slitting mills that flattened the wrought iron into strips and cut nail rods, from which iron nails were forged by hand. A few plantations possessed plate mills where red-hot bars were thinned under the beatings of trip-hammers, dipped into a tin alloy, and formed into pans, coffee pots, and other utensils. It was the growing number of these mills that frightened British manufacturing interests.

The conclusion of the colonial iron story came not only when the hundreds of people surrounding the industry became concerned over the new policy enforcing the ban on intercolonial trade and on the construction of finishing mills, but even more so when a new social and political force emerged at the time of the Revolution. This new class of ironmasters and owners of iron plantations was willing to do its utmost to be certain that Washington's army was well supplied with cannon and

Figure 3–3. Colonial Iron Works. These old drawings indicate the primitive nature of the colonial iron industry. Iron plantations were characterized by villages clustered near blast furnaces, always situated close to seemingly inexhaustible timber resources for charcoal fuel. The lower drawing, from *Old Scribners Monthly*, illustrates how cast iron "pigs" were formed in sand moulds at a typical colonial furnace.

shot, muskets and even bayonets from steel mills constructed earlier in defiance of the Iron Act.

Over and above these hostile reactions of a people under imperial constraints, a serious depression at the end of the 1760s and the new revenue-raising measures of the English ministries added their weight to documents, appointments, licenses, deeds, bonds, leases, playing cards, ship documents, newspapers and pamphlets. The Townshend Act of 1767 taxed certain English manufactured goods imported by America—glass, paper, tea, painter's colors, and white and red lead. The duties had to be paid in bills of exchange or specie at a time when specie could hardly be found to pay for legitimate imports. These laws were eventually repealed, but the Tea Act and the "Intolerable Acts" replaced them. Revolution, smoldering for years, was the colonists' response.

Limits to Growth

Nonetheless, even the victory of the colonies over England did not change the fairly simple socioeconomic, political, and technological apparatus of American society. So long as these institutions remained primitive and undeveloped, the possibilities of rapid resource exploitation, large resource surplus for trade, and consequent growth of local wealth that could be reinvested in further growth all stayed limited.

The technologies of agriculture, timber, and mineral extraction scarcely were improvements over medieval techniques. No common medium of economic exchange enabled large trading transactions to take place beyond "book credit" of the local merchant. Roads and river transportation were undependable at best, impossible at worst; this also placed curbs on trading activities. Colonies remained isolated and independent political units before the Federal Constitution was ratified. The colonies competed with one another for trade. Furthermore, by 1770, only five cities claimed more than 8,000 inhabitants each; the country was overwhelmingly agricultural. European cities could use American produce, but political obstacles hindered trading arrangements.

For rapid resource exploitation to occur, a way had to be found to distribute (Indian) land to settlers, and new political, economic, social and technological arrangements had to be developed. This story is the burden of the remainder of the book.

References for Further Reading

The classic treatment of early northern agriculture is the *History of Agriculture in the Northern United States: 1620-1860* by Percy W. Bidwell and John I. Falconer (1941). The most recent study of American agriculture is John T. Schlebecker's excellent *Whereby We Thrive: A History of American Farming, 1607-1972* (1975). Alice Morse Earle's *Home Life in Colonial Days* (1910) and *The Golden Age of Homespun* by Jared van Wagenen (1963) complement these books with a detailed account of everyday life on pioneer farms. The *Letters from an American Farmer* (1957) by eighteenth century immigrant J. Hector St. John de Crevecoeur presents a contemporary view of American frontier life. *Lands that Our Fathers Plowed*, edited by David B. Greenberg (1969), contains interesting and informative original accounts by early American settlers. It includes an excerpt from Peter Kalm's *Travels Into North America*. Lawrence H. Gipson has written an excellent background study of the American Revolution, *The Coming of the Revolution* (1954), including the role of natural resources and manufacture. *The Epic of Steel* by Douglas I. Fisher (1963) contains abundant historical material on the development of the colonial iron and steel industry. Louis M. Hacker's *The Course of American Economic Growth and Development* (1970) lucidly explains some of the economic causes of the American Revolution. William Cronon has written an extremely interesting ecological history of colonial New England, *Changes in the Land: Indians, Colonists, and the Ecology of New England* (1983). And Wilbur R. Jacobs' excellent treatise, *Dispossessing the American Indian: Indians and Whites on the Colonial Frontier* (1985), not only documents the powerful impact of whites on Indians through fur trade, but also covers such themes as the "noble savage" and the "land ethic" among American Indians.

Part Two

THE NEW NATION

Chronology of Major Events

1781	Articles of Confederation ratified by 13 states.
1784	Englishman Henry Cort patents iron puddling and rolling process.
1784-1788	First major American depression.
1785	Ordinance of 1785 for survey and distribution of public domain passed by Congress.
	First American turnpike authorized by Virginia.
1787	Northwest Ordinance passed by Congress.
	First American cotton mill founded at Beverly, Mass.
1787-1788	Constitution ratified by eleven states.
1788	Upper Mississippi lead deposits exploited.
1790-1791	Hamilton's economic program enacted by Congress.
1790	First U.S. Census: 3,929,627. Over 90% engaged in agriculture.
1791	First U.S. Bank established by Congress.
1792	American Robert Gray rediscovers the Columbia River in Oregon territory.
1793	Eli Whitney invents the cotton gin.
1800	Yankee ships cruise Pacific coast looking for sea otters.
	Harrison Land Law enacted.
1803	Louisiana Purchase and Lewis and Clark Expedition.
1805	First cattle drive from the Ohio Valley to the East.
1807	Fulton's steamboat makes successful Hudson River run.
1808	John Jacob Astor organizes the American Fur Company.
1811	Nicholas Roosevelt's successful steamboat run down the Ohio-Mississippi.
1812-1814	War of 1812 and stimulation of domestic manufacturing.
1816	The second U.S. Bank established.
1817	Henry Clay imports the first Hereford cattle into the U.S.
1818	Cumberland Road completed to Wheeling.
	Treaty of Joint Occupation of Oregon Territory between U.S. and Great Britain.
	Jethro Wood patents an iron plow with interchangeable parts.
1819-1822	First American banking crisis.
1820	U.S. Census: 9,638,453 (7.2% urban).
1821	Moses Austin receives a land grant to settle in eastern Texas.
	Mexico wins independence from Spain.
	William Becknell opens the Santa Fe Trail.
1824	First sample of Peruvian guano introduced to U.S.
1825-1860	Cotton remains largest U.S. export.
1825	Erie Canal officially opened.
1830	First Preemption Act passed.
	Ten thousand Anglos settled in eastern Texas.
1830-1845	Indians removed to west of the Mississippi River.
1831	First American railroads begin operation.

1832	First American clipper ship launched at Baltimore.
	George Catlin proposes national park.
1833	California Trail opened by Joseph Walker.
	Obed Hussey patents first successful horse-drawn grain reaper.
	Frederick Geissenhainer patents iron smelting process with anthracite coal.
1834	Cyrus McCormick patents grain reaper.
1836	Republic of Texas wins independence.
	Jackson's Specie Circular issued.
1837	John Deere develops steel plow.
	Henry Ellsworth of the Patent Office distributes foreign seeds.
1837-1843	Panic of 1837 followed by general business depression.
1840	Douglas Houghton discovers copper on Keweenaw Peninsula, Lake Superior.
	Agricultural Division of Patent Office established.
1842	Great Migration to Oregon country begins on Oregon Trail.
1844	Samuel F. B. Morse develops first practical telegraph.
	Lake Superior iron deposits discovered.
	Grain header patented by George Esterly.
1845	Texas annexed to the United States.
1846	Oregon Treaty with Great Britain.
1846-1848	War with Mexico. Treaty of Guadalupe-Hidalgo (1848) cedes Texas, California and New Mexico territories to U.S.
1847	Mormons begin irrigation in Utah.
1848	Gold discovered at Sutter's Mill, California.
1849	U.S. Department of Interior established.
	Mormon organization of Utah and Nevada territory.
1850	First of railroad land grants adopted by Congress.
1853	Chicago linked to New York by railroad.
1855	St. Marie Canal re-opened to link Lakes Superior and Huron.
1856	Englishman Henry Bessemer and American William Kelley independently develop converters for steel production.
1857-1858	Panic of 1857 causes sharp business depression.
1858	Silver discovered in Nevada.
	Marsh harvester for gathering grain into bundles patented.
1859	Colonel Drake successfully drills for oil at Titusville, Pa.
	Pikes Peak Gold Rush in Colorado.
1860	U.S. Census: 31,443,321 (19.8% urban).
	Secession of South Carolina.

Chapter 4

FRONTIER LANDS, INDIANS, AND SPECULATORS

The founding fathers realized that their infant nation's future was tied to its expansive reaches of land. A few among them conjured utopian dreams about its disposal to the downtrodden poor. They wanted to establish an agrarian paradise. The more practical ones would have been quite content to pay off the public war debts with one quick sale of all the land. Some of them saw in the land a golden opportunity to speculate; they hoped to pay long-overdue personal debts or to make a fast fortune. It hardly seemed to occur to any founding fathers that the land was already occupied.

It is true that in theory federal law recognized the Indians as owners of the land. The very first Land Ordinance of 1785 provided that title to a region be cleared by treaty with Indian tribes before the land could be surveyed and sold. In practice, whites occupied Indian lands long before the chiefs were called to treaty councils with government agents. The agents then bargained for the land with liquor and manufactured goods. Although some tribes learned later shrewdly to bid the price higher than any settler or land company would be willing to pay, Indians actually had little choice in the matter. If chiefs were not cooperative, their tribes could be forced out of their lands by the U.S. Army, which could be called in after fraud or persuasion failed.

A more basic conflict between Indians and whites lay in their fundamental cultural beliefs about the use of land. Despite a century and a half of white acculturation, most Indians still could not completely fathom the meaning of private property. Land was to be used in common, according to Indian understanding; it could not be bought, sold and traded for trinkets. A Cayuse Indian chief, Pee-o-pee-o-mox-a-mox, represented the Indian viewpoint to government negotiator I.I. Stevens at the Walla Walla Treaty council of 1855: "Goods and the earth are not equal; goods are for using on the Earth. I do not know where they have given land for goods." (Quoted in Carstensen.) A treaty might have signified the willingness of a tribe to share its lands but not fencing them off for the private and exclusive use of white settlers. Nor did most Indians understand why such a drastic action had to be taken.

Wars became inevitable as Indians were pushed farther and farther west. Finally, in 1823, President Monroe, accepting reports that lands west of the Mississippi were too dry and severe for white settlement, instructed his negotiators to promise the Indians that they would never again be bothered by the white man's intrusions if they moved peaceably to the western designated Indian regions. But even as the first tribes were moving onto the new Indian territory west of Missouri and Iowa, settlers were crossing their lands on their way to California and Oregon, helping themselves to wild game along the route. When western mining booms were reported back to the East, Monroe's promise died. It was buried when railroad construction to the west coast reached the high plains.

State Land Disposals

The sensitive feelings of Pee-o-pee-o-mox-a-mox notwithstanding, land was very much an article white Americans bargained over, especially after the Revolution, when "land jobbing," as speculation was called then, offered the greatest promise of financial gain. At that time, land speculators were not interested in developing the lands. They wanted only to resell them as quickly as possible at the highest rate of profit. Since the frontier remained within the borders of the original states after the Revolution, the first land schemes were hatched by influential state legislatures, the beneficiaries of estates confiscated from the Loyalists after the Revolution.

For land-hungry New Englanders the shortest route to lumber-rich and fertile lands west of the Appalachians lay in the Mohawk Valley, which cuts a groove between the mountains in New York from northern Massachusetts to Lake Ontario. In one generation after the war, New York added at least half a million new settlers to its population. Areas in the western regions had already been cleared of forests by Indians of the Six Nations, largely agricultural and sedentary tribes, and these clearings were well suited for farming. The Nations were cajoled, threatened, and raided by Generals John Sullivan and James Clinton until they sold their land and moved farther west or onto reservations.

New York's fast-running rivers and falls excited eastern capitalists looking for inexpensive new sites to develop logging and manufacturing plants. Reports of the magnificent falls at Niagara brought to its edge thousands of curious travellers, as well as financiers who brainstormed a hundred and one ideas for its exploitation.

Sale of New York Land

So much land jobbing was undertaken during the two decades after the war that its history defies a summary treatment. The selling of New York State gives some idea of the frenetic pace of the business. Much of it first belonged to Massachusetts, which claimed all of the western section. In 1786, Massachusetts ceded its claim in return for the right to sell 6,000,000 acres of the land in western New York. The sale took little time to execute, with two of its citizens, Nathaniel Gorham and Oliver Phelps, buying it *in toto* for a million dollars payable in three installments, on the condition that they reimburse the Indians for their land. Gorham and Phelps tried hard to unload the land quickly, but time ran out and they were forced to turn over two-thirds of their tract to Robert Morris, a signer of the Declaration of Independence.

From his banking operation in Philadelphia, Morris managed to earn the reputation as the "speculator's speculator" during a period of American history when competition for the title was formidable. With a low resistance to bargains, Morris continually performed juggling feats with hundreds of thousands of acres, paying for acreage in the northwest with money from southern land deals, and spending time in debtors prison when his machinations didn't work out. Morris couldn't hold his New York lands as long as he desired, hard-pressed as he was for cash, so he sold them to a group of English capitalists headed by Sir William Pulteney, and to an adroit Dutch banking syndicate, for lands known as the Holland Purchase. (Most post-Revolutionary speculators went first to wealthy Europeans for quick resale deals. Large amounts of venture capital were beginning to be accumulated from English burgeoning manufacturing enterprises and established Dutch trading profits.)

Pulteney hired one of the first promotion men of the new country, Captain Charles Williamson, who spread advertising literature of the "Genesee Country" widely over America, Britain, and France. No favorable detail was excepted: fertile farming land, thick forests, large salt springs, and a superior "healthy" climate. (Word had gotten out that people of the area suffered from many illnesses, perhaps because of the profusion of mosquito-bearing lakes.) Talk of the impending construction of a canal and the probability of world markets for the farmer's goods was a highlighted feature of the promotional tracts. This style was reproduced in a thousand pamphlets to apply to as many communities in the next half century. Even the buyers of the Holland Purchase, who divided their tract among themselves, caught on to the method in their attempts to sell land. Ad campaigns seemed to be at least partially responsible for the huge numbers of people who flocked to upstate New York between 1790 and

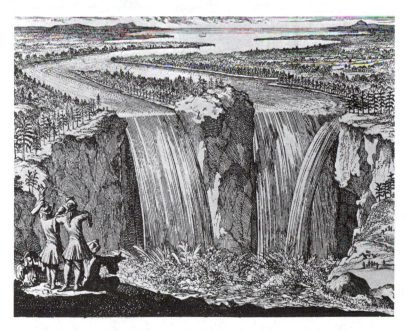

Figure 4–1. Niagara Falls. The wild gestures of the men in this early American engraving can be interpreted in two ways: either in ecstatic admiration for the wonders of Niagara Falls, or in entreprenurial excitement about the commercial possibilities of the falls.

1820—over 800,000 new settlers. Leading the rush were small farmers from southern New England who were discouraged about poor yields and high debts.

To protect the newcomers of their state from Indians and the British, many New York lawmakers sought to populate the buffer regions along the northern St. Lawrence frontier. These regions were offered as military bounty land to ex-servicemen, but they never rose to the bait. Heavily forested, the terrain was rough and well-known as the hunting grounds of several Indian tribes. The state went ahead with a surveying of the four million acres, named it "The Ten Towns of the St. Lawrence," and put it on the market in moderately-sized plots. Alexander Macomb finally bought most of the territory and resold it over a period of years.

Another new military tract of 1,500,000 acres east of the Pulteney Genessee purchase was opened for veterans in the 1790s, but virtually all of this valuable farmland was bought up from the ex-servicemen for a pittance by omnipresent speculators. This pattern was repeated whenever other military bounty land was opened along the frontier. In many instances, though, when speculators arrived at the sites, they found squatters who were armed with local support and encouragement, and who were fully prepared to defend "their" land. Litigation over land claims soon became a common feature of the new frontier. (Later, half of the population of one small town in the Missouri territory was said to have been made up of lawyers.)

Most of the New York lands were sold from between two and four dollars an acre depending on location and guesses about soil quality. Several years' credit was offered by land companies and speculators and only a small down payment was required, because other speculators and the Ohio companies were attempting to lure prospective buyers to their own regions. During bad times, as in 1807 or 1819, when buyers could not make payments, creditors sometimes accepted produce in lieu of payments, but more common were foreclosures, crop and livestock seizures, and a drift into tenancy. Huge manorial estates in the style of plantation owners of the South were common in upstate New York. Some landlords required bushels of wheat for rent much as had the medieval lords; they lent money at high interest rates to their tenants, and they operated the only local stores. The first decade of the nineteenth century brought violent rent wars in New York, unparalleled in the history of the country.

Southern Land Sales

From the Hudson River to the Georgia territory, the folded ridges of the Appalachians effectively slowed the westward movement. Old Indian paths winding around mountains and through gaps which followed the trails of migratory wildlife provided the earliest routes west. South of New York, pioneers headed for the forks of the Ohio at Fort Pitt or worked their way through the Cumberland Gap in western Virginia to eastern Kentucky and Tennessee. Many emigrants stayed in the mountains; others preferred to settle in the valleys between the mountain ribs where they found plenty of fresh springs for livestock and superb limestone, which produced calcium-rich soil. In central Pennsylvania the Amish came through after these first settlers, bought their farms, and conserved the yield of the land. Pioneers in the mountains everywhere found abundant game and fish to supplement the produce of their small farms.

On the southwest frontier, Indian tribes refused to sell their lands and move. This detail did not deter the Georgia legislature from selling all lands west of the Alabama River up to the Mississippi, about 22,000,000 acres, for about a half million dollars. The buyers, four Yazoo companies, lost no time reselling the land to other wealthy speculators in the Northeast. Seven years after the original land deals in 1796, a reform Georgia legislature declared the Yazoo transactions null and void because of "fraud, atrocious speculation, and collusion." Eventually the U.S. government gained control of the land, but it had to pay Yazoo speculators over $4,000,000 in settlements.

The Federal Public Domain

No sooner had Lord Cornwallis handed over his sword in defeat than a serious dispute arose among the new states of the Confederation over the disposition of lands west of the Appalachians. Older states—Massachusetts, Connecticut, New York, Virginia, North Carolina, South Carolina and Georgia—claimed that their original charters granted them sea-to-sea (i.e., the Mississippi) rights. Maryland led five other states without western lands in a fight to put western lands under federal control. The smaller states had a genuine fear of the power of the larger states, but an

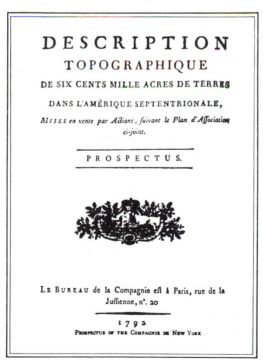

Figure 4–2. One of the first land promotion brochures in American history. This pamphlet was circulated widely in France to attract buyers and settlers to western New York State land. Like thousands of tracts which have followed it, it offered an objective, "scientific" description of the quality of the land and its commercial possibilities. Courtesy New York Public Library.

equally significant fear in the hearts of some influential land jobbers in the Maryland legislature was that they would be left out of the gains to be made on western lands if individual states administered them. Maryland refused to sign the Articles of Confederation until the larger states ceded their claims to the western lands. New York, then Virginia, and finally the rest of the larger states capitulated to the demand.

Thereupon over 200 million acres, called the public domain, had to be organized, distributed and somehow governed. By 1784, Congress was being pressured to act on the question of the public lands. But first they had to solve basic problems: How were the lands to be organized? Who was to get them and at what price, if any?

Colonial land policy had varied from region to region, but by the middle of the 1700s two traditional patterns had been established: the structured township system of New England and the scattered, individualized proprietary system of the middle and southern colonies. The two methods evolved into two ways of establishing land claims. In New England, lots were surveyed before they were occupied; in the South, a squatter or settler described his land in terms of irregular natural boundaries.

After a number of stormy sessions and a report by Thomas Jefferson, the Confederation government incorporated a variety of the New England land system in the Land Ordinance of 1785. The land was to be surveyed in townships six miles square, divided into thirty-six sections of one square mile each (640 acres). It was to be auctioned at a minimum purchase price of one dollar per acre with a minimum purchase of 640 acres. One section per township was to be set aside and sold to pay for the establishment of schools in the township.

In the first transactions, Congress sold a million and a half acres on the Ohio and Muskingum Rivers to the Ohio Company, a group of New England Revolutionary War veterans. Because the buyers used depreciated Continental certificates, their cost amounted to about eight or nine cents an acre. Then a group of Congressmen formed the Scioto Company and bought five million acres on the Ohio River near the Scioto for a similar price per acre. And yet another Congressman, Judge John Cleves Symmes, bought a million acres in the Ohio region, also using depreciated Continental certificates of indebtedness.

Because of the settlements these companies proposed to establish, it was necessary for Congress to provide for the government of the old Northwest. The Northwest Ordinance of 1787 vested authority in a governor, a secretary and three judges appointed by the national government until a region attained a population of 5,000 adult, free, male citizens. Then it could have a separate territorial government and send representatives to Congress. When the population reached 60,000, the territory could be admitted into the Union with full equality of statehood. The Ordinance also included a bill of rights and a provision encouraging the establishment of schools along with a prohibition against the extension of slavery. The bill of rights and slavery provisions were later written into the Constitution.

The Ohio River Country

Speculators in federal lands first focussed their attention on the Ohio River region. The river could be picked up in western Pennsylvania or reached overland from Lake Erie and navigated for a thousand miles to New Orleans with only a few serious rapids. Settlers could stop at a thousand points along the Ohio's serpentine route and buy land nearby. Future commercial centers of the territory were bound to be lucrative land investments.

Many Indian tribes, however, refused to sign treaties; they were challenged by the fledgling U.S. Army. Forts were built close to Indian lands north of the Ohio River, where the army suffered several humiliating defeats before General Anthony Wayne augmented his forces and in 1794 won the Battle of Fallen Timbers over the Miami warriors. He was then able to intimidate Ohio Indians into signing the Greenville Treaty, separating Indians and settlers along a boundary in north-central Ohio country. At the time it was believed that white settlements would remain in regions near the Ohio River, far south of the boundary.

For a decade before Fallen Timbers, thousands of pioneers each year were floating down the Ohio on their way to new settlements. The first seven ranges (sets of townships) had been surveyed in eastern Ohio country just west of Pittsburgh and the panhandle of what would be West Virginia. Southwest of the ranges was the land of the Ohio Company of Associates, who developed grandiose plans for settlement. One of their charter members, Rev. Manasseh Cutler, proclaimed that their development would provide a model for the settlement of the rest of America. In 1788, they named their first community at the mouth of the Muskingum on the Ohio "Marietta" in honor of Queen Marie Antoinette of France—perhaps a prophetic omen of the venture's future. The settlement had an auspicious inauguration with the building of the huge fort "Martius" and a celebration of the Fourth of July with venison, bear, turkey, and six-foot broiled pike. Around the fort the enthusiastic developers planned an expansive city with streets ninety feet broad and large sections reserved for civic, social, religious, and educational buildings. But by 1793, the Ohio Company had not sold enough of its land to make any payment beyond the first. Because of Indian problems and the hardships of the life, only a few hundred adults were attracted to the area. Nonetheless, by 1815 Marietta had established thriving shipbuilding and rope industries. The town boasted about two hundred dwellings. (The unsold land had reverted to the federal government.)

The Scioto lands underwent a more inglorious history because of overt fraud and deceit. Unable to find American buyers for their lands, the speculators succeeded in convincing the politically persecuted sponsors of about 500 French settlers to emigrate to Ohio. When the entourage arrived in 1790, they discovered that their deeds did not even apply to Scioto lands, but rather to those of the Ohio Company, for which they were obliged to pay an additional $1.25 an acre. The wealthy emigrants in the group, shocked at the primitive conditions of the frontier, soon departed for home or for French settlements in Louisiana. The poor were left in what was called Gallipolis to fend for themselves in an unknown country. In 1795, the federal government, which recovered the Scioto lands, offered 25,200 acres to the French as a substitute for their invalid titles, but only a few of the original settlers were still around. In the next two decades, though, the town built itself up and prospered because of the continued influx of pioneers into Ohio.

The Symmes tract in southwestern Ohio was more successful, owing largely to fertile lands and a bend in the Ohio where he founded Losantiville, renamed Cincinnati after the Society of Revolutionary officers. In the northeastern corner of the state

Connecticut had reserved the right to 5,000 square miles (the "Western Reserve") when it ceded its western lands to the federal government. Without large speculative gambles, these lands filled in slowly from east to west rather than south from Lake Erie, and the villages retained a New England flavor—town halls, village greens, and Georgian style churches. Failing agriculture and depleted soils contributed to the migration from Connecticut to the Western Reserve. Towns along the lake became flourishing ports for vessels sailing from New York State and for fur-bearing ships from Detroit.

New Public Land Policy

With the demise of the big Congressional speculators of the late 1780s, land jobbing subsided but made a strong comeback in the early 1800s along with a change in the credit policy of the government. The western territories were beginning to send representatives to Congress in the 1790s. These emissaries of western interests were instructed to tell Congress that government policy discriminated against poor settlers. Emigrants did not need 640 acres of farmland, nor could they pay $640 for land and have enough left over to pay for equipment and supplies until the farm began to produce goods. Largely because of the western influence the Land Law was revised in 1796, supposedly in the interest of the small farmer. The credit system was inaugurated, allowing the buyer a year to pay for half his land but at the same time raising the price to two dollars an acre. Since the settler still had to buy 640 acres, he had to come up with $640 in thirty days and the second $640 within a year—far too much to expect any farm to earn so soon. Furthermore, the value of government securities, with which most buyers paid for land, continued to rise until the turn of

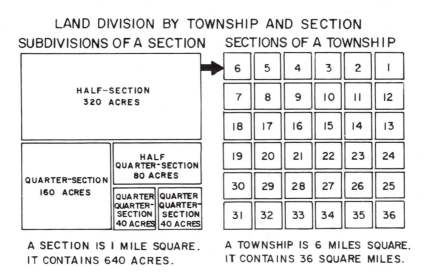

A SECTION IS 1 MILE SQUARE. IT CONTAINS 640 ACRES.

A TOWNSHIP IS 6 MILES SQUARE. IT CONTAINS 36 SQUARE MILES.

Figure 4–3. Land division under the federal Land Ordinance of 1785.

the century when they reached par. Land bought from the federal government after 1796, therefore, cost several times more than it did in the 1780s.

In 1800, the delegate from the Northwest Territory, William Henry Harrison, convinced Congress to change the provisions of the Land Law. Congress acquiesced, lowering the minimum purchase to 320 acres and extending the terms of credit to four years. In 1804, the minimum purchase was lowered again, this time to a quarter-section of land, 160 acres. Congress could afford to encourage settlement, however, since a year earlier it had purchased the Louisiana territory—523,446,200 acres of land—from Napoleon at about three and a half cents an acre.

The new land laws made western migration so attractive that wave after wave of easterners, mixed with increasing numbers of European immigrants, began the trek west. Land jobbers didn't miss the new opportunity to bid on land, and their presence assured the government of high prices for land. Since the land was fertile in the eastern Mississippi regions, credit terms were liberal, and prices for cotton and staples were high, potential buyers numbered in the thousands. Speculators succumbed to the temptation of overbuying. By the end of the first decade of the century, high inflation and a quick drop in cotton prices caught land buyers by surprise. Actual settlers found themselves in the same straits as jobbers, and both groups petitioned Congress for relief. Congressmen were loath to foreclose; instead they chose to give relief in the form of lower payments and postponements rather than revise a law that inevitably brought heightened speculation. Year after year, land relief bills were proposed and passed in Congress despite strong opposition from eastern manufacturing interests which feared "Ohio fever" and greater declines in the eastern labor supply.

Congress was not so generous to squatters on the frontier: Those who improved their lands were only to lose them at land office auctions to high-bidding speculators. Squatters wanted preemption rights: that is, they demanded the privilege of buying their improved lands at the minimum price per acre without competitive bidding. Conservative congressmen deplored the suggestion, arguing that a preemption law would reward lawbreaking squatters who were not supposed to be on the land until it was surveyed. Furthermore, they claimed that a preemption law would reduce revenues from the sale of lands at higher prices.

The Westward Movement

Meanwhile the eastern exodus continued: through the Mohawk Valley to Lake Erie and Cleveland, and overland to the Ohio River; through central Pennsylvania on the Kittanning Path to Pittsburgh and the Ohio, or to the same destination by way of the Forbes Road across southern Pennsylvania from Philadelphia; or through western Virginia via the Cumberland Gap near the upper branches of the Tennessee and Cumberland Rivers and on the Wilderness Road north to central Kentucky at Boonesboro; or all the way around the foot of the Appalachians in Georgia.

The Ohio River received the bulk of the traffic from northern migrations west. In 1804 and 1805, the Indian treaties of Vincennes and Grouseland signaled the extension of the western frontier into southern Indiana territory. Settlers were able to buy good farmland inexpensively there, since wealthy land jobbers were not found in abundance in Indiana and Illinois; the big money during the first generation of the century was to be made in the cotton lands of the eastern Mississippi region. The distinctive feature of the Indiana and Illinois settlements was their heterogeneity. It attracted Americans, French- and German-speaking Swiss, English, German, Welsh, and second- or third-generation French whose families were descended from Montreal trappers.

The landscape of the region also took on a more specialized distinctiveness. The Swiss attempted to set up vineyards and a wine industry in the southeastern Indiana community of Vevay along the Ohio, but drought, frost, and a decidedly unexceptional product discouraged its continuance. Seventy winding miles down the Ohio from Vevay, the pioneer found the notorious Ohio Falls, dropping about twenty-five feet in two miles. Experienced local boatmen could make it through two or three channels during the high water season, but most boats stopped at Louisville on the Kentucky side of the Ohio. A terminus for many boats whose freight was sold locally, Louisville flourished with travel and commercial activity. Boats unloaded their cargoes to be carried through the town to vessels on the other side of the falls, sometimes exchanging goods with their counterparts going down or upstream. A few boats lightened their loads while they ran the "chutes" or channels. Passengers usually stopped in Louisville for a rest in mid-journey.

Utopian Communities

For many years, the largest town in the Indiana territory was Vincennes, on the western border 120 miles up the Wabash River from the Ohio. It had been established as a French trading post and fort in the first quarter of the eighteenth century. In 1800, the Shaker religious sect settled north of Vincennes. By 1825, the Shakers had increased their spread to 1,500 acres, including livestock and mills as well as cropland.

More commercial interchange occurred with the Rappite communistic religious colony of Harmony on the lower Wabash River. The Rappites, or Harmonites, developed a prosperous agricultural community in western Pennsylvania before emigrating to Indiana. In both locations, they sold large quantities of surplus farm and manufactured goods. These Lutheran sectarians constructed over 200 superbly-built frame houses, dormitories, community halls, and manufacturing plants. The amazing community owned excellent farm equipment; it made flour, beer, liquor, wine, clothing, dyes, hats, shoes, linen and flannel. Their vineyards and orchards produced grapes and fruits unexcelled on the frontier, and their pastures supported as many as 2,000 sheep. Newly-settled farmers in a wide sweep around the community depended on Harmony's products to sustain them until their own farms began to yield produce. The Rappites did not look with favor on marriage, preferring celibacy on the way to perfection; thus other German-speaking immigrants were sought to augment their ranks. In 1822, Father George Rapp, leader of the community, convinced his associates of the spiritual need to move back east.

It took little time to find a buyer for the prosperous settlement. In 1824, the Scottish manufacturer-reformer-socialist Robert Owen bought out the Rappite village, equipment, and 30,000 acres of land, seeking to establish an egalitarian utopia. The community's constitution called for equality of labor and property as well as freedom of speech, but no wages were to be paid. Unfortunately his "New Harmony Community of Equality" did not begin to match the success of its predecessors. The intellectuals

Figure 4–4. Two early nineteenth century drawings of life on the Ohio frontier. The pioneer log house is built like a fortress with its characteristic second-story overhang; an early variety of steamboat is passing by on the Ohio River. The second drawing is a highly stylized (and romanticized version) of Cincinnati, also on the Ohio River, where an elegant gentleman calmly steers his flatboat downstream. Actually, early Cincinnati had its own fort for protection and the river was quite wild there. Long sweeps were used to steer the flatboats to maneuver around obstacles or to the bank for unloading or mooring. Courtesy the Ohio Historical Society.

and professionals in his following neglected to learn the skills of farming and home manufactures. Many did not feel like working at all, nor did any of the Rappites care to stay and teach their industries to the energetic ones of the lot. The town became an exciting cultural center, but never the smooth-functioning utopia Owen desired. In fact, he gave up the idea after two years of social chaos, willing the community to his sons.

At the time New Harmony was bought by Owen, Indiana, Illinois and Missouri were just beginning to show signs of settlement. Even in Ohio, most of the populated areas were confined to the Ohio and to rivers and streams flowing into it. The marshy, poorly drained north-central prairies were long avoided because of the illness which was associated with the region. The prairie soils would not prove their productivity until the subsequent generation when a way was found to drain and cultivate the rich, heavy humus.

The South

Ohio, Kentucky, and Tennessee were admitted to the Union before the Louisiana Purchase in 1803. By 1861, fifteen more frontier states were added—Indiana, Illinois, Maine, Missouri, Michigan, Iowa, Wisconsin, California, Oregon and Minnesota in the North and Alabama, Mississippi, Arkansas, Florida and Louisiana in the South. In that year, the population of Ohio had climbed to more than 582,000 people, doubling in less than ten years. Indiana was up to 150,000 and Illinois was over 56,000, while Missouri had a higher population than Illinois because of its slave population.

Land settlement in the South continued earlier patterns of plantation development. In the trans-Appalachian states of Kentucky and Tennessee, under the original jurisdiction of Virginia and North Carolina, a concentrated landownership tradition was begun by large grants. Sixty percent of the Virginia grants in Kentucky (until the latter achieved statehood in 1792) were for grants between one and five thousand acres; forty-four grants for forty to a hundred thousand acres; and four grants over a hundred thousand acres. When Kentucky became a state, it continued the practice by granting seven persons a total of 1,732,000 acres. Squatters who previously worked the lands often stayed on as tenants and continued to improve them until they were resold at a significant profit for the owners. The best farm land in western Tennessee was put into intensive cotton production.

King Cotton ruled over the deep South, particularly in the new territories. By the end of the 1700s, an unprecedented demand pushed up the price of cotton; land prices in the south rose concomitantly. The Whitney gin played an important role in the record prices for land sales, because it could effectively clean the seedy short-staple cotton of the upland areas in the new territories as cheaply as the long-staple variety of South Carolina and Georgia could be ginned.

Hardly any time elapsed between the violent eviction of the Creeks and Cherokees in the 1830s and the sale of their lands for as high as fifty to one hundred dollars an acre. At every land office, federal land sales attracted planters who were looking for new plantations or extensions of old ones; politicians who inevitably speculated for extra income; squatters who hoped to hold on to their land; and moneylenders who offered squatters the cash they needed at high interest or who bid up the price of the land and resold it to them.

With few notable exceptions of cleared lands known to be endowed with rich soils, most of the uncleared land in the cotton regions could not sell for more than five to ten dollars an acre because of the enormous investment in clearing and fencing the land before planting. Planters were accustomed to large-scale operations, utilizing dozens of slaves on hundreds of acres of cropland. The few small farmers who owned their land usually sold out because of the large capital investment needed in cotton production. With the big operations came big profits. In 1815 alone, $18,526,589 was grossed by southerners in cotton. The record profits bought more fields and slaves.

The cotton boom of the southern states was registered in their population figures. Alabama's population went up from a few thousand to 45,000 whites and 21,000 slaves in 1818; Mississippi rose to 56,000 whites and 10,200 slaves in 1820, up 89% in ten years. During this decade lands in these two states were selling for two to five times their value in normal years.

Sectionalism and Speculation

The bottom fell out of the land buying business after the enormous inflation of 1818-19. A number of reasons had encouraged speculative land buying: high prices for goods, especially cotton, at home and abroad; primitive efforts to set up state and private banks, which indiscriminately gave out credit; and the westward movement, especially after the War of 1812, when a small labor surplus developed in the East for the first time in the country's history, assuring land-sellers of eager buyers.

Then, because of overproduction, the price of cotton fell to half its former price and debtors could not make payments on their land. Fly-by-night banks failed and credit suddenly disappeared, along with paper money and specie. Land prices dropped. Crops rotted in the fields, and again appeals went to Congress. Every interest group from small farmers to bankers and speculators sent messages of distress to Washington, petitioning for extensions of credit, reductions in price, or the surrender of only part of the defaulted lands equal in value to the unpaid debt. Congress acted favorably to all of these requests; by 1832, eleven relief acts had been passed.

At the same time Congressmen were determined to apply quick remedies to the depression problem; they settled on the Land Act of 1820. Believing that the land credit system encouraged speculation and inflation, Congress abolished the credit provisions of earlier land laws. As a concession to small farmers, they reduced the minimum price to $1.25 and the minimum acreage to eighty. The law didn't stop speculation when times improved, but rather made it necessary for the frontiersman to borrow the liquid capital needed to pay for the land and start a farm. Congress aided their difficulty somewhat in 1832 when it permitted tracts as small as forty acres—a quarter quarter-section—to be bought from the federal government.

Because of a common interest in land policy, southern and western frontier states formed a coalition to lobby for changes in land policy in the 1820s. They were interested in control over federal lands within the borders of their states, arguing that older states enjoyed an unfair advantage because they could utilize income from the sale of their own state land for internal improvements and education. In new territories and states the financial burden of road and canal construction and education fell to the small landowner, who was not helped by the law of 1820. States complained that their internal improvements enhanced the value of federal lands and that they received no commensurate compensation for the work. If they could dispose of the land themselves, they would do it quickly and cheaply, and they could begin to collect taxes on it to pay for these improvements.

The demands of the western political alliance were compromised over the next two generations, but most of them were eventually written into legislation. Land was granted for the financing of education and internal improvements, as were preemption rights for squatters and finally free land to homesteaders.

The powerful agrarian coalition was feared and fought in the East by manufacturing interests and their Congressional representatives. Eastern efforts could not head off the formation of a new Democratic Party, which brought together agrarian interests of states south and west of the Appalachians, and which even included an incipient labor movement and Loco-Foco-ism, the agrarianism of the East. Andrew Jackson, fighter of the Indians and the British, common man and land speculator, carried the Democratic banner in the campaign of 1828 and defeated eastern banking and manufacturing interests. Land was a major issue of the campaign. If the exodus to the western states continued, eastern industrialists would have to continue to pay higher wages.

The first fruits of the election came in 1830, when the first preemption law was passed and renewed four times in the decade. Preemption laws forgave illegal preemption that had occurred before the passage of each law, but they did not ratify the right in principle. Squatters paid the minimum price of $1.25 an acre up to 160 acres. Although forbidden to do so, settlers were encouraged to find good lands beyond the frontier before Indian treaties were signed and surveying was accomplished. The Preemption Act of 1841 finally acknowledged this prospective preemption, establishing the right of anyone to buy public land if he settled on it and improved it.

The influx of new settlers in the west and southwest brought on renewed conflicts with the Indians. Georgia officials were annoyed with the federal government because it had not carried out its promise to remove Indians from its boundaries after the cession of Georgia's western lands. At the end of the 1820s, Indians still lived on rich lands that plantation owners were anxious to use for cotton. In 1828 the Georgia governor, pressured by mounting public opinion, ordered a survey of federal land, prompting the Cherokees to take legal action against the state. Chief Justice John Marshall upheld the Indian claims—to little avail, since Jackson was determined to use the Army for Indian removal. His Indian Removal Act of 1830 passed Congress by five votes, and the President sent the Army to enforce it. By 1835, over 50,000 Cherokees and Creeks of western Georgia and eastern Alabama; the Chickasaws and Choctaws of Mississippi; and the Seminoles of Florida had been forcibly taken from their ancestral homes and herded a thousand miles to Indian Territory west of the

Mississippi. The five tribes suffered 5,000 deaths due to disease, exposure, accident, and harsh treatment.

The Winnebago and Black Hawk Wars in Illinois and the unorganized Northwest Territory east of Lake Michigan cleared the new frontiers of Indian obstacles to settlement in those areas. In 1834, Congress set off the plains west of the western borders of Missouri and Iowa as Indian Country.

Until the 1830s, the federal government sold only a few million acres each year, but the wars, treaties and surveyings allowed land offices to dump 28,000,000 acres on the market between 1834 and 1835. By that time wildcat banking was well established again, cotton prices high, inflation rising and land sales booming. Immigration from foreign lands, spurred by European wars, religious persecution, and famine, increased enough each year to prevent depopulation in parts of the East. Nonetheless labor was scarce and eastern industrialists and their newspapers predicted economic chaos unless the westward flight was retarded. In 1836 Arkansas and Michigan were admitted to the union.

Innovative Speculators

One of the more unusual phenomena which occurred during this period was the rise of the town promoter. The bright young men of the day, emulating their elder speculator models, attempted a new route to material success—speculation in land and town promotion. A sprinkling of new towns accompanied each wave of settlers crossing the prairie. More than five hundred new town sites were developed in Illinois in the boom years between 1835-37, but the process had started much earlier in Ohio and Indiana.

The idea was to buy up strategic land sites, preferably near a river or a proposed road or canal, then set to work attracting people and small industries so that real estate would rapidly increase in value. The promoter had to lay out wide streets as had been done in Marietta and to donate whole blocks of land for churches, schools, city halls, court houses, parks, etc. Sometimes he built one or more of these structures himself, or bribed county commissioners to choose his own as the county seat. Capital and commerce were thus attracted. Soon the town bustled with markets and shops which in turn multiplied the capital. The promoter then sat back and collected large revenues from land sales and rents or from the marketing of essential goods and services. Thousands of townsites were planned on paper everywhere on the frontier during the era; hundreds were actually built; and many survived and thrived.

Traditional speculation in farmlands never lost momentum in the 1830s. With it, the traditional forms of corruption also stayed alive in the state legislatures, local justices and land office auctions. Public officials sold their influence and inside information to wealthy speculators. Surveyors and land-office agents formed land companies in conjunction with bank stockholders. Squatters were intimidated out of their lands, or induced into borrowing money at interest ranging from 30% to 110% above the allowable rates according to state usury laws. The latter was possible by using common banking bookkeeping tricks. Often speculators colluded to keep the price of land down, deciding before each auction which lands would go to whom.

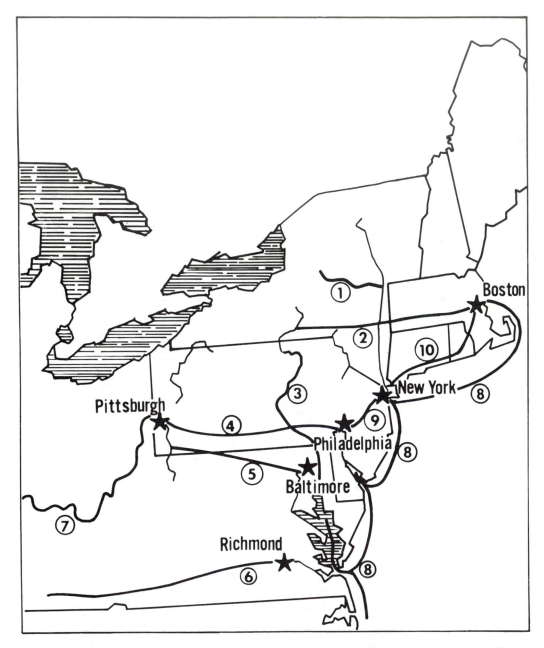

Figure 4–5. Major colonial settlement routes. (1) West from Albany along the Mohawk River valley by land transportation. (2) West from New England into lower New York State. (3) North into Pennsylvania by flatboats hauled or poled up the Susquehanna. (4) West from Philadelphia to Pittsburgh by Conestoga wagon. (5) West from Baltimore through the Cumberland Gap to southwest Pennsylvania. (6) West and south by the Wilderness Trail from Richmond into Kentucky. (7) South and west by flatboat on the Ohio River. (8) From port to port by coastal vessels. (9) and (10) Well-established roads, although scarcely highways by any modern definition, very early in the colonial period. In addition to providing commercial, military, and private traffic facilities, these roads linking Boston, New York, and Philadelphia also proved to be major settlement routes.

Another common fraudulent device grew from preemption laws, which in the case of conflict between two settlers claiming the same quarter section of land, allowed one of them a preemption float for another similar quarter section of unsold surveyed land. Any well-heeled speculator could hire dozens of pseudo-claimants—often Indians or slaves—for a few dollars and send them to preempted property, pick up preemption floats, and with the claims start a new town or two. One energetic speculator tried to lay claim to about half of Milwaukee by utilizing this method. Of course, collusion with the local justice of the peace or judge was necessary if the scheme was to succeed. Speculators and the great land companies could engross so much land and hold it for such high prices that poorer immigrants were forced farther west for free land in Indian territory. It was only a matter of time until the Army was called in to defend them and their land.

Even with preemption rights, settlers found that the cards usually were stacked against them, but finding strength in their collective woe, they formed claims clubs or settlers' associations to protect their claims at auctions. Word of the success of this device spread so fast along the frontier that by the 1830s, claims clubs were a common institution. In effect members of the clubs took the law into their own hands. They chose their own secretaries, who recorded members' claims, which were enforced at the auctions either by persuasion or force. The associations' activities served to deter speculators from bidding against the original claimant. Clubs also settled disputes among their own members and dealt with claim jumpers according to summary frontier justice.

During the 1800s, conventional wisdom considered land speculation as the short route to fortune's door. All manner of men enjoyed the game: squatters who made small improvements and sold their claims to later settlers who staked the claim for preemption privileges; small capitalists who invested in land companies; big eastern capitalists who bought large tracts of land, then quickly resold them to other big buyers; large land companies and individuals who developed and promoted tracts of land; moneylenders big and small; and townsite promoters who sometimes carried out gigantic projects on a shoestring.

In the first two generations of the nineteenth century, almost everything happened to the land that could have happened to it. It was bought, sold, bloodied. Its soil was mined and abandoned, picked over, passed around and abused. It was also nurtured and cultivated, divided into lots great and small. Crooks and honest men rubbed elbows over its disposal. But for all the stingy greed, silly foolishness, caprice and fickleness of land manipulators, mid-nineteenth century America found its white inhabitants substantially better off than they had been fifty years earlier. Someone had to pay the price for this progress, however: a very substantial price in land, culture, and deaths. Precedents established in the first half of the century continued in the latter half, except with greater numbers of settlers and a bigger army to subdue the Native Americans.

The very rapidity with which the land was occupied is a testimonial to the grid system recommended in the public lands report written by Thomas Jefferson and Hugh Williamson. The framers of the report, wittingly or not, developed an economic rationalization that was perfectly suited to the quick disposal of public lands. Thereafter America became a country of squares upon squares, easy to divide and subdivide, buy and sell. Thus the land came to be valued mainly for its economic possibilities rather than for its social, aesthetic, religious, or cultural importance.

Jefferson no doubt wanted only to simplify the process of disposing land and to avoid possible controversies over property then common in the South. Furthermore, the grid division fit into his political philosophy, for he hoped that the smallest squares or "wards" could govern themselves in the manner of early New England towns by direct democracy and send representatives to larger units (squares) corresponding to state and national governments. Because square grids are intrinsically democratic, Jefferson tended to overlook geographical differences between mountains and valleys or rivers and deserts, which could complicate both the economic and political aspects of his scheme.

Although Jefferson's political dream was not institutionalized, the grid system prevailed in the economic life of the country. In this way was the American land packaged as real estate—just another commodity. The development probably was inevitable, but it need not have been realized so early in American history.

References for Further Reading

The "Frontier Hypothesis" of Frederick Jackson Turner at the turn of the twentieth century ignited interest and much research on frontier lands and life. His *Rise of the New West: 1819-1829* (1962) embodies the spirit of the hypothesis and provides good background reading for the chapter. *A History of the Public Land Policies* (1965) by Benjamin H. Hibbard and *Our Landed Heritage* (1962) by Roy M. Robbins detail the interesting history of the public domain. Paul W. Gates has written extensively on the public domain; his *History of Public Land Law Development* (1968) embodies the most recent scholarship on the subject. The anthology, *The Public Lands: Studies in the History of the Public Domain* (1968), edited by Vernon Carstensen, adds depth on the subject by distinguished scholars, and *The Land System of the United States* by Marion Clawson (1968) lucidly explains how the American land systems developed from colonial times to the present. For a fascinating, scholarly volume on the social history, hardships, and daily travails of the people who came to the American colonies, read the exquisite account by Bernard Bailyn, *Voyagers to the West: A Passage in the Peopling of America on the Eve of the Revolution* (1986).

Chapter 5

RESOURCE ENTERPRISES

The Revolutionary War did not serve to solve all of America's economic problems with one sweep. Despite the political advantages of the Revolution, England was transformed into an economic enemy that did its utmost to cut its former colony's lifeline to the West Indies, America's source of hard money. She forbade the British West Indies to trade for American salted beef, pork and dried fish, or to accept shipments of naval stores and provisions in anything other than British ships. France and Spain enacted similar prohibitions. Neither would Great Britain allow her shippers to purchase American-built vessels. American shippers lost the profitable Mediterranean trade because they were no longer protected against pirates by the British navy. Foreign debts, inflated state currencies, bankrupt infant industries and a decided lack of political solidarity and confidence all led to a post-war depression.

Eventually, however, trade agreements were signed with major world powers, smugglers found new ways to avoid British restrictions, and old English trading ties were restrung. By the beginning of the nineteenth century the new nation seemed to find solid economic footing. Agriculture, particularly southern cotton, became the foundation of its strength and wealth.

The Cotton Kingdom of the South

After the Revolution the southern tobacco economy was in a state of near-collapse. Tobacco trade fell off drastically. Overcultivated, abandoned and eroded fields symbolized the decay of the Old South. Some Maryland and Virginia planters turned to wheat growing and subsistence farming on their old tidewater fields. Those who owned newer lands in the Piedmont regions continued to market tobacco, but uncertain and often depressed prices kept them in debt. Even without the secure income of a cash crop, though, planters of the Old South refused to give up their aristocratic life styles. Although their plantations deteriorated, they remained in their mansions and kept their slaves, waiting for a better day.

Farther south, in the Carolinas and Georgia, the planters on the coast grew rich on rice and long-staple (sea island) cotton. Rice growers had learned to use the tides to flood and drain their fields near freshwater rivers, and soils maintained their productivity in the process. Long-staple cotton, introduced into Georgia from the Bahamas in 1786, enjoyed a growing market each year. Its long fibers could be woven into fine cloths; a rolling machine easily separated its black seeds from the lint. The machine pressed the cotton between treadle-driven rollers, popping seeds out the back of the lint. But sea-island cotton could not be grown in the upland regions of the South; it needed a long growing season; it was sensitive to frost, and according to oldtimers, it thrived only in hot, humid salt air.

Short-staple cotton had been grown in the South for home use since the time of the Jamestown colony but not as a cash crop. Its green seeds stayed entangled in the lint and had to be picked out by hand. It took one person almost a day to clean out a pound, compared to the nearly twenty-five pounds of long-staple cotton he or she could process on a treadle-gin. Cotton growers were almost frantic in their efforts to market shortstaple cotton. Cotton material had gained in popularity in England; the new cotton spinning and weaving factories of Arkwright and other English capitalists could supply the demand—but only if they received enough cotton to make into the fabrics. Prices for the staple rose steadily after the Revolution.

It was Eli Whitney who turned things around for the South, and indeed perhaps for the nation. Whitney, a mechanic and graduate of Yale College, met Catherine Littleton Greene in 1793 onboard ship on his way to a tutoring position at a Georgia plantation. While Whitney was visiting Mrs. Greene at her "Mulberry Grove" plantation, the tutor of the Greene children, Phineas Miller, persuaded Whitney to attempt to solve the problem of ginning short-staple cotton. In ten days Whitney produced a model. Cotton was placed in a hopper, one side of which was slatted to permit wire teeth to pull through cotton lint but small enough to exclude cotton seeds. The wires were mounted on a roller, driven by a hand crank. A second roller turning in the opposite direction continuously cleaned the wire teeth. The original model could gin about fifty pounds of cotton a day. Whitney patented the machine and formed a partnership with Miller to manufacture gins in New Haven. Since the design of the machine was quite simple, though, it could be copied by every plantation blacksmith in the South. And it was. The partners fought patent infringements, but the slightest change of construction offered southern judges and juries an excuse for forgiving violations. The two collected sums of money from most southern states, but it was already spent prosecuting offenders. (Later Whitney contracted with the federal government for the mass production of muskets with interchangeable parts, another innovative breakthrough—and another moneyloser.)

Within a decade after Whitney put his gin into production, the stagnant southland had been returned to the height of its former glory. Even successful rice cultivation on the coastal plains was often abandoned in favor of the high profits in cotton. Tobacco planters of the old South rushed into cotton cultivation, even though their depleted soils had not yet naturally recovered or been restored by added nutrients. Before the War of 1812 with Britain, the Piedmont regions of the Carolinas and Georgia lived and breathed cotton on every available field. New waves of settlers poured into the southwest after the Harrison Land Act, then again after the War of 1812 when prices were high again. Hopeful cotton cultivators turned the corner below the Appalachians and filled in spaces around Indian lands all the way to the Mississippi, where levees were built at public expense to hold back flood waters from fertile alluvial land. The soil in the Southwest was rich black or brown loam capable of producing cotton for almost a generation without a significant drop in yields. Since only about six and a half months of frostless temperatures and about twenty-five inches of rain were needed each year to grow short-staple cotton, by 1850 the cotton belt reached from

Figure 5–1. Early cotton gins. The word "gin" probably came from "engine," and its earliest model, below, looked something like this double roller version, although it was more commonly driven by a treadle, not a crank. The reader may wish to speculate on the romantic nature of early engravings of this sort. It is not likely that the slaves enjoyed their work so much as this illustration would suggest. The older cotton gin could clear the seeds from long-staple cotton only. The wooly seeds of the more abundant short-staple cotton had to be cleaned by hand until Eli Whitney perfected his revolutionary gin. Whitney's simple device, depicted on top, utilized a small revolving drum equipped with wire teeth which reached through slats and pulled cotton fiber away from seed. This gin is a redrawn model of the original Whitney gin. Courtesy The Bettmann Archive and the New York Museum of Science and Industry.

the southern boundary of Virginia to northern Florida and straight west to Arkansas and eastern Texas.

Buyers bid for cotton each year in Liverpool, the port of entry for the world's textile center in Manchester, where the price rose or fell depending mainly on the size of the crop from the southern states, which grew three-quarters of the world's supply. At the turn of the nineteenth century the price boomed to twenty-three cents a pound. Oversupply, inflation, and depression near the end of the decade depressed the price, dropping it to a low of seven cents a pound at the outbreak of the war. Peace brought good prices again, up to thirty-three cents a pound in 1818. But in 1819, oversupply because of previous high prices and cheap new land brought the price down again, to eight cents. These cycles continued until the Civil War. America's economic growth during this time was in a large measure tied to the cotton economy. In 1792, the year before the invention of the cotton gin, the country produced about 6,000 bales. By 1859, 4,500,000 bales were grown, packed, and shipped. Cotton's value topped that of the next half dozen cash crops of the nation combined.

Plantations of the Old South

Cotton was usually grown with corn, an important staple on the plantation for slaves and hog-fattening. Corn was planted in March, cotton in April. Corn needed less care than cotton, which had to be hoed, plowed, thinned and watched for destructive insects. Corn came in first; it was picked immediately and husked. Forty to fifty bolls were common on each cotton plant, though the number could double on rich soils. Cotton did not ripen evenly on the plant; first the center whitened for picking; then the lower and finally the upper branches were picked. Pickers dragging long sacks tied to their waists or carrying baskets walked through the rows looking for ripened bolls. All free hands on the plantation were conscripted for cotton harvest, which lasted from the end of August sometimes into January. The good pickers could clear bolls around the plant with both hands at once. Since a planter's acreage was limited to the amount of cotton his workers could pick, he pushed his slaves to the limit during picking season. He encouraged, threatened, even gave money prizes to the the fastest pickers.

The large planters owned horse-powered gins, usually housed in a two-story broken-down shack of a building. A vertical shaft in the center of the bottom floor turned the ginning equipment on the upper floor. To this central shaft was attached a horizontal beam, onto which horses or mules were harnessed and driven in a circle. After the ginning, cotton was hand-tamped into sacks, and it took a person an entire day to fill a sack of about 250 pounds. By 1800 a screw press, which could pack about fourteen sacks a day, utilized a sweep and animal power to press down the lid in bale-shaped containers. Then the bales, later standardized at the weight of 500 pounds each, were stored in warehouses at southern port cities until slaves rolled them up the gangways of merchant ships.

The successful cultivation of cotton did not demand a large estate or dozens of slaves. The proximity of a river for transportation and good soil often were more important. Nonetheless, unless a small planter had the money for a number of slaves and capital equipment and started cotton cultivation at a time prices were high, he could not survive the lean years. Very often small planters were forced to sell out, or they lost their lands by defaulting on mortgage payments. Large plantations were dominant on the southern landscape by 1860.

The most depressing aspect of the cotton scenario was the slave trade. Although the African slave trade was legally outlawed by Congress in 1808, internal buying and selling of slaves among the southern states was continued under the impetus of a booming cotton market. A slave cost $300 in 1795 and $1250 to $1800 in 1860. Surplus slaves in upper southern states were sold to planters in the lower South. Thus developed a lucrative business supporting dealers, traders, agents and auctioneers. Some businessmen speculated in slaves, buying cheap and holding them for a rapid rise in prices. Others smuggled slaves from Africa. During good cotton years, Virginia exported about ten thousand slaves a year, Mississippi receiving about the same number.

As the plantation system spread through the South, the overseer took on more responsibilities on behalf of planters or absentee owners. The overseer rode on his horse behind gangs of slaves plowing or picking; he meted out the labor each day; wrote reports and inventories; made major crop decisions; and maintained the property of the plantation. Slaves represented a substantial investment and were generally well fed. Field hands ate at least a peck of corn meal each and from three to five pounds of bacon or pork a week.

Besides cotton, rice and sugar were important cash crops of the antebellum South. Strong competition from the East Indies and a destructive caterpillar ended indigo production by the time of the Revolution. It wasn't until 1794 that in Louisiana the process of sugar refining became advanced enough to be pursued on a large scale. A Creole, Etienne de Bore, built his own grinding and boiling mill, hired an experienced sugar-maker, and inaugurated successful production. Sugar cane plantations remained in the delta regions of southeastern Louisiana where the soil was productive and growing season long. Floods, frosts, fluctuating prices and changes in tariff protection closed down many large sugar operations; yet sugar crop tonnage in 1853 reached 220,000. Slaves worked most sugar plantations.

Cane stalks were planted in February, laid in deep furrows. They sprouted, grew, and were ready for harvesting by late summer. The first cane cut was not stripped of its leaves but matted in them and saved to serve as seed for the following year's planting. Then the regular harvest began. Stalks were slashed by heavy machete-type knives—first at the leaves, then at the ground. Finally the stalks were topped of green joints. The entire plantation worked feverishly trying to beat the frost, for if the frost came early, sugar juices often soured.

Every sugar plantation had its own mill for grinding and boiling. After pressing out the juice between rollers, the mill operator removed impurities from the liquid by heating it with limewater and pouring off the scum. The clarified juice was then boiled in a series of caldrons, with the heat increased as the juice thickened until the concentrate became thick, brown and moist. New varieties of cane and more efficient processes increased production and yielded better quality sugars as they were adopted during the first half of the century.

The Change in Northern Agriculture

Whitney's gin, together with a climate and soils encouraging cotton cultivation, affected a far wider sphere of industry and agriculture than only the cotton kingdom of the South. The advances in the technology of spinning and weaving developed in England found their way to New England's growing cities and rural industrial towns, close to water power sources which drove the machines of their textile mills. It took only a short time for expanding populations in America and England to begin wearing the less expensive, more comfortable cotton fabrics. The cotton gin reduced the price of cotton; spinning and weaving factories lowered labor costs; and urban populations on both sides of the Atlantic began to grow. By 1820 New York had 124,000 people; Philadelphia 113,000; Baltimore 63,000; and Boston 43,000. Close to 5,000,000 people were living in the New England and mid-Atlantic states then. By 1870 the number had increased to over 13,000,000. These people, not all living on self-sufficient farms, had to be fed and clothed.

Northern agriculture responded to the new markets. Even subsistence farmers of an earlier era had traded surplus goods for cash to buy necessities or to pay off loans on the land or tools. As time passed, farmers chose to buy land and raise crops with an eye to commercial markets. The first farmers to switch to commercial farming lived close to urban areas; then those near waterways used them to transport their goods east. Finally, by the mid-nineteenth century, as canals, roads, and railroads were completed, the changeover from subsistence to commercial farming in the North was fairly complete.

At the turn of the century, farmers attempted to continue to perform all their traditional subsistence activities and home manufactures and to engage in commercial farming as well. Markets increased for the farmer in proportion to his desire to capture a greater share of the business. New England and the western parts of the mid-Atlantic states had already phased out of a primarily subsistence agriculture by 1820. Even then most western farmers would have liked to be more involved in commercial farming, but transportation facilities were not yet built. The effects of the changeover were first a refocussing of farm families from subsistence concerns and home manufactures to those crops which were in demand at the marketplace, and second the hiring of additional labor if necessary. Log cabins had long since been replaced by frame houses, and additional income served to furnish the houses with manufactured furniture and consumer goods. Well-kept villages and towns grew out of ugly mud holes in New York and Pennsylvania, and later in Ohio and other regions of the old West. Parks and community buildings designed in the new wave of classical revival architecture were financed from taxes on valuable farm land.

Until the time of affluence arrived, however, the farmer had to solve many problems if he was to seize the opportunity to improve his material welfare. Widespread depletion of soils in New England, a chronic shortage of labor on farms, primitive agricultural tools, lack of marketing institutions, even competition from other farmers once the transportation problems had been solved—these obstacles hindered nearly every farmer through the first half of the nineteenth century. The farmer was kept from fully engaging in commercial farming.

Farmers dealt with the problem of soil exhaustion in New England by abandoning their lands in favor of the more fertile, low-cost lands of the West. They took their staples, wheat and corn, with them to their new lands. Wheat production flourished on the level prairie soils of Ohio, Indiana and Illinois. The soils of the region had been enriched by pulverized mineral rocks blown by westerly winds as the last glacier receded. The soils were overlaid with the accumulated decay of grass stalks. Wheat-growing had hardly changed for centuries: primitive plowing and harrowing, broadcast seeding, hoeing, sickle or cradle harvesting, hand flailing and winnowing. Primitive horse- or ox-powered gristmills ground the grain, or, where streams flowed, waterpower mills were employed.

Corn was the universal staple of virtually every state before the Civil War. It was cheap to buy, easy to raise, and good food for both the farmer and his livestock. Corn bread, hominy mush and corn fritters were put on the table of poor farmer and slave alike. It cost less to grow than any other popular food.

Corn also had salable value when it was distilled into whiskey or fed to hogs for winter fattening. Razorback hogs, the hardy foraging hogs raised at the time, were a fierce-looking, long-bodied variety of hog with heavy snouts and flap-ears. During the spring and summer they scavenged in the woods, living on nuts, acorns, roots and grass. Corn transformed their stringy muscle into delicious thick pork. Smokehouses to dry and flavor pork were common in the South and along the frontier. Hog lard could be sold in England for a fairly attractive price if a means of transport were close by.

Figure 5–2. The Conestoga wagon. Thousands of these freight wagons were built in the first decades of the 1800s to carry goods between the urban areas of the East and the Ohio River. The body of the wagon slants upward at each end to prevent the contents from falling out on the steep and uneven colonial roads. The Conestoga wagon typically used a team of heavy-draft horses which carried sets of bells on their harnesses. The colorful wagons, often painted with designs and colors from their Pennsylvania Dutch origins, made impressive wagon trains, and they moved enormous quantities of goods. A single wagon could carry as much as five tons of cargo. Courtesy Sperry New Holland Company.

Transportation Problems

There were never enough hands on the farm to do what needed to be done. Taking fifty to a hundred pounds of grain to market on the back of a cart could fill many days of a farmer's valuable time, even if passable roads or paths were available. If they were not, a lesser amount of grain went on the back of a horse or ox while the farmer walked. The Conestoga wagon was developed by German farmers in the back country of Pennsylvania to take large loads of wheat to markets in the East. Freight companies soon built them by the hundreds. With bottoms slanting inward toward the middle, the Conestoga wagon had the advantages of strong, broad wheels, wide beam, and wide interior. The wagon was a striking sight with its blue underbody, red woodwork and white canvas covering. In time, stockmen developed strains of heavy horses which could be teamed to pull Conestogas. Of course, the ideal solution for the farmer was to purchase land close to rivers, populated settlements, or prospective canals—if he had the money.

Transportation difficulties were partially the reason for the many attempts at new marketing arrangements during the period. If possible, farmers tried to market their own products at nearby settled areas. In the back areas, country merchants and millers bought the farmer's goods; the rural merchants supplied goods on credit from their retail stores, loaned money, and often even owned grist mills and sawmills. They also had contacts with wholesalers or middlemen who bought their produce in exchange for retail goods and cash. When their stock grew to uneconomic proportions, backwoods merchants usually limited their purchases of farm goods to the exact amount the farmer would buy from their stores. Other local buyers would then fill the need, sometimes paying cash for the farmer's goods, but more often taking his goods to market for a percentage of the sale.

At the same time, millers began to buy grain from the farmers and to process it for sale to grain buyers and wholesalers. Later, as transportation facilities improved, the millers preferred to send whole grain in bulk to their urban contacts, lessening the danger of spoilage en route.

Cattle drives had been part of the American colonial scene since the early 1600s, when the first recorded roundup and drive took place in Plymouth, Massachusetts. Large cattle drives began at the beginning of the century, to come from the back country of the mid-Atlantic states over the Appalachians to eastern markets. For a price, Pennsylvania Germans opened up pastures to drovers who wanted to fatten their cattle before they went into Philadelphia. Other farmers followed suit, and almost overnight pasture became available from Ohio all the way to Philadelphia, Baltimore and New York. The cattle industry moved west with the frontier. In the 1840s, cattle were driven east from Missouri and Iowa; in the fifties, from Texas. They came on foot, by canal, and across the lakes. Albany, the end of the Erie Canal and the gateway to New England and New York, was a major terminus of cattle movement by the time of the Civil War. Farmers in the West usually sold their animals to a drover who picked up hundreds or thousands of cattle and took them east, not without risks of animal losses or low selling prices. Drovers sold cattle to other farmers, agents and butchers on the way to Ohio, where the animals were fattened before continuing the trip east.

After the Civil War, Chicago became the largest livestock center, and cattle cars on railroads began to be used to carry livestock to destinations around the country.

Drovers usually handled small herds themselves along the way with the help of dogs and young boys who walked a day or two with the herd before returning home. Drovers had to know the best routes, roads, pikes, feeding spots and night shelters, river fording crosses and approaches. They also had to watch out for the lingering wolf as well.

Very often farmers slaughtered their own hogs, packed them in salt, and sold the pork to the nearest merchant. Or they drove the hogs to a nearby packing house for sale. Hogs were also driven over the mountains to eastern markets, as were sheep, though not nearly on such a large scale as cattle. When mutton prices were good, drovers often took mixed herds with them on their eastern drives. In the 1820s, probably fifty thousand sheep each year were driven to eastern markets to be sold for their mutton. But by 1848 Cincinnati meat packers had developed a kind of assembly line where slaughtered hogs hanging on conveyors were moved past lines of men who processed the meat into pork. In that year almost a half million hogs were packed and sold to eastern markets. Later Chicago would rival Cincinnati as the world's great meat-packing city.

Improving Agricultural Technology

The farmer accustomed to subsistence agriculture made his own tools from wood—plows, harrows, rakes, shovels, yokes, and the like. Occasionally a local blacksmith forged iron equipment, or the farmer improvised with iron scraps. But subsistence agricultural implements could not produce surpluses where a surplus of labor was absent. Productivity was linked to the improvement of tools and soil; it took years for farmers to accept this fact. Many were convinced that commercial farming itself did not necessarily represent a better life for them and their families; they cannot be faulted for their judgment. But if yields were to be increased and many hands were not available to tend the fields, a way had to be found to plow, seed, cultivate, and harvest more efficiently.

Two types of plows were commonly used at the beginning of the century: the shovel stirring plow and the moldboard turning plow. The common shovel plow looked like a thick, blunt shovel sheeted with iron; later models were forged from iron in one or two pointed shovels. Even the iron shovel plows could go no more than a few inches deep, nor could they break grass. The seed beds they prepared were barely adequate for a good-sized crop, nor did the plows weed the crops with much effectiveness. Moldboard plows, which turned the ground to a small degree, performed better but took at least two men and four oxen to operate. Both types needed constant repairs.

Cast iron was substituted for the wood in plowshares early in the century but, because it was high in carbon and brittle, it was easily broken and expensive to replace. In 1818, Jethro Wood patented a cast iron plow that was constructed in three separable pieces in a way that allowed the farmer himself to replace a broken part.

Wood's plow and scores more that were patented in the second quarter of the century utilized, at least in part, a mathematical formula suggested by Thomas Jefferson in 1798 at an American Philosophical Society meeting. New plows were designed to cut a furrow and gradually to raise and turn over the soil so that it would break evenly and flat. By 1850, 200 different kinds of plows were manufactured. Iron foundries replaced the village blacksmith; two factories in Pittsburgh claimed a capacity of 34,000 plows a year. One in Worcester, Massachusetts, actually produced 28,000 cast iron plows in 150 sizes and shapes in one boom year.

Cast iron plows worked smoothly and efficiently on eastern soils with the advantage of fewer man-hours and lower ox-power requirements, but they could not effectively break the heavy, root-toughened prairie soils. Sticky humus clung to the iron mold-board, so the midwestern farmer turned to new, hundred-pound wooden breaking plows until 1837, when John Deere, an Illinois blacksmith, constructed plows of sheet steel shares welded to wrought-iron moldboards. Tempered steel was smoother and soil did not stick to it. The steel cut through the matted grass roots which had stopped iron plows. By 1856, Deere's factory in Moline was turning out over 10,000 steel plows a year.

Until 1840, seeding was commonly done by hand depositing or broadcasting, with the seeds then covered by a sweep of the foot or a tree brush or primitive harrow in a rather haphazard fashion. Since the wheat grain was sown in the fall, sometimes among growing corn stalks, the method caused seed to be wasted and an uncertain yield. Seeding drills modeled after English designs and patented by Moses and Samuel Pennock in 1841 were marketed widely during the following decade. By the time of the Civil War, the construction of seed-drill machinery had become an important industry. Most drills utilized a perforated revolving cylinder or a vibrating box which deposited seeds through tubes to the soil. Neither variety always worked well but both could save much seed and improve yields nonetheless.

The invention of the cradle, which set down stalks gently, minimizing loss of grain, was important for the harvesting of grain, but it still required a large number of manhours to bring in a crop: perhaps two or three weeks of steady work for a forty-acre field if only one person was harvesting. Farmers had for years been working on a method to harvest grain utilizing horse-drawn devices, but could not find solutions to problems of uneven ground, uncut grain trampled by horses, easy retrieval for gathering and binding, and effective cutting devices. In 1822, an Englishman, Henry Ogle, invented a machine which partially met the challenge of these obstacles, but it was not until the mid-thirties that two American inventors, New Englander Obed Hussey and Cyrus McCormick from Virginia, were able to come up with a workable reaper. Even in the early years of experimentation, their machines could not be marketed widely because of snags in design or workmanship. In the forties the McCormick and Hussey reapers began to look alike and work along similar lines, precipitating an endless series of lawsuits brought against one another. McCormick had better business sense, setting up his plant in Chicago close to the large wheat producing states; by 1851 he was making 1,000 machines a year; they cost between $100 and $150 apiece. He also cashed in on the sale of licenses to other agricultural equipment factories. Most farmers bought their reapers in the fifties after the bugs

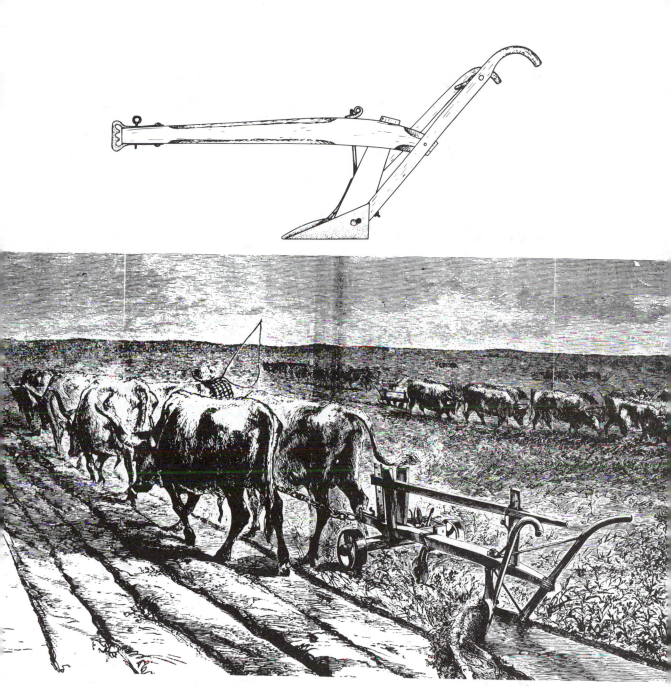

Figure 5–3. Two plows that broke the prairie soils. Having been unsuccessful with cast-iron plows, prairie farmers returned to hundred-pound, unwieldy "bull" sodbusting plows with wooden moldboards covered with wrought iron. These bull plows also had wrought iron shares and coulters, and heavy fifteen-foot beams. So great was the drag on such plows that they required as many as seven or eight yoke of oxen to pull them, along with the efforts of the plowman and a boy to prod the oxen. The illustration of the John Deere Plow is a drawing of a reconstruction of his 1837 model. Deere's innovation was to weld a cutting edge of steel to the wrought iron plow. The sharper, smoother steel then effectively cut the heavy prairie soils. Deere continued to modify his plow over the next generation until it gradually came to look like the moldboard design of James Oliver's famous chilled-iron plow. That design is now standard, but the innovations of Deere and Oliver literally opened up the West for the settlers. Courtesy The Smithsonian Institution.

Figure 5–4. Cradling wheat. Farmers have always faced time-consuming and often backbreaking labor at harvest time. Cutting stalks of grain is one such chore. Furthermore, the next steps in processing the grain dictate that as much as possible of the grain be kept accessible at the end of each bundle of harvested grain. The sickle and its long-handled relative, the scythe, allow the farmer to cut the grain stalks, but unless he takes special pains the grain will fall haphazardly. An important invention for handling grain was, therefore, the cradle: a series of bent wooden fingers attached behind the blade of a scythe. A harvester could swing the cradle in such a way that it cut the grain stalks off evenly and deposited them with the heads all facing in the same direction. The harvester could then lay the grain down in an even row for the binders who followed, tying the grain into manageable bundles or sheaves. A sheaf of hand-bound wheat can be seen in the foreground of this picture. The cradle increased a harvester's output geometrically, but it still was not efficient enough for the large farms of the expanding United States. Courtesy International Harvester Company and The Smithsonian Institution.

had been worked out of them and wheat prices were high. The horse-drawn self-rake reapers did ten times the work of two good workers with cradles. This meant that ten times more acreage could be put into the high-priced commodity. The Civil War brought a series of manpower shortages to the farm, almost forcing farmers to invest in reapers. By this time McCormick, who had been offering easy credit terms, had captured the lion's share of the market.

The self-rake reapers were deceptively simple devices. A serrated cutting knife, driven by the main axle of the reaper through cogs, moved back and forth between triangular iron guards which held the grain while it was cut; at the same time a revolving mechanical reel pushed the stalks into the guards. The grain fell neatly onto a platform. From there it was raked by a second operator; the cut grain was ready to be picked up and bound. In 1858, the Marsh harvester added a traveling apron which lifted the cut grain to two men on a platform, where they bound the grain as it was cut. McCormick eventually bought the rights to use this device on his machines.

Hand threshing, winnowing and bagging took proportionately much more time than reaping and binding, even in pre-mechanized farming days. Hundreds of beating devices and fanning mechanisms operated by crank, sweep or treadmill were worked on after 1820, but no successful machine was marketed before the late thirties when Maine farmers John and Hiram Pitts produced their thresher-cleaner, operated by horse-power on a treadmill. The mechanism was patterned after Scottish models. In an hour it did the work of seventy men using hand flails. Since the machines cost well over $200 each, many farmers preferred to hire out the threshing and separating to itinerant threshers working for owners of the machines. The cost was three to ten cents a bushel depending on the season and how much labor the farmer personally contributed. Threshing machines performed so much difficult and time-consuming labor that they were bought or employed through the wheat country almost as soon as they became available.

Theoretically the principles of mechanical threshing and winnowing were easy to conceive, but practically they were difficult to implement. Many mallet-beating threshers were sold earlier, but they wasted or crushed as much grain as they separated—an accusation which continued to be made against later threshers. The Pitts design utilized a revolving drum inside a concave slot to loosen the grain, along with a sieve which caught the straw and a fanning mechanism to blow it off the sieve. The horse treadmill which powered the device and the machine itself were simplified so that they could be mounted on wheels and drawn from farm to farm. In the fifties, steam power began to be applied to threshing when a few manufacturers placed steam engines on wheels. Steam engines offered more power and increased the lifespan of valuable horses.

Hay rakes drawn by horses could be driven by young people and they were an important labor-saving invention in the early 1800s. Later a baler or press came into use to compress hay. Baling facilitated transport. A host of other mechanized farm implements and items were invented and sold with varying degrees of success during the first half of the century: horse forks, corn planters, drain tile for fields, cotton seed planters, corn shellers, potato diggers, cultivators, cheese presses, churns, flax pullers, cob crushers, incubators and the all-important corn-shellers.

Inventions were a sign of the times. Money was to be made for those who could seize the opportunity to produce goods fast enough while prices were on the rise. However, although the new agricultural technology slowly became available, a relatively small proportion of the country's farmers utilized it. When the technology caught on universally, the increased output caused a drop in prices, throwing farmers debt-ridden for land and capital equipment into deeper debt. By the time of the Civil War, the pioneer who had pushed west a generation earlier could no longer declare himself an independent yeoman. Banks loaned him money for land; farm equipment firms advanced him credit for machinery; middlemen bought his produce at unpredictable prices; drovers took his livestock to market on commission; most of all, his crop had become specialized for cash value rather than home use. Along the eastern seaboard an incipient canning industry pressed even truck farmers to grow crops suited to their new factories. By 1860 over five million cans of prepared food were sold—mainly to immigrants and soldiers at that time. It took some time before the rest of America could be taught to eat from cans.

Soil Exploitation and Conservation

In New England and the old South, farmers cleared new lands when crop yields dropped so low from soil exhaustion that seeding became useless. Their rationale lay in the cheapness of new lands and the difficulty of soil management with a short supply of labor, time, and money. Moreover, it appears that they didn't really think the application of manure and fertilizers would help significantly.

The trend continued into the nineteenth century. Prairie farmers had an advantage, however, in that their soil endured much longer without any decline in yields. They also had pressures of shorthandedness, debts to pay off, lack of time to devote to the care of fields, and clearing of new lands. The productivity of their land never seemed to drop so low that it warranted a drastic change in farming habits. They stayed with what they considered to be the most economic plan: Maximum profits would be returned by cultivating as many acres of valuable cash crops as possible with the least amount of labor expended as possible. Long-term deficits to the land were not considered.

When yields declined, blame was assigned to everything except soil mining: weather, pests, overproduction, implements. So the land continued to be pressed for further yield, with even more disappointing results. The experience of New England and the old South became the experience of New York, Ohio, Indiana, Kentucky, Tennessee, and the states of the deep South. Farmers continued to move west for better lands. Rich bottom lands lasted longer, but even these were not an inexhaustible source of minerals. Cotton cultivation, like that of tobacco, was done in long rows which allowed run-off to form gullies through which the southern upland soils washed away with winter rains.

English farmers knew much earlier than the nineteenth century frontiersmen what was going wrong. Their message was carried across the sea by many vehicles with many sets of words: Soils need phosphorus, carbon, nitrogen, lime and even sulphur. Crops drain these elements from the soil slowly or quickly depending on the crop and the soil. If the land is not to be laid waste, care must be taken continually to bolster its mineral supplies. The task is not an easy one because minerals are often leached through the soil in solution so quickly that plant roots cannot utilize their value. Or the destruction of forest cover, crude cultivating methods, and overgrazing can lead to erosion, which washes away the nutrient-laden topsoil.

In America, the cause of instructing the American farmer was taken up by myriads of new institutions throughout the country: farm journals multiplying by the year; agricultural societies and fairs exhibiting the latest technologies and farm methods; and the resident farm columnist writing for virtually every newspaper in the country.

and the resident farm columnist writing for virtually every newspaper in the country. With few exceptions, writers deplored the destruction of forest cover, the absence of soil management techniques, the wasting of animal manure, and widespread disregard of fertilizer applications and crop rotation.

New ideas and old were expounded from the pulpit of the press. Jesse Buel, energetic advocate and journalist of progressive agriculture, summarized in the *Cultivator* the main tenets of the new system as "draining, manuring, alternating crops, the culture of roots and artificial grasses, the substitution of fallow crops for naked fallows, the application of lime, marl, and other earthly matters to improve the mechanical condition and the fertility of the soil, and the blending of tillage and grass husbandry—of cattle and grain." Buel and others particularly excoriated those who dumped millions of dollars worth of manure into rivers, swamps, and culverts every year. They called for the spring storing of manures in barn cellars and the building of compost heaps of manure, straw and organic wastes.

Pennsylvania German farmers had long utilized animal manures and red clover for their nitrogen and soil-building qualities; lime and gypsum applications; crop rotations of corn, oats, wheat and clover; meadow draining; and conservation of manures in the "blending of tillage and grass husbandry—of cattle and grain." From eastern Pennsylvania and small regions of Massachusetts and New York, these techniques were passed by word and example, and they took hold on isolated farms throughout the country. On soils which were depleted almost beyond repair, years of restorative practices had to be applied. Examples of this kind of diligence are rare, but as crop yields fell off drastically, farmers began to get the message. They began to save manure, to rotate crops, and even to purchase lime and guano—bird droppings from the Chincha Islands off the coast of Peru. Those who abandoned their worn-out fields and moved farther west left their lands to another kind of emigrant, one who was willing to patiently conserve, nurture and revive an abiding earth. The restoration of the land slowly came around, on the stony farms of New England; the tobacco-depleted coastal plains of Virginia; the eroded plateaus of Kentucky; the cotton lands of Mississippi and Georgia; in Ohio, Wisconsin and points west. However, it was a slow, almost imperceptible, occurrence in scattered parts of the country. So long as the continent appeared empty and cheap, very few people would worry about conservation of the soil.

Timber Use and Lumbering

Perhaps the most immediately useful resource of the country from its very beginnings was its thick virgin forests. The relentless manual energy that was focused on land clearing for two and a half centuries is impossible to calculate. Wood cutting by far required more time and energy of a pioneering family than any other activity. Wood was burned for fuel; used for building cabins and fences; converted into potash and charcoal. Its juices were tapped for sweetening and for naval stores. Many trees felled for clearing simply rotted on the ground.

Millions of forest acres were chopped and burned for dozens of domestic and commercial purposes before settlers crossed the Mississippi. With the coming of steamboats, ferries and railroads, and with the dramatic increase of housing for new settlements before the Civil War, wood consumption skyrocketed. The railroads alone probably used 3,000,000 cords of wood a year as late as 1860, a decade after the introduction of coal on Pennsylvania and New jersey lines. Even in the early days of railroads, the short lines linking communities of the east needed at least 100,000 cords of wood a year to burn in the steam engines. One southern line kept a continuous supply of 30,000 cords spaced along its route. By the mid-nineteenth century the hundreds of steamboats on the Mississippi and Ohio easily consumed over 4,000,000 cords a year. In the meantime, large families in wooden frame houses needed to keep warm in the winter; they also wanted the extra money from the sale of potash, pearl ash and naval stores, or even from chopped wood itself. Then there were new wood demands from railroad companies building new lines and from new communities in non-forested regions. As the century progressed, prices for chopped wood predictably rose, and along most rivers wood was stacked to be picked up by passing flatboats.

An important technological reason for the phenomenal rapidity of forest clearance east of the Mississippi River was the mass production of high-quality steel axes. In 1826, Samuel and David Collins inaugurated a makeshift ax factory in South Canton, Ohio, employing blacksmiths who utilized water-powered trip-hammers over their forges. In 1832, the brothers hired Elisha King Root to oversee their operation, and the new foreman standardized each stage of ax-making in an early effort as mass production. For instance, for uniform heating and tempering, 100 ax-heads were hung on a revolving drum over the furnace. The Collins stamp on ax-heads became common on the treecutting frontier.

It was natural that the lumber industry should grow and move west where large stands of timber lay untouched. Maine was the first big logging state, then New York, Pennsylvania, and other eastern states, next Ohio, and finally the Great Lakes States—Michigan, Wisconsin, Minnesota. Lumbering companies bought up for a few cents an acre thousands of acres from veterans who weren't interested in pioneering in the great northwest. For a generation military land bounty warrants were the major source of lumbering land, but later public domain timber lands could be bought for $1.25 an acre. In 1850 Congress passed the Swamp Act and 63,000,000 acres were given away, much of it to lumber companies. Only a few of those acres actually were swampy. Lumber companies also sent out their men to file homestead claims and picked up more free land. Then there was the "round forty" system, where the company bought and logged forty acres and as much government land around the forty as they could practicably reach. Lake Michigan and the rivers and lakes leading to it and the Mississippi provided their transportation to market.

Typically, a lumber king would gather motley crews of old and young lumbermen from the East, recent German and Scandinavian immigrants, French Canadians, Scottish and Irish. He would then send his group of foremen, axmen and teamsters into the pine forests of the lake country, build rickety camps, cut roads, and start to whittle away at the immense stands of timber.

Logging methods had hardly changed from the earlier New England period: hand tools, heavy lifting, brute strength. The ax was the basic tool, and expert axmen commanded comparatively high wages. In midcentury, the Yankee ax handle weighed seven pounds; it was oval and curved, with an enlarged end. By 1860, it developed a double bit with two sizes of edge, one thick side to cut into knots or possible embedded stones, which saved the sharp side for normal cutting. The crosscut saw, which could cut in both directions, did not come into use until after the Civil War, when it greatly increased lumber production.

Foremen notched trees on the side toward which they wanted the tree to fall and choppers went to work. The lie of a felled tree was important if it was to be hauled out of the forest easily. "Swampers" removed branches from the tree; logs were measured and cut to size, then dragged by oxen on a log skidway and piled beside a logging road. The teamster and his oxen or horses pulled sleds, sometimes sixteen feet wide carrying three to five thousand board-feet of timber, over crude logging roads to a river landing. At a slightly later period logging roads were gouged out and iced, so that fifteen- to twenty-thousand board-feet loads were the usual limit. Horses had to be used then, since their speed kept them ahead of the loads, especially down grades, where ingenious friction devices were developed to keep the loads off the horses' backs.

River Routes to Sawmills and Markets

At the river bank, a company stamper pounded his firm's registered mark into the end of each log with a huge mallet. The stamper also axed the mark into the tree's bark in a number of places so that ownership could readily be determined in the river or boom downstream.

After the ice had melted and rivers were high at spring freshet season—sometimes streams were dammed to give extra force to the drive—logs were rolled into the river and floated downstream to sawmills. River drivers guided the miles of logs, keeping them out of inlets and shoal water; jam crews patrolled channels to loosen key logs in the event of a jam-up. By 1860, a peavy, named for its designer in Maine, was used by all men on river drives. To its pointed iron jam pike was added a cant hook and a pole about sixteen feet long, making the peavy a useful tool to guide logs and break up jams.

Logs were steered into huge ponds near sawmills and tied off by booms. Sawmills had by this time become equipped with bandsaws arranged in gangs which could effectively cut several boards at one time. The mills were powered by water or later by steam. After the timber was rough cut, it was loaded into a sixteen-by-sixteen foot raft with twelve to twenty layers of lumber. Six of these "cribs" were tied together—untied in rapids—and floated to the nearest marketing city, perhaps Chicago, St. Louis or Cincinnati. As the quantity of lumber cut was compounded each year, every stage of the operation became more complex, and specialized companies began to take over river transport, milling, and marketing. Lumbering was on its way to becoming a big business.

The glamour stayed on in the myths of the lumber camp, Shanty Boy Ballads,

Paul Bunyan and his blue ox Babe. Day-by-day life in the lice-ridden bunkhouses was another story. The day's work started before dawn and continued till dark. Salt pork and beans with bread and molasses washed down with saltpeter tea was the lumberman's regular fare. The work was incredibly strenuous, the weather bitter cold in the winter. But at night the lumberman's feet could thaw out next to the fire in the center of the cabin, where yarns were spun and embellished, ballads sung and a great American myth created.

The rise of lumbering accompanied the rapid population increases in the country. Businessmen had to find ways to meet the demand for lumber from the hundreds of new western cities and expanding eastern cities which needed buildings by the tens of thousands. During the 1830s, the balloon-frame house, a light frame of sawed timbers nailed into a cage, was developed in Chicago. The mechanization of nail-making in the 1820s (greatly reducing the price of nails, which earlier were hand-made) along with economy of lumber, time, and expense in the construction of balloon-frame buildings—skilled labor and lumber were scarce and expensive—all contributed to the changing of the faces of nineteenth-century cities. People had neither time, money, wood nor skill to construct foot-square beamed houses or log cabins in their communities. They could put up a balloon-frame house with their modest savings and a little help from their friends.

Balloon-frame construction also proved a boon to western farmers who had been making do with makeshift barns until the new method swept the West. The new architecture democratized the construction of barns as barn-raising bees became established social events and practical innovations were made possible because of the flexibility of design. For example, the balloon frames enabled the farmer to open a gable in the front of the barn in order to hoist hay into its loft. Older eastern barns prohibited the horsepowered fork and railing arrangement because massive king posts blocked the gables. Eastern farmers stored hay on the ground floor and kept cattle in the barn cellar, where hay was pitched to them through trap doors. Despite the more convenient and economical design of the balloon frame, easterners considered them too fragile (though in fact they were not) and preferred the traditional huge, rough-hewn timber barns. Yet balloon-frame construction has withstood the test of time and the technique continues to be employed in homebuilding to this day.

The Pattern Established

The nation's first half-century of existence thus continued and intensified the patterns of the previous hundred years. Economic rationalization of natural resources kept pace with the development of markets, which lured planters and farmers into commercial enterprises with the prospects of high returns, then were glutted with goods after large investments of land, time and money were made. Early American capitalist gambles did not prove to be uniformly beneficial, especially for small farmers and planters who found out the hard way that it was difficult to stay in business on a shoestring and that it was only a matter of time before declining prices and high debts would bring in the banker with a foreclosure notice or a large planter or speculator willing to buy out the operation at a fraction of its cost. The same prospect of big profits spurred the development of agricultural technology and new banking arrangements and modes of transport. It even pushed political concentration into the hands of the federal government. The latter factors loomed large in early American resource development, and they will be taken up in the following chapter.

The essential fact at this juncture lies in the country's overwhelming commitment to economic development through the use of its cheapest commodities, land and labor, a purpose which has not lessened since that time. When business was good, the planter or farmer gave more thought to increasing his share of the market than to conservation practices. Neither did depressions and increasing tenancy force pre-Civil War Americans to examine their exclusively exploitative relationships to the land; they assumed that even if the soil was depleted of minerals at their present site, it would not be exhausted over the next hill. Forests were attacked again, soil mined, wildlife pushed farther west, erosion ignored. In general the possibilities of greater wealth and material gain overshadowed whatever conservation measures were suggested by foreign visitors or agricultural journalists.

The American landscape during this period was mainly characterized by small rural villages; picturesque cultivated fields (albeit monotonous with single crops); dirt highways, quiet towpaths along canals; river highways; water wheels by local mills; and clean water and air. Noise, congestion, and soot came in the fifties with coal burning, smokestacks of ironworks, growing cities, and the key to American development, the railroad.

The physical changes on the landscape symbolized the ideological tension between traditional Jeffersonian agrarianism and the flowering of American Enlightenment notions of progress. Jefferson long advocated the building of a nation of self-sufficient, independent farmers in tune with the earth that supported them. He even went through with the purchase of the Louisiana Territory, though he doubted the constitutionality of the action, because he wanted as much room for agricultural expansion as possible. He hoped to retard the growth of cities, commerce and manufacturing because he saw them as corrupting influences: "While we have land to labor, then, let us never wish to see our citizens occupied at a workbench or twirling a distaff," he wrote in his *Notes on Virginia*.

But the very expansiveness of the American land encouraged a departure from the historical constraints of a primitive agrarian simplicity and into ventures of materialist progress. The scientific, political, and moral ideas of the Enlightenment, stressing individual rights and human improvement or progress, tended to support the economic individualism of early American capitalism and spur an egalitarian quest for material gain. (Article I of the Constitution purposes the "progress of science and the useful arts.") As capital became available and important geographical and technological problems were solved, Enlightenment ideology was able to capture the collective American consciousness. American legal institutions now assume a superiority of individual private property over social or environmental good as well as the almost unchallengeable priority of scientific progress.

References for Further Reading

Besides Gray's *History of Agriculture in Southern United States*, already cited, Ulrich B. Phillips' *Life and Labor in the Old South* (1963) merits recognition as a classic treatment of the subject. A more recent, excellent exposition is *The Growth of Southern Civilization* by Clement Eaton (1961). *Slave States*, written in the 1850s for the New York Times by Frederick Law Olmsted (1959), offers informative insights into the life and customs of slaveholding states. Along with Bidwell and Falconer's *History*, already mentioned, Paul Gates' *The Farmer's Age: Agriculture, 1815-1869* (1960) is a superb, concisely written, scholarly account of agricultural life throughout the country before the Civil War. Clarence Danhof's *Change in Agriculture: 1820-1870* (1969) contributes a masterful essay of the changing institutions, technology and overall environment of agriculture from a subsistence to a commercial economy. The Agricultural History Society publication *Farming in the New Nation* covers problems in American agriculture and includes interesting chapters on outdoor farm museums such as Old Sturbridge Village, which interprets rural life in New England from 1790 to 1840. *Timber* by Manuel C. Elmer (1961) is enjoyable reading about both early and later big-time logging. Wilson Carey McWilliams' *The Idea of Fraternity in America* (1973) includes much more than the idea of fraternity in its sweeping intellectual history of American political and social thought. Many excellent books have been written about the textile mills and the young women who worked in them during the growth of early industrial New England. The actual story of these "mill women," the first female industrial wage earners in the United States, can be read in their own words in *The Lowell Offering*, edited by Benita Eisler (1982), and *The Factory Girls*, edited by Philip S. Foner (1981). A good case history of the ecological history of the forests of Minnesota can be found in Clifford and Isabel Ahlgren's *Lob Trees in the Wilderness* (1984), which begins with Native American and early white settlers' forest use up to the present time.

Chapter 6

SOLVING PROBLEMS
OF CAPITAL AND TRANSPORT

Given the new nation's geographical situation combined with an unstable economic condition after the Revolutionary War, it was by no means certain that the country would develop into the commercial power of later generations. In fact the odds against this eventual achievement were heavy. Geography and capital were primary obstacles. The larger measure of America's vast natural resources—fertile lands, virgin forests, mineral deposits—lay west of a formidable barrier, the Appalachian mountains, where population, roads and development capital were nonexistent. Furthermore, states competed with one another for foreign and domestic trade, issued their own notes and bills of credit, and were reluctant to yield any of their prerogatives to a federal authority. The economic and political climate seemed quite opposed to the development of an integrated, regionally-specialized market economy. Astute observers of the time, including British treaty negotiators, conceptualized the western frontier lands as generally uninhabitable, a wilderness cut off from civilization and fit to be occupied only by Indians and a few white trappers or social misfits. The seaboard states appeared to be embroiled with one another in endless strife over trade and money; they were connected merely in the interests of common defense.

From Confederation to Constitutional Congress

After the war, each state retained its complete sovereignty and independence, the Confederation Congress being little more than an administrative bureau for the states to solve problems of defense and communication. The states took care of their own taxing and regulated their own commerce. The Articles of Confederation provided for no executive or judiciary, only for a Congress which could make war and negotiate treaties or foreign affairs. It also could maintain a post office, establish coinage, and standardize weights and measures. At the same time, the Confederation Congress was burdened with a national debt and dependent on the states to contribute to its retirement at a time when specie was exceedingly rare in the country.

The Continental Congress and state governments had issued an overabundance of flat paper money to finance the war, causing an increasing depreciation of the value of this cheap money and creating public and private debts out of proportion to the real value of the currency in terms of specie. After the war, the gold and silver supply dried up and paper money became entirely worthless or was redeemed by speculators at a fraction of its par value. For private debts, however, creditors generally demanded full value even though debts had been contracted at a time of inflated currency. Small farmers were particularly at a loss to meet the demands of their creditors.

By 1786, the public outcry of small debtors reached seven legislatures, which issued greater or lesser amounts of new paper money. Massachusetts, one state that refused to reissue paper currency, was the scene of Shay's Rebellion in that year, and other states underwent similar upheavals. Yet most of the thirteen states elected enough backcountry representatives to influence legislation on the issuance of paper money and lenient bankruptcy laws in behalf of the debtor class. At the same time, individual states were gaining experience on how to regulate their currencies. Pennsylvania, for example, issued a restricted amount of paper money with no ill effects on its economy. But moneylenders and speculators in depreciated currencies began to worry that their enterprises might fail to realize anticipated profits.

Charles Beard, who pioneered the economic interpretation of American history, has pointed out that many of this group and the commercial or propertied class of the coastal towns were the original backers of a Constitutional Convention and a strong federal government. He has shown that of the fifty-five delegates who attended the Constitutional Convention, forty were holders of public securities; fourteen were land speculators; twenty-four moneylenders; fifteen slaveowners; and at least eleven entrepreneurs. No one represented the small farmers or artisan classes. Delegates to the Convention obviously wanted to protect their own financial interests, but were also determined to lay the foundations of an expanding national economy.

The new Constitution ultimately succeeded in both objectives, though the latter goal was not achieved until many other economic, social, political, and technological problems were solved. The power of Congress over interstate commerce stopped commercial rivalries and tariffs among the states. Without this power, each state could have sealed itself off effectively and the country would have become another European continent economically.

Congress was also given the power to coin money and regulate its value, depriving state governments of the right to issue their own bills of credit in anything other than gold or silver. Fiscal confidence thereafter was to be placed in the central government rather than the separate state governments. To underscore the shift, Congress was given the power to tax in order to "pay the debts of the United States." Alexander Hamilton, America's first Secretary of The Treasury, induced the first Congress to assume war debts, not only of the Confederation but even of the individual states, to be paid through tariffs and excises on whiskey. Eastern merchants, manufacturers, and money lenders profited from the federal largesse at the expense of small farmers, whose corn-whiskey stills were taxed, and at the expense of those who had to pay higher prices for imported goods. At the same time, the discharge of the public debt through forced savings put surplus capital in the hands of an aggressive entrepreneurial class eager to reinvest it in land speculation, manufactures, and even internal improvements, tying the states in a closer economic bond.

Other Congressional powers also led to a more-integrated national economy. Uniform bankruptcy and naturalization laws assumed a national rather than sectional interest in business and labor. Post office and post road construction and the right to grant patents and copyrights turned the course of American development toward national purposes. A federal judiciary was given the power to adjudicate rights between parties of different states or conflicts between the federal and state levels of government. A national army was constituted to defend American property rights by protecting western settlers and speculators from Indians as well as from foreign interferers. The prerogative of the executive to call out the militia to suppress rebellions assured property owners that their interests would be safe anywhere in the United States.

The Antifederalists

The new Constitution was bitterly fought by many leaders and members of the debtor class in every state. However, after some compromises (including the Bill of Rights) and protracted debate, it was ratified by all the states. The last holdout, Rhode Island, signed in 1790. The struggle continued, however, in the decades that followed. This conflict occurred among the three major groups of American society: eastern entrepreneurs, southern planters, and western farmers. Farmers and planters opposed efforts to take away the local state power which enacted lenient bankruptcy laws and could emit bills of credit. Western settlers, planters, merchants, and speculators all pushed hard for a strong national military to quell insurrection, put down Indian uprisings, oppose foreign competitors, or return fugitive slaves. Manufacturers sought alliances with western interests to pay off public debts with revenues from tariffs designed to protect their infant industries. Often western agrarians capitulated, since they were not opposed to economic expansion so much as they were resentful of a one-sided subsidy of manufacturing interests at a time when their own needs for financial security and transportation development were acute.

American politicians picked up Adam Smith's new doctrine. They saw *laissez-faire* free enterprise capitalism as the American ideal of self-sufficiency in the pursuit of private profits. But the mercantilist philosophy, which called for government promotion of the common national welfare, was too deeply embedded in the eighteenth century political mind to be so easily forgotten. Most leaders agreed that only a federal government could pull together so many divergent economic, social and geographic sectors and provide the necessary economic incentives for all these interests. The disagreement came in the discussion of how strong that central government should be.

The two philosophies which were to compete for generations over this question took their labels from the first president's major advisors, Thomas Jefferson and Alexander Hamilton. Jeffersonian democracy stressed agrarian yeomanry and shunned strong federalism in favor of local control and self-sufficient economic units. When Jefferson himself wielded the Presidency, however, his perception of the national interest grew to include a wider scope of federal intervention into these local units. Hamiltonianism, on the other hand, unabashedly sought to create a strong central government which could protect American industries, build a merchant marine, and maintain public credit through fiscal policies of banking, tariffs and taxes.

It was Hamilton who eventually won the day, not without much opposition and temporary setbacks. His Revenue Act of 1791 placed duties on a small number of imports and internal goods, but by 1795 he added substantially to both lists, the latter including distilled liquors, other alcoholic drinks, sugar, snuff and auction goods. An uprising of pioneers from western Pennsylvania who refused to pay the tax—the "Whiskey Rebellion"—shocked President Washington into calling out 13,000 militiamen in 1794.

Hamilton was also able to persuade Congress to pass the Bank Act of 1791 and the Mint Act of 1792. The National Bank was to act as the fiscal agent of the federal government. One-fifth of the private bank's $10,000,000 charter was underwritten by the federal government. The rest was owned by private capitalists, three-quarters of which they could pay for with government bonds. The bank was chartered for twenty years. The immediate effect of the charter was an additional subsidy to the people who speculated in government securities, since they were able to draw substantial bank stock dividends from formerly worthless currency. Jefferson and many of his supporters contested the Act because the Constitution contained no provision for the national government to give a private corporation power over currency and credit, but the Act was upheld by the Supreme Court. The Mint Act set up a bimetallic standard of money, with a metric or decimal system of coinage under the dollar. The market ratio of silver to gold was placed at fifteen to one. The Federal Bank operated as a central bank, issued its own redeemable paper money, and collected payments due the federal government, such as taxes or payments due on public land. Since so many notes from state-chartered private banks or state banks themselves passed through the federal central bank, which could demand redemption of the local notes and bills of credit with specie or federal bills at any time, the federal bank had power to expand the money supply by leniency or contract it by demanding payment on the notes.

The Hamiltonian course was set before Jefferson became President in 1801. By that time the nation's economy, impelled by the prodigious growth of the southern cotton trade, had advanced beyond the point of a self-sufficient agrarian simplicity. Surplus money from a recovered merchant class and loans from the national and state banks were invested in newly-protected manufacturing enterprises. Jefferson attempted to lift some controls of the central government, to reduce debts and taxes, but the nationalist die was cast. The economy was destined to take off and enjoy a life of its own, spawning sectional specialization of natural resource exploitation and manufacturing and national integration of banking, money, transportation and communication. The national supply of capital flowed to those resources that promised greatest return on investment.

The Beginnings of a National Hookup

The major obstacle to an integrated national economy in its beginnings was not the attitude of the frontier farmer. He knew that his income would rise if he could sell more goods to eastern or European markets. Subsistence farming was practiced more because of the impracticability of commercial agriculture than because of a desire for complete self-sufficiency. The problem lay in transporting farm goods to those who wanted them, and these transportation facilities could not be developed

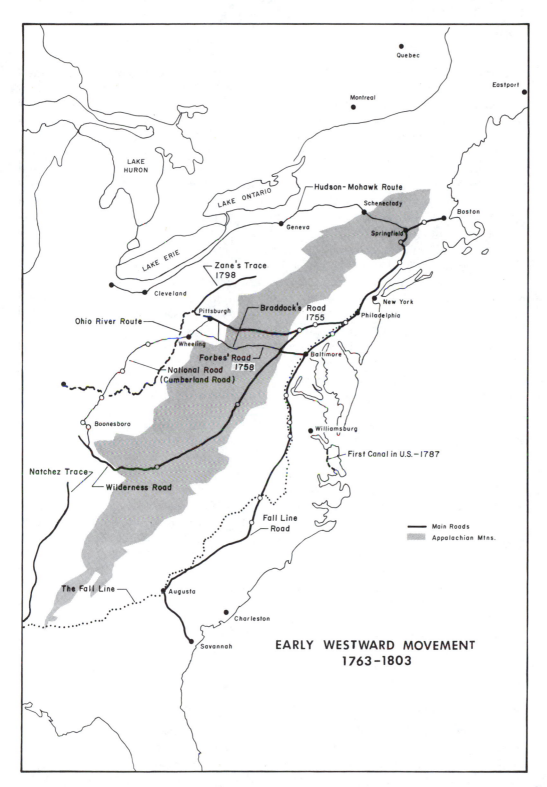

Figure 6–1. Main routes of the early westward movement. Note the fall line, which marked the upriver extremity of water that could be navigated.

by anyone alone. In hundreds of communities of the back country, farmers schemed and worked together to better their roads and canals. Through their representatives in the legislature or Congress, they sought help in building more of them everywhere.

Congressional action toward internal improvements was slight, but Congressmen indicated sympathy toward the idea. In 1803, Congress admitted Ohio into the Union with an enabling act which granted the new state 5% of the sale of its public lands to be used as a road-building fund. In 1806, the National Road, scheduled to begin at Cumberland, Maryland, and to go to Wheeling, Virginia (now West Virginia), on the Ohio, was authorized. Even President Jefferson in two of his annual messages encouraged Congress to utilize surplus revenues for building or improving roads, canals, and rivers.

Nonetheless, when better roads, canals, and other internal improvements were established throughout the first half of the 1800s, the achievement was as much the result of private as public enterprise. Farmers and their neighbors built their own roads to connect fields with markets, utilizing deer trails or clearing paths and filling muddy dips in the terrain with logs. In the early days of the country, road-building was accepted as a social responsibility, performed during slack seasons with crude farm implements and oxen. Local elected officials took charge of the task and were quite satisfied if there was enough of a path cleared to enable a cart or sled to get through in the snow or mud. These backwoods roads constituted no great engineering feats at the turn of the century, but a person could get to most settlements east of the mountains on them.

The "turnpike era" ushered in private enterprise and somewhat better road construction. Turnpikes often had a stone foundation with gravel layered over it and drainage ditches on each side of the road. Some turnpikes turned into elaborate operations if the builders decided to reduce steep grades with cut or fill; most pikes, however, offered no more travel comfort than the earlier homemade varieties. State governments granted charters to private corporations to exercise the right of eminent domain over specified routes and to charge tolls. The public at large—merchants and farmers—supported these corporations by the purchase of shares because both groups had a stake in improved transportation systems. States often bought large blocks of shares as an inducement to other investors. By 1822, Pennsylvania invested about $2,000,000 in turnpike companies—about a third of the total investment. South Carolina and Indiana built and operated their own turnpikes.

The Lancaster Turnpike in Pennsylvania, chartered in 1792, was completed between Philadelphia and Lancaster in 1794. The road cost a little less than $500,000 and eventually made money for the investors. Toll gates were erected every seven miles on the well-constructed road.

Road-building Enterprises

The moderate financial success of the Lancaster Turnpike spurred much private roadbuilding among the large commercial centers in the northeast. In 1807 Secretary of the Treasury Gallatin reported that sixty-seven companies had constructed 900 miles of roads in New York alone. The preceding year marked Congressional authorization for the National Road after an interminable chain of sectional conflicts and constitutional debates. The Road started at the terminus of the Frederick Pike, which came from Baltimore; by 1818 it reached Wheeling, and after several official starts and stops, it reached Columbus in 1833. About fifteen years later it reached Vandalia, Illinois. The National Road cost $13,000 per mile to build on its first leg to Wheeling, more afterward. Though sturdily constructed with gravel on solid stone foundations and excellent stone bridges, the road needed constant attention because of the heavy traffic. Considering the monumental obstacles hindering its continuation each year, it turned out to be a useful and remarkable success.

The turnpike era spanned the first thirty years of the century; most turnpikes were built in the northeast. New York and Pennsylvania led the nation, New York having completed 4,000 miles of turnpikes by the end of 1820. At that time, Pennsylvania had constructed 1,800 miles of road and another 600 by 1832. Southern and western states did not ignore construction, but they fell far short of the activity in the northeast.

The Lancaster Pike and later turnpikes were built by the macadam method, named after the Scotsman who devised it. First heavy rock was laid, then smaller stones, topped by gravel, crowned slightly to drain rainwater. Unfortunately, the roads did not hold their aesthetic shape for long. After 1844, plank roads, made of thick eight-foot planks set on stringers, became the rage; they could be constructed at comparatively little cost, particularly in forest areas. Hundreds of private corporations were granted charters almost overnight to construct thousands of miles of plank roads among hamlets and larger regional centers in the Middle Atlantic and North Central states. In the beginning, the plank road was a profitable investment, but heavy use and rot from the wet ground created unexpected hazards to horses and passengers. Skyrocketing repair bills dampened the enthusiasm of shareholders and potential new corporations.

Bridge-building corporations fared much better than turnpike companies financially. The art of bridgebuilding was enchanced during the turnpike era. It left many fine monuments. Stone piers and abutments provided a firm foundation for wood timbers protected by shingled roofs and clapboard sides. As bridge engineers gained experience, wrought-iron technology and the development of wire cable progressed to the point where long, safe suspension bridges could be erected. The Niagara Railway Suspension Bridge, built in 1855 with two decks and a span of 821 feet, could carry both railroad trains and highway traffic.

Financial difficulties plagued turnpike operations in every phase of their development. Estimated construction costs rarely measured actual expenses accurately; since state charters usually limited the number of subscribers, additional assessments had to be placed on shareholders in order to complete construction. Maintenance costs were heavier than the traffic. If tolls were raised to cover expenses, traffic and revenues dropped, though the less expensive pikes such as the National Road seemed always crowded with everything from mule pack-trains and hog droves to fancy stagecoaches.

Turnpikes encouraged the growth of freight companies which hauled goods between merchandizing firms in the east and commission men for farm goods in the west. However, their teamsters, professional drivers of the four-to eight-horse Conestoga wagons, found ways to avoid paying tolls by taking roads around tollgates

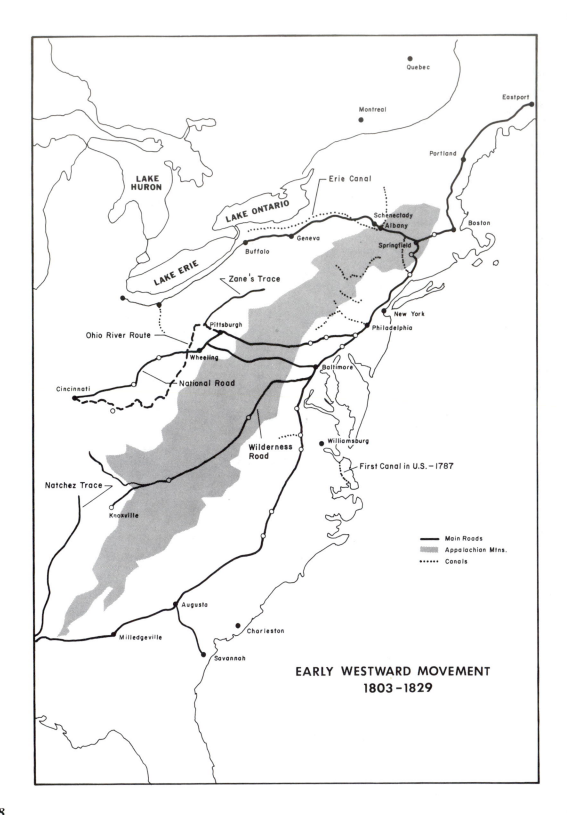

LAKE HURON

LAKE ONTARIO

LAKE ERIE

Quebec

Montreal

Eastport

Portland

Boston

Erie Canal

Schenectady
Albany

Springfield

Geneva

Buffalo

Zane's Trace

New York

Pittsburgh

Philadelphia

Ohio River Route

Wheeling

Baltimore

National Road

Cincinnati

Williamsburg

Wilderness
Road

First Canal in U.S. — 1787

Natchez Trace

Knoxville

Main Roads
Appalachian Mtns.
Canals

Augusta

Charleston

Milledgeville

Savannah

**EARLY WESTWARD MOVEMENT
1803-1829**

(shunpikes) or by waiting until after the gate had closed for the night. Turnpike firms even had trouble finding honest tollgate keepers, so that they often were forced to sell the concessions to individuals.

The final cause of the decline of turnpikes came with the rise of cheaper, quicker transportation on canals and railroads. Road-building would not be given new life until the automobile entered the picture in the next century.

Canals

Leading citizens of the major cities north of Baltimore were panicked by the idea of the National Road, since it was certain to divert commerce and people to opportunities in Maryland where the road began. A year before the National Road was completed to Wheeling in 1818, the newly elected Governor of New York, De Witt Clinton, convinced the legislature to provide revenues for the construction of the Erie Canal. His inspiration for the canal seemed to come from Elkanah Watson, who carried messages to Benjamin Franklin in Paris during the Revolutionary War. Watson was impressed with the efficient system of canals in Europe, and when he returned to the states, he promoted them as the best and cheapest method of transportation. Watson tried to show that the currents and depths of rivers were less dependable than canals for transport. Tow paths were either too high above the water or so low as to be flooded out. Canals constructed parallel to rivers could utilize the benefits of the river's waters, yet be controlled to a set level. Canals also were superior to land travel. Where a team of horses could carry a ton ten to fifteen miles in a day, a canal could transport ten times that amount twice the distance. As the members of the legislature knew as well as Watson, it cost a hundred dollars to carry a ton of goods from New York to Buffalo. They were ready to act.

Canals had been operating in the country since George Washington organized companies to build short canals around the rapids of the James and Potomac Rivers in the early 1790s. The Carondelet was opened in 1794 to provide New Orleans with a short-cut to the Gulf of Mexico through Lake Pontchartrain; in that year also the South Handley Falls Canal made the Connecticut River navigable. The Santee Canal, a much bigger project between Charleston and inland South Carolina, was completed in 1800. Three years later the Middlesex Canal connected Boston with the Merrimac River and the granite and timber quarries of New Hampshire, a distance of a little over twenty-seven miles. By 1817, when work was begun on the Erie Canal, fewer than 100 miles of canal had been constructed in the United States. Because of the great amounts of capital investment needed, early canals had not been profitable ventures for private corporations. Precedent was needed for state support, as well as a pool of trained canal builders. The Erie provided both.

Figure 6–2. Expansion of westward routes. The most significant canal to be built in this early period was the Erie Canal. Not only did it open up the West; it also served as a model for other canals in the North and South.

Figure 6–3. Burgeoning commerce to and from the West. The caption for this 1852 engraving claims that it is a true representation of the activity at Pier No. 1, East River, New York City. The canal boats were built with shallow draft and great sturdiness. It seems likely that the squaresails were not functional, but were advertisements instead, since canal boats did not carry fixed masts; they had to clear very low bridges on their journeys back and forth along the various canals. (The mast left foreground is a temporary one used for cargo handling—in this case, from one vessel outboard across a neighbor's deck to shore.) The artist had a little trouble with perspective, but in general managed to convey the kind of frantic activity that was to make New York a wealthy town for shipping and transshipping. Courtesy Culver Pictures.

Compared to the problems involved with building the proposed 363-mile Erie Canal, the earlier projects hardly deserve mention. The canal was to begin where the Mohawk Valley intersects the Hudson River: a navigable starting point. The route was to cut through the valley, much of it in a marsh known as the Montezuma Swamp, to the Finger Lake region of central New York, and westward to Lake Ontario.

The task appeared nearly impossible to sober observers of the time. Thick forests had to be cut, stumps uprooted, locks designed, cement waterproofing developed. Optimists countered that the highest point of the canal close to Buffalo rose only about 700 feet above the Hudson River in Albany, necessitating a minimal number of locks, and that ample water supplies were available to fill them.

Each year of work on the canal brought with it new difficulties. Malarial disease transmitted from mosquitoes and typhus by fleas and lice in the marshy areas struck down workers by the dozens. Workers hardly made any progress with their accustomed pick, shovel and ax so that engineers had to design a plow that could slice through tangled roots. Where a swamp was impossible to dig, the workers waited until winter when the ground was frozen solid. The engineers also developed special drums and cables to pull down trees and uproot stumps. They even worked on their own cement to seal the canal and found the limestone rock for it at Fayetteville and Lockport.

The engineers for the Erie—Benjamin Wright, James Geddes and Canvass White—learned on the job. Wright was chief engineer but was trained as a lawyer and did part-time surveying of canal routes in New York with Elkanah Watson. Geddes, a lawyer and New York county judge, learned to survey and became Wright's assistant. White was sent to England in 1817; he walked 2,000 miles of towpath studying canal construction. He returned to supervise lock construction, to work on the cement and to advise on the building of canal boats.

Canals were generally made so that the cross-section was an inverted trapezoid. The Erie Canal was forty feet wide at the top, twenty feet at the bottom and four feet deep. In most places water needed to be conserved; canal boats had rounded hulls and did not use as much space on the bottom as on the top. Locks in those days utilized wooden gates which filled up or let out water to take boats to the desired level. The sidewalls of the Erie locks were constructed of stone. They could pass boats through in the rapid time of about four minutes. The Erie engineers solved special problems of rises and dips in the terrain by cut and fill, and they built aqueducts to cross over streams and roads. They wrote their own books on canal design and construction, and they instructed a generation of American builders after them.

Simultaneously with the building of the Erie, the Champlain Canal was constructed north from Albany to connect with Lake Champlain and rich timber and trapping regions. Both canals were completed by 1825. The total cost ran a little over $10,000,000. The state paid for it by establishing a canal fund from taxes on salt manufacture, auctions, steamboat tickets on the Hudson, and lottery ticket sales. Additional funds came from loans and direct appropriations.

But the tolls from the boat traffic alone could have paid for the entire canal construction in less than a decade. Because thousands of canal boats passed through the canal each year, within ten years work was begun to enlarge its width and depth. The unalloyed success of the Erie encouraged the state to finance and build five more canals, these running north and south out of the Erie: from Rochester to Olean; from Oswego on Lake Ontario to Syracuse; and three connecting the Erie with rivers in upstate New York and the Pennsylvania North Branch Canal. Only the Oswego Canal approached the volume of traffic of the Erie itself, however. These canals were responsible not only for the booming grain farming of the west but also at least partially for the downfall of the grain farmers of the east. Eastern farmers responded either by moving west where soils were more productive or by turning to cattle feeding, dairying, or vegetable and poultry raising on their old lands.

Canal Building Enterprises

The booming triumph of the Erie Canal precipitated a mad scramble in the following decade to build canals from Maine to Virginia and west to Illinois. The West had begun to fill in and growing eastern populations needed foodstuffs. Every state sensed that its development was tied to canal building. Coastal states wanted to connect their harbors with inland areas and link themselves with the Ohio River. Western states built canals north from the Ohio to get to the Great Lakes, then east to the Erie Canal.

Many of these new canals, however, ran into unforeseen difficulties. In New England, one of the few good farming areas, near Worcester, Massachusetts, had no connection to Atlantic harbors. The Blackstone Canal from inland Massachusetts southeast to Narragansett Bay in Rhode Island filled the need, but the Blackstone River seemed to supply too much or too little water, and service was irregular. Similar problems arose for the $1,000,000 New Haven and Northhampton Canal, which was proposed to connect New Haven with the Connecticut River and the rich valleys of three New England states.

"Anthracite canals" did much better, though they were hurriedly dug to take the newly-discovered, valuable fuel from high ground in Pennsylvania to New York and Philadelphia. These two commercial centers were linked by the excellent Delaware and Raritan Canal. Baltimore tried to reach into the fertile central Pennsylvania valleys with the Susquehanna and Tidewater Canal in an attempt to draw some of the valley trade away from Philadelphia. The canal went forty-five miles up the river and cost almost $80,000 a mile. It made some money for Baltimore, but it also helped Philadelphia, which could connect with it through its already-completed Chesapeake and Delaware Canal.

Tidewater canals were built along the Potomac and James Rivers in Maryland and Virginia, but the most spectacular venture of the generation was Pennsylvania's Main Line Canal, almost 400 miles long, from Philadelphia to Pittsburgh. Philadelphia merchants promoted the project because of the outstanding successes in New York and the possibility of losing the Ohio River trade. Since Pennsylvania enjoyed no easy access through the state—much worse, a series of folded ridges and valleys of the Appalachian Mountains blocked the way—the engineering problems loomed large. Innkeepers, teamsters, and northern Pennsylvanians who wanted canals of their own mounted a campaign against the canal. Some farsighted critics even proposed that a railroad be built instead, but the success of Pennsylvania's neighbor to the north swept away all opposition. Work was started in 1826. The small Union Canal already connected Philadelphia with the Susquehanna, but a railroad was built to handle additional traffic. The canal proceeded west along the Susquehanna and the Juniata Rivers to the Alleghenies at Hollidaysburg, where the Allegheny Portage Railroad took over. Stationary steam engines drew boats up five inclined planes almost 3,000 feet and let them down again. Horses pulled vehicles on the level stretches between the inclines. The canal continued along the Conemaugh and Allegheny Rivers to Pittsburgh; it was opened in 1834. The total cost was more than $10,000,000. One hundred seventy four locks were required, as opposed to 84 on the Erie. Because of the slow-moving traffic on the Portage Railroad and in the locks, the canal never was able to make money; railroads being built elsewhere were cheaper and faster. The 350 miles of canal completed in other parts of the state by 1840 were no more successful than the Main Line. The legislature found out too late that the state's geography prohibited easy movement by canal throughout the region.

The Erie's reputation was also largely responsible for canal activity in the old northwest, where legislatures quickly approved projects linking the Ohio River to the Great Lakes. In 1825, before the Erie was formally opened, an extensive system of canals, with north and south arteries and branches, was approved in Ohio. Indiana followed suit. Traffic was heavy on the main canals until midcentury, but flood damage, economic depressions, and railroad competition forced both states into debt.

Were it not for the amazing success of the Erie, canal-building would not have been so widespread in the country. Mile for mile they cost ten times the amount of turnpikes and were less direct for many cargoes. Nonetheless most farmers and merchants preferred canals to turnpikes, for whatever reason, and turned to state governments for help in raising the large amount of capital needed to build them. By 1840 about 3,300 miles of canals had been constructed in the country. And about three-quarters of them were state-owned. Even the privately-owned ones needed considerable support of the states in the purchase of stock. Most states issued bonds and collected taxes to build canals, but few were financial successes. Eventually the federal government became accustomed to providing public domain land—more than 4,000,000 acres by 1860—for canal projects in western states. If nothing else, the heavy public subsidy by both state and central government indicates that neither body was adverse to the country's economic integration and regional specialization. And perhaps the canals, after all, were an improvement over the stomach-shaking, brain-rattling backcountry road system.

The American System

After the War of 1812, federal statesmen began to speak more of the government's role in developing a self-sufficient economy. By this time, even the most Jeffersonian of the western agrarian politicians were willing to support a moderate tariff policy so long as their sections received a slice of the federal pie, defined in terms of "internal improvements," but achieved practically from benefits in the public domain. Western congressmen worried about a third part of the new push toward self-sufficiency, a new charter for a second National Bank, because they feared a contraction of the existing easy money policy.

The three planks of Henry Clay's "American System"—the tariff, the U.S. Bank, and internal improvements—were proposed to "bind the Republic together," but they were the sources of heated debate for a generation after the war. As the measures came up for a vote, sectional interests became apparent. The West voted against the bank. The South opposed the tariff because it meant higher prices on manufactured goods. New England did not favor internal improvements because it did not appear that she needed more roads or canals than she already had. New York, which had surveyed the route for the Erie Canal and was looking for federal support, voted for all three bills. Pennsylvania and New Jersey did likewise, and these states carried the balance. President Madison, strict constructionist that he was, vetoed the internal improvements measure, much to the chagrin of many congressmen who realized that the West was closer to Europe by way of the Mississippi than to New York or Philadelphia by roads and rivers. It was left to New York to convince the country of the value of canals.

Judicial Authority over Sectionalism

The major judicial decision which confirmed the notion of national sovereignty over sectionalism came from Chief Justice John Marshall in March 1819, in a case concerning the U.S. Bank. The Bank had been observing an easy money policy and its branch officials were involved in corruption and embezzlement. A congressional investigation and the subsequent publicity brought a resignation by U.S. Bank President William Jones, who was not involved in the affair, but who was not a good manager either. The country already was falling into a depression, and the Bank was a convenient scapegoat; its new President didn't help matters, though, when he sharply contracted credit and demanded swift note payment.

The case brought before the Supreme Court, *McCulloch vs. Maryland* (McCulloch was a branch cashier who refused to pay a state tax), dealt with Maryland's right to tax a federally-chartered bank. Despite universal public opinion decrying the Federal Bank, Marshall, using the "necessary and proper" clause of the Constitution to which Hamilton had appealed when he proposed the First National Bank, upheld his earlier opinions of national sovereignty over the states. The controversial opinion brought a new public outcry against the Court as well as against the U.S. Bank, but the judicial course was set. Later the Federal Government could use the opinion and the "necessary and proper" clause to justify any activity not forbidden by the Constitution, *e.g.,* building interstate road systems, etc. The weakly joined Confederacy gradually became a nation, not of independent units, sectionalized or economically and politically self-sufficient. The decision confirmed what was happening economically and socially.

Steam Power and its Uses

Technological advances have long been known for their capacity to induce social or economic change. We have seen how improvements in agricultural technology increased yields for the farmer who was interested in commercial farming. In the early 1800s, improved machinery was preparing America's own industrial revolution. For instance, Francis Cabot Lowell's cotton mill could convert raw cotton into finished cloth within the walls of one noisy plant, with mechanized carders, spinners, and weavers "manned" by women and children, but powered by the swift waters of the Merrimac River.

Unlike England, America was blessed with myriads of rapids and waterfalls. While England needed the steam engine to begin the process of industrialization, northeastern American industrialists simply took their plants to the most rapidly flowing streams and falls. The receding glacier had left sedimentary fill in valleys through which streams had previously flowed. The pre-existing drainage system was disrupted, but the new falls over the sides of glacial fills proved a boon to operators of early textile mills, sawmills and gristmills.

For example, near Troy, New York, where the Mohawk and Hudson Rivers meet, one stream dropped 200 feet to the Mohawk, and pits, tunnels and channels called raceways were chopped out of bedrock along the edge of the stream. The water ran through pipes to water wheels or turbines which turned millstones or provided rotary motion to run textile machines. At this gorge, known as the Poesten Kill, the early water-turbine pits dropped only about eight feet, but later water turbines of the area were built on a much larger scale. The Mastodon Mill, for example, took water from 102-inch-diameter pipes into turbines on vertical shafts which provided 1,200 horsepower and which drove two miles of shafting, turning 10 miles of belts, operating 70,000 yarn spindles and 1,500 looms, all contributing to the production of 60,000 yards of cotton cloth a day.

The nation's first industrial development was planned by Alexander Hamilton and a few of his industrially minded friends who formed the Society For Useful Manufactures. The group bought up farms and land around the Great Falls of the Passaic River in New Jersey in the 1790s and sold them for factory sites or water power. The Passaic had a 70-foot drop then. Paterson, New Jersey, was born from the textile mills of the area, first for silk production, then for the production of textile machinery and eventually for locomotives and other machinery. Because water power was so readily available and easy to use, steam power would not become a necessity for industrialization until the mid-nineteenth century.

Furthermore, as long as Americans were fairly well concentrated on the coast, wind power could be utilized to carry their ships from north to south and back again, and up dozens of navigable rivers. The West could count on the Mississippi-Ohio system for the transaction of their commerce as long as the settlements were small. Most river traffic was confined to rafts and flatboats floating only downstream; shallow water, high banks that broke the wind, dangerous rapids, and curves prevented upstream navigation. At the end of the downstream journey, flatboats were broken up and sold for their lumber. If a hearty crew tried to pole, row and sail from New Orleans 2,000 miles upstream to Pittsburgh, they could count on at least a four-month journey.

As the population and commercial opportunities increased, western entrepreneurs sought faster and more efficient transportation routes and ways that could carry passengers and goods upstream as well as down. The solution had already been demonstrated by Robert Fulton's steamboat on the Hudson River in 1807, but the story had its beginning a hundred years earlier in the coal mines of England.

Early Steam Engines and Boats

The discovery of English coal in the 1600s prevented the complete destruction of forests, but as mining went deeper, water interfered and manual or horse-powered pumps became less and less effective. By 1712, Thomas Newcomen had developed a boiler-fired piston and cylinder engine which could pump the water out of mines. The next big step in the improvement of steam engines occurred in 1776, when James Watt increased the efficiency of the Newcomen engine. Great quantities of coal were needed for the Newcomen engine to reheat the cylinder continually and fill it with steam after it had been cooled by a jet of water to create the vacuum which sucked in the piston for each thrust. Watt kept the cylinder of his engine hot all the time and piped the steam into a separate condenser where the steam was cooled. Watt also used steam to push the piston; he combined that force with the condensing of steam

Figure 6–4. A water-power behemoth. This is the water wheel of the Burden Iron Company, Troy, New York. Built in 1851, the 60-foot-diameter iron wheel was once the world's largest. It developed 500 horsepower for Burden Iron, which at its peak turned out 50,000,000 horseshoes a year. The remains of this historic wheel were melted into scrap to feed munitions factories at the beginning of World War II. Note the flume construction overhead. Troy and neighboring communities enjoy sharp drops in the waterflow as streams fall to the Hudson and its tributaries. Many industries built factories nearby to take advantage of the water power. Courtesy The Smithsonian Institution.

to create a vacuum and pull the piston. A demand for steam engines came from the textile industry soon after Watt improved his model; Watt, at the request of his partner Matthew Boulton, developed steam engines which drove rotary machinery in 1781. Their engines were used to drive forge-hammers as well as to work winding machinery at coal and copper mines, or to power flour mills and cotton mill machinery. The stage was set for the application of steam power to shipping.

Many inventors tried to put steam to work on ships before Fulton. One of the more notable steamboats was demonstrated by John Fitch in 1790. After ten years of experimenting, Fitch built a steam-driven, forty-five-foot vessel which took its first passengers forty miles from Philadelphia to Trenton for the fare of five shillings or about $1.25. The steam engine sat toward the rear of the boat and its twelve-inch cylinder drove a set of paddles at the back. It could go eight miles an hour. Unfortunately the boat service lost money because the people of the area had been watching Fitch's failures for years and were not ready to accept a success, even though free drinks and sausage were served.

Robert Fulton was able to learn from the mistakes of Fitch and other inventors and developed the first commercially-successful steamboat in the world. Fulton's experiments on water resistance and steam efficiency on the Seine in Paris led him to utilize paddlewheels on the sides of his boat. With the strong financial backing of capitalist-landowner Robert Livingston, Fulton was able to produce a steamboat ready for its maiden voyage on the Hudson River in 1807. The boat was 150 feet long, with a thirteen-foot beam. Displacing 100 tons of water, Fulton's vessel was big enough for a passenger cabin containing twelve berths, a crew shelter, and a large engine area in its center. The *Clermont's* sensational upstream run of 150 miles from New York to Albany was accomplished in 32 hours. Steam power portended to forge another link between the commercial East and the agricultural West.

The Ohio-Mississippi River route was the next target of the Fulton team. One of the partners, Nicholas Roosevelt, grand uncle of Theodore, reported after a flatboat ride from Pittsburgh to New Orleans that despite rapids, snags and sandbars it would be possible to take a steamboat down the river. In 1810, Roosevelt went to Pittsburgh with machinery and a crew to build a steamboat for the run. He and his employees built the 116-foot boat out of timbers from nearby forests and used a Boulton and Watt steam engine imported from England. Roosevelt named the vessel the *New Orleans.* On September 26, 1811, he, his pregnant wife, servants, and a crew of seven started out from Pittsburgh. On the second night they stopped at Cincinnati to take on coal from their own mine. A few days later, in high water, they made it over the rapids at Louisville; Mrs. Roosevelt delivered her baby; and an earthquake shook the West. Their arrival in New Orleans on January 12, 1812, marked the beginning of a new epoch in Mississippi travel. Fulton and Livingston held a monopoly on steamship navigation on the Mississippi, but after years of litigation, the Supreme Court ruled in the 1824 *Gibbons vs. Ogden* case that the monopoly invaded the right of the Federal Government to regulate interstate commerce.

One of the men who fought the Fulton-Livingston monopoly, river captain Henry Shreve, devised an important modification which perfected the steamboat for Mississippi travel. The Fulton boats went deep into the water because of their heavy machinery and rounded hulls, which were liable to collisions with hidden snags or rocks and which unnecessarily took in a considerable amount of water. Shreve used a flatboat hull and designed a high-pressure steam engine with enough expanding steam pressure that it did not need the vacuum created by a separate condenser to pull the piston. The extra weight of the condenser could be eliminated. Even with

Figure 6–5. "Bound Down the River." A famous Currier and Ives print depicting midcentury life on the Ohio-Mississippi route where rivermen floated a thousand miles downriver, and either walked, poled, or rode a steamboat back. In the foreground we see a crew resting as the river supplies the muscle. A sailor is dancing a hornpipe to a fiddled tune while others look on. The sternwheeler steamboat seen right center is typical of the kind built for western waters. These were shallow draft vessels designed to float in very little water and to sail over the frequent obstacles dumped into the rivers by floods and rain runoff. Courtesy the Bettmann Archive.

the addition of a second deck, his *Washington* weighed less than other boats on the river and could make a round trip from New Orleans to Louisville in forty-one days: twenty-five days up and sixteen down.

On eastern rivers, Robert L. Stevens introduced other improvements which came to characterize steamboat navigation up and down the coast, especially on the Hudson, Chesapeake, and Delaware Rivers. The superstructure was enlarged; more efficient low pressure engines, transmissions, and gears made the boats more competitive and less likely to explode. In the forties, the use of anthracite became common in the East because of the escalating price of wood. The enlarged pistons drove walking beams attached to large paddle wheels on both sides of the vessel. Eastern steamboats were largely utilized for passenger travel. Gaudy decorations on encased paddlewheels advertised the steamboat lines. Luxurious bars, sumptuous berths and mirror-lined salons became common among rival lines, which were able to carry hundreds of passengers on their stronger vessels. Stern-wheeled boats pushed barges, and by the thirties steamboats did a good business on the Great Lakes.

But it was in the West that steamboats made their reputation; they were indispensable in the development of that region before the Civil War. Without them the thousands of loads of people and products—lumber, cotton, flour, lard, oats, coal, lead, furs, hides, whiskey, and salt pork—could not have been delivered to the East from farms and plantations. In 1860, 735 steamboats cruised the western waters, creating boom towns at Pittsburgh, Cincinnati, Louisville, and New Orleans, which was considered one of the great ports of the world. Steamboats had advantages of speed, economy and carrying capacity over flatboats and keelboats, though the latter often took loads to New Orleans and their operators returned home by steamboat. Steamboats in the fifties could carry 300 to 400 passengers on the decks alone. They traveled up western branches of the Mississippi—the Red, Illinois, Missouri—to pick up furs and carry supplies to government forts as far as Fort Benton in Montana, a 2,200-mile journey. By 1853, a good steamboat could make the trip between New Orleans and Louisville in four and a half days.

Because western steamboat lines wanted the greater power for upstream travel and the ability to use muddy river water, they utilized the lighter, high pressure engines (at first about 40 pounds per square inch; by 1840 almost 100 pounds), which tended to explode more frequently than the eastern counterparts. Other problems were common in western waters, especially snags—huge trees fallen from banks and hidden below the surface of the water. About a third of all steamboats running western

Figure 6–6. The *Natchez* explosion. The *Natchez* was a popular favorite of steamboat-racing enthusiasts until its boiler exploded during this night race on the Mississippi River. The artist's melodramatic presentation mirrors widespread popular outrage against the frequent steamship disasters caused by ineffective state and federal legislation for safety. The *Natchez* disaster prompted more stringent safety laws. Courtesy the Bettmann Archive.

waters were lost because of river accidents or explosions. At least 1,000 steamboats, valued at over $7,000,000, were destroyed one way or another on the rivers by 1850; about 3,300 persons were killed on them and 1,800 injured.

Government aid to steamboat companies was mostly confined to deepening rivers, removing obstacles or making harbor improvements. Steamboat transport thrived, however, without public help. It contributed to the business of canals, especially the Erie and the Louisville and Portland Canal around the rapids at Louisville, but the coming of the railroad spelled their eventual decline. Rail travel was more flexible, more direct, more dependable, and faster. Steamships could not operate in winter months. They had to proceed as the rivers wound; railroads could go where rivers and canals did not or could not go. Steam continued to pull the country together after the 1840s—but on rails rather than over waters.

The First Railroads

The United States had a few built-in advantages which encouraged the construction of railroads: cheap and abundant land, high demand for their construction from farmer and merchant alike, a growing iron industry for rails, and a plethora of forests for ties and fuel.

Nor was any special new technology necessary before railroads could be put into operation. The steam engine had many years of use before the railroad era; tracks had been laid to connect mines with waterways for a few hundred years. Even United States firms used wooden tracks surfaced with iron straps to connect the stone quarries at Quincy, Massachusetts, with the Neponset River wharf over a distance of three miles. Similar tracks had been laid at a stone quarry near Philadelphia and between anthracite mines and canals in northeastern Pennsylvania.

A Cornishman named Richard Trevithick put wheels on a steam engine and ran it over the ground as early as 1801. He developed rails for the engine three years later. By the 1820s, England had begun to construct railroad lines between city and country.

John Stevens, father of Robert L. and an important inventor in his own right, had suggested the idea of a railroad in 1812, utilizing tracks, flanged wheels and a steam locomotive. At the time there didn't seem to be an impelling motive. This came with the Erie Canal. Fearful that the Erie would draw most of their western trade, Baltimore merchants organized a group to plan a transportation scheme to the Ohio. They favored the idea of a railroad over a canal because of the troublesome ridges of the Allegheny Mountains. In a few weeks the citizens of the area, with the help of their municipal government, raised $2,500,000 for the Baltimore and Ohio Railroad. The Army Corps of Engineers surveyed the route, and in 1831 the B&O directors advertised for a locomotive. Phineas Davis, a watchmaker from York, Pennsylvania, won the competition with his engine, the *York*.

Before the B&O had its engine, however, the South Carolina Railroad was built to connect the cotton plantations of interior Georgia to Charleston harbor. Prior to the completion of this railroad, most of the cotton was floated down the river to Savannah, depriving the Charleston merchants of the lucrative cotton trade. Both the B&O and the South Carolina lines debated or experimented with horse-drawn cars before they ventured into steam power. By the thirties, however, steam had proved itself; technical adaptations for railroads proved minor. The South Carolina Railroad stretched for 136 miles in 1832; it was the longest railroad in the world. Other southern cotton areas quickly built railroads of their own to attempt to equalize the commercial advantage of Charleston.

Capitalists in other parts of the country began to turn with interest to the possibilities of the new form of transport. In the early thirties dozens of short lines were established in most of the populated centers including such railroads as the following: the Pontchartrain Railroad in New Orleans used to connect boats unloading at Lake Pontchartrain directly with the Gulf, avoiding the long route through the Mississippi Delta; the Lexington and Ohio in Kentucky to connect interior cities with the Ohio River; the Boston and Lowell, the Boston and Providence, and the Boston and Worcester, all set up with the purpose of joining to the Erie Canal at Albany. The trend continued in all parts of the country except in New York and Pennsylvania, where a commitment to canal construction during the early development of railroads allowed only a few short feeder lines. The two states fell so far behind the rest of the country in their transportation systems in the late forties and fifties that only massive public campaigns enabled them to put in necessary railroad lines.

Technological Developments

The early railroads had a few simple components. The engine usually had a long stack built in front of a horizontal boiler which rested on a frame. It was attached to pistons driving large iron wheels. A wood-and-water car came behind the locomotive, followed by stagecoach-type passenger coaches or flatcars for cargo. The early engines often sprayed a shower of embers on the passengers, who rarely had a ride without many jolts as the locomotive started up or slowed down to stop for water and wood. (Wood blocks were used as brakes, and stopping remained a major technical problem for some time.) A few train lines tried other experiments, such as cars equipped with sails or horses working treadmill engines. Necessary improvements like the cowcatcher came with time and experience.

Turns in the tracks caused many early derailments. An important innovation which enabled the train to take curves and bumps more easily was designed by John B. Jervis in 1832. The front set of four wheels was attached to the engine by a swivel, equalizing the weight and enabling the engine to follow a curve loosely. The next step, an 1842 development by Joseph Harrison, was the American equalizing beam, which allowed the wheels to "float" from a balance point without the constraint of the entire train car binding the wheels when tracks turned. Harrison's *Mercury* could travel at the speed of sixty miles an hour much more safely than earlier engines.

The earliest rails were made of wood, sometimes of stone, or of wood over stone, often surfaced with strap iron. Even covered with iron, the wooden rails tended to wear down rapidly and break. Early rails were flat or "L" shaped to hold the flat wheels of the locomotive. In the thirties Robert L. Stevens perfected the "T" rail to support flanged wheels. The gauge, or width of the track, varied widely—from

Figure 6–7. An early railroad scare poster. In the 1830s, the various teamster and canal interests opposed to railroads rallied the townsfolk to join in their efforts to stop the building of a "locomotive rail road" through a New Jersey town.

three to six feet—and connections from different lines were difficult to make until Congress decided on a gauge of 4' 8½" for the proposed Union Pacific. Eventually all roads conformed to this gauge. But during the early period of railroads, few were constructed with much similarity to one another.

By the 1850s, railroads had reached the western states where the flat terrain enabled lines to be stretched to nearly any desirable location. Railroads came out of the large western cities—Cleveland, Toledo, Cincinnati, Louisville, Detroit, Chicago, St. Louis, Memphis—and fanned in every direction. Cooled milk (stirred in cans with ice-filled tubes), vegetables, and fresh fruits were taken from upstate New York to Boston and New York City; from New Jersey to urban areas on the East coast; from Wisconsin to Chicago, St. Louis, Cincinnati and farther south. Grain was shipped to large eastern markets and to Europe, which returned manufactured goods and the trappings of wealth. The coming of the railroad cemented earlier tendencies toward regional specialization.

In the beginning of the railroad boom, American private capital provided most of the financing through the issuance of common stock. After 1850, European investors poured their money into railroad stock. English capitalists had lost much money in the 1837 panic and subsequent failure of canal companies, but confidence was restored when early railroads began to make money. The Illinois Central, Louisville and Nashville, Chicago and Northwestern, the Reading, and the Pennsylvania all received substantial amounts of foreign capital. (Huge federal land grant subsidies were not given on a large scale until after the Civil War.)

In the forties, public officials followed the new wave of railroad enthusiasm so that by 1860 about half the capital to subsidize new lines came from public governmental agencies. In 1824 Congress had authorized the right of the Corps of Engineers to survey roads and canals, and before the Act was repealed in 1838 about forty surveys had been completed for railroad companies. In order to increase iron stores for rails, English iron was taken off the tariff list, but was put back on again after eleven years because of pressure from home manufacturers. In 1850, millions of acres of public land were given by the federal government to the Illinois Central and over forty other private companies to subsidize railroad enterprises. States and local governments bought stock; made loans; guaranteed railroad bonds; and granted the power of eminent domain, monopoly rights, and tax benefits. The era of the railroad had arrived.

Jacksonian Capitalism

Between the twenties and the forties many people became rich because of the growth of production and trading, but also by means of thousands of speculative business deals through banks and financially-shaky corporations. After production and trade in agricultural regions increased enough to induce public support, state-chartered private banks sprang up throughout the West to offer easy credit to new enterprises. When trade dropped off, public confidence in banks fell as well, and a run on the banks' reserve of specie brought a contraction of credit throughout the West. Business cycles became a part of the western way of life.

In the meantime the Bank of the United States partially checked the tendency of private banks to overextend their credit by demanding redemption of state bank notes. A number of groups throughout the country resented this power of the U.S. Bank. Debtors (farmers as well as enterprisers) and the smaller western banks wanted local control of their credit policies. Most large eastern banks also opposed outside control of their credit policies. There was yet another opposing faction: working men and women who based their resentment of the Bank on different grounds. In the late twenties the working class began to oppose paper money from all banks, central or local, and to favor a hard money policy because they were so often paid with depreciated bank notes. In the South, too, planters feared more reduction in the prerogatives of the states to determine such matters as slavery. They fought the growing power of the central government, including federal banking.

Although very hit-and-miss in its effects, the early American banking system provided enough public and private venture capital to continue the economic integration

THE ILLINOIS CENTRAL RAILROAD CO., HAVE FOR SALE
1,200,000 ACRES OF RICH FARMING LANDS,
In Tracts of Forty Acres and upward on Long Credit and at Low Prices.

Figure 6–8. An advertisement of Illinois Central designed to lure settlers to their government-bestowed lands. The picture shows how McCormick's original reaper worked.

of the country. During this time, the independent American yeoman was not struggling to keep the rest of the world out of his simple life. On the contrary, he tended to move where the monetary action was, into land speculation and commercial farming, and to where transportation was available or assured. And the capital moved to where the profits were. These activities paved the way for a dramatically changed landscape.

It was the Illinois Central Railroad, endowed with 2,500,000 acres of federal land on both sides of its track, that created the new geographical entity of the 1850s, the railroad town. The railroad promoted rapid settlement on its land, blanketing the country and Europe with leaflets promising immediate prosperity in inexpensive lands in central Illinois. The firm even laid out 33 gridded towns along its 700-mile track from Chicago to Cairo at the tip of the state, each community sliced in half by the track and each endowed with a railroad station in the very heart of the grid. The railroad donated lots for schools, churches, and municipal buildings, and gave the towns exotic names like Onarga, Loda and Pera. Settlers bought lots from the railroad, started farms on the flat plains around the towns, and inaugurated a uniform economic pattern that emanated from the railroad. The situation was repeated on later railroad lands of the West after the Civil War.

Linearity from the railroad track and the beginnings of national economic integration, along with the accelerating tempo of a national transportation system which spawned a more regimented economic process, were clearly present in the nation at midcentury. People wanted to get to their destinations faster; the entrepreneurs and farmers wanted their products and produce delivered faster. So faster steamboats were designed and faster railroads constructed to compete with steamboats. Steamboats exploded by the hundreds; railroads, because of hasty and sloppy construction, outdid their river rivals in accident rates. Behind this phenomenon of linearity and speed was the economic imperative that motivated a country beginning to pursue its single-minded destiny.

Transportation development demanded liberal land policies toward railroads as well as toward settlers and, of course, rapid "Indian removal." Conservation or sharing of land and natural resources with Native Americans could not be included in collective attitudes and national policies that began to speak more and more of the necessity of material progress in the country. For this purpose, as a delegate to the 1850 Ohio Constitutional Convention declared, "The earth is to be subdued" and the state must help with the task. Thus new technologies for agriculture and transport were sought and developed while federal land laws became more liberal to encourage rapid western settlement and new banking arrangements assured equally rapid resource exploitation.

Changes in the modes of transportation in the generation before the Civil War symbolized the transformation of American society from subsistence economy to commercial economy and also symbolized its effects on the natural environment. Canals, with their charming locks, bridges, and tiny toll houses, blended in with their agricultural communities and allowed the landscape to remain open and clean. Railroad locomotives screeched, spread soot, and left a trail of sliced hilltops and cut-over landscapes as they hauled coal and iron to cities and factories built around their central stations. The economic imperative demanded the latter form of transportation, natural environmental values notwithstanding.

Daniel Webster noted the disturbing effects of railroad-building long before railroads became commonplace in America. On August 25, 1847, at Grafton, New Hampshire, on the day the Northern Railroad was opened, he described railroad builders as people who ". . . are no enthusiastic lovers of landscape beauty; a handsome field or lawn, beautiful copses, and all the gorgeousness of forest scenery pass for little in their eyes. Their business is to cut and slash, to level or deface a finely rounded field, and fill up beautifully winding valleys. They are quite utilitarian in their creed and in their practice. Their business is to make a good road. They look upon a well-constructed embankment as an agreeable work of art; they behold with delight a long, deep cut through hardpan and rock, such as we have just passed; and if they can find a fair reason to run a tunnel under a deep mountain they are half in raptures. . . ." (Quoted in Leo Marx, *The Machine in the Garden*, 1964.)

References for Further Reading

The Economic Origins of Jeffersonian Democracy by Charles A. Beard (1965) started the debate over the relative domination of financial interests in the affairs of the early United States. George Rogers Taylor's *The Transportation Revolution: 1815-1860* (1968) gives an excellent economic background of the period along with chapters on turnpikes, canals, steamboats and railroads. Older treatments of these subjects can be enjoyed with great educational benefit: Fredrick I. Wood's *The Turnpikes of New England* (1919); Alvin F. Harlow's *Old Towpaths* (1926); John H. Morrison's *History of American Steam Navigation* (1903); John W. Starr's *One Hundred Years of American Railroading* (1928). *The Age of Jackson* by Arthur M. Schlesinger (1953) remains a fine interpretation of the Jacksonian Era. Schlesinger's *The Cycles of American History* (1986) is an excellent companion volume to this text, as it illustrates how important a role business cycles play in environmental history.

Chapter 7

ADVANCING FRONTIERS

*I*n 1893, the noted American historian Frederick Jackson Turner put forward a new interpretation of the development of the American West. He attempted to prove that the availability of free land on the western frontier, which had advanced rapidly to the Pacific in successive stages, explains the American character and institutions more than inherited European institutions. He pointed out that the very geography of the wilderness demanded a new kind of society and personality, that the primitive environment in fact created a distinctive breed of men, women and institutions based on egalitarianism, individualism, love of freedom, self-reliance, materialism, crudeness, optimism and resourcefulness.

The hypothesis can be defended more as a poetic description of many mid-western communities which Turner had thoroughly studied than as a detailed explanation of nineteenth century Western America. Among other factors, Turner too easily discounted European ideological influences and technologies, eastern development capital, and emerging American factories and cities. He discounted particularly the all-pervading sensitivity to the demands of large eastern and European markets. If these markets had not existed, giant fur companies and mountain men would not have pushed far up the Missouri; timber companies would not have ventured into the wilderness of Minnesota; copper mining settlements would not have been built on the icy shores of Lake Superior; indeed, even farming would have been done on a much smaller scale, and the big cattle drives probably would never have been attempted.

Yet the Turner thesis points up the necessity of recognizing that the vast expanse of land, laden with rich natural resources, was not a neutral force in the shaping of American institutions. The land's varied resources were endowed with a pull that attracted settlers; equally strong was the push of personal or societal upheavals, depressions, religious persecutions, and countless other economic or political conditions. Emigrants took their habits and technologies, their customs and mores with them. The fusion of their cultural habits within the constraints of the new environment provided the foundations of the contemporary society of the American West. The beginnings of the process came with the Louisiana Purchase in 1803.

The Louisiana Territory

The Purchase came as a surprise bonanza to a country that wanted no more than the free use of the Mississippi to carry out furs and occasional farm goods from the western frontier, located just west of the Appalachians at that time. Spain, which in

1762 had taken the Louisiana territory from France and ceded it back in 1800 because of pressure from Napoleon, revoked the American "right of deposit" at New Orleans in 1802 before France officially reclaimed the territory. President Thomas Jefferson seized the opportunity to make an offer to buy the Island of Orleans from France, since that purchase would bring back America's right of passage to the Mississippi. When Napoleon offered him the entire territory, Jefferson hesitated because of scruples about Constitutional authority, but nonetheless accepted the $15 million land deal. An enthusiastic Congress quickly authorized the extraordinary purchase, the uncertain boundaries of which stretched all the way to the sources of the tributaries of the Mississippi in the Rocky Mountains, doubling the land area of the young nation.

Jefferson long had been interested in sending an exploring party from the Mississippi west to California, both to develop communication and commerce with the Indians and also to find out what kind of land, climate and wildlife lay in the far west. He secured a Congressional appropriation in 1803 for a "military" expedition to the Pacific for these purposes even before Spain had turned the Louisiana territory over to France and before the purchase was proposed. Besides collecting scientific data, the explorers were to determine whether or not the Missouri River could be utilized for transporting furs back to the United States and to find out the routes of Canadian traders. Friendly contacts with the native populations were also to be made, particularly for purposes of trading.

To lead the expedition, Jefferson chose his own private secretary, Meriwether Lewis, who in turn asked his friend William Clark, younger brother of George Rogers Clark, to share the duties of command. In May, 1804, the twenty-five members of the Lewis and Clark Expedition headed up the Missouri River. The current and "muscuiters" hindered progress, but the party successfully talked to dozens of Indian tribes and enjoyed their plentiful game—buffalo, elk, deer, antelope and turkeys—and cultivated crops—corn, beans, and dried squash. In return, the explorers gave the Indians gifts of coats, hats, flags, metal insignia, tobacco, and other trinkets and goods. The major effort was directed toward wooing Indian tribes away from trading their valuable skins, especially beaver pelts, with the British; but many rock and plant specimens were collected as well. The group was favored with special help from many Indians in finding the best route through the Northwest, but particularly from the Shoshones, who led them over the treacherous mountain trails for 300 miles from the three forks of the Missouri River to the Clearwater Fork of the Columbia River in Oregon country. The expedition reached the Pacific at the end of 1805 and started its return the following spring.

The pioneering work accomplished by the group was far-reaching. Later trappers and traders or Indian negotiators rarely engaged on a mission into the upper Missouri without a recommendation or counsel from Clark (Lewis died suddenly in 1809). Because of their exploration, the Missouri River almost immediately became an important route of western expansion and resource exploitation, mainly trapping and trading with the Indians. And the seeds of the later development of Kansas City, Independence, St. Joseph, Omaha, Bismarck, Fort Benton, Great Falls, Helena, Missoula and Portland were sown by two dozen hearty explorers. Their deed presaged the march of millions later fulfilling the white man's vision of manifest destiny.

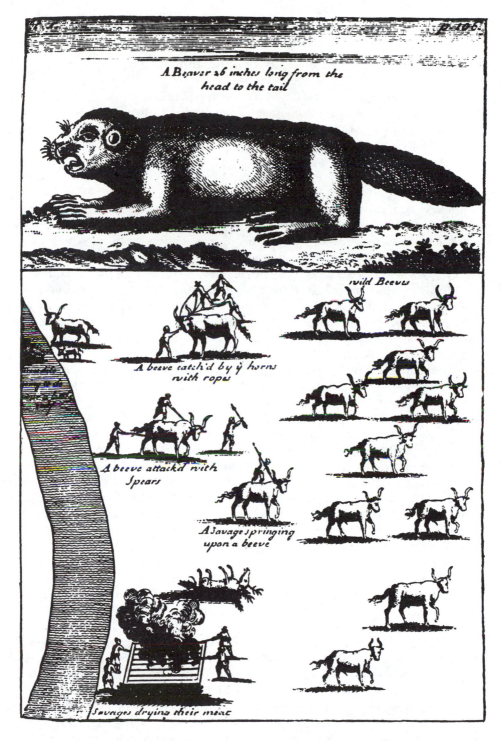

Figure 7–1. Conceptions of the Wild West. The fanciful illustration depicted here comes from the eighteenth century *New Voyages to North America* by the French Baron de Lahontan. The omnipresent western beaver is made to appear quite fierce, and the "wild beeves" are supposed to be buffalo in the process of being lassoed by Indians, speared and even being mounted. It is unlikely that the baron ever saw a beaver or a buffalo, much less Indians killing and preparing them.

Trapping, Fur Trading and Hunting

After the Revolution, the country west of the Appalachians began to teem again with traders and trappers seeking to reopen trade with the Indians for beaver and fox furs and deer and buffalo skins. Beaver still brought over three dollars a pound and a fur weighed about two pounds. The new center of the fur trade was St. Louis, a huge mud hole at the time, where trappers, traders, boatmen and Indians came from eastern and western river trading points and where large fur companies recruited their men. Along the Pacific coast, the sea otter's deep brown-gold pelt, costliest in the world, was already luring expeditions from British and American companies at the turn of the century. Within a hundred years, a million otter pelts were retrieved from coastal waters. Old sources of furs began to dry up as settlers invaded wilderness areas, pushing the advance guard of fur traders west of the Mississippi.

Fur trading was always an enterprise fraught with difficulties for the country. Either it was British soldiers in the Northwest harassing American traders, keeping them out of disputed territories, or it was the traders themselves in their dealings with the Indians—cheating them with inferior goods or bribing them with liquor to undercut competition. The federal government first tried to control the problem by licensing trappers and traders, requiring proof of good moral character and intention to obey Indian regulations. It didn't take long for officials to see the loopholes in the licensing system, so the government itself went into the fur trading business. Posts were built in Indian territories to insure Indians of a fair price and quality goods without the liquor incentive. The experiment was doomed to fail, however, since the operation was given only token appropriations each year. In the meantime, private enterprise provided liquor bonuses and easy credit to the Indians, neither of which government traders were permitted to dispense. By 1823 Congress decided to stop the operation of government posts, a decision helped along by strong lobbying from fur interests, i.e., John Jacob Astor and his Washington emissary, Senator Thomas Hart Benton.

The most significant of the fur trading companies was begun at the turn of the century by John Jacob Astor. Astor started in the fur business in 1786 with a small store on Water Street in New York City. Within five years he had dozens of trappers and agents working for him in the back country. By 1800, he moved his store to Broadway and probably was one of the richest men in New York. He bought his own ships and exchanged furs in England for manufactured products, making money at both ends of the transaction. He traded in France and in Venice, Leipzig, Trieste, and even Canton, China.

In 1808, Astor incorporated the American Fur Company (he was the entire corporation) with an initial capital investment of $500,000. He sent an expedition to the Oregon Territory, where his people were forced out by the British in 1812. He settled for control of the regions around the Great Lakes, then later expanded into the trans-Mississippi regions along the Missouri River north in a string of company posts almost to the Continental Divide, near the British Northwest possessions and about 2,000 miles from St. Louis. His domain extended into the southwest also; in both areas he bought out smaller trading firms and employed the most skillful agents to attract and keep his lucrative trade. Astor maintained three principal distribution and receiving stations, at Detroit, St. Louis, and Mackinac, and he owned keelboats and a steamship to take furs and supplies up and down the Missouri River. He sold out his interests in the Company after 1834 when he discovered silk stove pipe hats were beginning to replace beaver hats on the Continent; by that time his firm had monopolized the beaver export trade of the country. The company didn't last much longer, but the decimation of beaver had almost as much to do with the drop in trade as did the change in fashions. Buffalo robes, although worn widely throughout the West, had not yet become modish; their exploitation would come later.

During the life of the American Fur Company, the fur business was continually expanded and streamlined. Most companies, Astor's in particular, adopted the hierarchical organization of the early French companies: a chief trader in each area known as the "bourgeois;" junior executive clerks, the "commis," who were next in command and sometimes were in charge of small outposts; then the lowly "voyageurs" or "engagés" who performed all the manual work—canoe paddling and barge poling, portaging, hunting for daily meals, cooking, packing furs, all done in abject servitude to the "bourgeois." Usually French-Canadian peasants or children of trappers and their Indian wives, the voyageurs signed three-year engagements to the fur companies for minimal wages. The arduous daily labor, e.g., carrying 250-pound packs in portage or poling keelboats sun-up to sun-down, and the cruel treatment by their bosses occasioned regular desertions. The American Fur Company, noted for its especial harshness and severity to engagés, was finally compelled to import the young men directly from the back-country or Canada.

Forts and Mountain Men

A dozen fur-trading posts or military forts along the Missouri and its tributaries were built in the generation following the Lewis and Clark expedition. The forts served as trading posts for the fur companies, exchanging blankets, cotton goods, beads, brass wire, iron goods, butcher knives, axes, guns, powder, flints, lead, mirrors, kettles, beaver and muskrat traps, sewing equipment, horse equipment, and food and liquor, mainly for beaver or muskrat pelts and buffalo hides, but also for the furs of other exotic animals like martens, foxes, bears or an occasional panther. Book credit was given to Indian and resident worker alike so that both groups seemed to remain in perpetual debt to the post.

The forts greatly resembled each other. They were constructed and reinforced with timbers, with one main entrance and blockhouses on diagonal corners of the stockade. Inside, houses, shops and store and perhaps a garden were clustered together opposite an open court area where trading was done under the supervision of armed guardians in the blockhouse. Houses and entrance were fireproofed with earth or iron against flaming arrows. Indian attacks in scattered regions were regular occurrences.

Cross-country travelers frequently stopped at the forts, and in many of them Indians liked to congregate. Since supply trains from St. Louis were infrequent, the posts lived from their own gardens (irrigated with water from nearby rivers or streams) and the hunting of game, usually buffalo.

Besides those hunters and trappers who contracted with fur companies for salary, equipment and supplies, "free" trappers combed the streams and plains for pelts and skins, selling them to the highest bidders, Indian or white. These so-called mountain men travelled in groups, sometimes even pooling resources and proceeds in a collective organization. Their life and exploits became legendary in their own day, and even now are quite noteworthy.

They trapped in the spring and fall, working as long into the winter as the wildlife stayed out of hibernation. Most often the men trapped in tributaries and watercourses harboring beaver, wading in the icy streams to keep their presence and scent a secret from the nervous rodents. Since beavers travel the same path, or slide, up and down a bank to gnaw cottonwood trees and then return to their home in the water, traps were staked out in the water at the foot of the slide. Sometimes traps were baited with sticks dipped in beaver castor, produced in its musk-glands and saved as a precious byproduct by trappers. When a beaver was caught in the trap, it dove into the safety of deeper water but, weighted by the trap, it drowned, no shot marring its valuable pelt.

Mountain men lived off forest game—buffalo, elk, deer, antelope, and bear—but preferred delicacies like panther meat, dog meat, and beaver tail. Their staple, the buffalo, was eaten for meat and marrow; its skins were dried and tanned for clothing. Mountain men lived outdoors, rarely constructing shelters to protect themselves from rain or snow. Some Indian tribes were their friends, some their fierce enemies. In either case the trappers never rested easily, since even friendly Indians liked to rustle their horses and steal the fruits of the season's labor. Very often mountain men took Indian wives who shared the burden of their daily chores, cared for their children, and made peace with potentially hostile tribes.

In the mid-1820s, the rendezvous, a meeting for trade, began to replace the fort as a gathering place for trading and selling in the central Rocky Mountain regions each summer. The rendezvous were not unlike medieval fairs. Selling and bartering were accompanied by races, contests, much gambling, drinking, and exchanges of tall tales. Indian bands set up their lodges and joined the merriment with demonstrations of horsemanship and other hunting skills. Many a yearly income was drunk, gambled, or squandered away on beads or colorful gewgaws to decorate the buffalo-hide clothing of the mountain man or his Indian wife. The fur companies well understood the taste of their clients, and they parlayed this knowledge into good profits for themselves. Eventually as many as 2,000 people attended these rendezvous from 1824 to 1840. They were all set up at predetermined locations in the mountains east of the Great Salt Lake. From the rendezvous at the Great Salt Lake in 1826, Jedediah Smith, one of the most famous of the mountain men, blazed a trail to Los Angeles. He then trapped and hunted his way up California's central valley to the Sacramento area, and finally turned east across the snow-covered Sierras and scorched deserts of Nevada to join the Bear Lake Rendezvous of 1827.

The Struggle Over Oregon Country

After the Bear Lake gathering, Smith retraced his steps to California, then pioneered another trail north to the Columbia River, where his company was attacked by Indians. His furs were taken and ten men were killed. The chief trader for the British Hudson's

Bay Company at Fort Vancouver, John McLoughlin, aided the Smith party. While Smith stayed at the fort in 1828, he noted that 30,000 beaver pelts, valued at $250,000, as well as countless numbers and varieties of other furs, had been collected in the region during that season. (Just below the surface of American claims and negotiations for the Oregon Territory in the following generation was a sensitivity to the potential receipts from the Pacific Northwest.)

But seamen knew this fact much earlier than Smith. English Captain James Cook had alerted his merchant friends to the financial possibilities as early as 1778, shortly after he discovered the Hawaiian Islands and Vancouver as he was looking for the Northwest Passage. While wintering back at Hawaii, Captain Cook was killed by natives, but his successor on the expedition, Captain Clerke, returned to North America for sea otter pelts to sell in Canton, China. So great was their profit on the mission that

Figure 7–2. After whaling, sealing became the most profitable pursuit of the new pioneers of the Pacific, and during the nineteenth century seamen most often sought out seals and otters as well as whales. The amiable northern seals, shown above, and sea otters were easily clubbed to death so that their furs would not be marred by spear or shot. After whaler-seamen slaughtered over two million of the northern seal herds at the Pribilof rookeries in the Bering Sea (the inspiration for the 1867 sketch above), they descended upon the Guadalupe fur seals and sea otters in California, where millions more were killed to the point of extinction. In 1911 an international Fur Seal Treaty which outlawed pelagic sealing except by aborigines was signed, protecting Pacific seal herds.

the crew demanded to make another expedition so that they could all reap their fortunes and retire. The officers unsympathetically refused despite threats of mutiny. English merchants quickly took advantage of the trade; on one trip in 1785, James Hanna bartered a variety of trinkets with the Indians for 560 otter skins, which were worth over $20,000 at Canton.

Spain and England quarreled over the rights to the Oregon region, but Spain had backed out of the Northwest by 1790. New England Captain Robert Gray at the same time was introducing the commercial possibilities of the Oregon Territory to his own American merchant friends. The latter group tried their hand at the Canton trade. They were fond of establishing contact with Indians who had never traded with white men before along the Northwest coast; these would ask for even fewer goods for their skins. The Chinese, at least as shrewd as New Englanders at trading, soon managed to work the trades to their advantage. In either case the Northwest coast was overrun with Yankee ships and seamen by 1800. They sailed around the Horn, traded cotton goods for sea otter with the Spanish padres of California, picked up more skins in Oregon, and then sailed for China, where they obtained tea, spices and specie.

Although the animals had been living in Pacific coastal waters for perhaps 2,000,000 years, the sea otter population in the Northwest diminished so greatly in the 1790s that, without making an effort to get otter pelts, many ships traveled directly to Canton from Cape Horn. Instead, they stopped at the tiny islands near the tip of South America, where the crews clubbed thousands of fur seals to death for the trade. On just one of those islands, Mas Afuera, a few miles off the coast of Chile, more than 3,000,000 seals were clubbed in seven years, according to one captain who stopped there regularly. In Oregon, while the otters lasted, Indians did the work for both the English and Yankee merchants.

Meanwhile Englishman Alexander Mackenzie pushed to the coast overland from Montreal for the North West Company, sending word back to his firm that no possible water route through the Northwest existed. Therefore, the North West Company left the fur trade in Oregon to seamen merchants until they found out that John Jacob Astor planned to build his colony of Astoria at the mouth of the Columbia River. The Company immediately directed their employee David Thompson to build a fort there in 1811—too late to stop Astor's venture. However, British troops arrived at the beginning of the War of 1812, Astor's colony was ejected, and the North West Company retained complete control of the area. In 1818 the United States and England signed a Joint Occupation agreement, whereby citizens of both countries were permitted to settle in the Oregon Territory.

For at least a generation, English interests in the region increased while American influence diminished. Hudson's Bay Company absorbed the North West Company in 1821 and appointed John McLoughlin to oversee its trade at Fort Vancouver. McLoughlin also developed a small salmon industry and introduced the raising of vegetables, grains, fruits, cattle, and sheep, first for local consumption but soon for export. A flour mill and saw mill eventually were added to the prosperous fort.

The Oregon Trail

Americans did not begin to migrate to the Oregon territory until the mid-1830s, when missionary expeditions were sent overland to proselytize the Indians. The early missioners settled in the Willamette Valley but their endeavors for religious converts from nearby tribes went unrewarded. At the end of the 1830s emigration societies all over the country began to enlist recruits to fill in the Oregon territory. The land in the Northwest was depicted as the embodiment of the American dream, brimming with economic opportunities and social equality; it was further deemed as one's personal and patriotic duty to take the first wagon west.

Migrants over the Oregon Trail did not actually get started until 1841, when about seventy people left from the Missouri frontier at Independence. The trail went northwest to Fort Kearney at the south bend of the Platte River, following its north branch to Fort Laramie past Independence Rock and Devil's Gate, and through the South Pass of the Rockies. The trail went as far south as Fort Bridger before it turned northwest through Soda Springs to Fort Hall on the Snake River, which it followed to Fort Boise, through the Grand Ronde Valley, over the Blue Mountains to Whitman's Mission and down to the Columbia River into the Willamette Valley.

Pioneers usually waited until the spring when the grasses of the plains were high enough to provide forage for their animals en route. The 2,000-mile six-month trip was a difficult one; people, wagons and livestock had to pass through prairies, over mountains, and across deserts. At one point, after going through South Pass in the mountains, the wagoners had to cross forty miles of waterless desert to get to the Green River near Fort Bridger. From the fort, they had to reach the Bear River on their way to Fort Hall. Yet neither the long, arduous journey, nor the blazing deserts, nor the perilous mountain passes slowed down the tens of thousands of migrants, many escaping depressions and others looking for opportunities. The pressure of these early residents helped in 1846 to precipitate political action on a demarcation line between England and the United States. After Fort Vancouver of the Hudson's Bay Company was moved to the future Victoria on Vancouver Island, the British proposed to extend the forty-ninth parallel, which divided the United States from Canada at Lake Superior, across the Rockies to the Pacific Coast. The United States, already in a war with Mexico in 1846, wisely accepted.

The Southwest

At about the same time the English were sailing to James Bay, Virginia, the Spanish were moving from their Santa Barbara mines in Mexico seventy miles north into the Rio Grande region above El Paso. For about 200 miles along the Rio Grande in the area that would eventually become New Mexico, the colonizers found Indians they called "Pueblo" because of their characteristic villages of flat-roofed adobe huts, closely-packed and storied in three or four layers. There were perhaps 40,000 Indians along the river and several thousand more west of it scattered in villages on desert mesas. Every village was a self-sufficient unit, maintaining its own separate, irrigated fields. The pueblos shared a common culture, yet had minimal contact with one another and no real unity of language or political organization; they shared even less with the hunting and gathering Apache bands around them, except for some exchanges of goods or occasional attacks by the Apaches on the pueblos.

The Spanish intended to annex the pueblo region on behalf of the Crown. Their first wave of settlers moved in with several thousand head of cattle and sheep, about a hundred wagons loaded with missionaries, families and supplies, and a strong military unit on horseback. Their established procedure of setting up military presidios, missions, ranchos and even a few small farm villages was superimposed upon the Indian pueblos, from which the Spaniards conscripted labor and exacted taxes. The arid lands were pressed into agricultural use, but they could support only a small amount of irrigated cultivation; for the most part, the land was given over to grazing. When the supply trains came from Mexico every few years, district officials could trade for Spanish goods with sheep, wool, hides, pine nuts, blankets, and, when needed, Indian slaves.

The Pueblo Indians continually resisted the Spanish. Once, in 1680, they drove the intruders out completely and were not fully reconquered for another sixteen years. Yet the older Indian way of life was drastically altered, not only by their conquerors but also by the Comanches from the north, who regularly overran their villages. By 1800, well over half their villages had been abandoned, the number of pueblos down to nineteen from the sixty originally captured by the Spanish, and the population down to 8,000 from the original 40,000. The Indians who survived the wars, revolts, and epidemics gradually left the plains and sought out hidden valleys and secluded mesas in the harsher inland environment. Some of them were Christianized and integrated into the bottom levels of Spanish society, usually as cattle- and sheep-tenders. Spanish and Indians intermarried, and the mestizos eventually made up the overwhelming majority of the 20,000 Spanish-speaking people in New Mexico in 1800. Only a ruling body of a few hundred maintained what they considered to be the purity of Spanish blood and religion. By then, the village settlements grew grapes when they were not defending themselves from the Apaches in the south and west, or from the Utes on the north and the Comanches in the north and east—all now armed with rifles and on horseback. The original Pueblos lived on the fringes of the society, still performing domestic labor in the villages. One Indian group which prospered and grew in population during the 1700s was the Navaho tribe, which maintained contact with the old Pueblo Indians, became sheep and cattle raisers, developed new crafts, and from time to time, like their Apache brothers, went on raiding parties.

Anglo-American trading groups from Illinois and Missouri attempted to set up trade arrangements with the Spanish of the Southwest in the early 1800s, but official Spanish policy of that generation prohibited such relationships. A few groups managed to make a sizable gain on the sale of their goods, but more often the midwesterners were thrown into jail for several years by local Spanish authorities. After the Mexican Revolution succeeded in 1821, the Mexicans needed new sources of goods, and the era of prairie commerce was begun over the Santa Fe Trail.

The Santa Fe Trail

In the fall of 1821, William Becknell reached Santa Fe with his items for trade strapped to a string of pack animals. His welcome was so cordial and profits so handsome that he returned to Missouri immediately to prepare for a second trip, this time crossing the Cimarron Desert with twenty-one men and three wagons. They traded dry goods mainly for gold and silver, long the Mexican staple, but also for horses, mules, and beaver pelts. Within a few years large caravans from Missouri regularly arrived in Santa Fe, and hundreds of thousands of dollars worth of specie passed over to the aggressive Anglo tradesmen.

There were difficulties, of course, primarily from Indians over whose lands the traders passed with their tempting cargoes. Senator Thomas Hart Benton of Missouri, long the spokesman for his constituent fur traders and merchants, successfully appealed to Congress in 1825 for assistance. Three congressional commissioners were assigned to survey and to mark the Santa Fe Trail, and also to procure the privilege of safe passage from local tribes along the way. At the international boundary on the Arkansas River, the team received the consent of the Mexican government to continue marking the trail with mounds of stones en route to Taos.

In successive years trade and Anglo profits mounted, as did the frequency of Indian attacks. President Andrew Jackson calmed the western entrepreneurs with promises of military aid. Congress, however, refused to appropriate money for military expeditions, forcing the traders who used the Santa Fe Trail to provide their own military protection. By this time they could well afford it.

The Trail took a fairly direct route from Independence, Missouri, to Santa Fe, first through the humid prairies to Council Grove, where rainfall declines and the arid plains begin; Council Grove also marked the entrance to Comanche and Pawnee territory and the road to the Arkansas River. At a designated point on the river, the trail cut across the Cimarron Desert, a high, parched plain. Two rivers where water could be replenished intersected the trail, but the last jump stretched for sixty miles and was inhabited by Comanches and Kiowas. From the desert to Santa Fe, the terrain became hilly, grassy and less arid. Some caravans took the alternate route, avoiding the Cimarron cutoff, and travelled along the longer but no less difficult Mountain Branch of the Trail, which followed the Arkansas River all the way to Bent's Fort (Colorado) and then turned southwest through the mountains.

During the height of the Santa Fe trade, wagons assembled in Independence in the spring to prepare for the trek. Conestoga wagons had been adapted for prairie use, but were still pulled by four spans of mules or four yoke of oxen, sometimes hitching up longer strings to pull 5,000-pound loads. Provisions for each person amounted to about fifty pounds of flour, fifty pounds of bacon, twenty of sugar, ten of coffee; buffalo were killed along the way for additional food. Traders traveled singly until they reached Council Grove, at the edge of Indian country, then arranged themselves into caravans.

At Santa Fe, stocks of cotton goods and manufactured articles were traded for specie, beaver pelts and buffalo robes, Mexican blankets, and livestock—horses, jacks, jennets, and mules. It was the gold and silver, scarce in the United States, that the traders especially craved. This specie served as development capital for hundreds of other entrepreneurial projects during the middle of the century. The war with Mexico brought trade at Santa Fe to a halt, but it began again after the territory was incorporated into the domain of the United States. That changeover, of course, also signified the end of the easy flow of Mexican specie.

The Colonization of Texas

Early Anglo-American migrants to Texas also had specie-trading on their minds, as well as wild horses or cattle. Lands beyond the Sabine River on the western Louisiana border attracted farmers and ranchers because of their rich river bottoms, abundant, fast-running streams, oak and pine forests and high prairie grasslands. Spanish forces held the line on intruders, however—even when in 1813 a few adventurers recruited thousands of mestizo revolutionists in an attempt to drive the Spanish rulers out of Texas. Although Spain enacted an abrupt change of policy in 1820 with a liberal colonial land law (encouraging Moses Austin to apply to take 300 settlers into Texas), the Mexican Revolution intervened in 1821, and Mexican liberality far outdid that of the Spanish.

Thousands of homesteaders took advantage of Mexican generosity after 1820, though at the time Texas extended only to the Nueces River, less than half its later Anglo-American size. The United States land law of 1820 offered 80 acres for $100 plus surveying costs. The Mexican Republic provided a *sitio* of 4,428 acres for about $200. There were restrictions on land settlement around the borders, and settlers were required to accept Mexican laws. In 1825, a new provision of the land law granted agents called *empresarios* the right to collect entire colonies for settlement in Texas or Coahuila. Land was given in proportion to the number of families brought in—five leagues of grazing land (a league equaled 4,438 acres) and five *labores* of farm land (885 acres) for every hundred families.

Within six weeks of the passing of the new law, empresarios had contracted with 2,400 families to settle in Texas. By 1830, most of Texas was promised to empresarios, who began to speculate with their huge land grants, even attempting to sell them in Ireland and England after the six-year time limit of the grants had expired. The Anglo-American population in Texas expanded from about 1,800 settlers in 1825 to 20,000 in 1830. Cotton planters flocked to Texas, particularly those who had failed to recover from the 1819 depression, but also well-established planters who realized that they could do better on the fertile lands of east Texas. They took their slaves with them. Ranchers were equally enthusiastic about the inexpensive land in Texas, where land concentration by both ranchers and planters occurred within a few years after the 1825 law. A Mexican attempt to emancipate the slaves of Texas caused a slowdown of southern migration, however, and provoked Anglo friction and hostility toward the Mexican government.

But cultural, political and religious differences between Anglos and Mexicans were increasingly aggravated from the start of Anglo settlement. Anglo assertiveness and demands for political rights and representation, as well as their contempt for Mexican culture, were offensive. They precipitated suspicions that the new arrivals were out to take over the Texas government as soon as possible. The more the Anglos demanded, the more restrictions the Mexicans imposed, especially after the "Fredonian Rebellion" of 1826-27 over a contested land grant. Fearful that the United States would annex Texas, the Mexican government passed a new land law in 1830 forbidding more Anglo-American immigration. Later Mexican troops were placed in areas heavily settled by Anglos, and tariff regulations began to be strictly enforced. Arrests of Anglos became more frequent; even the prestigious Stephen Austin was arrested in 1833 after he had petitioned the new Mexican ruler, Antonio Lopez de Santa Anna, for separate Texan statehood. Although Santa Anna freed Austin and made temporary reforms in the state governments, within a year he disbanded state legislatures, deposed governors, and centralized his government in Mexico City. In 1835, war broke out, and within a year Texas had won its independence.

Texas had its independence but not economic or political security, because Mexican troops were encamped menacingly at its borders. The thousands of new migrants who flooded in after the war created additional problems, although President Sam Houston hoped that the sale of 180,000,000 unappropriated acres of land would take his government out of debt. Instead, forged land certificates, rival claimants to the land, land bounties for military service, speculation, and grants to encourage immigration all made it impossible to form a coherent land policy. Public indebtedness in Texas increased by the year; border wars flared up; and Indians were regularly provoked into battle. The empresario system was revived in an effort to fill out the state for protection and income, thus confirming earlier patterns of land concentration. Colonies arrived in Texas from England, Ireland, France, and Germany as well as the United States. Eastern abolitionists complained of what they called a southern plot to extend the plantation system into Texas. After ten years of public controversies and political power ploys, the United States offered statehood to Texas in 1845. In accepting the offer, the republic yielded up its public lands—and also its heavy debt—to the federal government.

Mexico had suspected the motives and activities of the United States from the time of the first rebellions in Texas, especially after Texan statehood, when the United States presumptuously extended the land area of Texas from the Nueces River to the Rio Grande. Mexico claimed that the disputed area never had been part of Coahuila-Texas but rather was a section of Tamaulipas, and therefore was patrolled by its troops. When the Mexicans attempted to drive a small Anglo military force from the disputed zone in 1846, Congress declared war. Within sixteen months Mexico was defeated and was forced to give up not only the disputed territory but also New Mexico and California. At Guadalupe Hidalgo in 1848, the Mexican government ceded all its lands north of the Rio Grande and Gila Rivers west along the line that separates upper and lower California. The United States paid $15,000,000 for the additional territory and assumed Anglo claims against Mexico, which totaled a little over $3,000,000. By the middle of the century, the United States land area had been extended to the Pacific. It had been a monumental imperialist adventure by any standards.

Early California Land Use

In California the earliest occupation and use of the land by Indian tribes was in balance with the region's variegated resources and climate. The widespread oak trees produced millions of acorns for the aboriginals, who pulverized them, leached out the bitterness, and prepared dozens of dishes from the meal, which they served with fish or wild game. The Indians did not cultivate crops, since there was really little need for more food than the land provided.

It was not California's resources that pushed the Spanish north from Mexico, but rather word that the Russians had penetrated into the North Pacific. A Dane, Vitus Bering, discovered and explored the Bering Strait for the Russians and reported the existence of a plethora of fur resources in the Pacific Northwest. Spain wanted to protect its hegemony over Pacific waters.

Thus soldiers and friars established presidios and missions along the California coast for dual political and religious purposes. Spanish culture and social organization went with them and were imposed on the often unwilling natives. In 1776, when Anglo-Americans were preparing the foundations of a new nation, the Mission San Francisco de Asis was established. A few years earlier in 1769, a mission was built in Monterey (named the capital of California in 1777). Spanish villages, or pueblos, had their beginnings in San Jose and Los Angeles. From these centers the number of missions, pueblos, and presidios grew steadily along the coast. In the beginning all were dependent on Mexico for grains, beans, meats, sugar, wine, and brandy.

The focus of the mission activity was the conversion of the Indians, but whether they were converts or not, the Indians were rounded up and put in the missions to tend flocks, vineyards, olive groves, orchards, and wheat fields. They were also taught to weave blankets and clothing; to embroider; to tan hides, render tallow, boil soap; to make shoes, saddles and pottery; and to operate flour mills. The presidios kept the native populations in check, though not always successfully, and watched for Russian, English, or American encroachments. The pueblos, refuges for many kinds of social outcasts, were scarcely able to acquire enough food to feed their itinerant populations. By 1800, only about 1,200 Spaniards inhabited California.

This was the period when Spanish authority did not permit trade with Anglos, but the prohibition did not discourage Boston traders from smuggling goods into California and trading for sea otters. The Yankees offered cotton dry goods, ironware, gunpowder, fishhooks, pepper, nutmeg, linen, Chinese silk, even crystal ware. Traders met padres at designated points of rendezvous—San Quentin, San Juan Capistrano, San Luis Obispo, Santa Cruz, and other hidden inlets along the California coast.

The famous California *ranchos* had their beginnings during the Spanish period. Although rancheros had no ready markets for their livestock before they began to send tallow to Lima in 1813, they could each hold from five to thirty leagues of land—up to 133,000 acres—as royal tenants. They received their allotment merely by applying to the district official, the *alcalde*, who piled a mound of stones to mark the property line and measured to figure the extent of the property by riding the appropriate distance on horseback. Within a few years, the rancheros usually owned from 2,000 to 10,000 head of cattle, 1,500 to 2,000 horses and mules, and 10,000 to

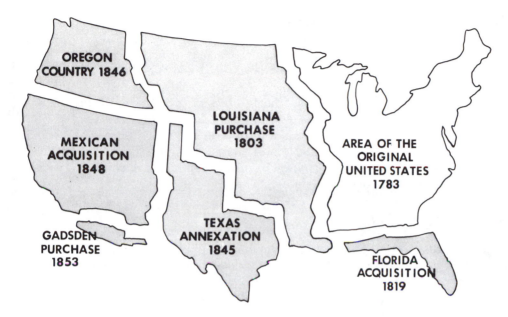

Figure 7–3. Land acquisition by the United States, through 1853.

20,000 sheep. Before tallow-trading, the cattle and sheep were raised to feed and clothe those who lived on the rancho and perhaps a nearby mission or presidio. After the Mexican Revolution, the rancheros secured title to the land and quickly enriched themselves on the hide and tallow trade with English and Anglo-American traders. Only about 20 land grants were given during the Spanish period, compared to 600-800 during the Mexican period.

The ranchero cultivated only enough grain to supply the needs of his household, utilizing the most primitive farming tools and methods. His interests centered solely on his cattle, which roamed wild on the still-verdant grasslands of the central plains and hills around them. At the grand rodeo each spring when calves were branded, the cattle which had been mixed on the plains were separated according to owner's brand. Then the number of cattle to be slaughtered was determined and skillful vaqueros rode past the cattle, deftly slitting a nerve in the nape of the neck. This act inflicted a quick death. Then hides were stripped; fat was cut off for tallow, melted and run into hide *bota* bags, and meat was cut up into strips and dried. Cattle fats were as important for domestic use as the beef. Manteca, fat near the skin, was used for cooking, while interior fat added flavor to Spanish dishes. Tallow was melted from kidney fat and other inedible interior fat.

Twelve years after the Mexican Revolution, the missions were secularized and the Indians were set free. The Indians were to receive a portion of the mission lands, but most often they ended up at a pueblo or a ranch in circumstances not much improved from life on the mission. They often assisted with the roundup by performing the dull and backbreaking labor of hide preparation—cleaning every particle of fat and meat from each hide, and stretching it to dry. Wishing to add to California's population,

Mexican officials encouraged the establishment of new ranchos, some on the lands of the former missions, by Mexicans or foreigners who were naturalized and converted to Catholicism. The Mexican period of California (1822-1846) was primarily the era of the great ranchos, which were then standardized at grants of eleven leagues (almost 50,000 acres). There was no limitation, however, on the amount of land a ranchero could purchase if he so desired, and in the days of high prices for his tallow and hides he often doubled his acreage. About 600-800 grants were doled out during the Mexican Period (26,000 acres —one quarter of California's land area), and a million head of stock trampled the grassy plains from San Francisco to San Diego. The perennial grasses, strong and perdurant from time immemorial, could not withstand the rapidly-multiplying herds indefinitely.

The California Trail

By the middle thirties, a substantial number of Anglos had migrated to California, many marrying into Mexican familes. The California Trail was carved overland from Soda Springs, in what was later to become Idaho, where one trail led to Oregon, the second to California. After descending from the mountains, the caravans had to cross almost 400 miles of blazing hot, barren desert northwest of the Great Salt Lake to the Humboldt River, which they then followed all the way to the Humboldt Sink west of Pyramid Lake. A westward route took the pilgrims to the Truckee River and on across the Sierras through Donner Pass north of Lake Tahoe, or they could follow a second trail into silver and gold country south of Lake Tahoe through Carson Pass and into the Mother Lode Country of California. This last was the trail of the Forty-Niners, and hundreds of them met their death along this route. Even before migrants reached Fort Laramie, the cholera-infested water holes spread dozens of diseases and struck down animals by the thousands as well as men and women. The alkali deserts further on claimed hundreds more. The gold fever of tens of thousands, however, drove wave after wave of them over Carson Pass into El Dorado.

The demand for meat during the gold rush changed the shape of the California ranchos, particularly in southern regions where the larger ones flourished. Before this period, cattle were primarily valued for their hides and tallow so that much meat was left to rot on the carcasses of dead cattle. The price of cattle increased twenty-fold, from two dollars to thirty or forty dollars for a full-grown steer. Thrifty rancheros were transformed into prodigal cattle barons overnight, and their ranchos into lavish estates.

Anglo newcomers picked up the idea quickly. Within a few years they drove thousands of head of beef cattle over the plains into the ranges near the mines, and their high quality beef undersold the tougher longhorn variety of the southern ranchos. Before long, overproduction led to low beef prices. Huge cattle herds also meant that the great bands of elk, wild horses, antelope, and deer were pushed out of the California plains forever. Lost also were the perennial grasses, especially during the drought of 1855-56 when the starving herds ripped out the last roots as 100,000 cattle starved in the southern coastal counties. A few years later, torrential rains flooded tens of thousands more head of livestock. In the early sixties, cattle populations increased again and rancheros overstocked to make up for declines in price, but droughts and overgrazing in two successive years wiped out many of the former cattle barons. Their estates were picked up by emerging new entrepreneurs of the mining era.

The disposition of ranchos during the Spanish and Mexican periods greatly influenced later land concentrations after California became a state in 1850. The Treaty of Guadalupe Hidalgo provided that Mexican property rights should be "inviolably respected." During the next generation, hundreds of lawsuits and countersuits over land claims were filed. Because of vagueness of language, technical loopholes, the lack of documentary proof, or merely the lack of financial resources to pursue their cases to the Supreme Court, many of the original Mexican claimants lost their land to American land speculators. The speculators managed to find justification to file for large tracts of land. Anglo lawyers also amassed valuable holdings as they took their fees in land from case after case. The American Claims Commission upheld 588 of almost 800 Mexican claims (for nearly 9,000,000 acres). The rest went largely to Anglo claimants, but in either case the vast tracts of land remained in the hands of very few owners. After the tens of thousands of individual gold-seekers ran out of money and sought small pieces of land to homestead, they found virtually all of it already taken. Although the state received over 8,000,000 acres from the federal domain which could have been sold to the emigrants in small plots for farming, it preferred, like the earliest Congress, to sell it off in large inexpensive tracts. Finally, the railroad companies received their share, more than 11,000,000 acres, to finance their operations, and the price of land became what the traffic would bear. Widespread fraud and local corruption by land engrossers compounded the land problem during the second half of the century, so that California was destined from its very beginnings to remain a state of large land concentrations rather than of small farm sites growing food for regional markets. In California, migrants were necessarily forced into the cities.

Mormon Settlement in the Great Basin

During the same period, in the Great Basin area near the Great Salt Lake where the Mormons settled, the disposal of land was not affected by engrossment, land speculation, market considerations, claim conflicts, foreclosures, or other land disputes which were common in California or in other parts of the country. Neither was there a relationship to a federal authority, and thus no special grants for schools, railroads, etc. The reasons for this unique situation lay in the special history and community organization of the Mormon religion.

Founded in 1830 in upper New York State, with a claim to a direct divine revelation by its founder, Joseph Smith, Mormonism's first generation was stormy and controversial. Smith's first adherents moved from New York to Ohio and later to Missouri. Because of local opposition in early settlements, Smith founded his own town, Nauvoo, Illinois, where he further tried to protect his church and the Mormons' property by entering national politics; he announced his candidacy for U.S. President in 1844, but he was murdered later that year. The church suffered further

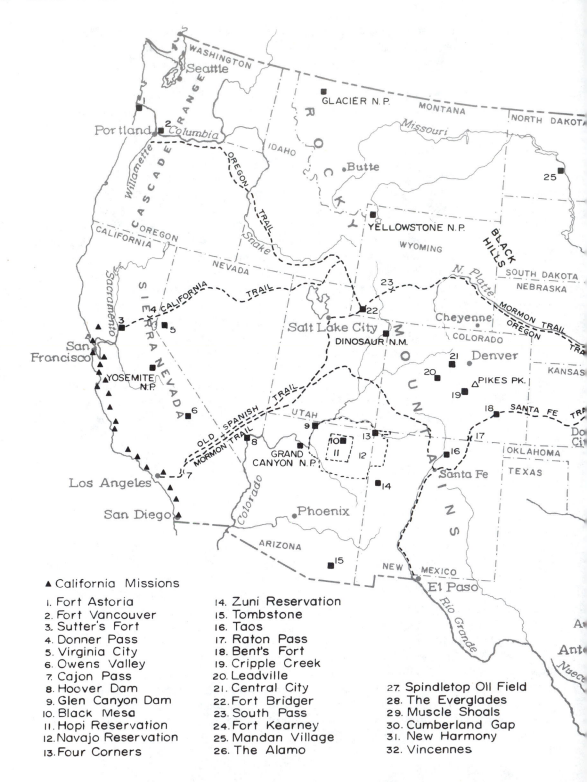

▲ California Missions

1. Fort Astoria
2. Fort Vancouver
3. Sutter's Fort
4. Donner Pass
5. Virginia City
6. Owens Valley
7. Cajon Pass
8. Hoover Dam
9. Glen Canyon Dam
10. Black Mesa
11. Hopi Reservation
12. Navajo Reservation
13. Four Corners

14. Zuni Reservation
15. Tombstone
16. Taos
17. Raton Pass
18. Bent's Fort
19. Cripple Creek
20. Leadville
21. Central City
22. Fort Bridger
23. South Pass
24. Fort Kearney
25. Mandan Village
26. The Alamo

27. Spindletop Oil Field
28. The Everglades
29. Muscle Shoals
30. Cumberland Gap
31. New Harmony
32. Vincennes

33. Nauvoo
34. Keweenaw Pen.
35. Sault Ste. Marie
36. Niagara Falls
37. Erie Canal
38. Drake Oil Well

39. Allegheny Portage RR and Mainline Canal
40. Hopewell Iron Furnace
41. Marietta
42. Williamsburg
43. Nantucket Island

persecution, finally being forced out of Nauvoo. Brigham Young then accepted the leadership of the group, led the Mormons into Iowa, and started west on the Oregon Trail. The Mormons travelled along the northern side of the Platte River rather than the Oregon Trail route on the south side, to Fort Bridger, from whence they headed southwest to the valley of the Great Salt Lake. The Pioneer Band was made up of 143 men, three women, two children, ninety-three horses, fifty-two mules, sixty-six oxen, nineteen cows, seventeen dogs, a few chickens, and seventy-two wagons loaded with farm equipment, seed grain, and a year's provisions. The group stopped at the Utah site in 1847, with Young's historic "This is the Place." It was an austere landscape, remote enough to discourage potential persecutors. Before winter, 1,500 more Mormons joined the community, which bought about 200 square miles of land from a trapper-squatter, Miles M. Goodyear, who claimed to have received a Mexican land grant there.

Water was scarce and the land was semi-arid and so isolated that Young realized that the community would have to become self-sufficient. Hundreds of new emigrants brought in stock, seeds, tools, spinning wheels and the countless instruments of self-sufficiency that were being discarded in the East at the time. Within a year, 5,000 acres were under cultivation. The land was surveyed and distributed according to need, labor, and status as in the early New England communities, and canals were dug into each family's five, ten, twenty, or forty-acre tract to provide irrigation. The larger units were given to those who raised livestock. The Mormons adhered to the principle that improvements to the land brought the right to ownership.

Most of their irrigation projects were built out of the streams flowing from the west side of the Wasatch Mountains into the valley. Other canals utilized water from the Jordan River, the American Fork River, and the Spanish Fork River, all of which flow in or out of Utah Lake. Water rights were not controlled by land ownership on a watercourse (riparian right), but according to social need or the most efficient benefit to the community. In the words of Brigham Young: "There shall be no private ownership of the streams that come out of the canyons, nor the timber that grows on the hills. These belong to the people: all the people."

Public ownership was applied to all the basic natural resources—water, forests, minerals, and, to a certain extent, land. Even in the exchange of surplus Mormon goods with those of their neighbors, social need was placed over market value. Without such arrangements, it is doubtful that the community could have survived in the harsh Utah environment. With them the group flourished. By 1860, the Mormons could boast of 40,273 people, 3,635 farms, and 77,219 acres of improved land in cultivation in Utah (named for the Ute Indians of the region). It was a living example of the strength of social good placed over individual profits. The idea deserves recognition, especially in a contemporary society torn apart by two centuries of social and economic competition.

References for Further Reading

The Journals of Lewis and Clark, describing the intriguing experiences of the early expedition, are available in several old hardback and new paper editions. Everett

Dick's classic social history of the Northern Plains and Rocky Mountains, *Vanguards of the Frontier* (1971), includes an interesting account of the mountain men, the big fur companies, and many other institutions of the early frontier of the West. *History of the Pacific Coast of North America* by J.W. Caughey (1938) provides a detailed account of early Oregon and California settlement. *The Commerce of the Prairies* (1967), written by Josiah Gregg in the 1830s, originally bore the subtitle "Journal of a Santa Fe Trader During Eight Expeditions Across the Great Western Prairies, and a Residence of Nearly Nine Years in Northern Mexico" and it is as fascinating as it sounds. A more specialized treatment of the historical geography of the Southwest is D.W. Meinig's *Southwest: Three Peoples in Geographical Change*, 1600-1970 (1974). A good development of much of the material in this chapter can be found in *Western America* by LeRoy R. Hafen and Carl C. Rister (1962), or John A. Hawgood's *America's Western Frontiers* (1967). The crucial importance of Spanish, Mexican and U.S. early water policies can be found in *Water in the Hispanic Southwest: 1550-1850* by Michael C. Meyer (1984).

Chapter 8

THE MINERAL
TREASURY OF THE WEST

That a few critical natural resources lie within the boundaries of a very few countries is the cruel prescription of fate. The United States and the U.S.S.R., for example, probably hold about three-quarters of the world coal resources. The Middle Eastern countries, the U.S.S.R., and China have about half the probable petroleum reserves of the world; America has also been blessed with large reserves of oil—perhaps 15%. On the other hand, other important natural resources—iron, aluminum, glass silica, limestone—are distributed widely in all parts of the world. Gold, silver, and copper are found where volcanic activity has forced them to the surface through crevices or geologic movement.

Why one nation or region should be so lucky regarding coal and oil and another so unfortunate is a question only very ancient earth history will answer. For millions of years the sun has radiated tremendous energy upon the earth. A small portion of it is captured by plants. Most of the energy is lost when the plant is either eaten by insects and animals or decomposed by microorganisms. If oxygen is not present, this is called a reducing environment. Complete degradation of plant remains cannot take place in a reducing environment. Often swamps lack oxygen, and plant remains accumulate there. Over thousands of years, the accumulation becomes quite thick. Eventually it gets buried beneath clay and sand. Heat and pressure form the organic matter into coal. There is no clear dividing line between the organic matter, which is peat, and the rock, coal. Under greater pressure and heat, the peat becomes lignite, and lignite becomes bituminous coal. A more severe metamorphism transforms the plant material into anthracite, the hardest coal.

Oil also needed long-term chemical and biological processes applied to decomposing microscopic marine organisms, algae and pollen. During the thousands of centuries that the remains of microscopic marine organisms accumulated with clay particles on shallow oceanic seas and continental shelves, pressure was built up to transform the aggregate into hydrocarbons. As the pressure increased, the hydrocarbons were forced toward the earth's surface and trapped beneath an impermeable stratum of limestone, waiting for a prospector's drill. Much coal and oil formation occurred over 200,000,000 years ago when Eurasia and North America were locked together before the continents began their northerly movement to their present positions.

Pennsylvania Coal

Pennsylvania, whose western half was thought of as the frontier after the Revolution, offers a good example of the country's resource needs and opportunities during the

APPALACHIAN BITUMINOUS FIELD

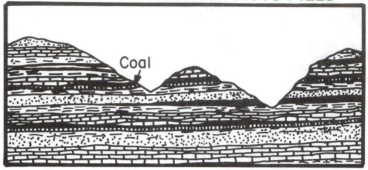

PENNSYLVANIA ANTHRACITE FIELD

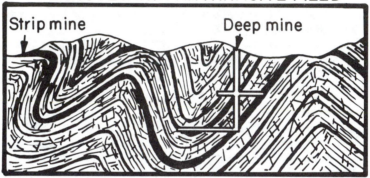

Figure 8–1. American coal formation. Bituminous coal was formed by simple layering of vegetative sediments, clay, and sand. The anthracite coal was formed when Appalachian mountain ranges were layered with accumulations of limestone, sandstone, and vegetation sediment. Then folding, thrusting, and metamorphism over a period of hundreds of millions of years brought about the present anthracite deposits.

first half of the 1800s. The depletion of forests near Pennsylvania's industrial areas caused enough concern to send the community leaders of these towns looking for other sources of fuel. Coal had been mined in Virginia for iron smelting since the mid-1700s, but few iron masters bothered to substitute coke for charcoal until they had an economical way to transport it. By 1800, local bituminous coal was being burned by Pittsburgh blacksmiths, small industries, and a growing number of homes outfitted with pot-bellied stoves. Nearby Kentucky coal operators floated their cargo down the Kentucky River to Frankfort's blacksmiths.

Northeastern Pennsylvania enjoyed large anthracite deposits, which, with 10 to 20% more carbon and fewer impurities, burned cleaner and hotter than bituminous coal, which was more difficult to ignite. Anthracite production picked up in 1812, when the war stopped the shipment of Virginia's bituminous coal to Philadelphia, but it did not continue after the war because of transportation difficulties. By the 1820s, canals from anthracite country were completed to carry coal to eastern cities, where its smokeless flame was preferred in the firing of increasingly-common heating stoves.

As the diminished supply of timber in the East drove prices up, both kinds of coal replaced wood on steamboats and locomotives; the latter began to string coal cars behind the engine.

Rail cars also carried coal from the mines to canals, running by gravity downhill to awaiting barges. Empty cars were hauled back to the mine by mules or horses. By 1829 locomotives began to carry coal directly to city markets, rendering some canals obsolete before they were finished. Coal created its own kind of boom towns in anthracite areas: Scranton, Carbondale, Hazleton, Wilkes-Barre. It was in this area that Abijah Smith, in 1818, first used black blasting powder (approximately three-quarters potassium nitrate, one quarter mixed sulfur and charcoal) to break down coal in the mines. His technique was later copied in western gold and silver mining until dynamite was developed.

Anthracite also boosted a depressed iron industry in the country. After the American Revolution, the cheap English iron which flooded the American market drove most of the larger iron factories out of business. Higher tariffs on iron and new iron technologies, which included the use of anthracite and coke (made from bituminous coal) enabled the American iron industry to recover.

Anthracite served as an excellent iron fuel because it was hard enough to withstand the weight of the ore without crumbling and having its fire smothered, as sometimes happened with charcoal or bituminous coal. Anthracite was used in the 1820s as a fuel in iron furnaces, but its superior qualities were not appreciated until 1836 when Frederick Geissenhainer, a German Lutheran clergyman living in New York, discovered that anthracite worked well with iron only when hot air was blown into the mixture. By 1846, forty-two anthracite furnaces in Pennsylvania and New York could produce 122,000 tons of iron a year, and because they supported any ore load placed over them, each could turn out over twice the tonnage of the best of the earlier charcoal furnaces. Before the Civil War, steam engines replaced waterwheels in providing stronger air blasts.

Development of the Iron Industry

Anthracite deposits are located almost exclusively in a concentrated area of one state, northeastern Pennsylvania, while new iron discoveries were being made throughout the old West, in upstate New York where blast furnaces were constructed in Buffalo, and as far as Indiana. When the high grade Lake Superior iron ores began to be surface-mined, transportation distances between eastern Pennsylvania and northern Michigan were too great at the time for a feasible cooperative arrangement between the two centers. A new solution had to be found.

Despite a century of coke-making in England and the availability of bituminous coal under half of Pennsylvania and throughout much of the old West, coke-making in America was not started until the 1850s. When western Pennsylvania was connected to the East by railroad and to the Great Lakes by steamboat, coke began to overtake anthracite as the leader of iron-making fuel. Connellsville, south of Pittsburgh, made large quantities of quality coke and was largely responsible for the industrial center's auspicious beginning. Before Connellsville coke, bituminous coal had been converted to coke by heating it slowly out in the open in large piles covered with turf. At Connellsville, seven-foot firebrick bee hive ovens were designed; doors at the top and side let in air and coal.

The iron industry was sensitive to the proximity of its fuel. In colonial times, where ore and timber were found together, furnaces were set up, usually close to a village or settlement. The furnaces were dispersed and numerous around the country. As the benefits of anthracite were realized, the iron industry became more centralized geographically to supply the growing markets of the eastern cities, although small charcoal furnaces continued near backcountry communities. The anthracite iron district came to be located in eastern Pennsylvania between Philadelphia and New York, close to anthracite, iron ore, and urban markets. After the Civil War, Pittsburgh, close to Connellsville coke, abundant limestone, and even good sources of iron ore, rose in prominence. Later, Lake Superior ore was taken to the Pittsburgh blast furnaces, with the ore going to the fuel. A blast furnace that needed 2,000 to 5,000 acres of timber to keep running in colonial times could be as productive with a half-acre, six-foot seam of coal.

The iron industry in America grew with the agricultural markets, since iron bars were increasingly necessary for the forging of tools and implements for farmers, mill operators, and teamsters. In the 1820s, small factories began to turn out farm implements, then more complicated machinery—plows, hay rakes, cultivators, reapers. Iron heating stoves and ranges spread; in 1850, 300,000 stoves were made. At the same time Pennsylvania was turning out over half the pig and rolled iron in the country.

The first major blast furnace innovation in America came in 1834, when a New Jersey iron works converted its cold blast furnace to the English hot blast method, which lessened the amount of fuel necessary to smelt the iron by over 40% and doubled the quantity of iron produced. The ironmaster piped a blast of air (later, steam engines were used) over the hot waste gases of the furnace itself, thereby heating the blast. The process was imitated by iron works in Pittsburgh, whose location at the head of the Ohio River helped the industry to obtain commissions to build boilers for steamships, stationary steam engines, and locomotives.

The Beginning of the Oil Industry

Another early Pennsylvania mineral resource, petroleum, had been used by Indians for medicinal purposes for centuries. Oil seeped to the surface, where it was collected and purified by boiling. Indians claimed it helped muscle strains, swellings, toothaches, rheumatism, and countless other maladies. The earliest settlers of northwestern Pennsylvania traded with the Seneca Indians for the oil, named it "Seneca Oil," and used it for more ailments than the Indians ever thought possible; animals were also the beneficiaries of the Seneca Oil treatment. Later it was called "Petroleum" (or "Rock Oil," as the word is derived from Latin), and by the early 1800s, petroleum had become a well-known item on the shelves of eastern apothecaries.

The steadily increasing demand for whale oil, beeswax, and tallow candles as illuminants through the first half of the century caused an even more rapid increase in the price of these commodities. Many artificial substitutes, such as alcohol and turpentine mixtures called camphene, were mixed up at home but most were either unsafe or ineffective. A Canadian, Abraham Gesner, derived an illuminating oil from coal in 1846, calling the derivative "keroselain" (from Greek for "wax" or "oil"). The later word, kerosene, was applied to all mineral illuminating oils. After Gesner's success, a number of Americans experimented with illuminating and lubricating oils, mainly from soft cannel coals (a bright-burning coal rich in volatile constituents) but also from petroleum. Samuel Kier decided to bottle the petroleum which continually and ungraciously appeared out of his father's salt water wells, and he distilled it in Pittsburgh for the growing illumination market in the early 1850s. By the end of that decade, its inexpensive and superior flame for a specially developed lamp had been proved. Supplies of the oil diminished; the price rose, and these two developments encouraged the inauguration of the first petroleum company in the small northwestern Pennsylvania community of Titusville.

Brewer, Watson and Company simply bottled oil from an old oil spring, first separating it from its inevitable companion, water. Three to six gallons a day were collected for shipment. In 1854 the firm formed a joint stock company, the Pennsylvania Rock Oil Company of New York, and expanded its land holdings to 1,200 acres, which included dozens of oil springs. However, the stock, having been issued during bad economic times and by promoters who did not inspire confidence, failed to bring in much capital for the fledgling operation.

Behind the scenes, a new firm, the Seneca Oil Company of Connecticut, was organized. It hired Edwin L. Drake, dubbed "Colonel Drake" to impress the locals, as general agent to set up a salt water drilling process in order to procure oil at Titusville. He bought a stationary steam engine similar to those on Ohio River steamers and built a thirty-foot wood derrick, twelve feet square at the bottom tapering to three feet square at the top, in which drilling tools could be raised and lowered. After many delays, monetary difficulties, water problems and cave-ins, Drake and his driller, "Uncle Billy" Smith, who developed an innovative drilling method, succeeded in connecting up his steam engine to the drill and digging three feet a day. After several months of drilling, everyone in the firm was out of money, and James Townsend, an early director and president, recommended that the project be dropped. However, a few weeks later, on August 27, 1859, Drake's well struck oil.

Almost overnight thousands flocked to Titusville and started to buy up land along Oil Creek near Titusville. A proliferation of derrick drills, some driven by steam power and others manually by men in stirrups on spring poles, changed the rural landscape for miles around the original well. Capitalists rushed to Titusville to invest in wells, land, and machine and barrel factories. This activity drew laborers, adventurers, and their families. A boom town atmosphere was created where the oil industry was born, and it prospered temporarily, even without the advantages of a gigantic automobile industry.

Midwestern Lead and Lake Superior Copper

Lead, however, was a metal resource which enjoyed immediate markets. Hunting and fighting constituted the regular fare of American pioneers, and lead bullets were

Figure 8–2. Beginnings of the oil industry in Pennsylvania. Edwin L. Drake (right) stands in front of the first oil well with Peter Wilson, a Titusville, Pennsylvania druggist who encouraged Drake in his venture. The Seneca Oil Company of Connecticut was organized to lease the oil farm on which the Drake well was built. The small buildings depicted on the certificates represent primitive refineries where oil was boiled and kerosene drawn off. The remaining gasoline and oil were dumped into streams and rivers. The sketch of Pithole, Pennsylvania for the *London Illustrated News* came in 1865 when daily oil production at the site reached 6,000 barrels a day, attracting 15,000 people to the area. This fairly romantic conception of Pithole should be compared to the usual landscape of early oildom here exemplified by the wells on Foster farm near Pioneer Run and Oil Creek. Early drillers rarely ventured far from Oil Creek with their portable steam engines which powered the drilling rigs. Oil Creek also provided the earliest form of oil transportation to its mouth at the Allegheny River, Oil City, where steamboats met the flatboats and transported the oil to Pittsburgh and points west. Photos Courtesy Drake Well Museum.

needed for both activities. Upper and lower Mississippi regions had yielded abundant supplies of lead as early as 1720, when the Frenchman Renault opened mines in Potosi and St. Francis, Missouri, southwest of St. Louis, with 200 French workmen and 500 slaves from Santo Domingo. At the end of the century, Moses Austin, the Texas colonizer, introduced the first shaft for lead mining and reverberatory furnace for smelting (where the flame from the side of the ore "reverberates" over it), as well as a tower for making shot. Molten lead was dropped through sieves in a copper pan from the tower. It would harden sufficiently by the time the lead pellets hit a cistern of water below. After the shot had cooled, it was loaded into a barrel fixed to a shaft and hand cranked until the pellets had polished and perfected themselves into spherical ammunition.

A hundred-mile lead mining area in Missouri began to fill up after the Louisiana Purchase in 1803. By 1819, several mining communities had been laid out and settled, with their county seat, Potosi, boasting of a courthouse built in Greek Revival style. The much older French settlement of St. Genevieve, on the Mississippi forty miles from the mines where lead was smelted and shot was made, was transformed from a quiet village into a roaring western town.

The upper Mississippi lead district, where Iowa, Illinois and Wisconsin now come together, did not increase its population dramatically until after the Black Hawk Indian war in 1832; a year later, settlement of the region was officially permitted. Another Frenchman, Nicholas Perrot, had discovered lead deposits in the region as far back as 1690, but it was Julien Dubuque who heavily exploited the area from 1788 until his death in 1810. He received permission from the Sac and Fox tribes to mine lead where Dubuque now stands, and hired Indians to do the labor, selling several hundred thousand pounds of lead ore to St. Louis smelters every year.

Determined to keep their lead resource to themselves after Dubuque died in 1810, the Indians forbade white entry onto their lands. They mined and smelted the lead themselves. After 1826, when the price of lead reached a new high, the white tide could hardly be contained. Pioneers mined on the eastern side of the upper Mississippi lead district until they could take over the Dubuque mines four years later.

Lead ore was mined in primitive fashion during these years: by pickaxe and shovel in a pit, sometimes with black blasting powder rammed into a hand-drilled hole. When the pit got deeper than ten to fifteen feet, a windlass and bucket set-up was constructed over the hole to take out dirt and ore. Rough-mined galena, the lead sulfide mineral, was then broken up and cleaned of quartzite matter by hand. The ore was smelted in a log furnace which looked much like a colonial iron furnace—a limestone hearth tapering to an open top with an arched opening in front to let in air, usually built facing the wind on the slope of a hill. Oak logs lined the bottom and sides of the furnace and covered the 5,000-pound charge of ore; the wood was fired, and at the right moment after at least twelve hours of roasting, molten lead was drawn into an iron pot from the rear of the furnace. Workmen then ladled the lead into iron molds which yielded fifty-pound lead bars. Lead smelting demanded much expertise and experience to prevent the high degree of waste which commonly accompanied the procedure.

Indians just north of the upper Mississippi lead districts had also been known to wear and use copper articles, as reported by Jesuit missionaries and explorers in the early 1600s. The last continental glacier had pushed some of the original rich copper deposits from the south shore of Lake Superior southeast into Wisconsin, Michigan, and even Ohio. The trail of Indian artifacts spreads as wide as that glacier, but the most copious reservoir of prehistoric copper goods came from their source in the Keweenaw Peninsula, which reaches claw-like far into Lake Superior from its south-central shore. The copper of that region exhibited such purity that the Native Americans could hammer it cold into whatever shapes they desired, and the copper would harden in the process.

The Keweenaw Peninsula

A number of eighteenth century adventurers, mostly English, sought to uncover that rich primordial mine and exploit it commercially, but they could scarcely penetrate the dense wilderness of the upper peninsula. Finally, in 1840, Douglass Houghton, first geologist of the frontier state of Michigan, took an expedition into the Keweenaw

Peninsula and wrote a glowing report on the commercial possibilities of copper mining there. The report was enough to lure prospectors over difficult terrain from the south or around the Ste. Marie Falls into Lake Superior (the canal there had been destroyed during the War of 1812), into the fascinating and beautiful region.

By 1850, more than 25 copper-development companies were looking for copper on the Keweenaw Peninsula. Only a few were very successful. Yet in the days before copper electrical wire, not much copper was needed to satisfy national demands. The reason for the prospectors' difficulties in finding rich veins lay in the fact that the copper appeared in so many different types of rock formations, and companies could not establish a regular procedure to find the elusive metal. "Mass" deposits of pure copper in cross veins were found irregularly in old cracks and fissures which had been sealed into the rock around them. At Keweenaw, the ore often was laid over 15,000 to 30,000 feet in volcanic rocks. Over a period of millions of years, as the earth moved and fissured, fluids carrying dissolved copper were forced upward into the crevices of volcanic and sedimentary rocks. This was the geologic process known as hydrothermal alteration.

"Bubble" cavities from magma—chambers of molten rock under surface rock—discovered later—contained much more copper, but most of it was so lean that special large stamp mills had to be constructed to crush the rock and separate out the crystals of copper for smelting. Copper crystals are referred to as porphyry copper, i.e., large crystals embedded in fine grained rock.

As magma cooled, the same process of hydrothermal alteration took place as through crevices, but the copper was spread out and more evenly distributed throughout the ore, so that large volumes of rock had to be crushed and milled. Gold, silver, and molybdenum are found with copper in the lodes. Bubble lodes were mined just after 1851, when thousands of miners, millers, and their families moved into the Keweenaw Peninsula and cleared the wilderness to build towns and villages. In 1857, the canal was rebuilt around the Ste. Marie Falls just as demand for Lake Superior copper was increasing. Railroads came in a few years later.

The third type of copper vein, the "conglomerate" lode, was discovered by E. J. Hulbert in 1861, also in the Keweenaw Peninsula. The rich conglomerate copper was originally a sedimentary deposit laid down under shallow water between lava flows.

After the Civil War, Hulbert sank his very profitable Calumet shaft; soon afterward, his Hecla shaft matched the performance and copper quality of the original Calumet. Although the ore body was superb, stamp mills and concentrating plants had to separate out the copper from other mineral rock by stamping and gravity before smelting. Other companies moved into the area at the time, but none matched the success of the Calumet and Hecla mines.

The copper barons and their huge firms in Butte, Montana, and in Arizona came later. But it was the copper mines of the Keweenaw Peninsula that prepared the country for the electrical revolution.

California Gold

The story of the California gold rush represents the next piece in the mineral picture of the West. The first wave of prospectors in the spring of 1849 brought 50,000 Americans

Figure 8–3. Early gold mining in California. This 1849 sketch shows the various steps in panning and rocking for gold in California creeks. Details of the illustration show the different kinds of back-breaking labor used by the miners to dig the alluvial soil and carry it to water—or to carry the water to the gold-bearing sands—to wash away lighter grains from the gold. The variety of primitive mining methods can be appreciated from the picture: riffle boxes, rockers, sluices, pans, picks, and shovels. Courtesy the Bancroft Library.

to California, which became the melting pot of mining lore to be taken back to mines elsewhere in the country. At a time when communication in the country was still in its primitive states, the gold rush served the mining industry as a thousand annual conferences rolled into a few years. The rush brought people to a land also rich in agricultural and lumbering possibilities. When gold fever subsided, California's greatly augmented population turned to these other resources for exploitation at a much faster rate than otherwise would have been possible.

The now legendary tale began in 1839, when a fast-talking Swiss adventurer named Johann A. Sutter convinced Mexican Governor Juan Alvarado to let him become a Mexican citizen and develop a 50,000-acre tract of land in the Sacramento Valley, where he later built Fort Sutter and New Helvetia. At the time, only a few hundred people who were not of Spanish or Indian descent lived in California, and the total population of the territory was less than 10,000.

Sutter collected a group of Mexican outcastes, Indians, and Hawaiians and started a rancho, which included a large amount of stock raising, some crude agriculture, a grist mill, and a distillery. He employed James W. Marshall as general handyman with the special assignment of erecting a sawmill. While testing the mill's undershot wheel at the end of January 1848, Marshall noticed a few gleaming crystals. He picked them up and spent several days, the last with Sutter, checking out their characteristics.

Figure 8–4. Results of mining the riverbanks for gold. This picture, which dates from about 1860, shows what happened when the California miners extended their digging and washing operations away from the banks of streams and back into the neighboring hills. Miners also built dams to dry up stream beds and make them more accessible and easier to exploit. The water was carried parallel to the endless-chain bailers to keep particular areas dry. This picture suggests the ingenuity of the miners in extracting ores. It also suggests what happened to the land where gold had been found. Courtesy the Bancroft Library.

In less than a week the two were convinced that Marshall had found gold on the property.

Although Sutter tried, he could not contain the news. Californians dropped whatever they were doing all over the territory and found samples of their own on his land. Even President Polk found out about the gold from the War Department and, anxious to prove that his settlement of the Mexican War had been astute, was delighted to spread the news in a message to newsmen in the East later that year. Before the snow melted that winter, thousands of Americans above and below the border began to storm the ports of California. By the summer of 1849, Sutter's bucolic paradise had been shattered by a horde of prospectors. About 100,000 people lived in California at the end of the year, having arrived from the Continent, Latin America, and China as well as the rest of the country.

Most of the prospectors first stayed in the valleys near rivers and streams close to where Marshall's original discovery was made. The primary deposits were hidden as specks in the granite core of the Sierras or caught in more concentrated form in fissures and faults of the mountain chain. For millions of years the Mother Lode had been subjected to rains and floods, winds and storms, snow and frosts, and the granite chunks had been loosened and gold increasingly liberated as it was sent coursing down ancient rivers and streams to the valleys below. Since gold is an inert metal, its chemical constitution was not changed for aeons. The gold was caught behind rocks or sand bars, on the insides of meandering stream loops, inside holes or potholes below waterfalls; then covered by sediment. During the millions of years, unobstructed gold continued its journey until streams dried up or changed their courses. The gold dust far from the mountains necessarily was fine-grained, since it needed so little energy to push it there; some of it undoubtedly was washed all the way to the ocean. But close to the mountains, prospectors expected to find much larger gold chunks. And sometimes they did find larger chunks.

The gold camps were situated just at the bottom of the mountains where streams began to lose their force. There the gold dust tended to sink toward the bedrock and accumulate, forming the "pay streak" which awaited the fortunate prospector. Along these ancient stream beds from the headwaters of the Mariposa River north for 200 miles to the north fork of the Feather River, not far from Sacramento, was the Mother Lode region of California—where grew Nevada City, Auburn, Placerville, Jackson, Sonora, Colombia, Coloma, and other boom towns—once a chaotic spread of tents, shacks, and diggings.

Mining the Gold

In the beginning, the neophyte prospectors mostly poked around here and there, hoping to find a million-dollar nugget. Soon they realized that their fortune would come from dust flakes and that it took hard digging and shrewd guessing to find even the dust.

The basic principle on which all California gold mining was based was derived from the weight of gold. Because it is eight times heavier than the gangue or sediment in which it is caught, gold can be separated out either by winnowing, i.e., by letting wind blow the sand from a sheet while the heavier gold falls back on the cloth, or by letting water wash the lighter sediment from a pan or through a device with bars designed to trap the gold. Panning was the liveliest art of the day. First the prospector picked out larger pebbles, then in gentle swirling movements washed out lighter sand until only heavier ingredients at the bottom of the pan could be examined. In gold rush days, a man usually washed out about fifty pans every day; sheet-iron "placering" pans eventually were uniformly designed 18 inches in diameter, four inches deep, with sides slanting outward.

Prospectors formed teams to dig down to the bedrock, one or two digging and one or two panning. If gold was found on a certain level of the ditch, that layer would be extended until the strike was exhausted or until it came to an adjoining claim. A "rocker" or "cradle" came to be used by four-man teams as the most efficient operating unit. The rocker was built in two parts, a removable hopper with a wire screen or punched iron sheet which cleared out gravel, sitting on a wooden riffle box, with bars across its bottom to catch gold. The whole contraption was mounted on rockers. While two men dug the claim, a third carried dirt and water to the rocker, dumping first sand and gravel, then water over it while a fourth man furiously shook the contents through the device.

A variety of schemes were hatched to wash out greater and greater quantities of pay dirt, all based on the principle of the greater specific gravity of gold, which does not float over riffle bars. Among the devices were artificial trenches laced with holes or gravel riffle bars; long wooden sluice boxes; similar boxes called "long toms;" and "sluice forks."

One problem connected with placering was the inadequate amount of rainfall during the summer months in California. For those who wanted to prospect the year round, independent water companies built dams in the mountains and delivered water over their own wooden flumes for miles, all for either a flat rate or a percentage of earnings. The Eureka Canal in El Dorado County had a 247-mile line.

As they did in other mining areas, California miners worked out their own legal code. Sutter and other landowners were not regarded as possessors of mineral rights. Neither were owners able to deny access to property or water. Miners' meetings determined specific rules for their own districts, but their laws were found to be quite uniform throughout California. Each person was entitled to one claim, usually a hundred feet along a river or stream, and each had to mark and record the claim clearly with a district recorder. Partners recorded claims alongside each other. Other rules dealt with minimum time lengths for working claims, water use, despoiling a neighboring claim in any way, and disputes. Miners meted out summary justice—whippings, exile, even hangings—to willful offenders of the common law.

After the diggings along stream and riverbanks had been worked out by 1853, new methods to wash out greater quantities of dirt closer to the primary lodes were sought. The first such experiment, hydraulicking, was carried out by Edward E. Mattson in 1853. He found a way to capture an intense amount of pressure in a hose and sheet-iron nozzle to wash down entire banks of gravel into gigantic riffles. Water was impounded high in the mountains and carried by flume to an iron piping and into the monitor, the nozzle mounted on a pivot which could be operated by a single

Figure 8–5. Hydraulicking. By the 1870s, miners had developed high-pressure water systems which they used to wash away waste rock and overburden to reach gold-bearing deposits. Aside from the immediate effect such operations had on the mine site, the silt that washed away caused streams to be clogged and brought about permanent damage downstream. Courtesy the Bancroft Library.

man. The pressure of water from the nozzle was built up to such an intensity that it could wash down countless tons of dirt, gravel, and boulders from a hillside in a few minutes. A river of mud rushed to a series of sluices with riffles of squared logs and flat boulders which separated out first large rocks, then stones and gravel, finally sediment and gold. At least one to two tons of rock had to be washed away for each ounce of gold. The mud and sluice tailings of hydraulicking ended up in the nearest river, which soon became silted and polluted from the outfall, which it carried into the valleys below. Rivers thus began to flood valley communities and camps every year. The California state engineer calculated that about 53,500,000 cubic yards of debris were washed into the state's creeks and rivers during 1880 alone.

Anti-debris committees from these farming communities in the Central Valley fought the hydraulic mine owners for a decade, but made no headway so long as mining interests controlled the state's political process. The Sawyer decision in 1884 required mine owners to stop the flow of materials detrimental to communities below, a requirement that meant either the construction of impoundment dams or the closing down of the operations. No mention was made, in the decision, of environmental damage to hills, so the giant monitors could be activated again a generation later in northern California's Trinity County mountains where agriculture and population were sparse.

Also, at the turn of the century, dredges were digging out left-over gold in the flat valleys of the Mother Lode region. Dredges separated gold and gravel more efficiently than the forty-niners did a half century earlier. They were built beside a river and skidded into it. The continuous chain of their iron dipper buckets hauled up the sand and gravel to be processed through a revolving perforated cylinder and into a separator with angle irons processed with mercury to catch gold flakes. Large rocks and gravel were sent out the back of the dredge through a stacker boom, which swung slowly back and forth creating miles of "earthworm" gravel tailings. Hundreds of thousands of tons of earth were sifted through to find the golden flakes. It was a profitable industry but it was devastating to the alluvial topsoil of the area.

After their small mining claims were exhausted in the 1850s, prospectors began to spread out, following up rumors coming from the Rockies of Montana and Colorado and from southern Arizona. The largest number headed for Colorado.

The Colorado Mines

The California argonauts started out in 1858 with the slogan "Pikes Peak or Bust." Many of the prospectors had tasted the fruits of the good life and learned the art of finding gold. They were ready to cash in on the next big strike. A hundred thousand men roared into what would be the Colorado territory, lured by titillating newspaper accounts. But after a year of hard work, the Peak had given out only a tiny amount of gold, and three-quarters of the group left the area. They admitted the Pike's Peak venture to be a "bust."

Then John H. Gregory happened upon a quartz outcrop that proved to harbor gold at Clear Creek (later Mountain City). The second Colorado rush was on, and Gregory made his fortune by selling out—prospectors like to find gold; they rarely stick around long enough to do the mining. Nonetheless, he left his successors a major problem of how to extract the gold.

Gregory's discovery originated at a primary lode, not in a placer deposit easily separated from sediment and gangue. The primary lodes of Colorado exhibited characteristics different from those of California, which eroded evenly out of faults and fissures. Since the ore was formed by hydrothermal alteration, the gold in the Colorado lodes stayed high in the peaks, fanning out from their centers indiscriminately and unpredictably. Only the free gold which signaled the outcrop could be easily recovered.

The manner by which the Rockies were formed during the Tertiary period of geological history, about fifty million years ago, supplies the reason for the peculiar formations. During that period, the central region of the continent was submerged under an inland ocean when the earth faulted into twin fissures where the Rockies later arose. Because of the heavy, cold oceanic cover, the molten rock, or magma, could not release and diffuse itself through the fissures, but rather cooled and stabilized in bubbles near the superficial crust. Forty-five million years later, in the Quaternary period, when the twin chain of the Rockies was uplifted at the site of the fissures, and the sedimentary layers began to erode, the massive gold-bearing quartz domes exposed themselves. Spread throughout and mixed within the quartz minerals were the elusive gold and silver treasures. Some of the precious metals were liberated by erosion and leaching; most were trapped in mushroom-shaped lodes. New mining techniques had to be learned by the oldtimers from California.

They found out how to deal with the Colorado deposits largely from Cornishmen, imported in great numbers by mine owners to drill, blast and timber their mines. The experience of these workers of the tin mines of Cornwall, England, was added to the collective mining experience of America. It contributed mightily to the prosperity of the Colorado gold and silver mines in Mountain City (later Central City), Leadville, Oro City, Fairplay, Hamilton, San Juan, Durango and many more.

The Colorado mines were tunneled out of solid granite. They needed little timbering for support. Neither was there a problem of flooding, since the mines were dug high above the water table. Difficulties did come with drilling, blasting, or hollowing out a main shaft and tunneling toward possible strikes.

Before steam engines were packed up to the mines on mules, simple manually-operated windlasses hoisted up ore-laden kibbles, iron barrels also used in the Lake Superior copper mines. Eventually elaborate headframes, topped by large pulleys powered by Cornish steam engines in small buildings of their own below, lifted elevators carrying mine cars or men.

The "drifts" or tunnels in the mines followed the ore. Veins were "stoped out" by drilling holes for blasting, setting the fuse for lunch time or before a change of shift, and staying out of the area until the noxious fumes had cleared. Miners tried to set up their operations so that they drilled into the ceilings of the drift, picked out the ore, and let it fall by gravity into mine cars below. Where the rock was strong enough to support the roof of the drift, rock pillars were left standing for this purpose. Otherwise notched log supports were set up along the tunnel or in a stope. Nine mules or ponies hauled five cars at a time through the drifts. They pulled one-ton ore cars on rails. These basics of drilling, blasting, stoping, supporting the roof and hauling by mule were followed in coal and copper mines in earlier generations and even today have only been changed in details of efficiency and energy utilization.

Mining has never been easy or safe work. Temperatures deep in the mines were ungodly hot (or cold); the labor was back-breaking, the hazards omnipresent. Temperatures in the Nevada mines climbed as high as 150°. Miners could work in such heat only a short time before they were hauled to the surface and rubbed down with ice, a resource as valuable as the silver they mined; ice was harvested from dammed-up ponds on the eastern slopes of the Sierras. Six times a shift, the mules also had to be rubbed with ice. One mine had a standing order for $1,700 worth of ice per day.

Until the days of elevators, miners climbed down slippery ladders to the tunnels, and before 1875, holes for blasting were pounded out manually with a sledge hammer and iron drills. Miners worked in semi-darkness. Candles or oil lamps provided some light. The miners depended on intuition and smell to sense impending dangers of fires, explosions or cave-ins. Only a minimal supply of air reached the farthest ends of the mine before blower engines and air-compressor drills.

Milling of the ore was learned on-site near the Colorado mines. Ore was sledged or blasted from large to smaller chunks and put into Blake or Dodge jaw-crushers, which smashed the rock into pebble-sized pieces small enough to be stamped out at the stamp mill. Each of the battery of five stamps was weighted with a shoe of a thousand pounds, enough to pulverize the once-heavy quartz into a pulpy mixture, which was then carried by water through a fourteen-mesh screen.

Next the ore had to be concentrated in a process which separated the worthless gangue from the gold, silver, or copper. The first step usually applied the principle that the metals are heavier than gangue; the pulp, still carried by water, passed over riffles, or later, over a concentrating table which was shaken in a way that forced the heavier metallic particles toward one end. Often mercury or salt was added to the pulp because gold and silver amalgamates with or attaches itself to these catalysts. Then the precious metals would be roasted or smelted, whereby they would be further purified of their sulfides, mercury or remaining gangue. As years passed, more sophisticated techniques of concentration were developed, but the entire process from the mine to the bar was always painful and time-consuming. The mine-owners seemed to think it was worth the trouble, Mark Twain's loud complaints notwithstanding.

The Comstock Lode

One of the most famous of all the early mining districts was the Comstock Lode of Virginia City, Nevada, often called "Washoe" between 1850 and 1860, after the name of the Washoe Indian tribe who lived in the region, east of Lake Tahoe where the Sierra Nevadas descend suddenly into the Great Basin flatlands. Prospecting was done there at least as early as 1850, when one member of a Mormon party, William Prouse, successfully panned for gold while the group waited for the winter snows on the Sierras to melt. Word of his good fortune took only a short time to leap the mountains, and less for a pack of California argonauts to find the location. The secondary gold deposits came from lodes in the hills above the stream bed and could easily be placered during the winter months when rain brought water to the Nevada deserts below. But the recoverable gold seemed to play out in a half dozen years. The monopolization of the mines as well as the torrid heat drove most of the prospectors out of the area.

The hundred-odd prospectors who stayed around didn't have much hope for the district because their rockers and sluice riffle-bars continually became clogged with a heavy blue-black sand they called "blue-stuff." Two of them, Patrick McLaughlin and Peter O'Riley, took on Henry T. P. Comstock, who managed to muscle his way into the Irishmen's claim with his partner, Emanuel Penrod, by asserting that they were trespassing on his property. The four looked for gold on their Ophir claim at Gold Hill, but had little success; they eventually decided to send a sample of the bluish sand to Placerville for an appraisal of its metallic content. Area newspapers received the word that the specimen had heavy concentrations of silver at the same time the

Figure 8–6. A pair of arrastras. This Spanish invention, which takes its name from the Spanish verb *arrastrar*, to drag, was used from earliest Spanish colonial times to crush gold and silver ore so that they could be separated from worthless substances. Horses or mules drew 150-200-pound stones over the ore. Water was mixed with the pulverized ores to form a slime which was taken off through sluices for roasting or for further processing. This illustration, a painting by a California native, J. Boot, was done in 1853. Courtesy the Bancroft Library.

happy partners heard, and a new wave of prospectors hustled over the mountains from California. Virginia City became a boom town overnight. The partners sold their claim to California capitalists, one of whom, George Hearst, began his fortune at the Comstock.

For the first few years the mines were worked on the surface. The ore was pulverized and amalgamated by the Spanish *arrastre*, a 200-pound stone dragged around a circular bed of smaller stones by mule, with water trickled through the circular device, turning the ore into a pulp slime so that mercury could be mixed in the amalgam and retorted off. But when the vein of high-grade silver on the surface dipped into the mountains, the miners turned their attention to the problems of extracting the ores deep inside the mountains. The quartz at Comstock was remarkably soft, easy to pick out, but difficult to tunnel. Traditional timber post-and-cap supports could not maintain the great weight and pressure of the rock even when posts of sufficient length could be found. Rock pillars caved in even more quickly than the supports.

Philip Deidesheimer, a German mining engineer working as a consultant in California, solved the problem by prescribing "square sets" of timber, four- to six-foot square cribs joined at the corners like tiny rooms, piled on each other as the ore was mined, and filled in with mining waste for reinforcement when lower stopes were abandoned. The innovation worked, necessitating enormous investment of transporting thousands of Sierra logs by flume to the mines where they were squared, framed, and installed. Even then, the ever-present danger of fire or dry rot threatened to undo the months of labor and materials put into the devices.

The second even more maddening problem came from water saturating the lodes, much of which rose from the earth's boiling interior. It flooded the mines with hot mineral springs. Drainage tunnels horizontal to the vertical shafts were dug to get rid of the water, but they were never adequate. The largest engines in the West at the time were designed to pump out the ever-present spring water.

By 1864, Adolph Heinrich Joseph Sutro, descendant of a long line of Wall Street financiers and brokers, proposed to construct a tunnel to drain, ventilate and explore the entire Comstock Lode from its entrance in Eagle Valley, and graded into Mount Davidson at a depth of 1,650 feet. A year later, he received a fifty-year franchise from the Nevada legislature to operate the tunnel. Furthermore, twenty-three mining companies temporarily agreed to pay his firm, The Tunnel Company, $2 for every ton of extracted ore after the tunnel was in operation. Men and supplies could be transported through the tunnel, which was also considered an important possible escape route in case of mine disasters. Sutro even managed to obtain Congressional rights to undeveloped lodes on both sides of the tunnel.

Sutro tried, doggedly and unsuccessfully, to get private and Congressional financing to complete the project. During the period, William C. Ralston, president of the Bank of California, set his sights on the tunnel. He had already monopolized the milling and the transportation of the ore through lavish loans which milling companies could not pay off during the depression after the Civil War. He had also taken over the

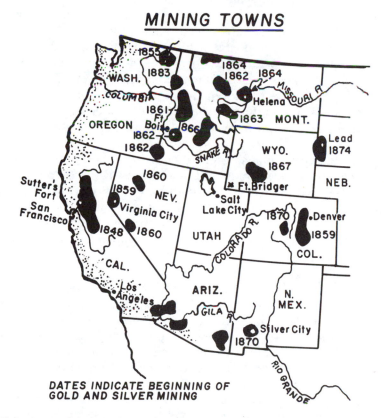

Figure 8–7. Mining areas of the American West. The dates show when miners began to extract gold and silver at the respective sites.

by building the Virginia and Truckee Railroad. The tunnel would make the mining companies completely dependent upon his auxiliary services so that then he could charge whatever the traffic would bear. Although Ralston spent millions trying to ruin Sutro and did succeed in a long delay of the project, he never managed to undermine the indefatigable German.

The man who indirectly saved the project was John W. Mackay, an experienced mine engineer who played a hunch on a possible new strike. At the point where the Comstock mines appeared to be played out, and their stocks had fallen to all-time lows, Mackay went into business with three other Irish partners—James C. Flood, James G. Fair and William S. O'Brien—and opened a mine that was found to contain an estimated $300,000,000 worth of ore. The news ruined Ralston, who was selling short on the stock exchange, but brought a large influx of investment money to the Comstock so that Sutro could complete his tunnel in 1879. When floods threatened to close down the mines, the mine operators, who had earlier reneged on paying Sutro the $2 fee per ton, capitulated to the royalty demand. Unfortunately, the tunnel was a generation too late; one by one the mines folded, either played out or hard-hit by flood and fire, and except for Mackay's Consolidated Virginia, the glory days of the fantastic Comstock Lode were over. Sutro had providently sold his shares in the tunnel before the Lode's impending eclipse was foreseen, and he moved to San Francisco as a millionaire. He became the city's mayor in 1894.

The beginnings of mining from the 1840s to the 1860s provided the first thrust toward a later Victorian capitalism of coal, iron, steel and heavy steam engines. Without the crude beginnings and sometimes blind experimentation of those intrepid early miners, later industrial developments might have moved much more slowly or along different lines. The early struggles of entrepreneur against entrepreneur for monopolistic dominance of a local resource also portended a later stage of American capitalism.

Western gold and silver mining, despite their contribution to the national treasury (to bolster the country's world trade and finance its Civil War), remained at best a mixed blessing. That half the world seems to have gone mad to collect a resource which in itself solves none of a people's basic needs cannot be explained outside of the fact that for centuries precious metals have been valued for themselves. The devastating effects on the land simply could not be compared to the possible exchange benefits of gold or silver.

A side-effect of the various mining rushes was to bring to western mining camps and their environs hundreds of thousands of seekers of a better life from dozens of countries and ethnic strains—Latin Americans, Cornishmen, Austrians, Chinese, Italians, Germans, Irishmen, and more. After over a hundred years since these groups were thrown together to work out their destinies, their greatgrandchildren have developed a relationship to other variegated and rich resources of the West: oil, agriculture, timber, and the like. Like their progenitors, contemporary Americans are still hell-bent on extracting the total value of these resources as fast as possible in the all-embracing philosophy of individual gain. In the stream of this tradition, it makes little difference whether one is extracting gold or oil. Environmental problems are certain to follow.

References for Further Reading

Peter T. Flawn's *Mineral Resources* (1966) covers the geology, engineering, economics and law of mineral resources. Parts of this chapter were greatly dependent on *Western Mining* by Otis E. Young, Jr. (1970), a book that not only gives a marvelous explanation of the technology of early mining in the West but also covers the geology, prospecting, placering, lode-mining and milling just as well. The classic treatment of the subject is Thomas A. Rickard's *The History of American Mining* (1932). *The Birth of the Oil Industry* by Paul H. Giddens (1938) and *Copper* by Ira B. Joralemon (1973) remain the standard references on the early history of those resources. Everyone should read Mark Twain's *Roughing It* (1902) on life in western mining companies. For those who are interested in the attitudes of the mining industry toward environmental protection and conservation, Duane Smith has written *America: The Industry and Environment, 1800-1980* (1987).

Part Three

AFTER
THE CIVIL WAR

Chronology of Major Events

1844	First sportsman's club, the New York Sportsman's Club, founded to protect and preserve game for purposes of hunting.
1862	Greenbacks issued by federal government. Department of Agriculture established. First Homestead Act passed. Morrill Land Grant College Act passed. Gold Rush at Tucson, Arizona.
1864	George Perkins Marsh publishes *Man and Nature*. Yosemite Valley, California, reserved as a state park. Siemens-Martin open-hearth steel-making process developed.
1865	Durum wheat introduced into Dakotas by Russian immigrants. Union Stockyards opened in Chicago. First state wildlife commission created (Massachusetts). Fifteen million buffalo living on the Great Plains.
1866	First drives of Texas cattle.
1867	Grangers (Patrons of Husbandry) founded in Washington, D.C.
1868	Refrigerator car patented by William Davis. John Muir arrives in California.
1869	First transcontinental railroad route completed. John Wesley Powell descends the Colorado River to the Grand Canyon.
1870	John D. Rockefeller establishes the Standard Oil Company.
1871	First U.S. Fish Commission established. First Granger law regulating railroads and warehouses passed in Illinois.
1872	Credit Mobilier scandal exposed. Creation of Yellowstone National Park.
1873	Timber Culture Act passed. Panic of 1873.
1874	Barbed wire perfected by Joseph Glidden.
1875	Black Hills Gold Rush. American Forestry Association organized. Bonanza machine farming begins in Red River Valley.
1876	Greenback Party makes first nomination for President. Nicolaus Otto devises internal combustion engine.
1877	Desert Land Act passed.
1878	Timber and Stone Act passed.
1879	U.S. Geological Survey established. Thomas Edison develops electric light bulb.
1880	U.S. Census: 50,155,783 (28.2% urban)
1881	Division of Forestry created in U.S. Department of Agriculture.
1882	Thomas Edison builds first central electrical power station. American Forestry Congress organized.

1884	Ladies' Protective Association organized.
	Charles Parsons patents steam turbine for electrical generation.
1885	New York establishes Adirondack Forest Preserve.
	Only 3,000 buffalo left in U.S.
1886	New York Audubon Society founded—forerunner of National Audubon Society.
1885-1914	Peak in immigration from eastern and southern Europe.
1887	Interstate Commerce Act passed.
	Hatch Act establishes Agricultural Experiment Stations.
	598 waterworks systems in U.S.
1890	Sherman Anti-Trust Act, Sherman Silver Purchase Act, passed.
1891	General Revision Act (Forest Reserve Act) gives President power to set aside forest preserves.
	Yosemite National Park established.
	National Irrigation Congress promoted and organized by William E. Smythe.
1892	Populist Party founded.
	Sierra Club organized by John Muir.
	German Rudolf Diesel patents his "rational" engine.
	First successful gasoline tractor built.
1893	Repeal of Sherman Silver Purchase Act.
	American Charles Duryea demonstrates his gasoline-powered automobile. First industrial use of electric motor in South Carolina.
1893-1896	Panic of 1893 results in failure of banks and commercial institutions.
	Waterclosets present overflow, collection, and disposal problems.
	Series of typhoid epidemics occur.
1895	E. C. Knight Anti-Trust case.
	Frederick Taylor popularizes "scientific management" principles.
1897	Secretary of Interior given jurisdiction over forest preserves.
1898	Gifford Pinchot becomes head of the Division of Forestry in U.S.D.A.
1899	"Refuse Act" section of Rivers and Harbors Appropriations Act forbids water pollution.
	Chlorine introduced to purify drinking water supplies.
	Engineers espouse dilution and filtration/purification methods for economic reasons. Physicians argue for wastewater treatment.
	3.5 million horses living in U.S. cities, representing monumental air/water pollution problems.

Chapter 9

THE RISE OF RESOURCE INDUSTRIALISM

*A*s an exploiter of resources, the United States was still a neophyte until the Civil War. A national market had emerged with the buildup of an urban population, but, with about 32,000,000 people coast to coast, the country was still quite small. Most regions had begun to specialize, but they managed to maintain a degree of self-sufficiency. Transportation took a dramatic step forward with railroad construction and point-to-point linkage unhampered by geographical limitations, but many railroads could not connect because tracks were built with different gauges; most lines ran between specific cities or a specific resource and its market. Water, human and horse power provided the mainstay sources of energy; the use of steam was still uncommon in America and electricity was not to come until the 1880s. Machine technology was quite crude, designed to process goods for small local rural or regional markets. America was still dependent on foreign countries for large amounts of capital investment, which tended to concentrate in companies or industries with the potential of yielding high returns, such as land companies, railroads, or gold and silver mines. Government vacillated in its role of resource developer—until the Republican Party gained control at the time of the Civil War.

After the South eliminated itself from national politics and could no longer voice its opposition, the Republicans began their program of development. It proceeded with such rapidity that by the end of the century the nation had undergone economic and social changes of considerable magnitude. The Republican platform, which was enacted before the Civil War, picked up much momentum after the war began. First, tariffs were passed to encourage more American manufacturing, and in 1862 the Homestead Act opened up new lands for development, for speculators as well as for those who wanted free land. Then the Congress passed the Pacific Railway Act which granted huge tracts of land and loans to the Union Pacific and Central Pacific Companies to build a transcontinental railroad. The first influx of greenback issues (see below) from the federal printer provided ready cash to entrepreneurs during that year. And the National Bank Act of 1863 bolstered the greenback economy. Tariffs continued through the Republican tenure, and a policy of non-taxation of the new captains of industry and their corporations assured a continuation of industrial growth.

The Greenback Era

The effects of the 1857 depression lingered into the sixties, but Republican military contracts brought business out of its slump. Nonetheless, by 1861, both government

THE CURSE OF THIS COUNTRY.

Figure 9–1. The greenback controversy. The pro-greenback cartoon of the 1870s above depicts the U.S. Treasury strangling workers, small business, and farmers. The government octopus is equipped with a gold coin on its nose, the symbol of evil to those who went deeply into debt when greenbacks were plentiful. The anti-greenback cartoon below suggests that paper money issued without proper backing will soon become worthless. Courtesy Culver Pictures.

and banks had exhausted their supplies of specie and possibilities of further note circulation. Hoarding and the outflow of gold to pay for imports exacerbated the difficulty.

To solve the problem, Congress authorized the Treasury to put $450,000,000 in greenbacks into circulation to pay war bills and another $300,000,000 in Treasury notes also to be utilized as currency. The National Banking Act enabled the Treasury Department to grant charters to participating banks which could issue their portion of the government notes, half of which went to the states according to population and the other half according to business demands. The national banking system was designed primarily to provide bonds, since chartered national banks had to cover all their Treasury notes through a market for government bonds. The new national banks were not, like the two previous U.S. banks, central banking institutions, but rather local private banks with charters issued by the federal government rather than by the state governments. Greenbacks and specie were utilized to pay off Treasury notes, in turn based on the issuance of government bonds. The country thus inaugurated its first experiment in a national paper currency, the greenback and national bank notes.

With so much money in circulation, war contractors could greatly expand their operations, particularly in textiles (with cotton from the South getting to the North by way of England) and steel. Farmers were offered generous credit terms to buy improved agricultural technology, which was more important than ever after their sons were taken off to war. By the end of the war, though, inflation had gotten out of hand, $100 worth of greenbacks buying about $60 worth of gold. The farmers and wage earners suffered most, since prices in general soared while farm prices or wages declined or remained the same. During the time farmers were paying off mortgages and loans on farm equipment, prices of wheat and cotton were cut in half. Many of these same farmers who later got into financial trouble thought their money worries were over earlier when Congress passed the Homestead Act of 1862.

The support for the Act came from an unusual alliance of western pioneers and eastern industrialists. The coalition wanted to strengthen western political resistance against the South by filling in the new territories as soon as possible. Both groups also wanted a transcontinental railroad along with the Homestead law so that eastern goods could be shipped west and western resources exploited and taken east. Without southern opposition these goals were easily and quickly accomplished. The instrument of implementation was the federal land once promised to the Indians as their perpetual heritage.

The Homestead Act of 1862 granted up to 160 acres to those who resided on and improved their land for five years, after payment of a small fee—$26, or $34 on the Pacific coast. After six months' residence the homesteader could claim title by paying $1.25 an acre. When word of the law's passage reached Europe, America's policymakers received high praise for their generosity and thousands prepared to move to the country that gave away free land.

Soon afterward, Congress authorized the Union Pacific to begin work on the transcontinental railroad at Omaha, Nebraska. Later the California component, the Central Pacific, was to start from Sacramento and the two lines were to join in Utah. In eight years seventy railroad companies were given charters to get railroads underway all over the country. They received varying amounts of land from both the state and federal governments, usually twenty alternate sections on either side of the track for each mile laid. Revenues from the land were to help finance construction, and the government granted loans totaling about $65,000,000 in addition to the approximately 40,000,000 acres of land. The latter figure climbed to over 131,000,000 acres before the middle of the following century.

The third act of federal largesse was a land grant measure, the Morrill Act of 1862, for the endowment of agricultural and mechanic colleges in each state. Eastern states without public lands were allowed to finance their schools with western land scrips to be sold for $1.25 an acre. Westerners took a very dim view of federal magnanimity which gave to the already developed eastern states their best lands—lands that could have been sold to finance internal improvements for the territories. Over 13,000,000 acres were handed over to the states and used to finance agricultural and mechanic colleges and state universities. These institutions promoted agricultural experimentation after the 1860s. The vocational schools also began to turn out practical crafts- men and engineers who later became the pragmatic technological cadres of industry. Technological efficiency; new methods of roadbuilding; an architecture based on the use of practical, safe, and cheap materials in housing and office buildings; and a generally new consciousness concerned with the efficient and economical were the direct or indirect result of the so-called A&M colleges. Resource exploitation was affected by the rapid training of professional technologists in both agriculture and the mechanic arts as economically-minded industries bid for the services of efficiency- minded professionals.

Homesteaders and Settlers

Although thousands of pioneers crowded the railroads, canals, and turnpikes to get to the free lands of the West, when they arrived at their destination it was difficult for them to distinguish between good and bad land on the open prairies. If they came in the late summer, prairie fires and devastatingly hot winds, perhaps a grasshopper invasion, would surely have accompanied them. Then they had to learn how to build a house without wood (with prairie sod), or what to use for fuel (buffalo or cattle "chips"), and where to find water. For the hearty, the community spirit was high. Settlers cooperated in the building of sod houses and well-digging. But many newcomers were not so hearty; they returned to the more familiar trappings of civilization.

Therefore, Congress was induced to offer further incentives to make western lands more appealing. It passed the Timber Culture Act in 1873, giving 160 acres to anyone (including homesteaders who already held 160 acres) who would plant trees on 40 of the acres. In 1878, the required number of acres to be planted was reduced to 10. By that time friction between cattlemen and settlers on western lands had developed to such a point that government officials recommended that the land on the high plains be disposed of as quickly as possible. In 1877, Congress enacted the Desert Land Act, whereby a settler could gain title to 640 acres at $1.25 an acre if he irrigated it within three years.

During the intensive mining years of the fifties and sixties, Congress did not intervene to enact mineral laws on the sale, lease or taxing of lands in the public domain. Finally, in 1870, the first of the mineral lands—those on which placer mining was done—were put up for sale at $2.50 an acre; lode claims went for $5 an acre. A few years later, iron and coal lands were put on the market, but many large companies had already found a way to engross these lands at a cheaper price.

The big losers of the story on land giveaways were the Indians. For a generation, settlers had been crossing their lands on their way to the Pacific but no attention was paid to the disruption of the lives of the Indians. Slowly, white settlement pushed farther and farther into Indian lands: into eastern Kansas and Nebraska, then into the gold, silver and copper regions of Colorado, the Dakotas, and Montana. The success of the Mormons encouraged farmers to move into the Rocky Mountain Territory, where trappers still combed the streams. Indians became more hostile to white incursions and began to fight more frequently. After the Civil War, the Union Army was moved to the far West, first to protect settlers, then to liquidate the Plains Indians' food supply, the buffalo. Little by little, Indians surrendered their vast tracts of tribal lands and were moved to reservations. If the reservations were later deemed too large for their use or needed for white settlement, a new treaty or "agreement" was made, and the tribe would move again. By 1863, the Winnebagos had been transferred five times. By 1877, the Indians had fought their last big battle. The white man had won the West, almost the full measure of the 175 million acres of Indian land.

Land Speculation and Engrossment

There was just as much tugging and pulling for land among settlers and speculators themselves as there was pushing Indians westward after the war. Land laws contained so many loopholes and pioneer land claimers were so immune to either law or loophole that it is a wonder that anyone survived the period. The more aggressive of the homesteaders took 160 acres (plus 160 for a wife). Then they claimed an extra 160 or more acres under preemption laws, perhaps more under the Timber Culture or Desert Land Acts. A settler could take advantage of the Preemption, Homestead, and Timber Culture Acts together and acquire 480 acres for about 50 cents an acre; in fact, this much land was necessary for successful farming to be done in the arid regions of the West. Local land officials conferred benefits of land on themselves and their speculator friends, who paid well for the service. Different territories applied the laws in different ways; different judges interpreted them according to whim, fancy, or personal interest. Land districts ranged from three to 20,000 square miles, with only a handful of officials to register and monitor the regions—and their salaries depended on the number and size of the fees. They naturally tended to interpret the law loosely: e.g., the law that demanded that a house at least "twelve by fourteen" be built on the land would be interpreted in a way that allowed a preempter to place a twelve-by-fourteen-inch cardboard replica on each of his claims.

The homestead and preemption laws also led to outright confiscation and leveling of the best prime forests of the country. The early Preemption Act of 1841 set the precedent for companies to move into immense forest stands of the Great Lakes and

Figure 9–2. Frauds on the prairie. These illustrations, from A.D. Richardson's book *Beyond the Mississippi,* show how enterprising (but dishonest) settlers circumvented homesteading requirements. At right a farmer is shown contemplating a house "twelve by fourteen," and below the land is claimed by a "habitable dwelling," although in the first instance the dimensions are in inches not feet, and in the second the inhabitants are crows and a garter snake.

Gulf States and legally or illegally to help themselves to whatever timber they could reach. The same practices were even more widespread in the pine and fir regions of Wisconsin, Minnesota, the Colorado Territory, and the Pacific Northwest, because increasing population demands and urbanization kept pushing up the price of wood. Gangs of men were rounded up by lumber companies in large cities like San Francisco or small towns like Duluth. They were paid a fee and taken to the claims office to file for 160 acres. One powerful lumber executive admitted he added thousands of acres to his domain by listing names found in Chicago and St. Paul directories at the local land office. Other lumber companies did not even go through the formalities of buying the land. They simply moved in, set up their mills and chopped and sawed timber. Then there was the practice of "round 40" mentioned in an earlier chapter; it was a profitable habit which continued until at least the end of the century. Wherever railroads or water flumes for mines were built, enterprising businessmen were ready to supply timber from the public domain for whatever price they could get, on those rare occasions when the railroads or flume companies did not take the timber for themselves. In this way, thousands of square miles were cleared and tens of millions of board feet of timber were taken from Washington to California, throughout the Rocky Mountains and upper Mississippi regions, and in a great sweep from Florida all the way to Texas.

What the homesteading and preemption laws did for timber kings, the Timber Culture Act and Desert Land Act did for cattle barons who sent cowboys to make multiple land claims near water holes and streams. That land which was not fraudulently taken was simply occupied as grazing land for thousands of head of cattle. The rest of the good land was usually taken very cheaply or free by area speculators who held it until a large influx of settlers pushed up the price.

In the same manner did the rich iron lands of Minnesota (as did the Lake Superior copper land under preemption laws) pass into private hands. Although mineral lands were not to be included in preemption or homestead claims, those who filed for their companies swore that no minerals were on the land. When iron lands were recognized by the law in 1873, they were to be sold at $1.25 minimum bid at auction, but much larger tracts were purchased for far less from the state or railroad companies. Great iron companies built up huge estates, mostly from homestead and preemption claims or Indian land scrip purchased for a few cents an acre. The Minnesota Iron Company, for example, picked up almost 9,000 acres from these sources alone, as did other iron companies of the region.

Although homestead laws were overtly passed to preclude speculation and corruption in western settlement, all previous and subsequent land laws undermined this purpose: i.e., preemption laws, desert and timber grants, cash sales, military bounty lands, giveaways to states and railroads, education grants to eastern as well as western states. This mixture of land policies made it quite simple for speculator or land companies to acquire very large holdings and to resell them in small plots to incoming settlers. Therefore when settlers arrived in Kansas or Nebraska, for example, instead of finding a homestead they were bombarded with leaflets advertising land sales from the State Agricultural College, or the local railroads, or a variety of land companies and speculators—millions of acres from $1 to $15 per acre with long-term credit arrangements available. Some remote pieces of land could be homesteaded, but the fact that neither speculators nor the state nor the railroads had bothered with them indicates their distinct undesirability. Conversely, it was not uncommon for a speculator or entrepreneur, such as William Chapman or Henry Miller in California, to acquire a million acres from state land sales, military warrants and, of course, dummy entrymen.

Almost 600,000 homestead claims were made, for about 80,000,000 acres, between 1860 and 1900. This represents about one sixth of all the public domain land disposed of during the period. Since many of the claims were dummy entries for land engrossers, probably only about a tenth of all public domain land went to bonafide homesteaders, and these people ran into other financial difficulties because of debts and inflation.

Yet the policy was geared for quick land disposal for quick exploitation, and this purpose was certainly achieved. By the turn of the century, 8,000,000 people had settled on farms west of the Mississippi, and timber and mining companies proliferated. Wood, coal, copper, lead, iron, and petroleum production increased from five to fourteen times between 1879 and 1900.

Industrial Growth: Steel

Even before Lincoln was inaugurated the Republican Congress pushed through a protective tariff on iron and steel products as well as on woolens, cottons, and carpetings. By 1864, again without the accustomed Southern dissent, the average import duty was up to almost 50%. One could say that the foundations of later long-lived prosperity of American industry were built in the steel mills of Pennsylvania, with quite a little help from Washington.

Steel was a critical material for railroads, which had become more and more subject to accidents because of faulty rails. Other developments after the Civil War spurred the steel industry and American business in general. The dramatic increase in and demand for stronger casings on boilers and steam engines on ships, in powerhouses of factories, and for a material to withstand higher pressures of larger machines provided a foundation for other potential industries. Steel also made safe bridges and higher buildings possible in growing cities of the time. Later precision tools were the result of the steel revolution—lathes, planers, machine tools, and, enormously valuable to the mining industry, the compressed air drill. After the introduction of electrical power, the number of these steel machines, cutting tools and presses multiplied each year. Later mass production techniques demanded interchangeable parts that would meet fairly precise tolerances.

It was relatively easy for pre-Civil War technology to make wrought iron, which contains less carbon than steel does, or cast iron, which has more carbon than steel. But it was very difficult to find the right formula for steel itself: from about 0.08% to about 1.7% carbon. An increase in the quantity of carbon makes the iron stronger but also more brittle. Steel, with just the right amount of carbon, is both very tough and also malleable. It took English steel-makers at Sheffield about two weeks to convert pig iron into cast crucible steel. Their method was too expensive and uncertain to be copied in America.

In England, steel was made from pig iron in a reverberatory furnace, where coke heated the charge from the side over the iron. The coke was not mixed with the ore. This process, developed by Henry Cort and patented in 1784, was called "puddling"; i.e., the iron-maker or puddler could "puddle" or stir and manipulate the iron while it was still hot, eliminating the need for reheating and hammering out the carbon and other impurities in order to make wrought iron. After most of the carbon was removed, the iron could be gathered up in a red-hot, pasty ball, which could be easily squeezed into bars through a grooved rolling mill. Bars were rolled through successively smaller grooves until they reached the desired width and thickness. All the while the process removed carbon and improved the quality of the iron. (If the wrought iron was not used to make steel for tools or cutlery, it was usually rolled into bars.) The puddling and rolling process saved labor and fuel. Such a mill began operation near Uniontown, Pennsylvania, in 1817; mills of this kind were not widespread in America, however, before the Civil War. The second step in making blister steel was the reintroduction of just the right amount of carbon into the molten wrought iron. The ironmakers packed charcoal with good wrought iron in a closed box. The shell-hardened blister steel could be converted into shear steel (by welding bars together) or the higher quality crucible steel (by melting pieces in small crucibles).

Two men, Englishman Henry Bessemer and Irish American William Kelley, independently came up with a much faster steel-making process in the 1850s but they were not ready to begin large-scale production until the sixties. They both worked from the same principle: Realizing that carbon and silicon (the second principal impurity in the furnace) unite with oxygen in molten pig iron, they simply blasted air through the iron and burned these impurities out, stopping the process part way to produce steel. Bessemer called his device a "converter." It was a cylinder with an open top and numerous holes in the bottom through which the air blast passed, holding up the molten metal. The cylindrical kettle could be tipped after fifteen or twenty minutes to pour out the converted steel. This process was a distinct improvement over the two-week process at Sheffield, but the timing of the stop was critical. The steel was often of very uneven quality.

Bessemer's converter worked fine with high quality Swedish iron ore, but not the English ore because the air did not burn out the excessive amount of phosphorus in the native ores. Kelley, who had started on the experiment eight years earlier than Bessemer and had used richer American ores, did not suffer the liability of a high phosphorus content. He called his method the "pneumatic process" and won an American patent over claims by Bessemer. But because the earlier steel rails imported in the country bore the "Bessemer steel" label, the steel from the Kelley process also came to be identified with the Englishman. Yet it was American ironmakers, rather than the English, who received the big contracts from the dozens of new railroad companies and their steel-making and rolling mills turned out enormous quantities of "T" rails during the era.

Figure 9–3. The "big blow" of a Bessemer converter. The converter can be rotated and tipped when the metal is ready to be poured out. It discharges a stream of sparks out of its spout when compressed air is blown through openings in the bottom of the converter. Pure oxygen was substituted for ordinary compressed air in the mid-twentieth century to make a higher quality steel. Otherwise the hundred-year-old process is the same. The model depicted above was put into operation by William Kelly of Eddyville, Kentucky in 1847, several years before Henry Bessemer conceived his similar process.

Simultaneously, a second, more efficient method of producing steel was in the final stages of experimentation on the Continent. Two German brothers naturalized in England, William and Frederick Siemens, found that they could utilize the heat from burnt gases of nearby coke ovens and blast furnaces as a new source of energy to charge the blast of air over an open hearth or reverberatory furnace and further intensify the hot blast. Their process was not entirely successful until they tried it with the open hearth furnace of the French father and son team of Emile and Pierre Martin. The Siemens-Martin process, based on the regeneration principle of hot bases (a logical development of the puddling process, increasing the heat even more), did not get a foothold in the United States until late in the century. It gradually replaced the Bessemer converter until World War II. It permitted greater control of the carbon content of steel; it could utilize steel scrap mixed with pig iron, and it had a larger capacity. Both processes used an acid furnace lining of burned limestone or dolomite, developed by Englishmen Sidney Thomas and Percy Gilchrist, to stop excessive phosphorus from combining with the steel.

Carnegie's Integrated Industry

The man who saw and exploited the potential of the steel industry was Andrew Carnegie, who, dazzled by the "big blow" of a Bessemer converter he saw in England, rushed back to America to invest in steel. Having started work as a bobbin boy for $1.25 a week, then as a messenger for a telegraph company, Carnegie invested small amounts, then increasingly larger amounts in very successful locomotive companies, sleeping car firms, bridge-building companies, and even oil companies. Along with his other ventures, he owned a number of iron mills and foundries in the Allegheny and Monongahela Valleys near Pittsburgh. After his Bessemer experience in 1872, he began to put together an organization in steel which itself outproduced Great Britain before the end of the century.

Carnegie was obsessed with cost-cutting through new technologies, and he pioneered integrated production methods; his blast furnaces, bloomeries and rolling mills all worked in a sequential and harmonious system. At the same time he bought out competitors, merged with some, drove others into bankruptcy, purchased key iron-mining companies, and pushed his workers harder and harder for higher production quotas. During the 1892 Homestead, Pennsylvania, strike, he hired an army of Pinkerton detectives to break the strike. Through progressive technologies and labor speedups, Carnegie was able to lower the price of a ton of steel from $65 a ton in 1872 to $20 a ton in 1897. Neither his profits nor his tonnage suffered, however. In 1900, he produced 3,000,000 tons of steel and pocketed profits of $40,000,000—without the disadvantages of an income tax.

Carnegie's firm was one of the first great monopolies of the country. He owned enormous reserves of ore, coal, and limestone and over half of the nation's coke ovens. He produced over half of the country's pig iron, 68% of its steel rails, 60% of its structural steel, and most of its steel plates, bars, wire, hoops, tin plates, tubes, barbed wire, wire nails, and the structural steel that went into most of the nation's bridges as well. He transported ore from his own mines on his 112 steamships and over the 1,000 miles of his own railroad line.

In 1900, Carnegie decided to sell the firm to J. P. Morgan (whose bank made $12,500,000 on the transaction) for $492,000,000, and the U.S. Steel Corporation was born. Carnegie devoted the rest of his life to philanthropic works.

With the spectacular expansion of the industry, new sources of iron ore were sought and found on the western end of Lake Superior. The Minnesota Iron Company, organized in 1882 by coal and railroad tycoon Charlemagne Tower, immediately built an eight-mile railroad from the rich ore fields at Tower, Minnesota, in the Vermillion Range to the docks at the present site of Two Harbors on Lake Superior. The field was soon one of the largest iron mines in the world, with good access to the steel mills at Buffalo and Pittsburgh. By the 1890s, the famous Mesabi (Chippewa for "giant") Range, sixty miles northeast of Duluth, was opened to iron production. The ore at the Mesabi was as soft as sand, and it could be scooped out with large steam shovels (developed in 1877 by William S. Otis to strip-mine coal) by first removing an overburden of earth. Within a few years, millions of tons of ore were taken from the Range to the Duluth harbor. The Mesabi Range remains one of the largest iron producing regions of the world. The Ste. Marie ("Soo") Canal between Lake Superior and Lake Huron handles more tonnage than any other canal in the world, most of it iron ore. The open pit method of mining was perfected at Mesabi, first with steam, then with electric power shovels.

Although practically all coal supplies were hand dug from Appalachian and Indiana mines, steam shovels were introduced to strip overburden and bituminous coal for the ever-hungry Carnegie coke furnaces. Among the first shovels was a reconstructed dredge, mounted on wheels, its hull removed. Its fifty-foot boom carried a dipper with a 1 1/4-yard capacity. It could remove overburden of thirty-five feet and strip-mine 400 yards of coal a day. In the 1890s, dragline shovels were put on 80- to 125-foot stationary booms; they were dragged across the pit until they were filled. Steam and electric shovels became larger, more powerful, and more widely used after the turn of the century.

In 1850, animals, water, and humans provided America's energy. After the war, the transition to steam and later electric power greatly increased the country's resource exploitation. No longer did factories have to be set up along falls or fast-running streams and rivers, nor did new industries have to confine themselves to the relatively small production of a water, wind, or animal power source.

Excessive exploitation of forests was one cause of the switch to steam, since tree stands no longer protected the watersheds. They were disrupted to the extent that stream flow was no longer predictable.

During the age of steel, the steam engine came into its own, and railroads were able to carry coal to the boilers of virtually every important factory town in the nation.

Edison's construction of a central power plant in New York City marked the beginning of the electric age. Here not a new energy source was discovered and put into service, but rather a new means of delivering energy, which still had to be converted from the energy in water flowing or fuel burning. Nonetheless factories

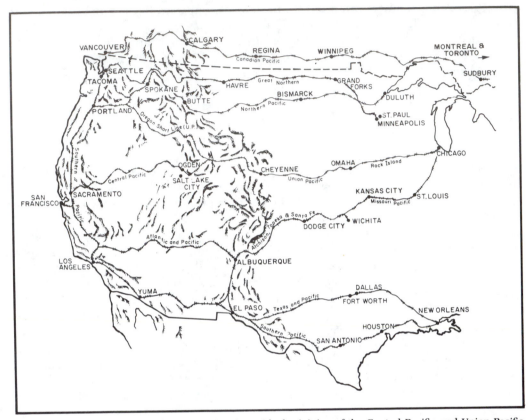

Figure 9–4. The western rail linkages. Beginning with the joining of the Central Pacific and Union Pacific in 1869 (at a point west of Ogden, Utah on this map), rail lines opening up the Far West were rapidly completed. These linkages served not only to connect east and west, but also to provide outlets to the world from the central areas that produced food and raw materials for the city factories. By the 1890s the phenomenal growth of city populations—775% for Omaha, 2000% for Seattle—demonstrated the influence of railroad growth.

could dispense with their own power sources, which were expensive to construct and maintain. They could then receive energy from a remote source. The full implications of electrical power were not to be realized for another generation, though.

The Railroads

In 1860, a little over 30,000 miles of railroad track were laid in America, all of it east of the Mississippi, most of it in the North. During the generation after the war, an average of 4,000 to 5,000 miles were laid each year—7,439 miles went down in 1872—and by 1900, almost 200,000 miles of railroad linked the country together and penetrated to remote villages, forests, and mines from the large cities. Railroad mileage reached 250,000 in 1916.

During this period, significant improvements were made on railroad locomotives and cars. In particular, George Westinghouse's compressed-air brake (1869) and his later electric signals speeded up railroad travel and simultaneously made it safer. When Congress chartered the Union Pacific Railroad, track gauge was standardized at 4'8½", which set the pattern for the rest of the nation's railroads. By the 1880s, locomotives and cars could transfer onto most of the rails of the country. The refrigerated freight car (1875) bolstered the cattle and meat packing industries, enabling them to ship their products from western ranges and stockyards to eastern markets.

The high point of railroad construction came when the Union Pacific joined the Central Pacific on May 10, 1869, at Promontory Point, Utah. The hoopla and celebration of the day followed hundreds of deaths and injuries of Chinese laborers on the Central Pacific and Irishmen on the Union Pacific. Few doubted the value of the transcontinental rail project at the time, however. Thereafter settlement quickened; economies of scale and regional specialization followed; national markets emerged; and eastern traders had their long-sought direct route to the Far East. Passenger cars were hooked onto loads of coal, timber, iron, and cattle. The railroad acted as a "multiplier" on economic development after the war, so much so that settlement of agricultural land thereafter almost assured agricultural overproduction and an uncertain future for farm families. The transcontinental railroad eventually would have been built even without the mighty boost of federal land and loans, but probably more slowly, and certainly without so much financial manipulation and corruption by railroad companies.

Examples of graft, stock-watering, and bribery among the federally-endowed companies are so profuse they seem commonplace. The most notorious case derived from the Union Pacific itself and its Pennsylvania construction firm, the Credit Mobilier Company. Oakes Ames, a representative of the firm and a Congressman, wheeled and dealed the contract through a maze of Congressional barriers. Ames offered many of his Congressional colleagues shares of the company at par, and even lent money for the purchase of the stock, which rose 400% in a few months. A congressional investigation found that company executives had pocketed millions of dollars in kickbacks, loans and other overcharge costs. At the other end of the track, the Central Pacific construction firm, the Crocker Company, charged an average of $100,000 a mile for their work, probably twice what an equitable price would have been. Other railroad companies of the west sold small farmers and investors watered-down stock which never could possibly pay dividends because of similar overcharges of their construction companies.

The railroad tycoon James J. Hill got his start in a syndicate that bought the deflated bonds of 2,500,000 acres of land with 500 miles of track. After the syndicate sold $8,000,000 worth of bonds to finance their new St. Paul, Minneapolis, and Manitoba Railroad and awarded themselves $15,000,000 worth of stock, they made a handsome cash profit and increased the track over their lands. *Land* values as the syndicate resold the lands soared, accruing further profits. Slowly Hill built up the Great Northern system, which spurred the resource exploitation of Minnesota, North Dakota and Montana. By 1908, he controlled 25,000 miles of railroad and had reached the Pacific coast. In the wake of his westward trail, Hill left a string of banks, farming, and ranching communities; he then proceeded west on his own fleet of ships to trade with Oriental merchants.

With the millions the railroad men made, they spent millions more on federal, state and local politicians, obtaining additional grants of land and subsidies or fighting bills for harbor and river improvements or winning lucrative mail contracts. Continual graft payments had to be made and competition from rival railroads or water transport firms stamped out.

When the depression of the 1890s finally hit the country, the railroads could still gain substantial income from land payments. For even after the Civil War, land grants to railroads from federal, state and local governments amounted to a quarter of the area of the states of Minnesota and Washington; a fifth of Wisconsin, Iowa, Kansas, North Dakota, and Montana; a seventh of Nebraska; an eighth of California; and a ninth of Louisiana—all of it among the most valuable land of the respective states.

The same iron and steel boom that raised railroad production a thousandfold brought iron, and eventually steel, shipbuilding to maturity in the half-century after the Civil War. Shipbuilders increasingly shifted their operations from timber regions to cities closer to iron and coke centers like Cleveland and Pittsburgh. In the 1880s steel ships driven by powerful steam engines began to replace wooden merchant vessels. By the end of the century the United States had its own navy of steel ships and was ready to flex its military muscle.

Industrial Trusts and Monopolies

It is obvious that in a country of growing cities spread along thousands of miles of track, a few railroad companies could set prices for long-haul transport and even charge high prices for the land along their track. It is not so obvious but probable that railroads were responsible for the extremely rapid growth of American cities, which were becoming centers of huge industrial enterprises that used the railroads to tie together their resource-producing, processing and marketing areas. In 1860 a little over five million people lived in cities; in 1900 a little under 25 million. Once the pattern of urban growth was established, railroads made further growth possible by transporting their food, building materials and consumer goods—sugar, salt, leather, whiskey, and kerosene, all of which were beginning to be mass-produced and marketed nation-wide from other large cities.

Small-scale resource processing for local markets by family operations remained for many years, but the trend toward large markets and rationalizing the process from production to distribution was set after the railroads made big industry possible. Rural craftsmen, blacksmiths, and even small mill operators closed shop and left their villages to find work in the cities, where they joined a labor force swollen with immigrants from all parts of Europe. There they worked in textile and leather factories, salt, sugar or kerosene refineries, flour mills and slaughterhouses that were beginning to sell their standardized products to the villages the workers had recently abandoned and to urban dwellers in other parts of the country.

It is also true that the railroads intensified the problem of competition for the new industrialists, since they were forced to compete with other firms who wanted to capture the national market. After the stronger firms managed to force their weaker rivals out of business, they began to form pooling agreements to control competition. Pools attempted to regulate production and markets among themselves, and even set up cooperative selling agencies to promote the industry as a whole, all to keep up demand and prices. Since each company maintained control of its own operations, many of them often broke ranks, especially during periods of good business. In the meantime a new kind of vertical integration appeared in isolated industries around the country whereby a central office in a large city close to markets controlled production, costs, marketing and distribution. Eventually, firms in pooling arrangements merged in order to adopt the more efficient form of vertical integration of production, processing, marketing, sometimes even transportation. When a few giant corporations captured the major share of the market, they could act together as an oligopoly and make joint pricing decisions. Railroads, the telegraph, and soon the telephone united the old industrial centers of New York, Baltimore, Philadelphia, Boston, Cincinnati, Cleveland and St. Louis with the new metropolises of Chicago, Indianapolis, the Twin Cities, Atlanta, Kansas City, Dallas, and San Francisco.

Some entrepreneurs established a system of national marketing and distribution before they concentrated on the production side. For example, Gustavus F. Swift set up outlets in every major city during the 1880s as he waged a monumental advertising campaign about the health benefits of western beef, which he shipped by refrigerated railroad cars from Chicago. He overcame the strong opposition and boycotts of local butchers, expanded his operation to include other meat and dairy products, and built new meatpacking plants in St. Louis, Omaha, and Kansas City. He continued to move into more cities as he changed the eating habits of American families. All the while, he systematized and bureaucratized the process at both ends of the operation—stock buying, processing, use of byproducts, advertising, marketing and accounting. Other meatpackers followed Swift's lead until only five large meatpackers dominated the national meat market—this accomplishment in the face of thousands of smaller producers serving local communities around the country.

James B. Duke set the example for the tobacco industry, also by concentrating on heavy advertising and a national sales organization. He merged with five smaller companies in the formation of the American Tobacco Company, which integrated the purchasing, manufacturing, marketing and accounting segments of the firm into one large bureaucratic and rationalized operation. The Washburn-Crosby Company similarly integrated the flour industry.

John D. Rockefeller

But it was John D. Rockefeller more than anyone else who prefigured a new age of market development and control. When oil was discovered in Titusville, Pennsylvania, Rockefeller was merchandizing produce in Cleveland. He and his partner invested in an oil refinery (for illuminants) there; it was a business that became so profitable

Figure 9–5. The development of oil refining and transportation. Because of the enormous influx of capital in the oil industry by early monopolizers like Rockefeller, refining and transportation technologies developed swiftly. Refining crude oil for kerosene was important because whale oil for lighting had become scarce and expensive. In the beginning of oil refining, crude oil was simply boiled, as is shown in the illustration above. The vapors from the boiling oil were drawn off through tubes which were cooled with water. The liquids thus distilled made excellent illuminants. The remaining oils were mixed with fish oils and animal fats to make machine and engine lubricants (labeled in the engraving), important for the American industrial revolution. Likewise, the primitive pipeline was the entrepreneur's response to exorbitant charges by early teamsters who carried oil barrels on carriages. This line was laid in 1865 from Pithole, Pennsylvania to the Miller Farm, a distance of 5-1/2 miles, and financed by Samuel Van Syckel, an oil buyer. The developments in oil shipment by railroad also came rapidly. The wood-burning Reno, Oil City and Pithold Railroad, shown at right, near Rouseville, Pennsylvania, first carried out oil in wooden barrels.

so quickly that the firm established the Standard Oil Company in 1870 with a capitalization of $1,000,000, increased to $2,500,000 in 1872, and to $3,500,000 a year later. It soon became the country's largest refinery, but suffering the competition of 250 other firms, it could garner only about 10% of the market. Within eight years, however, it did almost 95% of the oil refining in the country.

Standard Oil achieved this spectacular dominance in the industry through vertical integration, cost cutting, and a few ruthless methods of eliminating competition from independent oil refiners. The firm first formed the South Improvement Company to negotiate with railroad companies for special rates on large shipments of oil. Not only were they able to get rebates on shipments of their own oil, but they even obtained rebates on the oil of their competitors, who gamely tried to fight the oil titan. After the Ohio legislature forbade Standard's privileged state with the railroads, the company continued to receive special rates. Next, Standard began to take over independent refineries throughout the East. Rockefeller permitted the former owners of the refineries to operate the plants, but in each case they were required to yield their control to a voting trust which did all the purchasing, transporting and marketing of oil as one large firm. In a few years, independents saw that it would be impossible to compete with Standard Oil; they sold out. Rockefeller's success paved the way for voting trusts in the sugar, whiskey, match, steel, tobacco, and other industries.

Then the firm sought to control the pipelines, a deed accomplished in five years despite a bitter battle with independent producers of crude oil. Rockefeller built lines where his competition refused to sell out, and he brought the piping of oil under his aegis. All the while, Rockefeller was receiving lower prices from producers through bulk buying and sending his agents around the country with kerosene and lamps. The agents undersold big wholesalers and small country stores alike. He bought his own tank wagons, railroad cars, and ships, made his own barrels and bottles, and set up a research and development team to find byproducts of the refining process.

The Standard Oil Trust was organized in 1879 and 1882, when the new merger concentrated on the efficiencies made possible by vertical integration. Manufacturing was consolidated to meet specific marketing needs. But the Trust enjoyed an unyielding supply of cheap crude oil from small independent producers so that it was relieved of the high costs of exploring for oil and producing it. New layers of the company's bureaucracy were established, however, to coordinate production, refining, and marketing.

In 1892, the Ohio courts nullified the Trust agreement, but the company reorganized itself under New Jersey's holding company laws, capitalized itself first at $10,000,000 and soon afterward at $110,000,000. By 1904, Standard Oil once again controlled about 90% of the country's kerosene production; the rest of the market was shared among seventy-five companies. The Trust also determined the price of the commodity for the nation's users.

Creating a Demand

During the last decades of the century, increasing emphasis was placed on marketing and on creating a demand for special products. The Whiskey Distillers Trust streamlined their marketing organization through heavy advertising and packaging efforts; the Biscuit Trust and the Rubber Trust (for rubber boots and shoes) did the same, all three following leads provided by the concentrations in steel, oil, and meat. These companies not only cornered the markets on their commodities, but also greatly increased demand for them. The late nineteenth century trusts and monopolies set a trend which became the standard procedure for corporations of the twentieth century.

Industries of producers' goods were also able to concentrate and rationalize their production and distribution, mainly because of the enormous demands from growing cities. Carnegie saw the rise of cities as a boon to the steel industry, for in 1887 he shifted his mammoth Homestead plant from the production of rails to the production of structural steel; the plant was at full production immediately. He also was one of the first to save fuel by substituting electric motors for steam engines in the early 1890s. Power machinery was also needed for omnipresent urban construction, and even such new devices as steam rollers and other road and street construction machinery.

Thomas Edison's electric incandescent lamp and central power plant kindled this new round of resource development. Electrical urban lighting and power plants put overnight demands on the mining of copper, which possesses properties of high conductivity and rust resistance. The old copper mines at Keweenaw and new ones at Butte, Montana, and Morenci, Arizona, could scarcely keep up with requests for copper. Like most of the other ores of the period, copper passed into the hands of a few firms which were soon doing mining, smelting, and refining at one location. After the purer deposits were exhausted, copper oxides and sulfides were smelted and separated in a manner similar to gold and silver at the time, since any impurity in the copper spoils its conductivity. Unlike iron ores, which often are over 50% iron, copper ores are considered rich if they contain 4% or 5% copper.

Some mining companies before 1900 brought in Bessemer converters to smelt copper ores. The process became more sophisticated with the development of the electrolyte method of separating the ore, and later the "froth flotation" method enabled ores with a tiny amount of copper to be smelted. Gold and silver byproducts could be separated out as well. In the flotation process, the ore pulp is coated with oil in a tank and subjected to a stream of rising air bubbles which carry the purified metals to the surface as rich "concentrates."

The big copper companies entered into mergers—Amalgamated Copper; American Smelting and Refining; United Copper—and began to control the output of their mines to match demand. At the same time from their New York headquarters they closely watched mining production and processing, and they sought new markets for copperware and byproducts.

Neither the chaotic aftermath of the Civil War nor the depressions of the seventies and the nineties slowed mounting resource exploitation during the last decades of the century. Lavish federal land grants to railroads (whose construction opened up land and resource development as well as their markets) and a national currency led to the integration which prepared the way for efficiency-minded entrepreneurs. The rise of the engineers out of A&M colleges or trained on the job by entrepreneurs like Carnegie was also a major factor in developing more efficient technologies for extraction and processing.

New bureaucracies characterized the mineral and agricultural processing industries. A central office in a key city coordinated the various activities of each department, with special attention paid to marketing and advertising in a nation-wide context. Very often the distribution of processed resources was the first concern of a nationally-minded corporation, which aggressively endeavored to replace smaller local producers and retailers.

By the turn of the century, most key resource industries were controlled by one or a few large corporations, which could fix prices and increase production and productivity without fear of internecine competition. The vertically-integrated company then could zero its promotion guns on creating more demand for its products and exploit natural resources proportionately. The depressions of the seventies and nineties gave large firms the opportunity to force out weaker small companies by adapting cost-cutting technologies, particularly in power production.

Urban Pollution and Slums

The generation before the turn of the century also marked the beginnings of large scale pollution, especially from industrial sources. New York, then the country's largest city, started the trend. A pall of smoke and vapors from the city's 287 foundries and machine shops and dozens of refineries and tanneries hung over the region. Dirty soft coal was burned for hundreds of steam engines and pot-belly stoves; its smoke combined with the stench of horse manure and household wastes which putrefied in the streets. About 14,000 smokestacks belched soot and ashes in the Monongahela Valley around Pittsburgh at the time. The dirt and wastes of New York and Pittsburgh and the rest of the nation ended up polluting the cities, rivers, and streams of the country and destroying countless fish, vegetation and wildlife. The pollution also killed untold numbers of people and changed their unspoiled landscape into a desolate environment. H. L. Mencken commented on the Pittsburgh environs in an essay in the *Boston Herald:*

"Here was the very heart of industrial America, the center of its most lucrative and characteristic activity, the boast and pride of the richest and grandest nation ever seen on earth—and here was a scene so dreadfully hideous, so intolerably bleak and forlorn that it reduced the whole aspiration of man to a macabre and depressing joke. . . ."

Mencken knew, of course, that America still had its share of idyllic rural villages and small towns, but they began to lose their inhabitants to the cities during those decades after the Civil War, and more critically, they lost their separateness as well. The spreading railroad networks integrated town and city and carried increasing amounts of clothing and canned and consumer goods on their runs to the backcountry. Assured of regular deliveries, entrepreneurs opened chain stores in those small towns, thus planting the seeds of further homogenization of urban landscapes, specialization of manufactures, and an incipient consumer society.

The age which was inaugurated by the Civil War and which culminated in smoke-

Figure 9–6. One price of prosperity. These coke ovens, shown in a magazine illustration in 1887, were outside Birmingham, Alabama. In them coal was heated without sufficient oxygen to allow complete combustion of the coal. The heating fires produced quantities of smoke, soot, and ash, and the coking process itself also produced byproducts such as coal tar, which were discarded and which polluted the countryside and caused such high acidity in the soil as to make vegetation impossible. Courtesy Culver Pictures.

stacks and slums was marked by confusion and shifting values. The closed, certain ethics of the village began to be challenged by a new materialist "gospel of success," which placed material wealth above traditional social family and religious institutions. Powerful captains of industry like Carnegie and Rockefeller were emulated by young men on their way up the gilded ladder of success, and people came to expect to get or be gotten. The Republican Party responded to and represented this new breed of aggressive economic individualists, the so- called realists of the latter 1800s.

Commentators of the period lamented the new order; reformers campaigned for a return to the fraternity of village life. But the new industrial landscapes, the belching smokestacks, and the new slums inhabited by people who worked in steel mills turning out machines that would make consumer goods for subsequent generations, or who sweated in canneries or in plants producing tasteless food and standard-sized clothing for their own kind; the railroads on which Mencken could express his disgust at "the richest and grandest nation ever seen on earth": these forces of national economic interdependence, and profitability, wealth, and success would not so easily be contained by jeremiads from a nostalgic press or the pulpit. The "biological laws" of economic rationality explain, at least in part, the etiology of the madness about which Mr. Mencken complained.

References for Further Reading

Irwin Unger's *The Greenback Era* (1968) is a scholarly, readable social and political history of American finance, 1865-79. Those books on the public domain cited in a previous chapter also cover the period after the Civil War. Andrew Carnegie's life and corporation is fully documented in the two-volume work by Burton J. Hendrick, *The Life of Andrew Carnegie* (1932). Other important books on early business magnates and their practices are *Pioneering in Big Business* by Ralph W. Hidy and Muriel E. Hidy (1955) and Allan Nevins' extensive *Study in Power, John D. Rockefeller, Industrialist and Philanthropist* (1953). Of course, Ida M. Tarbell's contemporary account of the *History of the Standard Oil Company* (1969), originally published in *McClure's*, not only tells the seamy side of the Standard story but also is a model of investigative reporting by America's first muckraking journalist. *Stories of the Great Railroads* by Charles Edward Russell (1912) contains even more seamy dealings by three of the large railroads after the Civil War. The importance of the railroad's role as the primary promoter of economic changes is explored in depth in Alfred D. Chandler's classic study *The Railroads: The Nation's First Big Business* (1965). An important book which helps in an understanding of the role of technological development in the nineteenth century is W. Paul Strassmann's *Risk and Technological Innovation: American Manufacturing Methods in the Nineteenth Century* (1959).

Chapter 10

FARMERS AND CATTLEMEN

One striking disadvantage of the market system is its volatility. One year prices are high for particular goods, bringing to it large investments or transfers of money, labor and natural resources. Just as quickly it is possible for overproduction or unforeseen events like droughts, war, or dramatic changes in political policy to cause prices to fall and to occasion depressions. The tendency toward the development of monopolies or oligopolies is one result of this insecurity of the marketplace. Yet not even the greatest of industries is immune to market aberration or political foibles, as occurred in the 1860s when the South was specializing in King Cotton to the exclusion of subsistence crops.

The Southern Farmer

Although large plantations and small farms of the South continued to grow limited stands of corn and to raise hogs in the 1850s, they preferred to import most of their corn and pork as well as flour, beef, apples, butter, and cheese from the upper Mississippi Valley because growing cotton on their lands was more profitable than raising subsistence crops. Many southern journals and apologists deplored their dependence on northern states for basic foods, but planters and farmers followed normal economic procedure when they tried to increase their personal gain.

After war broke out in 1861, however, the South found it difficult to feed itself, and some northwestern farming centers in Illinois, Iowa, and Wisconsin temporarily found themselves with a huge surplus of goods because of displaced markets. The South suffered severe shortages, the Northwest a severe depression. Nonetheless, many southern planters refused to switch any of their lands over to subsistence crops because the price of cotton remained high and they were certain that the North would be quickly disposed of. In a short time the Confederacy was seriously threatened with famine.

Food scarcity in the South brought on highly inflated prices, food riots, and class strife between the aristocratic leadership and the rest of southern society. Bread rioting spread as fast as the inflation itself, with as many as 2,000 to 3,000 people raiding food and clothing wholesale and retail stores or quartermaster depots. Flour went from $20 to $250 a barrel in a little over a year; milk sold for $40 a quart in Atlanta, eggs $6 a dozen in Richmond. Hoarding and the extortion of high prices was commonplace. Confederate money became virtually worthless, specie unavailable.

Southern leaders tried to solve these problems by regulating the price of grain, vegetables, bacon, forage, horses, hay, molasses, and whiskey, and by impressing articles and goods needed for the Confederate Army. Although price control was badly needed in the South, regulated and non-regulated items continued to be sold on the open market for much higher prices. If a farmer strictly obeyed the law, he would never make enough to pay his own bills. Where the law was enforced, he hid his crops, mules and horses. The high death rate of Army animals brought a high rate of conscription from farms, already curtailed in their ability to support themselves since the Army took all able-bodied men between the ages of 17 and 50.

Civil chaos increased in proportion to shortages, pillaging, and looting. The scarcity of food became a major reason for the defeat of the South. Neither was there much cotton to show for the earlier choice of the planters. It had either been burned, or it rotted in hidden storage areas, or it was riddled with cannon shot on the southern lines of defense. The more compromising planters sold their crop to northern invaders who shipped it to New England for processing.

After the war, the southern people and their institutions were in near-ruin. Droughts in 1865 and 1867 impeded efforts by farmers with small acreages to restore southern agriculture. To the dismay of northern radicals, large estates and plantations were not broken up and distributed to slaves and poor whites, but rather most large land areas changed hands intact or stayed in the same hands with the addition of one or more partners. Some planters sold their second or third plantations to pay mortgages or taxes on their first. Although the number of farms in the South increased after the Civil War, so did tenancy and sharecropping, which was the condition of most freed blacks and poor whites.

The Sharecropping System

It is not surprising that the landowners remained in control of southern society after the war, but they were left with the major problem of how to replace slavery most profitably. Immediately after the war Black Codes allowed the marshalls of some states to convict unemployed blacks and have them sentenced to a year or more of work on the roads or plantations. These laws pushed many blacks and poor whites into accepting subsistence wages as laborers on plantations.

Simultaneously the sharecropping system was devised. The owner hired the share-cropper, with his family, before the spring planting to grow cotton, tobacco, or other cash crops on a specified number of acres according to the size of his family. In most instances, he was forbidden to plant his own garden since his sole preoccupation was to be directed to the cash crop. Furthermore, the owner sold groceries to the family. The landlord collected two-thirds of the crop at the end of the growing season, one third for land and a third for equipment and seed. The cropper received the final third to sell for his own needs. It was sharecropping, then, which solved the labor problem for the landowner in the predominantly agricultural southern society after the war.

The advantage of the arrangement for the owner or planter was the low-cost labor it provided, particularly since he could deduct store expenses from the cropper's share and end up with the entire crop as well as the cropper's indebtedness for the following season. Because sharecroppers had no legal right to occupy their shanties during the winter months, they suffered this additional insecurity, and rarely chanced incurring the owner's displeasure. Croppers usually just accepted the figures of the plantation bookkeeper, very often juggled to correspond with the harvest, and kept their mouths shut.

Although tenants enjoyed somewhat more freedom than sharecroppers, since they could choose to grow whatever crops they desired, even they were forced by circumstances to put in mostly cash crops in order to pay for seeds, rent, and other necessities. Local merchants, often the landowners themselves, advanced cash or merchandise in return for a lien on the farmer's entire crop. If the farmer did not grow enough cash crops, he would find his subsistence crops taken with the cash crops in payment for his bills. The prices of all farm goods dropped after the war, and the cost of everything else soared, especially in the South, entrapping both cropper and tenant in perpetual indebtedness. They were forced year after year to grow as much cotton as possible with neither the time nor the money or interest to restore the soil. Within a generation, most of the lands had been so depleted of their nutrients that they were abandoned, compelling the tillers to find other fields to work as a cropper or tenant. By 1900, over 1,000,000 poor whites and blacks worked in that capacity south of the Potomac and Ohio Rivers and in Texas. The gang labor of the plantation system had been replaced by tenancy and sharecropping, with the merchant or the landowner taking the role of the plantation master. And the isolated sharecropper lost the advantages of community support in the compact quarters of the former plantation.

The Prairie Farmer

Tenancy also became rather common in the prairie and plains states toward the end of the century, though the problem was not so chronic as in the South, nor were the reasons for its spread the same. The Homestead Act and the rich black soil between the 96th and the 100th meridian should have precluded this development in the Northwest.

Yet other geographical, economic, and political factors militated against the prairie farmer. The soil was excellent, probably the best in the country, but the climate and weather on the western prairies and plains were particularly fickle during the last half of the century. Summers were long and blazing hot, ending with a scalding wind, prairie fires and dust storms. Strong blizzards often came with winter, floods with spring. In the early days of settlement, stampeding buffalo herds were more of a problem than the Indians. After the plow broke the plains, heavy winds could quickly blow a farmer's black topsoil into the neighboring county and bank it around his sod house for good measure. Then in the 1870s, tens of millions of grasshoppers descended from the northern plains, riding the winds, and cleared the fields of their maturing crops. They even ate tree bark and wooden farm gear. A few exceptionally dry years could finally wipe out the savings of a decade.

Figure 10–1. An Iowa sod house. Long strips of tough sod were plowed up and cut into bricks of turf, which were laid upon each other for the walls. The owners of this sod house equipped their home with windows and supported its roof sods with sawed roof planks. Such features were signs of prosperity and elegance. Courtesy The Smithsonian Institution.

Even with these difficulties, prairie farmers could sell all the wheat and corn they could grow in the early sixties. In fact, farmers throughout the North did exceedingly well in the commercial arena from 1830 until the war ended, except for crop shortages in 1835 and 1837 and the depressions of 1837 and 1857. With the experience of such long-lived prosperity and the issuance of government greenbacks and easy credit, farmers did not hesitate to buy cultivators, mowers, and reapers and to work the fields with their wives and children while their sons were at war. Demand and profits were high, and farming had not yet passed the hundredth meridian.

However, the sudden disposal of millions of acres on the prairies and plains in the sixties, indeed the avid and widespread promotion of the lands by government agencies and land companies, pamphleteering throughout Europe, and the settlement of whole colonies of Irish, Scandinavians, Germans, and English and Scottish and Canadians all contributed to the rapid, unplanned expansion of commercial farming in the West. Before the end of the war two and a half million acres were added to the country's stock of cultivated farm land. After the war the land boom continued and millions of acres more were put under the plow. More farm machinery was bought to bring as many acres as possible under production.

By the end of the sixties the domestic agricultural market was glutted. Between 1867 and 1868 the price of corn went down from $.57 to $.32 per bushel, wheat from $1.45 to $.78. Fortunately, exports took up the slack for a few more years, even though the Suez Canal was opened in 1869 and railroads reached the Ukrainian wheat fields. Domestic surpluses did not slow down new farming activity or wheat production: From 1866 to 1880, 23,000,000 additional acres were cultivated, increasing the annual yield from 152,000,000 to 499,000,000 bushels of wheat. Exports increased until 1885, when foreign competition and overproduction pushed prices down.

New Farm Technology

In large measure the reason for the growth of production lay not only in additional cultivated acreages but also in continual improvement of farm technology. James Oliver perfected the design of a chilled-iron plow, which was able to scour the sticky prairie sod and was less expensive than cast steel. During the 1870s, he manufactured about 60,000 of them a year. He simply utilized an older method of placing iron or steel faces over sand-molds, a technique which provided density and hardness; but Oliver solved the older problem of brittle castings by circulating hot water through the chills and by reheating the finished cast plow. At the same time, seats were placed on the backs of plows, which were then called sulky or riding plows. Farmers could adjust them with levers according to the desired cutting depth. This was another innovation which speeded up the plowing of additional acreage. By 1870, dozens of models of the sulky plow appeared on the market and tens of thousands of them were sold each year. The spring-tooth harrow, patented in 1877, became nearly as popular because of its spring device, which allowed teeth to dislodge rather than to catch on rocks and roots. Disc harrows were also developed and used widely during the period.

Because of steadily increasing livestock and horse populations both in rural and urban areas, the growing of hay assumed greater importance. Mowing machines and spring-tooth rakes which tripped when full became necessary to speed up haying operations. Mechanical loaders for wagons, harpoon forks to lift hay into barn lofts, forked tedders to turn hay for curing in the fields, and baling presses came into frequent use after the Civil War.

Harvesting became even more efficient during the generation, though reapers solved basic problems a generation earlier. The Marsh Brothers harvester enabled two men on a platform behind the reel to bind grain as it was cut. Because of the thousands of harvesters operating during the war, shorthanded farm families were able to meet the needs of northern armies and cities. One hundred thousand Marsh harvesters were sold by 1879. In the same year, the twine self-binder proved itself on a Marsh harvester. It was a device that eliminated the necessity for two men per machine during harvesting. In the early eighties, the twine binder added to the impetus of expansion of wheat production in prairie regions and California. The number of harvesting machines on farms from 1880 to 1885 increased from 60,000 to 250,000.

California grain farmers rode behind headers which cut off only the heads of the grain and which deposited them loose on a conveyor belt leading to a wagon, which was unloaded when full. Crews then came by with portable threshing equipment and separated the grain from the chaff. In 1880, the two operations of harvesting and threshing were put together in the California combine. While the colorfully-decorated machine was pulled by horses or propelled by steam engines, 50- to 80-foot headers

Figure 10–2. Farming implements in the 1860s. As plowing techniques and efficient gang-plows, pulled by teams or even later by steam engines, made it possible for farmers to cultivate larger and larger areas, other equipment was needed to permit large-scale farming. The disc harrow was another such invention. The corn planter allowed the farmer to place corn seeds so that the rows of plants were evenly spaced on a grid. As the plants grew, the farmer could then cross-cultivate the fields with horse-drawn cultivators, killing off the weeds that competed with the corn. The operator inserted seeds at the intersections of the grid lines. Harvesting grain remained a painfully slow task accomplished by cradles well into the 1860s, but gradually reapers began to replace hand labor. The first harvesters required an extra hand to rake the cut grain from the platform.

The McCormick "Old Reliable" Automatic Self-Rake Reaper of 1867, shown here in an International Harvester Company photo, swept the cut grain aside, thus freeing a hand to help with binding the shocks of cut grain. Still to come was the twine binder, an astonishing device that gathered the shock together on the platform and then—without intervention by human hands—tied the shock with a length of twine and kicked it free. That device released as many as five workers to take up the threshing tasks. Power for threshing was provided by two kinds of steam-power sources, which gradually replaced horse-powered threshing machines. The "Eclipse" portable engine, in use since the 1850s, was pulled from place to place by horses. Courtesy The Smithsonian Institution.

lopped off tops into a thresher which squeezed grain into bags and threw straw out the rear. One firm, the Stockton Works, claimed that 280 of their "Hausers" cut and threshed 300,000 acres of wheat in 1886.

During the seventies and early eighties the new equipment inspired owners of great estates in the midwest to bring thousands of acres under cultivation in single operations called "bonanza farms." Landowners controlling thousands of acres, often with tenants, were frequently found in the country from its beginnings, but only when the technology and free labor were available could these estates be farmed as single units. The development of superfarms started in Illinois after the war, but did not become systematized until the late seventies when land was exchanged for

worthless railroad securities in the Red River Valley of the Dakota Territory. Oliver Dalrymple managed the first experiments of about 100,000 acres for the Northern Pacific Railroad. The Grandin brothers of Tidioute, Pennsylvania, put 61,100 acres of the land they received for their railroad securities into wheat. Other bonanza farms ranged from 17,000 to 40,000 acres, and smaller farms imitated the methods of the bonanza farms.

The huge pieces of land were broken into distinct units, each with its own farm buildings, boarding houses for up to 1,000 migratory laborers, and stables for horses which pulled the farm machinery. The arrangement was designed to keep the farm workers close to their work. Practically all the superfarms were supervised by professional managers like Dalrymple and owned by business interests from the East, since the capital investment of a bonanza farm was immense.

Double-plow sulkies pulled by four horses turned the soil. Spring or disc harrows preceded and followed the seeding machines. Harvesters and binders cleared the fields, then steam threshers took over. Bonanza farms used up to a hundred sulky plows, 200 harrows and 100 seeders, perhaps 150 harvesters, and twenty to fifty steam-powered threshers along with 800 horses and mules. The migrants who worked the farms started with the harvests in Kansas and worked northward, usually for about fifteen hours a day, sunup to sundown for room and board and about $18 a month. Twice as many men were needed for harvesting as for plowing and seeding. Besides wheat, feed crops of oats and barley were sowed. A few bonanza farms turned out over 600,000 bushels of wheat a year. After 1885, when prices dropped, bonanza farms found it difficult to pay taxes. Most of them slowly were broken up and rented as small tenant holdings.

Financial Problems of the Farm

Farm machinery developed after the Civil War and increased acreages under cultivation saturated the grain market by 1880, but the prairie farmers' woes began much earlier with deflation, credit problems and railroad monopolies. In fact, these earlier difficulties were the compelling forces of increasing production, since the farmer had to produce more crops to stay even financially. If he lost his mortgage he still tried to hold on to his equipment so that as a tenant he still might have a chance to buy back his farm.

But it was no easier to turn a profit as a tenant than as an owner. World prices for farm products declined steadily from 1870 to 1897 as new sources of food in

Figure 10–3. Large-scale farming of the 1880s. By the 1880s, horse- or mule-drawn combines enabled farmers to combine reaping and threshing in one piece of equipment. Most midwestern combines, like the two mule-drawn rigs shown working a Kansas wheat field, had 18-foot cutter bars and 20 horses or mules pulling the mechanism. The combine itself powered the cutting bar from one ground wheel and the threshing machinery from a second wheel. The driver sat on an elevated platform, and four men rode the rig to toss the sacked grain into wagons coming alongside. Such combines could harvest about 40 acres a day, but the California steam combines could double that amount by the 1890s with their 52-foot cutter bars. The giant steam combines and their crews could turn out as many as 1,800 sacks of grain a day. Mule combine photo courtesy The Smithsonian Institution; steam combine photo courtesy The Bancroft Library.

Algeria, Argentina, Australia, Canada, India, Mexico, and Russia were opened up by a revolution in transportation. While the farmer's goods were bringing in less money, prices for other goods, set more and more by trusts and monopolies, were rising.

The beginning of the farmer's heavy investment in land and equipment occurred during the war with the issuance of greenbacks. Because of the sudden increase of money in circulation, inflation accompanied the greenback, but credit was easy and demand high so that even large debts could be paid off. All farmers shared the expectation that their goods could be sold indefinitely since railroads were taking their goods to new eastern and western markets. After the war, however, much northern capital went south for investment, and the U.S. money supply declined, beginning a deflationary trend. Money—even greenbacks—became harder to obtain. The value of the greenback increased to closer parity with gold. Since the farmer incurred his debts when the greenback was worth less and had to pay back the same amount of dollars even though they were worth more, he had to produce more wheat to make up the difference in money value. Thousands of farmers attempted to solve the problem in the same way, and the collective overproduction caused the prices of farm goods to drop progressively lower.

The businessmen or military contractors in the East who had managed to garner large quantities of greenbacks were happy to see greenbacks rise in value. In fact, these and other hard money interests lobbied to have Congress retire greenbacks at par with gold. In response to this group, Congress passed the Specie-Resumption Act of 1875, which purposed to reduce the number of greenbacks in circulation by buying them back at par value. The Act cemented prices at their deflated gold value, a financially catastrophic policy for debt-ridden farmers. The Resumption Act came on the heels of the demonetization of silver in 1873, which limited the amount of silver in circulation, also tending to deflate currency. Until this time, silver mines were allowed to have as much "free silver" coined into money as they wished.

The farmers and their Congressional representatives raised a storm over these measures, bringing about new measures in 1876 and 1890 to allow the Secretary of the Treasury to purchase increased amounts of silver, and in 1878 the Resumption Act was repealed. By this time, however, almost half the total value of greenbacks in circulation had been retired. Money was tight and interest high, especially for the troubled farmers.

Transportation provided another kind of difficulty for prairie farmers. Only farmers with substantial capital to invest could afford to buy land near railroads. Most of them suffered the same transportation liabilities as did early eastern farmers, but without the advantage of an abundance of streams and rivers. (Roads remained a problem throughout the United States until well into the twentieth century.) Railroads were to have solved the farmers' transportation needs, and many farmers invested their life savings and the extra profits of the war years into railroad stocks and bonds. As was already pointed out, most railroads so watered down their stocks that the farmer's investment passed directly into the pockets of construction company executives and rarely were proportionate dividends paid. Occasionally construction was never begun on funded railroads, nor were bond investments refunded.

Railroad companies gave rebates to bonanza farms or large shippers to the East, and they charged inflated rates to farmers who shipped limited quantities of produce over short distances. Since the railroad companies built elevators near their depots, they were able to control marketing arrangements and prices offered to the producer. Wheat growers had few alternatives. If they did not sell to the railroad elevators, their wheat could spoil during delays often imposed on non-railroad-owned wheat. Farmers usually needed a quick sale to pay debts, and they could not wait for the grain to be sold at the central markets where prices were better. Whether or not they stored their wheat at the privately-owned elevators, they still had to pay an elevator toll in order to ship out grain. Elevator operators also tended to underrate the quality of the farmer's wheat, bringing down the price even more.

Farmers' Movements

In order to protect themselves against declining prices, farmers continued to over-produce. They also began to get together in social clubs to talk over their problems. Out of these clubs came the Patrons of Husbandry, popularly known as the Grange, in 1867. Although its constitution prohibited political activity, Grange meetings frequently turned into political strategy sessions concerning railroad battles, bankers who charged excessive interest or who foreclosed on their neighbors, elevator operators, farm equipment companies, and merchants or middlemen who bought and sold products directly to them.

Hundreds of local Granges in farm states around the country met the sorely-felt needs of farmers in the seventies. By 1875, Grange members numbered over 850,000, with the largest numbers in prairie states. Their major political focus centered on the realization of cheap transportation and cheap money. Granger literature abounded with attacks on railroad tycoons who had gotten rich from "people's land" and "people's money" given away by the government, and bemoaning the fact that the railroads had never reciprocated with equitable rates for the people. The silver law was denounced as the Crime of 1873 because of its deflationary effect. Railroad domination and extortion were targeted as a primary concern as early as 1868 by the Minnesota State Grange, and they remained so for the prairie chapters for at least the following decade.

In the 1870s, Grangers tried to solve their economic problems by cooperative buying and selling. District Granges pooled orders of supplies and staples, and contracted with jobbers or manufacturers for substantial discounts; hundreds of cooperative stores came out of these efforts. At the same time, many Granges contacted foreign ports for collective selling of livestock, cotton and grain. They even attempted to break up the "Harvester Ring," the "Plow Ring" and other "monopolies" by manufacturing their own farm machinery—headers, harvesters, threshing machines, and general farm implements. Grist mills and factories making cheese and butter, linseed oil, starch and hemp were not uncommon Granger projects. A few Granges established their own banks, and all state chapters set up fire insurance companies.

Unfortunately, root economic problems—overproduction, money and credit, railroad power—were not abated by the Granger cooperatives. Lack of business knowledge, capital, and cooperative experience along with the precipitously rapid growth of the ventures led to their equally rapid collapse. The farmers conjured up unrealistic expectations of the possible benefits of their projects, which provoked disloyalty and cynicism when the cooperatives suffered setbacks. Much good was done by the cooperatives for individual farmers, but long-term solutions could not be effected. Agriculture was locked into a larger marketplace—a function of political economy which foiled the Grangers' best efforts.

Through state and local farmers' clubs, Grangers were simultaneously looking for political solutions. Since many judges and politicians overtly or covertly worked for the railroads, farmers' associations nominated and elected their own candidates. In some states, they agitated for and won some railroad regulation of fares, freight rates, and warehouse fees, and in a few instances had state warehouse boards appointed. When railroads managed to find loopholes in the laws or when judges interpreted them contrary to their intent, farmers organized themselves with even greater determination, wrote tracts and books, and called state-wide action conferences.

A number of independent, anti-monopoly and reform parties were organized during the 1870s as a result of the political activities of the farmers. Platforms and declarations were drawn up by their organizations, and candidates espousing their principles were called Grange candidates. Sometimes third parties took their platforms to the Democratic party, eager for victory during those Republican years. In either case, Independent and Anti-Monopolist parties assumed greater importance in the West until the mid-1870s when the Greenback Party was formed.

The Greenback Party represented a popular response to difficult times. As general purchasing power declined (especially among farmers) at the end of the sixties and early seventies because of deflation, tight credit, and the curtailment of silver minting (the Crime of 1873), a depression came upon the entire country. In 1873 the first large scale foreclosures on farms occurred; many small businesses went bankrupt, and even railroad income dropped. The Act which demonetized silver signaled the rise of the Greenback Party, which demanded an increase in the amount of government Greenbacks. The furor over the Specie-Resumption Act of 1875 provided the Party with added impetus and strength, especially in agrarian regions. Throughout the seventies Greenback Party candidates were elected on local, state and national levels of government and issued the clarion call, "The right to make and issue money is a sovereign power, to be maintained by the people for the common benefit, not for monopolies and international syndicates which force government policies of dear money, cheap labor, and weak people."

The Party nominated General Weaver for President in 1880, and although he received only 308,500 votes, he waged a strong national populist campaign as he spread the greenback doctrine to every region of the country. In 1892, he was renominated by the Populist Party, a creation of the Farmer's Alliance, a conglomeration of a variety of farmers' organizations and clubs.

The first group of Alliances was formed in the mid-1870s in Texas for the purpose of catching horse thieves, finding strays, buying collectively, and opposing monopolist cattlemen. The Alliance stressed rituals, regalia, creed, and degrees more than politics for a decade. Then in the late 1880s, it took over the leadership of the farmer's movement. The Arkansas group began as a debating society; Louisiana's as a discussion group, until the groups from three states joined forces for political purposes late in the 1880s. At that time prices for agricultural goods were hitting new lows. Greater num-

Figure 10–4. "The Grange Awakening the Sleepers." This 1873 political cartoon shows a farmer, his hatband bearing the legend "Grange," sounding the alarm to ordinary citizens of the West, including local merchants and townspeople. The "Consolidation Train" bearing down on the unsuspecting citizens brings cars bearing "Food Monopoly," "Fuel Monopoly," "Oppression," and other unpleasant burdens. But the sleepers ignore the farmer's warning. The log ties upon which rails were laid were called "sleepers," a fact the cartoonist turned to his advantage. Courtesy Culver Pictures.

bers of farms—11,000 in Kansas alone between 1889 and 1893—were lost to mortgage companies, and interest rates soared along with the prices of everything except farm products. By the beginning of the 1890s Farm Alliances were found everywhere, very often as the successors of old Grange groups. State Alliances put up their candidates once again; they even met nationally on their common problems, and in 1892, they organized the Populist Party to make another bid for the Presidency.

The Populists ran on a platform of free coinage of silver; a graduated income tax; government ownership of railroads, telephone and telegraph; return of lands held by railroads; an eight-hour working day; tariff revision; popular election of senators; prohibition of alien ownership of land; abolition of contract labor; and the establishment of postal savings banks. The Populist ticket polled more than 1,000,000 votes, and many Populist candidates won local and state elections in 1892 and 1894. By 1896, the Populists merged with the Democrats and nominated William Jennings Bryan, who ran a hard campaign but was not identified solely with farmers' issues. William McKinley, his Republican opponent, won by only a half-million popular and 95 electoral votes. It was the high point of Populist politics.

By 1897, the effects of the Panic of 1893 had dissolved for business, and credit opened up again for farmers at lower interest rates. The prices for farm products started to rise and debts could be paid off once again. The world's supply of money was rapidly expanded, bringing the illusion of prosperity once more. These events—especially the rise in prices for farm crops—brought a return to traditional two-party politics. But the farmer's troubles were far from over.

Cattlemen

From the beginning of eastern colonization in America, cattle drovers stayed just ahead of the farmer on the American frontier. Long before Independence, colonies from the South and up as far as New York and on a smaller scale in New England, raised, branded and drove cattle to coastal towns. When the frontier was extended inland by the middle of the 1800s, millions of cattle were raised and driven for hundreds of miles through, over and around the Appalachian barricade from most frontier states including Ohio, Indiana, Kentucky, Florida, Alabama and Louisiana.

In 1860, the cattle frontier reached western Minnesota, Iowa, Missouri and into the Great Plains beyond. But it was Texas with its own separate cattle history and political history that endowed the cattle industry with its renowned characteristics. For Americans, cattle-raising has become associated with cowboys on horseback, dressed in chaps, six-shooter and wide-brimmed hat; corrals and western-style round-ups, and 1500-mile cattle drives over semi-arid deserts through Indian country. The solitary eastern drovers of cattle, sheep and hogs have become lost in history. It should be noted, though, that the trappings of the Texas cowboy were not designed so much for Hollywood as for the rigors of the West. Without horses and six-shooters, the cowboys could neither control the cattle nor intimidate Indians; without a sombrero-size hat and chaps they could withstand neither the sun nor the underbrush.

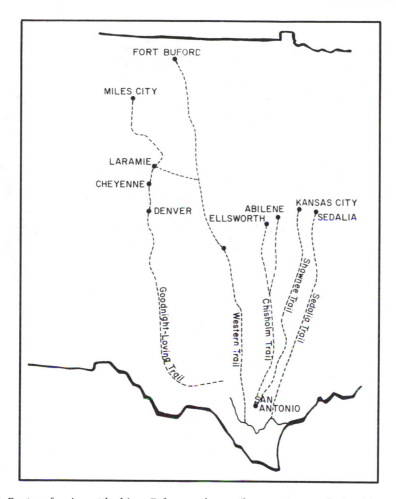

Figure 10–5. Routes of major cattle drives. Before southern rail connections made the drives unnecessary, huge herds of Texas cattle were driven north to established railheads. This map shows the major routes, the names of which still evoke the romance of the western cowboy.

The roots of both cowboy and range cattle go back to the wild and wiry Andalusian longhorns which rumbled off the Spanish galleon that brought Cortez to Vera Cruz in 1521. Descendants of these and later arrivals were gradually taken north and west on perennial gold-seeking missions. After the Mexican and Texas Revolutions and finally the Civil War, several million longhorns, some of which had interbred with eastern stock of Texas immigrants, roamed in the expansive plains of San Antonio to the tip of Texas.

Before the Civil War, western cattle were raised more for their hides and tallow than their beef. It is true that attempts were made to market beef on a few long drives from Texas to Ohio, New York, California, and Illinois, but myriads of obstacles impeded further efforts. Even during the war, while Texans were fighting for the Confederacy, few southern markets could be found for Texas Longhorns, particularly after the Union army gained control of the Mississippi. While Texas cattle were multiplying during the war, stocks of cattle in the North were depleted and demand in northern cities was pushing up the price of beef. The coming of the railroads made new efforts to drive cattle north from Texas worthwhile, and economically-depressed Texans began to think about cashing in on their major resource.

In 1866, the first western cattle drives started in the direction of the railroads in eastern Kansas, but they were blocked on their way to Sedalia by determined Kansas Jayhawkers who feared that the Longhorns would spread disease to their own livestock as had happened earlier. Soon afterward, entrepreneur Joseph G. McCoy created the first cow town of the West in Abilene, Kansas, where cattlemen could meet buyers and where railroad transportation to Kansas City was available. In a few months the first herds skirted Kansas farms and filed into Abilene's newly constructed stockyards, pens and loading chutes. Within a few years other cow towns, continually pushed west by homesteaders on the agricultural frontier, were built to accommodate the increasing number of herds and restless cowboys: Wichita, Newton, Ellsworth, Junction City, Caldwell, and the infamous Dodge City, all allegedly lawless and wicked, where socially undesirable elements of society devised unsubtle ways to capture the cowboy's yearly earnings. As they continued their western expansion, the Santa Fe, Kansas, Pacific, Union Pacific and other railroads met the herds.

Before long, established trails were trampled to the cow towns, the first one to Abilene holding a fairly straight line from southern Texas past Austin and Fort Worth, across the Red River into Indian Territory, then into Kansas. Later trails, each more westward than the previous ones, were added as settlement closed earlier paths; now came the Shawnee, Chisholm, and Dodge City Western Trail. The Goodnight Trail went from western Texas through New Mexico into Colorado, Wyoming, and Nebraska; this trail served local forts, communities, and reservations rather than external markets via the railroad. The northward drives also stocked ranches on the open range in Kansas, Colorado, Nebraska, Wyoming, the Dakotas and Montana.

Trail Driving Days

The first step of the drive north was the roundup, held in the spring and the fall when calves were branded and the herd of mature longhorns "cut out" to take to market. Cattle ran loose on the open range in those early days of cattle-raising, making roundups cooperative ventures, each owner participating with men according to the size of his holdings. In a large district of several thousand miles, two or three hundred men with a few thousand horses would gather together and work in teams scouring the range. One by one each range was combed for cattle until the entire district was covered, the men all the while separating cattle into herds of different owners and branding calves with the mother cow's brand. By the end of the exercise, the spectacular numbers of cattle, men and horses and consequent confusion and bedlam frayed the nerves of animals and humans alike.

Steers marked for eventual slaughter and calves were cut out of the herds by the best of the riders and horses, which had to know how to ease a calf or steer away from mother or herd, come to a dead stop or turn, twist, or hold while a calf was roped. After a calf was roped, it was dragged to a nearby corral fire where two cowboys held its feet on opposite sides while a third branded its hide.

Before the drive, enough horses had to be rounded up and broken to saddle and bridle, and preparations for the three- to four-month journey had to be made. Every cowboy needed six to ten horses for various purposes—cutting out, range and trail riding, night herding, and change mounts. The canvas-covered chuck wagon was filled with food, bedding, and camping gear: Supplies of flour, beans, coffee, sugar, salt, syrup, bacon, dried fruit, rice, soda, and condiments were packed in with a ten-gallon water keg, pots, pans, and a spade. Beef, of course, supplemented the regular fare.

About 3,000 head of cattle made up the usual herd, maneuvered by 16 to 18 cowboys, a cook and a teenage horse wrangler who handled spare horses (known as the *remuda*). Texas cattle were a multi-colored, striped and patched lot, and their lean frames were easily distinguishable from fattened eastern stock. The trail boss usually selected a large, outstanding steer to lead the herd, which fell behind it in an ever-widening column. The boss always rode a few miles ahead to find watering stops and campsites. Next followed the cook and the horse wrangler with his remuda. Finally came the herd, surrounded by riders, the youngest of whom trailed the herd, eating dust and gathering strays.

In the morning the cattle were moved out gradually as they grazed. From ten to fifteen miles could be made each day, but thunderstorms, swollen rivers, or nervous cattle could lengthen the trip by a month or two. Stampedes were sparked by any sudden noise, a clap of thunder or bolt of lightning, or perhaps by Indians dissatisfied with the number of steers paid as toll for crossing their land. Trouble also came from cattle thieves who could pick up lost, stampeded cattle. Cowboys standing watch at night sang low, mournful songs to calm fidgety critters, and mounts were always placed near sleeping cowboys in case of a stampede during the night. In such cases, the cowboys raced to the head of the stampede firing revolvers to attempt to turn the leaders so they could circle the mass of cattle.

When the group reached the cow town, the herd would be kept outside to graze while the boss made arrangements with a broker or a railroad for shipping. Sometimes young steers were driven to Kansas and sold to owners of ranches there or in Wyoming, Montana, or Dakota to stock the growing number of ranges of the North. If so, the young steers would continue their journey for another three to five hundred miles, often with the same group of cowboys. After all the business was completed, the crew enjoyed their annual riotous fling in town before returning to Texas. For twenty years cattle were driven north—probably over 5,000,000 of them—into Kansas and the northern plains. Cowboy institutions like the horse-ropings and cattle-brandings of the roundup reached this fullest development on the ranches of the central and northern Great Plains in the 1870s and 1880s.

Indians and Buffalo

During this generation the two major obstacles of the cattle empire's invasion of the north—hostile Indians and grass-eating buffalo—were removed. Forts had been established in Indian country for almost a half-century for purposes of trading and protection of trappers, travellers and miners. New priorities of the Civil War resulted in the military abandonment of most of them, but western settlers and politicians demanded their return after the war.

When the U.S. Army moved west after the war, it carried a new Indian policy to enforce. The federal government decided that those Indians who did not have definite limits on their lands were to be put on clearly-defined reservations and forbidden to hunt outside those limits. Washington's new decree brought on the Plains Indians' last struggle with the Cavalry, but within a few years the chiefs of practically all of the tribes agreed to settle on government reservations.

Because they supported and fought for the South during the war, the Five Civilized Tribes, originally from the Southeast, were required during the resettlement period to give up the western half of the Oklahoma Territory to the Kiowas, Comanches, Cheyennes, Arapahoes, Osages, and other tribes. These tribes bargained for a toll of a certain number of cattle when drives passed over their lands from Texas. If a trail boss was overly generous, he ended up with a greatly reduced herd by the time he reached Kansas. Thus the trail bosses tended to be stingy with their cattle, and unhappy chiefs sometimes sent out their braves to stampede the cattle of an uncooperative boss.

Figure 10–6. Buffalo hunting with the Colt revolver. In the early stages of buffalo hunting, Indians attacked the animals from horseback, with arrows or lances, or they drove them into stampeding over river bluffs where the buffalo would fall to their deaths. The advent of the American frontiersman with a rapidly firing pistol or carbine made it possible to kill many more buffalo (and Indians). Before long, professional buffalo hunters, whether alone or escorting hunting parties, killed hundreds of the buffalo in a single day for their hides, tongues, or meat—or just for the pleasure of killing. Courtesy the Bettman Archive.

Other Indian reservations were set up in the Dakotas, Wyoming, Montana, and Colorado for the Sioux, Northern Cheyennes, Blackfeet and dozens more of the Plains' tribes. Western and Southwestern reservations included tribes in Arizona, New Mexico, Utah, Nevada and Idaho. Although cattlemen found large government markets on Indian reservations, there was rarely enough food to provide an adequate diet for the Indians. Therefore, Indians often set out to find buffalo meat for themselves, sometimes raiding the livestock of nearby settlements as well.

This possibility did not last long. The animal that had been the Indian source of food and clothing for centuries was on its way to extinction. At the end of the war, thousands of ex-military men went west to collect land bounties or make their fortunes prospecting or buffalo hunting. Before the mid-sixties, Indians and whites killed about 100,000 buffalo a year for food, clothing and sport. Afterward, world demand for buffalo robes and the discovery that their skins made excellent machine belting pushed up the price enough to bring professional hunters and brokers into the picture. The newly-built railroads offered cheap transportation to eastern markets. Many fur trappers, having cleared beaver from western streams, joined buffalo hunters to rid the plains of its buffalo for fun, profit and western cattle interests. By 1870, when the big hunt rolled into full swing, 4,000,000 buffalo remained south of the Platte River and another 6,500,000 north of it. In five years, the southern buffalo herds were decimated.

Some of the hunters like William F. Cody, "Buffalo Bill," worked for the railroad companies building track west. The Kansas Pacific, which was extending its lines to serve the cattle industry, paid Buffalo Bill $500 a month to provide meat for its railroad construction workers. In 17 months he killed 4,280 buffalo. Buffalo Bill used the efficient Springfield rifle he named "Lucretia Borgia." On horseback he simply ran the leaders of a buffalo herd into a circle, then shot those which came out. The slaughtered prey lay close together; they were easy to retrieve. Other hunters set their rifles on tripods near milling buffalo, and, careful not to stampede the herd, picked them off one by one.

Because of the new rapid-fire rifles, hunters could average almost 100 buffalo a day. In a hunting party, one or two shooters took a crew of buffalo skinners who "peeled" skins from the buffalo, and who later cleaned and pegged the skins to the ground to dry. Before the buffalo were exterminated, Dodge City, five miles west of Fort Dodge on the Santa Fe Trail, served as a buffalo hunters' outpost. Tom Nixon from Dodge City held the record of 120 buffalo killed at one stand in 40 minutes; he set another record of over 2,000 buffalo killed in a month. (Dodge was a ready-made cow town after the day of the buffalo because of its rich grazing lands nearby.)

The demise of the buffalo both opened up the central and northern plains for cattle ranching and also compelled the Indians to stay on their reservations. Tighter control of rations meant tighter control of Indian behavior. After the plains opened up and were safely secured, the cattle industry was certain to flourish.

Cattle Ranching in the Northern Plains

Between 1870 and 1880, the northern ranges filled with cattle: from 374,000 to 1,534,000 in Kansas; from 80,000 to 1,174,000 in Nebraska; and numbers similarly mounting in

Colorado, Montana, Wyoming, and Dakota. From the tip of Texas to the Canadian border, cattle became king. Millions of cattle fed on the Great Plains for 1,600 miles. Most of the herds remained on the public domain, although a great deal of land had passed into the hands of the railroad companies, which leased some of their land for grazing. Conflicts over free grass among cattlemen themselves, sheepherders, and farmers were inevitable.

Individual ranchers and entrepreneurs, large cattle companies, and syndicates began to look for land on the western plains during the latter half of the 1870s. "Cow custom" of the range gave first occupation rights of public land to first arrivals. Cattle companies financed by eastern and foreign capital pushed the frontier farther west to virgin pastures not far from the mountains. Ranchers always looked for a stream or river on which to set up their ranches and water their herds, which roamed as far away from the water as they found forage. Ranchers and their cowboys then applied for homesteading claims to hundreds of acres along the water. Near the assumed boundary of the ranch away from the water, cow hands constructed their own camp from which they could watch the herds.

In 1880, the beef industry reached the edge of prosperity, not only because of free grass on the open plains but also because of the advertising effects of Swift, Armour, and other meatpackers. Investments in new cattle companies poured in with assurances of high returns from rising prices and low overhead. All prospective investors wanted to get in before public land was completely occupied by competitive firms, which were rumored to have made quick fortunes. Before long the ranges were stocked with cattle, owned largely by cattle barons or huge syndicates. In 1882, cattle were being sold at $30 to $33 a head, up from $7 to $8 a head in 1878-79. The hike induced further investment.

The invention of barbed wire also influenced changes in the cattle industry during the period. After Joseph F. Glidden marketed his barbed wire in Texas in 1875 (it was invented a year earlier), it came into widespread use in a few years by both farmers and ranchers. Western farmers who had earlier simply shot cattle trespassing on their lands began to put up the wire to protect their crops; on the Great Plains, no trees were available for fencing or building. At the same time gigantic ranges, some thousands of square miles, on private land in Texas were fenced with barbed wire. Although fencing was forbidden on public lands, big cattle companies defied the law and fenced land which could not be cheaply engrossed by the Timber Culture or Desert Land Acts. In order to keep out newcomers, owners would invest $175 per

Figure 10–7. Two inventions that changed the West. Two keys to controlling this western semiarid grassland frontier were fencing and water supply. Although earlier patents for cattle-discouraging barbs on wire had been taken out as early as 1867, in 1874 the Illinois farmer-inventor Joseph Glidden developed a process for keeping the barbs in place. The barbed wire that resulted was used by western farmers to fence their property against the depredations of herds of cattle. In some places the cattlemen cut the fences as fast as the farmers could put them up, but the farmers eventually prevailed. By 1883 80,000,000 pounds of barbed wire were sold annually in the West to both farmers and cattlemen who needed it to fence in their huge ranches. The Aermotor steel backed-geared windmill was one solution to the water problem. Where prairie winds blew constantly, the windmill could be used to power pumps that brought up subsurface water for the cattle. By 1879 westerners paid more than a million dollars for Aermotor windmills alone. Courtesy The Smithsonian Institution.

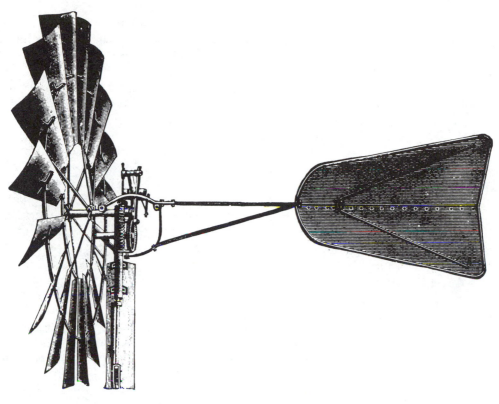

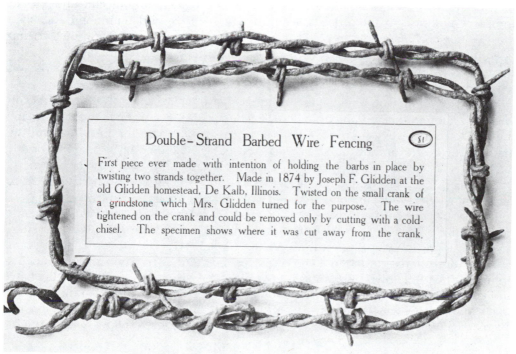

Double-Strand Barbed Wire Fencing   (81)

First piece ever made with intention of holding the barbs in place by twisting two strands together. Made in 1874 by Joseph F. Glidden at the old Glidden homestead, De Kalb, Illinois. Twisted on the small crank of a grindstone which Mrs. Glidden turned for the purpose. The wire tightened on the crank and could be removed only by cutting with a cold-chisel. The specimen shows where it was cut away from the crank.

mile to enclose the public land. Smaller ranchers organized themselves into "free land" fence-cutter groups to hold their stake on the open range. On the other hand, farmers lobbied for fence laws to require cattlemen to fence their property so that their crops would not be molested by cattle.

After the large ranches were fenced, windmills and tanks were installed to pump water for cattle on the far reaches of the range—a further investment of at least $1,500 per windmill watering about 400 head of cattle. Only well-financed ranchers could afford to build and maintain the required number of mills needed for a large ranch. The romance of cooperative roundups and long drives had passed. The cowboy's new duties dealt more with repairing fences and windmills or shooting coyotes and lobo wolves, even extending to the cultivating of corn and prairie hay for winter feed than activities like heading off a stampede. Cattlemen began to form associations to solve marketing problems, share breeding information, fight the power of the meatpacker monopoly, and deal with the problem of rustling. By 1885, bigtime ranching was the norm. Cattlemen's associations themselves held a firm grip on the economic and political power of the Great Plains states.

Also in 1885, big-time ranchers learned the meaning of overstocking and over-production. Prices dropped from $35 a head to $8-$10. Drought spread from Texas northward, leaving cattle without enough grass for food. Overgrazing placed an even heavier load on the limited amount of grass; what range was left was soon fenced and guarded. The final blow came with the blizzard of 1885-86, when frozen snow stopped cattle from getting to their winter grass. Millions of cattle died on the open range, and cattlemen decided that care would have to be extended to their herds during the winter months.

Through 1890, prices continued to drop for the cattlemen, but consumers paid the same amounts at the grocers. Swift, Armour, Morris, and Hammond stabilized meat prices and were able to reap huge profits from their packing and distribution operations. Since beef prices were so low, they had no need to raise cattle for themselves. They concentrated their efforts on obtaining rebates from railroads and advertising their products even more widely than earlier.

Those cattlemen who remained in business after the blizzard of 1886 had to reckon with new competition for land from homesteaders. Farmers and small ranchers (many of them former cowboys of the big cattle syndicates) moved onto public land, cut the cattle baron's wire, and put up their own, provoking the little range wars of Wyoming and Colorado. Small ranchers were accused of rustling the cattle of the large owners or syndicates. Cattle associations began to import gunmen or "range detectives" to ferret out rustlers, bringing on a new wave of violence up and down the ranges.

By the 1890s, free-range ranches passed out of existence, but the old-time cattle baron found a new source of wealth. As the railroad moved through his great estate, he sold out part of his pasture to prospective farmers who could, during good years, produce and market an abundance of wheat, hay and corn. Soon the big rancher enjoyed a bustling town on his former premises; he dispensed credit from his bank and goods from his stores. His cattle could be loaded directly onto the railroads and taken to Kansas City, Dallas, Omaha, Minneapolis, or Chicago. The weather on the plains remained unpredictable, however; good seasons were followed by drought, and bankrupt farmers would have to leave for the city to get jobs, or become tenants on the ranch property, or stay in town as wage-earners. The cattlemen's herds had long since been housed and fed during bad winters, so that blizzards did not wreak their former havoc.

Overgrazing

The vagaries of the weather; the open vulnerability of the public domain to a multitude of fortune-seekers when prices were high; and other economic irrationality all subjected the rich lands of the dry western states to continued overgrazing during the last quarter of the 1800s and the early 1900s.

Moderate grazing is healthy for perennial grasses and clovers, since centuries of grazing by wildlife have conditioned them to be stimulated to healthier growth when cut back by grazing. But moderate grazing was not practiced in the West. Perennial grasses, which normally continue to grow back year after year, were killed by overgrazing and were replaced by tougher but less nutritious annual grasses, which die and return from their seeds. In many areas of the West even the annuals were killed by further grazing pressure, and the land passed into bare and erodible deserts characterized only by clumps of sage-brush and other uneatable weeds.

When perennials and even less nutritious plants are lost, more land is needed for each animal to get an adequate amount of nourishment to live. On perennial grasses, a cow needs only about two acres; on annuals she needs at least five to ten acres, depending on the amount of perennials living among the annuals. Desert supports no cows. Thus, when too many cattle overgraze an area, it will support fewer and fewer animals. But the numbers do not shrink; instead the remaining cattle fight to survive on what is left as perennials, then annuals are killed off in the vicious cycle. In this manner was much of the rich western perennial grass lost and its soil eventually subjected to the violent winds that blew it away.

Sheepherders

The sheep industry on the western plains, particularly in the large herding areas of Wyoming, Montana and Colorado, shared some common origins with the cattle industry, in the sense that the first sheep came over with the Spaniards and were trailed a thousand or more miles from California, Oregon and New Mexico. (Before their sheep drives east to the markets and railroads after 1850, herders followed trails south into Mexico.) These drives, no less romantic than cattle drives from Texas, suffered the same hardships, stampedes, desert dust, swollen rivers and unfriendly Indians, farmers, and cattlemen. As the cattlemen, prosperity and adversity followed sheepmen, who tried to cover their losses by seeking corresponding benefits. Between 1865 and 1900 at least 15,000,000 sheep were trailed east to meet the railroads.

As to the cattlemen, the benefits to the sheepherder came from the free grass of the public domain. Sheepherders followed the practice of hiring dummy homestead entrymen in order to control water supplies of a range. But unlike the early cattlemen, sheepherders stored feed for winter use. Although sheepherders very often reached the public land before cattlemen, cattlemen refused to recognize their right to stay there. Between the halves of the sheep's hoof, they said, a gland secreted a foul-smelling fluid that poisoned the range; cattle would not graze on land occupied by sheep, they claimed. Therefore fighting broke out, most often in Wyoming and Colorado, over rights of access to the public land, which was becoming ever more scarce as the years passed. Of course neither had legal rights to the public domain, so cattlemen tried to intimidate sheepherders, mostly by stampeding or killing the sheep of their rivals, and thousands of the herders were killed or injured in the process.

As the cattle business became more of a risk and the prices of wool went up, cattlemen took to raising sheep themselves, and the same people who protested the presence of sheep earlier watered and fed cattle and sheep on the same range. Cattlemen also found that sheep were more hardy than cattle during cold winters, could reach grass on ranges higher than cattle could climb, and could chew grass left by cattle. Sheep were a good investment for them. The wool industry was not monopolized, and prices returned to normal after depressions, making sheepherding an especially good hedge against the practices of the meatpackers. Wool dealers sent representatives directly to the ranges during shearing season and bought from the owners or nearby merchants. Prices depended on supply and demand.

Yet sheepherding had its own cycle and never could be completely integrated with cattle raising. Special care had to be given to ewes and lambs during lambing season so that the lamb did not move too far away from its nearsighted mother; otherwise the ewe would not recognize its offspring and would refuse to feed it. From spring until fall, a herdsman took a few thousand sheep to mountain pastures to grow and be fattened, first on lower ranges, then to higher elevations. Owners usually provided their herders with covered sheep wagons in which they slept, cooked, and carried their provisions for the season. Herders followed a ritual from morning till night, keeping sheep together, moving them to watering spots and campsites, protecting them from coyotes and wolves, and capturing runaways.

Sheepshearing and dipping were done in the spring after the winter's growth, most often by professional sheepshearers who followed the season north from Mexico. They started on the southern ranges in early March and ended up on the Canadian border in June. Paid $.08 to $.10 a sheep, a good shearer could hand clip 100 sheep a day. Machine clipping came in the 1890s. Sheep were dipped in a nicotine, lime, or sulfur solution before and after shearing to clean the wool and to heal cuts. Wool was hauled in large bags holding over 300 pounds to railroad storehouses to await shipment. Some mutton was shipped by refrigerator cars to eastern markets, but until the turn of the century, sheep were more valuable for their fleeces than for their mutton.

Foods for the Urban Marketplace

Meats and crops were increasingly processed industrially for easier storing, transporting, and marketing to the new factory towns of the 1800s. Bread was the basic food and staple of the poor working classes of these towns. By midcentury, most cities had

Figure 10–8. The tombstone sketch was placed at the beginning of William T. Hornaday's *Our Vanishing Wild Life* (1913). Hornaday was one of the most vocal and energetic early twentieth century wildlife conservation spokesmen. The woodcut, from *Leslie's Illustrated Newspaper*, September, 1867, depicts Iowa farmers shooting passenger pigeons flying over their grain fields. Passenger pigeons were killed by the millions in America for two centuries, and the last of the species, "Martha," died in the Cincinnati zoo in 1914. The term "hog" has been a term of caricature for more than 100 years, and sportsman-conservationist George Oliver Shields applied it in his journal *Recreation* (1898) to "hoggish" hunters who overkilled game.

merchant mills which greatly expanded flour production and large bakeries which utilized mechanical kneaders to mix the dough in bulk.

After the Civil War, more efficient refrigeration for railcars with better insulation and ice storage enabled farmers and grain dealers as well as stock dealers to ship meat, fruits, and vegetables over long distances to city markets. Instead of shipping thousands of tons of live cattle, by 1880 half the amount of dressed beef could be sent in refrigerator cars from Omaha to New York. Carl Linde's ammonia compressor of 1876 was put to work in food plants and warehouses around the country in the handling, processing and distributing of foods. After 1870 refrigerated American ships were carrying meat, fish, dairy, fruit and poultry products to ports all over the world.

Louis Pasteur's low-level heat treatment to kill harmful organisms was a boon to the dairy farmers of the East, but canning, the hermetic sealing of highly heated foods, became the prominent food industry after the Civil War. Although canned foods were despised for many years—hapless immigrants consumed the large proportion of them—in fact canned products contained the basic nutritional requirements needed by the working class and helped control such nutritional diseases as scurvy. Solving the problems of canning technology received its greatest boost from demands of European armies and the Civil War, which brought soldiers and many other Americans around to eating canned foods. By the 1870s meats (especially corned beef) were canned in the Midwest; olives, salmon and tomatoes were canned in California, where fruits were dried in the open air, and all were shipped in abundance abroad at a good profit. Conveyer belts and soldering machines boosted production faster than markets.

Shortly before the Civil War, Gail Borden discovered how to concentrate milk in a vacuum. He added sugar and canned the milk for indefinite preservation. Within a generation, cheese factories, creameries, and condensed milk plants were well-established throughout the nation. During this period inexpensive fat substitutes like oleomargarine (beef suet converted into butter-like fat) were also developed as inexpensive foods for multiplying urban populations. Animal fats, no longer available in large enough quantities to satisfy the demands of the time, were soon replaced by vegetable fats like cottonseed oil, corn oil or coconut oil. At this time it was discovered that hydrogen added to oil—in the hydrogenation process—produced solid fats so that low quality fats and oils could be upgraded and made edible. Although salt remained the primary food preserver of fish, meat, butter and cheese, chemical preservatives came into use during the era: salicylic and benzoic acids for jams and fruit syrups, sulfurous acids for fruit pulp, and later formaline for the meat rations of soldiers of the Spanish American War of 1898.

All of these developments, however, hinged on the stability of a very unstable American agricultural system.

New Solution to Financial Woes

The perils of the marketplace showed themselves to farmers, cattlemen, and sheep-herders alike during the last decades of the nineteenth century. Although these groups tried to imitate the associations of other industries, they never managed to ally them-selves closely enough to control production and to stabilize prices; they knew that despite their fraternal organizations, they were in fact direct competitors of one another. Several generations had passed since farming was characterized by subsis-tence agriculture and since farmers marketed their own products. Middlemen played the critical role of marketing and pricing after the Civil War. When farmers became completely committed to commercial agriculture, their opportunities for material gain were enhanced—but so was their liability to bankruptcy or foreclosure. By the end of the century, the farmer, who was not as blessed as the cattleman with hundreds of acres to sell in order to remain financially solvent, began to think that the deck was stacked against him.

The problem of overproduction was solved in the 1870s with increased exports to Europe, then suffering from droughts and disease. American policymakers naturally were encouraged to expand foreign markets in the 80s and 90s to quiet farmers' protest movements and to balance foreign trade in favor of the U.S., but agricultural competition from Argentina, Russia, and India, as well as European protective tariffs, foiled their plan. The new solution involved military muscle. The roots of American expansionism, as William Appleman Williams has persuasively shown, go back at least as far as nineteenth century farmers' demands for economic justice. Although American farmers themselves were not militaristic, they did promote the Cuban cause against Spain in an effort to protect their markets in the Caribbean. They supported the war in 1898. As turn-of-the-century gunboat diplomacy became necessary for similar protection of industrial and agricultural markets, farmers joined corporate interests and backed an expansionist, i.e., imperialist, foreign policy which was necessary to continue an expansionist economy. Thus followed World War I, World War II, Korea and Vietnam, all of which were in some way connected with the exigencies of an expanding economy, full employment, and a subdued or satisfied population.

Of course, there always has been an alternative: social and political acceptance of limits to production, expansion, and profits. With this political alternative, decisions can be made regarding the conservation of natural resources.

References for Further Reading

Agriculture and the Civil War by Paul W. Gates (1965) presents a lucid account of food shortages and the inflation of the South during the Civil War. Holland Thompson's *The New South* (1919) is a much older but solid interpretation of tenancy and sharecropping after the war. The most extensive treatment of all agriculture during the period examined in this chapter is Fred A. Shannon's superb treatment, *The Farmer's Last Frontier: Agriculture: 1860-1897* (1968). *The Sod-House Frontier* by Everett Dick (1937) tells the story of pioneer life on the Great Plains. Carl C. Taylor's *The Farmer's Movement* (1953) contains abundant material on the farmers' economic and political struggles of the nineteenth century. Many excellent and colorful books have been written on the range cattle industry: Edward Everett Dale's scholarly *The Range Cattle Industry* (1960) and his popular *Cow Country* (1973); Ernest Staples Osgood's thorough analysis, *The Day of the Cattleman* (1968); Walter Prescott Webb's classic *The Great Plains* (1931) and Mari Sandoz's *The Cattlemen* (1958). *Trail Driving Days* by Dee Brown and Martin F. Schmitt (1952) contains an interesting text as well as dozens of well-chosen old photographs and sketches. *The Cattle Towns* by Robert R. Dykstra (1973) fills in the social history of the Kansas cow towns. *America's Sheep Trails* by Edward Norris Wentworth (1948) traces the development of the country's sheep industry. John T. Schlebecker's *Whereby We Thrive* (1975), already cited, has interesting information in it about food processing in the 1800s. *The Roots of the American Empire* by William Appleman Williams (1969) is the outstanding, pioneering study on the beginnings of American expansionism. *This Land, This South: An Environmental History* by Albert E. Cowdrey (1983) provides an environmental history of the South from colonial times to the present, showing the heavy impact of agricultural practices on the land.

Chapter 11

SEEDS OF THE CONSERVATION MOVEMENT

N**ineteenth century America was hardly the birthplace of the spirit of conservation. Expansion, waste, growth, political corruption, technological change,
and economic booms and busts manifested the century's almost total indif-
ference to the environment and its natural resources. The visible signs of change—the
building of cities and railroads; new trappings of affluence—tended to reinforce the
belief that the good life was possible for everyone. The raw materials of that progress
and change were the land, its natural resources, and cheap labor on the plantations
and in the proliferating factories.

The Enlightenment and Romantic Movements

Perhaps the eighteenth century Enlightenment was coming to roost in America. The
Enlightenment displayed optimism about the inevitability of progress and confidence
about mankind's advance over ignorance and the uncivilized. At the same time,
however, the Enlightenment also displayed a rationalist impulse toward scientific
analysis. Ironically, the rationalist impulse led to notions of conservation in the United
States—at least among a small number of the nation's educated elite. Newton's vision
of an order in nature led Enlightenment thinkers and their disciples in Europe and
America to scientific studies of soils, forest lands, water, and even the principles of
ecological relationships. As early as 1818, Benjamin Silliman of Yale had founded the
American Journal of Science, which included much study that later could be put to
use in the practice of conservation. Thousands of Americans studied at European
universities, and some of the great scientists of the Continent either emigrated to
America, such as naturalist Louis Agassiz in 1846; or corresponded with American
scientists, as did Alexander von Humboldt of Berlin; or provided pioneering research
into practical resource problems, as did Justus von Liebig, who worked on problems
of soil exhaustion; or Humphry Davy, whose experiments on soil fertility (tests for
calcium carbonate) guided Virginia planter Edmund Ruffin. (Benjamin Silliman's son
Benjamin, Jr. is believed to have given the first course in agricultural chemistry in
the country. In 1855, at the request of promoter George H. Bissell, Silliman wrote
the *Report on Rock Oil, or Petroleum, from Venango County, Pennsylvania*, which
recommended the distillation of crude oil for illumination and lubrication.) Tenuous
though it might have been, the first impulse toward conservation came from an elite
concerned with natural science.

The second strand of the conservation movement can also be traced to eighteenth century Europe in the romantic movement, which was in some regions a reaction against the critical analysis and rationalism of the Enlightenment. Rousseau and the romanticists gloried in the world of nature, especially the wilderness of the noble savage and the pristine simplicity of rural life. A few European romanticists—Goethe, Chateaubriand, Byron, Wordsworth, Blake—received a measure of their inspiration from the American wilderness itself. In the United States, as in Europe, the romantic sensitivity was also a reaction to the "progress" of industrialism and incipient urbanization. Nature was viewed as a corrective to the evil contaminants of civilization; nature purified and enhanced an individual weighted with the artificial culture of his age.

The cross currents of the Enlightenment and romanticism greatly influenced the elite of America's attitudes and activity, shaping its exploitation (the thrust of progress) and conservation (scientific utilization or a preservationist spirit) of the natural resources. It is significant that the forerunners of the conservation movement arrived at their conclusions from quite distinct starting points: "resource conservationists" from the scientific movement within the Enlightenment and the "nature preservationists" from the enthusiastic and worshipful preoccupation with the wonders of nature. Therefore, resource conservationists would later insist that resources be wisely used but used nonetheless; nature preservationists wanted nature to be left alone and untouched. The disparate awarenesses of the two groups would cause chagrin and conflict among conservationists from the beginning of their movement to the present day.

Resource Conservationists

Resource conservationists sought to utilize the land and its resources efficiently. The first major problem of this sort in the country dealt with the exhausted soils of eastern farms. Although most farmers solved it by moving west to richer lands, a few scientists and gentlemen farmers experimented with methods of enriching their soils. They received most of their information from Europe and attempted to circulate it among themselves. One means was the American Philosophical Society, founded in 1743, for which Thomas Jefferson wrote and delivered papers on agricultural problems. Another was the American Academy of Arts and Sciences, founded in 1780. Many local agricultural societies, such as the Philadelphia Society for Promoting Agriculture, popularized soil renewing devices such as crop rotation and composting. Agricultural societies, fairs, and journals began to proliferate after the turn of the nineteenth century; they were all interested in new methods of farming; sometimes they promoted soil conservation.

Frequent interchange among scientists, students, and travellers between Europe and America resulted in an increasing flow of information. Charles Lewis Fleischmann, who immigrated to the United States in 1832, was shocked at the state of agricultural practice in the country. He wrote widely about the need for agricultural colleges modeled after schools and universities in Germany and Austria. An American student of European agriculture and editor of the *New England Farmer*, Henry Colman, described English, Irish, and French agricultural schools and experimental farms in his two-volume work, *European Agriculture and Rural Economy*, in 1846. Colman included his own plan for agricultural schools in the United States.

Soil conservationists working after 1840, when the English translation of *Organic Chemistry in its applications to agriculture and physiology* appeared, looked for guidance mainly in the work of Justus von Liebig of the University of Giessen, later Munich. Liebig proved that particular minerals of the soil rather than the humus itself were responsible for plant growth and that these mineral constituents of the soil must be replenished as crops utilize them. Although Liebig discounted the value of manure as a soil additive and may have indirectly been responsible for great waste on the farms affected by publicizers and teachers of his theories, his method of chemical analysis of soils was the most significant contribution to soil conservation of the century.

Before Virginian Edmund Ruffin found out about the experiments of Davy, he successfully utilized marl (carbonate of lime mixed with clay) as a fertilizer. In 1821, Ruffin wrote it up in the *American Farmer*. He continued his experiments on soil improvement for over twenty years and was responsible for the restoration of hundreds of acres of southland farms.

A few years after Ruffin's article appeared, John Skinner wrote another article in the *American Farmer* noting the value of guano, the excrement of Peruvian seafowl. But not until 1843 did the first shipload of guano arrive from the Chincha Islands off the coast of Peru. By that time, many farmers were ready to try to revive their soils. Guano was used widely in the East until the Civil War, after which farmers, especially Southerners, turned to commercial fertilizers.

Ruffin's wide influence was derived from his simple but important postulate that soils with calcium carbonate tend to be fertile. The person whose work on soil analysis was far more sophisticated and important was Eugene W. Hilgard, who was born in Germany in 1833 and taken to a farm in Belleville, Illinois, three years later.

Hilgard studied geology and chemistry in Europe, where he became familiar with the teachings of Liebig and Boussingault. In 1860, as Mississippi State Geologist, he wrote his pioneering *Report*, which took up the cause of soil conservation through manuring, fertilizing, and contour plowing: "No land can be permanently fertile, unless we restore to it, regularly, the mineral ingredients which our crops have withdrawn." Later he became a proponent of the view that nations and empires rise or fall on the basis of soil fertility or exhaustion.

Most of Hilgard's life was spent on soil analysis in its natural setting, pioneering the scientific study of soil layer profiles. He assessed the physical constituents of a soil profile (structure, tilth, etc.) along with its chemical properties and developed methods for this work.

In 1875, Hilgard went to the University of California at Berkeley to become Professor of Agriculture and Botany. He immediately set up an Experiment Station on the Berkeley campus. It was the first in the country to combine theoretical and field research in agriculture.

By no means did scientific agricultural experimentation deal only with soil conservation. Much of it was concerned with pest control, a major problem of all farmers, and the improvement and distribution of new crop varieties.

Nor did any of these new ideas take hold very commonly among the nation's farmers. When a conservation mentality eventually began to take hold in the country, it was in large measure the result of the activity and new policies of the federal government.

The Department of Agriculture had its beginnings in the Patent Office in 1837, when Henry L. Ellsworth started to distribute seeds he received from abroad to interested farmers. After three years Congress appropriated $1,000 to Ellsworth for gathering agricultural statistics, conducting experiments, and distributing seeds. With the appropriation, Ellsworth was able to establish the Agricultural Division within the Patent Office. The division expanded its operations year by year until 1862, when Congress established an independent Department of Agriculture to continue the work started by Ellsworth.

At the same time, a movement for the federal underwriting of agricultural education was gaining momentum. Representative Justin S. Morrill introduced his first bill to grant lands for the establishment of agricultural and mechanics colleges in 1857. It was passed by Congress but vetoed in 1858. A bill with more liberal land grants was passed and signed in 1862. Although the nation was in no position to concentrate on educational innovations during the war, more than twenty states set up or added to their colleges of agriculture and mechanic arts. During that period, however, the quality of teaching and number of courses remained quite low. In spite of these deficiencies, for a number of years the federal government provided the initiative for the first important step toward universalizing advances made in agricultural conservation.

George Perkins Marsh

Studies by agricultural chemists in the 1800s were complemented by the publication of *Man and Nature* by George Perkins Marsh in 1864. Although trained as a lawyer, self-taught in languages and literature, and experienced with business affairs and politics, Marsh has become well known because he lucidly and graphically illustrated the devastating impact man has exercised on the natural world. *Man and Nature* presents nature as a fragile balance of interrelationships between plants and animals within an easily modified landscape. Whenever man domesticates plants and animals or clears a forest, or diverts streams, or interferes with some aspect of natural activity, the effects extend to a far wider sphere of the natural environment.

Marsh's genius lay in his ability to find dozens of studies in as many languages to confirm what he had observed in his own life. In Vermont, he watched the soils wash down from the overcut and overgrazed hillsides of the Green Mountains, clogging and flooding streams and rivers. In 1848, he travelled to the Near East as U.S. minister to Turkey, where he spent six years examining the historical marks of man's role in changing the face of the landscape around the Mediterranean. In 1861, when he was appointed minister to Italy by Lincoln, he had the opportunity to look at man-made devastation of Alpine regions where deforestation led to massive erosion; there, heavy rainfall or snow runoff prompted landslides into, and flooding of, villages in the valleys below.

Marsh begins his treatment by reaching back into history to the physical decay of the Roman Empire—deforestation, erosion, lands laid bare—and contends that because humans are able to interfere with the balance of nature, damage to the environment is less reparable even than great natural catastrophes. As mankind's technologies become more potent from hoe to plow and from ax to saw, so do successive alterations and damage to natural systems. In contrast, nature usually is able to restore itself after a natural catastrophe.

Marsh picked up a lively topic of his day—the domestication of plants and animals—and showed how even these developments have greatly disturbed natural environments. Long before the Industrial Revolution, simple peasants, shepherds and farmers were clearing forests, planting on hillsides, overgrazing, and little by little transforming the land from verdant fields and forests to "an assemblage of bald mountains, or barren, turfless hills, and of swampy malarial plains." He saw the importance of food chains; he perceived how the extermination of one link in the chain, such as small birds, could lead to gross imbalances on lower links, such as insects, which in turn change foliage interrelationships.

Over half of *Man and Nature* deals with the function of forests as critical agents of soil and water conservation. Forests are able to absorb much of the moisture of strong rains and melting snow. Without judicious cutting and replanting, Marsh warned, rains inevitably lead to torrents which sweep down hillsides, destroying undergrowth and topsoil, driving away wildlife, and flooding valleys. Therefore Marsh recommended that forests be managed scientifically, trees grown on farms, and only mature timber harvested. He further suggested that studies be undertaken to investigate interrelationships between animals and plant life and that the land be managed scientifically by draining, diking or damming, and irrigating. In his final chapter, he speculated about the possible side-effects of newly projected canals like the Suez Canal, in what must have been the first environmental impact report.

Marsh's treatise was widely read in America and Europe, but except for some influence on a few scientists and policymakers, his insights and recommendations were only rarely applied in the United States for the next half century. But he exercised great influence on a few important people.

Concern about Forests

While Marsh warned about the ecological effects of deforestation, logging in the Great Lakes states was taking its toll from the land. A sawmill typically lasted about twenty years in a region as it stripped the area of its trees, then moved on—eventually to the far West. Speculators then bought up millions of acres of denuded land from the government and resold it to potential farmers. In the Great Lakes states, the forest soils were thin, sandy and leached, unable to provide adequate yields very long for the thousands of new farmers who followed the loggers. By the end of the 1880s, poverty and incipient erosion problems characterized the North Central states.

In his "Natural History of the American Lumberjack," *Holy Old Mackinaw* (1938), Stewart H. Holbrook describes this scene at the time of the "Second Migration" of loggers from the Great Lakes states to the far West:

The nineties saw the Second Migration getting well under way. By 1900 the movement West was as marked as the Covered Wagon era had been.

In their wake the boys left camps and sawmills where they stood. They deserted entire villages, not even bothering to pull down the blinds or take down the stovepipes. Officials of formerly well-timbered and well-taxed counties were aghast to find nothing left to eat in the public trough.

Most of all, the loggers left stumps in their wake. And why not? That had been their job—to make stumps out of forests so that John Farmer, as lumberjacks somewhat disdainfully termed husbandmen, could get on with his work. No one had objected to stumps; both state and federal governments had done everything they could to get the timber cut as quickly as possible.

Now and again some crazy fanatic had raised his voice about a need for "conservation," or something like that; but the voice was weak and it wasn't a chorus until well into the twentieth century. Loggers were still useful pioneers, the very spearhead of Empire and Manifest Destiny.

In this atmosphere a few "crazy fanatics" did call for a stop to the plunder of the forests. As early as 1855, the Department of the Interior attempted to stop timber theft, but local land officers continued to ignore the trespassers, and many lumbermen eventually brought to trial were released by local juries. In 1873, Dr. Franklin B. Hough, Civil War surgeon and director of the National Census as well as an avid follower of Marsh, in a lecture entitled "The Duty of Governments in the Preservation of Forests" convinced the American Association for the Advancement of Science membership to lobby for legislative action on forest protection and preservation. In behalf of the AAAS, Hough pressed for legislation, claiming that lumbering practices were illegal. They would result in the despoilment of thousands of square miles in and around forested lands.

No legislation came from Hough's early efforts, but in 1875, Congress created the Division of Forestry under the commissioner of Agriculture to develop a report on U.S. forest production and consumption with an estimation of future outlook regarding the nation's forests. Hough was appointed to head the new division and to write the report; drawing heavily on Marsh's theoretical considerations and other secondary sources, Hough finished the first of three volumes in 1877. Congress distributed 25,000 copies of the *Report*, which set off new discussions of forest plunder and practices in at least a dozen influential journals around the country (which blamed railroads as much as lumbermen) along with several books and scholarly papers in the 1880s. Byproducts of the revived interest in forests and forest practices were the organization of the American Forestry Association in 1876 and the formation of several state forestry groups.

A groundswell of protest and recommendations to Congress accompanied the movement. By the early 1870s, lumbermen were already making sizeable cuts into the giant redwood groves of California. In an 1876 column for the Sacramento *Record-Union*, John Muir complained of government inertia in the face of wholesale

Figure 11–1. A logjam. This illustration of a riverman's nightmare is fairly recent but the problem is as old as river running logs. The river shipment of logs and pulpwood shown here was made in 1937, when low water, poor river channels, and lack of experienced driving hands contributed to the difficulties. Courtesy U.S. Forest Service.

destruction of the big trees, some of which lumbermen were blasting out with explosives. He advanced arguments similar to Marsh's, that destruction of the groves would disrupt water flow, alter local climates and destroy the land with its soils, flora, and fauna. A succession of fires in the groves alarmed Muir, who excoriated lumber millmen and sheepmen alike in the article, and called for government action to survey the extensiveness of the forest problems.

Many writers and professional and scientific groups made similar protests and called for the repeal of those land laws which were so blatantly abused. The American Forestry Congress, founded in 1882, led a new crusade for forest conservation. One of its leaders, Charles S. Sargent, professor of arboriculture at Harvard University, issued a series of bulletins which indicated the rapidity with which the forests were being cleared. Among other startling facts, he reported in 1880 that if cutting in the Great Lakes states continued at its present pace, the white pine would be depleted there within eight years. This statement and hundreds more like it prompted fears that a "timber famine" would soon befall the country if steps were not taken to stop the plunder and destruction of the country's forests. Public outrage began to make itself felt, particularly since the timber lands in question were either brazenly appropriated by lumber companies or bought for a pittance through preemption laws. Rural Improvement Societies were established all over the country to plant trees in order to renew what was thought of as a threatened important natural resource. Arbor Day, first celebrated in Nebraska in 1874, is an example of the sentiment.

With the nation suffering panic and depression in 1884, Democrat Grover Cleveland ran on a reform platform and won. He appointed populist William Andrew Jackson Sparks as land commissioner. Sparks was a man who wasted no time serving notices to railroads that their lands were liable to forfeiture unless all the terms of their grants had been met. Sparks sent special agents around the country to investigate preemption and homesteading irregularities and other land law violations by timber and cattle companies, as well as speculators. Although railroad, timber and mining interests organized a monumental bloc of opposition among their political allies, particularly in the Senate, and stopped conservation and land reform bills, Sparks bulled ahead until 1887, when he resigned because of a disagreement with Secretary of Interior Lamar.

Cleveland boasted that he recovered 80,000,000 acres of fraudulently-acquired public land in four years. He also appointed a professionally-trained forester, B. E. Fernow, to the Division of Forestry in the Department of Agriculture. Fernow followed N. H. Eggleson, another student of Marsh's work and successor of Franklin Hough. Fernow's excellent forestry training in Germany enabled him to suggest sound management practices at forestry conferences but did not equip him to deal with hundreds of lumbering operations spread from the South through the Rocky Mountain states and along the Pacific coast. Nothing short of the assistance of the U.S. Army would have helped him during that era.

The strategy of the forest conservationists lay in legislative proposals for forest reserves protected by federal forest patrols. They succeeded in persuading the New York state legislature that the reason for the drastically reduced flow of water into the Hudson River and the Erie Canal was increased lumbering in the Adirondacks. Fearing disastrous economic consequences if their important water routes were closed, the legislature created the Adirondack Forest Preserve of almost 800,000 acres in 1885, with a plan to increase it to 3,000,000 acres. Forest educators at Harvard, Illinois, Pennsylvania, Iowa, Michigan, and the American Forestry Congress, with Fernow himself participating, made steady headway in the education of a new generation of forest-conscious students and laymen. At the same time the land commissioner and the Department of Interior managed to stop some land fraud and engrossment by special interest groups.

The most radical departure from previous policy, and the biggest boon to conservation of the period, however, came under Republican President Benjamin Harrison,

Figure 11–2. A forest ranger on duty. This ranger, who is on fire patrol duty in Cabinet National Forest, Montana, in 1909, represented federal government efforts to preserve and protect the forest ranges of the West. Courtesy U.S. Forest Service.

who, with Secretary of the Interior John W. Noble, openly received the suggestions of numerous scientific societies, including the American Association for the Advancement of Science and the American Forestry Congress. All recommended repeal of the Timber Culture Act and preemption laws. On the eve of Congressional adjournment in 1891, Noble succeeded in obtaining the passage of a bill repealing these laws, along with an unnoticed rider granting the president the power to set aside forest reservations. President Harrison duly created six forest reservations including over 3,000,000 acres in 1891-92. Later he added nine more timber reserves totaling over 13,000,000 acres. Although sale of the forest reserves was forbidden, no Congressional appropriation was granted for their protection from fire or plunder. For a number of years both theft and fires were common in federal timber reserves, despite entreaties for appropriations from President Cleveland, reelected in 1892. Congress refused to appropriate money for this purpose, and Cleveland refused to set aside more preserves until money was appropriated. Finally, in the last days of his presidential tenure, he acceded to a plea from a group of conservationist and scientific societies led by the National Academy of Sciences to create thirteen new forest reserves. This goal was accomplished on Washington's birthday celebration, February 27, 1897.

In the same year of 1897, an amendment to the appropriations bill authorized the president to modify or suspend or revoke any forest reserves, and said that no reserve should be created unless it would improve and protect the forest, preserve the water flow, and assure a continuous supply of lumber; no lands were to be set aside as reserves if they were better suited for mining or agriculture. The act also gave the secretary of the interior the authority to permit cutting and use of timber and stone for firewood, building, mining and domestic purposes, and the use of waters within the national forests for mining, milling and irrigation. The act reestablished commercial access to the national forests, and also paved the way for Pinchot's multiple-use policy of grazing, lumbering and hydroelectric power generation in the national forests.

The Arid Lands of the West

A generation earlier, on April 1, 1878, another benchmark of resource-conservation thought reached the desk of the newly-appointed and zealous secretary of interior under Rutherford Hayes, Carl Schurz. Schurz was unsuccessfully fighting for land and timber reforms. The subject matter of the document before him that day did not relate to timberlands, or railroad corruption, or violations under homestead or preemption laws but rather it dealt with water problems on land west of the hundredth meridian. The document was entitled *Report on the Lands of the Arid Region of the United States, with a More Detailed Account of the Lands of Utah.* Its primary author was Major John Wesley Powell, then in charge of the Interior Department's Geographical and Geological Survey of the Rocky Mountain Region. The son of an immigrant Wesleyan preacher, Powell spent his young life in the western rural settings of Ohio, Wisconsin and Illinois, fashioning a homemade education in natural history, science and philosophy. He tried a few colleges, though none satisfied his scientific interest, and ended up fighting in the Union Army. He lost his right arm above the elbow at Shiloh. After the war he went back to Illinois to teach natural science at Illinois State Normal School where he formed a chapter of the State Natural History Society and he became the museum curator.

From this base, in 1867, Powell launched expeditions into the West, first to the Colorado Rockies, then to Utah and down the Green and Colorado Rivers. After his daring trip down the Colorado River in 1869, he received Congressional funding to lead a survey of the Rocky Mountain Region, though the appropriation was minimal and his crew utterly inexperienced. For the decade thereafter Powell studied western terrain, collected thousands of specimens of geology and natural science, codified Indian languages and cultures, drew maps, lingered at small Mormon and southwestern settlements, watched the filling of the Great Plains by cattlemen and farmers, but most of all observed the critical relationships among people, land, and water.

Behind the stark conclusions of Powell's report lay his analysis of the volatile climate of the plains west of the hundredth meridian. He contended that farming in those western regions would usually be hazardous because, with an average of less than twenty inches a year, the area lacked the necessary amount of rainfall to grow crops. Powell personally experienced the unpredictable and wide variety of weather patterns in the West, which received warm rains from the Gulf occasionally (violent storms occurred when these masses of air met cold, dry winds from Canada). But most often no rain fell at all. As farmers on the plains found out, blizzard blasts could follow blistering drought.

When settlers numbering in the hundreds of thousands rushed to the plains in the seventies, enough rain fell to encourage them to remain. Powell knew that their luck would not hold, and it didn't. Every manner of mishap—drought, blizzard, grasshopper, cyclone, and scalding heat wave—came upon the hapless homesteaders in the eighties. By 1900, two-thirds of them had given up and moved or lost their farms to mortgagees. The last generation of the century also brought money problems which compounded the settlers' woe. In the end, much of this land was monopolized by cattle barons or cattle companies with enough capital to wait out the weather.

Before more tragic events occurred, Powell recommended that because climatic conditions of land west of the 98th meridian were different, the land should be organized into different kinds of topographical and political units. The grid system of larger or smaller squares could work for farmers of the flat and regular plains of the midwest but, according to Powell, it was hopelessly irrational when applied to the western Great Basin region. Not only are many areas completely removed from any source of water, but land elevations and soil quality vary as dramatically as the weather. Lands should be designated according to the use to which they may be applied—farming, mining, lumbering, grazing—and surveyed as such. Powell suggested three classifications: Irrigable lands near rivers and streams; forest lands in the mountains; and pasture lands between irrigable lands and forested mountains.

Since he was most interested in indicating a viable method of irrigated farming, Powell's division was organized around watersheds. He noted that a practicable irrigation system demands a monumental investment of time and labor, making 160 acres of irrigated land about twice as much as a homesteader could reasonably farm; Powell recommended units of 80 acres of irrigated farming land. Without irrigation (his survey team found, for example, that in Utah only 2,262 square miles of land could potentially be irrigated), the land should be designated for pasturage in units of 2,560 acres (four complete sections). This minimal amount is necessary for a homesteading family to support itself without serious overgrazing of the perennial grasslands. In lands of scarce grass, 50 to 60 acres is needed to graze a single steer.

Development of American Water Law and Powell's Plan

Powell proposed that a grazing farm should have included in its 2,560 acres twenty acres of irrigable land for a garden, fodder raising, and watering of stock, with established and automatic rights to a source of water. This stipulation came from Powell's logic and observations of Mormon practice and the pueblos of New Mexico, not from the common legal code of the time. English common law of riparian rights allowed "riparian uses"—domestic and animal watering—to owners along stream or river banks, but the water could not be diverted, diminished or polluted to the detriment of a downstream owner. Riparian rights were developed in humid climates of rural life (where there was water for mills, stock watering, etc.). The same conditions applied to American lands east of the Mississippi, before Utah irrigation systems, California placer mining and Spanish pueblo rights modified the practice of American water law. In Utah, rights to water adhered in membership of the Mormon community, memorialized in the words of Brigham Young: "No man has a right to waste one drop of water that another man can turn into bread."

In California miners helped themselves to water on a first come first served basis whether or not their claims fell beside the streams; there water rights were assumed under the right of appropriation. The third approach in western water claims was found under Spanish law which granted the members of a pueblo the right to all water flowing into and under its community; this was a right which superseded all other claims. Thus the major factor in the determination of a pueblo was the water drainage pattern of a region.

Powell's plan followed the communitarian models of Mormon and New Mexico's pueblo communities rather than riparian or appropriated rights. The plan demanded a new kind of topographical survey based on watersheds rather than the grid system. The plan also assumed cooperative labor and capital of a group of settlers interested in the farming and grazing possibilities of an area. Sometimes small streams could be diverted and utilized by individual farmers, but most sections required the damming and diverting of larger streams for cooperative groups. Only groups of settlers could afford the cost of a planned irrigation system, and Powell suggested that Congress legislate that nine or more homesteaders could form an irrigation district (similar to Mormon irrigation wards) and make their own water laws, assuming that the right to water would adhere in the land.

Powell was convinced that his plan would preclude the already widespread evil of water monopolization along the scarce streams of the western plains. In its place, he attempted to institutionalize cooperative ranges and water supplies. This was a radical departure from the competitive individualism—not to mention range wars, widespread in the West. His midwestern background brought memories of communitarian practices—cabin building and barn raisings, husking bees—hearkening back to the closely-knit New England towns. Powell knew that the cooperative approach could work. Indeed, it would have to work, as it did in the Mormon settlements, if the West would become a permanent place for American families to live. Along with a hardheaded practicality, Powell possessed a sensitive idealism in his belief that men and women could work together with nature for their mutual benefit.

These notions, of course, flew in the face of every accepted national myth of the day—sturdy self-reliant yeomen farmers on their governmentally-bestowed 160 acres—particularly since many national figures claimed that the rains of the seventies, especially in Utah, were the result of settlement: "The rain follows the plow," went the myth. The concept of 2,560 acres was a preposterous notion to those bred in the humid climates of the East. Congress hardly considered Powell's land reform measures. Instead, in 1878, because of lobbying from the far West, they passed the much-to-be-abused Timber and Stone Act, permitting the purchase of non-agriculture timber and mineral lands, and with it a Timber Cutting provision allowing settlers and mining companies to take free timber from the public domain for their own uses. Although sale of the timber was forbidden, the law generated more small lumbering enterprises than homesteading, and license was granted the mining companies for a practice they enjoyed for well over a generation. The Desert Land Act, passed just before Powell submitted his report in 1877, had already enabled cattle barons to engross landholdings ten to twenty times greater than the amount suggested by Powell for homesteaders.

For his efforts Powell was awarded the first directorship of the Bureau of Ethnology in 1879 to continue his work on the codification of Indian languages and cultures. In the same year his survey group was merged into the newly-formed U.S. Geological and Geographical Survey, of which he was appointed director two years later. By the mid-1880s, blizzards and droughts struck the Great Plains, and panic came upon plains people and their Congressmen. The crisis brought forth a bill to establish an Irrigation Survey to map, survey and note possible irrigation sites, compoundment basins and canal routes. The task was as herculean as the Congressional charge was precipitous, but Powell seized the opportunity in an attempt to carry out his general plan. Indefatigably he traveled throughout the newly-established western states, suggesting that their counties be formed along watersheds so that political groupings could follow economic necessity. He underlined the importance of water rights inhering in land rights. By June 1890, Powell had isolated nearly 200 reservoir sites and about 30,000,000 acres of irrigable land, which he mapped and submitted to the General Land Office for reservation. The Irrigation Survey law specified that all settlement and existing land laws were to have been suspended until the irrigation districts could be determined. However, in October of the same year Powell's critics in the Senate managed to have his appropriation withdrawn. The general plan died with the funding cut-off.

Nonetheless, Powell's prophetic writing, lecturing, and work eventually bore fruit. At the very least he shook up the congealed mental patterns of a good many legislators.

Nature Preservationists

As Americans increased their frenetic economic and political pace up to a breathless sprint during the century, another movement grew in strength which took an alternative approach to conservation in the United States. The beliefs of the group sprang from European romantics, but they had a strongly American flavor. In general, adherents of the philosophy focused on the romantic value of nature as the ultimate restorer and purifier of a humanity corrupted by civilization. They were not so much interested in conserving the forests to protect watersheds or to assure America of future timber supplies, though these goals were not discounted, as they were in preserving wilderness areas, which possess their own aesthetic, spiritual and moral values. Beginning with "Thanatopsis" in 1811, William Cullen Bryant sounded the theme in behalf of American nature lovers for three-quarters of a century. His writing bespoke the wonders, divinity, delights, and soothing effects of nature. During the same period, James Fenimore Cooper's Natty Bumppo became a symbol of purity and excellence because of his lifetime exposure to the wholesomeness of the wilderness, where he was separated from the evil habits of civilized settlers.

Critics of American progress in that "enlightened" age were rare indeed. One man, Ralph Waldo Emerson, sought in 1840 to redress the social and spiritual errors of his time. At the outset of his Transcendentalist career he records in his *Journals*, "a question which well deserves examination now is the Dangers of Commerce. This invasion of Nature by Trade with its Money, its credit, its Steam, its Railroads, threatens to upset the balance of Man, and establish a new, universal Monarchy more tyrannical than Babylon or Rome."

Transcendentalism is of course more than a philosophy of nature, but its tenets cannot be completely understood without reference to nature, the reflection of eternal truth. If men and women would transcend the petty, dehumanizing, commercial burdens of their lives, they must maintain creative contact with the diffused presence of God in nature: "Behind nature, throughout nature, spirit is present," Emerson claimed in his maiden essay, *Nature*, published in 1836. Emerson, with Jefferson, believed in the objective superiority of agrarian over industrial life.

Henry Thoreau accepted the transcendentalist faith commitment of Emerson, his spiritual mentor. His unabashed bias fell on the side of Truth in nature and wilderness over the deceits of urban civilization. The countryside around Concord, Massachusetts, fascinated and exhilarated him as much as the commercialism of the city depressed him. In 1845, he decided to live in the country outside Concord to simplify and thereby to enhance his existence through direct contact with nature's "essential facts of life." Later Thoreau became actually terrified by the untamed wilderness of Mt. Katahdin in Maine and tempered his judgment about unalloyed wildness, but fear did not change his conviction that man needs his humanity replenished by the truths found in nature.

As the naturalist philosophy was being constructed, so were hundreds of new towns, cities, and industrial plants in the Northeast. The forests moved farther and farther west, and city-dwellers, some catching the transcendentalist or romantic spirit, began to take summer trips to the woods in the White or Adirondack Mountains. By mid-century, the Adirondacks were already thoroughly scarred by lumbering activity. The difficulty in finding unspoiled regions for camping eventually contributed to the movement for forest preservation. By the 1860s dozens of American journals were carrying nature, travel and camping articles, and illustrated travel books about the West began to appear. Photographers and artists, notably George Catlin, who first proposed the establishment of national parks, traveled the country and published the breathtaking scenes of American natural beauty. California's redwoods were well known throughout the nation by 1870. Natural history played a larger role in the nation's schools as well. Scientist Louis Agassiz trained a generation of teachers and scientists in the techniques of exploring, understanding, and appreciating nature through field trips and scientific investigations. He and his disciples set up museums of natural history and science in most of the large cities of the East, all utilizing the country at large to stock their collections. All of these events, small in themselves, together fostered a deepening consciousness of the values in nature, so that a movement for forest preservation had gained some popular momentum by the 1870s.

National Park Movement

Yosemite was already well publicized in 1864, when a group of California citizens approached Senator John Conness to request Congress to grant the state Yosemite Valley "for public use, resort and recreation." The bill granting Yosemite Valley to the state of California implied that the state was to act as a trustee for the federal government. This was the precedent-setting law for national park legislation. Frederick Law Olmstead, a landscape architect who earlier had written accounts about life in the South and had designed New York's Central park, was instrumental in obtaining the land for a park. He became the Yosemite Commission's first president. He spent a year preparing a management plan for the park ("for the free enjoyment" and "use of the body of people"), then left to continue work on Central Park and to inaugurate

THE VALLEY OF THE YOSEMITE.

Figure 11–3. A park is born. This 1874 engraving romanticizes the area that was to become Yosemite Park, but it does give the viewer an idea of the popular attitude toward such preserves. Passionate campaigning by writers such as Muir had convinced some readers that the national parks were earthly paradises. The conservationists did nothing to dispel such beliefs. Courtesy Culver Pictures.

more parks around the country. Olmstead's thought was deeply imbued with the conviction that natural beauty enhances human activity.

After 1868, the year of John Muir's arrival in California, the majesty of the Sierras and California's natural wonders were to become even more widely publicized and known. A convinced transcendentalist, Muir invited Emerson to "worship" in Yosemite Valley; 67 years old, Emerson accepted and withstood the rigors of travel for the experience. Cross-country trips to California became more commonplace during the seventies, prompting more books on the beauties of nature in the West, particularly the two- volume oversized set edited by William Cullen Bryant, *Picturesque America*, including the work of Catlin and other great American artists.

The land and geysers of Yellowstone were explored in the late sixties, and a Department of Interior official investigated the site. Within a few years enough attention was attracted to the natural scenes at Yellowstone to prompt a request that Congress create a national park in the territory. Since no state had as yet been carved from the region, Congress placed it under federal protection as a National Park, "as a public or pleasuring ground for the benefit and enjoyment of the people." Because it appeared that the region had no commercial value, the legislation was quickly passed by Congress. No management policy was provided, and its policing was at best haphazard, usually falling under the aegis of a nearby U.S. Cavalry unit.

Public opinion alone, even buttressed by scientific societies, did not move Congress to create National Parks. Railroad companies which hoped to run trains through potential park sites were quick to point out the "aesthetic" benefits of the legislation. For example, Jay Cooke's Northern Pacific, which had already floated a bond for a route through the territory, actively promoted Congressional action. E. H. Harriman, whose Southern Pacific and Central Pacific subsidiary had increased its passenger totals greatly because of the Yosemite Valley grant to the state, joined John Muir after 1900 in advocating an increase in the acreage around Yosemite. Yosemite remained under two authorities until 1906, when California ceded back its section of Yosemite to the federal government, but Congress could not agree on a management plan.

The Northern Pacific lobbied for the reservation of Mount Ranier as a National Park in 1899; the Great Northern for Glacier National Park in 1899. Sixteen national parks and eighteen national monuments had been set aside for recreation by 1916, when the National Park Service was established and given central management control over all the national parks and monuments.

John Muir

The person of John Muir himself was the final factor in the promotion of national parks. Muir embodied and spread abroad the transcendentalist idea that the wilderness mirrors divinity, nourishes humanity, and vivifies the spirit. A native of Scotland and pioneer of a Wisconsin farm, he never spent a great amount of time in civilization. He studied natural science and philosophy and read the naturalists at the University of Wisconsin, invented mechanical equipment, and worked at an Indianapolis carriage factory, where an accident almost cost the loss of his eyesight. Muir then decided at once to repair to the wilderness to become born again in the spirit. California

Figure 11–4. John Burroughs and John Muir, two giants of the conservation movement, in Yosemite Park. Burroughs, left, was a well-known naturalist and author, who, like his companion Muir in this picture, expressed the transcendentalist attitudes toward nature. Burroughs was widely regarded as an essayist. Muir used his powerful persuasive gifts to win over such influential persons as Theodore Roosevelt. Courtesy The Bancroft Library.

always seemed to be his destination, though he walked 1,000 miles through Kentucky, Tennessee, Georgia, and Florida first.

The Sierras provided Muir with the intense religious experience he was seeking. He never tired of repeating the story of his sense of fulfillment and exaltation at the shrine of nature's mysteries. It was his sense of oneness with nature that caused Muir anxiety, for he saw the plunder of his Beloved everywhere he walked. This horror drove Muir quickly into the public arena; he wanted to tell the world of his experience in the wilderness and what was happening to mankind's most precious gift.

Muir's message coincided with that of the Transcendentalists, except that his was filled with more enthusiastic missionary urgency. He tried to seduce Americans into leaving the cities for a while to enjoy the wilderness. Muir was certain that nature could almost magically transform over-civilized and urbanized men and women into their true selves if they let the power of nature overshadow them with its splendor.

Figure 11–5. The "Three Graces," Mariposa Grove, California.

When friends and visitors sat by his campfire in the Sierras, he would speak into the night about the quality of religious joy that nature brought to his life.

As quickly as Muir was enthused by nature, he was saddened by the men who exploited its commercial value. Sheepmen with their "hoofed locusts" stripped the hills of their luxuriant meadows and wildflowers, and lumbermen with their proliferating sawmills ate into redwood groves that had taken centuries to unfold. The article in the Sacramento *Record-Union* quoted earlier in the chapter was entitled: "God's First Temples: How Shall We Preserve Our Forests?" Muir believed that only enforced government control could save California's finest sequoia groves from the ravages of "fools." Muir's articles in the *Century* and other journals and papers of the East greatly assisted the movement for the establishment of forest reserves and National Parks, especially in California.

In the early 1890s, Muir took the lead in bringing together a group of twenty-seven west coast men whom he organized into the Sierra Club to "explore, enjoy, and render accessible the mountain regions of the Pacific Coast" and "to enlist the support of the people of the government in preserving the forests and other features of the Sierra Nevada Mountains." These men earlier became practiced at organizing a campaign to save Yosemite Valley when it became apparent that lumbering, grazing, and concessionaire interests were befouling the valley floor. Since state control proved inadequate, Muir's men convinced Theodore Roosevelt and the California legislature, with some help from the Southern Pacific, to turn the state section of the park over to the federal government.

In the early stages of the conservation movement, no strong division between the scientific, efficiency-minded resource utilizers and the resource preservationists developed. They worked together against unenlightened exploitation and corruption, and for the preservation of forests and parks. They articulated many of the same ideals and needs for nineteenth century America. The philosophical and ideological estrangement became clear at the end of the century, when a devotee of scientific management, Gifford Pinchot, became chief U.S. forester, split with Muir's ideals of forest preservation for itself, and began to apply his theories of resource management systematically. To Muir and the preservationists, Pinchot's management appeared to be a violation of a sacred trust.

Wildlife Conservation

Another transformation was gradually taking hold in the United States in the people's relationship to wildlife. Like their relationship to the wilderness, at first most Americans regarded game animals either as a nuisance that ruined their crops or as their rightful personal or commercial food source. One reason why thousands flocked to the shores of the new continent was the freedom to hunt and fish to their heart's content. Throughout Europe fish and game laws promulgated by the nobility or gentry prohibited peasants from access to game. In the New World game was so abundant that no one dreamed that it could ever drop to extinction levels. At the same time the immigrants were too preoccupied with wresting survival from a harsh environment to worry about the extinction of wildlife.

By the time of the Civil War a different environmental reality had evolved. Gold had been discovered in California and enormous population pressures began to be felt in the West. Buffalo, roaming the plains in the millions at the middle of the century, fell to a few thousand by the end of the 1800s. In the East wildlife populations dropped at an alarming rate. During the nineteenth century a few men and organizations started a movement that slowly changed the pattern of valuing wildlife.

Wildlife conservation was not a new idea in Europe; the nobility prohibited open access to their forests precisely because they wanted to keep their game for themselves, for sport and for food. But it was a struggle for the few American conservationists who spoke out early in the 1800s to get laws passed even to observe hunting seasons on endangered game. When sportsmen's clubs managed to have state laws passed, counties were usually permitted to exempt themselves. Game laws were considered an unwarranted infringement of liberty.

The prototype for many of the sportsmen's clubs, the New York Sportsmen's Club, was founded in 1844 to protect and preserve game for purposes of hunting. The club formulated laws for hunting seasons in the counties and later the state of New York, but much of their work was educational. The man who drafted the club's petition to the state legislature, Henry William Herbert, wrote articles on the outdoors and was one of the first writers who took up the cause of the depletion of wildlife in the country. He wrote under the pen name of Frank Forester in *The Spirit of the Times* and *Turf Register*, two well-known sportsmen's magazines. There were no game wardens at the time, so members of the New York club sought out and sued poachers who violated county game laws. Herbert wrote to club members in 1847, "I rejoice to hear of your success with the Game-killers; one or two more examples will work wonders."

A second influential writer was George Bird Grinnell, who became an editor of *Forest and Stream* magazine in 1876 and was a founding member of the famous Boone and Crockett Club. His lifelong crusade in association with the magazine, of which he became senior editor and publisher in 1880, was a campaign against market hunting and in behalf of realistic game laws. He worked with Theodore Roosevelt and others interested in big game hunting in the Boone and Crockett Club to fight for the preservation of big game in North America. Grinnell's investigatory articles on big game poaching in Yellowstone National Park in 1894 led directly to the enactment by Congress of the Yellowstone Park Protection Act, a pivotal piece of legislation for the many national parks that followed. He had great influence on later wildlife legislation and in 1886 founded the New York Audubon Society, forerunner of the National Audubon Society.

Forest and Stream magazine contributed another inveterate campaigner for game preservation in John Bird Burnham, who was its business manager from 1891 to 1897. Later he operated a game preserve, became the chief game protector of the state of New York, and was the first president of the American Game Protective and Propagation Association in 1911. By that time Theodore Roosevelt's presidency had established strong legal foundations of the long-term economic management of land and wildlife for the future use of the American people.

The most popular early figure to move somewhat from this pro-hunting position was William Temple Hornaday, who started his career as a taxidermist, working as chief taxidermist of the U.S. National Museum in 1882. He was instrumental in starting the National Zoological park in Washington, D.C. and later became the first director of the New York Zoological Park. Throughout his career his fame as a zookeeper was equaled by his notoriety as a champion of wildlife protection and as a vicious foe of sport hunting and all the manufacturers of sporting arms. He worked tirelessly for laws against the sale of wild game and importation of wild bird plumage. The frontispiece for his immensely popular book, *Our Vanishing Wildlife*, published in 1913, was a cartoon depicting a saloon loaded with hundreds of furs and game trophies with hunters caricatured within. He established the Permanent Wild Life Fund in 1913 and wrote about 20 books on wildlife preservation, including *30 Years War For Wildlife*.

A previous section discussed John Muir's role as a nature preservationist. While best known for his descriptions of mountain scenery, he included in many of his writings comments on bears, sheep, deer, squirrels, and even lizards and rattlesnakes.

Muir was an early advocate of animal rights, at least in the sense of treating them as equals. For example, in 1901 in *Our National Parks*, Muir wrote

Before I learned to respect rattlesnakes I killed two, the first on the San Joaquin plain. He was coiled comfortably around a tuft of bunch-grass, and I discovered him when he was between my feet as I was stepping over him. He held his head down and did not attempt to strike, although in danger of being trampled. At that time, thirty years ago, I imagined that rattlesnakes should be killed wherever found. I had no weapon of any sort, and on the smooth plain there was not a stick or a stone within miles; so I crushed him by jumping on him, as the deer are said to do. Looking me in the face he saw I meant mischief, and quickly cast himself into a coil, ready to strike in defense. I knew he could not strike when traveling, therefore I threw handfuls of dirt and grass sods at him, to tease him out of coil. He held his ground a few minutes, threatening and striking, and then started off to get rid of me. I ran forward and jumped on him; but he drew back his head so quickly my heel missed, and he also missed his stroke at me. Persecuted, tormented, again and again he tried to get away, bravely striking out to protect himself; but at last my heel came squarely down, sorely wounding him, and a few more brutal stampings crushed him. I felt degraded by the killing business, farther from heaven, and I made up my mind to try to be at least as fair and charitable as the snakes themselves, and to kill no more save in self-defense.

Muir often talks about animals as conscious beings. In *The Story of My Boyhood and Youth* (1912) he recounts how as a young man he was impressed by a goose who attacked him to defend another bird he had shot. After this time he rarely took firearms into the wilderness. Muir was different from even a kindred spirit like Hornaday in that he defended the so-called varmints or "bad" animals like alligators, snakes, and lizards. He wrote benignly about flies and revised his stern criticism of domestic sheep, "hoofed locusts" that destroyed the vegetation of mountain meadows. He deeply loved his dog Stickeen who accompanied him through difficult adventures across an Alaskan glacier, saying "through him as through a window I have ever since been looking with deeper sympathy into all my fellow mortals." At the time of this writing in *The Story of My Boyhood and Youth*, Muir began to advocate the rights of animals in and for themselves. He "never happened upon a trace of evidence that seemed to show that any one animal was ever made for another as much as it was for itself," and denounced the notion that "animals have neither mind nor soul, have no rights that we are bound to respect, and were made only for man, to be petted, spoiled, slaughtered, or enslaved."

Congressional Ineptitude

By the time the resource utilizers and preservationists came into open conflict over public land use, Congress had already legislated away most of the nation's forests, over which the government assumed no control for conservation purposes, and the intramural struggles were fought over the last remaining public forests. As historian Thomas LeDuc has pointed out, the most significant of the government land policies was the decision to dispose of the public domain quickly rather than to attempt to develop it or to retain any long-range controls over it. The major problems of conservation during the nineteenth and twentieth centuries have come from private lands, over which the government has eschewed jurisdiction even for purposes of the social good of all Americans.

Regarding the public lands themselves, conservationist and preservationist forces were united in their demands to Congress that federally owned lands be protected from criminal theft, trespassing, and despoilment. But pressured by a multitude of private interests which insisted that they be allowed free access to the resources of the public domain, Congress consistently refused to appropriate money for its protection and management until well into the twentieth century. Thus did Congress encourage the notion that the public domain existed for the benefit of anyone who wanted to take from its bounty both by tacitly tolerating the plunder of forest lands and the overgrazing on the plains and by legislating giveaways like the Timber and Stone Act provision. Nor would Congress agree to establish a national park or monument unless it could first be unassailably proved that the area could not be exploited commercially. It was perhaps in their frustration with the obduracy of Congress that conservationists split into opposing camps, each of which blamed the other side for the dismal state of environmental affairs in the country. Unfortunately, in so doing they further weakened their position in Washington. Given the belated and fragile character of the movement in the face of overweening economic, social, and political countervalents, they clearly needed all the solidarity they could muster.

References for Further Reading

Hans Jenny's excellent *E. W. Hilgard and the Birth of Modern Soil Science* (1961) not only presents Hilgard's life and contributions to soil science but also covers other soil theories of the nineteenth century. The most useful readings for this chapter are the original sources—Marsh, Powell, Emerson, Thoreau, Muir. Wayne D. Rasmussen has prepared an excellent collection of primary sources in his *Readings in the History of American Agriculture* (1960). David Lowenthal has written an outstanding biography and provided an introduction and edition of Marsh's original 1864 text of *Man and Nature* (1973). *Beyond the Hundredth Meridian* by Wallace Stegner (1954) recounts Powell's life and exploration of the Colorado in a steadily exciting account of the events surrounding the development of his General Plan. *The United States Forest Policy* by John Ise (1924) presents a detailed study of the entire period of conservation in the United States until World War I. Roderick Nash's *Wilderness and the American Mind* (1967) remains the standard reference for the history of American conservation attitudes. Other more popular but solid treatments on conservation history are Hans Huth's *Nature and the American* (1972), Stewart L. Udall's *The Quiet Crisis* (1970), *Man and Nature in America* by Arthur A. Ekirch 1973), *The Conservationists* by Douglas H. Strong (1971), *Speaking for Nature* by Paul Brooks (1980), and Wayne Hanley's *Natural History in America: From Mark Catesby to Rachel Carson* (1977). John F. Rieger's *American Sportsmen and the Origins of Conservation* (1975) develops a strong argument that sport hunters and fishermen played a crucial role in the development of the conservation movement in the nineteenth and twentieth century. On the same subject, see also James B. Trefethen's *American Crusade for Wildlife* (1975). Lisa Mighetto has edited a wonderful collection, *Muir Among the Animals: The Wildlife Writings of John Muir* (1986), which describes the evolution of his relationship to animals. Alfred Runte shows the interest of the railroad companies in the national park movement in his *Trains of Discovery: Western Railroads and the National Parks* (1984). Runte's *National Parks: The American Experience* (1979) further illustrates the context in which the parks were created, i.e., as being viewed as lands of little economic value. The scholarly biography, *Henry David Thoreau: A Life of the Mind,* by Robert D. Richardson (1986) traces Thoreau's intellectual development from his graduation at Harvard in 1837 to his death in 1862.

Camp near Round Lake (Adirondacks)

Chapter 12

URBAN ENVIRONMENTAL PROBLEMS

An environmental movement of a different character from the conservation movement of the nineteenth century developed simultaneously and slowly in U.S. cities. Environmental conditions in early American cities were primitive. In *The New Yorkers*, Smith Hart provides a graphic picture of living conditions in New York City at the close of the Revolutionary War:

The problem of sewage disposal rested lightly on the city fathers. Processions of slaves from the abodes of the town's first families wended their way to the river banks at dusk each with a tub of dung perched on his shoulder. The generality, however, still disposed of excrement by flipping it through the handiest window. In accordance with a city ordinance, on Tuesdays and Fridays from April to December, all good householders scraped it bi-weekly from sidewalk and gutter and pushed it into the center of the streets. In winter, they let it lay where it landed. There was a pleasant fiction current that these mounds of offal (known to the jocular citizenry as "Corporation Pudding") were to be removed by cartmen in the employ of the city and occasionally a captious critic would address a newspaper broadside to the Commissioner of Streets labeled "Awake Thou Sleeper," but it was generally felt that it was a small matter to make such a fuss about. Unless there was an epidemic, the "pudding" was left in the center of the streets where in due course of time it was kicked about by the feet of unwary passersby until it got lost.

The wells from which drinking water was drawn were situated for the most part in the middle of the extremely filthy streets. Much of the supply came from the famed Tea Water pump in Chatham Street (Park Row). The Tea Water was fed by seepage from the Collect Pond, once a beautiful limpid pool surrounded by hills, which had long since become a receptacle for dead dogs and cats and the contents of slop buckets. The white and black residents of the shanties on its banks laundered their odds and ends of linen and "things too nauseous to mention" in it.

Although the window was often the point of disposal at the time, in most small cities, human wastes and waste water were deposited into cesspools, in privy vaults and open lots or fields. Often the wastes were picked up and thrown into waterways or recycled by spreading on nearby fields.

Immigrants to Cities

By the time of the American Revolution, Philadelphia was the second largest city in all of the British colonies worldwide, with only 40,000 people. Within a generation, several dozen urban centers of 2500 or more dotted the Atlantic coastline. In the nineteenth century the influx of immigrants from peasant villages of Europe accelerated. More than 30 million people came into the country during the nineteenth century; most stopped in the coast cities and newer ones over the mountains. In 1910, immigrants accounted for at least 70% of the populations of New York, Boston, Buffalo, Detroit and Chicago. In Pittsburgh, St. Louis, Philadelphia, Newark, Milwaukee, and Cincinnati, the number ranged from 50 to 70%.

Between the Revolutionary War and the Civil War, cities became the magnet for tens of thousands of farmers who had tried to make a living from the land but were thwarted by the unpredictable boom and bust American economy, as well as by droughts, grasshoppers, and other hardships of the frontier. After the Civil War, tenancy became common in the prairie and plains states toward the end of the nineteenth century. The celebrated farm movements of the period could not protect farmers from inflation/deflation, railroad monopolies, declining prices, and credit problems. So they packed up what would fit on their family wagon and headed for the nearest city, where industrialists promised work for everybody. What they found were dozens of workers competing for every job, slums, tenement buildings, sewer backup (where sewers even existed) oozing onto filthy streets, and a steady stream of dirt particles floating from nearby smokestacks. Unions were weak or nonexistent, pay was meager, work hours extended into the night. They sometimes joined immigrants to live in discarded crates and other refuse in shantytowns on open land outside cities or shared rooms with other families in tenement houses that reeked with foul odors and disease.

The Road to Environmental Protection

American cities suffered dreadful epidemics until well into the twentieth century. Environmental and health problems developed in new industrial cities in Europe before they assumed grave proportions in the United States, and efforts to control them there were under way during the American colonial period. German kings assumed the role of protector of the land and health of their people. Health programs included the appointment of physicians and surgeons to protect against the plague and other contagious diseases and inspect food and water.

In England, protection policies rested with each local town or village. The poor laws offered a measure of social welfare but little environmental or health protection. Residents were forbidden to throw animal or human wastes into gutters and streams, but sewage and refuse remained a continual pollution problem, even when scavengers were hired to collect it. Because of rapid population growth in emerging industrial towns, the easiest way to dispose of any waste was to dump it into the streets and gutters, where rain eventually carried it into streams. Water supplies from wells and natural springs close to town dumps were contaminated from leaching wastes. Cesspools were usually dug near tenement buildings and seeped into the basements where very poor dwellers lived amid the stench and disease; in the mid-nineteenth century, at the beginning of the industrial revolution in Liverpool, 40,000 people lived in the cellars. Where privies existed they often served dozens of buildings; in

Manchester during the same period, 33 privies were set up for about 7,000 people. Dysentery was a fact of life throughout Great Britain and the Continent.

Early Urban Improvements and Health Reformers

Some cities in England, particularly London, were improved during the last half of the 1700s. Initial efforts were directed toward draining and paving streets, which were believed to be major causes of epidemics. The Westminster Paving Act of 1762 became a model for more than 200 British communities between 1785 and 1800. At the same time improvements were made in obtaining cleaner water supplies and disposing of wastes by new sewerage that gradually replaced wood mains with iron pipes. The iron industry was growing rapidly in England at this time.

But by early in the nineteenth century, the industrial revolution had taken hold in England and factory deaths were common, despite the fact that physicians had long studied occupational diseases of industrial workers, particularly in mining, metal-working factories, and textile mills. By the early sixteenth century, the Swiss physician Paracelsus wrote about the skin and lung disorders of miners, and in 1700 the Italian Bernardino Ramazzini wrote a book on various occupational diseases of the day.

Occupational/environmental diseases were lively topics in the press and novels of the mid-1800s. Elizabeth Gaskell, a popular novelist of the period, told the story of a young Manchester textile mill worker who was dying of byssinosis, a lung disease caused by inhalation of cotton, flax, and hemp dust. Charles Dickens referred to Manchester as "Coketown," a grimy industrial city that dehumanized its population, and in a newspaper report in 1868 he described the problem of a woman working in the mills in the words of one of her fellow slum-dwellers.

The lead, sur. Sure 'tis the lead-mills, where the woman gets took on at eighteen-pence a day, sur, when they makes application early enough and is lucky and wanted; and 'tis lead-pisoned she is, sur, and some of them gets lead pisoned soon, and some of them gets lead-pisoned later, and some, but not many, niver, and 'tis all according to the constitooshun, sur, and some constitooshuns is strong, and some is weak; and her constitooshun is lead-pisoned, bad as can be, sur; and her brain is coming out at her ear, and it hurts her dreadful; and that's what it is, and niver no more and niver no less, sur. ("Small Star in the East" 1868)

Beginnings of Modern Public Health

Until later in the 1800s, most physicians believed that most diseases were caused by the state of the atmosphere (miasma), from foul odors from excrement, privies, sewers, decaying carcasses or corpses, filthy streets and the like. Any kind of decaying organic matter from excrement to dead animals was seen to cause disease-carrying miasmas. Poor sanitary conditions were believed to be especially responsible for atmospheric conditions that brought about epidemics and infectious diseases. Throughout the nineteenth century, many studies were conducted that illustrated that animate contagion, living bacterial organisms able to reproduce themselves, were at the bottom of contagious diseases rather than the air, but the miasma theory directed physicians, chemists, health reformers and leaders from the mid-1700s until at least the end of the following century. At bottom it espoused environmental factors as the primary bearers of disease. In *The Cycles of American History*, Arthur Schlesinger points out that many Europeans in the 1700s believed that the air of the American continent was so bad that human beings could not grow in that atmosphere.

Alain Corbin mentions in his fascinating study on the sense of smell that doctors and chemists believed that diseases could be cured by a proper control of foul odors, particularly of excrement. They went so far as to classify smells that emerged from cesspits, latrines, etc., as well as other putrid smells from decaying carcasses and corpses.

The theory seemed to be confirmed by common observation. Many diseases in the factories were in fact caused by airborne pollutants. (In the quotation above, Dickens also noted that some people, because of genetic "constitooshun," were able to withstand the attack.) Furthermore, wherever epidemics spread, like the cholera epidemic of 1831 and 1832, the victims lived in poorer districts where foul smells, filth, and poor sanitation were characteristic features. Poverty and filth were seen as the primary threat to public health and morals, as well as to an ordered (free enterprise) economic system in an ordered society.

During this period, English philosopher Jeremy Bentham developed a utilitarian theory that illustrated how private interests could benefit from public order. His disciples were known as Philosophic Radicals, intellectuals who proposed a series of "rational scientific" reforms to solve public policy questions. Most were concerned with environmental causes of poverty and disease, and also how scientific/utilitarian policies can promote more efficient government and industry. The group believed that these reforms could be implemented most effectively on a national level by Parliament.

One of the most influential of the group was Edwin Chadwick, who became interested in public health as secretary of the 1834 Poor Law Commission. The commission was primarily concerned with freeing a large labor pool to work in new factories by removing people from local parish welfare lists, but Chadwick was also interested in the causes of poverty and the health of those living in slums.

The Report on Sanitary Conditions

Chadwick and two other disciples of Bentham, Southwood Smith and Neil Arnott, believed that disease was caused by the conditions of poverty, and that most of the problems of both poverty and contagious diseases could be eliminated by stamping out the environmental causes of sickness, i.e., the filth and stench of the slum. Chadwick's "sanitary idea" that the physical and social environment determines health and well-being was the conclusion of the most influential environmental health document of the nineteenth century, his own *Report . . . on an Inquiry into the Sanitary Condition of the Labouring Population of Great Britain*, appearing in 1842.

The report was commissioned because Chadwick and three medical inspectors who worked on the Poor Law Commission maintained that disease prevention could save the government and industry much money, a reason that remains a primary political motive for much environmental legislation. Chadwick wanted to collect public health data to find out which environmental conditions led to better health. Chadwick enlisted Arnott and Smith to the work on the report and also Philip Kay, known for his short tract, *The Moral and Physical Condition of the Working Classes of Manchester*, published at the time of the first cholera epidemic in 1832. All three were interested in epidemic outbreaks and had conducted surveys to determine their causes. The use of public health surveys (from reports of local physicians) to determine remedial action in regions, towns, and factories had been common throughout the Continent for about a century.

Chadwick's monumental work was published as a Report from the Poor Law Commissioners to the Home Department in London and was filled with survey material, rich in detail of environmental conditions related to mortality rates and economic conditions, as well as discussions about promising sewer technologies and disposal of sewage. The report concluded firmly that sickness and disease, especially contagious diseases, were directly connected to environmental filth and pollution from lack of drainage, polluted water supplies, and excrement and garbage in homes and on the streets. Chadwick especially blamed "miasmas" from decaying animal and vegetable matter, and other types of foul air. He quoted Villareme, who wrote for the Royal Academy of Medicine at Paris that the canton of Varregio was transformed from a disease-ridden, "barbarous and miserable" district into a model of industry, "moral character," and health by simply draining the swamp whose *aria cativa* (foul air) polluted the inhabitants.

He advocated the "great preventives" of "drainage, street and house cleansing by means of supplies of water and improved sewerage, and especially the introduction of cheaper and more efficient modes of removing all noxious refuse from the towns,. . . (all) operations for which aid must be sought from the science of the Civil Engineer, not from the physician, who has done his work when he has pointed out the disease that results from the neglect of proper administrative measures, and has alleviated the sufferings of the victims."

Note that Chadwick and his collaborating physicians agreed that the solutions for environmental-medical problems would come from the engineering, not the medical, community. The primary leadership role of the physician, however, was apparent in that they played the diagnostic role in uncovering community medical problems in the first instance by treating patients. Throughout that century doctors had a lower status and were often linked to health reform movements especially among the poor. Government and business hired technical experts or engineers to carry out their policies, which often had small budgets.

The report led to a wave of concern around the country. Groups were formed to deal with working people's problems of high mortality, disease, congestion, crime, and poverty—all found in slums. "The Sanitary Question" became the focus of discussion, locally and nationwide. A national Public Health Act was passed to establish a Chadwick-recommended General Board of Health, which was empowered to establish local boards of health to deal with local water supplies, sewerage, control of offensive businesses, and other matters. Each board was to appoint a health officer, a legally qualified medical practitioner, who would deal with the issues raised in Chadwick's report. Chadwick became leader of the first board, but found that local authorities were not so eager to implement costly reforms as he. Small water companies fought his efforts to set up central water systems, especially in London, where many members of Parliament held stock in private water companies.

In England, as early as the 1770s, the idea of using running water to carry off human wastes was born of the public concern over disease-laden miasmas. The invention of the water closet was designed to wash away foul odors as well as fecal matter and urine. Corbin calls this phenomenon the "privatization of human wastes." The notion has ancient roots (e.g., latrines of the Roman empire often were flushed by surface water) but not until Sir John Harington, a courtier and poet, published *The Metamorphosis of Ajax* in 1596, and persuaded Queen Elizabeth to install a water closet in her Richmond palace did the idea receive modern form. Sir John's book contained a complete plan of the first modern water closet. A few water closets were found in London and larger cities during the 1770s. At the time, unfortunately, the wastewater from water closets was dumped into cesspits, where it overflowed and often polluted springs, wells, and other water supply sources. The London water companies eventually flourished because of increasing demand for water to flush away the wastes out of sight, out of mind, and out of nose as well. However, the companies were not interested in consolidating their many systems in the interests of health reform.

Impact of the Report

Although sanitary progress in England continued in fits and starts, with much opposition raised around issues of costs of new sewerage and water systems, the report undoubtedly defined the important issues in Britain, the Continent, and the United States for almost a century. One reason for its importance and acceptance was that epidemics, infected food, and defective sewerage were beginning to reach crisis proportions in industrial cities. Not only were slums affected, but entire communities. The report was written at a time when it touched the nation's vital nerve.

One of Chadwick's central engineering recommendations was to apply sewage to agricultural land. He described a system of covered sewers that led from the city to a stream, which was diverted to irrigation ditches, increasing the land's productivity immeasurably. When the city attempted to divert the sewers away from the stream, the farmers fought the change in court, claiming that Edinburgh would lose the rich milk and butter from cows that enjoyed the grasses fertilized by sewage effluent.

Chadwick wanted to avoid contamination of the streams, in which towns typically dumped their wastes, so he recommended using covered sewers, flushed by water systems, to carry wastes directly to the countryside away from dense populations. Chadwick was among the first to recommend a combined water-supply and sewage-disposal system.

In 1858 the stench of sewage directly discharged into the Thames was so great (renown as the "great stink") that members of parliament could not bear to attend sessions. During that year they authorized the London Metropolitan Board of Works the power to build a main drainage system to intercept local sewers and transport raw sewage just far enough downstream that the incoming tide would not take the waste back to London. Within a generation Londoners realized that the pipe simply transferred the problem downstream, and a treatment plant was authorized. The new facility left the Londoners with a huge pile of sludge, which eventually was dumped from specially-constructed ships far out at sea (again transferring the problem).

Yet, throughout the nineteenth century land application of sewage remained the recommended form of disposal to protect rivers and streams and the water supplies of the towns and cities of Great Britain. Royal commissions and parliamentary committees were unanimous in four reports during the 1860s. They considered the use of chemicals in water treatment, rejected the possibility, and in 1871 a commission recommended legislation that would enable towns to seize land for the purpose of "purifying" sewage. In 1876, the Rivers Pollution Act forbade the discharge of sewage into a stream.

The Rivers Pollution Act is of great interest at least because it became an archetype of the history of many environmental regulations in the United States as well as England. Since the legislation potentially could affect hundreds of municipalities and industries, virtually all of its teeth were carefully removed before passage. Alleged offenders had to be given two months notice before enforcement could proceed, during which time the court could send "skilled parties" to advise treatment. Manufacturing interests were provided preferential treatment: local governing boards had to give special permission to the sanitary authority before the latter could initiate action against industry, making certain that the enforcement actions were "reasonably practicable." Industrial interests only had to claim hardship to be exempted from the law.

Critics in and out of Parliament said minimal progress was made to curb water pollution by the end of the century in Great Britain, and that land application of wastes, the primary means by which progress could have been made, was avoided because of the expense to cities. Instead, engineers began to recommend a "dilution" or "assimilation" method. First the sewage was chemically and biologically treated, then discharged in quantities that were believed to be in proportion to the stream's capacity of assimilation. The waterway thus became the chief means of water purification in modern times. It still is, on both sides of the Atlantic.

United States' Practice

American cities developed at least as haphazardly as London and other British cities and suffered similar environmental distress. The horse-drawn omnibus was the first of a series of transportation innovations in the 1830s that led to the hectic twentieth century city. Before that time cities tended to have their commercial activity clustered in one area, mostly at the waterfront, and people walked to work and back home. The physical expansion of the city then was limited to "walking city" dimensions. By 1850, commuter railroads began to appear to carry wealthier residents from newly built suburbs to their central city workplace. Streetcars, electric trolleys, cable cars and, ultimately, subways and elevated railroads changed urban land use patterns from "walking cities" to sprawling, densely populated, congested metropolises. Transportation lines served the underclass as well as the rich, taking everyone to downtown shopping and business districts. Noise, dirt, and smells from locomotives and other transporters were layered on the traditional smells in the city of horses and pigs (which were tolerated because they ate garbage).

Although responsible for most of the transportation, hauling, and much of the heavy labor of the era, horses represented a special environmental problem. There were 3.5 million of them in American cities at the turn of the century and they generated a monumental smell before and after evacuating their wastes. Every city had large horse populations: 83,000 in Chicago, 12,000 each in Milwaukee and Detroit. Environmental historian Joel A. Tarr remarked, "The faithful, friendly horse was charged with creating the very problems today attributed to the automobile: air contaminants harmful to health, noxious odors, and noise. The presence of 120,000 horses in New York City, wrote one 1908 authority for example, is "an economic burden, an affront to cleanliness, and a terrible tax upon human life." Experts at the time asserted that the normal city horse dropped 15 to 30 pounds of manure a day. The buggies spread it around and caked it to the streets. Tarr points to the calculations of health officials in Rochester, N.Y., which reported to the city that the 15,000 horses in the city produced enough manure every year to make a pile 175 feet high over a full acre of ground, enough to breed 16 billion flies and spread life-threatening sickness and disease. A strong demand for the "horseless carriage" existed very early in the large cities of America.

The Industrial City

City fathers of the time wanted flourishing, mechanized cities, so horses would have eventually disappeared from the scene even if they smelled like roses. By the twentieth century, most big cities, already crammed with a large, unemployed workforce and connected to each other by an elaborate network of railroads, were ready for the influx of capital from local and British capitalists that would transform them into full-fledged industrial cities. Older, small, local foundries, refineries, tanneries, etc., that were financed by merchant capital, were being pushed out of business by new, large corporations that strove for stable, monopolistic power in the marketplace. Municipal authorities welcomed their presence and never interfered with their operations.

New York was among the first to make the transition from a walking city to an industrialized city. Already in 1880 it had 287 foundries and machine shops, and another 125 steam engines, bone mills, refineries and tanneries. Its slums were among the most crowded in the world—more than 900 people were packed into every acre. By the turn of the century Pittsburgh had hundreds of iron and steel plants with (according to its publicists) about 14,000 chimneys up the Monongahela Valley. As early as 1862, Anthony Trollope described Pittsburgh as "the blackest place I ever saw." Shantytowns were common in the Pennsylvania steel and coal mining districts. Chicago's stockyards combined with eight railroads, a busy port, and heavy industry to assault its residents with smelly, cough-causing black smoke.

Most industrial cities reeked of sulfur, ammonia gases, offal rendering, bone boiling, manure heaps, putrid animal wastes, fish scrap, kerosene, acid fumes, phosphate fertilizer, and sludge. Garbage, kitchen slops, cinders, coal dust, and other unwanted litter was piled in the streets. Many cities had no official garbage collection practice.

New York hired street teams to handle its garbage, which was randomly and irregularly collected and barged for sea-dumping. Most other cities simply found a vacant lot or field in or out of the city where the open garbage lot became a breeding ground for disease, and it blew into nearby residents' windows. The rapid and huge population increases as well as the poverty and isolation of new immigrant groups crammed into tenement houses precluded the possibility of community cooperation or peer pressure to solve these problems.

After the Civil War

Industrialization did not accelerate until the Civil War when the Union government bought arms, food, and clothing, using millions of greenback dollars printed in lavish amounts. With this new kind of government financing of industries, cities began to spawn large companies that produced iron and steel for ordnance and later bridges and high-rise buildings, as well as textiles and food processing industries for their multiplying populations. Oil refining, chemical manufacturing, machine tool shops, engines and farm machinery followed. Most large metropolises grew rapidly and randomly with diversified economies, but many cities specialized with local resources, labor, and markets: steel in Pittsburgh, Youngstown, and Gary; glass in Toledo; textiles in Fall River and New Bedford; flour milling in Minneapolis; brewing in Milwaukee; farm machinery in Racine; meat packing in Kansas City and Omaha, and so on. The population in the cities grew 100 times from 1850 to 1900, with little thought, let alone planning and regulations, about the human and environmental effects.

Each city developed its own pollution problems as factories, furnaces, and warehouses were constructed amid a crazy quilt of streets, alleys, canals, and railroads. Urban immigrants from European farms and villages had been used to feeding their garbage to farm animals and spreading human and animal wastes on their fields. Industrial cities on the Continent and in the United States grew so rapidly that most people simply tossed their wastes into common dumps, cesspools, or dunghills in courts and alleys around which their tenements or houses were built. Besides excrement, in or out of cesspools, courtyards were filled with kitchen slops and other garbage, dead animals, ashes, street sweepings, and sometimes industrial wastes from nearby factories. People expected scavengers to haul away their garbage for a pittance. American culture still associates waste with low-life activity.

The Beginnings of Reform

So strong were the economic and cultural connections between England and the United States that the former colonies followed the economic pattern of English cities—laissez-faire growth and increase in wealth accompanied by rapid development of environmental and health problems. The intellectual bond also was tight, so American reformers and politicians looked to British practice for solutions to their own health problems, including epidemics that were related to urban decay.

Newspapers in the older cities at the beginning of the the nineteenth century blamed the accumulation of filth in the streets, poor drainage, and air pollution from businesses such as slaughter houses and soap factories for epidemic outbreaks. But at that period seaport towns still were growing too slowly to generate much action. After the heavy waves of immigration American cities reeled from recurring epidemics of yellow fever, cholera, smallpox, typhoid fever, and typhus fever. Then the country was ready for its own Chadwick report, and two of them arrived in the same decade, from New York and Boston.

The first was done in 1845 by John C. Griscom, a physician and New York city health inspector. Griscom launched his study at the end of 1842 when he appended a short essay, "A Brief View of the Sanitary Condition of the City," to his yearly health report. Three years later he published an expanded study, *The Sanitary Condition of the Laboring Population of New York*, a title that reflects the influence of Chadwick's report. Griscom analyzed the exploitive "system of tenantage" and its resultant poverty, and explained its relationship to filth, disease, and high mortality. The American Medical Association was founded in 1847 and its hygiene committee conducted sanitary surveys and collected other vital statistics that documented the need for reforms in urban practices.

Lemul Shattuck, a Boston bookseller and publisher, had already helped found the American Statistical Society in 1839. He issued a *Census of Boston*, which was prelude to another sanitary report, in 1845. The census documented the high general mortality, especially of infants and mothers, and the prevalence of communicable diseases such as scarlet fever, diphtheria, and tuberculosis. From these data Shattuck determined that a further study was needed and he convinced the Massachusetts Sanitary Commission to charge him with the task. Shattuck published his *Report* in 1850.

That study was pioneering in its attempt to standardize terminology and raise the quality of statistical material in reports of the day. He recommended establishing a state board of health and local boards of health to conduct and publish regular sanitary surveys. As did his colleagues in England and New York, Shattuck connected environmental sanitation to public health. Shattuck proved the importance of child health care, school health programs, mental health, health education, teaching preventive medicine in medical schools, alcoholism, and smoke control. Although little was done about these matters in his own time, Shattuck has had great influence on subsequent urban policies and reform activity.

However, politics and reform have not always gone together. While it was true that by the 1880 U.S. census more than 94% of the surveyed cities had set up a board of health, a health commission, or hired a health officer who controlled all aspects of environmental sanitation—water problems and sewage and garbage—these boards became political bodies and were not under the control of physicians. Rather, political considerations of money and influence played more of a role in local environmental affairs than considerations of public health until the late 1880s.

Sewerage Problems

Public reaction in the late nineteenth and early twentieth centuries increased as deteriorating air and water quality were seen to cause epidemics of typhoid, dysentery, cholera, and yellow fever. By the 1880s most cities had built sewerage systems that disposed of untreated wastes in nearby rivers, streams, lakes, harbors, and estuaries. Control of air pollution caused by smoke from factories, coal, and wood-burning stoves depended on heavy winds. Some cities' sewerage systems solved health problems caused by overflowing cesspools and privy vaults of their own residents, but downstream or lake cities usually drew their water supplies from these polluted watercourses. Even scavengers contracted by the cities to clean out cesspools and privy vaults (with buckets) often dumped the wastes into nearby rivers and streams. More often, cesspools were filled in with dirt and new holes dug, eventually contaminating water wells in all directions. At the same time, steel mills and other factories were built beside rivers or lakes because water easily purifies their products and then is handy for dumping metallic particles, oil grease, cyanide, ammonia and other waste products. Cities such as Pittsburgh, with chronic air pollution problems, also suffered from dying rivers and streams.

As the demand for clean water grew, not only for household uses but also for flushing to fight epidemics and for fighting fires in the tenement districts, cities built waterworks systems out of nearby rivers. Philadelphia built the first in 1802; by 1860, 136 systems had been built in the country; in 1880, there were 598 systems.

Citizen Reaction

During the 1890s, physicians, public health officers, and citizens' groups stepped up the pressure to do something about the "garbage problem," "foul smells," and resultant health hazards. The print media—newspapers, popular and technical journals—frequently featured articles about some aspect of the problem. Adding fuel to the early reform movement, William T. Sedgwick of the Massachusetts Board of Health proved the relationship between polluted water and typhoid fever. Writers and citizens groups cited the spread of diseases and stench as they appealed for action from their municipal leaders.

By the turn of the century, dozens of citizen groups, mostly made up of educated, middle-class women, were active in every large city. Among the most effective of the groups, the Ladies' Protective Association of New York City, was organized in 1884 to force authorities to clean up a smelly manure pile in a neighborhood. Later the women tackled a wide variety of urban sanitation, street-cleaning, and refuse disposal problems. So much media attention was given to these problems that most large cities had their own "public improvement" groups, very often formed by educated upper- or middle-class women. They were interested in health and aesthetics and involved themselves in littered streets, spoiled produce at markets, smoke pollution, sewage pollution, and other issues. They usually did not get involved in scientific debates or even specific control measures, as this argument from the New York group, the sentiments repeated often by other improvement groups, attests.

Even if dirt were not the unsanitary and dangerous thing we know it is, its unsightliness and repulsiveness are so great, that no other reason than the superior beauty of cleanliness should be required to make the citizens of New York, through their vested authorities, quite willing to appropriate whatever sum may be necessary, in order to give to themselves and to their wives and daughters, that outside neatness, cleanliness and freshness, which are the natural complement and completion of inside order and daintiness, which are to the feminine taste and perception, simply indispensable, not only to comfort but to self respect.

The contribution of women's clubs in conservation causes—particularly in refor-estation, forest preservation, and animal preservation—had been substantial from the mid-nineteenth century. The suffrage and Progressive movements added a sharper political edge to their work and brought many of their leaders to Washington to lobby the Congress and members of Theodore Roosevelt's cabinet. By the end of the first decade of the twentieth century hundreds of local women's organizations all over the country could mobilize hundreds of thousands of members in behalf of environmental legislation to protect the natural environment. Their day-to-day activities monitored the local environments in and around urban areas. The women's organizations' signal achievements established a solid tradition for environmental groups of the 1960s and 1970s.

Influence of the "Apostle of Cleanliness"

One of the more influential of the late nineteenth-century reformers, Col. George E. Waring, became involved in urban problems through his friendship with conserva-tionist and landscape architect Frederick Law Olmsted in the 1850s. Well known for research work in agriculture, Waring was appointed by Olmsted to do drainage and other agricultural work in New York's Central Park. Commissioned a colonel during the Civil War, and after the war continuing his studies in "scientific" agriculture, War-ing gradually turned his attention to drainage and sewerage problems, about which he wrote and on which he worked.

At Lenox, Massachusetts, in 1875-76, he built the first separate sewer system, called the "Waring system," one for channeled rain water and one for raw sewage. Waring believed it was necessary to build small-diameter separate sewers, one for storm water and one for wastes from homes, because a large combined system allowed fecal matter to accumulate and generate disease-inducing sewer gas. Chadwick, who also held to the miasma theory of disease, preceded Waring in this view. Many engineers, following the work of Rudolph Hering, believed that the combined single-pipe system brought no ill-health effects, but some advocates of the separate system contended that not all urban areas needed both flood drainage lines and a different sewage disposal system, which would have priority for any city's sanitary problems. The debate was carried in most engineering journals of the day, and their conclusions were derived mainly from cost considerations.

The National Board of Health appointed Waring to examine sanitary conditions in Memphis after 5,000 of its inhabitants died from a yellow fever epidemic and more than 25,000 more residents fled in panic. Waring was commissioned to build his separate system for the city, amid some controversy, and later built the system in other cities. His critics attacked him for promoting his own system and attempting to get rich from it (he held its patent rights), regardless of disputed sanitary value. Both separate and combined types led to a river or water course without treatment. The reason for the Waring system lay in a miasma theory of disease (influence of sewer gas), not that the sewage could be better treated separately from storm water.

By the end of the century, however, Colonel Waring was recognized as one of the nation's leading sanitary engineers. He worked with the short-lived National Board of

Figure 12–1. Col. George E. Waring placed this sketch at the beginning of his well-known *Street Cleaning* (1897), published three years after he was appointed to the task of street sanitation in New York. He apparently wanted to illustrate just how monumental was his charge. The photo from the N.Y. Department of Sanitation, taken a few years earlier, justifies his claim. Photo courtesy N.Y. City Museum.

Health and was able to interact with a variety of sanitarians, public health officers, engineers, and civic groups. He continued to publish widely circulated articles on sewerage, drainage, and other urban problems. He had worked on urban social statistics for the 1880 census, which introduced him to detailed statistics surrounding urban problems. In 1894 he was appointed New York Street-Cleaning Commissioner in reform Mayor William Strong's administration. Before the appointment, he was assistant engineer for the city of New Orleans.

Waring attacked problems of the city with steadfast discipline. He believed that all foul city odors had to be removed for the health of its residents: manure from the horses, sewer gas, garbage, factory wastes, human excrement. Meticulously dressed in his spotless uniform, pith helmet, and riding boots, and mounted on his prancing steed, the ex-military officer went to the most offensive parts of the city and gave orders to his street-cleaning corps. He checked and double-checked their work, gave pep-talks, fired them if they disobeyed or ignored his instructions, dressed them in white uniforms, and had his "White Wings" march in city parades. He repeated the talks at civic meetings and to journalists, who gleefully snapped his picture on his horse and gave Waring the publicity he wanted. The commissioner understood his position to be as much of a public educator as an engineer.

Waring reorganized every facet of the job from street sweeping and disposal collection to snow removal and "garbage-reduction" experiments. He also used ashes and street sweepings as landfill and collaborated in experiments to recycle ashes and organic materials into fireproofing blocks. Known as the "apostle of cleanliness," Waring greatly influenced other urban engineers for decades. His books and articles on urban engineering were considered authoritative long before and after he died in 1898. His work helped bring the field of sanitary engineering from England, where Edwin Chadwick created it, to the United States, where it became an important facet of municipal or civil engineering. Moreover, he was a media star, and he recommended cost-effective engineering solutions to a variety of sanitary questions.

Sanitary engineering developed early in the history of most cities because of the need to obtain water supplies for swelling populations, and some way had to be found to safely dispose of their sewage. By 1910, 70% of cities with 30,000 or more people owned their own water supply systems. With the flow of water into the cities came water closets and an increase in water consumption of 50 to 100 times. Thus did privy vaults and cesspools overflow, and new environmental problems were placed on the shoulders of sanitary engineers. With these new responsibilities for building sewer lines, the influence of the engineers grew in the cities. Soon they were handling the collection and disposal of garbage and refuse. People of the time hoped all these problems could be solved by good engineering and modern technology.

Influence of Germ Theory

For many centuries philosophers and physicians debated the causes of disease, especially dread plagues and epidemics. Several early scientists—Fracastoro in 1546, van Leeuwenhoek about 150 years later, and Spallanzani in the eighteenth century—suggested that a living contagion was the cause of infection. Most people were not convinced until Pasteur's experiments during the mid-nineteenth century. He was greatly assisted by improvements made on the microscope in the 1830s, as well as by the work of colleagues showing that fermentation was caused by microbes and by Bassi's proof that a particular microbe caused a certain silkworm disease.

Especially interested in disproving the ancient theory of spontaneous generation of life, Pasteur confirmed Spallanzani's experiments that microbes or germs floated in the air and set on applying his work to the origins of disease. After hearing Pasteur, the English surgeon Joseph Lister, son of the founder of modern microscopy, began to investigate bacteria present in the air and found that these bacteria often caused his patients' wounds to become infected with pus. Lister also found that he could control infection by applying carbolic acid, which at the time was used to disinfect sewage. In 1867, he wrote about his "antiseptic surgery" as a means of killing germs, and soon after germs were routinely excluded from wounds by cleanliness of person and environment. At the same time Pasteur was showing that microbes caused diseases in beer, wine, silkworms, hens, cows, sheep, and men; he also developed vaccination methods to prevent diseases.

Sanitary Engineering

By the turn of the century, the germ theory of disease was commonly accepted by public health officials on both sides of the Atlantic, but public policy continued to apply the miasma as well as the germ theory. Through the latter decades of the nineteenth century, most large American cities, to contain disease, used both quarantine (implying knowledge of contagion) and environmental sanitation, usually because of abhorrence of foul smells.

Sanitary engineering received respectability through the efforts of scientists and engineers associated with a number of research stations connected to state boards of health. Foremost among these was the Lawrence Experiment Station of the Massachusetts Board of Health, which brought together engineers, chemists, and biologists to solve problems of water purification and sewage treatment. One engineer at the experiment station offered this early definition of a sanitary engineer: "He who adapts the forces of nature to the preservation of public health, through the construction and operation of engineering works . . . (sanitary engineering) is the application of a new science to a new product of civilization. The new science is bacteriology; the new product of civilization is 'The Modern City.' "

After a reasonable consensus was reached on the germ theory of disease and particularly on the relationship between typhoid fever and water polluted by sewage, a deduction first postulated by Englishman William Budd in 1849 and later made at the Lawrence Experiment Station, sanitary engineers focused their attention on sewage treatment and "purification." The laboratory experimented with methods of sewage treatment—intermittent filtration and land application of wastewater—and showed they could protect water supplies. The experiment station rejected land application of wastes because of the enormous amount of land required for even a small city.

Meanwhile other experiments with mechanical filters at Louisville, Kentucky were proving successful. By 1900, *Engineering Record* reported, "The resources of the sanitary engineer are sufficient to bring about the purification of sewage to any reasonable degree. This costs money . . ., but not so much as is often believed."

The reason to treat sewage, of course, was to protect the water supplies of downstream cities. However, government and business did not favor sewage treatment, preferring water filtering and sometimes disinfection. By 1900, American sanitary engineers began to follow the British practice of water protection by combining stream dilution along with treatment of incoming water supplies. Americans developed a system of filtering water coming *into* the system rather than treating sewage going *out*, if the sewage did not create a "nuisance." The reason given was that it is more economical to purify water than treat sewage; people assumed that sewage was diluted, dispersed, and clarified as it moved down rivers and streams to the city receiving its waters. Purification measures by filtration made the water safe to drink after dispersion and dilution of sewage in waterways, they maintained. One of the first metropolitan areas to practice the method was Chicago, which first constructed a canal as an open sewer to dispose of Chicago's sewage to the Illinois River in 1848. Then, after a series of typhoid epidemics in the 1880s, a new Municipal Sanitary

District decided to solve the problem by expanding their drainage capacity with a new Chicago Drainage Canal in 1890. Designed by the famous engineer, Rudolph Hering, who traveled widely in England and the Continent, the canal carried sewage from Chicago to the Illinois River, which emptied into the Mississippi. Before long, growing cities around the country were emptying their wastes into nearby rivers, with water-carriage as the preferred engineering method. The water pollution or sanitary problems of the previous century were either diluted away or transferred downstream.

Until World War II, few municipalities interfered with the rights of business to dump wastes either into surface waters or on open lands. One reason was the common perception that industrial wastes did not carry the germs of disease; in fact, many believed that the wastes from factories killed germs in rivers and streams. More important was the extraordinary power that industry wielded in local governments.

An example typical of the period is the Calumet area of South Chicago, which was developed during the 1870s by the Calumet at Chicago Canal and Dock Co. The company received congressional appropriations to dredge the Calumet River and wipe out a lush marsh area. Soon the river was lined with steel mills and agricultural rendering plants. Into the river were poured acids, phenols, benzene, tars, oils, fat, and animal carcasses, along with domestic sewage. City officials were at first only concerned about the domestic sewage, not with industrial wastes. By the turn of the century when the volume of the wastes was multiplied by five, the stench and taste of the water made life on or near the river impossible. When local politicians realized they had to act on the crescendo of complaints, they did not consider a course of action that forced treatment of wastes or their reduction, but only further diversion and dilution.

Disputes over Methods and Policies

Early in the twentieth century, major public disputes about the need to treat sewage before discharge broke out between the engineers and public health physicians and their allies in the press. The issue was whether public health was being adequately protected. Politicians, business interests, municipal bureaucrats, and civic groups all became embroiled in the dispute. The Progressive movement supported treatment over dilution, not only for health reasons but for recreational and other purposes of waterways. The multiple resource use became a national plank in their platform. Most uses of water demand a fairly high degree of purity. Progressives also favored "rational" national planning to mediate special interests at the local level.

The federal government became involved with passage of the Public Health Service Act, which established research facilities to determine, among other things, the possibility of self-purification of inter-state streams. The act intensified the states' activities, mainly in monitoring sewage disposal and water quality through their state boards of health. Many times it took disease outbreaks like the typhoid epidemics of 1904 to galvanize state action.

A typical example of such policy struggles occurred in Pennsylvania, which passed its own 1905 law "to preserve the purity of the waters of the State for the protection of the public health" after serious typhoid epidemics. New municipal bodies were forbidden to discharge untreated sewage into state waterways, and cities that already discharged raw sewage had to receive state permits to extend their systems.

Pittsburgh, with a 500,000 population and another half million around its borders in 1910, had been suffering from recurring typhoid epidemics. For a century all domestic water had been drawn from the Allegheny and Monongahela rivers, where the city also dumped untreated sewage. In 1910, when Pittsburgh applied for a state permit to extend its sewer lines, the health director required a "comprehensive sewerage plan for the collection and disposal of all of the sewage of the municipality."

Pittsburgh hired the well-known engineering firm of Allen Hazen and George Whipple to do the study. Hazen and Whipple concluded that a new sewage treatment plant would offer no greater protection to downstream residents because the suburbs would continue to dump raw sewage. They also maintained that the cost of treating sewage far outweighed potential benefits. The state health department initially withheld the permit because the firm did not submit the comprehensive planning report the department required, but under political duress the state granted a temporary discharge permit, renewed regularly until 1939. No treatment plant was built in the region until 1959. Most engineers believed it was more cost effective for downstream systems to use sand or mechanical filtration methods developed in the 1890s at the Lawrence Experiment Station and Louisville, or to apply chlorine, which was introduced in 1908, than build new treatment plants at the source of the pollution. They agreed that a treatment plant was the better alternative when it was necessary to control floating solids and odors.

The nation's engineering community rejoiced over the victory with articles and editorials in engineering journals. *Engineering News* complained that the state board "joined blindly in . . . the doctors' or physicians' campaign against the discharge of untreated sewage into streams, with little or no regard to the local physical and financial conditions." The editors affirmed that engineering questions of water supply and sewage disposal should be left to engineers, not doctors.

After a series of typhoid epidemics in the late nineteenth century, several states, particularly in the East, attempted to regulate water quality, mainly by requiring cities to submit sewerage plans to the state. In the beginning, enforcement measures were rare, but after 1900, under mounting political and civic pressure and despite the difficulty in proving the source of waterborne diseases, state courts began to sue offending municipalities for creating downstream pollution. The first municipal treatment plants utilizing sand filtration and chlorine disinfectants were built during this era. During the entire period treatment for industrial wastes was ignored or believed to be too expensive to be considered. Engineers simply did not work on treatment systems for industrial wastes as long as health problems seemed to result only from undiluted domestic sewage. Fish kills rarely were significant political issues of the day.

Air Quality

The air of large U.S. cities during this period was no better than the water. Smoke was the bane of city life. Most cities were near waterways in order to receive and send out goods to market by boat, but these locations are especially susceptible to atmospheric inversions. Then cities built rail lines for trains that used cheap, available, and highly polluting bituminous coal. Soft coal was also used by factories that belched smoke and dirt so thick it covered everyone and everything, including the sun. By the turn of the century Dickens' "Coketown" was seen throughout America as the industrial revolution traveled at full speed.

Of course, many people became sick, and the foundations of buildings, viaducts, and statuary began to crumble. Foresters around several cities said smoke was killing large numbers of trees. Civic and women's groups allied with physicians to speak out about the effects of the "smoke nuisance." Relying on metropolitan statistics of the time, Dr. J.B. Stoner, an activist physician, outlined some of the problems caused by smoke:

. . . there are more people subject to nasal, throat and bronchial troubles in a smoky city than in a clean city. There are also more fatalities from pneumonia, diphtheria and typhoid fever owing . . . to the lowering of the vital forces as a result of the scarcity of sunshine, caused by heavy fogs of smoke. . . . Women living in sunless, gloomy houses and attired in somber clothes (were) also prone to be irritable, to scold and whip their children and to greet their husbands with caustic speech. . . . Children (were apt to become) dull, apathetic and even criminally inclined.

Health officers and the American Medical Association pointed to black lungs of dead city residents as evidence of deadly smoke pollution causing consumption and various bronchial disorders. Smoke Abatement Leagues and Ladies Health Clubs were organized around the country, again run by upper-middle class women. Most newspapers and journals took up the cause, attacking judges for being too lenient on industry (even Andrew Carnegie rallied the Pittsburgh Chamber of Commerce against smoke), and, responding to the power of their constituencies, politicians began to make statements about the smoke of factories and railroads.

Eventually, engineers became involved and also wrote articles, claiming the problem could be avoided with technical innovations like stokers and down-draft furnaces, or electrified transportation systems. These mechanical and stationary engineers even helped draft legislation to prohibit smoke nuisance, and wrote many technical reports to civic associations and local government officials.

Of course, this was an era when smoke was equated with progress and prosperity. Some good was accomplished by these turn-of-the-century reformers, but industry generally made changes in production equipment when and where it was expedient. The most successful arguments pointed to aesthetic degradation, health decline, and economic losses attributable to the pollution.

Dilution as the Solution

Most pollution problems in nineteenth century cities coincided with rapid population increases, urbanization, and the industrial revolution. Their solution was defined by nineteenth century utilitarians, led by Jeremy Bentham, who wanted to solve the

Figure 12–2. This steel and coke works in Pittsburgh was typical of most steel plants built at the turn of the century. Historically proximate to coal, iron ore, and limestone regions, the plant is built beside a river from which it takes water to cool and purify its products and into which it daily dumps back the water laden with hundreds of tons of metallic particles, oil, grease, cyanide, ammonia, and other waste products. Carbon and other substances, resulting from incomplete burning or heating of metals, form particulates, carbon monoxide, sulfur and nitrogen oxides, and toxic fumes and metallic dusts. Photo by Ron Rortvedt, courtesy Environmental Action.

problems by applying the same principles of rational "scientific" efficiency management as were governing the industrial revolution itself.

Chadwick's report, and its many successors on both sides of the Atlantic, was the prime example of utilitarianism in action. Chadwick's conclusions emphasized that efficient solutions to public health problems would lead to a healthier economy and a stronger England. The Progressives in the United States picked up the theme and applied it especially to problems of resource management and multiple-use policies for rivers and streams.

Special industrial and environmental interests only gradually were defined in opposition to one another, and government bureaucracies saw themselves mainly as serving the needs of emerging industries in England and the United States. A Royal Commission on Sewage Disposal report in London (1901) clearly shows the mainstream opinion in the testimony of A.D. Adrian: "You have to deal with this question from a common sense point of view. What is the object we have in view? The object is to make rivers as little of a nuisance as we possibly can. But that must be consistent with supporting industries of the neighborhood. If you go on to insist on conditions which it is impossible to carry out except to the detriment and destruction of these industries, then I say you are doing far more harm than good." As long as business interests and their engineers could demonstrate that their dilution and filtration technologies would prevent epidemics, they could hold back the more expensive treatment methods advocated by health reformers, conservationists, and Progressives.

References for Further Reading

A basic source for several sections of this chapter is references from the excellent scholarship of Joel A. Tarr: his "Search for the Ultimate Sink: Urban Air, Land and Water Pollution in Historical America" in Kendall E. Bailes, ed. *Environmental History* (1985). See also Tarr's "Urban Pollution-Many long years ago" in *American Heritage,* October 1971; and "Disputes Over Water Quality Policy: Professional Cultures in Conflict, 1900-1917" with Terry Yosie and James McCurley III, *American Journal of Public Health,* Vol. 70, No. 4, April 1980; and "Historical Perspectives on Hazardous Wastes in the United States" in *Waste Management and Research,* 3 (1985), 95-102. For a good case study, see Craig E. Colten, "Industrial Wastes in Southeast Chicago: Production and Disposal 1870-1970" in *Environmental Review* 10 (1986): 93-105. A basic source for the history of the "sanitary movement," especially in England, but also in other Western countries, including the United States, is George Rosen's classic *A History of Public Health* (1958). Hart's description of New York's streets is printed in a reference collection of documents, *Conservation in the United States; Pollution,* edited by Leonard B. Dworsky (1971). Edwin Chadwick's *Inquiry into the Sanitary Condition of the Labouring Population of Great Britain* (1842) still makes good reading. James Ridgeway's *Politics of Ecology* (1971) begins with an interesting treatment of the report and subsequent U.S. documents. The best source that documents original public works debates in nineteenth century London is *The Government of Victorian*

London, 1855-1889: The Metropolitan Board of Works, The Vestries, and the City Corporation by David Owen (1982). Alain Corbin has written a fascinating study of the social context of the sense of smell, *The Foul and the Fragrant* (1986), which includes excellent material on the extent of public concern over the threat of miasmas. Martin V. Melosi's *Garbage in the Cities* (1981) and *Pollution & Reform in American Cities, 1870-1930* (1980), also edited by Melosi, are excellent basic books. The latter contains an article by Suellan Hoy on the role of women in improving urban sanitation practices. A special issue of *Environmental Review* (8:1, Spring 1984), edited by Carolyn Merchant, points up the achievements of women's organizations in environmental history. For a survey and bibliography on urban history, see Howard P. Chudacoff, *The Evolution of American Urban Society* (1975); David Ward, *Cities and Immigrants: A Geography of Change in Nineteenth Century America* (1971); and Sam Bass Warner, Jr.: *The Urban Wilderness: A History of the American City* (1972). Most scholars utilize the U.S. Commerce Department study, *Historical Statistics of the United States: Colonial Times to 1970* for basic statistical data.

Part Four

THE
TWENTIETH CENTURY

Chronology of Major Events

1900	First quantity-production automobile factory built by Olds Company in Detroit.
	Mark Carleton returns from Russia with hearty durum wheat varieties.
	William Orton breeds disease-resistant strains of cotton.
1901	U.S. Steel Corporation founded by J. Pierpont Morgan.
	Oil discovered at Spindletop, Texas, by Captain Anthony Lucas.
1902	Newlands Reclamation Act passed.
1903	Serum for hog cholera developed.
1903-1910	Height of muckraking literature.
1905	National Audubon Society formed.
1906	Railroad Rate Bill, Pure Food and Drug Act, Meat Inspection Act and Antiquities Act passed by Congress.
1906-1910	Period of worst coal mine disasters in U.S.
1907	Inland Waterways Commission established.
	Forest Reserve Act repealed.
1907-1908	Panic of 1907.
1908	Theodore Roosevelt convenes Governors' Conference on Conservation.
1910	Mann-Elkins Act (interstate commerce) passed.
	469,000 automobiles registered.
	U.S. Census: 91,972,266 (45.7% urban).
1911	Fur Seal Treaty between U.S., Russian, Canada, and Japan.
	American Tobacco Company and Standard Oil of N.J. Anti-Trust cases.
1912	Marquis wheat introduced by Canadians William and Charles Saunders.
1913	Federal Reserve Commission established.
	Marion Dorset perfects serum for hog cholera.
1914	Federal Trade Commission established.
	Clayton Anti-Trust Act passed.
	Smith-Lever Act passed, providing for a cooperative federal-state Agricultural Extension Service.
1914-1919	Business boom fed by Allied war orders. Farm prices and production reach new heights. Sharp rise of aluminum industry.
1916	National Park Service Act passed.
	Migratory Bird Treaty between U.S. and Great Britain.
1920	Over 9,000,000 automobiles registered.
	Federal Water Power Act passed.
1921-1929	Rapid expansion of securities markets and investment trusts, with commercial banks branching into real estate and investment banking.
	Great expansion of automobile industry.
	Fourfold increase in gasoline production.
1921-1933	Farm depression becomes chronic.
1922	Izaak Walton League organized.
1925	Peak of Florida land boom. Collapse in 1926.

1927	John D. Rust invents mechanical cotton picker.
1928	Coolidge vetoes McNary-Haugen Farm Relief Bill.
1929-1933	Crash of 1929 leads to Great Depression with 15,000,000 people unemployed in 1933.
1929	Federal Farm Board established.
	26,500,000 automobiles registered.
1930	Oil strike in East Texas.
	U.S. Census: 122,775,046 (56.2% urban).
1933-1937	New Deal intervention attempts to increase business activity.
	Dust storms and drought in the West.
1933	National Industrial Recovery Act, Agricultural Adjustment Act, Civilian Conservation Corps, Tennessee Valley Authority passed.
	Soil Erosion Service established under Hugh Hammond Bennett.
1934	Securities and Exchange Commission established.
1935	Works Progress Administration established, National Labor Relations Act, Social Security Act passed.
1936	Soil Conservation and Domestic Allotment Act, and the Omnibus Flood Control Act passed.
	Completion of Boulder (Hoover) Dam.
1938	Second Agricultural Adjustment Act.
1938-1939	Recovery increased, but unemployment still at 10,000,000 in 1939.
1939-1945	World War II ends depression and gives enormous boost to economy.
1940	U.S. Census: 131,669,275 (56.5% urban).
	U.S. Fish and Wildlife Service established.
1941	Steagall Amendments for farm price supports passed.
1943	Enrico Fermi effects first atomic chain reaction.
1941-1945	Numerous war agencies established to direct resources, rationing, prices, labor, defense, censorship, intelligence operations, foreign relief.
1942	Alaskan Highway completed.
	DDT introduced into U.S.
1944	Soil Conservation Society of America founded.
1946	U.S. Bureau of Land Management established in Department of Interior.
1946-1960	Tide of affluence and prosperity except for three minor recessions.
1948	Donora smog tragedy; 20 people die from air pollution inversion.
1952	Truman's seizure of steel industry to prevent strike held unconstitutional by Supreme Court.
1956	"Soil Bank" agricultural plan enacted.
	$33,500,000,000 highway bill passed.
	Federal Water Pollution Control Act passed.
1959	St. Lawrence Seaway opened.
1960	U.S. Census: 179,323,125 (69.8% urban).
	Multiple-Use Act for National Forests passed.
1962	Rachel Carson writes *Silent Spring*.
	President John F. Kennedy hosts White House Conference on Conservation.
1963	Clean Air Act passed.

1964	Wilderness Act establishes National Wilderness Preservation System.
1965	Water Quality Act and Solid Waste Disposal Act passed.
1966	New York smog disaster; 80 die.
1969	National Environmental Policy Act (NEPA) passed.
	Major oil spill at Santa Barbara, California.
1970	U.S. Census: 203,235,298 (73.5% urban).
	Amendments to Clean Air Act passed.
	Earth Day celebrated.
	Water Quality Control Act and Resource Recovery Act passed.
1972	Amendments to Federal Water Pollution Control Act passed.
1973	Oil embargo by Middle East oil exporting nations.
1974	Alaskan oil pipeline approved.
1975	Federal standards for air and water pollution unable to be met by majority of industries, utilities and automobile manufacturers in regions throughout the country.
	President Ford vetoes second strip mining control bill. Congress fails to override.
1976	*Newsweek* publishes widely-circulated issue outlining environmental causes of cancer.
	Resource Conservation and Recovery Act (hazardous waste control) passes.
1977	Clean Air Act amendments strengthen enforcement and public involvement.
	Clean Water Act strengthens discharge requirements.
1978	Love Canal disaster exposes health effects of abandoned toxic waste dumps.
1980	Congress approves "Superfund" for abandoned toxic sites cleanup.
	President Reagan appoints antienvironmentalists Watt, Gorsuch (Burford), and Stockman to cabinet posts.
1981	Polls show large majority supports strong environmental laws.
	Water wells in the West found to be highly contaminated with TCE.
1982	Scandals force EPA Administrator Burford to resign.
1983	Times Beach, Missouri evacuated because of dioxin contamination.
1984	Major industrial accident at Bhopal, India kills more than 2,000 people.
1985	Major leak of toxic chemicals at Institute, West Virginia.
1986	President Reagan vetoes reauthorization of Clean Water Act.
1987	Congress overwhelmingly overrides veto of Clean Water Act.

Chapter 13

PROSPERITY, PROFITS, AND PROGRESSIVES

*T*he outward appearance of the country showed much abundance and prosperity after the depression which ended in 1897. In the heart of America, farmers began to receive good prices for their wheat and corn, and the increasing preeminence of the iron and steel industry manifested itself in hundreds of places: machinery in large and small factories, consumer goods in urban homes, transportation systems, bridges, buildings. Livestock, grains, timber, and iron ore provided the resources of the new prosperity, and in 1890 were ranked in that order according to their economic value. By 1900, iron topped the list in value, followed by livestock, machine shop products, lumber and grains. America had been transformed into an industrial nation with wealth accumulated from its natural resources through industrial organization. Moreover, consumerism was on the rise.

Resources came to be processed mainly in factories or plants. Despite one of the most devastating depressions in the country's history, commercial consumer output doubled in the decade preceding 1900: in clothing, leather goods, pottery, rubber goods, wines, gas and oil stoves and lamps, even in the processing of cheese, butter, condensed milk, sugar and the canning of vegetables and fruits. Yet these resources fell far behind the top five industries in 1900: iron and steel products, slaughtering and meat packing, foundry and machine-shop products, lumber and timber products, and flour and gristmill products.

The beginning of the twentieth century represented the birth of mass-production techniques. This birth was itself the completion of nineteenth century trends in the development of technology, especially in power generation, transportation, and national marketing, all dependent on vast quantities of natural resources, a large supply of cheap labor and an increasing influx of capital. The relationships among these factors which led to the accumulation of wealth in America indicate how America grew and who received the benefits of the growth. The material factors of fuel and power lay at the foundations of the nation's industrial revolution, particularly in the dramatic increase of the metal industries. That is, metal working and the generation of power depended on mining (of coal) and mining techniques, which conversely also needed efficient power sources. Another example: Electrolysis, which became very important in the extraction of copper and aluminum, was generally attainable only where electric power was in widespread use and easily available.

Because large investments of capital had to be made to equip factories and sell goods, a correspondingly large, inexpensive supply of labor power had to be found. Thus America's prosperity was built on the twin pillars of abundant natural resources

Figure 13–1. Getting the coal out. In the earliest mines, coal was broken from the seams with crude picks and tossed into baskets strapped on the backs of carriers. The carriers had to climb out of the mines on crude ladders. Later the coal was dragged to mine shafts by women and children who pulled sleds or carts through the dark mine tunnels. Eventually the mine carts were drawn by mules or even, as in this illustration, by goats. The draft animals were replaced at length by steam or electric engines. Mules or horses were also used to hoist miners out of mines on open elevators attached to crude capstan devices, as illustrated in the picture. Courtesy Bureau of Mines, U.S. Department of the Interior.

and cheap labor and shaped by capital, technology and the right political conditions. Big technology justified big business, which encouraged the growth of big government. It is important to understand something of all of these variables to interpret resource use in the twentieth century.

Fuel and Power

The most revolutionary technological feature of the new century was the harnessing of electrical energy, which can be converted into heat, light, and mechanical energy. It enjoys amazing versatility in its ability to power enormous machines as well as tiny instruments. But fuel and power development occurred before new methods of resource processing were devised. For the three decades before 1900, coal assumed an increasing role as the basic fuel for power sources; per capita consumption of it jumped from four-sevenths of a ton to three tons.

Mining techniques improved during the last quarter of the century with the introduction of the compressed-air drill, mechanized hoists, and nitroglycerine. Alfred Nobel had made the latter safe for use in the mines for blasting. Most persons unfamiliar with this powerful explosive do not realize that it is merely a by-product of soap manufacturing, treated with sulfuric and nitric acids. The compressed-air drill ran from a pipe off a compressor in a steam plant outside the mine. Its design resembled that of the double piston action of a steam engine, as air pushed the piston and drill forward, tripping a valve which shot air into the front of the mechanism, returning the steel to its original position, and so on. The device increased mining efficiency tenfold and improved ventilation as well, since it blew air into the mine—except that it took over a decade to discover that the coal or silica dust churned out by the drills lodged in the miners' lungs and was responsible for their deaths by the hundreds. Finally, around 1890, J. G. Leyner of Denver designed a machine which shot a stream of water into the cavity being drilled and wetted down the flying dust.

The new drills, mounted on steel columns held by jackscrews, demanded special hardened steels and bits, also developed in the last decades of the century. New lathes and cylinder-boring machines could turn out drills and machine tools with great precision. Chain and bar-type cutters, along with a disc machine, were used in coal mines; they were also powered by compressed air. An electric locomotive built by Jeffrey Manufacturing Co. in 1888 for bituminous coal-hauling inside the mines utilized galvanized-iron pipes as electrical conductors instead of wires. Finally, electricity was introduced as a power source for both drills and elevator hoisting machines, and coal production took another leap forward.

Michael Faraday discovered the fundamental principles of the electric motor as early as 1821 and those of the dynamo converting mechanical rotative energy to electrical energy in 1831. However, electrical production could not take place until engineering problems were solved. Two of them dealt with a high-speed turbine necessary for electricity generation and the loss of energy when the inefficient reciprocating motion of a piston engine transferred power to the rotary converter. Another was the problem of close-fit parts in a high speed water or steam turbine.

Figure 13–2. An indication of the kind of life lived by miners is the illustration of the boys in the breaker chutes. These children, called "breaker-boys" or "slate pickers," cleaned the flow of pieces of coal in the anthracite mines for a dollar a week. Their job was to separate non-coal rock from the anthracite. The chutes were an outgrowth of the development of coal-breakers at the mine heads—great toothed wheels that rendered the coal into usable chunks. Courtesy Bureau of Mines, U.S. Department of the Interior.

When steam was used, the turbine had to spin as fast as the steam passed through it; whenever steam was slowed down to match the speed of the turbine, there was not enough pressure to spin the turbine fast enough to generate electricity; when increased to high pressure, the turbine broke apart.

In 1884, Charles Parsons patented a steam turbine, to be used for electrical generation, which slowed down high-pressure steam without loss of power. His solution lay in utilizing multiple wheels on a single shaft with nozzles between the wheels. The compound steam turbine can be powered by coal or oil; it is still used in electrical generating power plants and large ships.

Electricity itself got its commercial start when Edison's carbon-filament incandescent lights were introduced to New York in the 1880s. By 1892, the General Electric Company was organized from smaller companies under the control of J. P. Morgan and, in combination with Westinghouse, it monopolized electrical generation for New York's streetcars, electric lights, and factory machines. In 1894, a hydroelectric plant of over 100,000 horsepower was set up at Niagara Falls, which later attracted factories. Within five years the power plant was ready to double its output of electricity. The electrically-powered hoisting engines at the Anaconda Copper mines in Butte, Montana, could raise four-deck cages at the rate of 2,400 feet a minute in 1896.

Nikola Tesla's polyphase alternating-current generation, developed in 1888, set the stage for a wider industrial and home use of electricity. The original Edison direct-current (DC) power plants could produce electricity only at very low voltages and distribute the power for a short distance (a mile or two); the system would have

Figure 13–3. At the turn of the century, electricity began to transform all phases of mining. This kind of trolley locomotive replaced women, children, and draft animals for hauling out coal. The power line can be seen directly over the left-hand operator's head. Courtesy Bureau of Mines, U.S. Department of the Interior.

demanded hundreds of power plants to service a city like New York. George Westinghouse's alternating-current (AC) plan allowed power plants to produce electricity at very high voltages and introduced transformers to reduce power at various points for industrial and home consumption. The Westinghouse system came to be commonly adopted around the country.

By 1900, entrepreneurs around the country were ready to go into the power business to satisfy the incalculable demand for electricity for street lights, electric tramways and subways, and individual electric motors which were replacing dangerous overhead shafting and belt drives in factories. Expensive and cumbersome power machinery was replaced by a simple electric motor which received the mechanical work of a water turbine through the miracle of electricity.

By 1902, there were 22,500 miles of electric urban and interurban railways in the United States. In the home, electric lights gained in popularity as fast as the new alternating-current power circuits could be installed, and items of an incipient consumer society got their start: fans, vacuum cleaners, even washing machines and refrigerators, and a little later irons, sewing machines, and electric stoves and space heaters. By this time electricity was helping to unify great areas in the country through the telephone and telegraph.

Figure 13–4. Generators in the first Niagara Falls power station, 1896. This system of eight 5,000 horsepower units distributed power over a distance of twenty miles. It was a financial success. Niagara proved the superiority of the Westinghouse alternating current system over the direct current system; it also pioneered the coming of large-scale centralized electric utilities in the twentieth century. Courtesy Niagara Mohawk Company.

Resource Processing

The electrical revolution greatly spurred the metals industries of the United States. By 1914, over a thousand companies were manufacturing machinery, apparatus, and supplies for electrical industries alone. New alloys of steel with tungsten and chromium (made in electric steel furnaces) were developed by Faraday and Mushet in England for the construction of power machinery and armor plate. Hydraulic forging presses for armaments were set up close to large hydroelectric power plants. Lathes, planes, and drilling, milling, and grinding increased in precision and cutting toughness. As early as 1890, 150-ton trip hammers could be forged to work gigantic pieces of metal. They made magnet frames for the large generators of power plants, which in turn could afford to lower the price of electricity to operate the giant equipment and other electric motors as well.

These improvements were made possible because of the experiments of Robert Hadfield, also in England, where he found that manganese steel becomes tougher under repeated impact and can be used efficiently for railcar wheels; later use of the metal expanded for profitable employment in power shovels, ore crushers and other mining equipment. Silicon steel, also invented by Hadfield, had the quality of retaining electrical current in the cores of transformers and generators. Electric motors improved the performance of all machine tools. Nickel-chromium steel armor won distinction for Admiral Dewey in Manila Bay in 1898; his sixteen-inch guns of nickel-steel fired chromium-nickel steel shells which tore gaping holes in Spanish ships.

The steel industry of Andrew Carnegie set the maddening pace of growth at the end of the century. Locomotives, bridges, skyscrapers, rails, ships, and finally the automobile needed larger and larger quantities of nickel and other alloy steels as well as iron ore itself. By the time of the Panic of 1893, the annual production of the sixty-ton locomotive reached 20,000. Steel bridges became common by 1900, when construction of steel skyscrapers gained momentum. Iron and steel shipbuilding, which had intensified with the naval introduction of steel ships and armor plate under President Chester A. Arthur, began to replace the wooden shipbuilding industry for coastal and international trade at the end of the century. The beginnings of American imperialism, the maturity of the hydroelectric power complex at Niagara Falls with its steel plants, and an incipient shipbuilding trust occurred simultaneously in 1898. The government would come to depend on steel industry to protect its interests abroad (and vice versa) as the twentieth century progressed.

Both natural gas, originating at Titusville, Pa., in 1872 and piped to the street lamps of nearby communities, and the petroleum business along with new urban water industries, needed safe and efficient iron pipes. By 1897, a price-fixing scandal shook the industry when the Addyston Pipe and Steel Company was taken to court in violation of the Sherman Anti-Trust Act. The pipe company lost its case, but monopolies of the day were not discouraged.

Wire-making grew in scope, especially after Joseph Glidden proved the effectiveness of his barbed wire in the 1870s. Wire-making also supplied the iron wire hoop industry for women's dresses; this industry, too, prospered. Crucible steel wire was woven for suspension bridges, the industry enjoying dozens of contracts after the construction of the Brooklyn Bridge from lower Manhattan to Brooklyn in 1883. By 1892, Elbert H. Gary had organized a barbed wire trust, later reorganized as the American Steel and Wire Company, which gained him the experience he needed later to act as J. P. Morgan's Chairman of the Board of U.S. Steel. Trusts were also organized in the steel-wire nail, the barrel hoop, and the screw industries in the 1890s. The American Tinplate Company and the stamping mill trust became monopolized in 1898.

The electrical, pipe, paint, steel and optical industries made increasing demands on copper, lead, zinc, and aluminum ores. Copper's primary use lay in its value as a conductor of electricity, but it also came to be utilized extensively in roofing and as an alloy because of its resistance to rust. Very lean veins of copper in the Rockies could be mined after 1890, when the electrolytic process enabled the refining of pure copper from an impure bar by means of an electric current. (The impure bar is dissolved in solution and the pure metal redeposited at the negative pole of the current, while other metals fall to the bottom of the tank as black slime.)

Uses of lead were extended beyond its traditional applications as shot, paint base, piping, and roofing to include solder base, printer's type, acid storage containers and electric cables. Zinc was not mined in any great quantities until after the Civil War when it was needed for galvanizing steel and as an alloy; later it became important as an electrode for the electrical industry, and at one period zinc was mined in great quantity in the manufacture of bathtubs and washboards. Aluminum production grew after the electrolytic process enabled the mining and refining of lean bauxite ores from Alabama and Georgia at Niagara Falls.

Lime, alum, phosphorus and borax were mined in Western deserts; building stone came from New England, the Carolinas, Georgia, Wisconsin, and Oregon, but brick and tile industries were spread throughout the country close to urban markets. During the last quarter of the century, paving bricks, along with enameled, pressed, vitrified and faced bricks, enabled the industry to proliferate. It even began to form trusts in the 1880s.

Meat, Grains, Timber, Textiles

Just behind iron and steel products in economic value were packing house products. Because of artificial refrigeration in cold storage plants and refrigerator cars (eventually even on ships), large companies concentrated their refrigerated and highly-mechanized slaughterhouses in Chicago, Kansas City, New York, and other metropolitan centers and shipped their products to smaller localities while advertising heavily around the country. The meat trust, consisting of the five largest meatpackers, was well established by the turn of the century.

Although grains and cereal products dropped from second in value to fifth between 1890 and 1900, the Midwest was established as the breadbasket of the country, and it was increasing its exports with greatly augmented production and new technologies. Charles A. Pillsbury learned how to use the iron-roller grain grinding process in Hungary, essential to the marketing of the hard kernel varieties of spring and winter wheats that thrived on the Plains, and applied the method in his own Minneapolis mills during the last quarter of the century. The Washburn Mills used revolving corrugated steel rollers, perfected at their plant in 1871. The National Biscuit Company took advantage of cheaper milling costs to integrate its operation vertically, merge with two other regional biscuit companies, advertise widely, and take control of the largest measure of the cereals market. The Corn Products Company did the same with starch and glucose.

With the rapidly growing cities calling for building materials as fast as they could be delivered, more forests and more efficient technologies were sought by lumber companies in the last decades of the century. Railroads opened up markets in the plains states for lumber products as well, and the sawmills of Michigan, Wisconsin and Minnesota turned out a third of the country's lumber in 1889. But the South and the Pacific coast were gaining prominence even then, also because of railroad lines built into the huge timber stands of those areas. The band saw, introduced in 1870 at Fort Wayne by J. R. Hoffman, replaced the double circular saw in the mills and in so doing eliminated much of the latter's waste by reducing the size of the kerf (cut) and by saving both power and time. Gradually large vertical bandsaws with blades up to twelve inches wide, and supporting logs with hydraulic jacks, were adopted by the more progressive mills after 1900. Automatic carriers, multiple edgers and trimmers, rotary planes, and kiln drying all contributed to the acceleration of lumber production of the time. The amount of lumber processed from 1869 to 1900 increased from 12.7 billion board feet to 35 billion. Almost the same quantity of timber was wasted on site or in processing. In 1902 the National Lumber Manufacturers' Association regulated the business by price fixing and standardizing products. Cutting, sawing and distributing lumber remained separate businesses, but nonetheless a few giant firms were able to monopolize certain types of timber in their own regions. The demand continued to rise in the far West and from foreign ports; in 1905, it was estimated that at least 80 acres of mature timber had to be cut every day to satisfy the needs of the Portland mills alone.

The steady growth of resource consumption and use can be seen in dozens of other industries. Sugar refining ranked close to grains in economic value. By 1890, commercial bakers and canners had an impact on American households since working wives and children no longer had the time to devote to traditional homemaking tasks. Mass-produced cans, mechanized food processing and mechanical filling and soldering of cans marked the beginning of the national food industry. Machinery also had been used in the processing of tobacco products for a decade before the end of the century, and the beginning of a trust was consolidating in tobacco.

The textile industry, the first to be mechanized in New England factories, continued its expansion into the South, where inexpensive cottons and labor were found. By 1880, America was producing a quarter of the total world output, but India then challenged U.S. supremacy. Greater technological efficiencies in cotton ginning and baling, frame and mule spinning, and weaving with the Northrop loom all greatly decreased textile costs by the end of the century.

Woolens were mechanized later than cottons, but by 1830 power mills were used in spinning, while carpet and blanket weaving were still done by hand. Even silk was manufactured with mechanized looms in Connecticut, New Jersey, and Pennsylvania

at the time; factories moved to Pennsylvania mining towns to take advantage of the cheap labor of the miners' wives and daughters, who worked spinning machines and looms.

Mechanical cloth-cutters, buttonholers, stitchers and pressers speeded the mass production of men's suits, and even the local dressmakers depended on pre-shaped clothes bought from factories. Machines made women's coats and knitted their hose, but for the most part clothing for men and women left the factory as flatwares to be cut and sewn in sweatshops.

Western cattle hides, softened with improved tanning agents, became more widely used in a large leather industry in the last generation of the century. The United States Leather Company attempted to monopolize the sole and leather markets in the 1890s, but too many beef packers arrived at the same notion. Shoemaking was also becoming mechanized, especially in Massachusetts, much to the discomfort of American wearers of new styles. By the turn of the century, thirty-five states had shoe factories where the manufacturers themselves conducted mail order and chain store businesses. Much rubber manufacturing of the time took place in overshoe factories, temporarily monopolized by the U.S. Rubber Company until the automobile boom brought competitors into the rubber industry. Charles Goodyear had solved the perennial problem of the instability of rubber (untreated it remains sticky in summer and brittle in winter) in 1839 when he treated it with sulfur in the heating process, later to be called Vulcanization.

The Internal Combustion Engine and the Automobile

Over and above the burgeoning consumer society of 1900, it was the automobile which presaged the new prosperity of American society. The technology of the internal combustion engine on which the auto depended was to be applied later to dozens of other devices, machines and gadgets in myriads of ways: e.g., the gasoline-powered portable chain saw which could clear forests fifty times faster and more efficiently than crews wielding Yankee axes, or the jet-fueled airplanes which further revolutionized transportation in the country. The automobile culture itself would come to mean the loss of the finest agricultural lands in the world to freeways and parking garages. But this point anticipates our environmental story by several decades.

Although the concept of an internal combustion engine is simpler than that of the one which involves the fire, boiler, and cylinder design of the steam engine, the practical problems are more difficult to solve. The very attractiveness of an efficient, lightweight, small, single engine which would eliminate the need for firegrate and boiler drew many inventors to work on its problems in the last century, but their simultaneous preoccupation with the steam engine and the transport systems which utilized steam deterred solutions to internal combustion difficulties. When

Figure 13–5. Pacific coast loggers. By 1900 the logging industry was cutting gigantic redwoods and Douglas firs, such as this tree, often 50 to 60 feet in circumference. First the loggers cut a deep notch with their axes to direct the fall of the tree. Then two men with the cross-cut saw cut into the wood from the other side until they met the notch. Teams of oxen, mules, or horses dragged the logs from the woods. Courtesy U.S. Forest Service.

Figure 13–6. Getting the logs out of the woods. The method of hauling enormous logs out of the forest called at first for large teams of horses, mules, or oxen. A better method, which originated in the Michigan forests, called for hoisting one end of the log in a set of wheels, or "bummer cart," with wheels as large as 12 feet in diameter. The dragging end of the log acted as a brake on downgrades. Western loggers sometimes constructed flumes, or troughs, in which water was used to float logs out of the forest. This steam engine was photographed in 1905. The Caterpiller tractor greatly increased the pace of logging in the mid-1920s. The first of such tractors was the steam-tractor patented by Alvin O. Lombard in 1901, a generation before caterpiller tractors were commonly used on farms. Courtesy U.S. Forest Service.

answers came, however, at the end of the century, practical production and utilization occurred almost overnight.

The early work on the internal combustion engine was done in Germany. In 1876 Nicolaus Otto mixed gas (not gasoline) with air in a converted steam engine cylinder, and the mixture ignited and pushed the piston without blasting the device to bits. He perfected his "Silent Otto" engine from this original experiment, and many small industries were able to use it effectively, though later development of electrical engines stifled the commercial possibilities of the engine. The Otto engine, however, illustrated the basic principles for later inventors: internal combustion; the idea of burning fuel inside a cylinder; the compression of gas before ignition to amplify the energy potential; and the four-stroke cycle of intake of gas and air, the compression stroke, the ignition and power stroke, and finally the exhaust stroke.

Petroleum was recognized quite early as the possible source of a combustible material in the cylinder, for as early as 1873 engines were built utilizing gasoline (which was easy to vaporize), paraffin, and heavier oils—all fractions of petroleum—but the engines ran at very slow speeds. Then in 1885 Gottlieb Daimler and Wilhelm Maybach, early associates of Otto, figured out how to rotate the piston explosions at high speed to achieve greater power in a gasoline engine, and Maybach added the float-fed carburetor in 1893. With Karl Benz's electric spark ignition system, developed also in 1885, the internal combustion engine had all the essential features which have served the automobile industry well for over three-quarters of a century. Heavy duty powering, however, fell to Rudolph Diesel's "rational" engine, patented in 1892 and able to use the crudest of the crude oils.

Daimler applied his gasoline engine to a bicycle in 1886, then to a four-wheeled carriage later the same year. By 1889, he integrated the best features of previous engines into one of the first gasoline automobiles. By the 1890s, a number of American mechanics became interested in the automobile, but they utilized many power sources—electricity, steam, gasoline, compressed air, carbonic acid gas, and alcohol. Most of the American inventors favored electricity from batteries, but Charles E. Duryea, a bicycle designer, preferred the gasoline engine. He demonstrated his model in 1893. He won so many of the automobile races of the 1890s that he became one of the most successful car men of the decade.

Duryea was followed by other automobile pioneers. In 1894 Elwood Haynes from Kokomo, Indiana, affixed a gasoline engine onto four wheels and drove around the natural gas fields he supervised. Ransom E. Olds, who had already run a three-wheeled steam horseless carriage in 1887, switched to gasoline engines in 1896. Olds was an early manufacturer of gasoline-driven cars. He was turning out 1,400 of them annually by 1900, up to 5,000 by 1904 after he began mass production techniques. Henry Ford entered the field in 1896, when he built his first car; he reached the speed of 25 mph in it—no small feat in those days.

Even in the late nineties many early auto manufacturers continued to use steam and electricity as power sources. In 1898, there were no more than 300 cars in the country, but by 1900 8,000 autos were registered. Olds and Ford set up production in Detroit close to steel factories, petroleum products and lake transportation routes. The rubber industry, skilled mechanics and the rest of the trade soon were drawn to that city for work. The industry continued a meteoric rise despite a nationwide road system eminently unsuited for mechanized vehicles. The highway accommodation would take decades.

Efficiency and Consolidation

By the turn of the century the "scientific" principle of production and marketing had begun to influence industrial organization around the country. Vertical integration was identified with scientific management, so that the oil, steel, sugar, tobacco, and meatpacking industries became models for other industries, which attempted to move from "pools" or trust arrangements controlling markets and prices to integrated monopolies or holding companies.

Individual factories began to be reorganized with a view to the "scientific management" principles of Frederick W. Taylor. Taylorism became a synonym for increased specialization, speedups, higher production goals and quotas, mass production, and interchangeable parts. Many of Taylor's efforts were directed toward conditioning machinists to keep up with the higher speeds of new lathes he designed, e.g., his carbon steel high-speed tools which could cut efficiently at white-hot speeds. In 1890, he invented the largest steel hammer in the country, and later he devised "time and motion studies" purposed to keep men and machines working in the same rhythm. In 1898, he was employed by Bethlehem Steel to reorganize their entire plant according to his plan. His *Principles of Scientific Management*, published in 1911, spread his ideas to industries around the world.

Figure 13–7. Charles Duryea. Driving a one-cylinder gasoline-powered converted buggy, Duryea won many races. He installed the first set of pneumatic tires on this vehicle in 1895. Racing attracted much attention, and news of innovations such as the pneumatic tires spread quickly, as did the word that the gasoline-powered vehicle drove faster than those powered by other kinds of fuel. Courtesy Oil and Gas Journal.

By that time Taylorism had been incorporated into the mass-production methods of the auto industry. Interchangeable parts necessitated the development of new machine tools: precision gear-cutters, die-casters and grinders, presses for stamping the chassis, bumpers and body panels, drilling and tapping machines. Then in 1913 Henry Ford experimented with the assembly line in an 84-stage assemblage of the engine, mounted in a chassis and towed on rails past a series of stations. Within a year the method was perfected, labor costs cut by at least a third, and the assembly line technique spread to other industries. This was the first step taken toward the automatic machine and automation.

The auto industry set the pace for the rest of the country. In 1910 469,000 automobiles were registered; ten years later well over nine million were on the road. Throughout the country other industries experienced the same kind of takeoff. In the fifteen years between 1899 and 1914, American industrial output went up by 76% with only 36% more workers and 13% more firms. In the first decade of the century, industrialists talked efficiency and insisted on it in their factories. Industrial

Figure 13–8. An early automobile assembly line. This photograph, taken at the Ford Motor Company in 1913, shows workers sliding magnetos from place to place for successive assembly operations, cutting labor time in half. Eventually conveyor mechanisms were set up and automatic movement became further rationalized. Courtesy of Educational Affairs Department, Ford Motor Company.

laboratories researched new methods and tools, Edison's well-known laboratory at Menlo Park, New Jersey, pioneering for dozens of others, such as Bell Telephone, Du Pont, Eastman Kodak, and General Electric.

Monopolies and Oligopolies

It was almost inevitable that monopolistic practices would come to be regarded as the most "scientific" and efficient goal of industrial development. The very size of corporations began to signify their ability to produce goods more cheaply, to increase profits for their investors, and to raise the standard of living for everyone, though in fact the reason for combinations lay more in the control of markets and prices for increased profits than in economies of scale which would enable the consolidation to lower prices. The smaller companies which joined consolidations were most of

Figure 13–9. A car with all the extras. This fully-equipped 1909 Model T Ford (with 1910 plates) was one of nearly one-half million vehicles registered in the United States. This particular car was a luxury model; nearly every piece of equipment other than the chassis and the wheels and engine had to be ordered separately. After this motorist repairs her low tire, she will re-start her engine by turning the crank at the front of the car. Courtesy Motor Vehicle Manufacturers Association.

all fearful of larger firms squeezing them out of business by price wars or other maneuvers. During the period of the rapid growth of monopolies and oligopolies, between 1890 and 1910, there was no firm antitrust policy pursued by the federal government, though the Sherman Act and legislation of several of the states were sporadically applied. The reason for government's failure was that its traditional "laissez faire" policy had not yet changed. Its role was accepted as protector and promoter, not as regulator, of business. Railroad land grants, high protective tariffs and dozens of pork barrel policies became the rule, not only permitting infant industries a fair chance in the business world, but also enabling well-established enterprises to set up monopolies just as easily. Neither was there any federal income or corporation tax to hinder monopoly development.

Monopolies, either as cartels of a number of companies setting prices and dividing the economic pie or as vertically integrated corporations controlling supply and distribution of a product, were encouraged because of different kinds of advantages. The American Tin-Plate Company, for example, could not have monopolized its product without tariff protection. The aluminum and oil monopolies, and to a great extent steel, simply engrossed the supply of resources at their sources. Others, like the glass bottle industry, monopolized machinery patents, while some grew in such strength, such as U.S. Steel, that they could dictate policy to the entire industry. All of them, as the railroads before them, catered to politicians for governmental favors.

Near the end of the century, a new kind of monopoly, the holding company, appeared. It was different from cartels and single, vertically-integrated corporations. Before 1889, state legislatures reserved the right to permit one corporation to hold stock in another. In that year New Jersey legislated the right of holding companies to maintain interlocking directorates and their freedom to trade in other states, so long as a general annual report was made to the legislature. By 1900 the trend was set among huge corporations toward holding companies. The individual companies kept their own charters but agreed to allow a board of trustees run the new consolidation as single business (in the interests of scientific management and increased profits). They received a proportionate share of the profits on the basis of new common stock certificates. New York, Delaware, Pennsylvania, West Virginia, Maine and Nevada joined New Jersey with liberal laws regarding holding companies.

In the decade between 1887 and 1897, at least eighty-six industrial trusts worth almost $1,500,000,000 were formed. By 1904, industrial analyst John Moody estimated that 318 trusts had been organized with capitalization of $7,000,000,000, most of them in basic resource industries such as copper, oil, steel, sugar, tobacco, and whiskey. After reorganization, the consolidation often attempted some kind of vertical integration with technological modernization in efforts to increase profits by market control and cost-cutting.

Monopolies were justified on the basis of the mature order which they allegedly brought to the American economy and the savings they assured investors in the purchase of machinery and resources, the transportation of goods, and even in obtaining credit. Those who integrated vertically could organize production "scientifically," control supply and demand flow, and concentrate on advertising the product. Although most small companies joined combinations because of a fear of price wars and the strength of their competitors, they were persuaded ostensibly by appeals to scientific management.

The procedure these turn-of-the-century trusts followed was uniform and simple. The directors of the new corporation paid for the assets of the member companies with new common stock, with which they also paid promoters and bankers (who received additional payment for loans) of the merger. New stock worth billions of dollars was issued in the first years of the century, and finance capitalists, a small group of financiers like the House of Morgan, were able to obtain controlling interest in dozens of new consolidations. They became known collectively as the "money trust," and with gigantic financial resources and insurance funds they became ruthless in their efforts to protect investments through further monopolization and "scientific management." Bankers spared no costs in buying out firms which could compete with their operations, even if the competitive properties were of little value, such as run-down railroads or outmoded iron factories, or even if they had to pay exorbitant amounts for companies like American Telephone and Telegraph. The money trust attempted to control new patents through purchases or through ceaseless litigation. With financial resources and credit potential in their hands, they could control national monetary policies and influence the direction of the national economy. In the name of efficiency, stability and scientific management, the finance capitalists determined what natural resources would be developed and who would develop them.

However, members of the money trust were far from infallible in their monetary judgments. During their tenure as keepers of the national economic stability, the panics of 1903 and 1907 took place; the effects of the latter endured until the First World War. Morgan and other financiers needed continuously rising security markets in order to keep selling their stocks, but whenever buyers thought that their stocks became overinflated, they started to sell and precipitated the panics. Often the sellers were correct in their judgments. No controls on the market could stop sudden downturns, and the financiers could not maintain public confidence in their stewardship of the national public good.

The Progressive Movement

Few Americans were surprised in 1902 when the U.S. Industrial Commission issued a report which stated, "In most cases the combination (i.e., trust or cartel) has exerted an appreciable power over prices, and in practically all cases it has increased the margin between raw materials and finished products. Since there is reason to believe that the cost of production over a period of years has lessened, the conclusion is inevitable that the combinations have been able to increase their profits."

The cost of living rose steadily between 1897 and 1913, up at least 35%. Although some of the material benefits of prosperity trickled down to the workers, they could not keep up with the galloping inflation. The new middle classes of small businessmen and professional people suffered from rising prices as well. The latter sometimes blamed aggressive labor unions for the price hikes, as happened after the anthracite coal strike of 1902, but the money trust and monopolies were more often accused. American society was experiencing a revolution of rising expectations along with the technological and financial transformations of the society. Millions of new dollars were added to the economy each year, and the lion's share remained at the top. One percent of the American families owned about seven-eighths of the wealth; seven-eighths of the families held only an eighth of it. About 20% of the population could live comfortably. Profits were high in the basic industries; widespread child labor and unrestricted immigration kept labor costs down to insure that profits stayed high.

It was easy to decry the evils of the day because there were so many of them. Reformers appeared in all walks of life, especially in the white-collar middle and upper-middle classes, the clergy, and the professionals. They were the heirs of the midwestern farmers' movements, but by the turn of the century, for the first time in a generation, farmers were enjoying a small measure of affluence. Agrarian problems were transferred to the cities, where the families of the processors of the farm goods lived. The Progressives took up the cause, but for all their training and education they were less sophisticated in their analysis than the farmers a generation earlier. What is more important is that both groups propounded a new principle in American political thought—that it is government's responsibility to control big business (or railroad monopolies). Theretofore it was almost unthinkable that the social good should be regarded as a higher value than private property.

Efforts to Regulate Big Business

In fact it was the Granger laws of the seventies and the eighties against the railroad monopolies that sent the progressive, reformist spirit surging through the nation. Although these laws were often repealed and although in 1886 the Supreme Court's Wabash case struck down state railroad regulation of interstate commerce, the Populists turned their attention to the federal government, in whose jurisdiction interstate commerce did lie. Year after year after 1874, their representatives introduced legislation to regulate interstate commerce. Finally, in 1886, the Cullom Committee investigated the problem and came to the conclusion that immediate action was incumbent upon Congress for regulation, particularly in light of the Supreme Court's Wabash decision. On February 4, 1887, President Cleveland signed the Interstate Commerce Act.

The Interstate Commerce Commission had no coercive powers even if it issued "cease and desist" orders to railroads engaging in discriminatory rates, rebates, or monopoly practices. The Commission simply gathered facts and appealed to the courts to enforce its decisions. The railroads suffered no obstacles in the continuation of their old practices, for when they were called to court for their offenses, they simply appealed the case all the way to the Supreme Court, and if they lost their case, no redress had to be made to the complaintant. The railroads won fifteen out of sixteen cases before the Supreme Court under the Interstate Commerce Act between 1887 and 1905. Railroads never changed a rate schedule, broke up a pool, or asked for a rebate to be returned. But the mild form of harassment by the farmers' groups called them into account, and the farmers' situation with the railroads could certainly have been worse if they had not organized to fight injustices.

Populist candidates were no less zealous against other monopolies in particular states during the period. In 1887, Louisiana initiated a suit against the Cottonseed Oil Trust, Nebraska against the Whiskey Combine; a year later New York took on the Sugar Trust, and Ohio even dared to attack the Standard Oil Company in 1890. In every case the trust was ordered dissolved, though each one reorganized under the protection of New Jersey's bountiful laws. It was more important, though, that the Populists instilled a "trust-consciousness." This legacy was inherited by Progressives. In the four years after 1889, sixteen states and territories had passed antitrust laws. In this climate, the reformers were able to have passed (in 1890) the Sherman Anti-Trust Act, which declared illegal any attempt to enter into a contract, combination or conspiracy in restraint of trade, or to attempt at monopoly.

The Anti-Trust measure was no more effective in legal terms than the Interstate Commerce Act, and no special enforcement agency was created; private individuals or the government were required to bring suits. Nor did industrial combinations have any difficulty in proving themselves blameless. They simply appealed to their own good works and the vague, undefined terminology of the Act. But once again, through the efforts of critics, the law pierced the armor of laissez-faire. Corporations began to feel it necessary to convince legislators and the executive of the rational and scientific necessity of consolidation.

The problem with the Sherman Act was that it did not precisely define what constitutes a "monopoly," "restraint," or even "trade." So when the *United States vs. E.C. Knight Co.* came to the Supreme Court in 1895, the judges ruled against the government, taking a narrow definition of the scope of interstate commerce. The case involved the American Sugar Company's acquisition of four independent sugar firms of the Philadelphia area, a deal that placed 98% of the country's sugar refining in its hands. The Court held that sugar refining within one state was not a matter of interstate commerce, even though the Company did business in all of the states.

In two other cases, the *U.S. vs. Trans-Missouri Freight Association* (1897) and the Addyston Pipe Case (1899), the Court declared the parties in violation of the Act. The western railroads attempted to fix rates by mutual agreement, and the pipe manufacturers controlled prices by collusive bidding and regulation of production. In these and other cases of the 1890s, the Court established that their purpose was to outlaw manifest agreements among competing companies to fix prices, divide up markets or otherwise restrain trade. Since the Court, along with the rest of the highest echelon of American society, believed that large corporations could attain the maximum economies of scale and pass these savings along to the public, no restriction was placed on growth itself as a restrainer of trade; only deliberate agreements among competitors were restricted.

The Progressives accepted this definition and understanding of the value of corporations and explicated it through their own writings, but especially through their representative, Theodore Roosevelt, the man who came to symbolize "trust-busting" for them. Roosevelt spent a half dozen years before 1896 on his Dakota Territory ranch, writing part of his four-volume treatise, *Winning of the West*. As a civil service commissioner appointed by Harrison and as New York police commissioner, he maintained a reputation as a reformer in the 1890s. As assistant secretary of the navy and organizer-commander of the Rough Riders, he manifested his leanings toward international American military supremacy. After the war in Cuba, Roosevelt was touted as a national hero. He became governor of New York on a reform platform, and he was nominated and elected vice president under William McKinley in 1900. Within a year after his inauguration McKinley was assassinated in Buffalo and Roosevelt became president.

Roosevelt wanted the trusts regulated, not necessarily broken up. A moralist at heart, speaking for many of his fellow Progressives, Roosevelt distinguished between "good" trusts and "bad" trusts. The former contributed to material prosperity, moderated prices, stabilized the country's economic life, and "on the whole have done a great good to our people," as he declaimed to Congress in his first annual message in 1901. "Bad" trusts charged extortionate rates and did not behave as their position in the captainship of industry befitted them. Roosevelt requested Congressional action to create a commission to investigate the great corporations and determine whether or not their activity needed regulation. Congress did not move on the issue until Roosevelt stirred up a group of Progressives in several speeches. Then Congress established the Department of Commerce and Labor, and with it the Bureau of Corporations. The work of the bureau greatly assisted the attorney general in the prosecution of trusts during the Progressive Era between 1900 and 1915.

Business and Government

The coincidence of the Progressive Movement, the beginnings of governmental regulation, and the presidency of Theodore Roosevelt, who strengthened the power of the executive branch, changed the relationship of big business to governmental bodies. Previously businessmen had stayed close only to Congress in Washington in order to cash in on handouts or to lobby for higher tariffs, but never had taken seriously the potential power of the Executive or even of Congressional lawmakers. The evangelistic tone and practical politics of the Roosevelt administration changed their attitudes. Moreover, the dominant business interests became gradually aware that the federal government could in fact support them in need. They became convinced that business and government could cooperate in "rationalizing" the nation's economy for everyone's benefit. By the end of the first decade of the century, businessmen were actually initiating social reforms or at least suggesting national regulation when the demands of individual states and their laws regarding rates, competition, or income taxes became oppressive.

The trend began with the personal diplomacy between the House of Morgan and Theodore Roosevelt. When J. P. Morgan heard in 1902 that Roosevelt wanted his attorney general to bring suit against his Northern Securities Company, he is alleged to have contacted Roosevelt with the complaint, "If we have done anything wrong, send your man to my man and they can fix it up." Morgan looked on government as another huge business with which one negotiates his differences. No meeting took place, and Morgan lost the suit—Roosevelt was convinced Northern Securities was a "bad" trust.

Three years later, in 1905, Commissioner of Corporations James Garfield was instructed to investigate U.S. Steel, but this time he took the initiative in arranging a meeting between Elbert Gary, Morgan's chairman of the board, and Roosevelt himself. Gary assured the president that his company would cooperate in every way possible for the benefit of the general public. Because of his cooperation, U.S. Steel turned out to be a "good" trust; later another Morgan company, International Harvester, cooperated, and through a special meeting Roosevelt's commissioner arranged another gentleman's agreement. What was happening in fact was that the personal diplomacy of Roosevelt and his commissioner acted as a buffer between the huge monopolies and the courts, all in the interests of "rational" policy, good order, high moral life, and scientific management of the public good. Even when Morgan was setting up the purchase of the Tennessee Coal and Iron Company, he sent his man to sound out the president first so that no suit would later be brought against U.S. Steel. The corporation received Roosevelt's blessing for its merger.

But Roosevelt's hand-picked successor, William Howard Taft, did not favor methods of personal diplomacy; rather, he preferred to work through the legal system. Although he broke with Progressive ideals, in his four-year term eighty suits were brought against trusts as opposed to forty-eight in Roosevelt's seven and a half years.

Anti-trust activity by the Supreme Court, however, was evolving more along Roosevelt's pattern of "good" and "bad" trusts than it was in the specific definition of monopoly. The notion was implicit in Justice Holmes's dissenting opinion in the Northern Securities Case in 1904. The case involved a railroad power struggle between Edward H. Harriman, who had control of western and southern lines and who was attempting to take over the Burlington lines into Chicago, and J. P. Morgan, who was putting together the Northern Securities Company with railroad magnate James J. Hill to protect the Burlington lines from further encroachments by Harriman. In 1901, Hill and Morgan formed a holding company that took over the stock of the Great Northern, Northern Pacific, and the Burlington lines.

To the shock, chagrin, and dismay of Morgan, Hill, and Wall Street in general, the holding company was ordered dissolved because of its intent to restrain trade in interstate commerce. The decision increased Roosevelt's popularity, but it did not change the balance of railroad power, since Hill and Morgan retained majority stock in the dissolved companies. But in his dissenting opinion, Holmes introduced the "rule of reason" in anti-trust judicial opinion. In opposition to Justice Harlan, who claimed that *every* combination restrains trade by its very size and to the public's detriment, Holmes stated that precedents should be sought in common law to distinguish between "reasonable" and "unreasonable" intent in restraint of trade. The rule of reason looked at motives, i.e., goodness or badness, behind the monopoly, rather than the *de facto* economic effects of the combination.

By 1911, when the Standard Oil Case was brought to the Supreme Court, the rule of reason was a generally accepted principle by the Court. The Rockefeller monopoly was dissolved because of its obvious and manifest intent to drive competitors out of business, not because of its size or market power. The court established that applications of the Sherman Act should be "determined by the light of reason." In the same year the American Tobacco Company was ordered broken up because of the "rule of reason" principle, which was elaborated in the St. Louis Terminal Railway Association Case a year later. In none of these cases was effective market control lost since majority interests remained in a few hands (e.g., Rockefeller's and Morgan's), and corporations were becoming more aware of the uses of the federal government.

The culmination of the anti-trust story of the Progressive period came with the passage of the Clayton Act in 1914 under President Woodrow Wilson. The new anti-trust law was written to remove the ambiguity of the older Sherman Act, particularly in the definition of what specific acts violate fair competition. Wherever discrimination in prices among different producers, or exclusive selling or leasing contracts, or acquisition of stock, or interlocking directorates lessened competition, all these practices were declared illegal. Directors of corporations were made personally liable for violations of their companies, and the law permitted individuals as well as government officials to secure injunctions to forbid continued violations while the case was in the courts. In another important clause, it exempted labor and agricultural organizations from provisions of the Act; the Sherman Act was utilized almost as much to hinder labor organizing efforts as it was used against monopolies, a precedent which dissuaded business interests from advocating its repeal.

Within the year, the Federal Trade Commission Act was passed, establishing a commission of five members to administer anti-trust laws by investigating any "corporation engaged in commerce" and "to require from them annual and special reports and other information." The commission absorbed the Bureau of Corporations established under Roosevelt. The group could issue "cease and desist" orders to stop unfair practices, while the commission pursued enforcement in the courts, and heard over 2,000 cases and issued 379 "cease and desist" orders during the Wilson administration. Among many other successful cases, they were instrumental in the dissolution of International Harvester and the Corn Products Refining Company.

What is more significant under the provisions of the Clayton Act is that it stressed the value of competition rather than attempting to strike down the huge monopoly conglomerates which by their very size prohibit entry into the market. From the time of the Sherman Act, the American elites—scientists, professional people, businessmen, politicians—believed that bigness and vertical integration assured more efficiency, stability and prosperity for society at large. Legislators and judges alike did not wish to discourage the growth of American corporations, even those which controlled resource production from extraction to marketing and distribution. They further believed that the American people would probably be served best by the corporate giants.

The next step in the logic of the elite groups was to assume that monopoly—or at least vertical integration—was the inevitable and desirable fulfillment of a capitalist society. Since excessive competition ruins business (the argument went), and business is the foundation of the social order, society is protected from chaos when large corporations can plan production and output from sources to home use. Efficiency of operation keeps down costs and prices as well. The notion was so widespread that Rockefeller, Morgan, Gary, Hill, and the rest of the monopolists of the day felt almost a sense of mission in bringing about the fulfillment of this natural law or manifest destiny of capitalism. Academicians followed business leaders in their reasoning, and politicians were led by both.

An even more outstanding fact of the period was that despite the control of capital by a small number of big-finance capitalists and despite enormous monopolistic activity, small competitive businesses grew in number faster and proved themselves more efficient than the giants. The upshot of this unexpected phenomenon was the reliance of the huge corporations on the federal government for the maintenance of their predominant positions in their industries. In the decade between 1899 and 1909, the number of manufacturing firms increased by 29.4%, and out of the nine largest industries only one of them—steel—had fewer than 1,000 firms in it. The steel industry had 446 different companies, despite Morgan's herculean efforts at monopoly control.

The smaller outfits serving local regions became so adept at marketing that the larger companies ran into trouble maintaining their production, and it is quite possible that the merger movement itself grew out of the unexpected difficulty that the large corporations were experiencing. In many cases, mergers were forced by price wars, blanket advertising, additional railroad rebates, and cornering of resources—all intensified by the largest companies in order to eliminate smaller firms from competition. In the end, the efforts of the great corporations were unsuccessful. As natural-resource availability and markets shifted, the conglomerates lost their relative strength. Competition multiplied in the iron and steel industry, oil, agricultural machinery, telephone, copper, meat packing, chemicals, paper, textiles, glass, tobacco, and others.

Business Dependence on Regulating Agencies

Because of the growth of serious competition, dominant businessmen began to utilize governmental regulatory agencies to protect their private price and market agreements by having prices standardized by the government, which would shield business from popular criticism. The Interstate Commerce Commission and the Federal Trade Commission played this role for big business after World War I.

As early as 1892, Attorney General Olney, a close friend of railroad magnate Perkins of the Burlington lines, wrote to him that it would be wise for the railroads to use the I.C.C. for their own purposes since "the older the Commission gets to be, the more inclined it will be found to take the business and railroad view of things. It thus becomes a sort of barrier between the railroad corporations and the people and sort of protection against hasty and crude legislation hostile to railroad interests. . . . The part of wisdom is not to destroy the Commission, but to utilize it."

Thus many railroads saw that, unless an interlocking directorate existed, there was no need to give special rebates to large corporate users so long as the government would legislate a floor for rates. They encouraged the passage of the Elkins Act of 1903, which held the railroads to prescribed rate schedules for all customers. And although the I.C.C. became an important regulatory agency for the government when its powers were expanded in 1909 and 1910 under the Mann-Elkins Act, Olney's words became prophetic for the commission; it did become inclined to take the railroads' view of things, and other regulatory agencies followed the same pattern. Their members usually came from or went to the regulated industry after their tenure on the agencies, as experts dedicated to preserving society's economic order and the best interests of the regulated business. Railroads never suffered rate wars after the I.C.C., and telephone companies were harassed by state legislation no more. It was the same story in resource regulatory agencies such as agriculture, forestry, and mining, among others. The tendency of regulatory personnel to work in (or for) regulated industries either before or after government service (lately termed "the revolving door syndrome") has persisted throughout the twentieth century.

The Progressive era and its attendant prosperity set the tone for both natural resource industries and conservation policies of the twentieth century. Technological, economic, and political change brought on societal upheaval and a chronic maldistribution of wealth. Savings from machines and cheap labor generated the trappings of prosperity but created enormous social problems as well. A system of big technology extracting massive amounts of natural resources by big business, which evinced a larger federal political apparatus, was brought to life during the period.

Figure 13–10. A progressive city, Chicago in 1905. The technological and economic forces which were portents of the future—the electric trolley and automobile in an industrial-commercial center (along with horse-drawn wagons from a former era) combined to result in a traffic jam that would rival any modern city. To judge from this picture, one could almost believe that environmental quality is improving rather than deteriorating. Courtesy Chicago Historical Society.

What is most astounding was that in the midst of great social distress the era was characterized by a moralistic and scientific optimism and a supreme confidence that these problems were soon to be dissipated. Progressives maintained that if men in office and business were honest, upright, good, and efficient, and if they applied the principles of science with a mind to the public good, the poverty, the slums, the dirty cities, sickness, political corruption, waste, and inefficiency would vanish. They proposed political reforms like the recall of judges, the initiative process, and the direct primary to make certain that their representatives stayed upright.

Progressivism blended Enlightenment notions that Progress was inevitable with a reformist morality, and this was its undoing. Progressives looked confidently to public servants in regulatory agencies, and to technical experts and social scientists in key bureaucratic positions, to restore the ideals of democracy, brotherhood, and fair play if politicians failed in their duty. Unfortunately, Enlightenment doctrine was born too early to account for the tenacity and power of corporate and legal institutions to maintain the status quo by corrupting or coopting public servants as well as public representatives. Big business soon convinced many "reformers" that only big enterprises could solve big social problems.

The deeper questions of privilege, of who would receive the major benefits of the nation's national resources and labor, or of how these benefits were to be distributed—issues that radicals like Eugene V. Debs raised—were swept under the rug by the moderate wing of the Progressive movement. In time Progressives became persuaded that scientific management and monopoly integration and power, if used wisely, could redound to the benefit of the whole society. This, it seems, is a perennial American myth.

References for Further Reading

An excellent overview of the period from 1877-1920 is Robert H. Wiebe's *The Search for Order* (1967). Likewise Richard Hofstadter's *The Age of Reform* (1955) examines the myths of progress and reform from Bryan to F.D.R. The business history of the age is well covered in *The Age of Enterprise* by Thomas C. Cochran and William Miller (1961). Gabriel Kolko's *The Triumph of Conservatism* (1967) defends the position that the economic and political reforms of the Progressive Era were shaped for their own purposes by the dominant business groups of the time. Harold U. Faulkner's *Politics, Reform and Expansion* (1968) provides a good historical background for the period leading up to the Progressive Era, between 1890 and 1900. In his *Private Power and American Democracy* (1970), Grant McConnell shows the foundations of the control of democratic institutions by corporate power in the Progressive legacy. William Robbins' books on American forestry—*Lumberjacks and Legilsators: Political Economy of the U.S. Lumber Industry, 1890-1941* (1983) and *American Forestry: A History of National, State, and Private Cooperation* (1985)—are persuasive illustrations of how economic problems led to political involvement by Progressives to rationalize and expedite the monopolization of the lumber industry, as well as to the cooperation that eventually embraced the goals of the conservation movement.

Chapter 14

STRUGGLES OF
EARLY CONSERVATIONISTS

By the turn of the century, the lines of the conservation and anticonservation forces were clearly defined. The conservationists, mostly Eastern professionals and scientists drawing support from Progressives who opposed land monopolists and speculators in public lands, were able to gain positions of authority under Roosevelt. They were determined to use the centralized policy-making powers of the federal government to stop waste and corruption in the West. Western interests fell on the anticonservation side, mostly because they wanted local control of their resources, but also because rapid economic growth could be most easily achieved through incentives involving the rapid exploitation of their natural resources. Grazing, lumbering, and mining interests were solidly behind the sectionalists. The preservationists and hunting clubs promoted conservation measures, though their purposes were quite different from those of the efficiency and "wise-use" conservationists in the federal branches of government.

Forest Reservation Controversies

The first conservationist battle was waged over the General Revision Act of 1891. Besides permitting the president to set aside forest reservations, the act repealed preemption laws and revised the Desert Land and homesteading laws. The Timber Culture and Timber and Stone Acts were left untouched, however, so that lumber companies enjoyed the privilege of engrossing or helping themselves to the timbered lands of the last frontier.

The West voiced little opposition to the first series of President Harrison's forest reservations. The next president, Cleveland, did not want to create more reserves until a comprehensive plan for their protection and use had been approved and financed by Congress. The McRae Bill of 1894 was proposed; it provided for the sale of mature timber to the highest bidder, and the income of these sales was to be applied to forest and watershed protection. Western interests, including lumbermen and miners who were used to getting their timber free, stopped passage of the bill.

After Cleveland created thirteen new reserves in 1897, the struggle between the Executive Branch and the West reached a new intensity. The debate over ownership, control, management, use, protection and development of public lands raged until the middle of the twentieth century. Some Westerners wanted the lands turned over to the states in irrigation and power projects; business interests insisted that the land be allotted to private developers; homesteaders and settlers wanted already-irrigated land parceled out in small lots.

In spite of all the land it set aside in reservations, the federal authority didn't amount to much until the Roosevelt administration. Congressmen, state legislators, and editorialists were shocked that Cleveland and later presidents continued to set aside forest reserves, land that the states customarily had regulated. Convinced that state governments necessarily bowed to moneyed interests and that waste and destruction of the public lands were inevitable unless strong federal action was taken, bureau and department officials, particularly under Roosevelt, adopted an aggressive posture in the preservation and utilization of the public lands. Westerners were as dismayed over the loss of political power—that they were not consulted in decisions regarding their lands—as they were over the actual reservations and management of the forests.

Congressmen from the West steadfastly refused to provide funds for forest and watershed protection that was tied to the federal government's control and sale of mature timber. Their spokesmen repeated that the only attraction their regions had in drawing venture capital for economic development came from liberal land, timber, and mineral rights. Their material prosperity depended on cheap land, they argued, which was little by little stolen from them by an arrogant federal executive and its bureaucracy. They also blamed Eastern banks and congressmen for controlling western development, claiming that if early settlers of eastern states had enjoyed the right to dispose of lands in their own way, the West should be entitled to the same privilege. Because of their continual pressure on Congress in the generation between 1897 and 1917, the West won many concessions: free timber to settlers (taken also by lumbermen and miners); new homesteading laws; federal financing of irrigation and power sites; liberal leasing and fee arrangements. But in the meantime, authority over land use and management was passing into the firm hands of the executive.

The Roosevelt Era: Reclamation

The Conservation movement of the early twentieth century is most often identified with Theodore Roosevelt's brand of Progressivism and his shrewd appointments to key positions. The mood of the age was moralistic and scientific, and the Roosevelt lieutenants assumed the moral and scientific posture of the time. They sought to stop the waste of the country's resources. They attempted to apply scientific criteria in their regulation, and they claimed to speak for the larger interests of society and its future generations instead of for the private appropriative profit-seeking of monopolists. But though the issues were clear in the minds of the early conservationists who wanted to implement a "wise and rational" policy of resource use, a practical program which would serve the needs of all the public was not so easy to work out.

The focal point of the Progressive conservationists was land—and the timber, water and grass upon it. Each of the latter loomed large in importance to state officials, settlers, and entrepreneurs alike. To conservationists, wood and water problems were linked; in his first message to Congress in 1900 Roosevelt viewed them as "the most vital internal questions" of the country. Yet until Congress legislated support for a land use program, neither Roosevelt nor his bureau chiefs could carry out their "wise use" policy. Their only tool was the locking up of public lands for potential future use.

The first conservation issue to which Roosevelt devoted himself was irrigation, known as the "reclamation" of arid lands for settling. The question had been discussed and fought over since the days of John Wesley Powell, who was just as concerned about preserving grazing lands as he was about opening up new agricultural home-steads. In fact, Powell was strong in his opinion that many lands of the arid West never could be utilized for farming.

Other irrigationists of the day, including advocates in the executive and legislative branches of government in Washington, were more optimistic. One effort toward the realization of a greening of the West came with the passage of the Carey Act of 1894, which authorized the secretary of the interior to grant up to a million acres to each state that would irrigate and settle the land; of every 160 acres given to a settler, twenty were to be irrigated. But neither the states nor private companies, much less individual homesteaders, were able to come up with the capital needed for the irrigation systems. Furthermore, local and sectional water laws and customs were so much in conflict and so many watersheds cut across state lines that, by the turn of the century, a number of Westerners were beginning to call for the intervention of a federal authority. At an important National Irrigation Conference in Phoenix in 1896, California water law specialist George H. Maxwell spoke forcefully in favor of a national irrigation law. He later organized the Irrigation Association for the purpose of pursuing this goal. Scientific and engineering groups around the country backed his plan.

At the same time, Frederick H. Newell of the U.S. Geological Survey, a student and associate of Powell who had been studying irrigation and water problems for over a decade (and with whom Roosevelt had consulted along with Gifford Pinchot on the protection of New York forests and watersheds), presented his water plan to the new president-in-succession, Theodore Roosevelt. Roosevelt endorsed it immediately and began to publicize the cause of reclamation. As a resident of the Dakota Territory, he understood the value of water in the West. Advocacy of irrigation, forest reserves, and homesteading in the West coalesced the Roosevelt conservation program. To him these issues were three sides of one conservation policy.

The Reclamation Act

Representative Francis G. Newlands of Nevada, hoping that irrigation would solve Nevada's chronic low population problem, presented the basic Reclamation bill to Congress. It was worked over, pulled apart, and finally passed in 1902, but not until Roosevelt saw to it that the interests of the small farmer and potential homemaker were protected. One important provision of the bill stated that landowners could apply for water on only 160 acres of their land and that absentee owners were to be denied federal water. The Newlands, or Reclamation, Act allowed receipts from land sales in the arid states and territories to be applied to the construction of reservoirs and irrigation works. The secretary of the interior was to set up the Reclamation Service in the Geological Survey to handle surveys, locations and irrigation development as

A GRAPHIC HISTORY OF THE PUBLIC DOMAIN

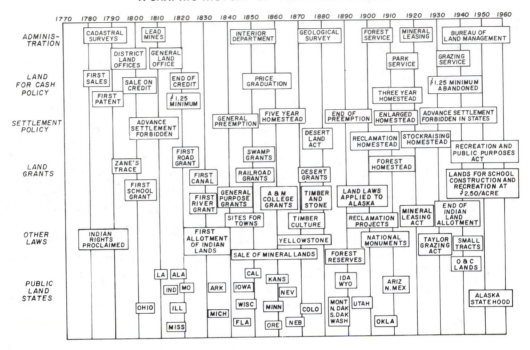

ORIGINAL LAND ENTRIES, 1800-1943

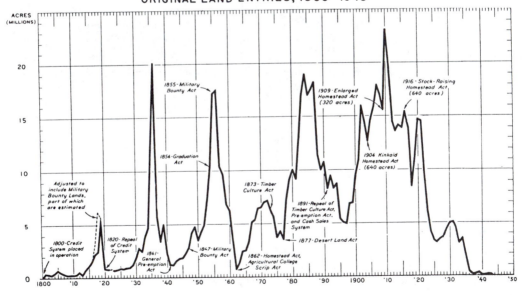

Figure 14–1. A graphic history of the public domain. The schematic above, adapted from Bureau of Land Management data, lists the various movements in American land management and the forces that have helped to bring those movements about. Land for cash policy, settlement policy, land grants, and depressions greatly influenced how much land was sold during each period of American history, as the U.S. Department of Agriculture chart below dramatically indicates.

well as payments from new landowners for construction charges of the irrigation projects (to be collected annually for ten years). Local water laws were to govern water distribution. Although the 160-acre limitation in the Reclamation Act reflected the intent to prohibit large corporations or monopoly interests from receiving an advantage from public monies, and conversely to encourage family farms, compliance with this provision, particularly in California, has been rare in the past eighty years.

Midwestern and eastern farmers were afraid of the possible competition from new agricultural lands, but eastern labor groups and conservationists applauded the bill along with representatives from all the western states. Former opponents of federal interference rejoiced that the government at least was replacing the lost land of the forest reserves and was making it possible for a new generation of family farmers to homestead on formerly wasted land. Newlands, himself an early irrigationist, had surveyed possible reservoir sites and bought them up to prevent speculation. He resold them later at cost plus interest to families who would benefit from irrigated land.

Roosevelt appointed Newell as director of the new Reclamation Service (in 1907 made an independent bureau under the secretary of the interior). The reclamation chief enthusiastically took on the new work, but he was faced with a never-ending succession of problems: thorny cases of water law, speculative activity, state jurisdictional rights, political imbroglios, engineering problems, and silting difficulties. Legal conflicts between the Reclamation Service and individual states often hindered effective water distribution since local water law was honored. Nor could the service transfer water over state boundaries, even when water could be most efficiently utilized in this way; e.g., California's Lake Tahoe outflow could not be used in irrigating the lands in the nearby Truckee Valley of Nevada.

Speculators often knew where proposed irrigation sites were planned. They bought up much of the land before the Reclamation Service approved the project for the region. Since speculators were not interested in farming, they did not make payments to the federal government for irrigation of their lands. When they did sell at greatly inflated prices, only well-financed farmers could afford to make payments to both the speculator and the government. If, as was often the case, the farmer did not have a number of good years growing and selling his crops, he would lose the land and farm. Not until 1908 did Congress withdraw from entry all western irrigable land, forestalling further speculative activity on possible irrigation sites.

The problem of speculation appeared with the first completed project in 1905, the Truckee-Carson ditch in Nevada, since much of the land had already been bought by private purchasers. Even more so did speculators control land in the area of the Roosevelt reservoir on the Salt River in Arizona near Phoenix, the second project of the service. Many public officials of the West decried the selection sites of these early projects, since their understanding was that the Reclamation Act purposed to develop public, not private, land. Reclamation head Newell disputed this opinion, saying that the law intended only the reclamation of arid or semi-arid lands, and made no distinction between private or public irrigable lands. Charges of corruption were aimed at the bureau when competing sites were chosen, but any decision could have been challenged since lands had been bought up by private interests throughout virtually every prime irrigable region of the West. Studies had been made of western lands since the 1880s, and knowledge of their conclusions was widespread. Thus did it happen that public lands were benefited only indirectly from the Reclamation Act. Of the twenty-four projects in the process of construction in 1910, the amount of the public domain affected was dwarfed by privately-owned sections.

Rapidly growing cities of the West viewed the Reclamation Service with some jealousy, since they were competing for water to supply their multiplying populations. For example, the Reclamation Service had planned a huge irrigation project in the Owens Valley northeast of Los Angeles, but the city's mayor, Fred Eaton, persuaded the Reclamation Engineer, J.B. Lippincott, a Los Angeles resident, to allow the city to take precedence over Owens Valley water for its future needs. In the meantime, Eaton was secretly buying up land along the Owens River to protect the city's rights to the water. Lippincott became convinced that the service, already burdened with many other problems, should abandon the Owens Valley project. The future farmers of Owens Valley lost their irrigation district, but Lippincott won a new job supervising the Owens Valley project for the city of Los Angeles.

Another potential conflict of the Reclamation Act lay in its omission of any provision dealing with hydroelectric power generation from the newly constructed dams. Instead, in 1896 and 1898, the secretary of the interior was given congressional authority to issue permits for the construction of power stations on public lands, along with private right-of-ways such as logging roads, canals, and water conduits. In 1901, the permit system was standardized and several power permits were granted. Within a generation, water and power corporations would achieve enough strength to begin to challenge policies that were inimical to their interests.

The Roosevelt Era: Forest Preservation

Roosevelt made it clear that water conservation was to be associated with forest reserves, which were known to preserve watersheds in timbered regions. The argument went back at least as far as George Perkins Marsh: it was developed in the Roosevelt administration by Gifford Pinchot, who had been head of the Division of Forestry of the Department of Agriculture since 1898. Suffering from acute staff and money shortages, Pinchot hired about sixty student assistants who did research on such problems as tree diseases, turpentine, and maple sugar extraction methods and who spent time with private owners educating them on forest management and sustained-yield practices (reforestation after cutting). Throughout his tenure at the Forest Service, Pinchot exhibited an extraordinary ability to overcome practical obstacles in order to achieve his objectives. Even after he resigned from the Forest Service he exerted great influence over federal forest policy through his programs and years of propaganda, and even through dozens of student aides who stayed in government service.

Pinchot studied forest management in Germany and other European countries that were attempting to bring back forest yields in seriously deforested areas and developing reforestation policies in other areas. During the 1890s, he had managed the forest on George W. Vanderbilt's Biltmore estate in North Carolina, and served on the Commission of the National Academy of Sciences, which had reported to President Cleveland in 1896 on the need for additional forest reserves. While Pinchot directed the Bureau of Forestry, Roosevelt consulted him on all matters relating to conservation, as did lumbermen themselves when it became apparent that the nation had run out of virgin timberlands to be exploited. From a staff of 123 in 1898, Pinchot gradually expanded the Forest Service to an organization of 1,500 people in charge of 150,000,000 acres of forests in 1908.

Pinchot early attempted to enlist the support of the large lumber firms. Believing that higher prices would encourage investment in sustained-yield forestry and more careful, unwasteful lumbering and milling practices, Pinchot privately supported the raising of tariffs on forest products. He was not opposed to the formation of regional timber monopolies so long as combinations agreed to practice scientific management. In return for support of a monopoly in the Southern yellow pine industry, which Pinchot knew would increase the profits of the combination and stabilize the industry of the region, the chief forester demanded a program of management directed by the Forest Service. The industry leaders refused and formed their combination, but it was soon afterwards struck down in the courts.

The forest reserves were left completely unmanaged from 1891 until 1897, when the secretary of the interior was given jurisdiction over the land. The Act of 1897 authorized the sale of standing timber to the highest bidder but made no reference to possible uses of the forest other than preservation, watershed protection, and timber growing. The secretary of the interior placed their management in the Division of the General Land Office, which attempted to organize a forest service unit but which suffered from severe shortages of funds and from untrained manpower.

From the time of his appointment in the Department of Agriculture in 1898, Pinchot fought for the transfer of the forest reserves into his Bureau of Forestry. He contended that the Land Office was too involved in political appointments to care about scientific management, and, furthermore, that it was far too stingy in its release of lumbering, mining, and grazing permits. The latter argument won commercial industries and their legislators to his side, and later the American Forestry Association and the National Irrigation Association supported Pinchot's leadership. Theodore Roosevelt spoke in favor of the transfer in his first message to Congress in 1901.

The Pinchot Program

Long before Congress approved the changeover in 1905, Pinchot privately intervened with Congress and the secretary of the interior in favor of greater commercial use of the forest reserves. When wildlife organizations attempted to lobby for game preserves in the national forests, a move vehemently opposed by stockmen, Pinchot dissuaded both Congressional and Boone and Crockett Club leaders from the legislation. After a personal investigation of forage conditions on grazing lands in the reserves, he encouraged the secretary of the interior to permit wider use of grazing privileges in the federal forests. The chief forester set the tone for conservationists of the decade—"wise use" and "scientific management" for the nation's long-lived material prosperity, not preservation for aesthetic considerations or wildlife habitats. Nonetheless, at this time Pinchot introduced the "multiple-use" concept in the management of the forest reserves; he tried to integrate the functions of the protection of watersheds and of grazing rights with timber management and sale.

Pinchot increased his forest programs in the new Forest Service created by the transfer of the forest reserves. He won increased appropriations from Congress and higher fees from grazing interests in the national forests, higher prices for timber, and more funds from power plant permits for power stations constructed in the Reserves. He reorganized the Forest Service after 1905 and set an example of commitment, excellence and professionalism among the young foresters on his team. And, of course, under his tutelage Roosevelt himself gained a widespread reputation as a conservationist, adding well over 100,000,000 acres and 118 reserves to reach a total of 150,832,665 acres in 159 national forests.

During this last flurry of conservationist activity, speculators and lumbermen were rushing to acquire as much forest land as possible while it remained open. One provision of the Act of 1897, the Forest Lieu Land Act, permitted holders of a bona fide claim in a forest reserve to exchange it for the same amount of vacant public land elsewhere. Therefore, speculators, railroads, and lumbermen held or bought under the Timber and Stone Act large tracts of inaccessible land on the tops of mountains or equally poor timberland in order to exchange it for the same number of acres of superb timber land elsewhere. Over 3,000,000 acres of prime timber land was handed over to large corporations under provisions of the Forest Lieu Act. Land-grant railroads used their free lands to special advantage in this way, quickly becoming outspoken advocates of a forest reserve policy and just as quickly adding almost a million acres of valuable timber lands, including the white pine forests of Idaho, to their holdings. Other large landholders joined the cry for greater forest preserves, knowing that their own lands would increase in value twentyfold.

Antimonopoly western Progressives demanded that the Forest Lieu and the Timber and Stone laws be repealed. Progressives were joined in their efforts by Western promoters of growth in denouncing the forest reserve policy, citing the same abuses of monopolists. Alert mining, lumber, and railroad companies seemed to win either way, but in the meantime they joined the cause of conservation. Pinchot was presenting himself as a genuinely concerned forester to lumbermen, who were given access to the national forests with their future supplies secured by sustained-yield forest management, and were picking up more private timberlands at the same time. But to other Westerners, the Roosevelt conservation program was a sell-out to corporate interests.

Not until 1905 was the Forest Lieu Land Act repealed, and a year later the Interior Department suspended all entries under the Timber and Stone Act so that these lands could be appraised and sold at their actual value. It was during this period that new leasing arrangements for grazing on national forests and permit charges for power plants were inaugurated in the Forest Service. Also in 1906, the Forest Homestead Act opened up certain agricultural lands for homesteading within forest reserves, and the secretary of the interior, under orders from Roosevelt, extended conservation policy to include coal reserves. Within two years over 50,000,000 acres of coal lands were withdrawn from public land entry. These preserves precluded further monopolization of coal areas under agricultural land laws. The coal lands were then appraised and sold for fifty times their former prices.

The Roosevelt Era: Range Conservation

Pinchot's early dealings with cattlemen regarding a range leasing policy on national forests precipitated a series of struggles with farmers' organizations and their representatives. Pinchot's arrangements conflicted with an earlier 1894 order (later mitigated) from the secretary of the interior forbidding livestock within the forest reserves. After Pinchot reversed the policy, the government was forced to play the role of intermediary among cattle, sheep, and agricultural interests. The Forest Division set up a system of priorities of range use. First priority was given to residents of the surrounding areas, then non-resident regular owners of ranges, then neighboring occupants at a further distance, etc. Sheepmen who trailed their sheep over long distances and sometimes through several states received low priorities, over their vociferous protests. Their continual complaints, particularly in states where they constituted substantial political power, forced continually changing priorities.

The farmers and cattlemen were locked in contest over whether large grazing or small homesteading would prevail in the West. In 1904, the small settlers won a victory with the passage of the Kincaid Act, which permitted 640-acre stock-grazing and small farm homesteading in Nebraska, with a five-year residence clause. Nebraska probably contained more illegally fenced-in cattle ranges than any other state in the West, and cattlemen earlier had hired vagrants to make illegal hobo filings of public domain land to keep their hold on vast acreages. The Kincaid Act was meant to satisfy reformers of that state and at the same time to act as an experiment which the West as a whole might follow later. Nebraska was symptomatic of the western range problem; the Interstate Land Company of New Mexico, for example, held over 1,000,000 acres of public land under fence.

After 1906 Roosevelt, Pinchot, and the new Secretary of the Interior James R. Garfield supported legislation setting up a leasing system for grazing lands of the public domain outside the national forests, just as one had been applied within the forests. Only with great reluctance did cattlemen begin to pay grazing fees, which they accepted only because the new system was a better alternative than denial of access to national forest grazing land. They also bitterly fought the idea of leasing the public lands outside the national forests until there was no other recourse, which did not occur until 1934, when the country was reeling from chronic erosion problems on the public domain.

Roosevelt's leasing plan divided his conservation team. Irrigationists wanted more irrigated homesteads carved out of fenced-in grazing land. Cattle interests opposed the irrigation movement because it turned grazing land into farmland. Only the professionals who surrounded Pinchot backed his plan. Farming, grazing, and western Progressive interests lined up against him, making Congressional approval impossible. When passage of a leasing act seemed imminent in 1914, Representative Edward T.

"*And What is to Become of Us?*"

Figure 14–2. An anti-conservationist cartoon. In this cartoon, from the *Seattle Post-Intelligencer*, the president is shown barring access to mines and forest reserves—the latter symbolized by a single tree. He is carrying a shotgun labelled "Executive Order," and his mount is blindfolded by a label that also identifies it to the reader as the Forestry Commission. Cartoonists of the time made frequent use of the noble animal here depicted because it was familiar to all as a source of strength even though it was both stubborn and lacking in sagacity.

Taylor of Colorado forestalled it by offering a law for the entire West modeled after the Kincaid Act. It was a 640-acre stock-raising homesteading bill. Although cattlemen adamantly opposed the measure, it was passed and signed into law in 1916.

The End of the Roosevelt Era

Another regrouping of conservation and opposing forces took place in 1907, when Senator Charles Fulton of Oregon attached an amendment to the Agricultural Department appropriation bill which in effect repealed the Forest Reserve Act of 1891. The amendment declared that the president could no longer create forest reserves in six of the most heavily timbered states of the West—Oregon, Washington, Idaho, Montana, Colorado, and Wyoming. It included a provision that 10% of the receipts from timber sales would be applied to schools and roads of the counties in which the reserves were located, and it officially changed the name of the "forest reserves" to "national forests." The enacted bill increased the Forest Service's appropriation, but did not, as Pinchot proposed, give him control over funds from the national forests. It is significant that the six states involved were large-scale sheep grazing states, and their senators had often complained that the Forest Service insisted on charging small-scale sheep herders to graze on forest reserve lands while it looked after the interests of large lumber companies.

Before Roosevelt signed the Appropriation Bill, he created twenty-one new forest reserves and 16,000,000 additional acres in the six states which would afterward be interdicted. The reaction of the West was predictable. Roosevelt and Pinchot were heavily assailed in tandem from the six states and other areas as well, by residents who were shocked at what all of them considered to be an arrogant abuse of power. The concern was not self-righteous. In the state of Washington, one newspaper claimed that, because of the new order, the Weyerhauser Timber Company and a few other large firms were able to monopolize the entire timber industry of the state. Not only did they own most of the timber country around the reserves, but the same companies were the few timber buyers which could afford to pay the higher prices charged by the Forest Service.

Another newspaper, the *Seattle Post-Intelligencer,* sarcastically queried, "Why not include the state?" and summed up the case for the rest of the West:

"The federal government assumes the attitude of the alien landlord, holding perpetually for its own uses millions of acres of land in this state, drawing revenues from them for expenditures elsewhere, and paying no taxes upon its vast holdings. . . . The growth of such a great state as Washington can no longer be hampered, and its development hampered, to please a few dilettante experimentalists, however well intentioned and patriotic in purpose they may be. Their idea that the greater part of this state must be kept in a primeval wilderness for the benefit of wealthy lumbermen and city sportsmen does not appeal to the people of Washington, who are inviting immigrants to build up the country."

The National Debate

The Act of 1907, Roosevelt's response, and the reaction of the West set the stage for a nationwide debate of the conservation question. Western anticonservationists, backed mostly by grazing interests of the six Northwestern states, called a meeting in Denver to protest federal conservation policies. Roosevelt sent Secretary of the Interior Garfield, along with Pinchot, and Newell of the Reclamation Service, but the agenda and speakers were fixed against their viewpoint. The president also wrote a message repeating his long-standing opposition to monopolies, his commitment to the settlement of the West by small settlers, and his dedication to the conservation of timber and water for future generations.

Since western interests remained divided throughout the conference—lumber, grazing, agricultural, power and mining companies and politicians—only general points of agreement could be reached. Almost unanimously they called into question the right of the federal government to retain title to state lands in perpetuity; to make withdrawals of state lands without their consent; to sell timber and coal in competition with citizens of the states; to regulate grazing by charging a fee; to control irrigation projects within the states; and to retard growth and development of the states because of large-scale withdrawals of land.

Of course these questions had already been settled by the constitutional provision granting the federal government power over the public domain, and also by a number of Supreme Court decisions which upheld that right. The conference organizers were well aware of these facts, but they raised states' rights questions again in order to challenge the unwonted aggressiveness of the executive during the previous decade. Yet they explicitly approved the president's record and efforts to bring defrauders of the public domain to justice.

At this juncture, the conservation movement passed from the hands of an elite corps of professionals on the east coast to a wider body of concerned citizens. The professionals themselves were the first to realize that they needed the support of a larger constituency. They went to great pains to attend every regional irrigation or forestry conference in order to explain the purposes of conservation and reclamation. Roosevelt expanded his propaganda campaign to include flood control, conservation, and reclamation in the East and appointed an Inland Waterways Commission to study rivers, navigation, power development, irrigation, flood control, and soil conservation throughout the country.

Roosevelt's interest was derived from a movement that was at the time promoting "multi-purpose use" of rivers similar to Pinchot's "multiple-use" of federal forest reserves. At the turn of the century many older communities situated on rivers, lakes, and streams turned to the possibilities of cheaper water transport once again because of the steep rise of rates stemming from the railroads' successful efforts to monopolize the transportation industry. Progressives supported new river and canal projects in Congress, but the Army Corps of Engineers, brought in as consultants, discouraged the projects. Nonetheless the movement reached a broader base of support under the "multiple use" concept. New proposals, including hydroelectric power generation, flood control, and irrigation were again on Congressional desks by 1907. The most notable, perhaps, was the idea for a Lakes-to-the-Gulf Waterway: a fourteen-foot channel that could carry ocean-going vessels from Chicago to New Orleans and open up potential Latin American trade.

Multiple-Use Water Policy

The Reclamation Bureau picked up the multiple-use notion discarded by the engineers and included it in their own plans for dam and irrigation works construction. W.J. McGee, former assistant to John Wesley Powell, popularized the concept in Roosevelt's behalf, capitalizing on the sentiment in favor of inland waterways, power development, and flood control. McGee's extraordinary background brought together work in the Bureau of Ethnology, in the anthropological section of the St. Louis Exposition and Museum, and as spokesman for the St. Louis Latin-American Club. It was McGee who convinced Frederick Newell of the value of the multiple-purpose use of waterways. Finally he also convinced Roosevelt of the necessity of forming the Inland Waterways Commission, a move which gained broader support for the Roosevelt program. Only a few of the commission's recommendations were approved by Congress immediately, but McGee's plan was revised and activated in the New Deal Conservation program. Multiple-purpose programs had become the standard approach in the Department of Agriculture at least as early as 1905, when Pinchot managed the national forests with a multiple-use policy.

Roosevelt's last major effort to appeal for national backing for his conservation program came when he called his historic Governors' Conference in 1908 to discuss the leading conservation questions of the day: state and federal rights and obligations in the context of conserving the country's natural resources. Roosevelt's Progressive flavor infused the conference with moral appeals to Americans and corporations.

He repeated his confidence in the ability of large corporations to extract resources and make profits without abusing the public trust. The administration viewed the conference as a grand success. All the important leaders of the country were present: the cabinet, the Supreme Court, and William Jennings Bryan, leader of the opposition party; governors of thirty-eight states and territories; captains of industry like Andrew Carnegie and James J. Hill; most of the prominent scientists, engineers, and leaders of scientific and engineering societies of the nation. (The engineers became the strongest advocates of hydroelectric power, more efficient mining techniques, utilization of byproducts in iron and steel-making, and "scientific" plant management.)

The Governors' Conference appointed a National Conservation Commission under the chairmanship of Gifford Pinchot to collect and publish information relevant to present and future resource requirements of the country. Roosevelt then set up a North American Conservation Conference, together with Canada and Mexico. At the end of 1908, the commission made its findings public in a three-volume report which served as a basis for future policy decisions and legislative action. The significance of the report lay in its compilation of up-to-date resource data in a single work. It stated, for example, that practically all of the public domain had been disposed of—less that 400,000,000 acres were left—and suggested that the remaining land be carefully classified according to potential use. Although four-fifths of all timber lands were privately-owned, the national forests contained 75,000,000 acres of salable timber. The commission recommended that the 65,000,000 acres of cleared forest areas unsuited for agriculture be reforested and protected for future timber supplies. The group noted the necessity of forestation of eastern lands to safeguard further erosion and of government control of grazing for the same purpose. Using Geological Survey records, the commission issued a warning that, except for coal and iron, the mineral resources of the nation could easily be depleted within the century if immediate steps were not taken to reduce excessive waste (especially in the oil and gas industries), substitute more abundant minerals for the rare ones, increase mining efficiency, and reorganize mineral land and mining laws.

Citing numerous frauds under the Timber and Stone Act, the commission recommended its repeal, but the Interior Department had already acted on the matter, and within a year the Land Office had recovered over 1,000,000 acres of fraudulently-acquired land. The sorry state of the nation's soils was treated, and the necessity of preserving phosphate rock on the public domain for future supplies of fertilizer was recognized. Just before the report was issued, Roosevelt and Secretary Garfield withdrew all the public lands which were thought to hold phosphate in Utah, Wyoming and Idaho, though the Franco-American Consolidated Phosphate Company, owned mainly by foreign investors, monopolized the industry and exported about half its product. Needless to say, the report of the commission and its recommendations bore the heavy imprint of its chairman's thinking.

The Roosevelt administration had been limited more to land reservation than land disposal and use. The president was responsible for 141,000,000 acres of the 167,500,000 in the national forests. He added five new national parks—213,886 acres. He introduced the National Antiquities Act of 1906 for the preservation of historic places on public lands. He withdrew coal, phosphate, and other mineral lands to prevent monopolistic acquisitions and to reappraise their value. He prosecuted hundreds of violators of public land laws and recovered millions of acres. But most of all, by his forceful personality and aggressive actions, he took conservation questions to the public forum and garnered wide public opinion to aid the cause of conservation in the generation following his retirement from office.

The Taft Approach to Conservation

Although Roosevelt's hand-picked successor in the White House had assured conservationists of a continuation of his predecessor's politics, sectional anticonservation interests in the Congress offered the new president no encouragement in the pursuit of such goals. But more important, Taft was not a showman or personal diplomat in executing his program. Trained in constitutional law, he found that his natural sentiments inclined him to those who interpreted the use of federal authority in a strict sense. In particular, he questioned whether the president actually held the power to reserve mineral lands and water-power sites, since this authority was not explicitly mentioned in the Act of 1891.

Taft appointed Richard Ballinger, a Westerner and former reform mayor of Seattle with a special sensitivity to western desires for development, as his secretary of the

Figure 14–3. A faithful public servant defends his charges. This cartoon, which appeared in 1910 in *The Newark News*, was drawn by Louis Wisa. It bears the caption, "Disguised as the faithful shepherd dog, a wolf is found within the corral." The marauding wolf in disguise is labeled "Ballinger," while the faithful collie sounding the alarm is labeled "Pinchot." The nearest and most likely victim for the wolf is labeled "Coal Lands," and the sleeping shepherd is President Taft. The artist has created a whimsical corral made of big sticks—an allusion to the conservation policies of Theodore Roosevelt. The corral gate is ajar, unfortunately, and through the opening may be seen a pack of wolves labeled "The Interests."

interior. Ballinger believed with Taft that those in the preceding administration had sometimes exceeded their constitutional authority in the withdrawal of water-power sites. Soon after his appointment, he restored those lands to entry. After Pinchot appealed to Taft, who reconsidered the question, the secretary withdrew again a fraction of the power-site lands which Garfield had previously taken from entry: i.e., 421,129 acres as opposed to almost 3,500,000 under Garfield. Of course Pinchot himself had influenced Garfield's lavish withdrawals, saying that he needed the land for ranger stations, but actually attempting to prevent monopolization of the land by power and water companies. Ballinger's attitude and actions soon antagonized Pinchot and the conservationist contingent of government so acutely that thereafter little cooperation between the factions was possible.

Ballinger also preferred private development over public reservation and reclamation, especially of irrigation projects, and openly criticized Newell's creative approaches. The secretary stopped Newell's program of funding irrigation farmers who taught new settlers how and when to operate the irrigation ditches on their lands; the instruction interfered with the business of private consultants and Ballinger claimed that there was no explicit permission for the procedure in the law. Ballinger further refused to allow settlers to pay for later irrigation fees with irrigation scrip, earned by working for the bureau while the irrigation works were under construction and before they could grow crops on their lands.

Although the Forest Service was in the Department of Agriculture, Pinchot had developed a close working relationship with the Department of Interior and Secretary Garfield. Ballinger sought to separate the work of the departments completely, even including the technical work of fire prevention and timber-cutting supervision on Indian lands. Ballinger would not give up jurisdiction over these lands, again arguing that the switchover was an unconstitutional act. The same problem occurred with forest landtitle questions, technically under both the General Land Office of the Interior Department and the Forest Service.

For these and other personal differences Pinchot sought to discredit Ballinger in Taft's eyes. A young agent of the Interior Department, Louis Glavis, reported first to his superiors in the department and then to Pinchot that Secretary Ballinger had used his influence to assist private corporations in the purchase of larger Alaskan coal holdings than permitted by law. Glavis was fired. He publicized the charges in *Collier's* magazine. Pinchot, convinced that the secretary had acted improperly but rebuffed by Taft for accusing Ballinger, defended himself and the Forest Service of charges made by the Secretary of the Interior. Taft then fired Pinchot for insubordination early in 1910, and Ballinger was later cleared of Glavis' accusations by a Joint Committee of the House and Senate. Nevertheless, a year later, largely because of outside pressure and the tight controls placed on him by a more cautious president, Ballinger resigned.

During the period of the controversy, however, both Taft and Ballinger continued a program of land withdrawal of critical resources. Fearful that the nation's supply of oil would be depleted within two generations because of wasteful extraction methods, Taft withdrew more than 3,000,000 acres of petroleum land from entry in California and Ohio in 1909, and another 2,700,000 acres in 1910, some of which were designated as naval petroleum reserves.

The president, however, was more eager to receive Congressional authority for his withdrawal practices and a validation of past withdrawals; he submitted such an authorization bill through Representative Pickett of Iowa in 1910. In this he perhaps was more the politician than is generally recognized, since by that time the country had been thoroughly indoctrinated by the Roosevelt conservation crusade, and despite massive Western opposition to the bill, a defeat could have cost the Republican party a large constituency. Civic and women's organizations all over the country supported the program of national conservation projects, and the movement gained corporate respectability from cattleman and lumberman organizations, along with scientific and engineering societies. Many conservationists, on the other hand, were displeased with the bill because almost a generation of legislative and judicial activity had justified the right of withdrawal. As they suspected, the act which Taft signed did not clear up with any more specific definition how the reserved lands could be utilized in the future. As had the original 1891 measure, the Withdrawal Act of 1910 left only two possibilities open for government agencies. Either it could release them for private development or it could lease them out and regulate their use. No provision was made in the bill for classification of the lands; priorities of use had to be redefined continually according to multiple-use philosophies.

Hydroelectric Power Struggles

The relationship between private and public jurisdiction received the most attention in the hydroelectric power question. By the end of the first decade of the century, the principle of regulation by leasing had become established in the national forests through timber sale and grazing rights. This precedent was not acceptable to the power industry, which wanted long-term franchises, renewal privileges, and minimal regulation. Until these terms were met, hydroelectric power investors were reluctant to build dams and power plants.

President Roosevelt threw up the first obstacle to the power industry in 1907, when he established his policy that navigable waters were to be put primarily to inland waterway use and that the construction of private dams and power plants were to be regulated and charged for the use of public waters. He and Taft vetoed every bill which did not meet these requirements. Although the 1901 Right-of-Way Act granted the secretary of the interior the right to permit electrical transmission lines to cross public lands and to permit the building of dams on public land sites, he or his successors could also revoke these permits. The investment seemed to be too insecure for entrepreneurs to build on public sites even at a time when the nation was clamoring for more electrical power.

The power industry never let up in its efforts to convince Congress to allow it to build dams with long-term leases but without fees levied for water use. They preferred to work through Congress for this privilege rather than through the less-amenable states, which claimed constitutional rights to the water of non-navigable streams in their territories. On the power question, Westerners fought for bills which would turn over power sites to the states. They fought against those providing for federal leases, franchises, of water-power sites.

The Roosevelt-Pinchot idea was for a comprehensive multiple-purpose river, irrigation, flood control development plan financed by the sale of water power. Pinchot continued his promotion of the plan through the National Conservation Congress, but many of the engineers and other delegates were beginning to support the power industry's point of view. Pinchot reiterated his fears of a developing water-power monopoly, then agreed to drop the question from the Congressional agenda to avoid creating a rift among its members. The struggle continued, in legislative circles, however, until 1920. Then, power company officials agreed to accept charges from the federal government in return for long-term leases.

The concept of leasing oil and coal lands, debated until 1920 as well, could not be settled even with the emergency situation brought on by the war. Finally, just before the water-power bill was passed in 1920, a comprehensive bill for leasing nonmetallic minerals was passed. These laws established federal policy and represented the culmination of the withdrawal or reservation policies, providing a procedure for natural resource use in the public domain.

Wilsonian Conservation

When, in a 1913 speech, President-elect Wilson declaimed, "A policy of reservation is not a policy of conservation," he seemed merely to be repeating a "Pinchotism," copying the most outspoken advocate of a "wise-use" policy. Yet Westerners hailed the new Democratic President, who said in the same speech that everyone should be equal in his right to natural resources and that locking up resources was tantamount to squeezing the little man between the government and the monopolies, which were the two large owners of the country's resources. The West jumped and clicked its collective heels in glee.

Idaho Senator Borah spoke for the rest of his western colleagues when he wrote Wilson a public letter pledging his support and looking forward to a new timber and water policy. He hoped that the federal government would grant free irrigation ditches to homesteaders: "We are putting millions into warships which rot upon the sea. . . . We are putting millions into great canals with no specific return to the Treasury. Why not put these lands, which are the property of the United States Government, in such condition as to make them available for homes?" Wilson responded by appointing two western men, Franklin K. Lane of California as Secretary of the Interior, and Clay Tallman of Nevada as Commissioner of the General Land Office.

Nevertheless, the Wilson administration instituted no new policies that unleashed the public lands from federal control or deferred in its interest in leasing arrangements. It did support the 640-acre homesteading law. In 1914 Wilson withdrew more mineral lands—3,000,000 acres of phosphate lands in Idaho, Montana, and Wyoming, and hundreds of thousands more which held coal, phosphate, nitrate, potash, oil, gas, and asphaltic minerals. Before long the West was brewing again with complaints from engineers and entrepreneurs, hydrologists, and politicians. They wanted action, but mainly they focused their attention on water and energy, without which growth and development in the West was impossible. Secretary Ballinger had recommended in 1911 that the federal government transfer water-power sites to the states for leasing but no legislation could be passed to effect the change. A commission was appointed to study the problem. Its 1911 conclusions found their way into the Federal Water-Power Act of 1920: fifty-year occupancy by private firms and a system of leasing for water-power development and occupancy.

One reason for the delay of passage of the bill was another report on water power in 1912 by the Bureau of Corporations, which publicized the rapidity with which the water-power industry was becoming monopolized. Two years later a House committee corroborated their findings with information that twenty-eight corporations and their subsidiaries owned over 90% of the water power on public lands, and that six of them owned 56% of those stations. Montana Power and Utah Securities locked up most of the power generation in four states, and the top power companies were connected by interlocking directorates, holding companies, and banking arrangements. If western politicians knew that electrical generation held the key to their states' development, it is clear that a few corporation heads shared this knowledge and were utilizing the public waterways to sell their scarce commodity.

The Hetch Hetchy Debate

It was water development—not timber or even grazing—that split the conservation movement into the "utilizer" and "preservationist" camps in the struggle over the damming of the beautiful Hetch Hetchy Valley in Yosemite National Park. Before 1902, San Francisco reform mayor James D. Phelan devised a plan with his water engineer to dam the Tuolumne River. He bought up water rights in the valley in his own name in order to avoid tipping off water and power companies. However, three years later, supervisors waived water rights on the Tuolumne and accepted a scheme by private speculators in the Lake Tahoe region. After Yosemite extended its park boundaries, the city renewed its application for Hetch Hetchy rights, this time in 1912, when it needed much more electrical power as well as water.

Then John Muir and the Sierra Club mobilized national opposition to the project. In the *Century* magazine Muir set forth an impassioned plea for saving the Valley: "Dam Hetch Hetchy! As well dam for water-tanks the people's cathedrals and churches, for no holier temple has ever been consecrated by the heart of man." Even the Pacific Gas and Electric Company (P.G.& E.) and other private utility companies, fearful that public power generation would become the cause of the loss of their biggest customer, spent enormous sums to aid conservation groups trying to save the valley from flooding.

Muir and his corporate allies were powerful but not so strong that they could stop an idea whose time had come. The Roosevelt men, especially Newell and Pinchot, had completely sold the country on a "wise-use" policy and multiple-purpose development. The preservationist forces were handily defeated, and Congress authorized the reservoir in 1914.

Before Congressional approval was given, the 1913 Raker Act was passed, granting the city and county of San Francisco sole water and power rights to Hetch Hetchy Valley and prohibiting the city from selling water or power to private utilities. After

Figure 14—4. The Good Life in California. Amid raging conservationist controversies, California Chamber of Commerce people (and their railroad company consorts) spread much promotional literature east to lure vacationers to their Sierra paradise. In this 1910 photo, tents and camping gear have been loaded on fender and running-board. The campers are poised at the exit of Yosemite's famous grove of redwood trees which, according to one wag, tended to develop holes at their base when they got to be 2,000 years old. Wawona blew over in 1969.

the dam and power plant were built at public expense, P.G.&.E. did manage to obtain the publicly generated power and is still selling electricity to San Francisco citizens at rates comparable to those for privately generated power.

The Hetch-Hetchy scenario has been replayed dozens, perhaps hundreds, of times since it first unfolded: private speculators or developers, conservationists, government technicians, and politicians all struggling over the "wisest use" of a beautiful stretch of ground. Hetch Hetchy precipitated a personal feud between Muir and Pinchot, who, following his own counsel, assured Roosevelt, Garfield, and other public officials that water supply (Muir claimed that the Tahoe area offered an excellent substitute) was a more important public use than preservation or recreation. Samuel P. Hays notes that Harry Slattery, a friend of Pinchot and Newell and secretary of the National Conservation Association, wrote to former Secretary Garfield in 1913, "Unfortunately, our good friends the nature lovers are still unreasonable in their attitude. There is grave danger that they will be able to block this necessary legislation." And California

Congressman William Kent wired Pinchot that a conspiracy was unfolding "engineered by misinformed nature lovers and power-interests who are working through the women's clubs." Little did Muir, Pinchot, Kent or even the man who started it all, Mayor James Phelan, realize that the ultimate victor would be the P.G.&.E. company.

Effects of the Progressive Conservation Program

Much of the ambiguity of the Progressive conservation program came from the many contradictions of the Progressive program itself. Although Progressives attacked monopolists as engrossers of the public domain, they allied themselves with monopolists who agreed on the necessity of a "wise-use" philosophy of scientific management and of economic growth and expansion. And although Progressives were committed to the fight for political and economic justice and to the idea of grassroots democracy, they did not hesitate to force the preservation of forests and mineral lands on smaller political units—the states and local governments—in the interests of a rational "wise-use" policy ("socialization of management") and in the name of all the people. In the final analysis they, rightly or wrongly, preferred their own ("scientific") counsel to that of the people, perhaps because they were convinced that powerful corporations would win out if these matters were put in the hands of the "people."

At the same time, however, Progressives insisted on a program of homesteading and reclaiming the arid regions of the West. The honorable goal of providing thousands of homesteaders a piece of land meant that the federal government could no longer dictate the terms of its conservation. Thus the Kincaid Act of 1904, the Forest Homestead Act of 1906, and the Enlarged Homestead Act of 1909 alienated tens of thousands of acres from government control, and large regions of the West were subject to overgrazing, plowing (the Act of 1909 actually required it) and inevitable destruction by erosion. At that point the land was useless to homesteader, government, and wildlife alike. Most Interior Department officials had enough experience at the time to oppose the legislation; a few predicted the consequences, but it was unthinkable to attack the high-minded motives inherent in Progressivist arguments. In time the homesteaders had to move off much of the land. They transferred the ownership to cattle companies or farmers who could hold the land until the federal government irrigated it.

Reclamation also wielded a two-edged sword but was the necessary corollary of homesteading arid regions. Again, by the beginning of the twentieth century, it was manifest that American farmers could produce enough food for their own country and many foreign lands as well. There was clearly no need to put more acreage under cultivation by means of irrigation at enormous public expense and continued subsidies, especially when the action assured future generations of farmers overproduction, lower prices, more lost mortgages, and tenancy. Moreover, dozens of scientists after Marsh pointed out that the disturbance of regional ecologies by irrigation and canals could lead to dramatic environmental changes and should not be undertaken without significant reason and intensive study. First the lofty Progressive ideals were embraced by early irrigationists and western Congressmen. Eventually they were even snatched up by the electric power industry and the Army

Corps of Engineers, who were converted to multiple-use arguments because they saw in them a wedge to Congressional appropriations for large-scale dam-building. The interaction among these interested parties was supposed to result in multiple-use national planning (democratic pluralism in action). Instead, the consequences provided a lesson in the survival of pork-barrel politics.

References for Further Reading

Earlier quotations in the chapter came from Roy M. Robbins' *Our Landed Heritage: The Public Domain 1776- 1936* (1942), already cited. The last two were taken from Samuel P. Hays, *Conservation and the Gospel of Efficiency: The Progressive Conservation Movement, 1890-1920* (1974), a splendid book which explains how the conservation movement was led by scientifically inclined professionals in the federal government. Elmo R. Richardson's *The Politics of Conservation* (1962) is another good book covering the same period of time. *The Closing of the Public Domain, 1900-1950* by E. Louise Peffer (1951) is another excellent reference on public land policy for the first half of the century. *The American Environment: Readings in the History of Conservation*, edited by Roderick Nash (1968), contains excerpts from many of the original sources mentioned in the chapter. *Origins of American Conservation*, edited by Henry Clepper (1966), also presents interesting information on the period. The work of John Ise, as always, is extremely helpful. *Forest and Range Policy: Its Development in the U.S.* by S. T. Dana (1956) contains a wealth of information on land, forest and range policy.

Chapter 15

THE BEGINNING
OF THE MODERN ERA

During the first decades of the twentieth century, earlier tendencies leading to the scientific rationalization of industry and government, to urbanization, economic expansion, and to the affluence of the modern consumer society established themselves. The process cemented the transformation from subsistence and regional and moderate resource use to a resource-processing economy dependent on the existence of large national markets. World War I accelerated the move toward a "rational" society. The nation was pushed into a more "efficient" and modern social organization in order to gear up for the demands of modern warfare.

Herbert Hoover later glowingly reported how well the country—industry, labor, agriculture, and government—responded to the challenge in their cooperation. Demand (and profits) from England, Russia, and France were so great and the cooperative spirit so uncommonly intense during that short emergency period that industrial management passed on a share of their material gains to their workers. The times seemed to vindicate those corporations who had proclaimed the organizational benefits of vertical integration and monopoly, for in order to "rationalize" production and distribution, industries during the war organized themselves into over 1,500 trade associations (organizations of firms in a single industry) which met yearly and published their own trade journals. As Republican secretary of commerce in the 1920s, Herbert Hoover organized hundreds more in the interests of "cooperation" and the rationalization of business.

The Extension of Monopoly Control

Predictable production and profits facilitated closer ties between labor and management, much to the surprise of those unions that had been so harassed before the war. Trade associations led to the revival of holding companies, once again thought to be the most efficient way of doing business. Since the Supreme Court had in 1911 announced that only "unreasonable" restraint of trade was to be considered illegal, new monopolistic ventures easily proved to the amenable Wilson and Harding (and even more so Hoover) courts that their activity redounded to the benefit of the nation. In the American Column and Lumber Company case in 1911, the American Linseed Oil Company case in 1923, the Cement Manufacturers' Protective Association case, and the Maple Flooring Manufacturing Association case in 1925, the Supreme Court upheld the legality of publishing cost and price information in order to standardize prices. Trade journals made it quite easy to arrive at common prices in any industry.

During the Coolidge administration the Justice Department reverted to the Roosevelt practice of holding personal meetings with offending corporations to indicate its displeasure with specific practices. It was then possible to negotiate differences and settle them without even bringing most cases to court.

If industries cooperated among themselves, shared information, divided markets, or established prices during the war and afterward, the Department of Commerce actively encouraged and aided the process in its new role as the dispenser of statistics on prices and costs to industry. The department increased its staffs in the Bureau of Standards and the Bureau of Foreign and Domestic Commerce in order to satisfy the needs of more demanding clients. Through the work of the Bureau of Standards, weights and measures, sizes, and designs were standardized in many industries. Even the already-standardized mass production equipment of the auto industry was made more efficient because of the bureau's suggestion that the industry adopt Johansson measuring blocks, i.e., gauges that measured machinery tolerances up to about a thousandth of an inch. The department also helped industries to secure foreign markets and advised investors in foreign enterprise about the security of their investments.

Other regulatory commissions also acted as governmental helpmates to industrial rationalization and cooperation. Bigger bureaucracies were set up in state as well as federal governments to handle new problems in the regulation of increased volume of trade and welfare. Each agency worked out its own procedures and set up the beginnings of long rows of documented files. Federal and state governments, in the previous century aloof and mistrustful of each other, began to assist one another. By 1920, both government and business were characterized by functional, rational, and orderly management and administration. Most of all, business had learned that government was its most reliable ally in achieving predictable economic goals.

Through the new bureaus and agencies in modern-minded governmental departments, no less than through judgments from the Supreme Court, holding companies received the favorable political atmosphere to dominate industrial life. By 1929, holding companies comprised all but four of the top ninety-seven corporations of the nation; the public utilities were among the most powerful of the newer arrivals. Ten holding companies controlled about three-quarters of the electric generating and transmitting facilities. The Van Sweringen brothers from Cleveland managed to gain control of eight mideastern and midwestern railroads (though they owned as little as .98% and .04% of the stock of two of them) through holding companies built on holding companies. They were hardly the only entrepreneurs who engaged in the practice: Corporations A,B,C would transfer 51% of their stock to holding company X; if holding company X gave 51% of *its* stock to holding company Y, the latter could control A,B,C with 25% of its stock. Many pyramids were built even higher, as the Van Sweringen episode attests.

The monopoly or oligopoly situations which characterized the resource-processing industries in the early 1900s maintained their holds on markets after the war. The Swift and Armour meatpacking companies were the second and third largest revenue producers in 1917. They introduced millions of dollars worth of labor-reducing equipment in their factories to lower labor costs, to keep prices low, and to force hundreds of small butchers out of business. At the same time, other packers joined with the giants in gentlemen's agreements to introduce market forecasting and oligopolistic pricing in the entire meatpacking industry in the 1920s.

Simultaneously, other areas of the food industry started on the road to oligopoly: Continental, General, and Ward in the baking industry; National Biscuit, United Biscuit, General Mills, and Pillsbury in biscuits and crackers, with the latter two dominating flour milling and competing in cereals with Standard Brands, Quaker Oats, and General Foods. National Dairy, Borden, Nestle's, Carnation, and Helvetia dominated the creamery industry. Food industries maintained their supremacy by marketing agreements as well as heavy advertising and packaging innovations, especially in the new grocery and variety chain stores, which expanded from 29,000 retail units in 1918 to 160,000 ten years later. Every year of the twenties saw the failure or absorption of hundreds of regional or small firms and so-called mom and pop grocery stores.

International Salt, Corn Products Refining Company, United Fruit, and American Sugar Refining all continued monopoly control of their industries from prewar years. After the Consolidated Tobacco Company was broken up in 1911, a competitive situation existed in the industry until the mid-twenties, when four companies—Reynolds, American, Liggett & Myers, and Lorillard—were able to control markets and prices with their leading brands.

From the time Andrew Mellon formed his Pittsburgh Reduction Company in 1888, the Mellon family's Alcoa managed to monopolize and vertically to integrate the aluminum industry from production to distribution and maintained a virtual monopoly on the production of the light metal by 1909. Alcoa held the few American bauxite deposits and all new discoveries while it developed new products, advertised mightily, set prices, and stifled potential competition. International Nickel used similar techniques to keep its top position in the industry. The copper industry was controlled by an oligopoly—Anaconda, Kennecott, Phelps Dodge, and Calumet & Arizona—and these firms continued to integrate their operations vertically.

Urban Culture

During the buildup period of industrial growth in the last third of the 1800s, the population shift from rural to urban areas was accelerating. Cities of 8,000 or more grew in number from 141 to 547 between 1860 and 1900, with the total urban population increasing from 5,000,000 to more than 25,000,000; the percentage of urbanites doubled from 16.1% to 32%. Most of the early migration occurred in New England, then in the northern mid-eastern states, where farms were abandoned for more secure factory work in nearby cities or for better lands farther west. Between 1900 and 1910, the population increased by 16,000,000 people, three-quarters of whom lived in towns and cities. The average American was no longer a farmer but rather an urban worker, shopkeeper, or clerk living in a tenement or tiny apartment. Almost 20,000,000 immigrants had sailed to the United States between 1820, when records were first kept, and the turn of the century; another 12,000,000 arrived before the war. Most of these new Americans lived in slums around factory cities. They were often deprived of economic and political opportunities by nativist groups that sprouted up during and after the war. Older urban populations became more middle class, but the city was less homogeneous than either the rural towns or foreign countries where the urban dwellers once lived.

The 1920 urbanites were serviced by the mass-production-consumption economy that was developing simultaneously with urban populations. The agricultural base of the society had been established for over a half-century, and the large industrial resource processors for several decades. Utility companies rose to the occasion in the 1920s, and the national retail chain stores began to offer discount products to city people.

One advantage large monopoly corporations held over smaller companies in the 1920s was their access to the radio and film industries. Already, in 1922, at least 3,000,000 homes possessed radio receivers. By the end of the decade, almost everyone had access to one; $852,000,000 was collected by their manufacturers in 1929 alone. Only the large national corporations could afford to "sponsor" radio programs and explain the virtues of their products to millions of listeners. Radio polls were taken by telephone to determine the popularity of programming. When the program of a sponsor did not draw enough listeners, it was quickly replaced by another hopeful.

The film industry influenced national tastes less directly but no less forcefully. In 1922, 40,000,000 tickets were sold every week to people who dreamed of a life like that of their screen heroes and heroines—luxurious, glamourous, adventurous, stylish, and glittering with jewels, furs, and the latest outrageously-decorated automobiles. Radio and the movies inaugurated the revolution of rising expectations and of conspicuous consumption. Necessarily, they homogenized American values. Nonetheless, the lion's share of the $1.5 billion spent on advertising in 1927, $690,000,000 went to newspapers, $210,000,000 bought space in magazines, $400,000,000 was spent on direct mailing, and even the burgeoning billboard business garnered $75,000,000. When corporate managers began to provide installment buying, raise wages so that wage-earners could afford their goods, and expand production sufficiently, the consumer society was ready for its take-off. These conditions were met in the twenties.

Banking and Prosperity

One basic prerequisite of the affluent society was the establishment of easy credit, a boon that came out of the Federal Reserve System inaugurated at the beginning of the European war. Federal monetary reserves and inexpensive loans made it possible for corporations to take a risk on the buying habits of the American public. Entrepreneurs could borrow at low interest rates and sell their products at high prices with credit. With the profits they could expand, do more advertising, offer more credit, and so on. And after the Reserve System was set up, business men were more confident that panics, such as the one that caused a run on the banks in 1907, could be more effectively contained.

In 1913, President Wilson signed the Federal Reserve Act creating twelve regional banks, centrally controlled by the Federal Reserve Board headed by the secretary of the treasury. Each federal regional bank held the reserves of its member banks. All national banks were required to join the Federal Reserve system. Others could attach themselves if they complied with federal stipulations. One purpose of the system was to control disturbances of the money supply by distributing federal reserves where they were needed. During most years of the preceding century, the federal government enjoyed an excess of cash, which could be redistributed where it was needed under the new arrangement. The system also acted as a central bank which could create money by issuing notes and credit to member banks and which could stop an inflationary flow of money by withholding credit.

When expansion of credit was necessary during the war, the system performed well. Federal Reserve banks were obligated to keep only a 3% reserve against time deposits—much less than had been required earlier for national banks. Member banks could also expand their supply of credit by rediscounting partially repaid loans, or by requesting an advance of future eligible money reserves.

After the war, speculators and investors used the low interest rates to finance new promotional schemes in the burgeoning consumer society. Although the Federal Board warned against the activity, they could not raise interest rates because the Treasury Department wanted to sell low interest Victory Loan Bonds, which encouraged easy credit conditions throughout the rest of the economy. In 1919, stock and commodity prices shot to high levels and a real estate boom pushed up land prices around the country. Credit passed on to consumers stimulated demand for more household goods. The bubble burst in 1921-22 but the Reserve System managed to sustain the member banks and the growth economy as well. Business interests were not at all discouraged from engaging in new enterprises after the depression, particularly since the Federal Reserve authorities embarked on another easy credit policy in order to bring the country out of its economic slump.

Because of these structural changes in banking and industry, for the first time in the nation's history large investments were poured into consumer goods—automobiles, radios, household fixtures, and appliances such as washing machines, oil furnaces, vacuum cleaners, electric stoves and iceless refrigerators. Earlier investment and production were largely confined to capital goods such as railroads or factory machines. Because of mounting wages and sales throughout the economy, real per-capita income increased from $543 in 1919 to $716 in 1929, both measured in 1929 dollars.

Besides banking and credit, the consumer industries relied upon a rapid growth of power-producing plants driven by oil, and upon scientific and technological advances in steel, oil, and agriculture—the latter called upon to feed a population increased by 17,000,000 people in the 1920s. Electric power production from 1899 to 1929 rose 331%, while production increased 295% and the population went up only about 62%. By 1929, 95.7% of machinery manufacturing was done by electricity and the U.S. produced more electric power than the rest of the world combined. Appliances needed electricity, and, of course, the radio and motion picture industries would have been impossible if electrification had not reached homes and theaters.

The Steel and Auto Industries

In the early 1920s, the production of large quantities of new all-steel autos and household consumer goods was made possible by the development of the continuous mass-production strip and sheet mills and cold reduction mills. Previously, auto bodies had been constructed by horse-carriage makers out of wood. They were painted with many coats of varnish. This took more than several weeks' time. The intense heat of the early car motors warped the wood and loosened the glue, often splitting auto panels. To solve these problems, auto body makers added more and more steel over the wood frame until it became almost completely covered with steel and weighted to a grotesque degree.

But in the first decades of the century, stamping presses for shaping steel sheet metal for lighter weight consumer goods had been spreading through the steel industry. When Edward Budd, a young Philadelphian, proposed in 1912 that his firm construct the automobile body completely from steel without wood frames, he was opposed in the effort. He then started his own steel auto-body manufacturing company. He successfully introduced an all-steel auto body for Oakland and Hupmobile cars in 1912, and he received a large contract from the Dodge brothers in 1913. Within a few years, other manufacturers picked up his idea despite heavy propaganda against it by carriage makers.

At this time, hand-sheet mills were manually turning out steel sheets one-sixteenth of an inch or less thick. Sheets were rolled from heated steel bars and run through rollers which were manually adjusted by huge screws to achieve various thicknesses. The varied thicknesses of steel sheets from hand-rolled mills constituted a big problem for the automobile industry, which needed standardized dimensions, temper, and quality on their production lines. Hand-rolled mills could never produce a completely standardized product.

In 1921, John Butler Tytus was provided by the American Rolling Mill Company with an experimental factory in Ashland, Kentucky to attempt to set up a continuous, hot-rolling steel process. Tytus designed a process of nineteen slightly convex rolls through which the steel, reheated four times in successive stages, passed. Tytus was left with problems of tension and slipping in the rolls, a difficulty solved by A. J. Townsend and H. M. Naugle of Columbia, which had contested Armco's patent, and which licensed other firms to use its process. The stage was then set for the production of lightweight metal consumer goods and of all-steel automobiles in numbers surpassing all previous records.

Cold-rolling mills gave the metal a smooth and shiny finish and more uniform gauge and temper. In succeeding years, mill operators could apply higher intensities of power to attain more speed and productivity and add to the steel's strength and versatility. At the same time, prices for a ton of the steel sheets declined from $100 in 1923 before the continuous rolling process was developed down to $80 in 1926, to $57 in 1939. Lower steel costs usually meant lower costs of consumer goods: e.g., refrigerators went from $475 to $169 in the same time span, and washing machines from $140 to $68. Henry Ford lowered the price of his Model T from $950 in 1909 to $290 in 1924, and he could raise wages and reduce working hours at the same time. Sheet steel came in time to bolster the sale of agricultural machinery and textile equipment. Before long it became important in virtually every large industrial use: electrical, drug, and chemical manufactures; aircraft; passenger trains; ships; petroleum refining; surgical and medical equipment; furniture; office desks and supplies; and other kinds

Figure 15–1. An early gasoline "tank wagon," predecessor to the modern gasoline tank truck. Electricity, steam, compressed air, carbonic acid gas, and alcohol were used successfully to power the many different early automobiles, but gasoline became the favored fuel, with an assist from the oil companies, as suggested by the sign on this tank wagon. Courtesy Sun Oil Company.

of machinery. Since sheets are easily galvanized with zinc for use as roofing, gutters, and pails, hundreds of manufacturers of household items became dependent on steel sheets. U.S. Steel, the largest revenue-producing corporation of the twenties, and dozens of new steel companies turned out the product as fast as their facilities permitted.

The Role of the Automobile

The demand for sheet steel was kicked off by the automobile industry, which dominated the 1920s more than any other manufacturing activity or consumer item. The number of registered cars jumped from 2,500,000 in 1915, a few years after the introduction of the Model T, to over 9,000,000 in 1920; to almost 20,000,000 in 1925; and 26,500,000 in 1929. The mass-production techniques of Ford, the development of sheet steel auto frames, and installment buying financed by the auto companies all played a role in the incredible saturation of the automobile into American society. The tempo of American life speeded up proportionately.

It is difficult to overestimate the geographic, economic, and social impact of the automobile revolution. The wilderness gave way to highways and their trappings—gasoline stations, roadside stands, restaurants, garages, tourist camps, wayside inns, and billboards. Towns and cities began their unstoppable sprawl into the countryside. Rural children were carried in buses to central schools. Americans took longer auto vacations and moved to new locations in search of new opportunities or jobs. Congress contributed its first substantial road-building subsidy with the passage of the Rural Post Roads Act of 1916, which granted the states $75,000,000 over three years; after 1920, $75,000,000 was provided every year until the depression. Between 1915 and 1925 the number of miles of hard-surfaced rural and suburban roads increased from 276,000 to 521,000; by 1945 there were 1,721,000 miles of rural surfaced roads in the U.S. Yet the great bulk of the highway funds came from local governments—about $2,000,000,000 a year during this period.

Towns, cities, and suburbs were newly designed with the automobile as the primary consideration. Suburbs existed before the auto; they were linked together by railroads, but usually did not expand farther than a mile or two beyond the stations. After the arrival of the car, suburbs pushed their way into the country. They were continually subdivided, and eventually they met one another. Since industrial and residential development depended on highways, the skyrocketing prices of land during the 1920s can be traced to auto fever. Agricultural land, not worth much then, was paved over with almost as much rapidity as it was twenty-five years later. Cars and trucks enabled farms, businesses, and industry to shift locations. No longer were the railroad towns or the land next to the railroad of such great importance. Commuting by car or truck was inexpensive. During the twenties, chain stores like Sears Roebuck built large stores with huge parking lots on the edge of town and began drawing off the trade downtown, already glutted with traffic. Railroad traffic was cut in half; many railroad companies fell into bankruptcy.

The 1920s also gave birth to the parking problem and its never-ending solutions: more parking lots and garages; more street space for parking; larger parkways and boulevards. Auto-accident figures already reached the tens of thousands in the twenties. The automobile took its place beside the telephone, the radio, and the movies in ushering in the modern era.

The automobile industry also followed earlier American models in its path to concentration. From twenty producers before the war, three firms ruled in 1927—Ford, General Motors, and Chrysler. These three attempted to win the final advantage by greater production and sales. Regional managers franchised retail distributors, divided according to districts. If a dealer did not meet his quota of cars each year, he risked the loss of his franchise—in much the same way that a person on the assembly line was forced to keep up with the pace of the mechanical equipment.

Of course the big three auto firms engaged in widely dispersed advertising through new advertising firms which guaranteed their results. The big three also made credit arrangements more attractive for the buyer. By the end of the twenties, the buyer needed only a 10% down payment. The auto makers switched to the hard sell, stressing the new models' latest styles and comfort. By 1927, the automobile had so much become a status symbol that Henry Ford had to drop his generation-old philosophy of economy-mindedness and incorporate some of the luxuries of his competitors' vehicles in the design of his new Model A. Later the firm added a bevy of gadgets and a multi-colored assortment of autos—a new model each year—in a desperate effort to make up for lost time. By 1932, the auto industry was buying up old cars for demolition in order to keep up the demand for new ones.

The industry also held the key to the nation's economic health. Automobile manufacturing represented over an eighth of all industrial activity in the country and employed over 7% of the wage earners. It consumed at least 15% of all steel production. Subsidiary industries like tires, upholstery, gasoline, oil, and glass were carried along with the fortunes of the auto industry. Some economists estimate that at least a tenth of the non-agricultural labor force was dependent on the auto industry in 1929. At that time, no other total industry, including subsidiaries, used up more natural resources or employed more people, and no other was more influential in setting the style of the mass-production-advertising-consumption society of the decades to come.

Oil Production and Waste

Petroleum tycoons were among the most grateful businessmen affected by the meteoric rise of the auto industry. Until 1901, when electric light bulbs were beginning to replace kerosene as the major illuminant, there was only one oil tycoon—John D. Rockefeller. At the time he didn't worry about the production of oil, an unpredictable

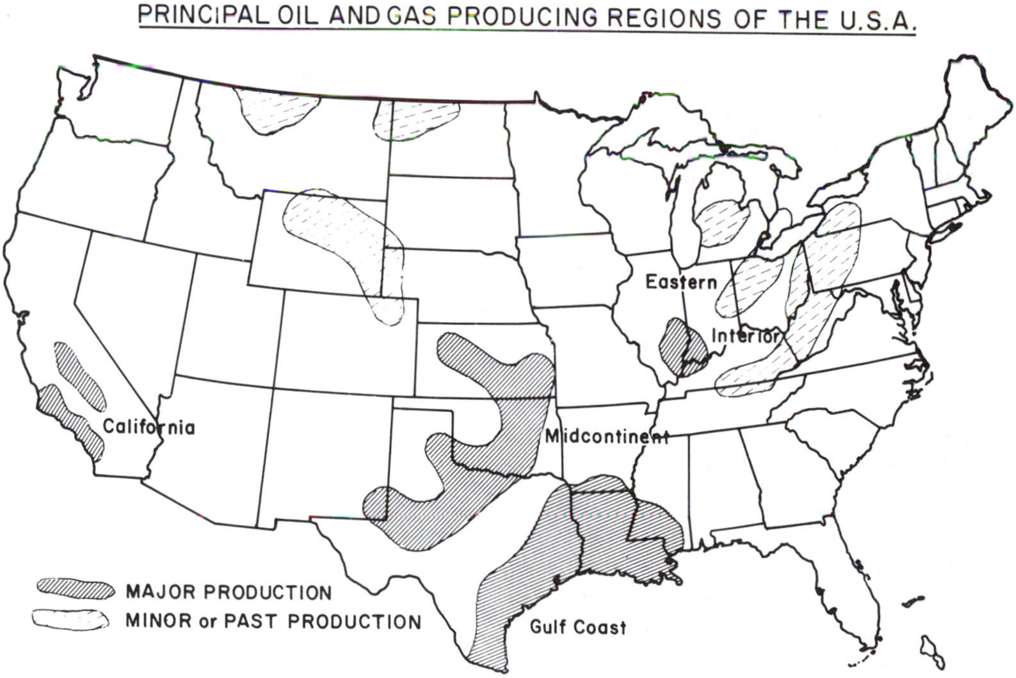

PRINCIPAL OIL AND GAS PRODUCING REGIONS OF THE U.S.A.

Figure 15–2. Continental sources of gas and oil to 1970. The map does not show offshore or Alaskan fields.

and messy occupation, since he controlled its refining and marketing. He allowed the independent producers of Pennsylvania and Ohio, the largest producing states until the turn of the century, to endure the risks and hazard of exploration and production.

As electricity was replacing kerosene, crude oil gained in popularity as a fuel, especially to heat factory boilers for steam engines and to heat the ship boilers of the British Navy. Oil was easier to get out of the ground, to transport, and to handle than the heavier, bulkier coal. Furthermore, oil flows through a pipe and leaves little residual waste when burned. And it was cheaper than coal. Even before the gasoline era, oil was considered an excellent investment.

So prospectors poured out of Pennsylvania into Ohio, where the Lima and other fields of northwestern Ohio began to produce millions of barrels of oil in the 1890s. Other sections of the state also yielded oil, and the Lima field was extended into Indiana. Virginia was producing a large amount of oil, as were Illinois and Kentucky after the turn of the century.

A new phase in the history of the oil industry was signaled in 1901 by Captain Anthony F. Lucas's fabulous discovery at Spindletop, in southeastern Texas near the Louisiana border and the Gulf of Mexico. The gusher spouted 200 feet high, carrying away a thousand feet of pipe, drilling tools, and derrick, and it blew off perhaps as much as 100,000 barrels a day for ten days before it could be capped. Within a few weeks, the lake of oil which had collected caught fire and burned skyward.

Throngs of promoters, investors, swindlers, and speculators rushed to the Beaumont district on specially chartered trains. Speculators bought land for dozens of miles around the tiny community of Spindletop for as high as $100,000 an acre. Representatives of one oil company who arrived in the first wave bought 1,000,000 acres and issued $15,000,000 worth of stock to pay for it. (But Spindletop oil was later found to encompass only 170 acres.) Another group of four companies pooled $14,000,000 and bought forty-five square feet of property. By the end of 1902, almost 400 wells were tightly bunched together on Spindletop mound, with the number increasing to 1,200 by 1904. By that time, however, total production at Spindletop dropped to about 6,000 barrels a day, less than a tenth of the original well's production. Only ninety-five of the 1,200 wells were producing oil, the lucky ones grossly overcapitalized. Only a few of the original promoters made big money from the episode.

The oil strike took prospectors to other areas out of Beaumont—for instance, down to the Matagorda field 150 miles southwest. This field included the rich Humble field eighteen miles northwest of Houston. In 1904, the oil fields of northern Texas near the Oklahoma line yielded high production levels; they continued on and off for a decade. The big problem for oil producers was price fluctuations stemming from the alternately gigantic to minimal supplies. Primitive oil production technologies could not regulate oil flow; natural gas-pressured gushers first blew tens of thousands of barrels into the air, then when capped and pumped, only a few hundred barrels daily could be coaxed from the well. Prices see-sawed between $.50 and $.10 for a barrel of Texas crude, depending on the available supply.

But the heavy sulfurous and asphaltic "sour" content of Texas oil made it difficult to refine, and the oil companies sold it mainly for fuel oil at prices far below those of the "sweet" crude from Pennsylvania. Although Standard Oil was in a position to refine and market the Texas oil, Rockefeller had earlier been expelled from Texas for illegal marketing practices, and he was not yet pushed into getting into the production end of the business.

The First Big Oil Companies

Rockefeller's twentieth century competition arose from the Spindletop strike. Lucas needed additional money during the final stages of his venture. He obtained it from John H. Galey of the Pittsburgh oil firm of Guffey and Galey. After the oil came in, Joseph M. Guffey in turn went to financier Andrew W. Mellon to help underwrite the new J. M. Guffey Petroleum Company. Mellon took 40% of the $15,000,000 worth of stock; Lucas sold out for $400,000, and Guffey gave one of his leases of acreage on top of Spindletop) to former Texas governor James Hogg, who was politically powerful in the state. Hogg formed the Texas Company (later Texaco), and the Mellon interests eventually squeezed out Guffey for alleged mismanagement in order to form the Gulf Oil Company. Before they took this step, the Mellons had second thoughts about the possibilities of the firm. They tried to sell out to Standard Oil, but the eastern monopoly was not worried about potential competition during the unstable period for the Texas oil companies. Therefore the Mellons decided to expand into a completely integrated oil company from exploration to marketing. They moved into Indiana where oil was sweeter, more easily refined, and closer to big city markets.

Spindletop was responsible for a third international oil giant, Shell Oil, known then as Shell Transport and Trading Company of London. Guffey (later Gulf) signed a twenty-year contract with Shell to transport fuel oil to the British Navy at a price of $.25 a barrel. When the automobile market drove up the price, Gulf Oil was almost ruined by the contract, but Shell flourished, bought more tankers, and eventually merged with Royal Dutch. Thus Standard, Gulf, Texaco, and Shell developed corporate strength even before the automobile was a significant factor in the petroleum business.

Much oil production was underway in California at the turn of the century. An oil craze swept the state shortly after oil was discovered in Pennsylvania in 1865, and the same cycle of prolific gushers, investment, speculation, fraud, and waste ensued. Promoters claimed that the famous Professor Silliman of Yale highly endorsed California oil from its southern fields and listed other scientific authorities on their promotional leaflets. By the end of the 1860s, shares sold for from $1.00 to $50,000 each in companies that drilled in every coastal county. One company paid $20,000 for 10,000 acres in Santa Barbara county, half of which was sold for $50,000 in the East, where it was resold for $450,000. That sum in turn was placed into the capitalization of the California Petroleum Company at a value of $10,000,000. Within a few years, California's wild enthusiasm died with the investments of the gullible and the prospects of finding oil.

Some oil development continued, though, throughout the seventies and eighties. In 1892, E. L. Doheny discovered high-quality oil in Los Angeles, and within two years hundreds of oil wells were lined up beside one another in town lots. By 1913, an estimated 1,300 wells had been drilled in Los Angeles, about 300 of them remaining in production. Yields rose from 500,000 barrels in 1899 to over 24,000,000 barrels in 1903.

Figure 15–3. California Oil field. This oil drilling site at Signal Hill, California, suggests the rush to exploit new oil strikes. Wells were sunk in such a manner that the oil could be extracted not only from the driller's property but from the neighboring property as well. Courtesy Shell Oil Company.

The overproduction pushed down the price of oil to $.10 a barrel and encouraged massive waste. Since storage tanks were rarely used in those days, oil was stored in open earthen reservoir lakes, where it evaporated, seeped into the ground, caught fire, or drained off. Because of low prices and financial difficulties of California companies, consolidation took place at a great rate, with most companies first selling their oil to Standard Oil and then finally selling out completely to the giant, which carried on widespread advertising campaigns for fuel oil and kerosene. More southern California gushers came in—one in Lakeview producing 8,000,000 barrels in eighteen months, with another 2,000,000 to 4,000,000 barrels lost.

Millions of barrels each year were wasted in seepage, transportation, and storage. The more sensitive public officials and citizens predicted an oil famine in a few years if some controls were not placed on oil drilling. In this context President Taft reserved several southern California oil fields for the use of the Navy and many more for the nation's future use. The waste was excessive, and it was also frightening enough to make the most conservative chief executive take steps which he believed to be quite drastic.

During the second decade of the century, the automobile industry and wartime demand made millionaire companies out of those which survived the earlier hard times. In 1911, almost 620,000 cars were on the road, but by 1930, almost 30,000,000 of them needed vast amounts of that gasoline which earlier had been drained off the kerosene and poured into rivers. Standard and its counterparts controlled prices regionally at whatever the traffic would bear. Standard of New Jersey, the third largest industrial corporation in terms of revenue in 1917, had to share the rapidly increasing markets with other large corporations: Cities Service, put together by stockbroker H. L. Doherty; Consolidated, built up by Harry F. Sinclair; the Philips Company from the gas fields of Kansas, Oklahoma and the Texas Panhandle; Skelley and Mid-Continent taking a piece of the center of the country. Sun and Pure had managed to stay in business while Standard was monopolizing the Eastern seaboard; on the west coast Union and Shell offered some competition to Standard.

The huge Standard Oil Company grew to even greater proportions, and although it was broken into smaller components after 1911, the company retained a strong grip on the marketing of its products around the country, especially in the industrial and urbanized East. Standard of New Jersey, New York, Ohio, Indiana, and California then began to buy up production facilities to assure themselves of an inexpensive oil supply. Too late did Standard of Indiana offer to buy Mellon's Gulf Oil, but the giant did manage to ingest dozens of small firms in the Rocky Mountain states and Texas, as did Standard of New Jersey absorb Humble in Texas and immediately become the largest of the southwestern oil producers. Even Standard of New York (Socony) penetrated the Texas oil fields by taking over the Magnolia Company. Standard of California earlier had bought up most of the larger independents of the state. By 1930, Standard companies enjoyed the lion's share of the market, and a dozen more corporations—headed by Texaco, Gulf, Shell, and Atlantic—were close behind. Since that time these companies have held on to the greatest share of an immensely-expanded industry.

The Waste of Oil

From the beginning of oil drilling, little thought was given to the value of oil as a non-renewable natural resource. Whenever a driller hit a strike, he extracted as much oil as soon as possible, for he knew that within days a swarm of other companies would be drilling dozens of wells along the boundaries of adjoining properties hoping to extract more oil than the original explorers could manage. Therefore, the first firm in the area quickly drilled along the property margins; in a very short time wells would be standing a few feet away on the next property, and every company sucked every available drop from the area with small care for the waste.

Hundreds of times an oil episode featured gushers, overproduction, depressed prices, abandoned wells, and incalculable amounts of oil and gas seepage, with the subsequent ruin of the small producers who could not stay in business for long receiving low market prices. It happened in every large producing area after the turn of the century: first in the Spindletop region; then in North Texas; then in the phenomenal strikes of Oklahoma; and often in California—Los Angeles, Huntington Beach, and Long Beach. Where the large corporations controlled markets, they often entered into curtailment agreements to slow down production.

Curtailment agreements kept up prices and profits. They were themselves further incentives to more wildcatting, prospecting, and waste. The tens of thousands of drill holes in abandoned wells in every oil region not only have led to wasted oil, but also to the loss of billions of cubic feet of natural gas. The Cushing, Oklahoma, oil field lost more in the potential value of its natural gas in 1913 than all its oil was worth! Bureau of Mines reports indicate that between 1922 and 1934 about 1,250,000,000 cubic feet of gas were wasted every day in the oil fields—the equivalent of 250,000,000 tons of coal. In those days gas was used simply to push oil to the surface. When this function was completed, the gas either was left to accumulate over the fields until it exploded, or was burned as it came out of the ground. As late as the 1950s, more than half the natural gas—trillions of cubic feet each year—was burned off in large numbers of the nation's oil fields. Low prices for natural gas did not warrant its capture and utilization by the oil companies.

The mad rush to profit from oil riches led to just as much financial waste. Geologists have estimated that 95% of the wildcat wells drilled until 1929 never struck oil. Even in the proved oil territory of east Texas the Natural Resources Planning Board estimated that 21,000 of the 24,000 wells drilled after 1930 were unnecessary—a $250,000,000 waste of financial resources. Behind the efforts, of course, stood the garish roadsters heaving for more gasoline and oil.

New Products and Technologies

The story is not completely depressing, however, even beyond the fleeting joy and individual freedom brought by the newly mobilized country's playthings. Oil was found to contain a veritable universe of possible uses. In the wake of the research and development movement that began before the turn of the century, Standard Oil began to experiment with new refining methods. When crude petroleum is refined, its hydrocarbons—molecules of carbon and hydrogen atoms—are broken up and recombined. Since petroleum hydrocarbons combine in hundreds of structural arrangements, the possibilities of separation and construction are almost limitless. Early refiners simply boiled the crude oil and distilled off the byproducts; This was easy to do because different hydrocarbons, e.g., kerosene and gasoline, have different boiling temperatures.

In the early 1920s, catalytic "cracking," subjecting the crude oil to great heat and pressure of 75 pounds in the presence of a catalytic agent and "cracking" heavy molecules into lighter ones, resulted in new petrochemicals including the lighter molecules of gasoline. Later the process of polymerization would arrange the lighter molecules in chains (polymers) and create synthetic petrochemicals. Thus basic chemicals like ammonia, ethyl alcohol, methyl alcohol, and glycerol, once derived from coal or agricultural products, could be synthesized from petroleum. Synthetic fibers—among them cellulose acetate, nylon, and dacron—are petrochemicals, as are

Figure 15–4. Home of a world-changing innovation. One of the great technological breakthroughs in the oil industry was the invention of the thermal cracking process by Doctors William M. Burton and Robert E. Humphreys. When put into operation in 1913, the new process doubled the yield of gasoline from crude oil. The oil industry was thereby able to supply a growing demand for gasoline which it cheerfully encouraged. The timely invention also helped provide fuel for the vehicles of the First World War. Shown here is the still used to test the thermal cracking process. Courtesy Standard Oil of New Jersey.

most plastics and synthetic tires. Even a high-protein ingredient known as Torula yeast, which grows on ethyl alcohol (made from ethylene), and which was eaten by German soldiers in cake form, is a petroleum product. It may someday help to solve world food shortages. Generally speaking, however, the synthetics have come to be a mixed blessing.

Although oil was a booming industry in the 1920s, textiles, coal and agricultural commodities suffered declines and financial losses. Styles changed so radically that world markets were lost, and dressmakers in 1928 needed only half the material required in 1918. Rayon, invented by the Frenchman Count Hilaire de Chardonnet in 1884, utilized wood chips dissolved in a chemical solution which was then forced through a spinnerette. Rayon was introduced in the United States in 1910 by the American Viscose Corporation, and it became very popular in the twenties. Acetate, a combination made from wood pulp and acetic acid, also was in vogue during the period. Nylon was not developed until the late thirties. During the twenties, the depressed textile industries, still geared for cotton and wool, moved into southern communities where labor was cheap and cotton close by.

Coal industries were hit hard because fuel oil was rapidly increasing in use, as were car and truck transportation as railroads in turn declined. A quarter of the nation's miners were unemployed, many because of new mining technologies at the end of the twenties, and those who did work had to live on lower wages than they had received a decade earlier.

Improvement in mining technology became more sophisticated after the establishment of the Bureau of Mines, separated from the Geological Survey in 1910. The survey reverted to its earlier work of classifying the minerals of the public domain (millions of acres of coal, oil, and phosphates were withdrawn to be classified after 1906). The bureau, formerly the Technologic Branch of the Survey, continued research on technological mining problems. Scientists at the bureau's experiment stations were eager to work out technical problems for the mineral industries during the 1920s, and they developed a number of new conservation techniques. All their innovations were gratefully received by cost-conscious industries.

The bureau pioneered new techniques of mineral extraction, refining, storage, and even of treating low-grade ores. The Bartlesville, Oklahoma experiment station, for example, worked on less wasteful drilling, refining, and storage processes. It discovered a way to recapture gasoline from still vapors at oil refineries, and it investigated new methods of repressuring oil fields which had lost their natural gasses. Bureau scientists showed industrial processors how to utilize lignite. They developed more efficient designs for blast furnaces that could use low grade ores, and they found new uses for coke-oven wastes and looked for ways to retort oil shale.

One of the primary original purposes of the bureau lay in the conservation of mineral resources, which as nonrenewable ores or oil can be conserved mainly in non-wasteful processing and wise use. The technological work of the bureau aided in this purpose, but because they were dependent on Congressional appropriations and good will, bureau chiefs became so closely allied with the purposes of industry, particularly in exploratory work, that their early conservation purposes became lost.

Agricultural Policy, Technology, and Science

The largest group that suffered economic distress was the farmers, who were never able to recover from the postwar depression. Despite progressive urbanization and growing populations, American agriculture greatly overproduced during the 1920s, an occurrence not solely due to greater acreage under cultivation because of reclamation projects. University, governmental, and experimental station agricultural scientists achieved important advances that increased output during the first decades of the century. New refinements of agricultural machinery and, of course, the tractor contributed not only to productivity but also to continuing declines in rural populations. The percentage of the rural population to the total U.S. population dropped from 60% in 1900 to 48.6% in 1920, down to 43.8% in 1930. Finally, federal policy factors loomed large in the plight of the farmer.

Before the war, American agriculture seemed to be in a strong economic position. The Smith-Lever Act of 1914 even provided for a cooperative federal-state Agricultural

Extension Service for instruction and practical demonstration for people not in residence at agricultural colleges. The law was the basis for the county agent system, which enjoyed funds from counties and states as well as the federal government. In 1917, county agents (working out of state colleges) were sent to every important agricultural county to teach farmers and their wives new ways to combat plant pests and animal diseases, as well as nutritional information and home economics. By 1915, farm production and prices had stabilized at high levels, and in 1917 farm incomes went higher. Even with Hoover's federally administered prices, farm prices rose again in 1918. Federal farmloan banks provided ready cash for agricultural equipment and arranged special contracts with Henry Ford for tractors to sell at $750. The Bureau of Markets standardized shipping and marketing arrangements to keep allies supplied with agricultural goods during the war.

With the additional income, many farm families were able to bring city comforts to their homes: automobiles, telephones, radios, household appliances, running water and electricity—all on the installment plan. Even without all these new luxuries, farm life was greatly improved in 1920. Then the postwar depression struck and the big market crops—wheat, corn, cotton—declined sharply in price. During the twenties the economic condition of farming did not greatly improve, and farm mortgage foreclosures became common once again. Land values dropped with those of the farms. Federal allowance of farm loans and credit during the 1920s could not solve the more chronic problem of indebtedness because of low prices. Land and farms were sold at one-half to one-quarter of their peak values. In 1928, the federal land banks owned over 5,000 farms; joint stock land banks owned another 1,000. Since so much land could not be disposed of so quickly, the farms were either abandoned or leased out to their former owners as tenants.

The wheatlands of Canada, Argentina, Australia, and Russia offered great competition to American wheat exports during those years. The first three countries processed eight times more wheat in 1928 than they did in 1900, and by 1928 world production of wheat actually exceeded consumption. World trade arrangements and American tariffs worked against the farmer after the war. European nations could not pay off their war debts to America or buy needed agricultural products from American farmers with their own goods because of the prohibitively high American tariffs protecting American manufacturers. Therefore these potential markets were lost to more remote countries that welcomed European manufactures. Lower world prices in wheat and corn determined deflated market prices at home, while the cost of living was rising for the farmer on other necessities. Substitutes for cotton and wool and other light clothing materials led to overproduction in the South as well. The tractor put thousands of horses and mules out of work, rendering obsolete much of the 15,000,000 to 18,000,000 acres of hay and grain land designated to feed them.

The demands on agriculture during the war and federal loans coincided with the improvement of gasoline-powered tractors. Earlier steam engines could do the work of 120 horses and draw as many as forty plows, turning over ninety acres a day, but they needed over two tons of coal and up to 25,000 pounds of water every ten hours to keep them running. The additional labor and teams of horses needed to carry fuel for steam tractors limited the latters' use to only very large farms.

Gasoline tractors, on the other hand, were economical for small operations so long as farm produce was marketable. Stationary gasoline engines had been used for pumping and threshing on farms since the 1890s, and they were put on tractors in the same decade. In 1910, over 4,000 tractors (which operated on one cylinder) were manufactured in the United States, and even in that year they compared favorably to the cost of horses and feed. Although the majority of farmers resisted the introduction of tractors, many into the forties, more than 250,000 tractors were in use by 1920; by 1929 a new tractor cost only $1,000, payable on the installment plan, and 853,000 tractors were being utilized. In 1945 there were 2,354,000 tractors working U.S. farms.

The phenomenon in the 1920s in many ways was a replay of the farm difficulties after the Civil War. As prices dropped and more goods had to be grown to make up for declining income, solutions were sought through additional mechanization, particularly in the wheat zones, where one tractor could replace the twelve to twenty horses needed to pull a combine. Even the sale of combines increased during the difficult twenties. Because of the effectiveness of the tractor-pulled combines in 1931, overproduction pushed the price of wheat down to $.25 a bushel in Kansas and Nebraska, though other factors should also be considered, e.g., weather and Russian durum wheats. Similar efficiencies were utilized by the corn grower, who could take care of his whole farm with the help of a son, a tractor and cultivator, a mechanical shucker, a corn binder, and silo filler (the corn harvester came later). And corn prices dropped correspondingly.

Agricultural Experimentation

At least one further variable should be considered in the discussion of overproduction of the American farmers during the 1920s. The turn of the century marked the beginning of some of the most significant scientific achievements, which contributed to the high yields of later American agriculture. The impetus came from federally funded experiment stations of the states, land grant agricultural colleges, and Department of Agriculture experiments themselves. The Hatch Act of 1887 had provided for a yearly grant to each state to support an agricultural experiment station, and within a few years the stations were providing direction to agricultural colleges and experimenting with new agricultural varieties, breeds, methods, and techniques. The county agents hired during the war tied in the farmers more closely with the work of the experiment stations, and they advised them on state and federal campaigns to eliminate the cattle tick, hoof and mouth disease, and bovine tuberculosis. Extension agents also kept farmers up to date on the latest high-yield or disease-resistant wheat and corn.

An early breakthrough for wheat production came at the turn of the century from the efforts of an Agriculture Department cerealist, Mark A. Carleton, who spent over a decade experimenting with and seeking wheat varieties which could withstand the fierce midwestern blizzards, droughts, and excessive temperature variations. His first clue came from Russian Mennonites who brought the hardy Turkey Red winter wheat with them into Kansas in the 1870s from Taurida in Russia. Carleton noted that topographical and precipitation maps of the Kansas and Nebraska regions corresponded with those of the Volga region of Russia. He was certain that the native Russian wheat of the Volga region could survive the tempestuous western climates. He

Figure 15–5. The rise of the gasoline tractor. Because the internal combustion tractor was comparatively light, because it became more and more powerful, and because it could provide power for other machines with its flywheel, it became one of the most revolutionary technological achievements in agricultural history. Farming productivity vaulted after the final development of the gasoline tractor. By the time this woman mounted her tractor in Riverside, California in 1918, she could start her engine effortlessly from the seat. Her tractor was also much stronger, with two cylinders rather than one. It was designed as a unit, not just an engine mounted on a frame. Tough steel improved both the engine and the gang plow the tractor is pulling. (Courtesy Laval Collection, Fresno, California.) As tractors became more available, a tractor culture developed. The greybeard is a student of the mechanic standing by the older hand-cranked tractor in a Kern County tractor repair school conducted by the California State Agricultural Cooperative Extension program in the 1920s. (Courtesy University of California Cooperative Extension.) The more modern tractors show pneumatic rubber tires, which cut fuel bills and which could be driven on roads, and the three-point hitch, developed by Harry Ferguson in the 1930s. The hitch made possible a flexible array of farming tools. Courtesy International Harvester Company and The Smithsonian Institution.

worked at persuading Agriculture Department officials to send him to Russia to bring back seeds of the best native wheats, sat down and learned the Russian language, and was ready to go in 1898. In Russia he found what he had been looking for—the durum Kubanka and its tough brothers, the Arnautka, the Gharnovka, the Pererodka—and brought them back to experiment stations on the dry fringes of the western prairies. As he expected, the Russian durum (macaroni) wheats survived the worst weather conditions the West had to offer.

Farmers began to plant Kubanka in greater numbers after 1904, when the dreaded black stem rust ruined every variety of wheat but the Russian durum. A few years later, wheat farmers discovered Carleton's hard red Kharkov, which was outyielding the very best of the old varieties on less than half the rainfall. The hard red Russian winter wheats spread beyond Kansas, Nebraska, and the Dakotas into Oklahoma, Texas, Montana, Colorado, and other states. By 1923, their total production reached almost 250,000,000 bushels, double the Northwest's hard red spring wheat crop.

Carleton's Russian wheats were improved through "pure-line" selection by such breeders as Herbert Roberts of the Kansas Agricultural Experiment Station, who developed the famous Kanred (Kansas Red) variety from the Crimean wheat. Pure-line selection, however, only sorts out the superior lines of a variety; it creates no new genetic combinations. New varieties are obtained by hybridization, whereby a breeder crosses two desirable varieties, such as one with a resistance to disease and one with a superior baking quality.

Hybrid Breeding of Wheat and Corn

One of the first achievements with hybrid wheat was the Marquis strain. Canadian scientists William and Charles Saunders, working with experimenter Angus Mackay, bred the very hardy and early ripening spring hard wheat, the Marquis cross, from the early growing Hard Red Calcutta from India and Red Fife from Poland. William Saunders started hybridizing wheats in 1888 and began the Marquis in 1892. The wheat was developed by his son Charles between 1903 and 1922. The early growing quality was important, since first frosts often killed Canadian wheat, but Marquis also possessed superior baking qualities. For these reasons the Marquis became popular in the U.S., and by 1918 over 3,000,000 bushels of it were produced in the nation. For twenty years thereafter, the Marquis became the standard by which other varieties were measured. It was utilized as the parent (along with Russian varieties) of many improved wheats, including Tenmarq, developed by John Parker in Kansas; Ceres, produced in North Dakota by L. R. Waldron; and Thatcher and New Thatch, bred by Herbert K. Hayes and his associates in Minnesota. Contemporary development of hybrid wheat is only now at the stage that hybrid corn was in the 1930s when it began to dominate feedgrain production, and, although hybrid seeds improve yields 20% to 25%, they cost five times as much as nonhybrids.

During the same period, Hardy W. Campbell systemized a method of dry farming for the semi-arid wheat growing regions where rainfall fluctuated between drought and abundance. As little as 12 inches of rain can produce a crop of hardy durum wheat; fourteen inches will often yield twice as much as twelve. A little water over the

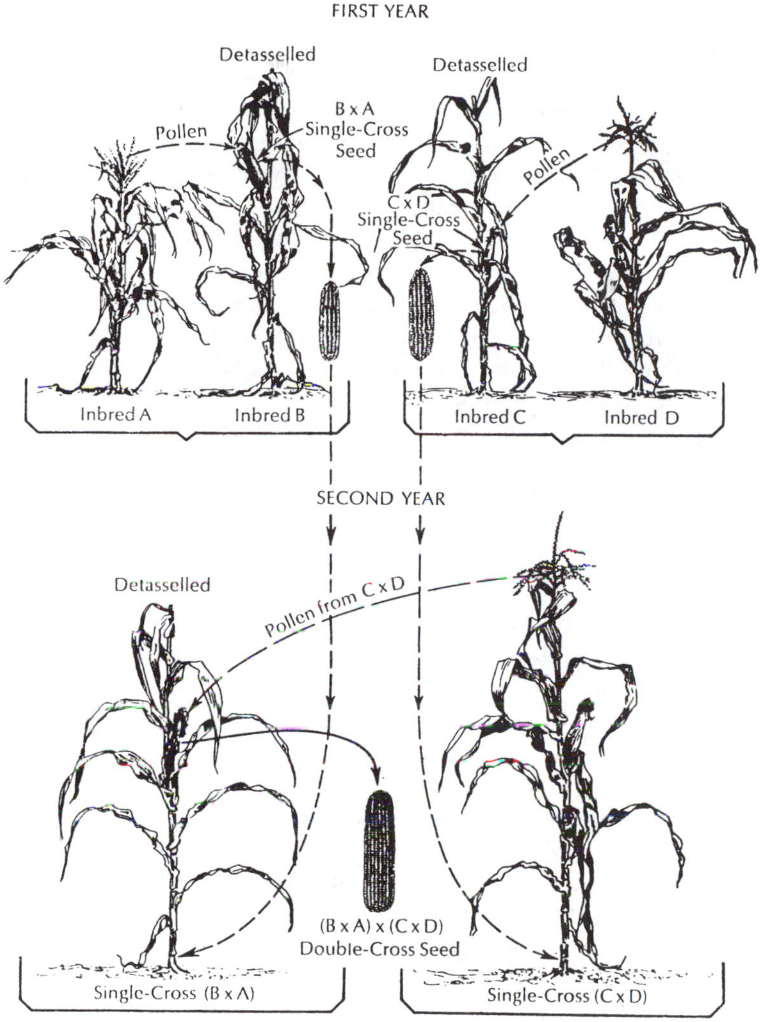

FIRST YEAR

Figure 15–6. Hybridizing corn. This drawing from the 1937 *Yearbook* of the United States Department of Agriculture, shows how corn plants are inbred to produce single crosses. The following year the single-cross plants are crossed again to get double-cross seeds. Plants from this elaborate procedure bear significantly larger crops and the plants show other genetic advantages.

minimum makes all the difference, and dry farming attempted to conserve any extra off-season precipitation by reducing runoff and evaporation, increasing the ability of the soil to absorb moisture, and allowing half the land to lie fallow to accumulate moisture each year.

A number of methods of dry farming were attempted in the 1880s and 1890s, especially because of its promotion by railroad magnate James J. Hill. Deep plowing, from twelve to fourteen inches in the fall, followed by replowing and harrowing in the spring, helped to conserve much of the yearly moisture, especially if a field was allowed to lie fallow on a year of scant rainfall. Canadian experiment station director Mackay promoted the off-year summer fallow with spring plowing because a two-year supply of moisture was carried into planting season.

H. W. Campbell, a Vermonter who homesteaded in the Dakota territory, invented a subsoil packer, and with its use developed a system of dry farming. Drawing on the work of University of Wisconsin agricultural physicist F. H. King, he showed how his implement could pack the subsoil in order to draw up deep water by capillary action, and how dust mulch after each rainfall could stop evaporation. With deep plowing and summer fallow, the practice proved extremely effective for the growing of such crops as sorghum, kaffir corn, and the durum wheats. The Bureau of Dry Land Agriculture in the U.S. Department of Agriculture was established in 1906 to continue experiments in dry land farming.

Turn-of-the-century experimenters did important work to increase yields for the corn belt as well. The corn story began in America with the widespread scientific discussion of Darwin's *Variations of Animals and Plants Under Domestication* and the long-hidden paper of Gregor Mendel, who had described the laws of inheritance with pea-crossing experiments. Two generations after Mendel and Darwin, plant breeders began to attempt to cross plants for resistance to specific diseases, heat, cold, and drought, for food value and eventually for adaptability to machine cultivation and harvesting. As early as 1870, Luther Burbank experimented with plant breeding by grafting, which itself is an ancient plant-propagation method. In the United States experimenters were more successful with corn than with wheat.

Animal breeders could more easily match quality pairs than plant growers could, since the breeder of plants was certain of only half of the line he was working on; the wind carried the other half. Nonetheless, in 1900 William A. Orton published in a Department of Agriculture bulletin a report on how he controlled the cotton wilt fungus disease by breeding disease-resistant strains of cotton. George H. Shull and Edward M. East at the same time were applying genetic research to agriculture by using corn plants, since the pollen of the tassel could germinate the silk of the ear on the same plant in controlled experiments. Shull worked at the Carnegie Institute Station for Experimental Evolution at Cold Harbor, Long Island, which was one of the old ironmaster's philanthropic scientific gestures. Shull inbred corn plants by covering them with paper bags, labeling them, and continuing the inbreeding over eight years. In 1907 he reported his findings to a meeting of the American Breeders' Association at Washington where East, of the Connecticut Experiment Station, listened with great interest. He too had been inbreeding corn plants. He pursued the work of Shull with his students, attempting to find a variety which produced the highest possible yield by breeding true types, then cross-breeding. One of the students on his research team, Donald Jones, invented the double-cross, marrying the children and grandchildren of a purebred line, bred for a desirable quality such as high yields. His result was a 20% yield increase over that of the nearest rival.

In the corn-hog belt, hog cholera plagued farmers for many years. Marion Dorset, biochemist for the Department of Agriculture at Ames, Iowa, worked for a decade on a preventative serum, which he perfected and released by 1913. Dorset combined injections of the cholera virus and a serum from hogs immune to the disease. By the start of the war, hog losses were cut to less than half those of the previous year.

Soil Experiments

An agricultural scientist at Purdue University, George Hoffer, paved the way for experimental research in soil and plant nutrition. Long before, Liebig had demonstrated that the earth needs nitrogen, phosphorus, and potash (potassium) to maintain its fertility, but no one advised the farmer when and how much of these essential ingredients were needed for his crops. Hoffer answered these questions, at least partially, while attempting to discover the causes of disease in corn plants. For a number of years during and after the war, Hoffer pieced together the puzzle of corn diseases by designing chemical tests which, when applied to the cut-open stalks, determined what essential element was lacking in the malfunctioning plant. Some soils, he found, contain too much iron, which the corn sucks into its stalk. The iron compounds plug up the sap tubes to cause root mold. By a series of happy accidents, Hoffer observed that the soil with too much iron needs potash additives. Where corn yields are low, Hoffer prescribed nitrogen; where the maize was stunted, Hoffer told the farmers to use phosphate to guard against aluminum. And the yields in the corn belt climbed each year.

There was more to learn about secondary food elements—manganese, boron, copper, zinc, iron, molybdenum, and chlorine. Researchers from California after the war found out a great deal about micronutrient plant food elements at the Delhi State Land Settlement Colony in northern Merced County, where war veterans were given undeveloped land to farm, mostly for peach and other fruit orchards. Peaches sold well all over the country during the twenties and were a good farming possibility.

Profits were good at Delhi for a few years, then the trees began to suffer from "little leaf" disease, which greatly lowers yields and is recognized by small yellow leaves in place of the fruit. Pomologist William H. Chandler began work immediately on the problem with plant nutritionist Dennis R. Hoagland, both University of California experimentation people from the Berkeley campus. They first tried well-known nitrogen applications, which had an adverse effect on the trees, then sulfur, and even sugar. They also dissected the trees and subjected them to chemical analysis to determine mineral deficiencies. In the meantime in the late twenties other parts of the state began to report "little leaf" symptoms on cherry, nut, and citrus trees.

Chandler found that ferrous sulfate applications checked or cured the disease, but could not understand why, since iron and sulfur had been tried earlier in other forms. His answer came when a Belgian shipment of ferrous sulfate produced no results on ailing trees at the Delhi. Using new methods of plant analysis, two chemists in the Department of Plant Nutrition, P. L. Hibbard and Perry Stout, discovered that the Belgian ferrous sulfate lacked zinc, present as an impurity in local sources of the compound, probably coming from galvanized iron or another scrap metal containing zinc used in its mining or processing. From this fortuitous occurrence the researchers discovered that it was zinc, not iron or sulfur, that cured "little leaf," and that the trees needed only tiny injections.

California's soils were rich with zinc, but when the supply close to the trees was depleted, "little leaf" disease resulted. In Florida, the same conclusion simultaneously was being reached at the orange grove regions of the state. Zinc thereafter became a common agricultural fertilizer, and the discovery of its importance led to more research on other trace elements. Dennis Hoagland continued experiments, using his water culture techniques, and performed pioneering work on the essential micronutrients by testing plants in solutions with different combinations of the trace elements. Most often his work was done in conjunction with practical problems brought to him from farmers through California experiment stations.

Politics and Agriculture

When farmers gave reasons for their economic distress during the twenties, few complained about scientific discoveries, research assistance, or even the new technologies of the era. They wanted to increase production, but they wanted to get paid for their increased yields. The political dilemma was fought in Washington. Those opposed to government aid to the farmers warned that raising farm incomes artificially imperiled free enterprise and economic freedom. Farmers claimed that they were not getting their fair share of the wealth in America they helped to create.

Between 1924 and 1929, Senator Charles L. McNary of Oregon and Representative Gilbert N. Haugen of Iowa introduced a series of bills to attempt to bolster farm income by separating exportable farm surpluses from the domestic supply. Their proposals put high tariffs on agricultural products. A fair exchange value based on prewar purchasing power was to be placed on agricultural commodities. A corporation chartered by the government was to buy enough goods at the fair price level to force the price of the domestic supply up to the fair price level. The corporation then would export farm goods at the world price levels, presumably lower than domestic prices, and farmers would pay the corporation's administrative costs through proportionate fees. The McNary-Haughen bills were passed by Congress twice and vetoed twice by President Coolidge.

Finally, because of President Herbert Hoover's campaign promises, the Agricultural Marketing Act of 1929 was passed and signed. Hoover and his associates were convinced that "rational" ordering of marketing arrangements in agriculture would solve most of the farmers' problems, just as scientific rationality had solved the problems of the business world. A Federal Farm Board was established to help with the formation of cooperative marketing associations, which owned "stabilization corporations" financed by the federal government to support farm prices. Unfortunately, 1929 was the year of the Great Depression, and the Farm Board did not have the financial resources to keep the farming community out of indebtedness and foreclosure. The farmers reacted to lower prices in the only way they knew how, by increasing production.

Thus the twenties gave birth to the modern era: in the crystalization of social and economic patterns of growth, standardization, and rationalization; in urbanization and industrial monopolization; in the pursuit of wealth; in affluent life styles and consumerism; in the formation of a media-oriented mass-consciousness and automobile culture; and in scientific research and technology. What came later, for the people as well as the natural resources, was simply a fulfillment of that beginning.

References for Further Reading

The Big Change by Frederick Lewis Allen (1952) is an insightful account by one who watched America transform itself between 1900 and 1950. Another excellent treatment showing the development from a small-government, small-town nation to a gigantic superstate is George E. Mowry's *The Urban Nation* (1965). David A. Shannon's *Between the Wars, 1919-1941* (1965) provides a solid social and political background for the material in this chapter, as Fred A. Shannon's *America's Economic Growth* (1951) and Robert Sobel's *The Age of Giant Corporations* (1972) fill in the economic interpretation and data. *The United States Oil Policy* by John Ise (1926) presents an extensive treatment of oil history in the U.S. from its beginnings to the mid-twenties. Two books which tell colorful stories of early and recent agricultural research are *Hunger Fighters* by Paul DeKruif (1928) and *Garden in the West* by George S. Wells (1969). The best treatment of conservation in the twenties is Donald C. Swain's excellent *Federal Conservation Policy: 1921-1933* (1963). *The Public Lands and the Conservation Movement* by William K. Wyant (1982) presents the history of public land law as a record of private enterprises exploiting the land. A very well researched history of the Owens Valley water controversy in California is *Vision or Villainy: Origins of the Owens Valley-Los Angeles Water Controversy* by Abraham Hoffman (1982). Lawrence B. Lee's *Reclaiming the American West: An Historiography and Guide* (1980) presents the literature of reclamation from the early irrigation movement in 1878 to the present debates about dam building. Paul Cartwright's *Theodore Roosevelt: The Making of a Conservationist* (1985) is "conservation" biography of the president. Two excellent biographies of Muir are *Son of the Wilderness: The Life of John Muir* by Linnie Marsh Wolfe (1978) and Stephen Fox's. *John Muir and His Legacy: The American Conservation Movement* (1981). The development of Leopold's ecological thinking is described in Susan L. Flader's *Thinking Like a Mountain: Aldo Leopold and the Evolution of an Ecological Attitude Toward Deer, Wolves, and Forests* (1974). Joseph M. Petulla's *American Environmentalism: Values, Tactics, Priorities* (1980) presents the intellectual traditions of environmental thinkers and their work as biocentric, ecologic, and economic.

Chapter 16

THE NEW DEAL
AND CONSERVATION

If the twenties were a preview of the modern era of growth, affluence, economic concentration, conspicuous consumption, and the rise of science and technology, those years were also a prelude to social and economic disaster. Implicit in the economic booms, the reckless pursuit of overnight fortunes, and the glamorous style of movieland fantasy was the risk of financial chaos. The tragedy of the period lay not only in the stock market crash of October 1929 but also in that, despite herculean efforts of New Deal economic engineers, the depression following the crash continued until World War II.

The Crash

The immediate cause of the Great Depression was the stock market crash of 1929, an event that was preceded by easy credit, mass speculation, and skyrocketing stock prices. Since the economy appeared to be slowing down in 1927, the Federal Reserve Board lowered the rediscount rate to its member banks so that more credit would induce investment and the purchase of more consumer goods throughout the economy. Instead, common people joined professional brokers to use the credit for gambling their savings or investment money in the hopes of larger gains from the stock market. Even Standard of New Jersey loaned money to stock investors at high interest rates in order to make more money than the company could garner by selling oil.

The flimsiest of rumors—expansions, dividends, mergers—would push up stock prices to undreamed-of levels. The average person was encouraged to buy on margin, paying for only half the stock price and borrowing the rest, because buying on margin allowed the purchaser to buy twice as much stock.

The stock market provided an easy way for holding company pyramids to increase their corporate assets. They could launch companies which produced nothing, yet they would recover millions of dollars from new stock investments. The infamous example of the Georgia Power and Light Company typified the practice. Georgia Power and Light was the only company which produced electricity among the dozens in its pyramid—including the Seaboard Public Service Company, the Middle West Utilities Company, and Insull Utility Investments. The rest existed to collect the savings money of thousands of private citizens. Samuel Insull, chairman of the board of sixty-five utility companies in thirty-two states, held together this billion-dollar paper empire.

Of course the companies could not earn enough to justify such high investment, so the bubble was bound to burst. The economy went flat, not only during 1929 but also for a decade following. During the same time, the stock market scarcely recovered; no one wanted to buy, only to sell. From 1929 to 1932 the average of 50 industrial stocks fell from 252.8 to 61.7; 20 railroad securities dropped from 167.8 to 33.6; 20 utilities from 353.1 to 99. Even secure investments paying over 10% on the market could muster only a few intrepid buyers.

The crash itself could not have exercised such a lasting impact on a fundamentally healthy economy, but chronic maldistribution of income and lack of capital investment enlarged the crash into a very great depression. The stock market catastrophe did wipe out tens of thousands of people who lost lifetimes of savings which could have been spent on homes or on durable goods, or consumer goods, or even capital goods. Instead, the capital ended up in the pockets of the very few on the top of the economic heap—a group unwilling to reinvest the money into the faltering economy. Even before the crash the top 5% of the population received over a third of the country's income. After the crash, these people did not want to risk their fortunes in capital formation, e.g., in manufacturing equipment or buildings to prime the economic pump and create jobs. Between 1929 and 1933, investments in capital goods dropped 88% Without investment in major industries, no wage earners would exist to buy goods from these industries. Thus, after the crash, very few entrepreneurs were investing, so few could purchase goods because few were working during this maddening downward economic spiral. To pay for food and shelter, people withdrew their money from banks. Around 3,000 banks, already reeling from unpaid debts, went out of business before the end of 1932.

Potential markets in the rest of the world could not help the country to get its economy started, for the whole world fell into a depression along with America, the creditor nation of the world after the war. When the United States, needing cash to pay bills, would extend no more credit to foreign nations, they had to stop buying American goods. Very soon their own production slowed down as they eased into the depression. In the twenties, America's prohibitive tariff had brought retaliations by the rest of the major world exporters, and no nation wanted to loosen trade restrictions when hard times came. A number of American policymakers suggested that European war debts be cancelled in proportion to trade favors, but Hoover's proposal for a year-long moratorium on the debt was passed instead. The high tariffs remained, as did high taxes and very high unemployment—the numbers increasing until 1933, when about 40% of the country's wage and salary workers were unemployed. Wages of those fortunate enough to work dwindled to practically nothing. Teachers regularly worked without pay. In New York City, 50,000 women and girls received wages averaging less than $3.00 a week.

The Great Depression

The nation only slowly recovered from a state of shock following the crash. The people became angry and demonstrative. In one march on Washington, 15,000 veterans had to be dispersed with tear gas, tanks, and bayonets. Farmers continued to overproduce; they received minuscule prices. When Progressives insisted that the entire wheat crop be bought by the government at fair prices and distributed to hungry Americans, the Hoover administration dismissed the proposal as disguised radical socialism. The Stabilization Corporations set up by the Hoover administration could not buy enough surplus agricultural goods to keep the farmers out of indebtedness. Thousands of farmers lost their land because of failure to pay taxes or mortgage payments. Often, though, farmers rallied to the aid of their neighbors either by forcibly halting the sale of foreclosed farms or by keeping out outside bidders so that the farm could be bought back for a few dollars. However, these tactics worked only in scattered areas of the country.

As months and years passed, farmers became more violent over low prices for their goods and foreclosures. They blocked highways, punctured tires with pitchforks, smashed windshields, stopped freight trains, roughed up sheriffs and lawyers, and even dumped milk on roadsides rather than accept the pittance of a market price offered for their goods.

Coal miners tended to even greater violence in strikes for higher wages. In many areas where they were desperate for food, miners smashed windows of company stores, or broke into self-service grocery stores. Ten thousand striking miners in southern Illinois formed a forty-eight mile coal caravan to dramatize their situation. In a few places, unemployed utility technicians helped them tap onto electric and gas lines which had been cut off from their homes; often they refused to pay streetcar fares, and they turned to violence when challenged by police. In many instances the police themselves refused to arrest offenders.

By 1932, the nation's leaders were completely bewildered by the stubborn continuation of the depression. Writer Stuart Chase spoke for almost everyone when he wrote that, given the country's impressive wealth, land, and relatively small population—125,000,000 people—"it seems incredible that anyone should be in want." He proved his point by calling on the research of Robert R. Doane, who listed the contemporary facts of America's material wealth in an article in *New Outlook:*

1,000,000,000 acres of farm land
500,000,000 acres of forests
100,000,000 acres of coal, iron, copper, and other mineral land
34,000,000 acres of rivers and lakes
100,000,000 acres of urban territory in various states of development
316,000 oil wells
6,500,000 farms with 105,000,000 horses, mules, cows, sheep and swine
500,000,000 chickens, turkeys, ducks and other domestic fowl
127,000,000 major machines—locomotives, turbines, motor cars, tractors, trucks, lathes,
    looms, etc.
700,000,000 installed horse power
2,000,000 miles of rural roads and 750,000 miles of surfaced highways
250,000 miles of railroads and 59,000 miles of navigable waterways
736,000 miles of pipe lines and 160,000 miles of electric transmission lines
88,000,000 miles of telephone, telegraph and cable lines

Yet millions of people *were* in want when Franklin D. Roosevelt came into the presidency in 1933. Although he was determined to utilize the wealth of the nation for the benefit of its citizens, he was left with the problem of how the goal should be achieved. Roosevelt called on dozens of college professors and experts in a variety of fields: Raymond Moley from Barnard College; Rexford Guy Tugwell, an agriculture authority; Adolf Berle, Jr., co-author of *The Modern Corporation and Private Property*; New Nationalism leftovers from the Theodore Roosevelt era such as labor attorney Donald Richberg; astute social worker Harry Hopkins; writers such as Charles Beard and Stuart Chase; Ben Cohen and Tom Corcoran, anti-monopoly disciples of Felix Frankfurter and Louis Brandeis; Progressive Senators Wagner, LaFollette and Costigan; Henry Morgenthau, Jr., Herbert Lehman, and many more.

The diversity of viewpoints and perspectives of the New Dealers pulled and tugged at the president throughout his long tenure. The majority subscribed to welfare capitalism. Unlike more radical reformers of the time, they supported the system of private profits but wanted to engage government in the task of unionization and welfare programs. New Dealers generally accepted the dominant position of monopoly and oligopoly, arguing with Berle and Gardiner C. Means that without price and production manipulation, the economy could never be stabilized. Roosevelt's Brain Trust generally rejected the ideals of Wilson and Justice Brandeis that the solutions to America's problems lay in breaking up monopolies and forming a nation of small proprietors; equally did they eschew the socialist alternative.

Nevertheless, the atomist Brandeisian view penetrated New Deal legislation somewhat through Cohen and Corcoran. Tugwell, Stuart Chase, and the Progressives agitated for more national planning through the federal government. Chase liked to quote Thorstein Veblen, intellectual mentor of his faction of the New Deal, to explain why poverty thrived in the middle of America's natural and material wealth: "Industry carried on . . . only in response to the presumptive chance of business profits. . . . The vital factor is the vendibility of the output, its convertibility into money values, not its serviceability for the needs of mankind." If the national economy were reorganized for the common good and needs of its citizens, rather than around expectations of massive profits, Chase argued, the country would be out of its economic slump and its poverty as well in a short time. Only the national government possessed the resources to accomplish this objective of national planning, he concluded.

The New Deal: Banking and Agriculture

When President-elect Roosevelt took his oath of office in March, 1933, most of the nation's banks were closed because of fear of failure. Roosevelt immediately pronounced a bank holiday and called Congress into a special session to pass a new bank bill. The Emergency Banking Act gave financial assistance to banks in danger of failure, provided for reorganization or reopening of others, and issued new Federal Reserve notes. In June the Glass-Steagall banking bill was passed, granting insurance on deposits up to $2,500 and replacing the Federal Reserve Board, until then controlled by private bankers, with a more centralized seven-member Board of Governors. Furthermore, the bill separated investment companies from banking firms so that deposits would be more secure against risky investments by investment companies.

During the first few months of 1933, the Senate had been investigating banking and the stock market under chief counsel Ferdinand Pecora. The committee turned up countless abuses by financial interests. This influenced the passage of the Truth-in-Securities Act of 1933, requiring a firm selling stock to reveal all pertinent financial data about itself. A year later, over powerful objections from Wall Street, the Securities and Exchange Commission was empowered to carry out the stipulations of the Act in the regulation of all securities. The power of the SEC was enhanced by the Wheeler-Rayburn Act of 1935, which ordered the commission to break up interstate utility holding companies and to obtain information about corporate structures of all holding companies. This act, which also empowered the Federal Power Commission to regulate interstate electric rates and the Federal Trade Commission to control interstate gas rates, indicates the influence of the atomist, anti-monopoly wing of Roosevelt's Brain Trust. Because of this wing's prodding, railroad holding companies were already called into account in 1933.

Soon after the Emergency Banking bill was passed, Secretary of Agriculture Henry A Wallace of Iowa set to the task of drafting farm legislation. He, as well as the president, believed that the farm problem could be solved if agricultural production could be cut back, so that prices on farm goods would rise. Although the notion seems strange in the face of a poverty-laden country where the people were suffering from a chronic shortage of purchasing power, New Dealers thought that subsidizing farmers could represent the beginning of national recovery, since they could then buy more goods from ailing industries. The Agricultural Adjustment Act never was able to effect such a dramatic change, but pressure from farm groups and a threatened general farm strike spurred the bill's passage early in the first hundred days of New Deal activity, despite heavy lobbying against it from millers, packers, and commodity middlemen.

The act granted price supports for wheat, cotton, corn, hogs, dairy products, leaf tobacco, and rice by taxing the processor and turning the money over to farmers who reduced their acreages proportionately to their payments for the following year. Processors then passed the additional costs on to consumers. When prices got high enough, farm imports under severe tariffs became cheaper than American produce. The purpose of the program was to bring the prices of industrial and agricultural goods into the same ratio, or parity, which existed in good farm years between 1909 and 1914.

Many objections were raised to the parity program as it became clear how much agricultural production had to be curtailed to keep prices up in a country where millions could not afford the higher cost of food. Since the program was passed in 1933 after planting and breeding seasons, in the first year of the program hogs had to be slaughtered and acreages, mainly cotton, had to be plowed under to push up prices. Even after farmers promised to restrict production, however, results were unsatisfactory. Farmers managed to increase yields on smaller areas because of larger applications of fertilizer and high-yielding species, but drought intervened to save the program for a few years. The act also had a detrimental effect on the competitive position of American cotton as well as on southern sharecroppers who were eased off their lands, which landlords inevitably chose to take out of production because of federal payments.

In those same first hundred days of the New Deal the farmers were extended federal credit through the Farm Credit Act and Farm Credit Administration loans to refinance mortgages at lower interest rates. Prices of wheat, corn and cotton doubled by 1935, and farm income went up 53%. But in 1936, in the Hoosac Mills case, the Supreme Court struck down the processing tax feature of the act, setting the stage for the Soil Conservation and Domestic Allotment Act. Congress appropriated $500,000,000 to the Agricultural Adjustment Administration to redistribute to the states for the purpose of taking land out of production and sowing soil-enriching grasses and green fertilizers like clover and soybeans. Grants were distributed to the farmers through local units—counties or farmer organizations—and attempts were made to protect sharecroppers.

The soil conservation program remained in a new Agricultural Adjustment Act passed by Congress in 1938. This was the final step in guaranteeing direct federal support to maintain farm prices. The vehicle of administration was a Commodity Credit Corporation, established in 1933 to guide price fluctuations in corn, wheat, and cotton by making loans to farmers who took commodities off the market until prices were established. The stored crops were used as security. If the price remained low, the government wrote off the debt and took possession of the crops. If the price rose, the farmer repaid the loan and sold his crops at a higher price. Loan rates became base prices for each commodity. Loans were rarely made on wheat during those first years because drought kept the grain in short supply, but some loans were made from 1933 to 1938 on cotton and corn, which the government sold at low prices on the world market.

The Act of 1938 made it mandatory for the Commodity Credit Corporation to make loans on corn, wheat, and cotton at rates between 52% and 75% of parity. Thereafter, Congress specified the percentage of parity to be guaranteed as the government began to accumulate overflowing granaries and storehouses of wheat, corn, cotton, and tobacco. Also in the thirties, marketing agreements between producers and processors of commodities such as fruits, vegetables, and milk were legalized, establishing minimum prices, quantity, and division of markets for the goods. In 1936, the secretary of agriculture was empowered to specify the upper limits or quotas for growers of listed crops. All of these agricultural policies of the thirties have remained substantially in effect to our own time.

The Program to Fight Depression

When Roosevelt assumed the presidency, over 15,000,000 people in the country were out of work. The states and local governments, overwhelmed with applications for assistance, were the first to send representatives to Washington seeking financial aid. Congress quickly granted the states $500,000,000 for relief purposes, and the president engineered patchwork solutions representing pressures from a spectrum of interests and viewpoints. The history of the period is as complicated as Roosevelt was inconsistent. He held to the ideal of a balanced budget, but spent uncommonly massive amounts of federal money, sometimes looking for an alliance between government and big business. At other times, he was suspicious of large corporations, often looking for voluntary cooperation but usually instituting mandatory controls.

The times called for speedy action, which Roosevelt provided but without an overall plan. The Department of Labor coordinated a national employment service to distribute information regarding the availability of jobs. A Home Owners' Loan Act helped people with defaulted mortgages refinance their homes through the federal government. The Civilian Conservation Corps was established to employ young people to plant trees, to maintain national parks, and to work on erosion control or localized rural problems. The CCC lasted until the draft of World War II It aided millions of young workers who received food, clothing, and $30 ˙a month to share with their families at home.

Roosevelt and his Brain Trust put most of their hopes in the National Industrial Recovery Act (NIRA) of June, 1933, and the National Recovery Administration (NRA) it set up. The occasion of the bill came from legislation sponsored by Senator Hugo Black of Alabama, which would have prohibited interstate commerce on goods that were processed by laborers working more than thirty hours a week. Black was interested in distributing the available jobs more evenly and retarding technological unemployment.

Along with the nation's corporate establishment, Roosevelt opposed the bill and put together one which both business and his brain-trusters could accept. Roosevelt's NIRA indicated the diversity of the bill's input. A Public Works Administration was created in the Department of Interior, with a budget of well over $3,000,000,000 devoted primarily to employ laborers on highways, waterways, public buildings, low-cost housing, and army or navy vessels. The bill also granted the nation's workers the right to bargain collectively for better wages and working conditions. For the business interests, industry trade associations engaged in interstate commerce were authorized to draw up codes of fair competition and to fix minimum wages and maximum hours in provisions that suspended conflicting anti-trust laws. After the voluntary industry codes were drawn up, they were to be approved by NRA administrators.

Immediately after his appointment, former cavalry general Hugh S. Johnson, chief administrator of the NRA, began to bring basic industrial spokesmen together to draw up codes. Despite overall industrial cooperation, the program did not boost industrial production, except within a few months after the bill was passed, because industrialists wanted to stock up before wage codes were written and enforced. At the time, however, few people had the money to purchase these goods, which were immediately marked up in price in anticipation of the higher wages workers were to get. But because the companies had overstocked, many factories had to lay off employees when higher wages were mandated by industrial codes. It took almost a year to get about 4,000,000 workers back on the job, and this was a fraction of the unemployment problem.

Small businessmen and labor complained that big business interests managed to dominate codewriting for the NRA. Competition was stifled, production restricted, employment kept down, and profits increased. Roosevelt appointed a review board headed by Clarence Darrow to look into the problem, and the committee confirmed the monopolistic bias of the codes, particularly through price and production schedules set by the corporations; in effect economic governments were legalized. Darrow and a former law partner wrote a supplementary report recommending socialized ownership as a way to solve both cutthroat competition and monopoly control. As prices began to skyrocket during those lean years, consumers protested loudly through their Congressional representatives.

By the beginning of 1935, Roosevelt requested Congress to amend the monopolistic features of the bill, but in May the Supreme Court nullified the entire act, declaring that Congress could not grant legislative powers to the executive as it had done through the NRA. With or without the law, however, industrial trade associations had developed procedures to standardize production and distribution, and the Wagner Act a few months later established the National Labor Relations Board to uphold the right of free collective bargaining through organizations of labor's choosing rather than the customary unions.

In the spring of the same year, the president realized that the NRA was not working and that the unemployment problem had not been solved. He sensed the need for a new approach. Steered by Senate Progressives Wagner, LaFollette, and Costigan, he convinced Congress to appropriate almost $5,000,000,000 for the Works Progress Administration (WPA) under Harry Hopkins, with more money appropriated in each succeeding year. Public building, conservation projects, artists, and writers' works all were funded in an unprecedented variety of public service employment tasks. In June the National Youth Administration was established in the WPA to fund part-time jobs for 400,000 students in the country. For six years the WPA operated and employed over 8,000,000 people, spending $11,400,000,000.

That same summer of 1935 brought passage of a social security bill, a banking bill, a public-utilities holding company measure, and a wealth tax. The latter bill levied excess profits, estate, gift, and capital stock taxes, but it did little to redistribute income. Roosevelt leveled his anti-monopoly offensive against the electric companies, notorious for corrupting the political processes and for exorbitantly high rates. The power companies mounted a lobbying counterattack in Congress, unparalleled up to that time, but nonetheless received a setback in the already-cited Wheeler-Rayburn Act.

The Strength of the Oligopolies

As can be surmised from the struggles among the economic and political blocs of the thirties, not all industries suffered great economic declines. The firms which had developed oligopolies earlier—in petroleum, chemicals, automobiles, steel, aircraft, and food—managed to restructure and grow by the end of the decade. For example, the big five oil companies—Standard of New Jersey, Gulf, Indiana Standard, Texas Company, and California Standard—solved the problem of competition and overproduction as early as 1926, when the major companies entered into price and territorial agreements. Two years later, the American Petroleum Institute added a code of ethics to the agreements that rationalized the action. It was thought that agreements would discourage waste, price wars, rebates, concessions to preferred customers, gifts, and employee bribing. The Federal Trade Commission approved the code in 1929, with the blessing of President Hoover. The Bureau of Mines assisted the major refiners by quoting monthly market demand figures.

Despite some new competition from the East Texas fields in the thirties, the majors developed a stronger oligopoly and continued to cooperate in technological research as well as in market agreements. All the firms at least doubled their assets, oil production, and profits during the twenties, and they could afford to lose money during the early years of the depression. During this period, they refinanced to take advantage of lower interest rates; decentralized for greater efficiency of marketing; expanded their operations; developed better refining methods; did more advertising; and began to make money again by the end of the decade. The higher gasoline prices supported their greater capital investments.

Although the automobile industry was hard hit during the depression, only the many small independents went bankrupt quickly. A few of them, like Packard, Nash, Hudson, and Studebaker, hung on to challenge the big three—General Motors, Ford, and Chrysler—which were able to capture larger shares of the depression market. (Since most of the nation's money was in the hands of the rich during the depression, Cadillac sales went up.) The giants increased their shares yearly until the end of the 1960s, when foreign competition began to make inroads on their territory. At the same time, they have strengthened their oligopolistic hold on the American economy.

The aircraft industry also tightened and made solid gains during the 1930s because of post office contracts and continued investments in the larger companies—United Aircraft, Curtiss-Wright, Lockheed, Douglas, and Martin. These firms continued to grow during the 1940s and 1950s because of big government contracts. The same kinds of temporary setbacks, consolidation, and growth were apparent in the chemical industries (Dow, Du Pont, Allied Chemical, Union Carbide, Monsanto), where in any one product or process only a few companies controlled the majority of business. The large food industries also maintained their positions.

This fairly intensive economic activity, unfortunately, did not trickle down to the throngs of unemployed factory workers in the cities or to the sharecroppers in the South or to the migrants in Southern California or to confused immigrants everywhere in the country. But the New Deal of welfare capitalism tried to include something for everyone. It

- [ ] continued earlier government-industry cooperation
- [ ] attempted to underwrite farmers for the costs of their production
- [ ] offered relief to the unemployed
- [ ] assumed responsibility for some of the costs of growing old, through social security
- [ ] safeguarded many mortgages on homes and farms
- [ ] attempted a public employment program
- [ ] guaranteed deposits of banks
- [ ] put a regulatory hand on Wall Street and holding companies

The basic failure of the New Deal was its effort to be all things to all people. Material benefits or political favors were given to rich and poor alike, but the rich, as always, were in a better position to utilize their share of the economic and political pie. Although the haphazard program of the New Dealers did have some short-term good effects, and did give a modicum of hope and help to many of the downtrodden, the fundamental cause of the depression—chronic maldistribution of wealth—remained to do its damage again.

While many of the New Deal measures touch natural resources only indirectly, their enactment established the context of America's later affluence, and many of the bills intertwined their philosophies with conservation objectives, such as soil restoration and reforestation or multiple-use water development and the creation of new national parks and forests. New approaches to fish and wildlife management also became embodied in legislation of the period.

New Deal Conservation

Franklin Roosevelt's personal interest in conservation problems began long before he became president. While serving in the New York State Senate in 1910, he was chairman of the Fish and Game Committee, which once recommended regulating timber cutting on private lands where wildlife appeared to be threatened. As head of the Agriculture Committee he became thoroughly grounded in the problems of the farmers of his state and the practices of soil restoration. After 1913, while in Washington as assistant secretary of the Navy, he maintained contact with Pinchot and water conservationists; on one occasion he visited the lower Mississippi region, an area buffeted yearly by severe flooding, where he suggested reforestation as a more permanent solution than the levee system. Roosevelt worked on reforestation on his own Hyde Park estates while sidelined with polio and out of public life, 1920 to 1928. During this period he promoted private financing of large-scale, sustained-yield forest farming.

Roosevelt's first struggles with the private power companies occurred in 1928 when, as governor of New York, he encouraged the New York State Power Authority to develop plans for inexpensive public hydroelectric power in the northern region of the state. The private companies fought the proposal, saying that only the federal government had the right to develop international waters. After Roosevelt became president, they would argue that power development should be left to the states.

It was no surprise then that Roosevelt surrounded himself with a number of conservationists when he was elected president, and had not the nation been

Figure 16–1. Dust storms. Semi-arid plains show the results of poor farming practices in 1933. As a great drought continued year after year, the loss of topsoil through the drying out of land and consequent wind erosion destroyed farms and wiped out the resources of the farmers, who were already sorely beset by the Depression. The photos depict scenes from the Dust Bowl: Billowing clouds of dust engulfing entire counties; tiny trees without foliage; home-made windmills without slats; farmhouses without life; chickens scratching for food in dust; automobiles, harvesters, wagons, hayrakes and plows—all buried in a sea of sand. Courtesy USDA, Soil Conservation Service.

immersed in such troubled times, a conservation program would have been much more important on his agenda. As it happened, the men who worked with him kept conservation issues alive: his Secretary of Interior Harold Ickes; agricultural experts Henry Wallace and Rexford Tugwell; Henry Morgenthau; and the "father of soil conservation," Hugh Hammond Bennett. Within a year of his appointment, Ickes dealt with the pressing need of classification of natural resources, and continued with the project of listing lands under headings of crop, range, forest, and mineral until it was completed. The secretary, under Roosevelt's authority, retired 25,000,000 acres of submarginal lands, mostly privately owned, that could not qualify for irrigation because of water scarcity, so that hopeful farmers would not again be duped by changeable western climate. One acre of irrigated land, however, was provided for every five acres of submarginal land retired into the public domain.

Agriculture Secretary Wallace's commitment embraced the land as well as the farmer. Like hundreds of conservationists around the country and in Roosevelt's own circle, Wallace greatly feared the destruction of the drought which started in 1933, when scorched brown fields began to lose their topsoil; springs and wells started to dry up,; and thousands of cattle died of thirst and hunger after they ripped out the last strands of grass. The dusty ground was left exposed to wind storms that came later. Throughout the plains states of western Texas, Oklahoma, Colorado, Nebraska and Wyoming, a huge dust bowl was created. Since the drought and dust bowl areas encompassed thousands of acres of farm land, the Wallace Agricultural Adjustment Act purposed to allow much of the land to lie fallow and enrich itself. At the same time the farmers took it out of economic production. The Roosevelt conservationists were concerned that the dust bowl portended what would become of the entire American landscape within a short time unless they acted quickly. In the period from 1933 to 1935 a sense of impending natural disaster punctuated the economic gloom spread throughout the country.

Roosevelt appointed Ickes to oversee the Public Works Administration in the first hundred days of the New Deal program. Although Ickes sat on more projects than he financed, he lost no time appropriating $5,000,000 for erosion control terracing projects. Tugwell gave Hugh Hammond Bennett's name to Ickes for the job of administering the soil conservation program, and the secretary of the interior appointed him to a new bureau in his department, the Soil Erosion Service.

Soil Conservation

Bennett had a lifetime of experience in preparation for the job. He came from an old farm in the Pee Dee Basin of North Carolina, worked his way through the University of North Carolina, and went to work for the Bureau of Soils in the U.S. Department of Agriculture. In 1905, he was sent to Louisa County, Virginia, to make a soil survey and find out why crop yields were so poor. Where the soil lay in woodlands, he found soft, mellow, deep loam; nearby where it was cutover and many-times plowed, hard clay surfaced without topsoil. It was evident to Bennett that rainstorms had washed away the rich topsoil layer by layer. Many years later, in his book on soil conservation, he would note, "The red, yellow, and black floodwater running away to the sea are no reflection from the sky; the color of such floodwater is produced by the color of

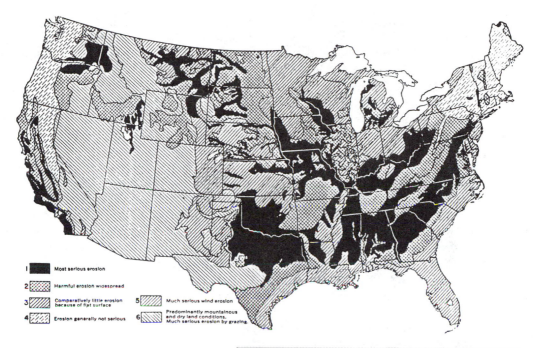

1 ■ Most serious erosion

2 ▨ Harmful erosion widespread

3 ▨ Comparatively little erosion because of flat surface

4 ▨ Erosion generally not serious

5 ▨ Much serious wind erosion

6 ▨ Predominantly mountainous and dry land conditions. Much serious erosion by grazing.

Figure 16–2. Soil erosion. The gullies of Stewart County, Georgia, here depicted, are noted for their enormous size and depth. In that area more than 100,000 acres were affected by gullies and chasms over hundreds of miles of the southern Piedmont region. Not only have the soil and the subsoil been lost forever to agricultural use, but adjacent soils have also been covered by coarser, less-fertile accumulations of the eroded material. The map, prepared by H. H. Bennett's Soil Conservation team in 1933, shows the extent of soil erosion around the United States then. Courtesy USDA, Soil Conservation Service.

the soil material in suspension. This material comes from the surface of the ground, the best part of our fields, and thus impoverishes the land."

In 1911, while working in Fairfield County, South Carolina, Bennett became alarmed when he found that 136,000 acres, or 44% of the once-fertile county land, was lost to cultivation. This left its inhabitants living in one of the first belts of rural poverty.

By 1918, Bennett made soil conservation into a crusade. Under the auspices of the U.S. Department of Agriculture in 1918, he wrote an appropriation of $160,000 for soil erosion research, and Bennett was permitted to set up ten erosion stations around the country. From information gathered at the stations, Bennett estimated that over 500,000 acres of topsoil were lost to erosion each year. That is, if a train of freight cars were loaded every year with the soil washed out of American fields and pastures, it would encircle the earth eighteen times at the equator. By the 1930s, 9,000,000 acres of U.S. farmland were destroyed and 80,000,000 acres seriously damaged. Eighty percent of the country's farmland was eroding at that time.

Then the dust storms hit Washington. In 1935, while western sand and dust blew over the darkened Washington sky and out to sea, where it bothered mariners far from land, Congress created and funded a permanent Soil Conservation Service in the Department of Agriculture under Bennett, eliminating Interior's Soil Erosion Service. Within a year the service operated 147 demonstration projects with about 25,000 to 30,000 acres at each project; 48 soil-conservation nurseries; 23 research stations; 454 Civilian Conservation Camps. Over 50,000 farmers on 5,000,000 acres requested aid that year and Bennett's team taught them his techniques: terracing and contour-plowing hill lands; crop rotation; fertilizing; and soil-strengthening with enriching grasses and legumes.

In 1937, Roosevelt requested the states to assume the administrative details of the Soil Conservation Service through local soil conservation districts organized by farmers and ranchers so that the federal role could be confined to technical assistance. Almost 3,000 districts have been set up since that time. The local districts exist under the state law, but they sign agreements with various governmental and private agencies for particular services. After the Supreme Court struck down the first Agricultural Adjustment Act, the Soil Conservation and Domestic Allotment Act became the legislative foundation that supported financial and technical assistance in soil-building programs. Continuing research on soil conservation by the Department of Agriculture has been utilized as well by bureaus of the Department of the Interior.

The problem of overgrazing on public lands was dealt with by the Taylor Grazing Act of 1934. Representative Edward T. Taylor of Colorado had been advocating a strong states' rights stand in Congress since 1909 and fighting federal regulation and grazing fees. Nevertheless, as the population increased in the plains states in the 1920s and violence between cattlemen and sheepherders intensified and erosion became a serious problem because of overgrazing, Taylor changed his mind and became a

Figure 16–3. Controlling soil erosion. Through the efforts of H. H. Bennett and the Soil Conservation Service, a nationwide campaign to conserve and rebuild the nation's soil was waged during the Depression. Here three of their methods of erosion control are illustrated: strip cropping, terracing and wind breaks (shelterbelts). Farmers traditionally planted fields in rectangles to correspond to property lines, but where rain was heavy they were taught to cultivate in strips following the contour of the land. Terracing also usually follows the contour but includes shallow channels designed with enough fall to carry off excess water that could begin gullying. The contoured-terraced picture was taken in Iowa, and the aerial photo was taken in Nebraska, where heavy winds and fine soils make belts of several rows of trees around fields and homes desireable. Some shelterbelts have been as wide as 165 feet with 20 or more rows of trees and shrubs. Courtesy USDA, Soil Conservation Service.

zealous exponent of federal control. During House testimony long after his bill was passed, he explained the reasons for his conversion:

I fought for the conservation of the public domain under Federal leadership because the citizens were unable to cope with the situation under existing trends and circumstances. The job was too big and interwoven for even the States to handle with satisfactory coordination. On the western slope of Colorado and in nearby States I saw waste, competition, overuse, and abuse of valuable range lands and watersheds eating into the very heart of western economy. Farms and ranches everywhere in the range country were suffering. The basic economy of entire communities was threatened. There was terrific strife and bloodshed between the cattle and sheep men over the use of the range. Valuable irrigation projects stood in danger of ultimate deterioration. Erosion, yes even human erosion, had taken root. The livestock industry, through circumstances beyond its control, was headed for self-strangulation. Moreover, the States and the counties were suffering by reduced property values and decreasing revenues.

Taylor's arguments, even strengthened by statements from Roosevelt and Ickes, did not sway other sectionalists and homesteader advocates, who successfully stopped passage of the bill in the first Congressional session of 1934. Later that summer, the eastern migration of western dust broke down this opposition. The bill gave the secretary of the interior the power to create grazing districts, collect fees, and to issue permits for up to ten years, preferences being given to settlers and landowners living near the ranges. A Grazing Service was created to administer the act, and public lands not organized into grazing districts became leasable. One of the distinguishing features of the bill included the requirement that the secretary of the interior cooperate with "local associations of stockmen" to solve area problems.

The local control concept had been in effect in national forests for over a decade. Often two or more permit holders herded their cattle in common on the same tract, where it became necessary to work out problems of salting, watching herds, and range management. When such situations arose, the Forest Service helped in the organization of local groups that solved their own difficulties. The groups and their Congressmen have exercised a great deal of influence over fees and appropriations of the Grazing Service, reorganized into the Bureau of Land Management in 1946. Whereas the national forests have included competing uses of timber production, grazing, recreation, and watershed protection, the grazing districts have only one purpose; thus, there is only one commercial interest lobbying for benefits. Overgrazing continues to be a problem on the western plains grazing districts, and grazing fees remain significantly lower than lumbering fees in the national forests. Thus, because of budget inadequacies and political weakness, the Bureau of Land Management has encountered difficulties in bringing about a complete restoration of the plains.

Under the Taylor Act, the president closed the remaining unreserved and unap-propriated public lands to settlement and development, but left them open to mining, hunting, fishing, camping, and outdoor recreation. These lands are now the battlefield for conservationists against strip-mining of coal or the motorcyclists' lobby, which seeks the easing of restrictions on their use of the desert for cycling. The Bureau of Land Management is the agency which usually moderates these struggles, when the groups were not contesting in Congress or the courts.

Forest and Wildlife Conservation

During the dust bowl period, a flurry of new conservation activity dominated government bureaus: the establishment of national parks at the Olympic rain forest and in the Shenandoah; national monuments at Joshua Tree and the White Sands; and a big-game refuge in Oregon; a Shelter-belt Program through which 18,000 miles of shelter-belt forests were planted by 33,000 farmers in the plains states after 1934; the purchase or acquisition of millions of acres of cutover or tax delinquent lands in the South, Central, and Lake states. Most of the federal purchases included cutover, badly managed timberland, that was immediately placed under intensive management by the Forest Service.

During the depression, the Forest Service also expanded its forest research program authorized by the McSweeney-McNary Act of 1928. The service set up tree-growing experiment stations on the lands of private lumber companies and taught growers, among other things, how to manage cut-over lands. The service's Forest Products Laboratory extended its research into the chemistry of wood, but it was mainly interested in showing timbermen how to save wood and money. However, the major technological breakthrough of the period took place in Georgia, where a chemist discovered a sulfate process by which the southern pines could be used for the making of paper. From that day the southern timber industry, extending over many of the old cotton lands, began its dramatic rise.

It was for reforestation and soil conservation as much as the acute unemployment problem that Roosevelt established the Civilian Conservation Corps, an idea he cherished for at least two years before its implementation in 1933. Within two years, 500,000 young men in 2,600 camps were in the CCC, and another 2,000,000 would enroll before the war. They built fire trails, lookout towers, roads, and fire breaks in the national forests. They thinned 4,000,000 acres of trees, stocked streams and lakes with about 1,000,000,000 fish, set up over 30,000 wildlife shelters, dug irrigation canals, restored old battlefield sites, and engaged in pest control in grassroots localities. Most of all they planted trees—hundreds of thousands of them—in the plains, on eroded hillsides, over cutover mountains, and in burned-out forests. When fires broke out in the forests, CCC brigades were rushed to the scenes.

The fish-stocking activity of the CCC also stemmed from the widespread fear of complete fish depletion in the lakes and streams of the country during the decade. A crescendo of lament came from fishermen, especially the growing Isaak Walton League, blaming dams and industrial pollution for the declining fish populations. By the 1930s, studies were published showing methods by which fish could bypass dams through fish screens, ladders, and other devices. The Institute for Fisheries Research at the University of Michigan under Carl Hubbs did pioneer experimental work in fish conservation, management, stocking, and habitat management. The institute published management bulletins, and other universities followed its lead in experimental research dealing with marine ecology.

After two centuries of open season on American wildlife, the 1930s brought a different kind of wildlife problem—natural overstocking and congestion. It took many years of lobbying for groups like the Boone and Crockett and Sierra Clubs, and of course, work by preservationist elements within the Forest Service itself, particularly Robert Marshall, to influence the service in 1924 to set aside wilderness areas in the national forests, where no permanent structures, roads or development were to take place. Many species of wildlife flourished in national forests and in these areas, but at the same time, stockmen continued to exterminate the predators of their cattle and sheep—coyote, bobcat, and mountain lion—so that other animals, especially deer, upon which they preyed, were left without natural enemies, and the numbers of deer or other wildlife without natural enemies increased until food supplies became exhausted in their habitats. The same phenomenon occurred in areas where bounties were given for foxes; and the overstocking of quail followed. When deer in Pennsylvania died off by the thousands for lack of food, and similar problems were reported in other parts of the country, new questions about wildlife were raised.

Aldo Leopold, who had worked for a wilderness policy in the Forest Service, answered many of these questions about game management in the late 1920s while serving in the Forest Service in the Southwest, especially through the *Bulletin* of the American Game Association. He told game officials that the amount of acreage and the type of forage of a wildlife habitat determine the number of animals that can be supported in an area. Furthermore, he said that regulated hunting can maintain a proper balance of wildlife in a habitat.

When droughts hit the country during the twenties and thirties, game management proved especially difficult for declining waterfowl-breeding areas, and although Congress appropriated money to set up a national system of waterfowl refuges under the Norbeck-Andresen Act of 1929, the depression slowed its implementation. Then Roosevelt appointed Jay N Darling as the first head of the Bureau of Biological Survey. He was a man interested in waterfowl conservation for many years; he immediately cracked down on waterfowl hunting violations. He utilized the Duck Stamp tax to expand the bureau's program of waterfowl refuges. By 1935, Darling had increased the bureau's funding enough to inaugurate the Cooperative Wildlife Research Unit Program, housed in land grant colleges for advanced students of wildlife management. Matching funds were given by the colleges, the state fish-and-game agencies, and the American Wildlife Institute to enable students to gain professional training while doing wildlife research. Aldo Leopold continued his research in such a program at the University of Wisconsin.

The most significant New Deal wildlife legislation was the Pitman-Robertson Federal Aid in Wildlife Restoration Act of 1937. The bill reallocated the 11% excise tax on sporting arms and ammunition to the states in proportion to the number of their licensed hunters, to be applied to wildlife research, land acquisition, and other approved projects. The law also required the states to designate their own hunting license fees to programs of the fish-and-game agencies rather than to other state projects as was the common practice of the time. Then, in 1939, the Bureau of Biological Survey from the Department of Agriculture and the Bureau of Fisheries from the Department of Commerce (which did fish-culture experiments, restocked streams, and regulated salmon fishing) were consolidated into the new U.S. Fish and Wildlife Service of the Department of the Interior. Among other duties within the national forests and wildlife refuges, the service negotiates treaties with Canada and Mexico regarding migratory bird regulation and research.

The Tennessee Valley Authority

Roosevelt began the most far-reaching of his conservation ventures when he made a request to Congress in 1933 that it approve the Tennessee Valley Authority (TVA), involving the states of Tennessee, Kentucky, Georgia, Alabama, Mississippi, North Carolina, and Virginia. The area suffered from depleted soils, rampant erosion from cutover hills, recurrent flooding, chronic poverty, and economic desolation. The solution called for a massive program of economic and social revival. Senator George Norris and some of his fellow Progressives had worked for a decade to obtain government operation of the lands at Muscle Shoals, Alabama, on the Tennessee River, a development started during World War I to supply hydroelectric power for nitrate production (for explosives). The Norris Bill for a hydroelectric-nitrate plant (for fertilizer) was twice vetoed by Republican presidents, but Roosevelt saw in it the beginnings of a vast multi-purpose project to control floods that end up in the Mississippi delta and to provide inexpensive power for the poverty-stricken region. The project could also experimentally indicate a reasonable yardstick by which private power rates could be measured. The public corporation was to manufacture nitrogen fertilizers; dig a channel 650 miles from Knoxville to Paducah for navigation; set up a reforestation and soil conservation program; and develop social experiments in local community economic control.

The bill was passed and signed within a month of its proposal. The president chose Antioch College President Arthur E. Morgan as his first appointee to the three-man board of directors, and Morgan helped in the search for the other two—Harcourt A. Morgan, President of the University of Tennessee and David E. Lilienthal, a lawyer who specialized in public utilities law. Arthur Morgan enjoyed a wide reputation as an outstanding flood control engineer who set up water conservancy districts in Ohio. He was a utopian educationalist with strong interests in conservation and social reform. Harcourt Morgan, former agricultural college dean, filled the need for a regional person who could lead its conservation projects. Lilienthal worked for Governor Philip LaFollette as chairman of the Wisconsin Public Service Commission.

Arthur Morgan made certain that the first laborers of the project came from the valley; that they would learn construction skills; and that the residents would build their own dams. Harcourt Morgan was responsible for the fertilizer plant and land improvement program, and Lilienthal took over the hydroelectric and legal sides of the project. The three decided to wholesale power to nonprofit public municipal distribution systems from the already-constructed Wilson Dam plant. The price of TVA electricity was less than one-fourth that of the private companies. Thus Lilienthal was forced to spend much of his time arguing the many suits brought against TVA power distribution.

The TVA story is packed with drama and intrigue in its web of intramural struggles and differing ideologies along with the devious attacks of its enemies from the private utility companies, to which—much to Lilienthal's chagrin—Arthur Morgan often capitulated. The program was stalled, and it never lived up to the dreams of Roosevelt or even the original board, but it did offer a glimpse of what a planned social-economic program could look like. TVA gave cheap power and fertilizer; it also started significant reforestation, soil-conservation and flood control programs. Moreover, it began to set up regional programs in everything from public health planning and adult education to a comprehensive recreational plan and a master architectural design. Unfortunately, because of a greatly strengthened Republican-conservative Democratic coalition and consequent lack of funding, the implementation of the larger scheme never managed to get off the ground.

A spinoff of TVA, the 1936 Omnibus Flood Control Act, confirmed and extended for the entire nation the Flood Control Act of 1928, which originally applied only to the Mississippi and Sacramento Rivers. The act institutionalized a policy of multipurpose dams for power, flood control, and irrigation—the intent of the Hoover Dam project approved in 1928. The thirties gave rise to planning resource-use in large river basins (with as many as 16,000 watersheds) such as the Tennessee, the Missouri, the Columbia in Washington and Oregon, and the Arkansas. The planning often included navigation possibilities and relationships between soil and water resources. In the forties and fifties, more emphasis was placed on small watershed planning with local and state organizations assuming major responsibility for reclamation projects.

TVA and the many scandals in private utility holding companies of the time set the stage for new demands by rural areas to receive electricity from the federal government. Only one farm in ten had electricity and running water then, and private companies would not extend facilities to rural localities because their investment did not yield high or fast returns. A report written by conservationist Morris L. Cooke on the problem of the Mississippi Valley recommended government-funded rural electrification. Cooke, a veteran of public power fights in Pennsylvania, had done consultant work for Roosevelt on power policy in New York State.

Roosevelt established the Rural Electrification Commission in 1935 with Cooke as its director. Private power companies lobbied to have REA funds turned over to them for rural development, but it soon became clear to Cooke that very few farms would benefit by the hundred million dollars given to private companies. He proposed instead that local nonprofit cooperatives be set up to string their own electric distribution lines into the country. They were to be financed by low-cost government loans. The REA bill was quickly passed, and within a few years, farm families began to enjoy electrical power. In 1941, four out of ten farm families had it; by 1950, nine out of ten.

The New Deal is nearly impossible to summarize. It was not a consistent program so much as it was a response to everchanging situations by an extremely talented presidential political broker. This is not to say that the protagonists around Roosevelt, or that the president himself, were not committed to particular ideologies or programs, whether trust-busting or utopian planning, "sound-money" or inflationist, free enterprise or "monopoly-efficiency." In fact, Roosevelt and his aides were often autocratic or authoritarian. For our purpose, it is sufficient to note that a strong conservationist thrust underlay most of the political and economic approaches of the New Deal Program.

In the words of Arthur M. Schlesinger, Jr., the New Deal was to begin drawing the "lineaments of a new land." Sad to say, the lineaments of a new land were soon to be scarred by strip mining, and the lineaments of far-off lands were to be devastated by American bombs and napalm, both under the impetus of renewed economic growth and expansion spurred by World War II. It has become increasingly clear that the drive of the American economy continually to expand will necessarily take its toll on the natural environment. Even the shelter-belt forests which came to symbolize the great work of soil conservation over the sand hills of Nebraska began to be cut down in the 1970s to put more land under cultivation in order to pay for foreign oil with American wheat and corn. And the conditions which brought about the dust bowl are being repeated.

References for Further Reading

Arthur M. Schlesinger's *Coming of the New Deal* (1954), the second volume of his "The Age of Roosevelt" series, and William E. Leuchtenberg's *Franklin D. Roosevelt and the New Deal* (1963) are both superb in establishing the context of New Deal activity. *The Politics of Conservation* by Frank E. Smith (1966) encompasses most of the federal involvement in conservation history and has several excellent chapters on TVA and Roosevelt's conservation program. The incisive contemporary writer of the period who is quoted in the chapter, Stuart Chase, set down much of his political and conservation philosophy in *The Economy of Abundance* (1934). Already referred to in previous chapters and helpful in this one are *The American Environment* (Nash, ed.), *Origins of American Conservation* (Clepper, ed.), and *The Closing of the Public Domain* (Peffer), from which the Taylor quotation is taken. A good case study in the context of changing environmental philosophies of two major California environmental groups is Susan R. Schrepfer's *Flight to Save the Redwoods: A History of Environmental Reform, 1917-1978* (1982). Joseph V. Siry's *Marshes of the Ocean Shore: Development of an Ecological Ethic* (1984) shows the struggle of fishing and development interests, local, state, and federal agencies over marshes, estuaries, and tidal areas. Donald Worster's award-winning *Dust Bowl: The Southern Plains in the 1930s* (1979) underlines the strong connection between the market economy and environmental degradation in the southern plains during the great depression.

Chapter 17

SOURCES OF AMERICAN ABUNDANCE

What the New Deal could not do in six years—revitalize the nation's economy—World War II did in two. By 1944, half the country was engaged in production for war; in 1945, the federal government spent over $100,000,000,000, compared to the largest New Deal expenditure of $8,500,000,000. In 1944, full employment returned; by 1945, there was a labor shortage, sending 5,000,000 women to work. The war increased production to 60% over the 1940 gross national output. Practically everyone was working for the government or was the indirect recipient of federal money. If anyone harbored serious doubts about government intervention in the economic life of the country, the misgivings disappeared during the 1940s. The nation's material transformation was total.

The economic, social, and cultural institutions of the twenties were so well established and their models so impressed in the American consciousness that when good times returned in the forties, American society continued along the course interrupted a generation earlier. But because of government financial controls and two more military excursions into Southeast Asia, along with vastly expanded world markets and money supplies, the inevitable recession was retarded until the seventies. In the meantime, sophisticated technologies, particularly because of their ability to generate enormous quantities of energy, brought new dangers of resource depletion.

War Mobilization

A price had to be paid for the new affluence after World War II: the cruelties of war itself; higher taxes; unprecedented national debt; and massive population dislocations. Over 15,000,000 servicemen were shipped to military training camps and the front lines for battle. The rural jobless, especially southern blacks, pulled up stakes and moved to the booming new urban war industrial centers. Over 1,000,000 farm people migrated to the cities between 1940 and 1950 and stayed there after the war. Urbanization became an accomplished fact during this time, bringing additional housing shortages, congested streets, inadequate transportation facilities, and crowded classrooms.

Bureaus in Washington proliferated. The Office of War Mobilization, under former Supreme Court Justice James F. Byrnes, coordinated and supervised the War Production Board, the Oil Administration, the Office of Economic Stabilization, the War Labor Board and War Manpower Commission, and the Food Administration. The War Production Board bought $16,000,000,000 worth of industrial facilities, disposed of or rationed millions of tons of natural resources, controlled national transportation routes and labor practices, set prices and rents, and even had a strong influence on profit margins and wages.

The large corporations received most of the contracts. Forty-five percent of them were granted to six firms in 1941. A third of the war orders during the rest of the war went to ten corporations—one of them, General Motors, capturing $14,000,000,000. Of course these corporations had to subcontract much of the work. (The War Production Board believed that big operations were more efficient than small ones.) Boosted further by tax laws and capital-gains regulations, mergers picked up again. Perhaps as many as 500,000 smaller companies were swallowed up by larger ones during the war. By 1947, the 113 largest firms, with assets over $100,000,000 each, owned about half the manufacturing facilities of the country, according to a Federal Trade Commission report. But because of the huge government expenditures, thousands of new small businesses also got their start during and after the war.

The accomplishments of war mobilization can hardly be faulted. Armies and countries around the globe were outfitted with equipment, airfields, and highways and were supplied with food. Every year production goals were set higher, and most of them were met. Iron, copper, coal, and oil production skyrocketed. The steel industry was bursting at the seams. Great demand for food products spurred mechanization of agriculture. This process was also encouraged by high prices and government loans. The war cost about $360,000,000,000 and precipitated a monumental drain on the country's natural resources. It also kicked off the era of affluence.

The Postwar Economy

Although New Deal leftovers in Washington after the war were prepared to continue federal funding of public works projects to head off the expected return of unemployment after the war, they needn't have worried. Americans had been forced to save their money—probably as much as $150,000,000,000—during the war because of the scarcity of consumer goods. For instance, people had to wait for months or years for automobiles, refrigerators, and appliances. Even with an enormous supply of ready cash, a wary government pursued easy-credit, deficit-spending inflationary policies after the war. Very cheap loans were available for housing, especially for veterans, who received millions in benefits and payments.

Corporations which leased the $16,000,000,000 government industrial facilities bought them and retooled quickly in an effort to gear up for the insatiable consumer demand that lasted for a generation. Housing, automobiles, and thousands of new gadgets were easily supplied by a larger, trained work force, supplemented by returning soldiers. More jobs meant more spendable income, which new marketing and advertising methods and expanded consumer credit attempted to channel into corporate accounts. As the consumer society of the twenties restructured itself, TV became an increasingly important vehicle; almost 90% of American homes had a set by 1960. New and changing roles and ideals were presented to Americans in their living rooms. A population explosion contributed to consumer demand, and median family incomes rose from $3,083 in 1949 to $5,657 in 1959, even though the bottom 13%

Figure 17–1. The interchangeability of land under the grid system, promulgated by Congress almost two centuries ago, enabled this agricultural and orchard land near San Jose, California to be quickly converted to residential subdivisions by a simple financial transaction. The two photos were taken in January, 1950 and June, 1956 during the economic boom after World War II. Since that time hundreds of acres more of this valuable land has been taken for urban expansion, roads, freeways, and interchanges. Photos courtesy U.S. Department of Agriculture.

of the population—mostly nonwhite—was living on less than $2,000 a year. By 1955 America was producing almost half of the world's goods with 6% of its population.

But the war had effected a serious imbalance in the deployment of the nation's human, economic, and natural resources. Military considerations weighed heaviest during the Cold War period of the fifties and sixties. "The military-industrial complex" is what the postwar defense industries came to be called, and the man in whose presidency the complex grew most quickly, Dwight Eisenhower, warned of the potential political and economic dangers of the new defense elite. The Pentagon grew to monstrous proportions long before the country's involvement in Vietnam. In the decade after the war, its budget exceeded $325,000,000,000, more than industrial capital investment during the period.

The Korean War, the Cold War, competition to reach the moon before the Russians, Vietnam and southeast Asia, atomic and space programs—all directed hundreds of billions of dollars toward a tiny, nonsalable segment of the economy: military hardware. A relatively small number of highly technical research and development teams working on sophisticated weaponry or specialized space projects also claimed billions of dollars. At the same time, the armaments industry was contracted by the government to continue to spread weapons around the globe to allies and friendly nations.

Other activity of the government in the economy was more socially beneficial. Huge subsidies were granted to colleges and universities which enlarged science facilities; student scholarships increased. The New Deal was revived by Harry Truman in programs like urban renewal; extended social security and welfare benefits; higher minimum wages; and attempts at a full employment bill. Later the Federal-Highway Acts of 1956 and 1958 projected construction of 40,000 miles of roads financed by federal gasoline taxes; $40,000,000,000 was spent by 1970. This was an amount undreamed of in 1916, when the first federal highway program was enacted.

Federal cooperation with the automobile boom followed the "automobilization" of the American economy and culture. There were 4.5 people for every car in 1930; by the 1970s, fewer than two people per car, and over 100,000,000 registered cars. A fully geared auto industry could turn out about 12,000,000 cars a year if the demand existed for them now. More significant is the fact that one out of every six jobs in the United States is connected with the production or use of the automobile, especially in such natural resource exploitation as that of lead, iron, zinc, steel, aluminum, copper, and oil.

During the war, the list of basic commodities supported by the government's Commodity Credit Corporation was expanded; the Steagall Amendment gave the secretary of agriculture the authority to support the price of nonbasic commodities; and price ceilings were placed on farm products at 110% of parity. When farm prices started on a downward trend after the war because of overproduction, Congress renewed its commitment to support basic farm commodities and the principal Steagall commodities at 90% of parity. This policy greatly increased government stockpiles of food commodities. In the fifties, the total inventories hovered around $10,000,000,000. These stocks were disposed of with a view to varying social considerations: as fertilizers (potatoes); sent abroad to "friendly" nations; and used in school lunches.

Industrial concentration kept pace with government centralization. A massive amount of capital was needed for the technologies of the lucrative new aerospace industries, or for retooling the basic industries with automated, self-regulated machines able to turn out goods more rapidly and precisely than ever before. The large corporations could reinvest their soaring profits in this equipment because of tax advantages afforded such enterprises. Even banks were needed less for sources of capital investment than they had been at the first of the century. The old business tycoon was replaced by a corporate, managerial class of professionals educated in the latest techniques of efficient management. The changes permeated not only industrial or processing firms, but also resource-production industries like agriculture, mining, and logging. Small stockholders retained virtually no voice in the decisions of the latter day corporations. Conglomerate corporations, groups of businesses having no direct relationship to the parent company, became attractive investments after the war, especially in those diffuse industries which wanted a hedge against the possibility of peace "breaking out."

The economic source of the affluent society resulted from the war. It increased both government expenditures and economic concentration. Appendages of the new society were high-pitch advertising competing for higher incomes; bigger automobiles to be driven over hundreds of new highways; slick supermarkets for the suburbs; dozens of new credit devices for thousands of new consumer items. Inflation came in the wake of a transformed America, and a growing class of the poor and the elderly were left out of the mainstream of abundance.

The Centrality of Energy

Almost every characteristic of modern American society—from intercontinental air or highway transportation to communication devices and computer-run industrial and office equipment—depends on an increasing supply of energy, the ability to convert the locked-in power of fossil fuels into mechanical work. The war and government sponsorship of major scientific research pushed ahead the nation's capacity to do immeasurably more work than was done in the prewar period. But it was not the innovation—the nuclear reactor—that proved most useful; rather it was the high-pressure steam turbine, designed first by Charles A. Parsons in 1884, that was steadily improved in size, strength, and efficiency for American ships and electrical dynamos during and after the war.

Tough alloy steels and sophisticated engineering of new steam turbines have contributed to new electrical generating capacities of 1,500,000 kilowatts. Over 75% of the electrical power generated in the world (83% in the United States), annually equivalent to about 75,000,000 horsepower, is produced by steam turbines; most of the remaining electricity comes from the turbines of hydroelectric power plants. This great work capacity makes the simplicity of the turbine's design even more amazing. Its basic construction is carefully spaced blades on a shaft through which superheated water under great pressure passes.

Steam turbines are also used in nuclear power plants where the fission of uranium or plutonium in a controlled chain reaction is used to superheat steam. Enrico Fermi effected the first continuing chain reaction in 1943, and the military found its first practical function in an atomic bomb. After the war, the Atomic Energy Commission promoted the possible harnessing of atomic fission for peaceful uses. Within a generation, the atomic plant industry was ready for commercial production, but by this time fears about dangers stemming from dangerous radioactivity delayed the AEC's full-scale adoption of nuclear reactors to solve the nation's energy problems. Nuclear power presently represents only about 8% of the electrical energy of the United States.

With or without nuclear reactors, the maintenance of America's comfort and convenience level requires enormous quantities of energy and a bottomless pit of natural resources to fuel boilers and to manufacture consumer goods.

The Steel Industries

Of all the resources affected by the war, iron and its conversion into steel played the most significant role. Operating at less than 20% of capacity in 1932, the steel industry—even with price-fixing legalized by the New Deal—could not be pulled out of chronic depression. With the war came overwhelming government demand for products of tough alloy steels—armaments of every variety; millions of shells; over 70,000 ships; steel helmets; and hundreds of other exotic steel items like landing mats for planes, etc. Thanks to the war, the steel industry regained economic health overnight and returned to almost 100% capacity by 1943.

Steel products remained scarce after the war, when the scramble began for automobiles, kitchen sets, and everything from railroad locomotives and rails to razor blades, tin cans, wire fences, pipelines, and bridge and skyscraper structural steel. The industry was exempted from the operation of antitrust laws so that steelmakers could allocate and ration the short supply to various processors—often their own subsidiaries. The Korean War in 1950 brought government allocation systems and price controls again, but when these constraints were lifted in the mid-1950s, the top twelve steel firms were found to control well over 80% of the industry's four principal branches—iron ore mining (85%); pig-iron production (87%); steel-making (83%); and steel-rolling (82%). Since then the same firms have operated as an oligopoly. A related industry, aluminum, remained even more tightly controlled, with 96% of all sales made by the top four firms.

That a few companies could control an industry which derives its basic resource, iron ore, from such a variety of locations can be understood only from a historical perspective. Before the Civil War, iron production was still a localized industry. Although dozens of independent firms operated profitably after the turn of the century (despite Morgan's U.S. Steel merger), the 1920s were marked by a return of consolidations through holding companies. The weakest steel companies were wiped out by the depression, leaving comparatively few firms to reap the advantages of wartime production. Where steel facilities were lacking, the government was willing to finance new construction—$770,000,000 in fifty-two new steel plants. These operations were sold to their wartime managers, the same large integrated producers that survived the depression—U.S. Steel, Republic Steel, Armco—at colossal bargains. For example, the Geneva Works at Geneva, Utah, near Salt Lake City was erected at a cost of $202,000,000 and sold to U.S. Steel for a little over $47,000,000. The sale enabled the giant to control western markets for the first time. Since outlays of capital for steel works are massive, only the very few experienced steelmakers can afford to set up operations. They were obviously aided by contract and capital subsidies from the federal government.

The oligopoly in general and U.S. Steel in particular received a legal boost in 1948 from the Supreme Court's Columbia Steel decision allowing U.S. Steel to acquire Consolidated Steel and with it to dominate the West Coast market of rolled steel products. The minority opinion of the Court that the merger "makes dim the prospects that the western steel industry will be free from the control of the eastern giants" has become an accomplished fact.

Figure 17–2. Improved mining technologies. Birmingham iron ore is extremely hard, in contrast to that of the northern open-pit mines. A drill crew is shown here in the Birmington, Alabama, Number 9 mine drilling blast holes to free some of the ore. Note the compressed air hoses and the power turrets, a process developed over a hundred years ago, which are used here to drill two blast holes simultaneously. Also note the overhead which is treated to prevent collapse. Courtesy Bureau of Mines, U.S. Department of the Interior.

Since the war, the concentration of control over iron ore reserves has remained in the hands of a handful of integrated steel producers, especially the rich Lake Superior district where the integrated producers retain more than 95% of the ore. Although the steel industry now imports about a third of its iron ore from Canada, Venezuela, Brazil, and Peru, the large firms alone are capable of buying fleets of ore-carrying vessels and expensive heavy mining equipment. As the secretary of the interior observed to a Subcommittee on the Study of Monopoly Power in 1950, "I do not think it would make any difference whether you had five companies in the steel business or 500 companies . . . if one or two companies controlled the source of raw material. The monopolistic feature would be there in the controlling point." The small companies have never been certain of a continued supply of ore at a price they could afford to pay.

Since the war the largest steel firms have moved forward toward finishing and fabrication of steel products. Through mergers and acquisitions, they have been able to monopolize such specialized industries as drum barrels, wire, pumps, and structural steel. In the past two generations, the top steel companies have determined their own price policies which neither government nor potential competition have been able to challenge successfully.

New Technologies

At the same time, their techniques of exploration, extraction, and processing have become increasingly sophisticated. Large corporations employ teams of geophysicists to search for ores around the world with magnetometers, which measure the intensity of the earth's magnetic field. (Iron or chromium ores exert a more powerful pull than non-mineralized rock.) Helicopters, airplanes, and government satellites map large areas, and infrared-sensitive film indicates rock structures that may bear valuable minerals. In searching for minerals or fossil fuels, geologists, including a few from the US Geological Survey, have devised methods like the application of electrical currents to find sulfide minerals; the use of Geiger counters to locate uranium; and the use of such devices as mercury "sniffers," berylometers, and rock drills which recover ore samples deep in the earth.

Iron ore has generally been accessible on the earth's surface and easy and inexpensive to mine. Underground mining suffers from problems involving water, ventilation, temperature, and physical dangers to miners added to the technical difficulties of removing and hoisting the ore. But the high-grade ores in the United States found on the surface have already been extracted, so that at districts like Lake Superior, the mining companies are beginning to extract billions of tons of low-grade ores known as taconites, some with only 25% iron. Huge earth-moving equipment can scoop up to 350 tons a bite and dump the ore directly into trucks or railroad cars. This kind of mining cannot be duplicated underground even with the fastest diggers or the strongest hoists.

Low-grade taconite ores are now mined primarily because of a recently-developed pelletizing process, the making of pellets of iron near the mine. The ore is blasted and scooped out of the hills, then crushed; iron oxide particles are concentrated magnetically; waste is discarded; and iron-ore particles are cemented together with bentonite in a 1094°C oven into marble-like pellets. The process speeds refining and cuts out the needless and expensive transporting of millions of tons of waste materials to the steel mills. For every ton of iron-ore pellets shipped, three and one-half tons of taconite are processed.

Alloying elements which change the mechanical or physical properties of the metal have multiplied the uses of iron and steel in the past fifty years. Elements that form alloy steels when added to carbon steel are called ferro-alloy metals. They include chromium, cobalt, manganese, molybdenum, nickel, niobium (columbium), tantalum, titanium, tungsten, vanadium, and zirconium. Most alloy steels are made in electric furnaces where mixtures and temperatures can be carefully controlled. The basic ferro-alloy metals, except molybdenum, are imported by the United States.

Industrialized nations need alloy steels in great quantity for their special properties. Stainless steel is made from chrome because the alloy does not oxidize. Cobalt-iron alloys are indispensible for magnets in modern tools and communication systems—radio, television, guided missiles, jet aircraft, gas turbines, high-speed tools. Manganese also contributes to strong, durable steel. Molybdenum steel is corrosion-resistant; nickel steel is a high-temperature and electric-resistant alloy. Niobium strengthens pipes and truck and railroad-car frames. What is significant about many of these ferro-alloy metals is their irreplaceability. There are few suitable substitutes for cobalt in magnets for communication systems, and only a small portion used by the United States is mined here—in Cornwall, Pennsylvania, as a byproduct of iron mining and in the Blackbird district of Idaho. Most of its limited supply comes from Zaire, Finland, Belgium, Norway, and Canada. The essential manganese is mined in Brazil, Gabon, South Africa, and Zaire, though an American firm has begun plans to attempt to mine it from the floor of the Pacific Ocean. Tungsten comes from Canada, Bolivia, Peru and Thailand. The origins of the ferro-alloy metals partially explain the reasons for American interest and political relationships with these countries; but it should also be noted that the U.S. Bureau of Mines and a number of research centers throughout the country are continually developing new mining techniques, processing methods, or substitutes for these vital minerals.

Coal Production

By 1920, coal supplied over two-thirds of the energy of the country. Since the rise of oil, the use of coal has dropped off greatly, but it still is needed by many power plants, and coal for coking maintains a primary role in the steel industry. After the war, by-product coke ovens replaced beehive ovens which burned up and lost in smoke a third of the value of the coal. By-product ovens capture valuable volatile products—ammonia, tar, and ammonia gas vapors—as they are driven off enclosed chambers heated by flues. Every ton of coal yields about eight gallons of tar, two gallons of benzene, three-tenths of a gallon of toluol and 20 pounds of ammonium sulfate.

These byproducts of coal, like those of petroleum, provide raw materials for chemical industries in the contemporary synthetic era. The coal chemical benzene is required in the manufacture of synthetic rubber, DDT, and the many products of nylon. Sulfa drugs, aspirin, novocaine, barbiturates, certain vitamins, and antiseptics are derived from coal chemicals. At least 250,000 products could be put on the list: telephones, stereo recordings, pens, appliances, many types of plastics, dyes, ink, quick-drying enamels, perfumes, adhesives, cellophane, photographic chemicals, creosote, and of course, food colorings and flavorings. Ammonium sulfate from coal is used in fertilizers; toluol, in TNT.

Even before the oil shortages of 1973, the electric utility companies bought almost half the coal produced in the country. Price boosts in oil since that time have made

Figure 17–3. American coal deposits. This map shows only the known coal deposits in the contiguous forty-eight states.

coal a competitive fuel. This fact has induced large oil companies to invest heavily in coal; Standard Oil of California, for example, paid $33,000,000 in 1975 for only one firm, Ames, which had 3,000,000,000 tons of coal reserves. These recent developments have spurred wider mechanization of underground deep mining with continuous cutters, timbering machines, and conveyor belts, eliminating older methods of drilling, blasting, and hauling.

Although the newer, safer, and cleaner underground coal- mining machinery can produce hundreds of tons per man per day, strip mining is far cheaper, more capital-intensive, and more profitable. Two dozen men can operate a strip mine that will produce millions of tons of coal a year. Thus older coal companies like Peabody (now the country's largest stripper) and new firms established by oil firms like Chevron, Shell, Atlantic Richfield, and Exxon, or conglomerates like Westmoreland Resources (which also includes big oil companies such as Gulf and Continental along with construction and energy firms), all have begun to lease hundreds of thousands of acres in eastern Montana, northern Wyoming, and the western Dakotas where one of the largest coal deposits in the world lies just beneath the surface. About 34,000,000,000 tons of low-sulfur subbituminous coal and lignite in the region make up over a third of the country's coal reserves, according to the North Central Power Study done by the Bureau of Reclamation in 1971. While the coal seams in the East are usually less than five feet thick, northern plains' seams run from 70 to 200 feet thick.

The bureau recommended the construction of forty-two power plants, burning 42,000,000 tons of coal a year in eastern Montana, and a complex of dams, reservoirs, and aqueducts storing and delivering water for boilers at the power plants and for coal gasification plants that would convert the coal into gas as a heating fuel. (The coal is changed to gas by adding hydrogen, which is supplied by water in the form of steam.) The Intake Water Company, a subsidiary of the Tenneco conglomerate, has already filed a request for more than 80,000 acre-feet (one acre-foot is 325,851 gallons) from the Yellowstone River in Montana—an amount equal to about a quarter of the average annual low flow of the river. About 10,700,000 acre-feet of the Yellowstone were requested in 1974 by private firms and the states of Montana and Wyoming. The American Natural Gas Service wants to reserve 375,000 acre-feet of the Missouri River in North Dakota, where the company plans to strip-mine 1,400,000,000 tons of coal for twenty-two projected gasification plants, each one of which would use about 30,000,000 gallons of water per day. Other large firms with public leases have likewise requested hundreds of thousands of acre-feet for gasification, prompting a team from the National Academy of Science in 1974 to report that electrification and gasification projects in the northern plains portend "staggering" water problems. And Montana Governor Thomas L. Judge complained that the Bureau of Reclamation was giving preference to industrial applicants over agricultural users.

The electric utilities of the region plan to imitate Peabody Coal's strip mining and transporting arrangement at Black Mesa, northeastern Arizona, a 3,300 square-mile plateau in a Navaho and Hopi reservation. After stripping the coal (22,000 tons a day) at Black Mesa, Peabody crushes it and sends it through a slurry pipeline to the Mojave power plant at the tip of Nevada, which service Los Angeles, Las Vegas, Phoenix, and the rest of the blooming Southwest with electricity and send about 350 tons of fly ash into the atmosphere every day. The pipeline takes 2,700 gallons a minute from underground water sources; in addition, thousands of acre-feet are drawn from the Colorado River to supply the power plants every year. Utah, New Mexico and Colorado also have thousands of acres of strippable coal. New coal-fired electrical generating plants are already under construction all over the West and Southwest to use nearby supplies of coal. Texas utilities are beginning to haul Wyoming coal 1,500 miles to Texarkana, Beaumont, and Amarillo. Much western coal is also going east and into the deep South.

The railroads—especially the Burlington Northern—the U.S. government, and the Cheyenne and Crow Indians own most of the coal lands in the northern plains. The railroads received 15,000,000 acres from the federal government in Montana alone during the last century, and the Burlington Northern is about to reap a bonanza from its own 2,400,000 acres and the 6,000,000 on which it has mineral rights. Although the 1906 Hepburn Act forbids railroads from transporting commodities in which they have an interest, BN is expected to mine or lease their lands and to monopolize the carrying of the coal to utility furnaces around the country.

The Department of the Interior has leased over 700,000 acres of public land, holding about 15,000,000,000 tons of coal. A 1973 study by the Council on Economic Priorities states that public land rent and royalty rates set in 1920 and 1938 and applied to the present are so low as to be token payments; that leases have not been competitive—in 59% of the public coal sales only one bidder appeared, in another 10% no bidder was forthcoming, and the average bid was $3.31 per acre; that lease-holdings are concentrated in a small number of large corporations—fifteen firms are

Figure 17–4. A modern mammoth. This 3850-B stripping shovel removes over-burden from strip mines. It has a 210-foot boom; its dipper bites out 115-cubic yard chunks. The bulldozer beneath the bowels of the stripper provides some idea of the gigantic size of the machine. Courtesy Bucyrus-Erie Company.

holding the land until the price of coal goes even higher; and that social, economic, and environmental impacts of coal development of the lands have not been studied adequately. Leasing companies paid the federal government from $.17 to $.25 per ton of mined coal in royalties.

The northern Cheyennes and the Crows, recently concerned about the potential impact of the strip mining and gasification development on the 300,000 acres of land they leased in the late 1960s and early 1970s, have begun a legal battle to cancel the lease, just as sixty-two Hopi spiritual leaders in Arizona have challenged the Peabody contracts. If the agreements over the Cheyenne reservations hold, 56% of their land would become transformed into strip mines, gasification plants, power plants, rail lines, and new towns. The Cheyennes would have little to say about the development. Consolidation Coal Company, for instance, planned a town for 30,000 coal workers—ten times the present population of the Cheyenne reservation. The lessors in the northern plains' reservations are Westmoreland Resources, Consolidated Coal, Shell Oil, Gulf, Peabody, and American Metals Climax.

What makes these reserves so attractive is the simplicity of extraction. Mountains and hills are few; the overburden (the earth and rocks above the coal seam) is shallow, and strip-mining equipment is enormously powerful. Topsoil is scraped before holes are machine-drilled in the overburden for blasting. After the overburden is scooped out, the process is repeated for the coal, which is carried by truck to railroads. Coal companies use huge shovels or $20,000,000 draglines, mounted on 250- to 310-foot booms, which can pick up from fourteen to 220 cubic yards of overburden per bite once a minute, or from fourteen to 350 tons every scoop. Smaller mechanical equipment usually is used for scooping out coal.

Reclamation of Strip-mined Land

Besides water requirements, serious questions remain about the possibility of reclaiming the land. Nine out of eleven states with the greatest amount of strippable coal in the country now require that strip-mined land be restored to its original contour, but regulation is often weak or vague. Although the corporations have begun reclamation of some of the plains lands, the final determination of their efforts has not yet been made. The states require strip-miners to preserve topsoil, but much of its gets blown or washed away before reclamation of an area begins. More important, critical water tables that distribute moisture throughout the plains have been disturbed by strip-mining, and nobody is certain of the capability of spoils to hold water for long. Small streams have silted up after earlier reclamation projects, and minerals loosened by the broken overburden are quickly dissolved by rain so that they leach into ground waters and streams, leaving them hard and sometimes foul. A 1969 Report by the Appalachian Regional Commissioner indicated that about 5,700 miles of streams have been polluted in areas of Appalachia where aquatic life has been reduced or eliminated. The water quality of 10,500 miles of streams has been affected as well.

This phenomenon has been responsible for the pollution of the once-soft Kentucky River with concentrations of magnesium, calcium, sulfates, and sulfur. It is expected to occur in the mineral-rich western land. Strip mining breaks open soils that have been compacted for thousands of years; iron, copper, manganese, zinc, and dozens of other minerals will probably dissolve into water systems and threaten aquatic life. Unfortunately, certainty about strip-mining's effect on regional ecologies does not exist.

In the traditional coal regions of Appalachia, where most lands have not been reclaimed since stripping started in the forties, strip mining has intensified. In that region, mountain tops are flattened to clean out the coal, and adjacent valleys are filled in for "development." This method is designated as "mountain-top mining." Appalachian coal companies have also developed contour-stripping and auguring, the latter a technique by which sets of giant augur drills eight feet in diameter gouge into hillsides and pull out coal. The effect on the age-old ecology of Appalachia has approached devastation. Ironically, the Tennessee Valley Authority, which was advanced the responsibility for environmental and social planning of the region, has commissioned much strip mining to obtain fuel for its power plants. TVA is the world's largest purchaser of strip-mined coal, and its earlier aspirations toward multi-purpose regional development have been all but forgotten.

Former Kentucky legislator Harry M Caudill, author of *Night Comes to the Cumberlands*, notes in a 1973 article in *Atlantic* magazine that even in England where stringent regulation of strip-mined lands is practiced, restoration has proved difficult:

Restoration extends over five years and costs about $5,000 an acre, but even these stringent measures leave the land sunken and maimed and the groundwater charged with enormous quantities of minerals.

The American stripping companies, even where required by law, have not begun to emulate the exact carefulness of the English in restoration practices. In a Geological Survey Bulletin in 1970, Paul Averitt estimated from coal producers' data that coal had been strip-mined from about 2,450 square miles in the U.S. With about 128,000,000,000 tons of strippable coal left in the country (71,000 square miles), Averitt assumed that 100 square miles of land would be stripped each year. (In fact, the increased efficiency of strip-mining equipment, the oil crisis, and lenient government policies have greatly increased the tempo of strip-mining.) Strip-mining measures are justified, as the Bureau of Reclamation's North Central Power Study emphasizes, because the country's demand for electrical energy doubles every ten years.

In his 1975 State of the Union message, President Gerald Ford called for an additional 250 major coal mines, another 150 coal-fired power plants, and at least twenty new synthetic fuel plants by 1985. During 1974-75 President Ford vetoed two strip-mine control bills that would have required (albeit with weak provisions) nationwide reclamation of strip-mined lands as closely as possible to their original contour. This bill was passed and signed by President Carter in 1977, including a provision which imposes a tax of 35 cents a ton to pay for land damaged by strip-mining in the past. Nonetheless coal made its mark on the alluvial valleys of the West and especially the Northern Great Plains, where thousands of immigrants flooded into previously tranquil towns in a great new coal rush.

The Oil Industry

Steel, coal for coking, oil, and even highways and suburbs find their common denominator in the automobile. The major outlet for steel in America is the auto industry, (over 20%, as well as 45% of all malleable iron); the major use of oil goes into the refining of gasoline, which is responsible for almost 45% of all U.S. oil consumption (fuel oil uses for utilities and homes comprise about 37%). Although coal has suffered economic setbacks and fluctuations, oil has not. In the thirty years between 1940 and 1970, domestic production of crude oil rose from 1.3 billion barrels (1940), to 1.9 billion (1950), to 2.5 billion (1960), to 3.3 billion barrels (1970). Automobiles use over 80 billion gallons of gasoline each year. The automobile industry has expanded and has been monopolized even faster than the oil industry. By the early sixties, the top four firms controlled 99% of American auto sales, though foreign cars have cut down this

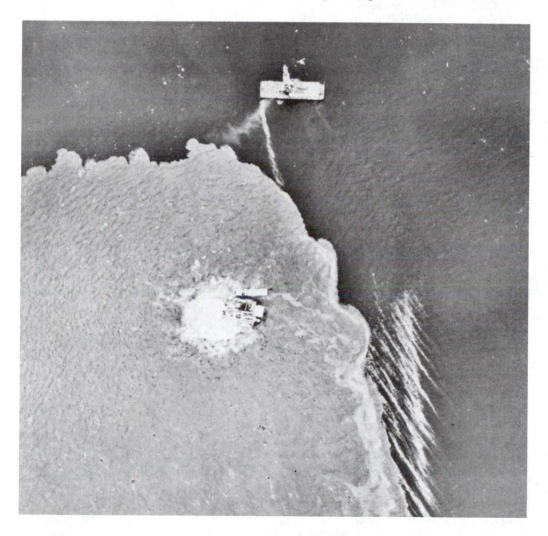

Figure 17–5. The Santa Barbara oil spill. A leak developed from a well at the bottom of the Santa Barbara Channel early in 1969. Before the leak was stopped, thousands of gallons of oil floated to the surface, polluting nearby shorelines as well as the water itself. This view is taken from 1,800 feet. It shows the Union Oil Company drilling rig (center), a barge that attempted to counter-drill to relieve pressure (top), and the enormous slick spreading down and away from the site. Courtesy U.S. Environmental Protection Agency.

margin since then. In 1956 and 1958, Congress's Federal Highway Act institutionalized the community of steel/auto/oil/highway/development interests.

These industries did not have to conspire to establish America's dependency on the auto and its exigencies. As far back as the twenties, suburbs had been preferred because cities were noisy, dirty, unhealthy, and unsafe. In the affluent society, especially since highway construction has been subsidized by federal and state government, those who could afford to and were not prevented from moving away from socially undesirable areas have done so. As long as gasoline prices were reasonable and commuters did not have to pay the social costs of pollution, it paid to move away from the city. Subsidies came from taxpayers who built highways, from a government that did not tax for polluting the air, and even from the oil industry that kept gasoline prices low as long as profits stayed high.

Despite continuous control of the oil industry by a few companies since the 1930s, gasoline prices did stay fairly low. In the early thirties, a brief flourishing of competitive producers and refiners from the new fields of east Texas sent very cheap gasoline to the depression-hit cities, eager for anything to keep their prized autos running, but New Deal and state "conservation" laws soon laid production quotas on the wildcatters. Prices were pushed up to pre-depression levels, and the U.S. Bureau of Mines quoted "market demand" figures each month so that the industry would not overproduce. Unable to produce enough for a decent living, most of the small operators sold out. The war turned modest profits into great returns and some minor competitors returned to the industry.

The minors did not seriously threaten the majors' control of the industry, which had been limiting production and fixing prices (indirectly and legally through the U.S. Bureau of Mines) for over a generation. Even outside the United States, Jersey Standard, Shell, and Anglo-Iranian's predecessor signed an agreement in 1928 to limit production, share markets, arid fix prices. The seven major oil companies (the "Seven Sisters") of Standard Oil of New Jersey, Royal Dutch Shell Group, Gulf, Texaco, Standard Oil of California, Socony Mobil, and British Petroleum as early as 1950 owned every major pipeline in the world, 70% of the refining capacity, and excluding the Soviet Union's, two-thirds of the world's oil tanker fleets. By 1955 they had captured 90% of the world markets, and had made enormous profits at the wellhead, particularly from foreign oil. Until 1950, 20% of the oil profits went to the oil producing nations for their oil; after that time until 1973 profits were split evenly between the majors and the oil producing countries. Generally, profits from crude oil came to at least $1.40 per barrel out of a $2.50 world market price in 1950, $.70 a barrel going to each side. Since the foreign share of the profits was accounted as a foreign tax credit rather than as a royalty, the oil companies could deduct the payment directly from their own taxes, in effect not losing the full profit at all.

Because the majors received such generous returns at the wellhead, enjoyed a tight hold on refining capacity, pipelines, and transportation, and retained a majority of retail outlets, a small number of competitive refiners and independent service station dealers could be tolerated. During these years the majors increased their profits by employing cost-cutting measures in production and transportation, even if they were wasteful or if they carried the risk of environmental damage. New oil fields,

Figure 17–6. A very large crude carrier on the ways. *Esso Northumbria,* shown here sliding down the ways at her launching, is one of a class of gigantic oil carriers now plying the world's oceans. Some idea of scale may be obtained from the fact that the ant-like creatures at the bow rails are men. While such ships, with sizes of 250,000 or more tons deadweight, may seem to offer savings because of their huge capacities, they also present unprecedented danger in case of grounding, collision, or fire. Courtesy Exxon Corporation.

for example, provide cheaper oil production because gas pressure is high, and oil companies will often use the gas to push out the oil before gas pipes are installed in order to gain short-term cost advantages. Much natural gas is wasted, but since its price is governmentally regulated, profits are not high enough to warrant conservation measures.

The same kind of cost-expediency over conservation was evident during the sixties, when mounting numbers of pipeline breaks, up to 500 a year, spilling from 5,000 to 12,000 gallons, began to upset environmentalists and legislators. In February 1970, a *New York Times* article widely publicized three oil-spill accidents committed by Standard Oil in a single month: 15,000 gallons off the Florida coast; 3,000,000 gallons into Nova Scotia Bay over twenty-six miles of shoreline; 50,000 gallons a day for several weeks into the Gulf of Mexico because Standard had not complied with minimal federal safety regulations requiring "safety chokes" to shut off malfunctioning wells. In each case, from twenty to fifty miles of shoreline was covered, and wildlife, marine life or important oyster fisheries were devastated. In California, the huge Santa Barbara channel oil spill from a drilling platform also provoked a widespread outcry.

The Seven Sisters market percentage dropped from 90% in 1955 to 70% in 1969, largely because of the gradual influx of independents. And although profits remained substantial, new environmental regulations demanded large capital outlays as did expansion to increase production. Consumption of gasoline rose about 5.2% a year. World markets were increasing, especially in industrialized nations like Japan, and greater profits were being realized at the gas pump because of gradually rising prices. The majors were interested in drilling in Alaska to increase production. They also wanted to regain control of the retail business. Environmentalists had successfully retarded the former, and minor competitors, the latter.

The Oil Crisis of 1973

Their opportunity came during the Mideast oil embargo and alleged oil shortage of 1973. Although America imported only 7% of its oil from the Mideast, and although refineries operated at less than capacity throughout 1972 and 1973, and even though the embargo did not stop hundreds of re-routed tankers from coming into the country for months after the embargo, bringing about a 6% increase in the total 1973 U.S. supply, oil and gasoline prices soon doubled. Claiming a shortage of gasoline, the majors stopped supplying off-brand independent dealers with their surpluses as they had done in the past. Simultaneously they "deactivated" a large percentage of their own brand stations leased to independent dealers. Within six months of the "crisis," a quarter of both the leased and privately owned independents were driven from business. Slowly, though, the majors began to reintroduce their own self-service "independent" stations, which sold gasoline for a few cents less than the major brand but did not offer credit or extra services.

During the year after the energy crisis, the majors increased their profits each quarter from 40% to 85% By 1975, Exxon (Standard Oil conglomerate) with $45.1 billion in revenues during 1974 had replaced General Motors as the nation's richest corporation, and five out of the top seven companies were oil firms. The Federal Trade

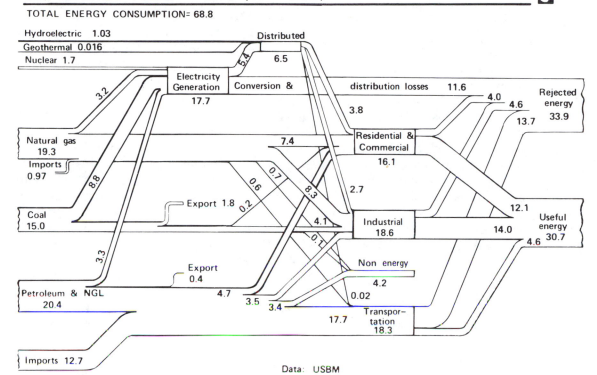

Figure 17–7. Energy-flow patterns from original conversion through the United States environment. All values are in units of 10^{15} British Thermal Units. As the chart indicates, more energy was rejected (wasted) than was used. The United States has about 6% of the world's population, but it uses about 35% of the energy used in the world and nearly 40% of the world's natural resources. Courtesy the Energy Research group, Lawrence Livermore Laboratory.

Commission released a study in July 1973 indicating that the majors were attempting to manipulate prices, and a Federal Grand Jury reported that five of them—Exxon, Mobil, Shell, Gulf, and Texaco, along with smaller firms—overcharged utilities by millions of dollars by mixing cheap with expensive oil and by making complicated paper transactions as a tanker was enroute to an oil port so that customs invoices and records could be doctored and prices raised. The price gouge was passed on to electric customers in Jacksonville, Boston, Los Angeles, and other localities.

Gasoline customers suffered long waits at service stations, during which times they heard on their radios that only higher production levels of oil at home could assure the country of adequate supplies in the future. Within a year after the embargo, the Alaskan pipeline was approved and the majors used some of their billions of dollars of extra investment money to pour into expansion.

Part of the extra money went into new fleets of gargantuan supertankers called VLCCs (very large crude carriers), most weighing over 300,000 tons and carrying over 500,000 deadweight tons (six barrels to a ton, forty-two gallons to a barrel) of crude oil. Although VLCCs cost upward of $60,000,000, they represent the most profitable way to carry oil. But they are involved in over a thousand accidents a year, a few every day somewhere in the world. In *Supership*, Noel Mostert tells an Orwellian tale of how VLCCs blow up or split asunder and spew millions of gallons of crude oil into the sea, sometimes running aground or pulverizing small ships. Risks involved with VLCCs dwarf anything before them; whatever beaches were befouled and millions of birds or marine life killed before the oil crisis will most likely be compounded a hundredfold in the future. More ominous is the difficulty with which the toxicity of the larger spills is dissolved, since a large quantity of the protein of the world comes from the fish which live in the continental shelf waters over which the VLCCs float.

Unlike the first half of the century, when virtually every town had a good public transportation system of electric trolleys, the post-oil-crisis commuter has few options other than the automobile. Because of a complicated concatenation of events, subsidies, rapid social affluence, and the personal freedom the automobile brings, the 1970s brought commuters to a point where they can scarcely afford to drive to their jobs. It should be noted that the auto/oil complex had a hand in this dilemma also. For example, National City Lines—a holding company owned by General Motors, Firestone, Phillips Petroleum, Standard Oil of California, and Mack Truck—bought out forty-six transportation systems across the country during the forties, then began to dismantle rail operations and switch over to busses manufactured by the owners. Although convicted of criminal conspiracy in 1949, National continued to reduce service until it divested itself of the remaining fragments of the system in the sixties. Only the auto was left—and a sparkling highway system.

The most damaging constraint of the Highway Trust Fund is that federal gasoline tax money must go into the construction of new highways, just as the gasoline taxes of most states are earmarked. Public transportation systems which could lower pollution levels may not partake of these funds. Instead, rich and valuable land is covered with highways which cut wider and wider swaths through wilderness areas, benefiting a relatively few trucking companies or residents who can save a few miles with a new highway. More than 60% of the total land area of most American cities is devoted to the movement and storage of automobiles.

Federal Leases

As long as production in Alaska or the outer Continental shelf of the United States is expanded—now accomplished facts—the power of the oil cartel will be strengthened, since only the majors have the immense amounts of capital needed for exploration and production. As an incentive to further competition, some Congressmen have recommended royalty bidding for new exploration sites rather than bonus bidding, which requires a large initial lump sum paid to the federal government. Other legislators have insisted on the purchase of foreign crude oil by the federal government in order to prevent swindles and also to increase public revenues rather than cartel coffers. Still others want the enforcement of the Clayton Act, which forbids mergers of coal and oil industries. None of these alternatives have been yet seriously considered by Congress, however.

A study done for the American Public Power Association, the National Rural Electric Cooperative Association, and other consumer groups has shown that in the 1970s many oil companies have used surplus profits to buy out coal companies, and four of the top fifteen coal companies, which control half the nation's production, are owned by oil companies. Coal prices jumped 282% between 1955 and 1974 (670% between 1973 and 1974), and as oil and coal ownership consolidates, the oil companies will be able to determine energy prices from either source, independent of costs, demand, or usual economic criteria. Furthermore, major oil companies have begun to dominate the nation's geothermal resources—underground reservoirs of steam which are harnessed to power electrical dynamos. Shell, Gulf, Union, Standard of California, Getty, Philips, and Sun all have large lease holdings on the geothermal fields of California.

The increased riches of the oil companies have not stopped the widespread practice of cheating the government out of millions of dollars of oil and gas royalties from federal leases. The US Geological Survey administers 12,400 producing oil and gas wells on federal and Indian lands, and a 1975 Department of Interior audit of royalty-accounting practices showed the government to be regularly shortchanged because no checks exist to determine the exact amount of oil or gas that is extracted and because oil and gas companies often report and pay royalties late, a practice which boosts interest rates for the government, since it must borrow to make up for late payments.

Oil companies also have been able to reach left-handed into the rich navy oil reserves in Elk Hills and Buena Vista Hills, California (created in 1912), Teapot Dome, Wyoming (1915), and an area near the North Slope of Alaska known as "NPR-4" (1923). Teapot Dome, of course, was the site of an earlier scandal involving navy reserves. In 1921 President Harding's secretary of the navy, Edwin Denby, transferred their control to the Department of the Interior, where the secretary, Albert Fall, secretly leased Teapot Dome to Harry Sinclair and Elk Hills to Edward Doheny. The Supreme Court eventually cancelled the leases in 1927.

In the early 1960s, the oil companies found a much simpler way to get at the navy oil by drilling around the edges of the pool. Because drilling into a common pool has the effect of creating a liquid "landslide," the navy had no alternative but to sink "off-set wells" on its side of the property to maintain a balance of pressure and not lose its own oil. The navy lost a court suit against Standard of California (Socal) over this practice at Elk Hills in 1973, but at the same time hired Socal to do the drilling for the government when it was forced to drill offset wells. The game also was played at Teapot Dome and in Alaska, where the now-famous North-Slope oil fields are being drilled. Finally, late in 1975, Congress approved a bill to start pumping oil from the Elk Hills reserve.

One of the few Federal Trade Commission lawsuits of the 1970s was against the vertical integration of the majors, i.e., their control from the wellhead to the filling station. The argument of the cartel was strikingly similar to that of the 1911 Standard Oil case: that monopoly is more efficient, that it brings better products less expensively, that the organization of the oil industry helps the country maintain its standard of living.

Timber in the United States

In 1973, complaints about timber shortages echoed the louder, more deafening alarms sounded because of the oil crisis. The prices of both commodities doubled their 1970 levels, and allocations were forced on unhappy buyers. But unlike the oil crisis, the shortage of available lumber was real. And also unlike oil, timber is renewable. Other parallels can be seen in the dual crisis. Part of the problem involved a foreign nation; small loggers are being squeezed out of business; technology has made far greater resource exploitation possible; some increase of economic concentration has occurred; and the Forest Service is currently defending its policies in a legal battle with the preservationist wing of the conservation movement.

The timber story began after World War II. Japan's forests had been severely over-cut during the war and the country could not meet its reconstruction needs. In an attempt to forestall trade agreements between Japan and Communist nations, General Douglas MacArthur, commander of the Allied Powers in Tokyo, requested timber from the Alaskan national forests on behalf of Japanese leaders. In 1957 the Forest Service was directed to contract with a Japanese firm, the Alaska Lumber and Pulp Company, to lumber and process 5,250,000,000 board feet of timber over a period of fifty years from the Baranof and Chichagof Islands in the Tongass National Forest in Alaska. Since that time Japanese firms have begun to cut private forest lands and presently to import almost three-quarters of the entire Alaskan forest yield.

During the same period, other events and factors have led to increasing U.S. exports to Japan. For example, Japan was eager to buy young-growth trees that foresters had cut in regular thinning operations to let in sun for the healthy trees. California law, which made timber taxable after forty years, spurred many owners to sell the same kind of young-growth trees to Japanese buyers. Then, in 1962, a Columbus Day storm blew down more trees along the Pacific coast than mills could handle, and these were readily exported. Before long, well-established commercial timber connections, based on higher prices and foreign policy commitments, were made between the United States and Japan.

Exports continued to rise in the 1970s, up to 2,500,000,000 board feet and 2,500,000 tons of wood chips a year to Japan and 1,000,000,000 board feet to other countries of the world. In the late sixties, retail prices for lumber in the United States began a rapid acceleration because of unforeseen increase of housing starts following lower government interest rates. From 1 1/2 million units a year in the sixties, the number went up to two million in 1971, and 2.4 million in 1972. During that year, the United States used 14.2 billion cubic feet of wood, enough to pave the country with two-by-fours. A third of it was needed by the housing industry; another third went to wood products; and the final third to pulp mills for paper, rayon, cellophane, explosives, and plastics.

Corporate Technologies

In the seventies, the small "peckerwood" logger found it hard to compete with large firms which owned the expensive equipment needed to cut all marketable timber

SOURCES OF AMERICAN ABUNDANCE **395**

economically and quickly with a minimum of mill loss in sawdust and chips. The big timber companies use chipping headsaws that can slice up logs as large as eight inches in diameter into usable lumber and electronic scanners which measure the log and feed exact information into computers that plot critical cuts maximizing lumber yield. Electromagnetic controls prevent new razor-thin saw blades from developing destructive and wasteful wobble and at the same time increase efficiency by 10% or more. This kind of outlay runs into millions of dollars but can make the difference between a year of profits or losses.

Since the revolutionary portable chain saw was introduced in the 1940s, timber cutting has become increasingly mechanized. Loggers are capable of clearing and shipping hundreds of acres of small pines in a few weeks with tractor-like harvesters, operated by a single person, which cut down, clean limbs, saw trunks into measures of 6 1/2 feet, and bundle them for later pickup by truck. In larger fir forests, powerful chain saws make short work of the huge trees and giant diesel yarders carry hundreds of logs a day to landings where lifts load them onto trucks.

Although thousands of small firms still cut and manufacture timber throughout the country, large corporations like the Pacific coast Weyerhauser Company, which owns 5,700,000 acres (1% of all commercial forest land, including national forests), are extending their forest land holdings to a greater extent each year. In the decade after 1963, they added 10,300,000 acres of land to their 22,000,000 acres in the South. Yet industrial lumber corporations own only 14% of the total commercial forest land of the nation. The national forests hold 18%; other public land 9%; and small farms and miscellaneous holdings, 59%.

The large firms usually clear-cut large areas, burn over the ground to sterilize it, plant seedlings, fertilize, use repellents to keep away deer, and thin the growing trees. In this way, corporation forest managers figure that they reduce growing time from 80-100 to 40 years. University experimenters often assist corporations in their efforts to breed tall, straight, fast- growing, genetically improved trees for plantations that can be easily machine-harvested.

Rise in Demand for Timber

Even with reforestation and timber plantations, the United States imported the equivalent of almost 3,800,000,000 cubic feet of timber in 1982, more than double the 1,700,000,000 exported by the nation. Hardwood, veneer, and plywood from Japan, the Philippines, Taiwan, and Korea made up 60% of America's total consumption of those products, and Canada contributed 22% of the softwood (pine, fir, etc.) products used by the country. Net imports totaled 11% of the country's consumption of wood in 1972.

Between 1942 and 1982, timber demand has risen by 85% and the figure continues to soar. The Forest Service hopes American output will increase by means of expanded tree planting with faster-growing timber, more efficient technologies, reforestation, and more intensified management on small private holdings where most of the nation's forests lie. Increased pressure on the Forest Service, which holds discretionary power over public timber, to release more public forest lands for commercial purposes has been thwarted primarily because of their "even-flow" policy and the Multiple Use-Sustained Yield Act of 1960 which requires the service to allow only as many trees cut as can be indefinitely sustained by replanting. Furthermore, during the 1970s, Congress has refused to appropriate money for additional reforestation despite an annual revenue of upwards of $500,000,000 for timber from the national forests.

Despite claims of sustained-yield practices, the total amount of standing timber in large lumber-company holdings has declined by 32% in the past twenty years. In the heavily lumbered state of Oregon, for instance, a Library of Congress study shows that lumbering of virgin timber is going on at a rate five times greater than new timber can grow. This imbalance is one reason for pressure for government timber.

Conservationists have opposed further cutting than present levels and have held up the cutting of over 8,750,000,000 board feet in the Tongass National Forest of Alaska, claiming that the Forest Service violated the Multiple Use-Sustained Yield Act of 1960, which requires that the national forests be managed for recreation, range, watershed and the enhancement of wildlife as well as for timber supplies, "not necessarily (for) the greatest dollar return or greatest unit output" of timber. The Sierra Club and Sitka Conservation Society argued, "the Tongass has great resources of deer, bear, and eagle, has magnificent hunting and scenic splendor, and has streams vital to the watershed." The plaintiffs also appealed to the Organic Act of 1897, repealed in 1976, which states that only designated, mature trees are permitted to be cut, challenging the Forest Service's permission for clear-cutting the area, slightly larger than the state of Rhode Island. They further argued the possibility of damage to the soil from erosion brought about by the use of heavy logging tractors and by exposure to heavy winds and rains.

The 1969 National Environmental Policy Act, which requires an environmental impact statement and a public hearing on any federal act which may have an impact on the environment, has also been utilized to stop clear-cutting operations. NEPA has become the mainstay piece of legislation for environmentalists wishing to stop timbercutting, or canal, highway, and other construction or marshland drainage, but such actions are only stop-gap. The deeper question deals with long-range planning and whether or not American society is willing to pay the price of continued economic growth and abundance. National guidelines for future forest use would permit a clear assessment regarding how much timber would be harvested; how it would be harvested; how much timber would be exported; and which forests would be preserved for wilderness. Both alternatives—monopoly control by timber interests and the Forest Service, and the criteria of economic growth—have proved inadequate determinants for forest use in the past.

Conservation of Resources of the Sea

The conservation of sea resources has proved to be even more problematic than timber or fossil fuel questions, since the matter involves the interests of great and small world powers. Because the oceans beyond the territorial limits of nations are considered "high seas," no one country can unilaterally decide whether or not to conserve or protect the fish and whale resources of the oceans.

Whales are more vulnerable to over-exploitation in the open seas, since smaller fish are confined to areas over the continental shelves where plankton is abundant. Since the invention of the harpoon gun and the utilization of the steam-powered whale catcher in 1864 by the Norwegian Svend Foyn, whale populations have declined. Blue and finback baleen whales, for example, had been too huge and fast to be chased and killed by handthrowing harpoons from small whaleboats at a time when whalers could take in only about one whale a month.

By the end of the 1800s the bowhead and right whales, both baleens, were close to extinction. The blue (the largest animal ever known to have existed on earth), humpback, and gray whales have been reduced to less than 10% of their nineteenth century numbers. In the past fifty years, about 200,000,000 whales have been killed for fertilizer, cosmetics, mink food, and lubricating oil. As the larger species have been decimated, the whaling industry has begun to exploit smaller sei and sperm whales. The industry uses helicopters to scout, sonar scanners to detect, and speedy catcher boats to run down and kill whales with powerful weapons. Catcher boats then transfer the whales to giant factory ships that process whale meat and oil, and even can, freeze, and package their cargoes en route to home ports.

In 1970, Secretary of the Interior Walter Hickel placed eight species of whale—the finback, sei, sperm, bowhead, blue, humpback, right, and gray—on the endangered species list under the Endangered Species Preservation Act of 1966, amended in 1969, which forbids buying, selling, or importing fish or wildlife (and products made from them) threatened with extinction. The secretary of the interior is authorized to compile a list of the endangered animals or fish. By the end of 1971, the last of the U.S. whaling licenses were cancelled. Although the International Whaling Commission has banned whaling throughout the world, commission has no enforcement power over nations such as the Soviet Union and Japan, which continue whaling activities at reduced levels. Conservation groups have continued to pressure the United States government to boycott goods from countries that kill whales.

According to whale experts, it is likely that the bowhead whale, which lives in Alaskan waters, will fall to extinction by the end of the century. Native Alaskan Indians are permitted to hunt the bowhead amid great controversy among conservationists and government officials.

The Soviet Union and Japan lead in the extraction of other fish throughout the world each year and account for almost a third of the world commercial fish catch, according to U.S. Marine Fisheries figures, recorded in millions of pounds. In 1950, only plaice, halibut, and salmon were overfished. By 1968, tuna, cod, and ocean perch had joined the ranks of depleted fish stocks.

Like the efficient technologies of the whalers, the heavily capitalized foreign fishing fleets are capable of processing hundreds of thousands of tons of fish, with factory ships traveling alongside trawlers many thousands of miles away from their home ports. Also as in the whaling industries, sophisticated technologies like sonar devices detect schools of fish for small- mesh nets to drag in entire colonies, enclosing young and mature fish alike. Soviet vessels also attract crustaceans such as the krill by utilizing an electrical field around an underwater pipe which sucks in the fish.

United States fishermen are only fifth in the world fish-catch standings, but American wholesale fish processers and buyers purchase two-thirds of their fish from foreign sellers each year. Fish processing is a lucrative business. It has lured many of the great food corporations like Heinz, Borden, General Mills, Consolidated Foods, Westgate Foods, Ralston Purina, and others to the enterprise. Often American processers and wholesale buyers own their own fleets or purchase fish from small American fishermen, who not uncommonly receive less than 10% of the price consumers have to pay for the fish. Fish can pass through three to five middlemen before it reaches the customer. Yet less and less of the world fish catch is eaten by humans. Between World War II and 1967, the percentage of fish converted to fishmeal for livestock and chicken consumption (to a lesser extent for fertilizer, soap, and oils) increased from 10% to 50%. The U.S. poultry industry depends on fishmeal for a third of its broiler feed, though chicken begins to develop a fishy taste if over 10% of its feed is fishmeal. Of course much of the protein value of fish is lost to humans as it passes through chicken or hogs, just as the protein value of grain is lost as it is consumed by livestock, which people prefer.

The Soviet Union and Japan have dominated world-wide competition to extract more fish from the oceans because of their willingness to invest huge amounts of money in gigantic ships and sophisticated technologies while they pursue a single-minded commercial and diplomatic policy to become the top fishers of the world. Other countries have attempted to protect themselves and to extract enough protein to feed their populations (though much of it goes to North American dogs and cats or to chicken and hog raisers) by establishing 200-mile territorial water limits. General agreements among the 148 member nations of an international Law of the Sea Commission has already been reached that each country should be empowered to forbid foreign fishermen from entering its 200-mile coastal water boundries. But implementation has been slow because of diplomatic red-tape and corporate lobbying. Many corporate processers get bargain prices from foreign fishers in U.S. waters.

The big fishing tug-of-war is only in its beginning stages and probably will become the source of future struggles. Protein from fish costs half that of the production costs of beef (though the price of fish is equal to or higher than beef in the U.S.). Fishing is becoming more profitable as farming costs go up. Thus the money flows into fishing enterprises, which are supported by the persistent myth that the world fish supply is inexhaustible. The result is the continued extraction of more fish than can replenish themselves, especially among cod, flounder, tuna, ocean perch, and other traditional stocks. Even stocks of dolphins are depleted—well over 100,000 of them each year—because fishermen gather them in with schools of yellow fin tuna which instinctively swim just below three species of dolphin in the South Pacific. Dolphins indicate the places where tuna may be caught; high powered speed boats are launched from the mother ship and chase the frightened dolphins into a tight circle; the mother ship then throws a net over the entire area and draws it in, drowning dolphins and killing tuna together. Despite federal regulations limiting gill net fishing, thousands of dolphins are killed along with tuna every year.

Agriculture and Agribusiness

Two outstanding facts dominate the riddle of contemporary agriculture. The first is that the Jeffersonian values of an agrarian democracy of small landowners—ideals that have so strongly influenced public policy since the 1700s—have faded into the background of American society and been replaced by values of the superfarm and supermarket. The second is that no economic segment of the nation has contributed to much wealth to the country by its man-hour productivity and yet received so few economic rewards as the farming community.

That the agrarian ideal has collapsed can be demonstrated by looking at rural population declines: from 13,600,000 in 1920, down slightly to 11,000,000 in 1940, 10,000,000 in 1950, then all the way to about 4,000,000 in 1970, while the total population of the country was climbing to 200,000,000. About 22,000,000 people migrated from rural to urban areas between 1940 and 1960, after which time the rate slowed to about 750,000 a year. In 1935 there were 6,800,000 farms in the country; the number dropped to below 3,000,000 in 1970. Before World War I, agriculture accounted for 30% of the work force; in the 1970s, less than 5% work on farms. The number is steadily declining and will probably hold at about 3%. This group is called upon to feed over 230,000,000 Americans and many millions more around the globe; more remarkably, they manage to pile up surpluses each year. Despite this achievement, the few people left on family farms often live in pockets of poverty or near-poverty conditions in sections of each farm belt. The reason for the demise of the family farm and the Jeffersonian dream lies in the difficulty of earning a decent living on a small scale farming operation.

Nonetheless, the rise in agricultural productivity between 1940 and 1970 has been remarkable. Using the years 1957-59 as an index of 100, in 1940, farm output per man-hour was 36, in 1970, it shot to 190. In 1940, crop production per acre was 76; in 1970, production was up to 130. During this time the cropland utilized fell from 103 to 94. In the non-farm sector, productivity was less than three-quarters that of agriculture from 1957 to 1970.

Research, mechanization, and enormous capital investments account for many of the gains. For example, research on corn yields has continued since the 1920s and yields have averaged about twenty-six bushels an acre until World War II By the late fifties, the average rose to forty-nine bushels, in 1969 up to eighty-four. In the 1970s, many areas average over a hundred bushels an acre. Furthermore, before the war 108 man-hours were needed for every hundred bushels; by 1970, fewer than nine.

Other factors have made such productivity possible, especially irrigation. When irrigated, new strains of cotton have yielded over 1,000 pounds an acre. But not all areas of the country enjoy the benefits of publicly funded irrigation works. In the South, for example, small farmers cannot compete with large irrigated cotton operations in California, Arizona, and west Texas. In the western states, irrigated areas covered 18,000,000 acres in 1939; the total was over 40,000,000 acres by 1970.

Between 1934 and 1970, all farm inputs except labor increased. Using 1957-59 as an index of 100 again, mechanical power rose from 32 to 118; fertilizer and lime use from 14 to 220; feed, seed and livestock purchases from 24 to 149. Farm labor dropped

Figure 17–8. Modern agricultural equipment. Sophisticated technology is needed for corporate farming. This fleet of five grain harvesters remains in formation as it cuts and threshes more than 700 acres of wheat a day—a far cry from the plodding harvester with his cradle. Trucks drive alongside the harvesters to receive the threshed grain, while chaff and straw are ejected behind the machines. In the photo to the left, trucks are used to haul rice already cut and threshed by rice combines.

from 190 to 65. In 1900, every farm worker could feed seven people; by 1940 he could provide for eleven; in the early 1970s he could supply at least forty-five. In 1976, one farm worker supplied food for 56 people.

The Rise of Corporate Farming

Mechanization and mass-production have characterized agriculture since the late 1950s. Celery harvesters can cut, trim, wash, and crate thousands of plants a day. The new combines cut, separate, and bag more than a hundred acres every day; owners of huge wheat farms often contract fleets of combine operators who start in Texas and cut their way to the Dakotas harvesting the nation's wheat. The tomato harvester cuts the plants underground, pulls them into its bosom with metal fingers, and shakes off the fruit into troughs where workers sort them out. The machine took

Modern tomato harvesters use a driver, a foreman, and a crew of a dozen workers who package the tomatoes and place them on a conveyor to a tractor-drawn loader. In order for these and similar harvesting operations to work, plants had to be bred that ripened crops simultaneously and that otherwise had to be adapted to the machines. Courtesy California Cooperative Extension.

a dozen years of research at the University of California at Davis by plant geneticist G. C. Hanna, who had to breed a plant whose fruit would ripen all at once and would stand being firmly and easily shaken off. Agricultural engineer Colby Lorenzen, whose problems with dirt and tomato smashing were endless, worked with Hanna. By the mid-1940s, after a generation of development, a new spindle cotton picker (utilizing a large spindled drum) was marketed, an accomplishment which needed the breeding of a variety of cotton whose bolls matured uniformly and simultaneously. Man hours on cotton fields were cut from about 150 to 25 per acre.

Examples could be multiplied. Farms with 2,000,000 egg-laying hens demand 100,000 gallons of water every day. Those crops which have not yet been completely mechanized are already at experiment stations or in laboratories where researchers are patiently solving the last few problems.

Small farmers have a difficult time paying for the higher costs of essentials like fertilizer and gasoline for their tractors or the increasing taxes on their land. Some

LAND USE IN THE 50 STATES

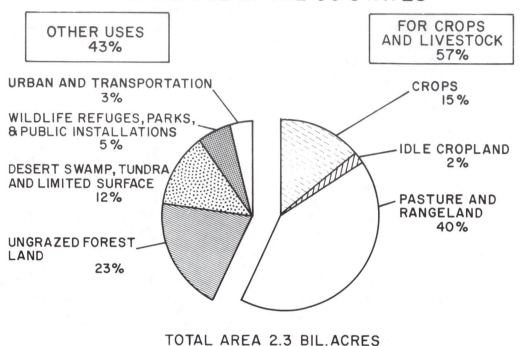

OTHER USES
43%

FOR CROPS
AND LIVESTOCK
57%

URBAN AND TRANSPORTATION
3%

WILDLIFE REFUGES, PARKS,
& PUBLIC INSTALLATIONS
5%

DESERT SWAMP, TUNDRA
AND LIMITED SURFACE
12%

UNGRAZED FOREST
LAND
23%

CROPS
15%

IDLE CROPLAND
2%

PASTURE AND
RANGELAND
40%

TOTAL AREA 2.3 BIL. ACRES

Figure 17–9. American land use. This graph, from United States Department of Agriculture sources, suggests that the working cropland of this country supports many millions of people with a comparatively small commitment of land because of capital-intensive agricultural techniques, mechanization, pesticides, and fertilizers. The environmental problems are increasing, however, along with the number of corporate farms.

manage to expand; most move out of farming and sell out to larger neighbors. Thus, although the number of farms is decreasing, their average size has been increasing—from 155 acres in 1935 to 380 in 1970. More revealing is the fact that less than 5% of all farms own well over half the nation's land under cultivation.

The movement toward mechanization and mass-production has led to corporate farming, with billion-dollar corporations now buying and farming vast tracts of land, especially in California; and agribusiness—corporations which are vertically integrating agriculture by both buying the farmer's goods for processing and marketing and selling farm goods like fertilizers, pesticides, machinery, etc., and giving credit to boot. Agricultural researcher A V Krebs defines agribusiness as "the combination of corporations engaged in the cultivation of land for the raising and production of crops and livestock (agricultural production); corporations which finance agriculture or are engaged in the manufacturing, transporting, wholesaling and distribution of farm machinery, fertilizers, pesticides, seed, feed and packaging material (agricultural inputs); and corporations engaged in the manufacturing, processing and marketing of food (agricultural outputs)."

Corporations like Standard Oil of California, Aetna Life and Casualty Co., RCA, U.S. Steel, Burlington Northern, LTV, Pacific Lighting, Tenneco, Greyhound, Occidental petroleum, Dow Chemical, Boeing, and Connecticut General Life Insurance have gone into farming. Tenneco, an oil and pipeline conglomerate, now has the biggest farming operation in the country and is the thirty-eighth largest corporation as well. They boast that they control a complete food supply from "seedling to supermarket."

According to 1964 U.S. Department of Agriculture figures, in five states corporate farms do the preponderance of agricultural business: 89% in Arizona; 79% in California; 70% in Nevada; 63% in New Mexico; and 57% in Colorado. When a large corporate farm specializes in a product, it can undersell its competition. In California, for example, the Federal Trade Commission has charged United Brands and Purex for attempting to monopolize the production of fresh vegetables. Many smaller lettuce growers of the Salinas Valley of California have sold out to United, Purex, and Bud Antle (Dow Chemical) because of the pressure of the corporate farms.

With their large financial reserves these companies are determining the future of agriculture in the United States; and as in other monopolistic ventures, if they are wasteful or inefficient, they need not sell out to a corporate competitor, as a small farmer would be forced to do.

Most agribusiness firms are connected to food processors and distributors, the top end of the vertically integrated system. These groups are tending toward oligopolies. They manage to charge higher prices, though farmers continue to receive low payments. Concentration in the food industry has developed particularly in grains and milk. As early as 1966, the four largest firms in cereal preparations controlled 87% of the market; the four largest in bread and prepared flour, 75%; biscuits, crackers and cookies, 70%; wet corn milling, 67%; fluid milk, 60%. In 1972, a Federal Trade Commission report asserted that consumers are overcharged $2,100,000,000 a year because of monopolies in thirteen food lines including the abovementioned grains and milk plus meat-packing, canned fruits and vegetables, frozen fruits and vegetables, cane sugar refining, and others.

Monopoly control in canned and frozen fruits, nuts, and wet milk is achieved primarily through co-ops of growers who have limited production through yearly determined marketing orders. Growers in cooperatives can set artificially high prices while they collectively control markets, as they do in fruit, nut, and milk production. The Federal Trade Commission reported in 1975 that the California Canning Peach Association dominates the canning peach industry with 46% of the market share; the California Almond Growers hold 70% of the market; Sunsweet Growers Inc. has 50% of the dried-prune market; Sunkist Growers maintains a hold on 88% of the California-Arizona lemons and 75% of the California-Arizona oranges; Ocean Spray Cranberries dominates 85% of the cranberry industry. The Commission found that because of marketing orders, retail prices have been artificially raised in these industries, and tens of thousands of tons of fruit have been left on the ground to rot each year. Thus even these representatives of the cooperative movement, which stands for one of the few hopeful possibilities of a rational and equitable use of resources in the future, manifest irrational economic concerns of monopoly power as management-oriented giants rather than the common good of small growers. Voting power of these cooperatives is not based on a one-person one-vote system but on size and production capacity.

However, most small farmers do not enjoy monopoly protection. Rather, both as consumers and buyers, they have been at the mercy of monopolies. Farmers are no longer the self-sufficient yeoman of colonial days. They need capital equipment that runs into the hundreds of thousands of dollars, lots of credit, wire, seeds, fertilizer, and dozens of other items. Large corporations are ready to sell them what they need: Bank of America (production loans), Upjohn Co. (seeds), the Williams Companies (fertilizer), International Minerals & Chemical (pesticides), Ford Motor Co. (machinery), Firestone (tires), Ralston Purina (feeder pigs), Merck & Co. (poultry stock), Cargil (feed), Dow Chemical (cartons and wrappings), Eli Lilly (animal drugs), Exxon (farm fuels) and Burlington Northern (rail transportation). Many of these corporations, especially in petroleum, tires, chemicals, and rail transport, have oligopolistic control of their markets. On the other side of the contract, as we have seen above, farmers have to sell their products to monopolized companies such as the four largest grain companies, which do most of the buying and selling of grain in the world, or agribusiness firms, which sometimes offer them credit deals.

Therefore the spectacular productivity of agriculture has not redounded to the material benefit of the producing farmers. Even the $20,000,000,000 worth of farm commodity price supports have helped small farmers very little, since subsidies are paid in proportion to production, with the largest subsidies going to corporate farms. California millionaire grower J. G. Boswell received over $6,000,000 in subsidies from the federal government in 1970, and about $10,000,000 in 1986. The corporate farmers also benefit from federally funded irrigation projects, which the unenforced Reclamation Act of 1902 stipulates must service only 160-acre holdings. Land grant college research has mostly benefited large growers in its bias toward mechanization for very large tracts of farm land, and profitability studies for food processors and distributors. Little effort by researchers serves the needs of small producers on limited acreages, e.g., methods of cooperative buying and selling, improving and farming small tracts, etc.

With the weight of economic concentration against them, it is small wonder that small farm operators find it difficult to maintain their holdings. When farmers move out of depressed rural communities, the small businessmen who served them have to close down as well. It is clear that even after a hundred years of struggle, small farmers as a class have not been able to achieve economic justice.

References for Further Reading

A good summary of contemporary American natural resource use can be found in Robert Estall's *Modern Geography of the United States* (1972). *The Structure of America's Industry*, edited by Walter Adams (1961), illustrates the development of monopolies in resource and other industries after World War II. *Scientific Technology and Social Change* (1974), a collection of articles from *Scientific American*, traces the influence of scientific discovery and technological innovation on society and is particularly valuable for its essays on energy and the trenchant introductions to each section written by the book's editor, Gene I. Rochlin. *Affluence in Jeopardy: Minerals and the Political Economy* by Charles F. Park (1968) shows the distribution of mineral resources in America and the rest of the world and the political implications of their depletion. *New Energy* by James Ridgeway and Bettina Conner (1975) and *Making Democracy Safe for Oil* by Christopher Rand (1975) provide an excellent background to the oil crisis and the major energy producers. Three books on the recent struggles of the National Forest and Park Service are Dennis C. LeMaster's *Decade of Change: The Remaking of Forest Service Statutory Authority during the 1970s* (1984); David A. Clary's *Timber and the Forest Service* (1987); and Ronald A. Foresta's *America's National Parks and Their Keepers* (1987). *Playing God at Yellowstone* by Alston Chase (1986) investigates the role of Park Service policy changes at Yellowstone that the author blames for a widespread decline in wildlife in the park. A.V. Krebs' monumental synthesis of agricultural history and policy, *The Corporate Reapers: Eradicating the Family Farm System in America* (1987) (Myndseye, P.O. Box 171, The Plains, VA 22171), contains an exhaustive survey of past agricultural policy impacts as well as a trenchant contemporary analysis. *The Unsettling of America: Culture and Agriculture* by Wendell Berry (1977) highlights the connections between agriculture and human institutions such as the family farm in a book that complements Krebs' argument.

Chapter 18

THE POLITICS OF POLLUTION

After World War II a new constituency began to emerge in the American environmental movement, outside of the inner circle of conservation thought. Urban sprawl and industrial pollution began to take their toll on the populace, and events pushed Americans little by little to a deeper concern for the natural environment. Conservation of natural resources gradually became transformed into environmental protection, less at the level of local politics, more on the level of a wider national consciousness.

Before the 1950s and 1960s, the policy emphasis, particularly in the federal government, was on efficient use of natural resources, especially land (soil), timber, water, and minerals, rather than on environmental protection of water, wilderness, and air, or even protection of human health. Very few efforts were directed toward environmental protection on a national level. It is remarkable that so few policymakers even suggested it, considering the widespread outcries about the possibility of "timber famines" or other natural resource disasters. The vast majority of Americans did not perceive clean air and water as threatened, though many scattered local efforts were made in the cities to protect the public health with better and safer water systems.

But after the war, such social developments as rapid population growth, increased air and water pollution and traffic congestion, and much faster consumption rates of dozens of new products made of new chemical compounds took conservation consciousness into a new stage of political activity—the efficient use of natural resources but also a new politics of environmental pollution. But the fact that the federal government was not accustomed to addressing environmental problems, even those that crossed state lines, restrained its involvement in local or state problems. So the unhappy result has been two generations of uneven, overlaid environmental regulations and equally erratic state and local enforcement. The reasons can be found in the nature of environmental politics since World War II.

Urban Growth and New Consumerism

Early in the 1950s, dozens of new metropolitan areas in all sections of the country suddenly emerged. From 1950 to 1960, U.S. cities with over 50,000 people grew by an average of 65 percent. Many cities doubled or tripled in size seemingly overnight. The forced saving during the war, when consumer goods were not available, created a pent-up demand for appliances, housing, and consumer goods. This led to a quick retooling of war industries to peacetime production. On the promise of jobs, former servicemen took their families to these large urban areas. Cheap GI loans enabled tens of thousands of ex-servicemen to buy homes, and they also received funds to attend college.

The idea that the American masses were entitled to a wide range of consumer goods was fairly new. Some of the emerging middle classes had gotten a taste of the good life and home conveniences during the 1920s with the inauguration of easy credit and the siren portrayal of consumer values in newspapers, magazines, and, especially, the movies. A growing inventory of items—homes, wringer washing machines, gas stoves, carpet sweepers, indoor plumbing, automobiles, watches, and others—became within credit reach of virtually all of the expanding middle class.

The 1950s were marked by massive federal redevelopment efforts to wipe out slums and other old sections of large cities and to spend billions on highways connecting the growing metropolitan regions. The entire country caught freeway fever, and within a generation many of the nation's old downtown sections were torn down, rebuilt, or paved over.

The required land and resulting congestion of streets, highways, housing, waste disposal, airports, new factories, commercial areas, and other ingredients of modern metropolitan regions soon provoked political reactions and generated new environmental controversies. Farms, increasing their production to feed a new, increasingly affluent, hungrier population, used more and more artificial fertilizers and pesticides, mainly DDT It was a short generation before problems of the natural environment, ranging from a new burst of air, water, waste, and land-fill pollution to a variety of wilderness despoilments, touched every corner of the nation.

One of the first national battles of the decade took place over the proposed damming of the Green River at Echo Park in the 320-square-mile Dinosaur National Monument of the Colorado-Utah border. The area, designated by Woodrow Wilson as a national monument in 1915 because of its prehistoric dinosaur fossils, also was blessed (or cursed) with the kind of deep, narrow gorge at Echo Park that hydraulic engineers seek out for dams, especially in the West. As the country grew, engineers and planners kept looking for newer and larger sources of water supplies and hydroelectric power. Per capita use of water in the cities grew at exponential rates, doubling every 6 to 10 years.

During the 1940s, the federal Bureau of Reclamation developed a comprehensive plan for a 10-dam Colorado River Storage Project to meet the water demands of the booming Southwest. Political support for the project after the war seemed universal. Secretary of the Interior Oscar L Chapman held a public hearing on the Echo Park Dam in 1950 and recommended that, "in the interest of the greatest public good," Echo Park be included in the project. The entire Colorado project, however, had to be approved by Congress.

The Sierra Club and the Wilderness Society both were active during the period. Urban chapters steadily increased their memberships because people were becoming more interested in getting out of noisy, hot, congested cities for trips into more peaceful, refreshing wilderness areas. Gradually, beginning in the 1940s, more and more people were looking for non-material amenities. In an effective national campaign against the proposed Echo Park dam, through articles in publications such as *Life, Newsweek,* and the *Saturday Evening Post,* as well as in conservation magazines,

THE NUCLEAR FUEL CYCLE

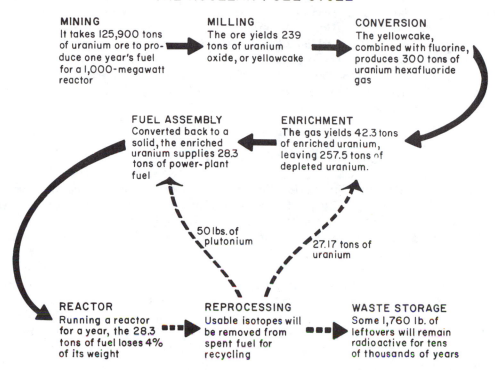

MINING
It takes 125,900 tons of uranium ore to produce one year's fuel for a 1,000-megawatt reactor

MILLING
The ore yields 239 tons of uranium oxide, or yellowcake

CONVERSION
The yellowcake, combined with fluorine, produces 300 tons of uranium hexafluoride gas

FUEL ASSEMBLY
Converted back to a solid, the enriched uranium supplies 28.3 tons of power-plant fuel

ENRICHMENT
The gas yields 42.3 tons of enriched uranium, leaving 257.5 tons of depleted uranium.

50 lbs. of plutonium

27.17 tons of uranium

REACTOR
Running a reactor for a year, the 28.3 tons of fuel loses 4% of its weight

REPROCESSING
Usable isotopes will be removed from spent fuel for recycling

WASTE STORAGE
Some 1,760 lb. of leftovers will remain radioactive for tens of thousands of years

Figure 18–1. Environmental risks of the nuclear fuel cycle. Risks involved with nuclear energy include more than plant explosions, as at Chernobyl. Note the item returning to "Fuel Assembly" from "Reprocessing." Those 50 pounds of plutonium are now the subject of strenuous debate. Transportation proves very difficult, and security nearly impossible, in the face of extremists and terrorists who now have the technology to convert the plutonium into nuclear explosives for blackmail. Also, note the "Waste Storage" item. Nobody has yet found a safe and satisfactory way to store the waste, some of which has a half-life of over 20,000 years.

club leaders tapped this desire for wilderness. They used non-economic arguments in full-page newspaper ads and direct mail campaigns: "Wilderness areas have become to us a spiritual necessity; an antidote to modern living"; they are needed "for our spiritual welfare;" they present a prehistoric "reservoir of stored experiences in ways of life before man;" "we deeply need the humility to know ourselves as the dependent members of a great community of life." Thousands of wilderness advocates wrote letters to congress and the secretary of the interior to protest the damming of Echo Park.

Supporters of the dam were, of course, shocked that anyone would question the desirability of economic growth, but the new environmentalists managed to have Echo Park struck out of the project bill, and Congress stated its intention that "no dam or reservoir constructed under the authorization of the Act shall be within any Park or Monument." The bill became law in April 1956. The environmentalist victory spurred further efforts for wilderness protection and other issues of wildlands, open space and outdoor recreation.

A Wilderness Act, establishing a national system of wilderness protection, took another eight years, but in 1958 Congress was ready to create the National Outdoor Recreation Review Commission. A commission report led to the Land and Water Conservation Fund, which established for the first time a continuous source of revenue for the acquisition of federal outdoor recreation lands. The momentum of the incipient wilderness movement of the Fifties gathered strength in the Sixties and led to millions of wilderness acres set aside, including not only forests, streams, and rivers but also wetlands, swamps, and pine barrens.

Water Quality Issues

Compared with dam building under the Bureau of Reclamation, the federal government role in the water pollution field had been minuscule since the turn of the century. A few states had taken the lead in pollution technology development, notably at the Massachusetts Lawrence Experiment station, and local and state boards of health were set up to regulate water pollution. The federal responsibility, however, was defined by three limited acts: the Rivers and Harbors Act of 1899, forbidding the discharge into waterways of anything hazardous to navigation; the Public Health Service Act of 1912, which authorized investigations of water pollution related to disease and public health; and the Oil Pollution Act of 1924, forbidding oil discharges in coastal waters. None of these laws was extensively utilized for water quality protection, nor were notable efforts made to enforce the laws.

During the 1930s, spurred by continued epidemics caused by known water-borne bacteria, New Dealers attempted to bring water pollution control under federal regulation through public works programs. Many states and cities were granted monies to construct waste treatment plants. This activity laid the groundwork for the Federal Water Pollution Control Act of 1948, legislation designed to expire in five years but later extended until 1956. The legislation stipulated that the primary responsibility for controlling water pollution rested with the states but gave the federal government an advisory and support role under the surgeon general of the U.S. Public Health Service. During this period, many civil and sanitary engineers, particularly those who had formed consulting firms (or those who were unemployed), joined forces with doctors, health reformers, and conservationists to lobby for water quality protection by means of water treatment plants rather than the older dilution methods.

The federal government's charge was to develop comprehensive programs with the states to reduce pollution in interstate waters, to make loans for treatment plants, and to fund state and interstate water pollution control agencies. The federal public health agency could also take enforcement action against polluters but only if a polluter in one state threatened the health or welfare of someone in another state, and if action was requested by the governor of either state. Such cumbersome action was rarely attempted.

During the 1950s, more people began to notice water pollution from both municipal and industrial sources. Sickening odors and pollution slicks in rivers and streams and fish kills, obviously from industrial sources, forced beaches and recreation areas to close. Thus, there was only scattered opposition in Congress to the 1956 Federal Water Pollution Control Act amendments, and that was regarding the nature and the amount of financial assistance, not whether aid should be given. The Isaak Walton League and other sportsmen's groups kept the pressure on Congress to stop the increasing pollution of rivers that once provided a rich harvest of fish.

The 1948 legislation was strengthened with more funds available to the states, and the laws were made permanent. The approach remained cooperative with the states, but grants instead of loans were allotted for the construction of municipal sewage treatment plants. A grants section, originally part of the 1948 bill, had been deleted because of a widespread fear of inflation at the time. Although the 1956 law had strong support in Congress, the Eisenhower administration strongly opposed the 10-year $500 million grant program and considered a veto. Instead, Eisenhower attempted to stop funding of the program through the budgetary process, again failing because Democrats in Congress—overwhelmingly in favor of the program—outnumbered Republicans two to one.

A Quickening Pace: The 1960s

Although the forties and fifties water pollution legislation was a start toward federal cooperation in cleaning up the nation's waters, it hardly scratched the surface of the problem. Democratic President John F. Kennedy wasted no time in 1961 requesting an increase in waste treatment grants. With the strong support of his party, he quickly signed a bill that doubled the previous authorization, and which expanded the federal jurisdiction over both interstate and navigable waters (including their tributaries). At the same time the bill enabled the U.S. attorney general to prosecute cases for the secretary of health, education and welfare. Thus, virtually all U.S. waters were brought under the control of the federal government pollution control program, with the power of the attorney general behind it.

The unwillingness of either the federal government or the states to assume responsibility for stringent water quality standards was one reason for building only treatment plants and continuing to research water quality. Very few states developed pollution control programs, and none contained recommendations for enforcement. During the forties and fifties, only a few pollution abatement cases reached the federal government.

These problems came to public view between 1959 and 1961 because of congressional field hearings and press reports. The Senate Select Committee of National Water Resources in 1959 and 1960 held hearings in 22 states, with dozens of witnesses calling their state's water pollution abatement efforts a dismal failure. These comments were noted in the leading newspapers, and amplified by conservation groups and the League of Women Voters.

Widely publicized at the time were: pollution in the Passaic River in New Jersey that killed thousands of fish and threatened drinking water; sewage-contaminated water in Colorado; and an HEW report that warned southwestern Colorado and northwestern New Mexico that their Animas River water was 40% to 160% above permissible levels of radioactive content. Futurist Alvin B. Toffler reported these episodes in the *Reader's Digest* (March, 1960). He concluded, "The time has come to mount an all-out effort to protect our water supply. Every citizen can play a vital part." A *U.S. News and World Report* article (Feb. 29, 1960) quoted conservationist Bernard Berger, warning that residential and industrial water pollution threatened the nation's future.

Sportsmen complained about rapidly depleting fish stocks in lakes and streams (e.g., Rusty Cowan, "Mystery of the Walleyes and the Water," [*Sports Illustrated*, Nov. 6, 1961] among many such articles in most sports magazines). A Rachel Carson article in *Redbook* (August, 1961), asked "How Safe is Your Drinking Water?" Her monumental *Silent Spring* was published in 1962 and reviewed by well-known naturalist Loren Eiseley in the *Saturday Review* (Sept. 29, 1962). Eiseley called the book a "relentless attack about human carelessness, greed, and irresponsibility—an irresponsibility that has let loose upon man and the countryside a flood of dangerous chemicals. . . ." Another significant article, "Wastes Spoil Once Pure Sources," appeared in big-circulation *Life* magazine (Dec. 22, 1961). The National Wildlife Federation, the National Audubon Society, and the Izaak Walton League mounted campaigns for a strong federal water bill.

The Water Quality Act of 1965

Congress held five public hearings for new water quality amendments, introduced by Senator Edmund Muskie, beginning in 1963 and continuing through February 1965. Muskie proposed that a new division be created inside HEW and made responsible for water quality standards by approving the states' standards. His proposal worried the oil, chemical, and pulp and paper industries, all of whom said water standards would cost them money. Many state health and water agencies also spoke out against what they considered an infringement of traditional states' rights authority on pollution questions. Industry agreed that because the states were closer to the problem than federal authorities, they could better solve it. Neither states nor industry wanted a damper on inexpensive economic expansion, even if the expansion was environmentally foolish and dangerous.

Environmental organizations and such public-spirited groups as the League of Women Voters and the National Council of Mayors spoke in favor of the bill, although most wanted a stronger bill. Finally, after two years of inter-House sparring, Congress passed the Water Quality Act of 1965, giving the HEW secretary and his new Federal Water Pollution Control Administration the power to set standards in states that did not file a letter of intent to do so within a year. Grants for waste treatment plants doubled, and a new demonstration program investigated a combined system of storm and sanitary sewers.

The following year a presidential reshuffle sent the new agency to the Department of the Interior, with HEW keeping only health-related issues of water pollution. At earlier hearings and in the press, there had been a great debate over the need for an environmental agency. Industry and state agencies said they had built up good rapport with the Public Health Service and insisted a new agency was not needed. Environmentalists and their allies responded that health personnel were not sensitive to ecological, recreational, and aesthetic concerns and, furthermore, had not proven adequately aggressive in pursuing water quality standards with the states. The concerns of the new environmentalists went beyond efficiency, and emphasized environmental amenities and responsiveness to broader public interests over matters of individual health.

The 1965 act set up for the first time a federal agency whose specific charge was water pollution control. For the first time the federal government proposed to establish and enforce, with the states, water quality standards. The agency's move to the Department of Interior was intended to enable the federal government to carry out the provision of standards more independently. The primary reason President Johnson agreed to the transfer of authority was the influence of Stewart Udall, a strong environmentalist and then secretary of the interior. Of course, the issue was far from settled. Many sportsmen and conservation groups complained that the states continued to drag their feet on major pollution problems.

Many in Congress wanted pollution control responsibility in the hands of regional watershed agencies rather than with the states. Muskie fought off these proposals, considering them too radical, but organized a coalition that pushed for more government construction grants. Congress then passed the 1966 Clean Waters Act, which also amended the 1924 Oil Pollution Act.

Oil Spill Problems

The 1966 law, mainly because of the influence of the oil industry and Rep. James Wright of Texas (elected speaker in 1987), redefined the term "discharge" to require that the discharge of oil had to be "grossly negligent or willful" before the government could bring suit against the polluter. Since willful negligence is hard to prove, enforcement against oil polluters became extremely difficult.

During 1967, a number of oil spills received wide publicity. The most notorious was the Torrey Canyon spill of 119,000 tons of crude near Great Britain. Also receiving publicity were ten miles of the York River in Virginia, several beaches fouled by oil, 30 miles of Cape Cod National Seashore, and a spill of six million gallons of diverse petroleum products near Wake Island in the mid-Pacific.

The largest and most infamous spill occurred in California in late 1969 in the Santa Barbara channel. As a drillstem was withdrawn from a drill platform six miles off shore, more than 250 million gallons of crude oil escaped to disfigure a huge section of coastline. Over 800 square miles of ocean was covered with the sticky, black mixture and thousands of seabirds were killed, as were several California gray whales in the middle of their northern migration to Alaska. Once again, thousands protested what they perceived as minimal government effort to protect the natural environment.

Finally, in June 1969, the Cuyahoga river near Cleveland, Ohio, burst into flames because of an unidentified oil discharge of thousands of gallons. The stench and filth of the river had long been the butt of local jokes—among them that it should be declared a fire hazard. But the damage the fire caused was no joke and it spurred more people into action. The press began to cover environmental issues with new zeal. Everyone seemed interested in the environment. Environmentalists pointed out that millions of gallons of oil are discharged into U.S. waters every year, with no adequate controls placed on the polluters.

The 1967 oil disasters precipitated a popular mandate for Congress to develop new amendments to cover oil accidents and discharges. But throughout 1968, until Congress adjourned, they failed to pass legislation acceptable both to Muskie environmentalists and industry lobbyists. Environmentalists turned up the heat on Congress during 1969, especially after the Santa Barbara blowout and the Cuyahoga River fire.

The new bill covered oil and thermal pollution, acid mine drainage pollution, and pollutants leading to eutrophication. Ship owners were liable for oil spills up to $14 million and there was no limit on the owner's liability if there was willful negligence or misconduct. Permits were required for any facilities that might pollute waterways, certifying that the facility would not violate water quality standards.

By 1970, after passage of the National Environmental Policy Act and the national celebration of Earth Day, public opinion against pollution, particularly water pollution, had risen to an all-time high. As early as Feb. 10, President Richard Nixon, who had been advised that his chief Democratic political rival in the 1972 election would be environmentalist Sen. Edmund Muskie, recommended to Congress new effluent standards for cities and industries.

Muskie's committee began work on a new bill in early 1971. The new national goals, called "policy" in the Senate bill, were to be that "the discharge of pollutants into the navigable waters be eliminated by 1985." Further it said: "wherever attainable, an interim goal of water quality which provides for the protection and propagation of fish, shellfish and wildlife and provides for recreation in and on the water be achieved by 1981."

Besides authorizing more than $24 billion in construction grants over three years, the new bill required a three-fold approach to water quality: "technology-based" standards; "receiving water" standards; and discharge permits for effluents directly discharged into surface waters. The "technology-based" standards was a new legislative approach. Municipal treatment plants had to have secondary treatment facilities built before 1977; industrial sources were required to install the "best practicable technology" (BPT) available, also by 1977, and upgrade them to "best available technology" (BAT) economically achievable by 1983. BPT technology represented the known treatment methods already in use for conventional pollutants; e.g., biochemical oxygen demand (BOD), total suspended solids—non-filterable (TSS), fecal coliform bacteria, pH (acidity or alkalinity), and oil and grease. BAT refers to the newer treatment technologies needed to control unconventional toxic pollutants, or more advanced techniques for conventional effluents.

In these sections, the act was "technology-forcing" in that it gradually mandated more and more limited discharge levels and assumed that technology would develop in time to achieve the goal of no discharges by 1985. Adopting a new approach to water cleanup was necessary because of the difficulty in getting the states to develop adequate "receiving water" standards, and especially to enforce them. Environmentalists believed that streams were getting dirtier, not cleaner, under the 1965 legislation. They were convinced that "technology-forcing" standards, with federal oversight and enforcement powers, would push industry to make pollution-control advances faster and more effectively than state-initiated standards based on gradations of cleanliness.

Yet, the states were still required to develop a "water quality standard" for each water body within their boundaries, indicating a limit for each pollutant at "designated water use," e.g., drinking water, fisheries, industrial water supplies, etc. These standards were to go beyond the technological approach of the federal requirements because they considered public health and ecological protection according to "designated water use."

The act required every public and private facility that discharges wastes directly into US waters to have an NPDES (National Pollutant Discharge Elimination Systems) permit, issued through an EPA regional office. Moreover, the act instructed the newly established Environmental Protection Agency to make up a list of "toxic" chemicals and to develop effluent standards for each of the chemicals, allowing an "ample margin of safety." Industrial discharges were to be allowed one year to come into compliance with the standards, as they were promulgated by the agency. Enforcement for all of the provisions of the bill was local, state, and federal in scope, but the EPA had the authority to veto individual permits and the EPA administrator could sue polluters. A provision in the 1970 law allowed citizen suits against violators.

On the day before adjournment, President Nixon announced his veto, which was overridden by a wide majority. Thus did the Water Pollution Control Act Amendments of 1972, among the most sweeping, innovative environmental legislation ever considered, become law. Their history has been eventful.

More Wilderness Issues

While the League of Women Voters and environmental groups were waging their Clean Water Crusade during the 1960s, much related environmental work also was occurring. The Sierra Club waged campaigns on wilderness issues, and more battles were being fought over urban developments. Events throughout the decade led to the National Environmental Policy Act as well as Earth Day in 1970.

When the Bureau of Reclamation unveiled its Pacific Southwest Water Plan in 1963 at the same time as the Wilderness Act's controversies were beginning to untangle, wilderness advocates were horrified to learn dams were planned for Bridge Canyon and Marble Canyon, both inside the Grand Canyon. Just upstream from the Grand Canyon on the Colorado River, water was beginning to fall in behind the new Glen Canyon Dam, covering a wilderness of breathtaking beauty, all the way to Rainbow Bridge National Monument, which supposedly had been protected under the Colorado River Storage Project Act.

An enraged David Brower, head of the Sierra Club, and a small army of supporters took out full-page ads in newspapers with such headlines as: "Should We Also Flood The Sistine Chapel So Tourists Can Get Nearer The Ceiling?" and "Now Only You Can Save The Grand Canyon From Being Flooded . . . For Profit." This ad concluded, "There is only one simple, incredible issue here. This time it's the Grand Canyon they want to flood. *The Grand Canyon.*"

All the forces of wilderness organizations were mobilized—tens of thousands, perhaps hundreds of thousands of letters of protest, telegrams, phone calls to Washington, and bumper stickers. Newspaper and magazine articles and books were published in an overwhelming display of political force. Even ultra-conservative Rep. Wayne Aspinall, chairman of the House Interior and Insular Affairs Committee, who fought to keep the dams, could not get enough support to stop a 1968 bill that deleted both Grand Canyon dams from the Pacific Southwest Water Plan. The bill went further, prohibiting construction of any dam within the entire Grand Canyon. A few days after that bill passed in October, 1968, President Johnson signed a bill establishing the National Wild and Scenic Rivers System.

The National Environmental Policy Act

Not long after Richard M Nixon became president in 1969, he was reportedly read a poll showing that protection of the environment was the third most-important issue to American voters, behind the Vietnam War and jobs. So he instructed a staff member to prepare an environmental program and in 1970 gave the first of two environmental messages to Congress. In the meantime, at the end of 1969, Congress passed the National Environmental Policy Act.

The bill redirected the priorities of the federal government to

1. Fulfill the responsibilities of each generation as a trustee of the environment for succeeding generations
2. Assure for all Americans safe, healthful, productive, and aesthetically and culturally pleasing surroundings
3. Attain the widest range of beneficial uses of the environment without degradation, risk to health or safety, or other undesirable and unintended consequences
4. Preserve important historic, cultural, and natural aspects of our natural heritage and maintain, wherever possible, an environment that supports diversity and variety of individual choice
5. Achieve a balance between population and resource use that will permit high standards of living and a wide sharing of life's amenities
6. Enhance the quality of renewable resources and approach the maximum attainable recycling of depletable resources

These generalized aspirations of the landmark law have found their way into a number of significant court cases, but the more powerful lever of the law in Section 102 (2) (c) mandated environmental impact statements for all federal projects. Government agencies were required to set up an environmental review process that was to evaluate the impacts of such federal projects as new highways, power plants, coal mines, oil rigs, and hundreds of other projects. Agencies such as the U.S. Forest Service and the Army Corps of Engineers were pressured to hire their own staff people to look at environmental impacts of agency projects. And a number of states passed their own versions of NEPA. Within a few years the law was used to attempt to stop the Alaskan pipeline, and many dams and development projects.

The Environmental Protection Agency

During Nixon's first year, a blue-ribbon presidential council on governmental reorganization was set up to promote more efficiency in federal agencies. The council began its work on natural resource programs in early 1970, and by late spring made its recommendations. Proposals included forming a new agency called the Department of Natural Resources and the Environment, that would deal with natural resources, pollution control, public lands and energy departments and programs. The reorganization touched many agencies, especially the Department of the Interior, and it was expected new agency would be housed there.

The reorganization plan caused jockeying and politicking because some departments would lose and others gain influence, but in the end President Nixon created the Environmental Protection Agency as a separate entity. Initially, the EPA had divisions of water pollution, air pollution, pesticides, solid wastes, and radiation.

Not all of the natural resource or environmental programs were placed in the EPA Because of the special friendship that Secretary of Commerce Maurice Stans enjoyed with Nixon, several programs were organized into a National Oceanic and Atmospheric Administration in his department. Secretary of Agriculture Clifford Hardin managed to keep the Forest Service in his department. Secretary of the Interior Water Hickel, who had criticized the Nixon administration for its handling of a war protest at Kent State University, lost the new agency as well as water pollution control programs.

Given all the political maneuvering at its birth, and that it began its life without the tradition or support of a parent department, it is amazing that the EPA was able to survive and be effective. That it grew in strength is a testimony to the ability and charisma of its first hard-working director, William D Ruckelshaus, a committed staff, the support of powerful members of Congress, and a persistently active environmental movement.

Clear Air Legislation

The movement for clean air had been developing momentum at the same time as other environmental activity. But environmental legislation seems to be enacted only as crises occur, and it was difficult to see the effects of invisible toxic pollutants in the air.

For most of the nation's history, polluted air simply seemed to be a necessary inconvenience and a cost of local prosperity. If you were a white-collar worker in Pittsburgh during the 1940s, you simply took an extra white shirt with you to work, knowing the one you put on in the morning would be gray by noon. You got used to washing the grime off your face in the morning in the summer because you had to open the window at night when local factories blew out their smokestacks, and coal-burning locomotives passed your neighborhood.

These nuisances were either ignored or addressed in some feeble way by city and county regulations. Chicago and Cincinnati had smoke regulations as early as

1881, and Albany County, New York, wrote a smoke law in 1913. Ohio passed a state law in 1897 to limit smoke emissions from steam boilers. In 1907, the International Association for the Prevention of Smoke, later to become the Air Pollution Control Association (APCA), was established to lobby for smoke prevention regulations and controls.

New efficient boiler designs that reduced black smoke and saved money for fuel were developed during the 1940s. The designs were phased into many factories, but because boilers can last for decades and few if any regulations required the switch to newer models, progress was slow. Meantime, the first signs of more toxic air pollution from smog and fog were emerging.

In 1948, a temperature inversion (an unusual meteorological occurrence in which a layer of warmer air overlies a heavier cooler layer that holds down pollution) lasted eight days in the tiny town of Donora, Pennsylvania. Twenty people died and hundreds more were hospitalized. Four years later a widely publicized "killer fog" in London was responsible for about 4,000 deaths. As urbanization crowded more and more people into smaller areas, air circulation decreased, temperatures increased, and pollution from the cities could not be easily dispersed by natural processes. The early smog incidents resulted mostly from burning coal in home heaters and in factories.

In 1949, the U.S. Public Health Service reported on the Donora incident, recommending that the federal government research the nature of air pollution. Several congressional resolutions supported the recommendation after the London "fog" episode brought a renewal of the effort. Finally, in 1955, seven years after Donora, a bill was passed authorizing a federal program of research, training, and demonstration. The program was renewed in 1959 for four years.

Throughout this period most legislators and bureaucrats considered air pollution a local problem. An HEW official told the Senate Public Works Committee that "instances of troublesome interstate air pollution are few in number;" and also an internal Bureau of the Budget memorandum stated that "unlike water pollution, air pollution . . . is essentially a local problem."

A few hard-hit metropolitan regions did act on their own. Los Angeles County, for example, set up an air pollution emergency plan in 1955 with a "first alert" when ozone levels reach .5 parts per million (ppm), and a "second alert" when the level reaches 1.0 ppm. Later the county set up a "forecast system." Also in 1955, the California Legislature created the first of its pollution control districts in the San Francisco Bay Area to monitor stationary sources of air pollution; in 1961, it set up a program to control auto exhaust under the Motor Vehicle Pollution Control Board. A few other cities and states began to act on the air pollution problem, but minimal efforts were made either locally or nationally to work toward a comprehensive program.

However, during the 1960 presidential campaign a number of big-city Democratic legislators reported their constituents' environmental concerns to candidate John F. Kennedy. Then, as president, he called for a federal air pollution control program in 1961 and again in 1962, when a number of air pollution bills were introduced. The president's bill authorized, under the Public Health Service of HEW, more grants for research and financial help to state and local air pollution agencies, for interstate air pollution studies and for enforcement of interstate air pollution laws along the lines of water pollution laws. President Kennedy was assassinated before his Clean Air Act was passed at the end of 1963.

Sen. Edmund Muskie took up the task of further air pollution regulation with hearings around the country during 1964. By this time, most residents of large cities were aware of the role of auto emissions in air pollution and clamored for controls. Most of the testimony concerned the need to regulate automobile emissions; some people complained about the burning of garbage and trash as well. Muskie soon introduced a bill defining federal standards and authorizing enforcement of auto emissions. The bill also dealt with solid waste disposal.

HEW, having followed the nationwide Muskie hearings, was also ready to present an auto emissions proposal to President Lyndon Johnson, but Johnson wanted the auto industry to comply voluntarily. HEW relayed the president's objections to the Senate subcommittee considering the bill. The outrage expressed by the country's major newspapers, environmental groups, and political organizations caused Johnson to reverse his decision and to support the Muskie bill. In fact the auto industry wanted federal, not state, standards to incorporate into their auto designs but lobbied for weaker provisions than the original proposals. Soon after the bill was passed in 1965, the secretary of HEW agreed to have the same emission standards that California developed for 1967-model cars applied throughout the country, beginning with 1968 auto models.

The Air Quality Act of 1967

The following year, in 1966, New York City suffered a temperature inversion for four days. Hundreds of people reported dizziness, nausea and eye irritation; many were hospitalized for respiratory and heart ailments. Eighty people died. Again the incident was widely reported.

A month later, HEW's third National Conference on Air Pollution met in Washington. Secretary of HEW John Gardner gave the keynote, emphasizing the need for national air quality standards for an essentially national problem. The agency proposed legislation for regional control agencies as well as national standards. Within another month, in January, 1967, President Johnson proposed new legislation that incorporated national standards and regional monitoring of "airsheds," financed by the federal government, along with federal aid for auto inspection and research.

The bill generated heated opposition from industry spokesmen during the hearings on national standards for selected industries, especially when they found out the regional organizations were to develop their own standards. The question of sulfur standards raised the ire of congressmen from coal-producing Eastern states worried that high-sulfur coal would become unsellable, and Johnson's bill was modified considerably.

Sen. Muskie followed the precedent of the 1965 Water Quality Act, which required the states to write letters of intent within 90 days and to establish standards for specific pollutants within another 180 days as applicable in air quality control regions designated by the secretary of HEW. Another lively debate ensued over whether

California would be permitted to have more stringent auto emissions standards than federal air quality standards. California legislators and their many supporters won the floor fight, and the Air Quality Act of 1967 was passed. Although the secretary of HEW was given the power to review and modify state standards, the agency was only to look into the desirability of establishing its own national emission standards from all sources of air pollution. The high-sulfur coal states won the first round of many legislative battles, but eventually the argument prevailed that, without federally mandated air quality and emission standards, states would lower standards to attract "dirty" industries.

With the states' lack of response on air quality standards, history repeated itself. By the end of 1970, HEW had yet to approve a state implementation plan; indeed, only 21 plans had even been submitted. Public opinion on environmental issues, however, was at an all time high—with many news stories on oil pollution and polluted cities. *Life* magazine suggested in 1970 that probably by 1980 people in the cities would have to wear gas masks or die because of smog inversions. It was time of great suspicion of industry in general, and the auto industry in particular. In 1969, the Justice Department began an investigation to determine whether the automobile manufacturers had conspired to prevent an air pollution control device program from being established. The consent decree implied that the big three auto companies (GM Ford, Chrysler) had attempted to do so.

When the 1967 authorizations expired in 1970, environmentalist forces began to gear up to close the loopholes in the new law. President Nixon had realized the political importance of the issue and wanted to take it from his potential rival for the presidency in 1972, Sen. Muskie. In his major speeches during the year, Nixon sounded like a lifelong environmentalist. He began to assert the need for national emission standards, including for new or hazardous air pollution sources. Earth Day, celebrated in April, 1970, added the clout of hundreds of thousands of letters to Washington in favor of stronger environmental regulations.

The 1970 Clean Air Act was similar to the 1967 bill except stronger. Auto emissions were to be cut 90% by 1975 compared with 1970 emissions; national air quality standards were to be established; and the states were to have their implementation plans in place by 1975. Citizens' suits were permitted in the same manner as in water quality legislation, and appropriations for research and local air quality agencies reached a record high. In general the 1970 Act continued the federal-state partnership idea. The federal government maintained its oversight role and established minimum standards for ambient air quality. The states could supplement the federal regulations with their own rules if they desired. Few foresaw the difficulties to come.

The 1970s

The seventies brought frustration and dismay not only to environmentalists, policy-makers, and agency personnel but also to a wide variety of industry and citizen groups. Enforcing the law was extraordinarily difficult because of the complicated history of environmental regulation and the jealous protection of local governing rights. Very often the states withheld power to enforce the laws and delayed setting up a suitable structure to do so. And because it so difficult to determine precise standards to protect human health and the environment, the regulations themselves have allowed firms to request delays or challenge the standards. The inflexible time schedule required for industry implementation of rules lent credence to the requests for delays. Economic recessions supported industry claims that the regulations placed undue hardship on the private sector. Public opinion itself became very fickle when Americans were asked to change irresponsible environmental behavior, particularly when it involved the automobile.

The effort to cut auto emissions 90% by 1975 well illustrates the difficulties of the decade. The act allowed car makers to request a one-year delay in implementing emissions standards if they had made "good faith" efforts yet could not develop the necessary pollution control technologies. In 1972 public hearings, the auto companies called catalytic converters ineffective and unsafe if they caught fire. Other witnesses testified they had used converters for thousands of miles safely and effectively. Some witnesses said the devices caused excess gas consumption; others denied it. A few feared a strong regulation would shut down auto production.

According to former deputy EPA administrator John Quarles, it was David Hawkins, an attorney from the Natural Resources Defense Council, who provided the convincing argument—that for all their protestations the auto companies did not present firm evidence that they could not meet the 1975 deadline. Knowledgeable about recent technological improvements, EPA Administrator William Ruckelshaus denied the applications for the delay.

The auto makers then filed suit in the US Court of Appeals to overturn EPA's decision, and early in 1973 the court agreed with the auto companies that economic factors were not given enough weight at the hearing. At new hearings it became clear that the technology was adequate and safe, but it was not certain that the auto firms could gear up adequately on the massive scale necessary. This time Ruckelshaus granted the delay.

Later in 1973, amid war with Israel, Arab nations placed an embargo on oil exports to the United States. Congress passed emergency legislation to cut energy consumption and expand energy supply. Power plants were required to switch from oil to more polluting coal. At the same time, large coal strip-mining operations sprang up in western states. The Energy Supply and Environmental Coordination Act of 1974 temporarily suspended emission limit of stationary sources, including power plants. Public support of environmental rules began to fade in the wake of the energy crisis, gasoline shortages, high prices, and economic recession.

The catalytic converter got another setback in 1975 when a study indicated that the converters could produce potentially dangerous sulfates that could interact with water vapor in the atmosphere. Congress mandated that final auto pollution standards be reached by the time the 1978 models were marketed. At the same time, the EPA administrator lifted the requirement for the desulfurization of gasoline because of rapidly rising prices and continuing inflation. Critics began to mount a campaign claiming that high prices were the result of pollution control costs.

Then, in early 1979, the EPA decreed that the permissible amount of ozone in the air may rise to 0.12 part per million parts of air, up from 0.08 part per million, the earlier standard. EPA Administrator Douglas Costle said that the change was "based on a careful evaluation of medical and scientific evidence." Immediately, the American Petroleum Institute filed a suit, contending that the rule was more stringent than necessary, and the Environmental Defense Fund and other environmental groups claimed that the new standard would seriously affect people's health.

Despite the cooling of environmental enthusiasm during the 1970s, Congress passed 1977 Clean Air Act Amendments, which attempted once again to obtain compliance from polluters. New "non-compliance penalties," equal to the costs of cleanup, were enacted upon those who would not install necessary control equipment. Permit fees were to be charged by the states as well, and state boards were to include a majority of their members from people who represent the public interest, i.e., those who do not derive a significant portion of their income from anyone subject to the permits or enforcement orders. States also could adopt more stringent emission limitations than federal standards required, and, especially, were guaranteed the right to prevent significant deterioration of state air resources.

In general, the EPA played research, advisory, and watchdog roles over the 247 air quality control regions, reviewing state implementation plans, overseeing monitoring, and penalizing such stationary sources as power plants and highly polluting industries. At the same time, the agency struggled to get the auto industry to meet national emissions deadlines.

Even during the difficult seventies, much environmental work was accomplished: inventories of polluting industries, which were monitored and forced to develop pollution control plans by certain deadlines; primary ambient air quality standards to protect human health (sulfur oxides, particulate matter, carbon monoxide, photochemical oxidants, hydrocarbons, nitrogen dioxide) were established, as well as secondary ambient standards to protect property and the environment—crops, plants, wildlife, soil, water, etc. Separate standards were set for hazardous air pollutants—asbestos, mercury, vinyl chloride, and beryllium, and new ones like benzene during the 1980s.

Clean Water Act of 1977

The Federal Water Pollution Control Act of 1972, retroactively renamed the Clean Water Act, was subject to the same problems of non-compliance, lack of enforcement, and delay in meeting deadlines as the Clean Air Act. One difference was that the water quality legislation had been much longer in the making, but intergovernmental cooperation and other factors of environmental legislation made it subject to the same kind of obstacles as the Clean Air Act.

Another difference in the Clean Water Act was Congress' deliberate effort to require dischargers to limit their pollutants in two steps, upgrading pollution control technologies at the designated deadlines of 1977 and 1983. The first water quality standard was to include the *average* of the best existing performance of plants within each category of industry. However, the second standard imposed the best performance level in existence on all dischargers in the industry. The first standard required the EPA administrator to perform a cost-benefit analysis to determine whether the costs of treatment were justified by the quality of effluent control. The second standard did not make this requirement since the goal of the act was to achieve zero pollution discharge by 1983, presumably at any cost. The agency assumed that if some dischargers were polluting at very low levels, the technology exists for others to incorporate in their operations.

By 1977, at least 16% of the major non-municipal dischargers did not meet the first-step water quality standard, and about 53% of the publicly owned treatment plants failed to meet the deadline as well. Congress attempted to introduce some flexibility into the deadline structure in its 1977 Amendments to the Clean Water Act.

The 1977 Amendments to the Clean Water Act first links compliance deadlines for publicly owned treatment works into federal funding for secondary treatment facilities. A federal court earlier had maintained that the law mandated public treatment work deadlines whether or not the facilities received federal funds. The amendments further authorized the EPA administrator to extend the deadline if the discharger has made a good faith effort to comply with the law. The earlier law stipulated an inflexible deadline and it was upheld by the court. And, finally, in response to court cases brought by U.S. Steel and Republic Steel, the act gave the administrator veto power over state-issued NPDES permits whether or not effluent guidelines formally had been issued. The question was whether industry had to meet Congressionally mandated environmental deadlines or could fall back on weaker state standards.

Toxic Pollutants

The most controversial aspect of the 1977 amendments dealt with the mandate EPA was given in 1972 to develop a list of chemicals it considered "toxic," then within six months establish standards for the chemicals. Dischargers of the toxic pollutants were given a year to meet the requirements. However, the agency was unable to promulgate the list, not only because of the massive proportions of the undertaking but also because the scientific information about the health effects of the chemicals was either unavailable or too complex to translate simply into regulations. Industry and environmental groups provided the EPA with studies that canceled each other out. Realizing it would be impossible to base their rules on "toxicity" to human health, the agency concentrated on the actual discharges of six suspect chemicals.

In 1973 and 1974, the Natural Resources Defense Council sued the EPA administrator four times to force the agency to come up with the list and standards. Finally, in 1975, the cases were consolidated in Judge Thomas Flannery's U.S. District Court, and the EPA offered to settle the suit with the environmental group through a consent decree. The parties in the case negotiated for several months over what constituted a "toxic" pollutant and came up with a list of 65 chemicals, now know as the "priority pollutants," derived from dozens of agency and private sources. The list was not compiled chemical by chemical, based on a consensus of toxic specialists, but was haggled over starting with several hundred and cut down to a number the NRDC felt the EPA could enforce.

At the same time, 21 major industrial categories were selected as "primary industries" to be regulated in intervals until the end of 1979. Since agreement regarding health and aquatic effects had been impossible to reach, the EPA was to concentrate on the "best available" treatment technology for standard-setting, based on availability and cost. Meantime, the EPA would develop a data base of information about the priority pollutants, from which numerical, ambient criteria could be derived so that specific standards could be put in place by the states in future years. The consent decree took the EPA off the hook in their inability to develop standards for toxic pollutants, but did not change the way the Clean Water Act was to work.

The Flannery Decree (of the NRDC court case) had been signed by the time the Clean Water Act Amendments were passed in 1977. The Best Available Technology requirements were already in the law, to be enforced for conventional pollutants by 1983. It was generally assumed by the committee that drafted the 1977 amendments that the Flannery Decree would be sufficient to control toxic pollutants as well.

In 1979, in response to the amendments, court decisions, and evolving EPA policy, the EPA recodified the National Pollutant Discharge Elimination System (NPDES) permit system, under which clean-up requirements are given to individual discharge sources through the permits. The purpose of most environmental regulation had been

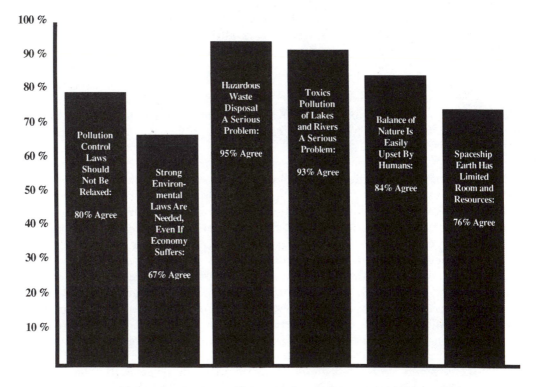

ATTITUDES ON ENVIRONMENTAL CONCERNS
EARLY 1980s

Figure 18–2. Public Opinion Polls of the 1980s. The graph illustrates the dramatic shift in public opinion favor of environmental protection, regardless of cost.

to establish uniform, nationwide requirements for categories of pollutants. Variances were given for special reasons and for special periods of time while dischargers attempted to comply with the regulations.

Under the new NPDES rules, EPA expanded the applicability of a special variance—the "fundamentally different factors" (FDF) variance. The variance authorized the EPA to establish different effluent limits for a particular facility if factors relating to that facility were "fundamentally different" from the factors EPA had considered when developing that industrial category's uniform effluent limit regulations.

The new FDF variance authorization was applied to pretreatment standards for industries that discharged wastes into municipal treatment works, and to the next set of requirements for direct dischargers of toxic pollutants, i.e., those who were to comply with the "best available technology" requirement. What followed was a tie-up of agency personnel on case-by-case determinations of effluent requirements and more serious delays in application of the requirements. Industry again wanted variances for what it claimed were the economic burdens of the requirements, and began to look to a more friendly federal administration. Their hopes were not long in becoming fulfilled.

The Reagan Administration

After Ronald Reagan was elected president in 1980 and began to choose his cabinet, a headline in *Science* magazine read, "Environmentalists tremble." They had reason to. The new secretary of the interior, James Watt, immediately disclosed plans to develop the resources of the public lands of the West and the oil offshore around the country. And the new EPA administrator, Anne M Gorsuch (later Burford), proposed a budget about one-fourth the size of the Carter administration's. Over them all, at the center of power at the Office of Management and Budget, David Stockman claimed regulatory oversight and examined the cost-benefit consequences of regulations. In his widely publicized "Dunkirk" planning document for the newly elected president, Stockman lost no time attacking what he described as "burdensome" rules on carbon monoxide, industrial boiler emissions, hazardous and toxic waste, and, especially, the Clean Air Act Amendments of 1977, which he characterized as "staggering excess built upon dubious scientific and economic premises."

Simultaneously, President Reagan fired the entire 45-member staff of the Council on Environmental Quality, the executive oversight organization created by the National Environmental Policy Act that prepares legislation for the president, to make room for a tiny staff of about a dozen. The president had no plans for environmental legislation beyond minimizing the cost of current legislation. In Reagan's opinion, environmental protection cost too much money, and it wasn't his issue.

Gorsuch began her term by dismantling the enforcement division, then announced that the White House wanted a weakened Clean Air Act, including a two-thirds reduction of the program to prevent deterioration of air, a rollback of emission standards for new automobiles, and a lifting of some deadlines for achieving clean air. Next, the administrator said that the EPA would no longer support nationally uniform, technology-forcing controls that amounted to "treatment for the sake of treatment."

Decisions were to be left to comparisons of the cost of treatment against cleanup benefits, largely left in the hands of state and local agencies.

In practice, the "best available technologies" Flannery consent decree was tossed aside, and the new pattern would allow industries to retain their "best practicable" technologies and phase into ambient, geographically limited (on a case-by-case NPDES permit) regulations. In defense of its new policy, the EPA cited an agency-funded study by JRB Associates, which found that BPT-level technologies can remove about 70% of toxic pollutants from primary industries. At the same time, Gorsuch asked the federal court to let the EPA out of its five-year-old consent decree with the Natural Resources Defense Council on the ground that its smaller budget did not permit it. Judge Flannery did not accede to the request but an aggressive OMB a shake-up of agency organization, and declining morale, along with politics as usual on Capitol Hill, held up new amendments to the Clean Water Act for more than six years.

The Clean Water Act controversy was an old one. Because local industries and agencies had stalled for a decade, environmentalist remained unconvinced that local "receiving water" standards would clean up the nation's waters. For them it was far better to demand best available technological standards (BAT) than leave the matter to local politics and standards that might not be enforceable. Furthermore, environmentalists wanted standards that would make the water "really" clean, not just adequately clean. That is, clean enough everywhere for people to swim in, and for fish to stay free from buildups of toxic pollutants.

Environmental Problems and the Media

During the last years of the Carter administration in the late 1970s, new environmental problems began to surface and absorb the attention of the entire country. The first national exposure came in the summer of 1978, with heavy media coverage of disturbing health effects of chemicals seeping into homes around the old Love Canal in Niagara Falls, N.Y. Local health officials found higher-than-normal rates of miscarriages, birth defects, and liver ailments among the residents. The abandoned, never-completed canal had been used for chemical-waste disposal in the 1940s by Hooker Chemicals & Plastics Corporation, which subsequently sold the filled-in site to the Niagara Falls Board of Education for one dollar. A school was built, and families settled in around it.

In August, 1978, the New York health department stated publicly that the lives of Love Canal residents were endangered. President Carter declared a national emergency. The government agreed to buy 240 homes of the "inner ring." By the time President Reagan came into office in 1981, more than $30 million had been spent by the local, state, and federal governments on clean-up and relocating the residents. Many more worried locals wanted to get out of the area as well, and a national controversy developed over the health studies done on the residents.

This episode was just one of hundreds of public outcries over toxic-waste dumping and groundwater contamination that have remained on newspaper front pages and prime-time television. A number of television documentaries on the environment and health were produced in 1979 with titles that suggest their content: "A Plague on Our Children" (Nova, WGBH, Boston); "Serpent's Fruits" (WNET, New York); "The Politics of Poison" (KRON, San Francisco). *Time* (Sept. 22, 1980) presented a lengthy cover story entitled "The Poisoning of America" about the environmental and health effects of omnipresent toxic chemicals.

Most of the media coverage of environmental pollution quoted such scientists as Dr. Samuel Epstein, who wrote *The Politics of Cancer* in 1978 and Harvard biologist Dr. Matthew Meselson, interviewed in "A Plague on Our Children," to point out the connection between cancer and toxic pollutants. The discussion had been alive as early as 1976, when *Newsweek* (January 26, 1976) reviewed research done at HEW and the National Cancer Institute on the causes of cancer that indicated higher rates of cancer occur in petrochemical industrial zones. Another milestone occurred June 22, 1976, when Leslie Stahl stated in a CBS Report Special: "It's now known that increased contamination of our air, water, and food is contributing to our soaring cancer rates." A few years later, even Jane Fonda would say in her *Jane Fonda's Workout Book*, "Cancer is a byproduct of the petrochemical age." The idea had become conventional wisdom.

In 1979, 17,000 rusty steel drums were found leaking chemicals in an open field in "the Valley of the Drums," Kentucky, and an EPA survey disclosed hundreds of similar problems around the country. In 1983, the entire town of Times Beach, Missouri, had to be closed and bought out by the EPA for $30 million because dioxin had contaminated a mixture of oil and industrial wastes that were sprayed on roads to hold down dust near the town in the early 1970s. Many other unpaved roads around the country regularly had been sprayed with oils saturated with highly toxic polychlorinated byphenyls (PCBs), toxic metals, and sometimes dioxin as a way to dispose of waste oils.

The chemical revolution of the twentieth century that introduced so many home and personal conveniences—textiles, drugs, steel, papers, electronic equipment, appliances, paints and dyes, and cultural artifacts—brought hundreds of different toxic wastes in garbage and hazardous waste dumps and underground storage drums near neighborhood factories, all located near somebody's back yard. At the 1.2 million gasoline stations occupying every nook and cranny of the country, hundreds of thousands of underground storage containers were rusting and leaking; the tanks have a 15-year life span and 350,000 were projected to be leaking by 1987. Eventually, these toxic chemicals (300 in gasoline) and wastes found their way into groundwater, were spread or illegally dumped on back roads, or were mishandled and exploding near family homes.

Though fires and factory explosions once were relegated to the back pages of newspapers and left out of TV coverage, the media began to report these events. One such example occurred in July, 1980 in northern Meade County, Kentucky, near Louisville. TV audiences around the country watched black clouds of burning vinyl chloride billowing from 10 railroad tank cars. About 10,000 people were evacuated from the area, which was sealed off for days.

Another example indicates how huge numbers of people have been drawn into the problem of dumping of hazardous wastes. By the end of the 1970s, through the persistence of environmental groups, the media, and a personal sailing boat campaign by folksinger Pete Seeger, the millions of people who live along the Hudson River suddenly became aware that their river, so rich in cultural history and scenic beauty, was dying because of decades of dumping by hundreds of factories and municipalities. What seemed to catalyze action was the discovery that more than 1.5 million pounds of non-biodegradable PCBs were poisoning the fish.

By the early 1980s, dozens of wells throughout California, Arizona, and Washington were found to be contaminated with high levels of carbon tetrachloride, trichloroethylene (TCE), both suspected carcinogens, and other chemicals, pesticides, and industrial cleaning agents or degreasers. Most of the contaminated wells were near garbage or hazardous waste dumps, abandoned dumps, or factories that stored wastes on their own sites.

These problems, plus scandals in the top of the Environmental Protection Agency that eventually caused the administrator and others to resign, brought public shock over new federal environmental policies that threatened a decade of environmental activity. Environmental organizations received a sudden infusion of new members and money to fight the administration.

In June, 1981, a Gallup Poll for *Newsweek* concluded: "A large majority of the public believes that government regulation and requirements are worth the extra costs they add to products and services. Three-quarters believe that it is possible to maintain strong economic growth and still maintain high environmental standards." A *New York Times CBS News* poll published October 4, 1981, confirmed that 67% of the people polled said that they wanted environmental laws maintained even if the economy suffers. A September, 1981 Harris poll said 80% of the people opposed relaxing pollution control.

Then in 1982 a Harris survey showed that 95 percent of a national sample considered "disposal of hazardous waste" a "serious problem" and 93 percent thought that "pollution of lakes of lakes and rivers by toxic substances from factories" also constituted a "serious problem." Furthermore, the public was beginning to grasp the underpinnings of the environmental movement, as can be seen in a 1982 *Research and Forecasts for the Continental Group* survey. Seventy percent of the people interviewed said they were hurt by the recession, yet 60 percent believed pollution to be one of the most important problems facing the nation. Eighty-four percent of the sample agreed with the statement, "The balance of nature is very delicate and easily upset by human activities," and 76 percent agreed that "the Earth is like a spaceship with only limited room and resources." Finally, an *ABC News/Washington Post* poll of April 1983 found again that "Even though the large majority of Americans believe compliance with antipollution laws costs business firms at least a fair amount of money, more than three out of four say those laws are worth the cost."

The Resource Conservation and Recovery Act

In 1980, the EPA estimated that more than 70,000 chemicals were being manufactured in the U.S., with about 1,000 new ones added every year. From industrial wastes, most of them utilizing these chemicals, about 260 million metric tons of hazardous wastes are generated each year. Most states and cities had had laws regulating waste for decades, and because solid and hazardous waste regulations occurred in a number of federal laws, even the earliest organization of the EPA included divisions for Hazardous Materials and Waste Management. The Resource Conservation and Recovery Act of 1976 attempted to control the disposal of hazardous waste by establishing a "cradle to grave" tracking system from generation to disposal. The EPA was given 18 months to issue regulations on the identification, generation, transportation, storage, treatment, and disposal of hazardous waste. The task was monumental, but the agency managed to publish the first set of federal regulations on the generation of hazardous waste in May, 1980. In 1982, the EPA published further regulations on the design and operation of hazardous waste land-disposal facilities.

In the meantime, the EPA released a study that estimated that more than 750,000 businesses generated hazardous wastes and 10,000 transporters moved them to 51,000 dump sites—municipal, hazardous, and thousands already abandoned—that contained hazardous wastes and represented a threat to the groundwater of nearby residents. Since World War II, because of increased manufacturing of consumer goods, the wastes grew from about 4 million metric tons to about 260 million metric tons a year. Contaminated groundwater was reported from landfills, underground injection wells, and surface impoundments of wastes in unlined pits and lagoons.

Soon after Love Canal and related episodes, the EPA developed a plan for a fund to pay for cleaning up abandoned waste sites that threatened groundwater supplies. Congress responded by passing the Comprehensive Environmental Response, Compensation, and Liability Act of 1980 (CERCLA), to be commonly known as Superfund, with an initial funding of $1.6 billion. Over a period of five years, the fund was debated in Congress, at the General Accounting Office, and on the state level (How much is needed? Who is to pay? How should responsibility be divided among joint industry users?, etc.). In 1985, the Office of Technology Assessment released its "Superfund Strategy" report, which projected cleanup costs of $100 billion to clean only 10,000, of a possible 22,000 sites, over a period of 50 years.

To control the problem of leaking landfills in the future, Congress passed a reauthorization of RCRA in 1984, which banned land disposal of certain wastes, gradually over a period of five years, in those cases where the wastes could threaten human health and the environment. The EPA was to make such designations by specific dates for specific categories (bulk noncontainerized liquid hazardous wastes were banned quickly, then dioxins and solvents, etc.). If the EPA did not make a designation by the given dates, the waste would automatically be banned. This provision came to be known as the "hard hammer" approach, pounding home the importance of action and speed. Another interesting implication of the amendments was that the EPA was to make its determination about the safety of land disposal of a specific waste exclusively on the basis of the environmental and health impacts, without regard to possible alternative ways to dispose of the waste. The assumption was that the requirement will create a market for new technologies, such as recycling or clean incineration, and, of course, new manufacturing processes that generate less waste.

The Bhopal Tragedy

The modern period of environmental politics began December 3, 1984, when a poison gas, methyl isocyanate, leaked at the Union Carbide factory at Bhopal, India, killing more than 2,000 people and injuring another 200,000 in the world's worst industrial accident. About 3,000 people a day were treated in 20 medical dispensaries nearby, and billions of dollars of claims have been filed against Union Carbide.

The following year on August 11, another leak of toxic chemicals occurred at Carbide's plant in Institute, West Virginia, and memories of the Bhopal disaster shook residents there and near many American chemical plants. Soon after, in the fall of 1985, an EPA draft study reported that in the previous five years almost 7,000 accidents, involving the release of 420 million pounds of toxic chemicals, had occurred in the United States, killing 139 people, injuring 1,478 and leading to the evacuation of 217,000. Then, in April, 1986, following a nuclear power plant accident in Chernobyl, experts placed 100,000 Russians at high risk of contracting cancer, and five European countries found high levels of cesium-137 in their produce and soils and will suffer the effects for many years.

By this time most multinational corporations had conducted safety audits on all their plants; nonetheless, insurance rates, soaring since Superfund made many companies potentially liable for hazardous waste contamination and accidents, suddenly became prohibitively expensive for companies generating, storing, hauling, or disposing of hazardous materials.

What Does It All Mean?

After two generations of modern environmental regulation, basic questions remain. For example, the nation still lacks an effective, workable definition of hazardous waste to determine what should be landfilled or treated. Further, by any definition, the number of hazardous pollutants in waste, water, and air far exceeds the regulators' ability to identify and control them.

It has proven next to impossible to define a "safe" level of exposure, a fact that has tied the hands of legislators and regulators alike. For example, it would take two to four years and cost up to $1 million each to test all the 1,000-plus chemicals introduced into commercial use every year. About 1% of all commercial chemicals, 10% of the pesticides, and about 18% of all food additives are now tested each year. At least another 10,000 untested separate chemical entities are in widespread use.

This uncertainty about basic standards allows industry to continue to press to weaken environmental regulations, arguing that many required discharge reductions are not worth the capital and operating costs and, in many cases, could put companies out of business. Industry scientists point out that analytical measurements, on which their priority-pollutant standards are based are often incorrect or unreliable. Industry gets its strongest support from state and local governments, which are responsible for enforcing federal laws.

Environmental groups and their supporters, now an unquestionable majority of the country, claim that scientific answers to the questions of toxic risks slowly and surely have been emerging and that the conclusions support community and environmentalist experience and fears about toxic pollution. Furthermore, they deny that the costs of complying with regulations is excessive, resent industry's polluting just to save money and claim the health costs of pollution are far more significant. Each industrial disaster adds to the environmentalists' political, and, therefore, agency, support.

Perhaps the most significant fact of modern environmental history has been the rapid development of political muscle by environmental groups, which have been largely responsible for the laws and regulations. The environmental constituency cannot be ignored in the legislative process. Nonetheless, environmentalists, who have had to fight for everything they've gained, have reason to believe that environmental quality is far from ideal—from the standpoint of any measure they would want to apply.

The world, not just the United States, faces a monumental environmental problem. The atmosphere and oceans carry pollution around the globe. When millions of acres of forests are cleared, global carbon dioxide levels are increased and erosion cripples the world's soil bank. Wildlife and plant species depletion accelerates year by year. Yet in one generation, the American people, and committed people in many other countries, have proved steadfast in their commitment to improving environmental quality. They will continue to struggle in behalf of that goal in the years to come.

References for Further Reading

The title of this chapter, "The Politics of Pollution," is taken from the excellent book by the same name by J. Clarence Davies III (1970), revised with Barbara S. Davies in 1977. A critical original source is the U.S. Congress, Senate Committee on Environment and Public Works, *A Legislative History of the Clean Water Act of 1977*, Committee Print 95-14, 95th Congress, 2d Session, October, 1978; as well as the committee's *A Legislative History of the Clean Air Act Amendments of 1977*, Committee Print 95-16. Three further sources are also extremely helpful on the history of this legislation: Philip P. Micklin's "Water Quality: A Question of Standards" in *Congress and the Environment*, edited by Richard A. Cooley and Geoffrey Wandesforde-Smith (1970); James Banks' "Dumping into Surface Waters: The Making and Demise of Toxic Discharge Regulations" in *Beyond Dumping*, edited by Bruce Piasecki (1984); and Fredric A. Strom, ed., *Land Use & Environment Law Review—1979* (1979), a tome that surveys the environmental legislation of the 1970s. John Quarles, deputy administrator of the EPA during its early years, offers "an insider's view" of the EPA in his lively *Cleaning Up America* (1976). *Environmental Policy in the 1980s: Reagan's New Agenda*, edited by Norman J. Vig and Michael E. Kraft (1984) illustrates the impact of the Reagan administration on environmental policy. A more specific anthology dealing with the impact of Reagan's order mandating benefit-cost analysis for new environmental regulations is *Environmental Policy Under Reagan's Executive Order: The Role of Benefit-Cost Analysis*, edited by V. Kerry Smith (1984). Riley Dunlap's "Public Opinion: Behind the

Transformation" (*EPA Journal*, Vol. II, July/August 1985) traces the development of public support for environmental pollution control policies from the mid-1960s to the early 1980s by examining surveys from the major opinion research organizations. On the development of environmental consciousness, see Samuel P. Hays, "From Conservation to Environment: Environmental Politics in the U.S. Since World War II," in K. Bailes, ed., cited earlier. J.M. Petulla, *American Environmentalism: Values, Tactics, Priorities* (1980) traces the biocentric, ecologic, and economic traditions of thought in American environmentalism in their past and present applications.

Index

WE VALUE YOUR OPINION—PLEASE SHARE IT WITH US

Merrill Publishing and our authors are most interested in your reactions to this textbook. Did it serve you well in the course? If it did, what aspects of the text were most helpful? If not, what didn't you like about it? Your comments will help us to write and develop better textbooks. We value your opinions and thank you for your help.

Text Title _____ Edition _____

Author(s) _____

Your Name (optional) _____

Address _____

City _____ State _____ Zip _____

School _____

Course Title _____

Instructor's Name _____

Your Major _____

Your Class Rank _____ Freshman _____ Sophomore _____ Junior _____ Senior

_____ Graduate Student

Were you required to take this course? _____ Required _____ Elective

Length of Course? _____ Quarter _____ Semester

1. Overall, how does this text compare to other texts you've used?

_____ Superior _____ Better Than Most _____ Average _____ Poor

2. Please rate the text in the following areas:

	Superior	Better Than Most	Average	Poor
Author's Writing Style	_____	_____	_____	_____
Readability	_____	_____	_____	_____
Organization	_____	_____	_____	_____
Accuracy	_____	_____	_____	_____
Layout and Design	_____	_____	_____	_____
Illustrations/Photos/Tables	_____	_____	_____	_____
Examples	_____	_____	_____	_____
Problems/Exercises	_____	_____	_____	_____
Topic Selection	_____	_____	_____	_____
Currentness of Coverage	_____	_____	_____	_____
Explanation of Difficult Concepts	_____	_____	_____	_____
Match-up with Course Coverage	_____	_____	_____	_____
Applications to Real Life	_____	_____	_____	_____

3. Circle those chapters you especially liked:
   1   2   3   4   5   6   7   8   9   10   11   12   13   14   15   16   17   18   19   20
   What was your favorite chapter? _____
   Comments:

4. Circle those chapters you liked least:
   1   2   3   4   5   6   7   8   9   10   11   12   13   14   15   16   17   18   19   20
   What was your least favorite chapter? _____
   Comments:

5. List any chapters your instructor did not assign. _____

6. What topics did your instructor discuss that were not covered in the text?_____

   _____

7. Were you required to buy this book? _____ Yes   _____ No

   Did you buy this book new or used? _____ New   _____ Used

   If used, how much did you pay? _____

   Do you plan to keep or sell this book? _____ Keep   _____ Sell

   If you plan to sell the book, how much do you expect to receive? _____

   Should the instructor continue to assign this book? _____ Yes   _____ No

8. Please list any other learning materials you purchased to help you in this course (e.g., study guide, lab manual).

   _____

9. What did you like most about this text? _____

   _____

10. What did you like least about this text? _____

    _____

11. General comments:

    May we quote you in our advertising? _____ Yes   _____ No

    Please mail to: Boyd Lane
                      College Division, Research Department
                      Box 508
                      1300 Alum Creek Drive
                      Columbus, Ohio 43216

    Thank you!

DATE DUE			
NOV 1 8 1991			
MAY 0 4 1992			
DEC 1 8 1992			
MAY 0 9 1998			
JUL 3 1 2008			
JUL 0 8 2010			